# BACK TO DARWIN

# BACK TO DARWIN

*A Richer Account of Evolution*

*Edited by*

John B. Cobb, Jr.

WILLIAM B. EERDMANS PUBLISHING COMPANY
GRAND RAPIDS, MICHIGAN / CAMBRIDGE, U.K.

© 2008 William B. Eerdmans Publishing Company
All rights reserved

Published 2008 by
Wm. B. Eerdmans Publishing Co.
2140 Oak Industrial Drive N.E., Grand Rapids, Michigan 49505 /
P.O. Box 163, Cambridge CB3 9PU U.K.

Printed in the United States of America

13  12  11  10  09  08        7  6  5  4  3  2  1

ISBN  978-0-8028-4837-6

www.eerdmans.com

# Contents

*Preface*

The title *Back to Darwin* was not on the mind of any contributor to this volume, including me as editor, as we worked on this volume. Nevertheless, in reading through the proofs, it occurred to me as an appropriately suggestive, if not a rigorously precise, characterization of the thesis of the book. Perhaps, given that the editor is a theologian, I should stress that no one is proposing a return to Darwin's theological views. It is his demonstration of the fact of biological evolution that we all affirm.

There are occasional criticisms of Darwin's scientific formulations in the book, and no one would agree with everything he said. For example, he shared with the scientific community of his time a deterministic view of nature, whereas some contributors reject this metaphysics. He insisted that evolutionary changes are all very gradual, and we do not all agree.

Nevertheless, none of us questions Darwin's major, distinctive ideas. All of us accept and admire his immense achievement in showing that all living forms, certainly including human beings, evolved from common ancestors in a process in which natural selection has played a central role. The problems highlighted in this book are with certain assumptions and overstatements in the post-Darwin development of evolutionary theory. The book implicitly proposes that we go behind *those* developments—back to Darwin—and evaluate the later evolutionary theories more critically.

Not all contributors are committed to "going back." Some would be satisfied to go forward, enriching mainstream theories with new research. Indeed, the one who has contributed most to this volume, Francisco Ayala, does not see a need to go "back." The role he has so generously played has been to present the actual course of mainstream development in evolutionary thinking in a way that suggests that what is required is to keep moving forward. What others see as missing in the mainstream development, he believes is being responsibly assimilated into it. Thus within the book there is an implicit debate as to whether there is need to go back to Darwin. However, I, as editor, have structured the book as a whole so as to argue for such a new start.

The term used by most authors to describe the position of the mainstream of evolutionary biology today is "neo-Darwinism." As pointed out by Ayala, contemporary biologists use this term rarely, and chiefly as a historical designation of the synthesis of Darwinian natural selection with Mendelian genetics. This synthesis has been taken for granted in most of the further development of evolutionary theory.

No contributor to this volume questions the important role that genes play in evolution. Nevertheless, there is much criticism of neo-Darwinism. The accurate teaching of the importance of genes has led to extreme statements about them and their role. For example, gene mutation is presented as random not only in the sense that it is not directed by an end or purpose but also in the sense that genes are unaffected by their environment, especially by the life-form in which they are located. In common formulations, the activity of these life-forms disappears from view. They are treated as the means by which the genes reproduce themselves. Also, in the usual formulations, mechanisms of genetic change other than random mutation are little considered. One argument of this book is that much empirical evidence is neglected as a result of the tight and extreme formulations of neo-Darwinism.

If we go back to Darwin, we will clear the slate of these restrictive theories. That does not mean that we will reject the brilliant achievements they have guided. But we will lay alongside them other theories. For example, there is evidence for the importance of epigenetic factors within the cell. There is evidence for lateral transfer of genes and even complete genomes as well as mutation. There is evidence that what happens to the life-form influences the selection of genes. There is evidence that the activity of these life-forms affects the environment in ways important to what is naturally selected. This evidence is not denied by mainstream evolutionary biologists, but it is not given an adequate place in their standard explanations of evolution. The "nothing but" formulations of leading neo-Darwinists are profoundly misleading and destructively restrictive. None of the enrichments of evolutionary theory that we propose conflicts with Darwin; he left such matters open to further research.

Neo-Darwinism reflects the dominant scientific community in its rigorous exclusion of subjectivity from science. Prominent spokespersons are especially emphatic in asserting that the science from which subjectivity is excluded is in principle complete. Darwin was less rigid on these points. For some of the writers in this book, this is the most important issue of all. To return to Darwin is to open the door to a serious discussion of this fundamental philosophical issue.

The conference out of which this book emerged was on evolution and religion. For some contributors to this book, the most important question is whether belief in God can be reconciled with affirmation of evolutionary theory. That some sort of belief in God can be reconciled with Darwin's teaching is hardly in doubt, since Darwin himself was a deist. Some of us believe that a richer theism is also compatible with Darwin's scientific thought and fits even better with the richer account of evolution this book offers.

JOHN B. COBB, JR.

# Acknowledgments

My chief acknowledgments are of the remarkable cooperation of all those whose writings appear in this volume. I especially emphasize that of Francisco Ayala, whose extensive contributions are explained in the introduction. I would also express my appreciation to Bill Eerdmans and Tom Raabe. It has been a pleasure to work with both of them.

Working with a lot of essays is made much easier by computers, but for those uncomfortable and incompetent with these machines, there are many problems. At various stages along the way I have been helped by persons much more competent than I in such matters. Often the help has extended beyond the use of computer skills to other aspects of editing. I want to acknowledge here the assistance of Jonathan Cobb, J. R. Hustwit, Steven Lee, Robert Vincent, and Michael Wehry.

JOHN B. COBB, JR.

# Contributors

**FRANCISCO J. AYALA** is University Professor and Donald Bren Professor of Biological Sciences at the University of California, Irvine. He has published over 900 articles and is author or editor of thirty-one books. He is a member of the U.S. National Academy of Sciences and the American Philosophical Society, and received the 2001 U.S. National Medal of Science. *The New York Times* named Ayala the "Renaissance Man of Evolutionary Biology."

**IAN BARBOUR** has been professor of physics, professor of religion, and Bean Professor of Science, Technology and Society at Carleton College in Northfield, Minnesota. A recipient of the Templeton Prize for Progress in Religion, his most recent publications are *Nature, Human Nature, and God* (2002), *When Science Meets Religion* (2000), and a revised version of his Gifford Lectures, *Religion and Science: Historical and Contemporary Issues* (1997).

**L. CHARLES BIRCH,** until retirement Challis Professor of the University of Sydney, specializes in ecology. He is a Fellow of the Australian Academy of Science, a member of the Club of Rome, and for twenty years a leader in the World Council of Churches. He received the Eminent Ecologist Award of the Ecological Society of America in 1988 and the Templeton Prize in 1990. In addition to scientific publications, he has written on science and religion.

**PHILIP CLAYTON** is Ingraham Professor at Claremont School of Theology, and Professor of Philosophy and Religion at the Claremont Graduate University. He is author or editor of some sixteen books in philosophy and theology, with a specialization in relations between science and religion. His newest work, *In Quest of Freedom: The Emergence of Spirit in the Natural World,* will be published this year by Vandenhoeck & Ruprecht.

JOHN B. COBB, JR., is Professor Emeritus of the Claremont School of Theology and Founding Co-director of the Center for Process Studies. He has written on a number of theological topics and has also examined several other academic disciplines, such as economics, from a Whiteheadian perspective. His previous work on biology was in collaboration with Charles Birch: *The Liberation of Life: From the Cell to the Community.*

JOHN C. GREENE is Professor Emeritus of the University of Connecticut. He is best known for his books on the history of evolutionary thought—*The Death of Adam: Evolution and Its Impact on Western Thought, Debating Darwin, Darwin and the Modern World View, Science Ideology and World View*—and also for *American Science in the Age of Jefferson.*

DAVID RAY GRIFFIN is Professor of Philosophy of Religion and Theology, Emeritus, at Claremont School of Theology and Claremont Graduate University and a co-director of the Center for Process Studies. His thirty-three books include *The Reenchantment of Science* (1988), *Religion and Scientific Naturalism* (2000), *Reenchantment without Supernaturalism: A Process Philosophy of Religion* (2001), and *Two Great Truths: A New Synthesis of Scientific Naturalism and Christian Faith* (2004).

PETE A. Y. GUNTER has written widely on the philosophies of Henri Bergson and Alfred North Whitehead as well as on environmental issues. Among his books are *Bergson and the Evolution of Physics* (1969), *Henri Bergson: A Bibliography* (1974; 2nd ed. 1986), and *Texas Land Ethics,* with M. Oelschlaeger (1997). He has published over 130 book reviews and numerous articles, concentrating on process philosophy

JOHN F. HAUGHT, Ph.D., is Senior Fellow, Science and Religion, Woodstock Theological Center, Georgetown University. His area of specialization is systematic theology, with a particular interest in issues pertaining to science, cosmology, evolution, and ecology. He is the author of numerous books, including *God and the New Atheism: A Critical Response to Dawkins, Harris, and Hitchens; Christianity and Science* (2008); and *God after Darwin* (2nd ed. 2007).

LYNN MARGULIS, Distinguished University Professor in the Department of Geosciences at the University of Massachusetts–Amherst, was elected to the National Academy of Sciences in 1983. She received the National Medal of Science in 1999 from William J. Clinton. Her publications are mainly in cell biology and microbial evolution. She is best known for her work on symbiogenesis and her support of the Gaia hypothesis. Among her many publications, the most recent book is *Dazzle Gradually: Reflections on Nature in Nature,* coauthored with Dorion Sagan.

REG MORRISON is a Sydney-based author-photographer who has specialized in evolutionary and environmental matters for the past twenty-five years, and has most recently written two science resources on geological and biological evolution for use in Australian high schools. His last general-market book, *The Spirit in the Gene,* summarized the impact that humans have had on the biosphere, and explored the genetic origins of the behavior that produced this impact.

DORION SAGAN is author or coauthor of numerous books and articles on topics ranging from cybersex and philosophy to the evolution of bacteria. He has written for *Wired, The New York Times, New York Times Book Review, Pabular, Cabinet, CoEvolution Quarterly,* and *BioScience.* His books include *Microcosmos, What Is Life?, Dazzle Gradually, Into the Cool,* and, most recently, *Notes from the Holocene: A Brief History of the Future.*

JEFFREY P. SCHLOSS is Distinguished Professor of Biology and Director, Center for Faith, Ethics and the Life Sciences at Westmont College. He received his doctoral training in Ecology and Evolutionary Biology from Washington University. He has taught at the University of Michigan and Wheaton College, and been a Danforth Fellow and Director of Biological Programs for the Global Stewardship Study Program. He has long-standing interests in the theological implications of evolutionary theory, particularly Darwinian accounts of morality, religion, and human purpose.

ROBERT J. VALENZA is Dengler-Dykema Professor of Mathematics and the Humanities at Claremont McKenna College, Claremont, California, where he has taught for twenty years. His primary academic interests are algebra, number theory, and metaphysics. He is author of *Linear Algebra: An Introduction to Abstract Mathematics,* coauthor of *Fourier Analysis on Number Fields,* and most recently editor of *The Best of Civilization,* an anthology of essays from one of his courses.

HOWARD J. VAN TILL is Professor Emeritus of Physics and Astronomy at Calvin College in Grand Rapids, Michigan. He earned his Ph.D. in physics from Michigan State University in 1965 and has research experience in millimeter-wave astronomy. Dr. Van Till has served on the Advisory Board of the John Templeton Foundation and is a member of the editorial boards of both *Science and Christian Belief* and *Theology and Science.* One of his books is *Portraits of Creation: Biblical and Scientific Perspectives on the World's Formation.*

# Introduction

JOHN B. COBB, JR.

## The Science/Religion Problematic

Today we are accustomed to think of scientific affirmations and religious beliefs as in tension, if not in strict opposition. The news media are full of accounts of a struggle over the teaching of evolution in public schools. It is important to realize that this tension has not been characteristic of the relation of science and religion through most of Western history.

For many centuries Christian teaching coexisted with the best science of the time. In the medieval period this was Aristotelian science, and the theology was well integrated with this science. Protestant theology adjusted rather easily to the new science of the seventeenth century. It did so based on the Cartesian dualism of matter and mind. Theologians accepted the mechanistic view of the physical world, while holding, along with most scientists, that the human world, the world of mind, was fundamentally different. Further, the mechanical character of the material world pointed, in the view of both scientists and theologians, to an external Maker.

This comfortable shared vision came under philosophical attack, in the late eighteenth century, from David Hume. Hume accepted the empiricist view, shared by most scientists, that the only source of knowledge of the world was sense experience. He then examined that experience closely and showed that ideas central to the sciences, especially that some events *cause* others to happen, were not justified. We have no sensory experience of such causality. The most that we can discover in our sense experience is regular, predictable repetition of succession. Whenever one type of event occurs, another follows.

This change of meaning of causality was problematic for science. Its acceptance would have been disastrous for the theology of that day, which depended on affirming a causal relation of creation between God and the

1

world. Obviously, this act of creation was totally unobservable and unrepeatable.

Immanuel Kant was deeply troubled by the implications for science of Hume's conclusions. He did not dispute Hume's accuracy, but he thought science required the notion of necessary causal efficacy. This notion, he decided, is provided by the human mind. We necessarily organize the phenomenal world, that is, the world as it appears to us through our sense organs, in terms of causal relations. But this enriched understanding of causality did not improve the situation for theology. Since this contribution of the human mind applied only to the phenomenal world, causality in Kant's sense was irrelevant to any possible relation between God and the world. The mechanical character that Kant believed necessarily characterized our understanding of the phenomenal world provided no reason for affirming a Creator. The human mind took over the creative role from God.

Unlike Hume, Kant remained interested in belief in God. He found reason for this belief in ethical experience. He argued that ethical experience provides warrant for affirming the reality of God, but he made it clear that this affirmation is fully disconnected from any scientific account of the world.

Kant thus substituted an epistemological dualism for the metaphysical dualism of Descartes. However, most people, including most scientists, especially in the English-speaking world, continued to think in terms of Cartesian dualism. They viewed science as the source of knowledge of a material world that operated on mechanical principles. It was composed entirely of matter in motion. The matter was usually understood as composed of atoms that changed only in their relative location. God was the creator of the atoms and provided the laws that governed their motion. Moral and religious concerns, on the other hand, belonged to a sphere that was metaphysically different, that of mind or spirit. Science and religious knowledge lived together happily.

It was Darwin's teaching of evolution that threatened this relation as a culturally satisfactory one. Evolution showed that human beings, including their minds, are part of the natural world. If this world is a machine, consisting entirely of matter in motion, then human beings are part of that machine. Our humanistic and religious ideas have no basis in reality.

At this point the *Kantian* dualism gained practical cultural importance. Kant had shown that science in fact deals only with the world of appearances or phenomena, which it necessarily interprets in mechanical ways. Hence, from the point of view of science, human beings, insofar as they are objects of sense experience, also belong to that machine. But since this is an account only of the phenomenal world, not the real or noumenal one, believers are free to posit God; and an analysis of ethical experience provides the warrant for doing so.

This Kantian dualism requires more sophisticated thinking than did the

Cartesian dualism that had been undercut by evolutionary thinking, and for many people it was not convincing. Hence many who were concerned about humanistic and religious values continued to oppose the new teaching. Some appealed to the Bible as a counterauthority to science, arguing that the creation of human beings was distinct from the creation of other species. Thus the warfare between science and some sections of the religious community began.

The mainline Protestant churches were not willing to participate in this "war." Accordingly, for the most part their leaders adopted some form of dualism influenced by Kant. A more readily accessible formulation, the distinction between fact and value, was called neo-Kantian. Some drew the dividing line between reason and faith, or between the natural and the supernatural. After the "linguistic turn" in philosophy, the distinction has sometimes been made in terms provided by Ludwig Wittgenstein: science is one "language game" and theology is another. Each language game has its own rules, and there is no conflict between them. The meaning of what is said in one language game does not affect the meaning of what is said in another. None of them can claim to describe a reality that is beyond or outside of language.

The universities were already structured around a dualistic understanding. They distinguished between the sciences and the humanities. In general the sciences were not influenced by the humanities, and the humanities paid little attention to the sciences. The study of religious phenomena and beliefs belonged to the humanities. Theology staked out a claim either within the humanities or in professional schools.

This new dualism reestablished peace between the leaders of the church and the scientific community. When proponents of less sophisticated forms of Christianity objected to the teaching of evolution, the leaders of the mainline churches came out in its support. This pattern continues even today. It is the basis on which traditional religious leaders join the scientific community in opposing the teaching of "creationism" and of "intelligent design" in the schools, and it is the basis on which the courts also reject it.

In 2006 a group of Christian clergy from many different traditions signed "An Open Letter concerning Religion and Science." They are troubled by the association of the church in the public mind with opposition to scientific teaching of evolution. Hence they conclude their letter as follows: "We urge school board members to preserve the integrity of the science curriculum by affirming the teaching of the theory of evolution as a core component of human knowledge. We ask that science remain science and that religion remain religion, two very different, but complementary, forms of truth."[1]

1. See http://www.uwosh.edu/colleges/cols/religion_science_collaboration.htm.

## Problems with the Dualistic Solution

However, with the passage of time the situation has become much less stable. It turns out to be rather difficult for scientists to formulate their views without implications for theology and for theologians to formulate theirs without implications for science. Further, the idea that this separation is the ideal solution is under siege from three directions.

First, many of the scientists who accepted the dualistic compromise so as to have a free hand in doing their work did not really believe that science dealt only with appearances, leaving beliefs about reality to others. Nor did they believe that what they learned about "facts" was irrelevant to what could reasonably be said about "values." The idea that they were playing one language game among several of equal status did not appeal to them. Some of them did not think there was a sphere of reality about which science had nothing to say.

Some of them have said quite vocally that scientific knowledge alone is reliable and that anything said about mind or spirit or values must be harmonious with it. Some have spelled out the implications of their scientific findings for these discussions. Among these, evolutionary biologists have often been very forceful. The synthesis of Darwinian evolution and Mendelian genetics that in this book we call "neo-Darwinism" accented the reductionist and deterministic character of evolutionary theory. Some of its advocates have strongly asserted both that science now shows that human beings are to be understood in these materialist terms and also that there is no other valid form of knowledge. A few of them have published their reductionist views of human beings in widely read books, forcing the public to deal with them. In chapter 17 David Griffin provides a detailed summary of their position.

Second, on the religious side, most conservative Christian communities have always assumed that their beliefs deal with the whole of reality. These beliefs include the doctrine of God's creation of the world as described in Genesis. Accordingly, from the first, there has been popular opposition to evolution. In the early twentieth century, largely in reaction to the acceptance of evolutionary science by the mainline churches, fundamentalism arose as a distinct movement within Protestantism. It rigidified the most conservative Protestant views of the Bible. Today, what were then the "mainline" Protestant denominations have lost membership and public status, so that their support of the freedom of science has diminishing effect. Groups that were once on the margin are now the mainstream of Protestantism. It is their voice that dominates the presentation of Christianity in the media. Some of them have sought and gained political power. Between this rigidly biblicist Protestantism and strict neo-Darwinism, no compromise is possible.

Also, even within the denominations that are committed to the freedom of science, many are uncomfortable with the dualistic understanding. The theology that leaves the natural world out of its scope altogether seems seriously truncated. The teaching of this theology has contributed to the neglect of nature that allowed the ecological crisis to intensify unnoticed. It has also contributed to the general loss of strength of these denominations. Further, some members of these churches who are accustomed to respect the thinking of scientists are impressed by the negative implications of neo-Darwinism for traditional Christian teaching and values and feel the need to rethink their faith, if not to abandon it altogether, in light of these assaults. Simply declaring that science is irrelevant to theology does not suffice.

Third, dualisms are difficult to justify philosophically. Despite the continuing influence of Kant, few fully accept his interpretation of either science or ethics. The simpler dualisms formulated later are even harder to maintain under close examination. For example, it seems that our values are influenced by our factual beliefs. Indeed, there seem to be patterns of relationship among our beliefs in all spheres.

## Toward Integration

These difficulties with the *dualistic* solution have led to the question of whether a new *integration* between science and religious belief is possible. From the beginning, some religiously oriented thinkers argued that evolution could be interpreted as clarification of the way God works in the world. Some Protestants went on to speak of the evolution of religious understanding expressed in the Bible. Instead of interpreting biological evolution as showing that human beings should be understood in materialistic categories, some argued that the earlier stages of evolution should be interpreted in light of what we know of reality in our own experience. This line of thought was most effectively and influentially articulated several decades later in the writings of the Catholic paleontologist Teilhard de Chardin.

Teilhard was widely respected as a paleontologist, and some scientists have supported his proposal for integration of evolutionary science and religious faith. On the other hand, few scientists have seriously internalized his vision in such a way as to affect their research. On the religious side, the initial response was negative. Teilhard was not allowed to publish his speculative writings during his lifetime because of their challenge to normal Catholic teaching. However, they were published after his death and received enthusiastic support in many Catholic circles. They were influential in Vatican II, and they continue to have great influence both directly and through the work of Thomas Berry. However, today they have been marginalized in official Catholic teaching.

Despite this marginalization, Teilhard's efforts to find a synthesis have not been abandoned. This book is one of those that take up this task. Such a synthesis requires major adjustments both in theology and in the formulation of scientific theories — in this case, the theory of evolution. Since most religious people and most scientists are resistant to change, gaining support for integration of science and theology remains difficult. This book is intended to push this program forward. Since more of the needed revisionist work has already been done in theology than in the sciences, this book concentrates on the revision of scientific evolutionary theory.

The resistance to current teaching is elicited at three levels. One of these levels is biblicism. The first chapter of Genesis depicts God as creating the currently existing species separately in a brief period. Evolutionary theory shows that the present order arose gradually over hundreds of millions of years. No contributor to this book questions that evolutionary theory is correct on this central point. Those of us who are interested in the Bible have long since come to terms with its prescientific character.

The second level is the one most often mentioned. Evolutionary theory as typically presented today depicts human beings as part of a nature that is understood as machinelike. It is not possible to fit human freedom and responsibility into this picture. Traditional humanist and religious values are undercut. Many of the contributors to this book are concerned about this.

The third level is the relation of evolutionary teaching to belief in God. As normally presented, it systematically excludes God from any role in the course of worldly events. For some contributors to the volume this is a matter of primary importance. The systematic discussion of this question constitutes part IV of the book.

The writers contributing to this book are quite diverse. Nevertheless, none are either full-fledged neo-Darwinians or proponents of creationism or Intelligent Design. Some have no particular interest in the struggle between neo-Darwinism and the defenders of traditional humanistic and religious values. If they criticize neo-Darwinism, it is for reasons quite independent of this controversy. Most, however, are interested in the relation of science and religious faith, and the book is organized with this question in view.

This means that the book as a whole is a critique of neo-Darwinism and of the extent to which the dominant community of biologists describes evolution in its terms. The book is organized in such a way as to call for revisions in the now standard formulation of evolutionary theory. These revisions would account for evidence that the current theory neglects. It would also allow for integration with humanistic and religious concerns, including a role for God. The book suggests how such integration is possible without any distortion of the scientific evidence.

One danger in engaging in this project is that the views criticized will not be understood in their richness and full potential. It is easy to caricature what one opposes. To counteract this tendency, we are fortunate to have the participation of Francisco Ayala, a respected biologist. At my request he has contributed several essays giving creative expression to mainstream evolutionary thought. His scientific formulations, like those of most evolutionists, largely follow the theories that in this book are called "neo-Darwinian."

However, Ayala is not himself a neo-Darwinian in the full sense. He is, instead, an articulate representative of the dualism that to this day remains the basis of such peace as we have between science and religion in the United States. He is a Christian believer who is committed to the fundamental difference of the spheres in which science and faith operate. Accordingly, he sees no need for Christians to criticize the currently dominant formulations of evolutionary theory. Humanistic and religious concerns belong to a separate sphere and are, in his view, not affected by what is accepted as scientific truth. Accordingly, one role Ayala plays in this book is to remind us that it is quite possible to stand in the mainstream of current evolutionary thought and remain a committed Christian.

Ayala's contributions will enable readers who care about both science and faith to judge between two approaches: (1) Ayala's acceptance of the standard formulations of evolution, on the one side, and of Christian teaching, on the other, as reflecting two ways of knowing, and (2) an integrationist approach that requires revisions not only in theology but also in the formulation of scientific theory.

In saying this I have neglected an intermediate position that is today widely adopted. Ian Barbour has shown that in addition to the three positions I have identified — conflict, the mutual independence offered by Kantians, and full integration — there is a fourth: the possibility of dialogue.[2] This dialogue has been vigorously and effectively promoted by the Templeton Foundation. The advocates of dialogue typically emphasize the integrity of both science and the various theologies and then seek reformulations and adjustments that avoid conflict. For the most part the adjustments are on the side of theology, but the interests of religion may also give support to movements among scientists that are more congenial to the affirmation of religious values and insights.

2. Ian G. Barbour, *Nature, Human Nature, and God* (Minneapolis: Fortress, 2002).

The dialogue sometimes advances toward integration, but it can end in mutual respect not far removed from mutual independence.

The book as a whole makes no pretense to neutrality between these positions. It is directed toward the advancement of integration. That in no way excludes dialogue as a means, but it directs that dialogue toward integration. This differentiates the argument of this book from the mainstream dialogical emphasis of Martinez Hewlett and Ted Peters as expressed in their editorial in *Theology and Science*.[3] They "presume that the Darwinian model in its Neo-Darwinian form represents the best science" and move "from there to set this science into dialogue with theology." They recognize that this means the exclusion of purpose from the scientific explanation of evolution, and accordingly propose: "God has a purpose *for* nature, even if the methods of scientific research cannot discern purpose *within* nature." This allows theology and science to avoid conflict, but it does not move in the direction of integration.

The integration at which I as editor aim is not possible without overcoming the limitations imposed on contemporary teaching of evolution by the strong, continuing influence of neo-Darwinian theory. Some of the changes the book calls for can be viewed as supplementary to the currently dominant way of thinking or simply as further developments within it. Ayala's contributions already point in this direction. Fortunately, neither he nor the currently dominant thinking he represents so well is rigidly bound to all the elements of neo-Darwinism as described by Griffin in chapter 17. Most working biologists, like Ayala, are open to various modifications and developments.

The most encouraging recent development among thoughtful practitioners in evolutionary studies is the growing acceptance of the idea of emergence. It is increasingly recognized that genuinely new things emerge in the evolutionary process and cannot be accounted for in the categories appropriate to that from which they emerged. If evolution is presented to the public in this way, many of the negative implications of rigid neo-Darwinian formulations are overcome. This is currently the most promising integrationist way to deal with the controversy about public school education. That in the course of evolution new levels emerge can be accepted by many biologists, and this recognition opens the way to understanding human beings nonreductively. If this idea were clearly integrated into the teaching of evolution, its offense to humanists and religious people would greatly decline. For this reason, chapter 18 by Philip Clayton may be, practically speaking at least, the most important in the book.

However, the exact meaning of "emergence" is of great importance. Clay-

---

3. Martinez Hewlett and Ted Peters, "Who Sets the Evolution Agenda?" *Theology and Science,* March 2006, pp. 1-3.

ton describes the range of meanings and their implications. He points out that neo-Darwinists can accept some forms of emergent evolution. But when this acceptance leaves intact the materialistic metaphysics that comes to expression in most scientific formulations, the disconnect between evolutionary theory and the concerns of humanists and religious people remains. Although it may be possible to moderate the current controversy without dealing with the underlying philosophical question, the empirical discussion cannot finally be separated from the metaphysical one.

Accordingly, the book as a whole calls for more radical changes in the assumptions and habits of mind expressed in contemporary mainstream biology. Some of the essays emphasize phenomena, neglected by the currently dominant evolutionary theory, whose incorporation would significantly change the nature of the theory. Other essays deal directly with the philosophical assumptions needed for a more adequate theory. Some of us are convinced that the loosening and broadening of evolutionary theory, even though based on empirical evidence, require a challenge to the materialistic metaphysics that dominates most scientific thinking, including that in biology. The empirical and philosophical challenges go together in this book as a whole.

## Whitehead as Resource

The conference out of which this book has come was held in Claremont, California, in October 2004. It was organized by the Center for Process Studies and partially supported by a grant from Metanexus. The "process" thought that informs the work of the Center is primarily the philosophy of Alfred North Whitehead, a mathematical physicist who believed that both the materialistic and the dualistic metaphysics that continue to pervade Western science are seriously misleading. He proposed a metaphysics of organic events. The Center for Process Studies has investigated the adequacy of this different metaphysics in a variety of fields, in this case evolutionary thought.

We view "energy" as pointing more helpfully to what is basic in the physical world than "matter," and we think that the units of energy are events rather than objects. Accordingly, instead of viewing the units of physical reality as tiny lumps of matter that act on one another only from without, we emphasize the advantages of understanding them as momentary happenings or energy events, largely constituted by their relations with events in their past. They are interrelated occurrences of energy rather than self-contained material atoms. Whereas the individual entities posited by the metaphysics underlying neo-Darwinian theory are bits of matter affected only by external physical forces, the energy events posited by process metaphysics are affected internally by their environments.

This idea of internal relations leads to viewing the world with a different set of glasses. For example, the common depiction of genes in neo-Darwinian literature as largely unaffected by their environment arouses immediate skepticism. One looks instead for evidence of environmental influences. One calls attention to the fact that genes function differently according to their location in the sequence and to their relation to other genes. One expects interaction between DNA, RNA, and proteins. One looks for ways in which the condition and activity of the cell as a whole affect the genes, and one also examines how the cell is affected by its relation to other cells. The idea that genetic changes are entirely random, in a sense that denies the relevance of the local environment of the genes, is difficult to swallow. Of course, the amount and importance of the influence of the immediate environment in comparison with such things as cosmic rays or quantum effects is an empirical question, so that a process thinker must be open to the possibility that it is negligible. But reluctance to make this judgment leads to examining some forms of evidence with greater care than is characteristic of those who are committed to the view that all mutations are random.

The doctrine of internal relations is connected with an emphasis on subjectivity. In the moment of their happening, all energy events are subjects in the sense that they are acted upon and also act. The act is their self-organization out of their contexts for the sake of realizing some value in themselves and in future occasions. In this sense they are purposive, and together they constitute the world as aiming at increasing value. The vast majority of these events make up the solids, liquids, gases, and plasmas that constitute the inanimate physical world; others make up living organisms; and a few, made possible by central nervous systems, include conscious feeling and even thought.

In this philosophical vision, the emphasis is on the flux. As soon as an energy event has occurred, it becomes an object for subsequent events. It participates as a datum in the self-constitution of new energy events out of such past subjects. From the point of view offered by this understanding of reality, any science that totally excludes subjectivity and purpose from its consideration cannot fully account for its data. This is especially true for biology, which deals with creatures, beginning with unicellular organisms, in which subjectivity and nonconscious purpose play a significant role.

The implication of this position is quite radical. From this point of view a science that fails to acknowledge any role for subjectivity and purpose can provide only a partial explanation of its data. One response would be for science to acknowledge that it gives only a partial explanation of natural events. The alternative is for science to expand in such a way that it includes, for example, the feelings and purposes of animals in its explanatory account of animal behavior. If in fact such feelings and purposes influence animal behavior, as most people actually believe, then an account of behavior that leaves these out cannot be complete. And if animal behavior affects the evolutionary process, as many of us believe, then the way in which evolution is now explained needs to be subsumed in a more inclusive account. A number of the essays in this volume point in this direction. I develop this argument systematically in chapter 14.

This change would be of profound importance for the relation of evolutionary theory and theology — even if the question of God were omitted. However, some of the writers in this book are keenly interested in the integration of theism with evolutionary theory, and once the subjectivity and purposes of creatures are acknowledged as contributing to evolution, new possibilities for such integration arise. The idea that creaturely aims at the realization of value are influenced by a divine aim at the realization of value need not imply an intervention by God in any sense that violates the natural order. The issue is, instead, the character of the natural order. This order, in Whiteheadian perspective, grounds the spontaneity and the self-organization of creatures, on the one side, and the restrictions on creaturely behavior identified by what are called physical constants and the "laws" of nature, on the other. It also leads over time to the actualization of such value as the physical conditions allow.

## Teaching Evolution in Public Schools

Whitehead's comments on evolution were made seventy to eighty years ago. Hence the proposals for relating theism and evolution sketched above and developed later in this book were formulated with no thought of the contemporary debate about the teaching of evolution in the public schools. A word about the implications of process thought for that debate is in order.

We process thinkers find the established position somewhat difficult. That position is that the public schools should not promote any religious views. This makes good sense for those who accept some form of Kantian dualism. If science is taught simply as the only account possible of the phenomena with the additional clarification that it does not tell us anything about what is truly real, the noumenal world, then religious issues can be seen as untouched by science. But process thought does not separate the phenomenal (that which appears in sensory experience) and the noumenal (that which is real in itself) in this way. Similarly, if people believe that facts are value free, then schools can teach facts while avoiding any implications about values. The latter are left to the home and religious institutions. Process thought denies that fact and value can be separated in this way. From the perspective of process thinkers, no education can be completely neutral on all religiously important matters.

Nevertheless, there is practical wisdom in the commitment to keep religious instruction out of public education. It is also important that historical and scientific facts and well-established theories be taught as honestly and accurately as possible even if they conflict with the teaching of one religious community or another. Any attempt by a religious community to slant public school teaching in a way favorable to its particular teaching must be resisted. The need for such resistance was clear in regard to "creationism."

In the current cultural situation, "Intelligent Design" appears to many as a fallback position for "creationists." Accordingly, many oppose teaching it in the public schools on the same grounds. Even though its appeal to empirical facts is far more responsible than that of the creationists, its claim to be scientific is highly questionable and is rejected by the great majority of scientists. Its specific arguments have not stood up well under close scientific examination. None of the participants in the conference that produced this book support the introduction of this theory into the public schools. Even some proponents of the theory oppose this political move.

Nevertheless, process thinkers are sympathetic with the concerns of conservative Christians about how evolution is taught in the public schools. We agree that schools should avoid teaching that evolution shows signs of being directed or guided by an intelligent purpose. Theories adequate for science can be provided that do not make statements favorable to theism, and public school teaching should stop with these. But this does not mean that we approve teaching that says or implies that the evolutionary process is wholly undirected and purposeless. It is as important to exclude antitheistic teaching as theistic teaching.

This is more difficult because the systematic exclusion of God from any role in the course of events has characterized the goal of the scientific community for a long time. For many scientists it is part of science, precisely that science they claim should determine what is taught in the public schools. A major thesis of this book is that this radical denial of any role for God in the course of events is the consequence of the metaphysics with which science has been so closely associated rather than any requirement of science as such. It is the metaphysics and not the empirical facts that leads to the conclusion that the evolutionary process is directionless and to the widespread tendency of scientific formulations to support metaphysical materialism and reductionism.

Many of the contributors to this book affirm a theistic interpretation of evolution. This means that when we separate the theoretical issue from the practical one about what is to be taught in public schools, we should engage the advocates of Intelligent Design as serious conversation partners. We do have areas of agreement. For example, both process theologians and advocates of Intelligent Design view the current neo-Darwinian orthodoxy as inadequate to account for all the data and hold that a divine intelligence affects the course of events. Also, for both, the negative implications of neo-Darwinian teaching for religious faith are important considerations.

Nevertheless, there are also differences. Whiteheadians do not like the idea of "design." The course of events has been far too chaotic for this term to ring true. "Design" suggests that the realization of certain patterns is predetermined. A Whiteheadian sees a large role for contingency as to what patterns are realized. Contingency arises, as neo-Darwinians rightly note, in gene mutation, but also from the intersection of various chains of events and from creaturely decisions. The outcome is not built into either the intentions of a designer or the inevitable outworking of mechanical forces.

Advocates of Intelligent Design tend to accept some phenomena as mechanistically explained while arguing that others cannot be. This leads toward a view of "a God of the gaps" — a God whose actions are "supernatural." Whiteheadians also use examples that seem most strongly to call for explanations other than the neo-Darwinian one, but the point is to offer a different approach to the whole explanatory process. In our view God is present and active everywhere. We see this activity as part of the natural order. There is no "nature" from which God is absent. God is a factor in all complete explanations of natural events.

Although only Ayala's and Griffin's essays comment directly on the contemporary discussion of what should be taught in public schools, the book as a whole does have implications for this important, practical question. I will state my own conclusions. We should teach biology as a whole, and evolutionary theory in particular, with a clear recognition that living creatures are subjects with their own feelings and purposes. These organisms affect their environments and are affected by them. Genetic changes take place in this context, so that the environment that selects the mutations that survive is affected by the organisms among which it selects. Evolution understood in this way is one in which emergence is a prominent feature. Ultimately it is better understood as resulting from the interaction of subjects rather than only as the emergence of new patterns of matter. Locating human beings within this context is neither demeaning nor reductionistic.

Presenting evolution in some such way would leave the question of theism and atheism quite open. The process can be presented descriptively without raising the question of the deepest causes of its remarkable characteristics. This account would include an emphasis on random mutation of genes and show the role played by such mutations in the generation of complex patterns of order. But it would discuss other contributors to the evolutionary process as well.

In contexts other than the public schools, atheists could describe the process as self-contained and self-explanatory and either maintain or deny humanistic values as they wish. They need not ask questions about the source of novelty or the order that grounds this process. But theists would be free to ask these additional questions and to propose a plausible answer that would not be disconnected with what people learned in their biology classes at school.

## The Organization of the Book

The book is organized in four parts along with an important appendix. Part I provides background material. It is unwise to plunge into the work of resolving the problem of evolution and theology without some knowledge of the history of this discussion and of the positions taken on the topic in recent times. John Greene provides the requisite account. Greene writes as one convinced that a fairly traditional theology can be reconciled with the facts of evolution.

It is also unwise to plunge into criticism of the currently dominant formulation of evolutionary theory without understanding it well. The second chapter is a revised and expanded version of the paper Ayala delivered at the Claremont conference. It well represents the views of those mainstream evolutionists who are also open to allowing a parallel place for humanists and religious thinkers.

To ensure that the contemporary mainstream evolutionary thinking of active biologists is well understood by readers of this book, I requested that Ayala take a larger role in the volume. I suggested that he write responses to some of the critical essays, especially where he felt criticisms misrepresented standard biological teaching or could easily be taken into account within it. He chose not to engage in direct discussion with individual authors. But he generously agreed to contribute additional material that did express how mainstream biologists can and do understand many of the issues treated in this book. Implicitly he does respond to some of the subsequent critique. Two additional chapters in part I are of this sort, as are two chapters in part II.

The reader of these additional essays by Ayala might wonder what all the fuss is about. Surely sensible religious people do not wish to interfere with biologists exploring these frontiers! Certainly none of the contributors to this book have such a wish. However, many mainstream spokespersons for evolutionary biology draw conclusions from it that are deeply disturbing not only to religious people but also to humanists generally.

Part I concludes with an essay by Jeffrey Schloss that examines the neo-Darwinist literature. Much of it makes fully explicit the challenge to religious and humanistic values that many draw from the biological theories. He makes it clear that much of the widespread interpretation of evolution is based on neo-Darwinian theory that is in deep tension with theistic faith. He points suggestively to doctrines commonly associated with neo-Darwinism that remain controversial among biologists, suggesting that a different take on the data could lead to conclusions that are not so antithetical to theistic beliefs.

Schloss's formulation of the tension between humanistic values and neo-Darwinian evolutionists is mild compared to that of some neo-Darwinians. Schloss drew my attention to the following statement near the beginning of a recent article in a leading journal on the philosophy of biology.

> Darwinism thus puts the capstone on a process which since Newton's time has driven teleology to the explanatory sidelines. In short it has made the Darwinians into metaphysical nihilists denying that there is any meaning or purpose to the universe, its contents and its cosmic history. But in making Darwinians into metaphysical nihilists, the solvent algorithm should have made them into ethical nihilists too. For intrinsic values and obligations make sense only against the background of purposes, goals, and ends which are not merely instrumental.[4]

Part II turns from exposition of the past discussion and the current mainstream to those who believe that this mainstream is still too narrow. A. Y. Gunter identifies six topics where research calls for broadening or modifying mainstream theory. Three of them have to do with setting biological evolution in a wider context and bringing other sciences to bear in its explanation. In the succeeding chapter Dorion Sagan discusses one of these: thermodynamics. The third approach is from quantum theory, and Gunter discusses this more fully than the other two. Since chemistry is a kind of bridge between physics and biology, Reg Morrison contributes a brief piece on that topic.

Gunter's other three topics focus on types of biological occurrences that some believe contribute significantly to the evolutionary process but which they see as inadequately incorporated into mainstream theory. Of these, evidences for neo-Lamarckian evolution are discussed only by Gunter. Symbiogenesis is treated at some length in a chapter by Lynn Margulis and Sagan, and Ayala provides an account of the Baldwin effect. Margulis also pro-

---

4. Tamler Sommers and Alex Rosenberg, "Darwin's Nihilistic Idea: Evolution and the Meaninglessness of Life," *Biology and Philosophy* 18 (2003): 653-58 (653).

vides a chapter on the Gaia hypothesis, and Ayala argues that so-called punctuated equilibrium makes little difference for basic theory.

In his chapter on the Baldwin effect, Ayala affirms that it is well established, but he believes it has already been adequately integrated into an expanded neo-Darwinism. Barbour's essay, somewhat like Gunter's, surveys developments in biology that are in tension with neo-Darwinism. He includes the Baldwin effect, and his discussion brings out features that would be more difficult to incorporate within neo-Darwinism. I offer a concluding chapter to part II, trying to put together some of the implications of what has been said by others in the context of Whitehead's philosophy. Overall, the reader is given the opportunity to consider the possible validity and relevance of a variety of reflections about evolution, the full incorporation of which would certainly change the way the story is told.

Part III is a collection of essays that focuses on the limiting consequences of the worldview or metaphysics that neo-Darwinism shares with most science. Charles Birch as a biologist has taught evolution in terms of the standard theories of the biological community. These are largely shaped by neo-Darwinism. But he is troubled by its implication that human beings are zombies. If science can, in principle, explain human behavior exhaustively without referring to subjectivity, then it seems that such subjectivity is irrelevant to what goes on. Birch believes that science should acknowledge the reality and efficacy of subjectivity.

Robert Valenza approaches this same issue as mathematician-physicist-philosopher. He offers a sustained argument as to the necessary incompleteness of any account of reality that omits subjects. The fully developed argument may prove too demanding for many readers of this book, though it should have particular importance for philosophers. It constitutes the appendix. However, the basic theses are stated succinctly and accessibly in a short article included in the body of the work.

Griffin provides a detailed and systematic analysis of the philosophical assumptions that neo-Darwinists share with many other scientists. It is these assumptions more than their specific scientific statements that lead to the conflict between their theoretical formulations and humanistic and religious concerns. He shows that although some of these commitments were present already in Darwin, they are more fully and rigidly developed in neo-Darwinism.

An essay by Clayton on emergence concludes this part. I have noted already that this holds special promise for easing the tensions with regard to teaching in public schools. Even if, currently, most biologists took only a few steps into emergence thinking, these steps would open the door to discussions with humanists and religious thinkers that could have a very different character from the current confrontation.

That a thoroughgoing neo-Darwinism excludes God from any role in evolution is one of the reasons for objecting to it. Part IV deals directly with this question. Can a scientific account of the world be incorporated into a theistic one? What difference, if any, will this make to the scientific formulations?

For John Haught and Jeffrey Schloss the primary question for this is whether the evolutionary process reveals any trends or tendencies. Haught shows that if we view matters on a sufficiently broad scale, the trends are inescapable. However, he seems little concerned whether this can be shown for biological evolution. Philip Clayton has recently commented that "theism *should* lead us to expect order in physics, directionality in biology, and moral responsibility in the social sciences."[5] Schloss contributes a technical biological study arguing that there is evidence of such trends. Both judge that these trends show, or at least allow us to affirm, that divine purpose is at work in the world.

Neither Haught nor Schloss says much about the way God's purpose affects events in the world. Howard Van Till tells how, as an evangelical Christian, he developed a theory that was too close to deism. Griffin showed him how, with reasonable adjustments, he could move toward a fuller theism. Griffin provides a detailed account of how Whitehead's philosophy explains the role of God in the world. I conclude with some Whiteheadian remarks of my own on how God influences events in the world.

Participants in the conference generally felt that the papers presented were very rich, but also that a significant book could not be simply a collection of these essays. If the conference had a distinctive contribution to make, it would be to introduce a Whiteheadian voice into the present discussion of evolution and religion. The papers could contribute to this goal only if the editor took a strong hand in organizing the book. I have accepted this responsibility and, accordingly, have gone beyond the usual editorial role.

To make the material more comprehensive I have invited contributions from Ayala, Morrison, and Clayton that were not part of the conference. I have also arranged the papers into a sequence that enables me to make my argument, and I have added my own materials in order to do so. I have written not only this introduction to the book as a whole, but also essays at the ends of parts II and IV. I have also written introductions to each of the four parts clarifying how it contributes to the argument of the book as a whole.

My contribution is not, regrettably, based on extensive knowledge of biology or on intensive research into evolution. I am viewing the discussion at the conference and in these chapters from the perspective of one biased by the in-

---

5. Philip Clayton, "Biology, Directionality, and God: Getting Clear on the Stakes for Religion-Science Discussion," *Theology and Science* 4, no. 2 (2006): 123.

fluence of Whitehead to see interaction among organisms rather than only the changing positions of bits of inert matter. Accordingly, my comments throughout are heavily dependent on the other contributors to this volume.

I have not, of course, altered the formulations of any of the contributors. I certainly do not intend by my editorial intervention to detract from the diversity of beliefs and arguments of the individual contributors, not all of whom agree with my views, and thus with the conclusions I draw from the whole corpus of writings. I hope that this emphatic statement of my editorial purposes will safeguard the integrity of each contribution, distinguishing it from the use I have made of it in the volume as a whole. But I do intend to provide the reader with a clear indication of the way a theistic evolutionary theory can be coherently developed from a Whiteheadian point of view — a theory that takes account both of the extensive evidence rightly cited in favor of the now standard formulation of evolution and also of the limitations of this theory that are highlighted by its critics.

I have given a great deal of time to developing the conference papers into a book because of my conviction that there is nothing in the empirical evidence for evolutionary theory that requires those now dominant theoretical interpretations that are hostile to humanistic and religious convictions. I am convinced that a shift from Cartesian and Kantian thinking to Whiteheadian thinking could resolve many current problems. The result would be a better biology, in strictly scientific terms, as well as one that is fully open to humanistic and religious insights.

# I | BACKGROUND MATERIALS

# Editor's Preface

The debate about evolution has been going on since the late nineteenth century. One portion of this debate has been about whether there has been any such thing. However, for some time now it has been difficult for most of those who have investigated the evidence to take this debate seriously. The fact of evolution is not seriously doubted by those who approach the evidence with an open mind. All participants in this book are convinced evolutionists.

Nevertheless, a serious and worthwhile debate continues. What does the fact that human beings have evolved from other species over aeons of time say about matters of human and religious importance today? Scientific developments in evolutionary theory have changed the landscape somewhat, but the basic issues remain much the same. The range of answers given a century ago does not differ drastically from the range given today. Our current reflection will be enriched by awareness of the past.

John Greene has studied the history of this conversation and has been personally involved in it. He writes as a theist who does not think that what we know scientifically requires drastic revision in traditional thinking about God. His personal views, no doubt, influence his selection of historical material, but he presents this in a way that allows readers to draw their own conclusions. Overall his account is supportive of us Whiteheadians in our desire to achieve an integrated account of evolutionary science and religious beliefs and even in the way we go about it. On the other hand, Greene thinks we modify traditional teaching about God too much. I believe that a full integration of evolutionary theory and traditional Christian theology requires quite drastic changes in both.

For those who want to be faithful to the needs of science while maintaining human and religious values, the alternative to changing science and religious belief is to keep science and theology in quite separate compartments.

Francisco Ayala adopts this dualistic (or pluralistic) view. In the introduction to the book, I emphasized that dualism has been the chief way in which peace has been achieved in Western cultures. It remains an important strategy today.

Adopting the post-Kantian version of dualism allows Ayala to stand squarely in the dominant tradition within the community of evolutionary biologists. In chapter 2 he lays out the standard doctrine clearly and succinctly. He does not flinch at its reduction of humanity to matter in motion, a reduction that is responsible for much of the concern of humanists and theologians. By this he means chiefly that science should view the world only objectively, and that the categories appropriate for this objective description suffice for understanding everything. For him, however, this comprehensiveness of science does not preclude other ways of knowing, and when ethical, aesthetic, and religious questions are in view, these other ways come into play. However, Ayala is convinced that they do not, and should not, affect scientific research or theories or imply that there are any aspects of reality that are off-limits to scientific inquiry.

At the conference Ayala heard many criticisms of the standard scientific formulations. Even those he could take seriously tended, in his view, to abstract from the thinking of evolutionary biologists to such a degree that their actual thinking and practice were misrepresented. His lecture at the conference did little to alleviate that situation. Accordingly, at my request, he has revised and expanded that lecture and also prepared additional papers.

One of the reasons biologists do not recognize themselves when their views are described and criticized by philosophers and theologians is that they find themselves labeled, also in this book, as "neo-Darwinists." Ayala explains that they use this term only for a position developed a century or more ago. It is not a label biologists now apply to themselves. That I have chosen, anyway, to use the term indicates a difference between the typical interests of biologists, on the one side, and philosophers and theologians, on the other.

From the point of view of the latter, most biologists today, even those who belong to diverse schools of thought and differ on many points, work out of the tradition that was initiated as neo-Darwinism. It was a new form of Darwinism with greater explanatory power. Darwin had emphasized natural selection among organisms. By synthesizing natural selection with Mendel's work on genes, the new Darwinism was able to explain the changes in the organisms among which nature selected. Their differences were then seen to result from random mutation of genes.

Because the philosophical and theological issues raised by Darwin are sharpened by this move, and still more by the way the resulting theory has usually been formulated by many biologists, for philosophical and theological purposes the label remains useful. In chapter 17 David Griffin provides a detailed analysis and criticism of the philosophical assumptions characteristic of many thinkers in this tradition. But it is important to recognize that the assumptions he identifies are rarely thematized by working biologists, and that many of them do not draw from these assumptions the consequences that are so controversial among philosophers and theologians.

This is true in Ayala's own case. Early in chapter 2 he states that the central importance of Darwin is that he showed that human beings are part of the world studied by natural science, a world composed of matter in motion. This appears to affirm a straightforward metaphysical position that is offensive to many philosophers and theologians. However, Ayala does not draw these conclusions. First, in a footnote he makes it clear that his use of the word "matter" does not have all the meanings that philosophers and theologians find in it. Secondly, he distinguishes his materialism as methodological rather than ontological or epistemological. And thirdly, he emphasizes that there are other ways of knowing about reality besides science. The neo-Darwinism criticized by David Griffin includes none of these qualifications. If they were fully articulated in the typical presentations of evolution by biologists, and if these biologists drew out the implications of these qualifications, the current controversy might lose much of its intensity. The currently heated debate about the teaching of evolution might be transformed into a more thoughtful discussion of the best formulations of the theory.

That discussion would remain important, however, and most of this book is devoted to it. Ayala's own formulations indicate why more such discussion is needed. In the section entitled "Natural Selection and Mutation" we find a statement that expresses standard neo-Darwinian explanations of evolution. "The variables determining which direction it will go are the environment, the preexisting constitution of the organisms, and the randomly arising mutations." A number of contributors to this volume disagree that evolution can be adequately described in this way. I am one of these, and I have developed my Whiteheadian alternative theory in relation to this statement, arguing that the activity of organisms is an additional variable that is not reducible to the three Ayala identifies.

Much of the disagreement is moderated by Ayala's next paragraph, which begins: "The process of mutation that provides the raw materials for natural selection is now known to be much more complex than it was thought a few decades ago." He then provides a remarkable list of ways in which genomes are changed. He asserts that "full genomes may be acquired, even within a preexisting genome," and that "lateral transfer of genes among distantly related organisms went on for millions and millions of years." One wonders whether these phenomena can properly be understood as examples of "randomly arising mutations." Does there not come a time when the standard language of the neo-Darwinian account should be modified? Perhaps the third variable determining the direction the process takes could then simply be called "genetic change." This would leave the theory open for discussion of the respective roles of the acquisition of genes and genomes by lateral transfer, on the one hand, and random mutation, on the other. The work and theories of Lynn Margulis would no longer be marginalized.

That Ayala does not envision such a level playing field is indicated by the fact that his discussion of what is meant by randomness, which follows this paragraph, has in view only mutations in the ordinary sense. The other forms of genetic change, so comprehensively identified, play no further role. The advocates of their importance in the evolutionary process, including the authors of some of the later chapters, cannot be satisfied. To them it appears that the mainstream of biology, here represented by Ayala, is still too heavily shaped in its standard formulations and arguments by neo-Darwinism. The critical discussions in the later parts of the book are still needed.

The relation of mainstream evolutionary theory and neo-Darwinian orthodoxy is similar at other points. The "central dogma" of that orthodoxy was that genes are not affected by their environment, specifically that, while DNA affected RNA, there can be no influence the other way. In a footnote Ayala points out that exceptions to this "dogma" have been demonstrated. Also, in the paragraph describing the many forms of genetic change he lists several that indicate that genes are affected by their environment. He returns to this in an essay on the Baldwin effect in part II.

From the point of view of process philosophy, one of the main problems with materialism is that it treats causality as unidirectional. Although neo-Darwinian biologists recognize complex interactions among the entities they study, the influence of materialism on their thought leads them to neglect these interactions in their typical formulations. They know that what happens at the level of organisms affects both the environment and the genes, directly or indirectly, but Ayala's formulation, quoted above, speaks only of the one-way effects of genes and environment on organisms. Everything else is treated as negligible. I will take up this discussion in chapter 14.

Some who do study the effects of organismic actions on the environment judge that some of these actions express animal intelligence and purpose so that the subjectivity of animals also plays a role in the evolutionary process. If so, there may be a problem about holding that animals, including human ones, are adequately understood, even for scientific purposes, as matter in motion. Ayala's dualism of approaches to knowledge does not answer all the questions that can be asked about the place of subjective experience in nature.

As editor of this volume, I am pointing out these possible limitations in Ayala's formulations because I hope the accurate, comprehensive, engaging, informative, and largely convincing accounts he provides in this part will not lead the reader to think that all the more critical discussants are arguing with a straw man. Certainly, some of them have in view less careful and nuanced presentations of mainstream theories of evolution than what Ayala gives us here. But his position, too, calls for debate.

In chapter 3 Ayala explains the mainstream view of reductionism and other topics discussed by critics. His explanations do not end the discussion, but they should help prevent readers from supposing that mainstream biologists are rigidly committed to all the positions attributed to neo-Darwinism in later chapters. They are aware of many of the issues raised in these chapters and have responded to them. Although Ayala does not reply directly to what critics of neo-Darwinism say in subsequent parts of this book, readers are encouraged to review his comments when the same topics are discussed from a more critical point of view.

Chapter 4 describes current frontiers in biological research, the results of which may lead to further revisions of theory. They show that mainstream biologists are fully open to expanding the boundaries of research in many directions. These chapters make richly rewarding reading quite independently of the arguments developed in this book.

Most of the authors in parts II and III are aware of the considerable degree of variety and fluidity among mainstream evolutionary biologists. As Ayala points out, few of these identify themselves as neo-Darwinist. Criticisms of neo-Darwinism, therefore, are not necessarily criticisms of mainstream biology. Reading these essays by Ayala enhances this understanding. It shows the rich potential of the dominant community to respond to many new developments flexibly.

On the other hand, it is unlikely that the revisions to which Ayala is open will give a significant role to many of the alternatives discussed in part II. His essay there on punctuated equilibrium displays his tendency to minimize the significance of such features of the evolutionary record as its large gaps and relatively abrupt changes. It is even less likely that his flexibility will extend to changing his view of science to take account of subjects as well as objects. It is interesting that when he deals with the Baldwin effect in part II, he describes it in a way that omits any reference to the subjectivity, or even the activity, of the animals involved.

Accordingly, reading his essays confirms the influence of what we are calling "neo-Darwinism" in Ayala's work and in the dominant community of biologists he represents. On the scientific side, despite his awareness of the complexity of the actual situation, he modifies very little the view that natural selection among randomly mutated genes is a sufficient explanation of evolution. Like the neo-Darwinists, he seems to take the Cartesian picture of nature as an inherent part of science itself, so that he does not seriously consider metaphysical revision. Accordingly, many of the criticisms of neo-Darwinism in succeeding chapters do challenge Ayala, and through him, contemporary mainstream biology as well.

What Ayala writes here also makes clear that he is quite capable of responding thoughtfully to all such challenges. This book does not do justice to the full scope of such responses. Its role and purpose is to develop a Whiteheadian alternative to the presently dominant form of evolutionary theory. I deeply appreciate Ayala's willingness to participate as dialogue partner in a one-sided enterprise in which I, as editor, have the last word.

Finally, it is important to remember in reading these chapters by Ayala, and especially chapter 2, that his neo-Darwinian science does not involve him in the implications that Jeffrey Schloss draws in chapter 5 and David Griffin, in chapter 17, from the standard neo-Darwinian position. He does not consider science as the only, or even necessarily the most important, way to understand the world in which we live. He does not treat ethical, aesthetic, and religious values reductively. Instead he treats them as valid alternative ways of approaching life and the world. This is his chief difference from the full-fledged neo-Darwinists, an extremely important one for those with humanistic and religious interests.

However, this book is not about Ayala's irenic and generous views, but about those we call neo-Darwinist, which continue to dominate the discussion from the side of biology. It is these teachings that arouse the concerns of many of the contributors to this book. Chapter 5 brings us back to these issues. Some of the assumptions widely held by mainstream working biologists, and accepted by Ayala as part of biology, seem to have implications for the understanding of human beings that are disturbing to many religious and humanistic persons.

Some of the most articulate biologists have gone to great lengths to draw out these implications and to insist that the general public take account of them. Much of the opposition to neo-Darwinism has been evoked by this literature. Schloss surveys the issues raised in this literature, especially those that arise from particular, widely held biological theories. He makes it clear that the general public has a stake, indeed, an enormous stake, in debates about biological theories.

# 1. *Balfour versus Huxley on Evolutionary Naturalism: A Twenty-First-Century Perspective*

JOHN GREENE

## The Balfour-Huxley Debate

In 1895 Arthur James Balfour, a philosophically trained Scottish politician-statesman then serving as chancellor of the exchequer, published a book entitled *Foundations of Belief: Being Notes Introductory to the Study of Theology* containing a searching criticism of the evolutionary naturalism that Thomas Henry Huxley had labeled "scientific naturalism." The naturalism underlying positivism, agnosticism, and empiricism, Balfour argued, rested on two grounds: (1) it reduced human experience to sense perception with the result that the only knowledge available to human beings was knowledge of phenomena, the things that appear to our senses, and the laws connecting them; and (2) it viewed human nature in all its aspects as a product of natural processes — that and nothing more. (Balfour clearly had in mind not evolutionary theories in general but Darwin's attempt in *The Descent of Man* to view the whole of human nature as a product of natural and sexual selection.) The first of these assertions Balfour had dealt with in an earlier book, *A Defence of Philosophic Doubt* (1879), purporting to show that the picture of nature depicted by the physical science of his day — a world of colorless, tasteless, soundless vibrating atoms acted on by forces — could no more be perceived or correctly imagined than the deity represented to humankind by theologians. In both cases, said Balfour, we must content ourselves with symbolic images. "There is not a single particle of matter that we can perceive or picture to ourselves as it really exists." The reconciliation of science and religion, therefore, was to be achieved, not by setting up the logic, method, and findings of science as the test of religious truth, but by recognizing that both science and theology were systems of belief resting ultimately on faith and that both were forced to represent to the human imagination in anthropomorphic language an ultimate reality transcending the power of human reason to grasp fully.[1]

As to naturalism's second assertion — that human nature in all its aspects is a product of natural laws and processes — Balfour argued that this view deprived the basic values of Western civilization, values shared by Darwin, Huxley, and Balfour himself, of any rational justification. Reason became a mere instrument for survival; the passion for truth an emotion with no foundation in the nature of things; art and aesthetics mere by-products of the machinery of nature; morality a matter of natural appetites; self-condemnation, repentance, and remorse emotions without any reasonable foundation.[2] Huxley might rhapsodize about the liberally educated man as "one who is full of life and fire, whose passions are trained to come to heel by a vigorous will, the servant of a tender conscience; who has learned to love all beauty, whether of nature or of art, to hate all vileness, and to respect others as himself," but where was there place for these moral and aesthetic intuitions in Huxley's "web and woof of matter and force interweaving by slow degrees, without a broken thread, that veil [of sense impressions] which lies between us and the Infinite, that universe which alone we know or can know"?[3] The exalted values of the champions of naturalism, Balfour perceived, were derived from conceptions of reality and the place of humans in it that were totally incompatible with the picture of the universe they professed to draw from science.

This "inner discord" between the values and intuitions associated with traditional conceptions of nature, man, and God and the implications of an evolutionary naturalism claiming the sanction of science, Balfour predicted, would be resolved in one of two ways. Either evolutionary naturalism would be abandoned in favor of a philosophical and religious view of reality that recognized the essential similarity of the scientific and theological ways of picturing reality and the need to postulate a rational Author of nature as the source of the order, beauty, and goodness in the world, or Western culture would descend to a level consistent with Huxley's depiction of nature as "a realm of matter and law . . . co-extensive with knowledge, with feeling, and with action."[4]

1. Arthur J. Balfour, *A Defence of Philosophic Doubt: Being an Essay on the Foundations of Belief* (London: Hodder and Stoughton, 1926), p. 245. Original edition 1879.

2. Arthur J. Balfour, *Foundations of Belief: Being Notes Introductory to the Study of Theology*, 8th ed. (London, New York, and Toronto: Longmans, Green, 1933), p. 27. Original edition 1895.

3. "A Liberal Education" (1878), in *Selections from the Essays of Thomas Henry Huxley*, ed. A. Castell (New York: Appleton-Century-Crofts, 1948), p. 18; Huxley, "The Origin of Species" (1860), p. 58.

4. "The Physical Basis of Life" (1868), in *Selections from the Essays of Thomas Henry Huxley*, p. 21.

Huxley, combating an illness that would end his life in that very year, mustered strength to reply to Balfour's prophecy with his own vision of the future course of Western civilization. In the future as in the past, wrote Huxley, it would involve a "struggle for mastery" between the scientific spirit originating in Greek philosophy and the opposing spirits of postprophetic Judaism and the prophetic Judaism transformed by Hellenic speculation into the elaborate complex of dogmatic Christianity. At long last, said Huxley, "the scientific spirit, freed from its early wrappings, stands in independence of, and, for the most part, in antagonism to, its ancient rivals. Its cosmology, its anthropology, are incompatible with theirs; its ethics are independent of theirs."[5] This was a strange utterance coming from the Huxley who, two years earlier in his Romanes lecture, had declared war on the idea that ethical progress depended on imitating the cosmic process and had championed instead the Hebrew prophet Micah's injunction to love mercy, do justly, and walk humbly. Where or how Micah had obtained this knowledge of human duty Huxley did not say. Some men, he observed in a letter to a friend, have "an innate sense of moral beauty and ugliness," from whence acquired who could say. Huxley was a humanist at heart, but his head and his heart were at war with each other.[6]

Having introduced the protagonists in the story we are about to tell, let us now review in broad outline some major twentieth-century developments with the idea of determining to what extent the conflicting prophecies of Balfour and Huxley have been fulfilled. In physics and cosmology the scientific spirit achieved notable successes in formulating increasingly abstract mathematical models capable of predicting striking results. The history of these speculative and technological triumphs and reverses, leading from Planck's discovery of the quantum effect to Einstein's special and general theories of relativity, Schrödinger's development of quantum mechanics, Niels Bohr's interpretation of the wave-particle duality, Heisenberg's uncertainty principle, E. O. Lawrence's cyclotron, Hubble's expanding universe and the consequent big bang theory of the origin of the universe, and the successive theories of supergravity, supersymmetry, cosmic inflation, and superstring theory — this history has been told with admirable lucidity by physicist David Lindley in his book *The End of Physics: The Myth of a Unified Theory*, published in 1993. What Einstein and Stephen Hawking were seeking, Lindley says, was a theory of everything, a theoretical physics so complete that God would have had no choice in deter-

---

5. "Physical Basis of Life," p. 21.

6. Thomas Henry Huxley, *Evolution and Ethics and Other Essays* (New York: Macmillan, 1895), p. 109. See also Leonard Huxley, *Life and Letters of Thomas Henry Huxley* (London: Macmillan, 1900), pp. 223-24, and Thomas Henry Huxley, *Science and Hebrew Tradition: Essays* (New York: D. Appleton, 1898), pp. 160-61.

mining the character of the universe. Reason, logic, and physics would constitute the unmoved mover, the uncaused effect.

Not surprisingly, Lindley was skeptical of this ambitious scientific dream.
The clues these scientists needed to guide them on their search were scarce,
Lindley noted. The microworld of particle physics had been exposed by particle
accelerators, but further progress was inhibited by the size and cost of the machinery required to test theoretical predictions. The macroworld of cosmology
would be explored further as bigger and better telescopes were built, but no
amount of technical ingenuity would permit the astronomers to see other universes, or our own universe at any other time than the present. What the search-
ers for a final theory were trying to find, Lindley concluded, was something that
could be grasped by reason alone, urged on by a passionate faith in a universal
order of nature discoverable by human reason.[7]

In the same year Lindley published his book, 1993, Sylvan Schweber, a
physicist and historian of physics and of evolutionary biology, published in the
journal *Physics Today* an article announcing that "The reductionist approach
that has been the hallmark of theoretical physics in the twentieth century is being superseded by the study of emergent phenomena." Einstein's dream of ar-
riving at a unified theory of universal elementary laws from which the cosmos
can be built up by pure deduction has given way, says Schweber, to a realization
that the sciences of nature are arranged hierarchically, each level — particle
physics, solid-state physics, chemistry, biology, and the like — having its own
emergent laws that cannot be reduced to the laws governing lower levels. This
realization, says Schweber, has produced a sense of crisis in the physics community and a fear that this challenge to the privileged status of high-energy physics
may diminish Congressional support for the high-cost equipment needed in
pursuing the dream of a unified theory still further.[8]

## The Rise of Neo-Darwinism

Turning now to the life sciences, and especially to evolutionary biology, we see
Darwin's theory of evolution by natural selection, long neglected by the founders of experimental Mendelian genetics and by paleontologists with evolution-

---

7. David Lindley, *The End of Physics: The Myth of a Unified Theory* (New York: Basic
Books, 1993), p. 209. See also John Horgan, *The End of Science: Facing the Limits of Science in the
Twilight of the Scientific Age* (Reading, Mass.: Addison-Wesley, 1996), for a collection of inter-
views with leading scientists on the future of science.

8. Sylvan Schweber, "Physics, Community and the Crisis in Physical Theory," *Physics Today*, November 1993, pp. 36-39.

ary theories of their own, emerging triumphant in the 1930s and 1940s as three mathematical population geneticists, R. A. Fisher, J. B. S. Haldane, and Sewall Wright, joined hands with geneticist-naturalist Theodosius Dobzhansky, field naturalists and systematists E. B. Ford, Ernst Mayr, and Ledyard Stebbins, paleontologist George Gaylord Simpson, and T. H. Huxley's grandson Julian to produce a neo-Darwinian evolutionary synthesis based on changes in population gene frequencies brought about by natural selection operating on the organisms produced by those genes. No common worldview united these men. Fisher was an Anglican, Haldane a Communist sympathizer, Wright and Julian Huxley panpsychists; Simpson was an agnostic, Dobzhansky a Christian of Russian Orthodox background, Mayr and Huxley atheists. But all subscribed to traditional Western values, and all looked to Darwin's theory of natural selection to unify biology and cast light on human duty and destiny. Their efforts reached a grand climax when the devotees of the neo-Darwinian synthesis assembled at the American Philosophical Society in Philadelphia, the University of Chicago, and elsewhere to celebrate the 100th anniversary of the publication of Charles Darwin's *On the Origin of Species*.

At this point my narrative of events becomes more personal, for it was in 1959 that I attended the Darwin centennial celebrations in Philadelphia and Chicago, where I began a friendship with Theodosius Dobzhansky and saw Julian Huxley, Sir Charles Galton Darwin, and other notables in action. In that same year the Iowa State University Press published my first book, melodramatically titled *The Death of Adam: Evolution and Its Impact on Western Thought*, in which I took issue with Dobzhansky's suggestion that man, as the most progressive animal on earth, was now in a position, if he so chose, to take conscious control of his own evolution and thus become, as Julian Huxley predicted, "business manager for the cosmic process of evolution." As a free, intelligent agent, I observed, man could plan all sorts of things, himself included. But who was to plan the planners? Who was to prevent them from establishing a tyranny of mind and body over their fellow human beings? Was man, in truth, a Prometheus unbound, ready to assume control of his own and cosmic destiny? Or was he, as the Bible represented him, a God-like creature who, having denied his creatureliness and arrogated to himself the role of Creator, now contemplated his handiwork with fear and trembling lest he reap the wages of sin, namely, death? The planned society, I noted, looked less inviting in its grim reality than it did when still a dream. The conflict of nations and races, far from raising mankind to ever higher levels of freedom, virtue, and culture, threatened to accomplish the destruction of the human species. Science and technology, which were to have led the way to a bright new future, were now increasingly preoccupied with devising new and more dreadful weapons of obliteration. The historical Adam was dead, a casualty of scientific progress, but the Adam in whom all men die was alive and well, a moral being whose every intellectual triumph was at once a temptation to evil and a power for good.[9] When Dobzhansky saw me in Chicago after having read this closing passage in my book, he exclaimed, "Professor Greene, why are you so pessimistic?"

My dialogue with Dobzhansky, which continued through the sixties, turned mostly on the question whether the creativity of the evolutionary process, conceived as a continuum linking cosmic, biological, and human evolution and conveyed to the public in value-laden figures of speech such as "progress," "trial and error," "blind alleys," "opportunism," "success and failure," and the like, could be reconciled with the mechanistic view of nature inherited from the seventeenth century. I argued that it could not, that biologists must *either* discard these teleological, value-laden figures of speech and the notion of progress associated with them *or* revise their conceptions of science and nature to make sense of a natural, creative process, perhaps along the lines suggested by Alfred North Whitehead. Dobzhansky disagreed. "I refuse," he said, "to believe in 'direction' in any other sense than that the Alpha and Omega of evolution are simultaneously present in God's eyes (like to Laplace's universal intelligence). . . . I cannot believe that God from time to time becomes a particularly powerful enzyme."[10]

In many ways the Darwin centennial celebrations marked the apogee of the neo-Darwinian synthesis launched in the 1930s. Among biologists the synthesis had no significant challenger, although there were internal disputes among its advocates. Among the anthropologists, represented at Chicago by Alfred Kroeber, Clyde Kluckhohn, and Sol Tax, among others, human nature was still conceived as shaped by nurture and culture, not by nature, and grand theories of cosmic-biological-social evolution in the manner of Herbert Spencer were out of fashion. On the religious front the Catholic Church, under Pius XII, had given Catholic scholars permission to discuss evolution as a hypothesis and to take account of ancient Near Eastern literary forms in interpreting the Bible, and the long-suppressed writings of Pierre Teilhard de Chardin appeared in print, notably his book *The Phenomenon of Man,* which so enchanted both Julian Huxley and Dobzhansky. In the Protestant world new interpretations of the doctrines of revelation and inspiration issued from Anglican and neoorthodox spokesmen and even from some self-styled "conservative Chris-

---

9. John C. Greene, *The Death of Adam: Evolution and Its Impact on Western Thought* (Ames: Iowa State University Press, 1959), pp. 338-39.

10. John C. Greene, *Debating Darwin: Adventures of a Scholar* (Claremont, Calif.: Regina Books, 1999), p. 98.

tian" members of the American Scientific Affiliation in a volume edited by Russell Mixter of Wheaton College.[11]

## Renewed Controversy

But this relatively calm situation could not long withstand the powerful forces, military, social, and intellectual, that were transforming the character of science in the Western world. The rise of Hitler to power in the world's leading scientific nation, the outbreak of World War II, the Japanese attack on Pearl Harbor, and the ensuing Korean War and Cold War had changed the scientific scene dramatically, giving rise to Big Science, the Manhattan Project, and the military-industrial-academic complex and bringing scores of refugee scientists to English and American laboratories. Physicists and biochemists, spurred on by Erwin Schrödinger's book *What Is Life?* entered the biological sciences, pushing aside the founders of the evolutionary synthesis in the competition for government funding and bringing with them the experimental, reductionist point of view that produced the Watson-Crick discovery of the structure of DNA, soon to be conceived as nature's secret code containing information and instructions for building organisms.[12]

As Howard L. Kaye, professor of sociology and the history of social thought at Franklin and Marshall College, has shown in his searching criticism *The Social Meaning of Modern Biology,* the molecular biologists were much less respectful of the traditional values of Western civilization than the founders of the evolutionary synthesis had been. The soul, said Francis Crick, was a figment of the human imagination, the mind simply a way of talking about the functions of the brain. Morality was a biological phenomenon. It was time, said Robert Sinsheimer, chancellor of the University of California at Santa Cruz, for man to take charge of his own evolution and move toward a "higher state" through the systematic practice of eugenics. To this end he suggested in 1985 the idea of sequencing the human genome to discover the entire set of instructions for producing a human being. Professor Walter Gilbert of Harvard University was skeptical of the project at first but eventually declared it to be the "Holy Grail" of biology. James Watson of double helix fame agreed. "We used to think our fate was in our stars," he said.

11. See *Proceedings of the American Philosophical Society,* April 1959, p. 103; and S. Tax, ed., *Evolution after Darwin: The Evolution of Man* (Chicago: University of Chicago Press, 1960); also John C. Greene, *Darwin and the Modern World View* (Baton Rouge: Louisiana State University Press, 1961), lectures given at Rice University in the wake of the Darwin centennial celebrations.

12. See Howard L. Kay, *Who Wrote the Book of Life? A History of the Genetic Code* (Stanford, Calif.: Stanford University Press, 2000), for a full account of the rise of molecular biology.

"Now we know in large measure our fate is in our genes." Since human genetic instructions were designed by natural selection to adapt human beings to conditions in the Stone Age, conditions that no longer prevail, why should we not make ourselves a little better suited for survival? "That's what I think we'll do. We'll make ourselves a little better." Here at last was Julian Huxley's dream of "a rational applied biology" teetering on the brink of realization.[13]

The successes of the molecular biologists, the renewed interest in Darwin's long-neglected *Descent of Man,* and William Hamilton's mathematical demonstration of the validity of the concept of kin selection inspired evolutionary theorists to stake a biological claim to the social sciences under such titles as sociobiology, ethology, bioanthropology, evolutionary psychology, cognitive psychology, and the like. Human nature and behavior, it was claimed, were shaped, not by culture, imitation, and learning, but by random genetic variation and natural selection of those types of brain structures best suited to promote survival of the hominids inhabiting the savannas of Africa in the Stone Age — the so-called ancestral environment of the species *Homo sapiens.* Since that time, it was said, the human species had spread over the whole earth and then, about ten thousand years ago, had invented entirely new social and cultural environments involving farming, city life, and empire. But the human brain and the genetic predispositions to behave in certain ways remained the same, driving this now badly adapted species to uncontrolled population growth and genocidal warfare, endangering not only the survival of the human species but also that of millions of other species. This grim saga was conveyed to the public in anthropomorphic figures of speech portraying hordes of selfish genes selfishly manipulating the behavior of the robot humans they had created for one purpose only, namely, to insure the passage of the genes themselves into succeeding generations by hook or by crook. Commenting on these grim portrayals of the human situation, Howard Kaye writes:

> From Spencer's inflation of evolution into a "total theory of existence" . . . and a "scientific morality," to Julian Huxley's "Religion Without Revelation" and "Evolutionary Ethics," to E. O. Wilson's sociobiological quest for life's "ultimate meaning" and a "biology of ethics," the search for moral certainty, individual meaning, and communal purpose within a scientifically comprehensible universe has been central. Burdened with such metaphysical baggage, the science of evolutionary biology passes over into myth despite the avowed materialism or even reductionism of its leading theorists.[14]

13. Howard L. Kaye, *The Social Meaning of Modern Biology: From Social Darwinism to Sociobiology,* 2nd ed. (New Brunswick, N.J., and London: Transaction, 1997), p. 184.
14. Kaye, *Social Meaning,* p. 157.

Howard Kaye's critique made sense to me; for I had expressed similar views a few years earlier in the final essay of my book of essays *Science, Ideology, and World View.* There I described the books by Julian Huxley, George Gaylord Simpson, and Edward O. Wilson on the meaning of evolution as the Bridgewater treatises of the twentieth century in that they sought to find in science answers to questions of ultimate meaning and value, answers that would take the place of what Simpson called "the lower and higher superstitions," which had hitherto served as answers to these questions. These writers, I suggested, were caught on the scientistic horn of the positivist dilemma.

> Whoever regards science as man's sole means of acquiring reliable knowledge must eventually confront that dilemma. If science and the scientific method are defined narrowly so as to exclude value judgments and all non-logico-experimental statements . . . it then becomes impossible to say why anything, science included, is important or valuable, why the passion for truth is to be inculcated and respected, or why human beings have any more inherent dignity than starfish or stones. But if, on the contrary, science is declared competent to discover human duty and destiny, as those who choose the other horn of the dilemma assert, one is soon confronted with the conflicting claims of Huxleian science, Freudian science, Marxian science, Comtean science, and a host of other scientisms. In the ensuing struggle the central idea of science as an enterprise in which all qualified observers can agree as to what the evidence proves vanishes from sight. Thus, whichever horn of the positivist dilemma one takes, science is the loser.[15]

## Dialogue with Mayr

These opinions, and others like them, had already brought me into correspondence with Ernst Mayr, a founding father of the evolutionary synthesis. Mayr had responded to the invasion of biology by reductionist physicists and biochemists by turning his attention to the history and philosophy of science in order to refute the reigning philosophers of physics, to develop an autonomous philosophy of biology, and to vindicate the concepts and methods of the systematist-naturalist against those of the supposedly more scientific mathematical and experimental biologists. Our correspondence ranged over topics in the history and philosophy of science as well as the bearing of science on ques-

15. John C. Greene, *Science, Ideology, and World View: Essays in the History of Evolutionary Ideas* (Berkeley, Los Angeles, and London: University of California Press, 1981), pp. 162-63, 188.

tions of meaning and value, of human duty and destiny. As a historian I found Mayr's idea that the development of evolutionary ideas in the Western world had been impeded by the successive "false ideologies" of Platonic essentialism, Christian dogmatism, and Cartesian-Newtonian "physicalism" not only ahistorical but also antievolutionary. It ignored the interweaving of all three of these worldviews, and of ancient Greek atomism as well, in the transition from Aristotle to Darwin and the influence on Darwin himself of the Christian doctrine of creation and the mechanical view of nature inherited from the seventeenth century.[16]

In the philosophy of science, Mayr tries to define a middle ground between the reductionism of the physicists and biochemists and the holistic perspective of the vitalists and the believers in Aristotle's final causes. He does this by conceding the biology of proximate causes (physiology and embryology) to the reductionists while reserving the realm of ultimate causes for the evolutionary biologists with their "organic-historical" conception of nature's progress from monad to man. To me, however, Mayr's version of evolution as a natural creative process (which he describes in the usual anthropomorphic, teleological figures of speech) seemed subject to the same difficulties encountered by Dobzhansky and Julian Huxley, but without the benefit of either Dobzhansky's Alpha and Omega or Huxley's panpsychism. For Mayr the key to evolutionary progress is the concept of emergence: "the emergence of unanticipated properties at higher hierarchical levels." What the underlying nature of reality must be to give rise to emergences like these Mayr does not say. Somehow or other all these properties and capacities of what Mayr calls the "substrate" of the world are perpetually there in potency, waiting for the law-bound transformations of mindless, valueless, purposeless matter-energy to actualize them in its random combinations. The vast, unthinking, value-blind complex of matter-energy, euphemistically called a "universe" by the only beings capable of conceiving it as such, has become aware of itself, so to speak, in that peculiar form of human consciousness known as "science," and it has done so by what Mayr calls a "sequence of improbabilities." "It is," he declares, "a miracle that man ever happened."[17]

But what could be more implausible than this emergentist scenario? In one breath Mayr dismisses the biblical miracles and tells his readers that Darwin, Ernst Haeckel, and T. H. Huxley exploded "the traditional anthro-

16. John C. Greene, "Reflections on Ernst Mayr's *This Is Biology*," *Biology and Philosophy*, 1999, pp. 113-16.

17. Ernst Mayr, *Toward a New Philosophy of Biology* (Cambridge, Mass., and London: Harvard University Press, 1988), pp. 12, 5, 21.

pocentrism of the Bible and the philosophers." In the next he pictures the evo-lution of mankind as unique, unrepeatable, and unpredictable and warns that the future of mankind is not something dictated by the laws of nature; rather "it is we ourselves who hold the fate of our species in our hands."[18] What a par-adoxical situation for the chance product of a sequence of improbabilities!

## Scientific Criticisms

As the twentieth century drew to a close and the twenty-first dawned, both gene-based reductionism and the evolutionary synthesis defended by Mayr were subjected to trenchant criticism by biologists and others. In a little book entitled *The Triple Helix: Gene, Organism, and Environment*, Richard Lewontin mounted an all-out attack on the machine metaphor that had dominated biol-ogy ever since Descartes first introduced it and on the development metaphor, of equally ancient origin, which pictured embryological development as pre-formed in the sperm or egg or, in modern terms, in the genes. In an opening passage reminiscent of Arthur James Balfour's ideas, Lewontin wrote:

> It is not possible to do the work of science without using a language that is filled with metaphors. Virtually the entire body of modern science is an at-tempt to explain phenomena that cannot be experienced directly by human beings, by reference to forces and processes that cannot be perceived di-rectly because they are too small, like molecules, or too vast, like the entire known universe, or the result of forces that our senses cannot detect, like electromagnetism, or the outcome of extremely complex interactions, like the coming into being of an individual organism from its conception as a fertilized egg.[19]

In biology, Lewontin argued, it was time to stop conceiving the organism as the passive nexus of independent environmental and genetic forces, the changing environment generating problems for the organism in its struggle to survive, and random genetic mutation providing solutions to those problems. Instead of conceiving the organism as adapting to a randomly changing envi-ronment in this random fashion, biologists should recognize that the organism *constructs* its environment by its activities, and that the effective environment consists of those aspects of the external world that are relevant to those con-

18. Mayr, *Toward a New Philosophy*, pp. 176, 293-94.
19. Richard Lewontin, *The Triple Helix: Gene, Organism, and Environment* (Cambridge, Mass., and London: Harvard University Press, 2000), pp. 3-4.

structive activities. As for embryological development, it was best conceived, not as preformed in a genetic blueprint, but as the outcome of a unique interaction between the organism's genes, the temporal sequence of external environments through which the organism passes in its life cycle, and random events of molecular interaction in individual cells. Evolution, Lewontin concludes, is "an historically contingent wandering pathway through the space of possibilities."[20] As a convinced Marxist, however, Lewontin might be hard pressed to explain how such a "wandering pathway" could produce a being capable of writing *The Triple Helix.*

In a more recent book, *Acquiring Genomes: A Theory of the Origins of Species,* Lynn Margulis and Dorion Sagan agree with Lewontin's view that evolution is a historically contingent wandering pathway, but they reject the neo-Darwinian thesis, essential to Lewontin's work in population genetics, that the evolution of new species results from the gradual accumulation of mutations favorable to survival and reproduction in particular circumstances. Genuine novelty, they argue, arises spasmodically from stress-induced occasional symbiotic mergers of unlike organisms, especially (but not only) microbes. "The hegemony of R. A. Fisher, J. B. S. Haldane, and Sewall Wright is gone forever. . . . The language of evolutionary change is neither mathematics nor computer-generated morphology [nor] statistics. Natural history, ecology, genetics, and metabolism must be supplemented with accurate knowledge of microbes."[21]

Like Lewontin, Margulis and Sagan "feel no need for the supernatural." Their God, or rather goddess, is Gaia, "the interactive system on the surface of the Earth, supplied with solar and geothermal energy gradients, that maintains the temperature close to 18 degrees Centigrade." Professing complete agnosticism as to the origin of the big bang, the resultant cosmic expansion, and the laws of thermodynamics, they find in Nietzsche's "will to power" and the operation of thermodynamic laws ("nature abhors a gradient") a full explanation of the apparent purposefulness and emergent novelty in nature. "The key point," they write, "is that living and non-living 'selves' come into being to reduce gradients naturally." As for such novelties as human beings with their inflated self-esteem, they are Johnny-come-latelies whom Gaia can dispose of with a shrug of her shoulders, leaving Earth to the creative microbes that gave them birth.

Another trenchant critique of the evolutionary synthesis owes its origins to developmental geneticist Stuart Kauffman, creator of computer models of the dynamics of complex systems. M. Mitchell Waldrop describes Kauffman's

---

20. Lewontin, *The Triple Helix,* pp. 47-48, 88.

21. Lynn Margulis and Dorion Sagan, *Acquiring Genomes: A Theory of the Origins of Species* (New York: Basic Books, 2002), pp. 201-2. See also pp. 44-50, 68-69, 134-35.

views as follows: "Living systems are not deeply entrenched in an ordered regime. . . . [They] are actually very close to the edge of chaos transition, where things are much looser and more fluid. And natural selection is not the antagonist of self-organization. It is more like a law of motion, a force that is constantly pushing emergent, self-organizing systems toward the edge of chaos."[22]

## Biology and Human Culture

This approach to emergent phenomena in evolution has been warmly endorsed by David Depew and Bruce Weber in their masterful survey of the history of Darwinian theories, *Darwinism Evolving.* Kauffman's ideas, Depew and Weber believe, suggest the mutual dependence and interpenetration of chance, selection, and self-organization in evolution, a dependence and interpenetration revealed by nonlinear dynamic models of complex systems, thereby giving the Darwinian tradition a new lease on life. The same models, these authors suggest, indicate that scientific naturalism is not only expanding to deal with complex systems but is also poised to achieve a reconciliation between the natural and the human sciences, a reconciliation outlined at some length in Depew and Weber's long essay "Evolution, Ethics, and the Complexity Revolution."[23]

If ethics is to be reconciled with scientific naturalism, say Depew and Weber, it must break loose from old philosophical debates stemming from Plato and study instead what modern "interpretive" social scientists have discovered about the moral practices of human societies. Evolutionists, for their part, must embrace the complexity models that are revolutionizing all science. The natural scientists must abandon the scientistic myth that progress in the human sciences requires branding much of human culture, and especially religious beliefs, as illusion. The humanists, in turn, must stop thinking that any culture worth having must transcend nature, natural science, and philosophical naturalism. Only in this way, conclude Depew and Weber, can the perennial battle between naturalism and transcendence be transcended.

This view of what Depew and Weber call the "interpretive" social sciences does not agree with the views I set forth in my lectures at Rice University, published as *Darwin and the Modern World View*, where I wrote:

22. M. Mitchell Waldrop, *Complexity: The Emerging Science at the Edge of Order and Chaos* (New York: Simon and Schuster, 1992), pp. 302-3.

23. David Depew and Bruce Weber, "Natural Selection and Self-Organization," *Biology and Philosophy*, 1996, pp. 11, 54-55; Depew and Weber, "Evolution, Ethics, and the Complexity Revolution," in *Evolution and Human Values*, ed. Robert Wesson and P. Williams (Atlanta: Rodopi, 1995), p. 63.

In the effort to deal with man by the methods of natural science, we must perforce overlook those aspects of human nature and culture that do not readily lend themselves to formulation in scientific terms. We concentrate on those aspects of the subject matter that are amenable to our method — man's animal organism, his social needs, and the stabilizing influence of religious and moral beliefs. After a while we forget what we have left out. . . . Culture becomes simply a mode of adaptation to the environment, morality simply a matter of preserving social solidarity, religion nothing but a way of discharging individual and social tensions, and so on. This goes along very well until we are recalled to the concrete world by the necessity of action. Then we can no longer evade such questions as whether there are dimensions of reality inaccessible to science, whether some truths can be known only from the point of view of a responsible moral agent, whether religious beliefs relate to a reality which is more than social. If there are such truths, such dimensions of reality, the apprehension of them may be a cause of action. But how can science hope to calculate the influence of such causes on the total action situation?[24]

The attempt of modern social science to avoid questions of this kind, I argued, is fraught with danger because there is no neutral ground with respect to them. The assertion that science can neither verify nor disprove them gives rise imperceptibly to a conviction that there is *no* way in which their validity can be tested. But where there are no tests of validity, there is no truth or falsity. There is only the bare fact of belief. If the ultimate ends of action have no basis in the structure of reality, there is little point to science. The passion for science then becomes an odd preference for a certain kind of activity. This is precisely the situation in which Darwin found himself at the end of his spiritual evolution. Science had become his passion, the only thing that made life bearable, but its larger significance was no longer clear to him. He was sure he had been right in devoting his life to science, but he could not say why.

What shall we say, then, concerning the conflicting prophecies of Balfour and Huxley as to the probable course of Western culture in the twentieth century? Without doubt the spirit of science extolled by Huxley achieved notable successes in the physical and biological sciences and in applied science as well. In so doing, however, it developed a severe case of hubris, overweening pride. Some of its devotees claim the whole field of rational inquiry, from physics to the humanities, as their legitimate bailiwick. Science aspires, says Ernst Mayr, to understand and explain "everything known to exist or happen in the universe." Next to

24. Greene, *Modern World View*, pp. 126-28.

art and music, say Mayr and Karl Popper, science is "the greatest, the most beautiful, the most enlightening achievement of the human spirit."[25] But there are other equally or more qualified contenders for this honor. What about Chartres cathedral and the other medieval cathedrals built by the labor of thousands? What about the achievements of the black peoples of Africa brought to this continent as chattel slaves yet maintaining their human dignity and dream of freedom and equality through pain and suffering and, at the same time, contributing priceless art and music, scholarship and leadership despite the slings and arrows of discrimination and outright violence? Science is indeed a noble achievement of the human spirit, but scientific theory, as such, has no room for the concept of spirit. The human spirit cannot be weighed, quantified, predicted, or genetically engineered. It is, in short, spiritual, a word that some spokesmen for science seem to want to banish from our vocabulary.

I conclude, then, that science needs to be seen in a wider philosophical and religious context that can make sense of the human spirit scientists love to talk about. A first step in this direction would be to discard T. H. Huxley's notion that "there is but one kind of knowledge and one way of acquiring it."[26] There are many kinds of knowledge — the scientist's, the artist's, the craftsman's, the philosopher's, the seer's — each of which is acquired in its own way. And there are truths, important truths, that can be tested only by faith-inspired experiments in living, doing, and dying, as the lives of Gandhi, Martin Luther King, Jr., and a host of other nonviolent revolutionaries testify. Science yields a kind of knowledge, but not this kind.

Balfour had hoped that the twentieth century would produce a philosophy of nature and science that would reject evolutionary naturalism and recognize the essential similarity of the scientific and theological ways of picturing reality. His hope has been partially realized, but to a very limited extent. The philosophy of science was dominated for six decades by the reductionist logic of physics. Ernst Mayr then led the way in claiming autonomy for the philosophy of biology on the basis of emergent phenomena, but without granting a similar autonomy to the philosophy of human nature. By the end of the century the position of many philosophers was aptly summed up by the title of Werner Callebaut's book, *Taking the Naturalistic Turn; or, How Real Philosophy of Science Is Done.*[27]

25. Ernst Mayr, *This Is Biology: The Science of the Living World* (Cambridge: Harvard University Press, 1997), p. 41.

26. "The Advisableness of Improving Natural Knowledge" (1860), in *Selections from the Essays of Thomas Henry Huxley*, p. 15.

27. Werner Callebaut, *Taking the Naturalistic Turn; or, How Real Philosophy of Science Is Done* (Chicago: University of Chicago Press, 1993).

## Whitehead

There were a few dissenting voices, however. Instead of attempting to derive the complex nature of humans from the law-bound transformations of matter-energy, these writers argued, we should look for clues as to the general character of the evolutionary process by examining our own experience, of which we have firsthand knowledge. This was the method adopted by the mathematician-logician-philosopher Alfred North Whitehead. Whitehead extended the concept of experience to embrace all natural entities down to the level of electrons and protons, each entity prehending (taking into its own being) in some degree the rest of the universe in its successive occasions of experience. As I wrote to Ernst Mayr in response to his statement that he believed that man was somehow higher than the chimpanzee: "I think Whitehead would say that man is higher because he prehends the universe more fully than the lower animals or plants. The knower is higher than the known unless the known is also a knower. That is why I think that all science is anthropocentric. We may not be physically at the center of the universe, but *mentally* we grasp the galaxies, the dinosaurs, and the like into our own being, and that being transcends the objects known in thus knowing them."[28]

The population geneticist Sewall Wright adopted an approach similar in many ways to Whitehead's. In his view the primary reality for human beings was "the kind of knowledge provided to each person by his own stream of consciousness." The scientist's knowledge of the external world, said Wright, was wholly derived from bits of the streams of consciousness of many observers and was restricted to those aspects that could be communicated in terms of the so-called primary properties of matter, a restriction that stripped the stream of consciousness of its original richness. Moreover, all the common knowledge of these "primary properties" was based on units of measurement — centimeter, gram, second — with operational definitions that were recipes for *voluntary* actions. "Reality," Wright concluded, "clearly consists primarily of streams of consciousness. This fact must take precedence over the laws of nature of physical science, even though it must be largely ignored in science itself."

> We must acknowledge the necessity of dealing with the universe as the world of mind, within which all subordinate minds must be included in some sense. . . . The question is . . . whether the mind of the universe is all knowing and omnipotent, or . . . merely that which is superimposed on the

28. Greene, *Debating Darwin*. p. 244.

point-to-point interactions of the minds of the components as the integrating factor. . . . As one concerned with the philosophy of science rather than philosophy in general, I must take the latter view, recognizing that there is a great deal that science does not and probably never can know.[29]

Other writers, too, followed Whitehead's lead. The Catholic philosopher Bernard Lonergan sought insight into the common human experience of obtaining a sudden insight into the solution of a problem (the "Eureka!" experience). His analysis led him from mathematical physics to evolutionary biology and the concept of "emergent probabilities," and eventually to a philosophy of nature supplying a basis for theology.[30] The Catholic theologian John Haught views the religious experience of being grasped by "that which is yet to come" in the context of Whitehead's process philosophy. This experience, says Haught, cannot be expressed in scientifically specifiable concepts because science attributes efficacy only to the causal past. "Nevertheless, if we follow Whitehead's great insight that human experience may be the source of metaphysical categories that by analogy we can assume to characterize the experiential events that make up the rest of nature, then theology can infer that the same 'power of the future' that grasps us in faith must also be effective and persuasively present in the entire cosmos."

If, Haught argues, biologists are permitted to resort to metaphor and analogy, as biologists from Aristotle to Darwin to Dawkins have done, why should not theologians be granted the same privilege? "By employing metaphors for God's influence such as 'Ground of Being' or 'Absolute Future,' theology can in principle account for the fact of evolutionary novelty at a deeper if less precise level of explanation than the scientific. And such metaphorical explanation would not contradict or compete with evolutionary biology any more than evolutionary biology's own metaphorical 'explanations' at its own level conflict with the chemical or physical explanations at another."[31]

29. Sewall Wright, "Panpsychism and Science," in *Mind in Nature: Essays on the Interface between Science and Philosophy*, ed. John B. Cobb, Jr., and David R. Griffin (Washington, D.C.: University Press of America, 1977), pp. 79-80.

30. *Insight*, in *Collected Works of Bernard Lonergan III* (Toronto, Buffalo, and London: University of Toronto Press, 1997).

31. John C. Haught, "Darwin's Gift to Theology," in *Evolution and Molecular Biology: Scientific Perspectives on Divine Action*, ed. Robert J. Russell, W. R. Stoeger, and Francisco J. Ayala (Vatican City and Berkeley, Calif.: Vatican Observatory Publications and the Center for Theology and the Natural Sciences, 1998), p. 411.

## Evolution and God

Returning now to the conflicting prophecies of Balfour and Huxley concerning the future of Western culture, it might seem that Huxley's vision of a struggle for mastery between the spirit of science and the Judeo-Christian tradition has been realized in the evolution-versus-creationism wars that have dominated the public press in the United States from the Scopes trial onward. From the Balfourian point of view informing this essay, however, these wars seem a sideshow to the main issue in the dialogue between the scientific spirit and the religious spirit. I can agree with Philip Johnson and his colleagues that the writings of many evolutionary scientists are deeply impregnated with implicit materialistic metaphysics and dubious epistemological claims as to the all-sufficiency of science and scientific ways of knowing. But I disagree strongly with Johnson's view that evolutionary science is nothing but that. And I disagree equally strongly with attempts to present William Paley's natural theology as creation science and to picture the Bible as a textbook of science. On the other hand, I am equally critical of those scientists who regard scientific explanations as total explanations and the scientific way of seeking truth as the only acceptable way. If the critics of evolutionary science are misguided in trying to convert Paley's natural theology into science and the Bible into a textbook of science, the partisans of the all-sufficiency of science are equally misguided in presenting the Bible as a compilation of outdated folklore and in seeking to convert evolutionary science into ethics and natural religion, as Edward O. Wilson and many others do. Here we have the strange spectacle of the advocates of religion presenting themselves as scientists and the champions of science presenting themselves as ethicists and purveyors of natural religion.

I am happy to say that Niles Eldredge, a paleontologist and ecologist at the American Museum of Natural History, agrees with me in finding this spectacle distressing. "The tired old creationism debate," he writes, "simply has not prepared us for the kind of positive interaction that I see as eminently possible as we enter the new millennium and grapple with tough environmental issues."[32] In speaking engagements at colleges and universities across the United States, Eldredge has discovered among the younger members of conservative Christian communities a growing realization that, if we do not address our environmental problems effectively, there won't be much of creation over which

---

32. Niles Eldredge, *The Triumph of Evolution and the Failure of Creationism* (New York: Freeman, 2000), pp. 167-69. For a comprehensive, well-balanced, sociologically informed account of American theories of origins, creationist and otherwise, see K. W. Giberson and D. A. Yerxa, *Species of Origins: America's Search for a Creation Story* (Lanham, Md., Boulder, Colo., New York, and Oxford: Rowman and Littlefield, 2002).

to enjoy dominion. Environmentalists, Eldredge notes, have frequently dispar-
aged the biblical passage in which God promises the Israelites dominion over
the beasts of the field as justifying the rape of the earth. But, says Eldredge, the
concept of dominion yields easily to that of stewardship, and this is what he
hears from many conservative Christian students as they reinterpret the biblical
passage in the light of ecological research on the global ecosystem. Eldredge
himself interprets concepts of God as reflections of the way different peoples at
different times have interpreted their ecological situation. Thus, he interprets
the dominion passage in Genesis as a reflection of the early agriculturist's sense
of newfound human freedom to step outside the confines of the local ecosystem, but he concedes that the apparent correlation between views of the spirit
world and the viewers' ecological situation does not invalidate any particular
concept of God.

For my part, I think this is a meager and inadequate concept of concepts
of God. A deeper and more adequate concept is developed by Colorado State
University philosopher Holmes Rolston, in *Genes, Genesis, and God: Values and
Their Origin in Natural and Human History*. Rolston writes: "Ours is an age of
many doubts but no one doubts that there has been a remarkable genesis on
our planet. . . . [T]here are in broadest outline two complementary or competing explanations of this genesis: a scientific account, for which we take the title
word 'genes,' and a religious account for which the symbolic word is God. The
term 'genesis' mediates between the dual accounts in dialogue with other philosophical and metaphysical possibilities for the explanation of Earthen fertility."

Evolutionary history is interpreted as the generating, conserving, and enrichment of value and its eventual appreciation in human terms, philosophical
and religious as well as scientific. "The questions here become ultimate ones,
though they are born in the phenomena of natural history and human culture,"
Rolston explains.

> The religions, including those of the monotheistic West . . . have steadily
> thought to detect a Beyond in the midst of the here and now. They have
> found neither nature nor history in and of itself final or fully self-
> explanatory. They have claimed a Presence immanent and transcendent,
> stirring in Earth history. The evidence for such transcendence is the strik-
> ing emergence, or genesis, of information and value. There are genes, there
> is genesis, but explanations are not over until one has reckoned with the
> question of God.[33]

---

33. Holmes Rolston, *Genes, Genesis, and God: Values and Their Origin in Natural and Human History* (Cambridge and New York: Cambridge University Press, 1999), pp. x, xiii.

On that great question the scientific jury is still out. Physicist Steven Weinberg, no friend of religion, still cherishes the dream of a final theory of everything, "an understanding of all the regularities that we see in nature, based on a few simple principles, laws of nature, from which all other regularities can be deduced." He concedes, however, that science can never explain any moral principle. "There seems to be an unbridgeable gulf between 'is' questions and 'ought' questions. We can perhaps explain why . . . the human race has evolved to think that certain things should be done, but it remains open to us to transcend these biologically based moral rules."[34] How we are able to transcend these rules, Weinberg does not say.

Among evolutionary biologists the question of God raised by Holmes Rolston has been a subject of serious discussion by some writers, but not in sufficient numbers to alter the dominant ethos of the biological research community taken as a whole. As we have seen, Ernst Mayr claimed autonomy for the philosophy of biology on the basis of emergent phenomena but refused to grant a similar autonomy to the philosophy of human nature on the same grounds. As for theology, Mayr views it as totally different from science. Theologians, he says, "invoke the supernatural to explain how the natural world works." Unlike scientists, they never abandon or modify their dogmas when a better interpretation is offered, and they believe in a "metaphysical or supernatural realm inhabited by souls, spirits, angels, or gods," a realm totally outside the scope of science. By contrast, virtually all scientists known to Mayr "have religion in the best sense of the word." Moreover, they bring to the study of nature a "set of first principles": that there is a real world independent of human perceptions, that this world is structured in such a way as to yield to scientific investigation and explanation, "that there is a historical and causal continuity among all phenomena in the material universe," that the "legitimate domain" of scientific study includes "everything known to exist or happen in this universe."[35]

A quite different picture of scientific first principles informs cell biologist Kenneth R. Miller's book *Finding Darwin's God: A Scientist's Search for a Common Ground between God and Evolution.* Quantum mechanics, says Miller, has discredited the idea of an objective world existing independently of human perception. It has also rendered untenable the idea of an unbroken causal continuity linking all events in the material universe. "What matters," Miller writes, "is the straightforward, factual recognition that matter in the universe behaves in

34. Steven Weinberg, "Can Science Explain Everything? Anything?" *New York Review of Books,* May 31, 2001, p. 50.

35. Weinberg, "Can Science Explain Everything?" p. 50.

such a way that we can never achieve complete knowledge of any fragment of it, and that life itself is structured in a way that allows biological history to pivot directly on these tiny uncertainties. That ought to allow even the most critical scientist to admit that the breaks in causality at the atomic level make it fundamentally *impossible* to exclude the idea that what we have really caught a glimpse of might indeed reflect the mind of God."[36] Despite Einstein's dislike of giving chance a real role in physical events, says Miller, the indeterminate nature of quantum reality won out, leading Niels Bohr to comment: "Who is Einstein to tell God what to do?"

Obviously, Miller does not share Mayr's view that a dialogue between science and theology is impossible. Having established the quantum nature of the material world, he goes on to discuss at length how this discovery affects the basic theological doctrines shared by Jews, Christians, and Muslims concerning miracles, the problem of evil, the nature of God, and the like. Whether the God Miller believes in as a Catholic is, as he tells his students, "Darwin's God" is doubtful. The God of Darwin's *On the Origin of Species* is a deistic God operating through "laws impressed on matter by the Creator." He lost faith in this God when, after writing *The Descent of Man,* he experienced the "horrid doubt" whether his "inward conviction" that the universe was not the result of mere chance had any validity in view of man's shared ancestry with the apes.

Kenneth Miller's belief that theology must engage in dialogue with modern science is shared by the biochemist Arthur Peacocke, who is also an Anglican priest and until recently director of the Ian Ramsay Centre (Oxford) for the study of religion in relation to the sciences. But Peacocke's conception of that dialogue is quite different from the one Arthur James Balfour had in mind. In Peacocke's view, science provides the model and the findings to which theology must conform if Christianity is to have relevance for modern life. "This is one world," Peacocke writes in his essay "New Wineskins for Old Wine: A Credible Theology for a Scientific World." "A monistic naturalism is overwhelmingly indicated by the sciences. This need not be reductive about the many levels of the world, and in human beings; but the only dualism now defensible appears to be the distinction between the Being of God and everything else. Talk of the 'spirit' or the 'soul' as distinct entities appears to be precluded." Likewise, says Peacocke, the doctrines of original sin, the fall of man, a "new heaven and a new earth," and traditional ideas of eternity and God's timelessness must be discarded as inconsistent with modern science. "So what is left? The belief that God is merciful Love and has, through the resurrection of Jesus, taken at least

36. Kenneth R. Miller, *Finding Darwin's God: A Scientist's Search for Common Ground between God and Evolution* (New York: HarperCollins, 1999), pp. 213-14.

one human being fully open to God's presence into the divine life."[37] However unlikely it seems that Peacocke's proposal for a revised theology will prove acceptable to his fellow theologians, it certainly gives the lie to Ernst Mayr's view that theologians never revise their ideas in the light of new evidence.

In contrast to Peacocke's views is a long tradition among British evolutionary biologists working within a framework of traditional Christian theology. Donald MacKay, the late neuroscientist, interpreted the evolutionary process within a strongly providentialist framework that emphasized God's sovereignty over all events.[38] The historians James Moore and David Livingstone have drawn attention to the way in which such a theology has often provided a congenial worldview for evolutionary theory.[39] Other evolutionary biologists, such as R. J. Berry, professor of genetics at London University and a previous president of the Linnaean Society; Ghillean Prance, for many years director of the Royal Botanic Gardens at Kew; Prof. Malcolm Jeeves, formerly president of the Royal Society of Edinburgh with R. J. Berry; Denis Alexander, chairman of the Molecular Immunology Programme at the Babraham Institute, Cambridge;[40] and many others that space does not allow to list, provide a significant ensemble of scientists who have seen little problem in baptizing Darwinism into a robust Christian theism. It is intriguing that the tendency to absorb Darwinism into a conservative Christian theology has been most pronounced in Darwin's own backyard. The correlation may not be accidental. For a sampling of theological responses to modern science on the continent of Europe, Mayr might begin with Niels Gregersen's *Rethinking Theology and Science: Six Models for the Current Dialogue.*[41]

As we have seen, in its search for clear comprehension of natural causes, science strips nature of everything — so-called "secondary" qualities, value, meaning, purpose, human freedom, and spirituality — not amenable to its

---

37. Arthur Peacocke, "New Wineskins for Old Wine: A Credible Theology for a Scientific World," *Science and Spirit* 10, no. 2 (1999): 1-4. See also John Polkinghorne, ed., *The Work of Love: Creation as Kenosis* (Grand Rapids: Eerdmans; London: SPCK, 2001).

38. Donald MacKay, *The Open Mind and Other Essays* (Leicester: InterVarsity, 1986).

39. James Moore, *The Post-Darwinian Controversies: A Study of the Protestant Struggle to Come to Terms with Darwin in Great Britain and America, 1870-1900* (Cambridge: Cambridge University Press, 1979); David Livingstone, *Darwin's Forgotten Defenders* (Edinburgh: Scottish Academic Press, 1987).

40. R. J. Berry, *God the Biologist* (Leicester: Apollos, 1996); Ghillean Prance, in *Real Science, Real Faith* (Eastbourne, E. Sussex, England: Monarch, 1991); Malcolm Jeeves and R. J. Berry, *Science, Life, and Christian Belief* (Leicester: Apollos, 1998); Dennis Alexander, *Rebuilding the Matrix: Science and Faith in the Twenty-First Century* (Oxford: Lion, 2001).

41. Niels Gregersen, *Rethinking Theology and Science: Six Models for the Current Dialogue* (Grand Rapids: Eerdmans, 1998).

methods of investigation and creates its own specialized world of particles, forces, genes, and the like described metaphorically and related mathematically and presented as the real world that somehow or other produces the apparent world of meaning, value, and purpose inhabited by human beings. So conceived, science renders incomprehensible its own discovery of the emergence of new levels of being exhibiting new laws and properties irreducible to the laws and properties of lower levels. Equally incomprehensible is the scientist's passion for truth; her love of nature for its beauty, diversity, and majesty; and her sense of moral obligation as a scientist.

Faced with these incomprehensibilities, what shall we conclude? Shall we conclude with Einstein that the most incomprehensible thing about the universe is that it is comprehensible? Or shall we conclude with Johannes Kepler that "God who founded everything in the world according to the norm of quantity, also has endowed man with a mind which can comprehend these norms"? Or shall we conclude with the absurdist existentialists that the world makes no sense at all or, alternatively, whatever sense we decide to give it? Or, finally, shall we conclude with Balfour that science and theology are enterprises based ultimately on faith and struggling mightily to comprehend and portray in human figures of speech a reality that transcends the power of human thought to grasp fully? On the evidence herein presented, Balfour's view of these issues seems to have been truly prophetic.

## 2. From Paley to Darwin: Design to Natural Selection

Francisco J. Ayala

I argue in this paper that science encompasses all of reality and that we owe this universality to Charles Darwin, who completed the Copernican revolution by extending to the realm of life the Copernican postulate of the natural world as matter in motion governed by natural laws.[1] The Copernican revolution had left out the diversity and configuration of organisms, because organisms and their parts manifest to be designed. Natural selection acting on spontaneously arising mutations can account for the diversity of organisms and their design. Evolution is a creative process owing to a fruitful conjunction of contingent and deterministic processes.

The argument is preceded by a presentation of William Paley's brilliant exposition of the argument-from-design, the most articulate and biologically expert case made to date for the existence of the Creator, elicited from the complex functional design of organisms. Paley's argument suffers from a fatal flaw, namely, the pervasiveness of deficiencies, dysfunctions, oddities, and cruelties in organisms.

I start with two disquisitions: one on the origin, use, and disuse of the term "neo-Darwinism," the other on the validity and limits of science as a way of knowing.

1. Here and elsewhere I speak of the universe as consisting of "matter" and affirm that science encompasses all of reality without implying materialism. Philosophically, my position could be named "methodological naturalism," a position taken, at least in practice, by scientists, implying that science seeks to explain the natural world by formulating hypotheses, laws, and theories that can be tested, by observation and experiment, against the world of nature. Methodological naturalism does not imply epistemological naturalism; that is, it does not imply that science is the only way of knowing. Indeed, as I write below (and I would consider obvious), I uphold the validity of knowledge acquired by nonscientific modes of inquiry, such as common sense, literature, art, philosophy, and theology. That is, epistemologically I am a dualist (or pluralist, if one may prefer).

## On "Neo-Darwinism" the Moniker

Evolutionists and other biologists generally accepted two forms of biological heredity early in the nineteenth century, and well into the early 1880s. Hard inheritance was "founded upon the idea that heredity is brought about by the transmission from one generation to another of a substance with a definite chemical and, above all, molecular constitution."[2] Soft inheritance transmitted modifications acquired by the organism during its lifetime, mostly by use and disuse (as the muscle enhancement that might happen by strenuous exercise) as well as those induced by the environment. Darwin, even if reluctantly and doubtfully at times, accepted soft inheritance but minimized its role in evolution. Lamarck had taken the idea for granted and allowed soft inheritance to play a significant, although not central, role in his theory of evolution. According to Lamarck, the inheritance of acquired characteristics accounts for variation among individuals of the same species, although it is of no consequence in determining the direction or pattern of evolution. The evolution of lineages through time was determined, according to Lamarck, by an inner drive for perfection in all life. Lamarck's theory of evolution was indeed metaphysical,[3] like Henri Bergson's a century later.[4]

Soft inheritance was rejected as a consequence of August Weismann's experiments and his theory of the "continuity of the germ track."[5] Weismann established that there is a separation between the "germ track" and the "soma track" from the very beginning of an individual's life, and thus nothing that happens to the soma can be communicated to the germ plasm. Weismann adopted wholesale Darwin's central idea of natural selection, but exclusively based on hard selection. This theory of evolution was designated by Romanes (1896) as neo-Darwinism.[6] This is how the moniker entered the evolutionary literature.

The term "neo-Darwinism" was frequently used in the late nineteenth century and early twentieth century by proponents of Darwin's theory of natural selection. Interest in the subject and use of the term increased after the re-

---

2. August Weismann, *Essays upon Heredity* (Oxford: Clarendon, 1889), cited by Ernst Mayr, *The Growth of Biological Thought: Diversity, Evolution, and Inheritance* (Cambridge, Mass., and London: Harvard University Press, 1982), p. 699.

3. *Philosophie zoologique,* "Zoological Philosophy," was the title of Lamarck's 1809 book.

4. Henri Bergson, *Creative Evolution* (New York, 1911). Originally *L'Évolution créatrice.*

5. August Weismann, *Die Kontinuität des Keimplasmas als Grundlage einer Theorie der Verebung* (Jena: Gustav Fischer, 1885).

6. See G. J. Romanes, *An Examination of Weismannism* (London: Longmans, Green, 1893), and *Life and Letters* (London: Longman, Green, 1896).

discovery of Mendel's laws of heredity in 1900. Early in the twentieth century, however, an acrimonious controversy arose in which the term "neo-Darwinism," although not a main player in the debate, was largely replaced by the terms representing the two contentious camps and, thus, their theories: "mutationists" (also referred to at the time as Mendelians) and "biometricians." According to Hugo de Vries and other mutationists, notably William Bateson in England, variation in organisms comes in two kinds. One is the "ordinary" variation observed among individuals of a species, which is of no lasting consequence in evolution because it could not "lead to a transgression of the species border." The other consists of the changes brought about by mutations, spontaneous alterations of genes that yield large modifications of the organism and give rise to new species. According to de Vries, a new species originates suddenly, produced by the existing one without any visible preparation and without transition. Mutationism was opposed by the biometricians, led by Briton Karl Pearson, who defended Darwinian natural selection as the major cause of evolution through the cumulative effects of small, continuous, individual variations (which the biometricians assumed passed from one generation to the next without being subject to Mendel's laws of inheritance).

The controversy between mutationists and biometricians approached a resolution in the 1920s and 1930s through the theoretical work of several geneticists who used mathematical arguments to show, first, that continuous variation (in such characteristics as size, number of eggs laid, and the like) could be explained by Mendel's laws; and second, that natural selection acting cumulatively on small variations could yield major evolutionary changes in form and function. Distinguished members of this group of theoretical geneticists were R. A. Fisher and J. B. S. Haldane in Britain, and Sewall Wright in the United States.

The interest of geneticists and other biologists in evolutionary studies was spurred by the publication in 1937 of *Genetics and the Origin of Species,* by Theodosius Dobzhansky. Dobzhansky refashioned the formulations of the mathematical evolutionists in language that biologists could understand, dressed the equations with natural history and experimental population genetics, and extended the synthesis of genetics and natural selection to speciation and other cardinal problems omitted by the mathematicians. *Genetics and the Origin of Species* had an enormous impact on naturalists and experimental biologists, who rapidly embraced the new understanding of the evolutionary process as one of genetic change in populations. Interest in evolutionary studies was greatly stimulated, and contributions to the theory soon began to follow, extending the synthesis of genetics and natural selection to a variety of biological fields. Important contributors to evolutionary theory during the ensuing years were the zoologists Ernst Mayr (*Systematics and the Origin of Species*, 1942) and Julian Huxley (*Evolution: The Modern Synthesis*, 1942), the paleontologist George G. Simpson (*Tempo and Mode in Evolution*, 1944), and the botanist George Ledyard Stebbins (*Variation and Evolution in Plants*, 1950). These researchers contributed to a burst of evolutionary studies in the traditional biological disciplines and in some emerging ones — notably population genetics and, later, evolutionary ecology.

This largely expanded theory of evolution has been, since the 1950s, generally referred to as the synthetic theory of evolution, the modern synthesis of evolutionary theory, or the modern theory of evolution. These labels are still used among biologists, although evolutionary biologists most often simply speak of the theory of evolution.

The term "neo-Darwinism" has little currency among evolutionary biologists. A quick perusal of several recent issues of the five specialized journals where I publish most often (*Genetics; Evolution; Molecular Biology and Evolution; Journal of Molecular Evolution;* and *Phylogenetics and Molecular Evolution*) has failed to discover the term "neo-Darwinism" or any of its cognates among the 400-plus articles examined. A direct Internet query of "neo-Darwinism" has, however, yielded a handful of papers that have used the term since the year 2000 in scientific journals, such as *Heredity, Molecular and General Genetics, Environmental Biology of Fishes,* and *Annals of the New York Academy of Sciences.* Two widely used textbooks (Douglas J. Futuyma, *Evolutionary Biology*, 3rd ed., 1998; Stephen C. Stern and Rolf F. Hoekstra, *Evolution: An Introduction*, 2000) do not include the term in the index; another textbook (Monroe W. Strickberger, *Evolution*, 3rd ed., 2000) uses the term twice in the text and once in the glossary. An advanced but dated treatise (Th. Dobzhansky, F. J. Ayala, J. W. Valentine, and G. L. Stebbins, *Evolution*, 1977) uses the term once, but only historically, in the context of Weismann's theory.

Historians of evolutionary theory use the term "neo-Darwinism" sparingly, and usually only as a term of past currency. Ernst Mayr's monumental, 974-page *Growth of Biological Thought* (1982) uses the term twice, in reference to Weismann in both cases. *The Evolutionary Synthesis* (E. Mayr and W. B. Provine, editors, 1980), a multiauthored historical investigation, refers to neo-Darwinism or neo-Darwinians about a dozen times, but always in the context of early-twentieth-century evolutionary theories, particularly in France and Germany. In current use, it seems that the term "neo-Darwinism" and its cognates are mostly confined to the writings of philosophers and theologians.

## Science as a Way of Knowing: Power and Limits

I do not intend to engage in a full epistemological exploration of the nature and methods of science in this section. My goal is much more modest, limited to stating my views about the significance and bounds of scientific knowledge.

Science as a mode of inquiry into the nature of the universe has been successful and of great consequence. Witness the proliferation of science academic departments in universities and other research institutions, the enormous budgets that the body politic and the private sector willingly commit to scientific research, and its economic impact. The Office of Management and the Budget (OMB) of the U.S. government has estimated that 50 percent of all economic growth in the United States since the Second World War can directly be attributed to scientific knowledge and technical advances. Indeed, the technology derived from scientific knowledge pervades our lives: the high-rise buildings of our cities, thruways and long-span bridges, rockets that take humans to the moon, telephones that provide instant communication across continents, computers that perform complex calculations in millionths of a second, vaccines and drugs that keep bacterial parasites at bay, gene therapies that replace DNA in defective cells. All these remarkable achievements bear witness to the validity of the scientific knowledge from which they originated.

Scientific knowledge is also remarkable in the way it emerges by consensus and agreement among scientists and in the way new knowledge builds upon past accomplishment rather than starting anew with each generation or each new practitioner. Surely scientists disagree with each other on many matters, but these are issues not yet settled, and the points of disagreement generally do not bring into question previous knowledge. Modern scientists do not challenge that atoms exist, or that there is a universe with a myriad stars, or that heredity is encased in the DNA.

Three traits jointly distinguish scientific knowledge from other forms of knowledge.[7] First, science seeks the systematic organization of knowledge about the world. Common sense, like science, provides knowledge about natural phenomena, and this knowledge is often correct. For example, common sense tells one that children resemble their parents and that good seeds produce good crops. Common sense, however, shows little interest in systematically establishing connections between phenomena that do not appear to be obviously

---

7. See Francisco J. Ayala, "On the Scientific Method, Its Practice and Pitfalls," *History and Philosophy of the Life Sciences* 16 (1994): 205-40; see also Ayala, "Biology as an Autonomous Science," *American Scientist* 56 (1968): 207-21, and Ernst Nagel, *The Structure of Science* (New York: Harcourt, Brace and World, 1961), pp. 1-14.

related. By contrast, science is concerned with formulating general laws and theories that manifest patterns of relations between very different kinds of phenomena. Science develops by discovering new relationships, and particularly by integrating statements, laws, and theories that previously seemed to be unrelated, into more comprehensive laws and theories.

Second, science strives to explain why observed events do in fact occur. Although knowledge acquired in the course of ordinary experience is frequently accurate, it seldom provides explanations of why phenomena occur as they do. Practical experience tells us that children resemble one parent in some traits and the other parent in other traits, or that manure increases crop yield. But it does not provide explanations for these phenomena. Science, on the other hand, seeks to formulate explanations for natural phenomena by identifying the conditions that account for their occurrence.

Seeking the systematic organization of knowledge and trying to explain why events are as observed are two characteristics that distinguish science from commonsense knowledge, imaginative literature, and artistic expression. But these characteristics are also shared by other forms of systematic knowledge, such as mathematics, philosophy, and theology. A third characteristic of science, and the one that distinguishes the empirical sciences from other systematic forms of knowledge, is that scientific explanations must be formulated in such a way that they can be subjected to empirical testing, a process that must include the possibility of empirical falsification. Falsifiability has been proposed as the criterion of demarcation that sets science apart from other forms of knowledge.[8]

New ideas in science are advanced in the form of hypotheses. Hypotheses and other imaginative conjectures are the initial stage of scientific inquiry. It is the imaginative conjecture of what might be true that provides the incentive to seek the truth and a clue as to where to find it. Hypotheses guide observation and experiment because they suggest what to observe. Imaginative conjecture and empirical observation are mutually interdependent episodes. Observations made to test a hypothesis are often the inspiring source of new conjectures or hypotheses.

Testing a scientific hypothesis involves at least four different activities. First, the hypothesis must be examined for internal consistency. A hypothesis that is self-contradictory or not logically well formed in some other way should be rejected. Second, the logical structure of the hypothesis must be examined to ascertain whether it has explanatory value, i.e., whether it makes the observed phenomena intelligible in some sense, whether it provides an understanding of

8. See Karl R. Popper, *The Logic of Scientific Discovery* (London: Hutchinson, 1959).

why the phenomena do in fact occur as observed. A hypothesis that is purely tautological should be rejected because it has no explanatory value. A scientific hypothesis identifies the conditions, processes, or mechanisms that account for the phenomena it purports to explain. Thus, hypotheses establish general relationships between certain conditions and their consequences or between certain causes and their effects. For example, the motions of the planets around the sun are explained as a consequence of gravity, and respiration as an effect of red blood cells that carry oxygen from the lungs to various parts of the body.

Third, the hypothesis must be examined for its consistency with hypotheses and theories commonly accepted in the particular field of science, or for whether it represents any advance with respect to well-established alternative hypotheses. Lack of consistency with other theories is not always ground for rejection of a hypothesis, although it often is. Some of the greatest scientific advances occur precisely when it is shown that a widely held and well-supported hypothesis is replaced by one that accounts for the same phenomena that were explained by the preexisting hypothesis, as well as other phenomena it could not account for. One example is the replacement of Newtonian mechanics by the theory of relativity, which rejects the conservation of matter and the simultaneity of events that occur at a distance — two fundamental tenets of Newton's theory.[9]

Internal consistency, explanatory value, and consistency with preexisting knowledge are tests also used in philosophy, theology, and other modes of systematic knowledge, in addition to science.

9. Examples of this kind are pervasive in rapidly advancing disciplines, such as molecular biology at present. The so-called central dogma holds that molecular information flows only in one direction, from DNA to RNA to protein. The DNA contains the genetic information that determines what the organism is, but that information has to be expressed in enzymes (a particular class of proteins) that guide all chemical processes in cells. The information contained in the DNA molecules is conveyed to proteins by means of intermediate molecules, called messenger RNA. David Baltimore and Howard Temin were awarded the Nobel Prize for discovering that information could flow in the opposite direction, from RNA to DNA, by means of the enzyme reverse transcriptase. They showed that some viruses, as they infect cells, are able to copy their RNA into DNA, which then becomes integrated into the DNA of the infected cell, where it is used as if it were the cell's own DNA.

Other examples are the following. Until very recently, it was universally thought that only the proteins known as enzymes could mediate (technically "catalyze") the chemical reactions in cells. However, Thomas Cech and Sidney Altman received in 1989 the Nobel Prize for showing that certain RNA molecules act as enzymes and catalyze their own reactions. One more example concerns the so-called colinearity between DNA and protein. It was generally thought that the sequence of nucleotides in the DNA of a gene is expressed consecutively in the sequence of amino acids in the protein. This conception was shaken by the discovery that genes come in pieces, separated by intervening DNA segments that do not carry genetic information; Richard Roberts and Philip Sharp received the 1993 Nobel Prize for this discovery.

The fourth method of testing a hypothesis, and the one that is distinctive of scientific knowledge, consists of putting the hypothesis on empirical trial, by ascertaining whether or not predictions about the world of experience derived as logical consequences from the hypothesis agree with what is actually observed. Scientific hypotheses cannot be consistent with all possible states of affairs in the empirical world. A hypothesis is scientific only if it is consistent with some but not with other possible states of affairs not yet observed in the world, so that it may be subject to the possibility of falsification by observation. The predictions derived from a scientific hypothesis must be precise enough to limit the range of possible observations with which they are compatible. If the results of an empirical test agree with the predictions derived from a hypothesis, the hypothesis is said to be provisionally corroborated; otherwise it is falsified. The requirement that a scientific hypothesis be falsifiable has been called by Karl Popper the *criterion of demarcation* of the empirical sciences because it sets apart the empirical sciences from other forms of knowledge.

Science is a way of knowing, but it is not the only way. Knowledge also derives from other sources, such as common sense, artistic and religious experience, and philosophical reflection. In *The Myth of Sisyphus,* the great French writer Albert Camus asserted that we learn more about ourselves and the world from a relaxed evening's perception of the starry heavens and the scents of grass than from science's reductionistic ways. One need not endorse such a contrasting claim in order to uphold the validity of the knowledge acquired by nonscientific modes of inquiry. We thus learn about ourselves and about the world in which we live and also benefit from products of nonscientific knowledge. The crops we harvest and the animals we husband emerged, millennia before science's dawn, from practices set down by farmers in the Middle East, Andean sierras, and Mayan plateaus. Philosophical inquiry and theological reflection have for millennia illuminated human nature and its relationships to the world beyond. And so have imaginative literature and the plastic arts. Legal codes and political systems have guided and aided human life, at least since the beginning of agriculture.

It is not my intention here to belabor the extraordinary fruits of nonscientific modes of inquiry. But, in the pages that follow, I will set forth the view that nothing in the world of nature escapes the scientific mode of knowledge, and that we owe this universality to Darwin's revolution. I wish here simply to affirm something that is obvious but becomes at times clouded by the hubris of scientists and the timidity of philosophers and theologians. Successful as it is, and universally encompassing as its subject is, a scientific view of the world is hopelessly incomplete. There are matters of value and meaning that are outside science's scope. Even when we have a satisfying scientific understanding of a natural object or process, we are still missing matters that may well be thought by many to be of equal or greater import. Scientific knowledge may enrich aesthetic and moral perceptions, and illuminate the significance of life and the world, but these are matters outside science's realm that are all-important for understanding human nature and our place in the universe, and for conducting a meaningful life.[10]

## Natural Science as Natural Theology

The English clergyman and author William Paley (1743-1805) was intensely committed to the abolition of the slave trade and had become by the 1780s a much-sought public lecturer against slavery. He was also an influential writer of works on Christian philosophy, ethics, and theology. *The Principles of Moral and Political Philosophy* (1785) and *A View of the Evidences of Christianity* (1794) earned him prestige and well-endowed ecclesiastical benefices, which allowed him a comfortable life. Illness forced him in 1800 to give up his public speaking career, which provided him ample time to study science, particularly biology, and write *Natural Theology; or, Evidences of the Existence and Attributes of the Deity* (1802), the book by which he has become best known to posterity and which would greatly influence Darwin. With *Natural Theology* Paley sought to update John Ray's *Wisdom of God Manifested in the Works of the Creation* (1691), taking advantage of one century of additional scientific knowledge.

William Paley's *Natural Theology* is a sustained "argument from design" claiming that the living world provides compelling evidence of being designed by an omniscient and omnipotent Creator. Paley's keystone claim is that "There cannot be design without a designer; contrivance, without a contriver; order, without choice; . . . means suitable to an end and executing their office in accomplishing that end, without the end ever having been contemplated."[11]

Paley elaborated the argument-from-design with greater cogency and more extensive knowledge of biological detail than had any other author, before or since. Paley brings in all sorts of biological knowledge, from the geographic distribution of species to the interactions between predators and their prey, the interactions between the sexes, the camel's stomach and the woodpecker's tongue, the compound eyes of insects and the spider's web. He explores and re-

---

10. Socrates stated that the unexamined life is not worth living. Socrates surely was not primarily thinking of the scientifically unexamined life.

11. William Paley, *Natural Theology* (New York: American Tract Society, n.d.), pp. 15-16. I will cite pages following this American edition, which is undated, but seems to have been printed in the late nineteenth century. The page numbers have been placed in the text.

jects the possibility of a sort of "natural selection": organisms may have come about by chance in an endless multiplicity of forms; those now in existence are those that happened to be functionally organized because they are the only ones able to survive and reproduce. Paley's evidence for intelligent design and against chance derives from a notion that some contemporary authors have named "irreducible complexity," that he calls "relation": the presence of a great variety of parts interacting with each other to produce an effect, which cannot be accomplished if any of the parts is missing.

Chapters are dedicated to the complex design of the human eye; to the human frame, which displays a precise mechanical arrangement of bones, cartilage, and joints; to the circulation of the blood and the disposition of blood vessels; to the comparative anatomy of humans and animals; to the digestive system, kidneys, urethras, and bladder; to the wings of birds and the fins of fish; and to much more. For 352 pages *Natural Theology* conveys Paley's expertise: extensive and accurate biological knowledge, as detailed and precise as it was available in 1800. After detailing the precise organization and exquisite functionality of each biological object or process, Paley draws again and again the same conclusion, namely, that only an omniscient and omnipotent Deity could account for these marvels of mechanical perfection, purpose, and functionality, and for the enormous diversity of inventions that they entail.

Paley's first example, in chapter 3, is the human eye, which he compares with a telescope: they are both made upon the same principles and bear a complete resemblance to one another, in their configuration, position of the lenses, and effectiveness in bringing each pencil of light to a point at the right distance from the lens. Could, he asks, these attributes be in the eye without purpose? I will quote him at some length, for there is no better way to display his knowledge of the anatomy of the eye or his skill of argumentation.

I know no better method of introducing so large a subject, than that of comparing a single thing with a single thing: an eye, for example, with a telescope. As far as the examination of the instrument goes, there is precisely the same proof that the eye was made for vision, as there is that the telescope was made for assisting it. They are made upon the same principles; both being adjusted to the laws by which the transmission and refraction of rays of light are regulated. . . . For instance, these laws require, in order to produce the same effect, that the rays of light, in passing from water into the eye, should be refracted by a more convex surface than when it passes out of air into the eye. Accordingly we find that the eye of a fish, in that part of it called the crystalline lens, is much rounder than the eye of terrestrial animals. What plainer manifestation of design can there be than this difference? What could a mathematical instrument maker have done more to show his knowledge of [t]his principle, his application of that knowledge, his suiting of his means to his end . . . to testify counsel, choice, consideration, purpose? (pp. 20-21)

It is worthwhile to follow Paley's argument a bit further:

The lenses of the telescopes and the humors of the eye bear a complete resemblance to one another, in their figure, their position, and in their power over the rays of light, namely, in bringing each pencil to a point at the right distance from the lens; namely, in the eye, at the exact place where the membrane is spread to receive it. How is it possible, under circumstances of such close affinity, and under the operation of equal evidence, to exclude contrivance from the one, yet to acknowledge the proof of contrivance having been employed, as the plainest and clearest of all propositions, in the other? (p. 22)

He brings in, to his argument's advantage, the issue of dioptric distortion:

In dioptric telescopes there is an imperfection of this nature. Pencils of light, in passing through glass lenses, are separated into different colors, thereby tinting the object, especially the edges of it, as if it were viewed through a prism. To correct this inconvenience has been long a desideratum in the art. At last it came into the mind of a sagacious optician, to inquire how this matter was managed in the eye, in which there was exactly the same difficulty to contend with as in the telescope. His observation taught him that in the eye the evil was cured by combining lenses composed of different substances, that is, of substances which possessed different refracting powers. Our artist borrowed thence his hint, and produced a correction of the defect by imitating, in glasses made from different materials, the effects of the different humors through which the rays of light pass before they reach the bottom of the eye. Could this be in the eye without purpose, which suggested to the optician the only effectual means of attaining that purpose? (pp. 22-23)

The functional anatomy of the eye is, later on, summarized as follows:

[We marvel] knowing as we do what an eye comprehends, namely, that it should have consisted, first, of a series of transparent lenses — very different, by the by, even in their substance, from the opaque materials of which the rest of the body is, in general at least, composed, and with which the whole of its surface, this single portion of it excepted, is covered: secondly, of a black cloth or canvas — the only membrane in the body which is black — spread out behind these lenses, so as to receive the image formed by pencils of light transmitted through them; and placed at the precise geometrical distance at which, and at which alone, a distinct image could be formed, namely, at the concourse of the refracted rays: thirdly, of a large nerve communicating between this membrane and the brain; without which, the action of light upon the membrane, however modified by the organ, would be lost to the purposes of sensation. (p. 48)

Could the eye have come about without design or preconceived purpose, as a result of chance? Paley had set the argument against chance, in the very first paragraph of *Natural Theology,* arguing rhetorically by analogy:

In crossing a heath, suppose I pitched my foot against a stone, and were asked how the stone came to be there, I might possibly answer, that for any thing I knew to the contrary it had lain there for ever; nor would it, perhaps, be very easy to show the absurdity of this answer. But suppose I had found a watch upon the ground, and it should be inquired how the watch happened to be in that place, I should hardly think of the answer which I had before given, that for any thing I knew the watch might have always been there. Yet why should not this answer serve for the watch as well as for the stone; why is it not as admissible in the second case as in the first? For this reason, and for no other, namely, that when we come to inspect the watch, we perceive — what we could not discover in the stone — that its several parts are framed and put together for a purpose, e.g. that they are so formed and adjusted as to produce motion, and that motion so regulated as to point out the hour of the day; that if the different parts had been differently shaped from what they are, or placed after any other manner or in any other order than that in which they are placed, either no motion at all would have been carried on in the machine, or none which would have answered the use that is now served by it. (p. 1)

The strength of the argument against chance derives, Paley tells us, from what he names "relation," a notion akin to what some contemporary anti-evolutionist writers have named "irreducible complexity" (and that some of them have given themselves credit for discovering). This is how Paley formulates the argument.

When several different parts contribute to one effect, or, which is the same thing, when an effect is produced by the joint action of different instruments, the fitness of such parts or instruments to one another for the purpose of producing, by their united action, the effect, is what I call relation; and wherever this is observed in the works of nature or of man, it appears to me to carry along with it decisive evidence of understanding, intention, art . . . all depending upon the motions within, all upon the system of intermediate actions. (pp. 175-76)

The outcomes of chance do not exhibit relation among the parts or, as we might say, organized complexity:

> The question is, whether a useful or imitative conformation be the produce of chance. . . . Universal experience is against it. What does chance ever do for us? In the human body, for instance, chance, that is, the operation of causes without design, may produce a wen, a wart, a mole, a pimple, but never an eye. Among inanimate substances, a clod, a pebble, a liquid drop might be; but never was a watch, a telescope, an organized body of any kind, answering a valuable purpose by a complicated mechanism, the effect of chance. In no assignable instance has such a thing existed without intention somewhere. (p. 49)

## In Praise of Imperfection

Paley's natural theology fails, even in his time, when seeking an account of imperfections, defects, pain, and cruelty that would be consistent with his notion of the Creator. Chapter 23 is entitled "Of the Personality of the Deity," and it would surprise many by its well-meaning, if naive, arrogance, as Paley seems convinced that he can determine God's "personality." This is how the chapter starts: "Contrivance, if established, appears to me to prove . . . the personality of the Deity, as distinguished from what is sometimes called nature, sometimes called a principle. . . . Now, that which can contrive, which can design, must be a person. These capacities constitute personality, for they imply consciousness and thought. . . . The acts of a mind prove the existence of a mind; and in whatever a mind resides, is a person. The seat of intellect is a person" (p. 265). Paley proceeds in the next chapter to set "the natural attributes of the Deity," namely, omnipotence, omniscience, omnipresence, eternity, self-existence, necessary existence, and spirituality. All these Paley infers from the observation of natural processes!

Paley raises the question of organs or parts seemingly unnecessary or superfluous. He considers two possible states of affairs: "in some instances the operation, in others the use, is unknown." Examples of the first kind include the lungs of animals, which we know to be necessary for survival, although we are not "acquainted with the action of the air upon the blood, or in what manner that action is communicated by the lungs" (p. 46). Instances "may be numerous; for they will be so in proportion to our ignorance. . . . Every improvement of knowledge diminishes their number" (p. 47). Examples of organs whose use is unknown include the spleen, which seems not to be necessary, for "it has been extracted from dogs without any sensible injury to their vital functions." But the part may serve some unknown function, says Paley, even if it is not necessary for survival in the short run. In any case, "superfluous parts do not negative the reasoning which we instituted concerning those parts which are useful" (p. 47).

This last comment seems to me remarkable in that it is so unconvincing and so inconsistent with Paley's conceptual framework. Yet this is his general explanation for nature's imperfections: "Irregularities and imperfections are of little or no weight . . . but they are to be taken in conjunction with the unexceptionable evidences which we possess of skill, power, and benevolence displayed in other instances" (p. 46). But if functional design manifests an intelligent designer, why should not deficiencies indicate that the designer is less than omniscient, or less than omnipotent, or less than benevolent? Paley cannot have it both ways. Moreover, we know that some deficiencies are not just imperfections, but they are outright dysfunctional, jeopardizing the very function the organ or part is supposed to serve. We now know, of course, that the explanation for dysfunction and imperfection is natural selection, which can account for design and functionality but does not achieve any sort of perfection, nor is it omniscient or omnipotent.

Organs with unknown functions, Paley points out, correctly, may be attributable to our limited knowledge; a function may eventually be discovered. His suggestion is that, for example, the function of the lungs or of the spleen might eventually be discovered, as indeed it has been for these two organs. For actual irregularities, dysfunctions, and imperfections, his claim that "they are of little or no weight" seems to me totally unsatisfactory.

Michael Behe, one recent author who has reformulated Paley's argument-from-design, responds to the critics who point out the imperfections of organisms in a different way.

> The most basic problem is that the argument [against intelligent design] demands perfection at all. Clearly, designers who have the ability to make better designs do not necessarily do so. . . . I do not give my children the best, fanciest toys because I don't want to spoil them, and because I want them to learn the value of a dollar. The argument from imperfection over-

looks the possibility that the designer might have multiple motives, with engineering excellence oftentimes relegated to a secondary role. . . . Another problem with the argument from imperfection is that it critically depends on psychoanalysis of the unidentified designer. Yet the reasons that a designer would or would not do anything are virtually impossible to know unless the designer tells you specifically what those reasons are.[12]

So, God may have had his reasons for not designing organisms as perfect as they could have been.

A problem with this explanation is that it destroys "intelligent design" as a scientific hypothesis (which is what Behe claims it to be), because it provides it with an empirically impenetrable shield.[13] If we cannot reject intelligent design because the designer may have reasons that we could not possibly ascertain, there would seem to be no way to test intelligent design by drawing out predictions logically derived from the hypothesis that are expected to be observed in the world of experience. Intelligent design as an explanation for the adaptations of organisms could be (natural) theology, as Paley would have it, but, whatever it is, it is not a scientific hypothesis.

I would argue, moreover, that it is not good theology either, because it leads to conclusions about the nature of the designer quite different from those of omniscience, omnipotence, and benevolence that Paley had inferred as the attributes of the Creator. It is not only that organisms and their parts are less than perfect, but also that deficiencies and dysfunctions are pervasive, evidencing defective "design." Consider the human jaw. We have too many teeth for the jaw's size, so that wisdom teeth need to be removed and orthodontists make a decent living straightening the others. Would we want to blame God for such defective design? A human engineer could have done better. Evolution gives a good account of this imperfection. Brain size increased over time in our ancestors, and the remodeling of the skull to fit the larger brain entailed a reduction of the jaw. Evolution responds to the organisms' needs through natural selection, not by optimal design but by "tinkering," as it were, by slowly modifying

12. Michael J. Behe, *Darwin's Black Box: The Biochemical Challenge to Evolution* (New York: Simon and Schuster, Touchstone, 1996), p. 223.

13. See Robert T. Pennock, ed., *Tower of Babel: The Evidence against the New Creationism* (Cambridge, Mass., and London: MIT Press, 2000), p. 249. The implications of this point for the teaching of evolution in the schools have been drawn in the public arena. In the *Washington Times*, March 21, 2002, U.S. Senator Edward Kennedy, who has publicly supported the teaching of alternate scientific theories when there is diversity of opinion among scientists, writes that "intelligent design is not a genuine scientific theory and, therefore, has no place in the curriculum of our nation's public school science classes."

existing structures. Consider now the birth canal of women: it is much too narrow for easy passage of the infant's head, so that thousands upon thousands of babies die during delivery. Surely we don't want to blame God for this defective design or for the children's deaths. Science makes it understandable, a consequence of the evolutionary enlargement of our brain. Females of other animals do not experience this difficulty. Theologians in the past struggled with the issue of dysfunction because they thought it had to be attributed to God's design. Science, much to the relief of many theologians, provides an explanation that convincingly attributes defects, deformities, and dysfunctions to natural causes.[14]

One more human example: Why are our arms and our legs, which are used for such different functions, made of the same materials, the same bones, muscles, and nerves, all arranged in the same overall pattern? Evolution makes sense of the anomaly. Our remote ancestors' forelimbs were legs. After our ancestors became bipedal and started using their forelimbs for functions other than walking, these became gradually modified but retained their original composition and arrangement. Engineers start with raw materials and a design suited for a particular purpose; evolution can only modify what is already there. An engineer who would design both cars and airplanes, or both wings and wheels, using the same materials arranged in a similar pattern, would surely be fired.

Examples of deficiencies and dysfunctions in all sorts of organisms can be endlessly multiplied, reflecting the opportunistic, tinkerer-like character of natural selection, rather than intelligent design. The world of organisms also abounds in characteristics that might be called "oddities," as well as those that have been characterized as "cruelties," an apposite qualifier if the cruel behaviors were designed outcomes of a being holding on to human or higher standards of morality. But the "cruelties" of biological nature are only metaphoric "cruelties" when applied to the outcomes of natural selection. Examples of

---

14. Examples of theologians who account for the evolution and "design" of organisms in terms of natural causes, without special intervention of God or any "intelligent designer," include Ian Barbour and John F. Haught, among the participants in this volume, as well as Arthur Peacocke, who has referred to Darwinism as the "disguised friend" and has quoted, with approval, Aubrey Moore's 1891 *Lux Mundi*: "Darwinism appeared, and, under the disguise of a foe, did the work of a friend" ("Biological Evolution — a Positive Appraisal," in *Evolutionary and Molecular Biology: Scientific Perspectives on Divine Action,* ed. Robert J. Russell, W. R. Stoeger, and Francisco J. Ayala [Vatican City: Vatican Observatory; Berkeley: Center for Theology and the Natural Sciences, 1998], pp. 356-76). In a similar manner, see in the same volume John Haught, "Darwin's Gift to Theology" (pp. 393-418): "The challenge of Darwin to theology, I shall argue, will in the end prove not to be a damper, but a gift" (p. 395).

"cruelty" involve not only the familiar predators (say, a chimpanzee) tearing apart their prey (say, a small monkey held alive by a chimpanzee biting large flesh morsels from the screaming monkey), or parasites destroying the functional organs of their hosts.

Cruelties are found also, and very abundantly, between organisms of the same species, even between individuals of different sexes in association with their mating. A well-known example is the female praying mantis that devours the male after coitus is completed. Less familiar is that, if she gets the opportunity, the female will eat the head of the male before mating, after which the headless male mantis thrashes in spasms of "sexual frenzy" that allow the female to connect his genitalia with hers.[15] In some midges (tiny flies), the female captures the male as if he were any other prey and with the tip of her proboscis injects into his head her spittle that starts digesting the male's innards that she then sucks; partly protected from digestion are the relatively intact male organs that break off inside the female and fertilize her.[16] Male cannibalism is known in dozens of species, particularly spiders and scorpions. Diverse sorts of oddities associated with mating behavior are described in the delightful, but accurate and documented, book by Olivia Judson, *Dr. Tatiana's Sex Advice to All Creation.*[17]

The defective design of organisms could be attributed to the gods of the ancient Greeks, Romans, and Egyptians, who fought with one another, made blunders, and were clumsy in their endeavors. But, in my view, it is not compatible with special action by the omniscient and omnipotent God of Judaism, Christianity, and Islam. The American philosopher David Hull has made the same point with shrill language:

> What kind of God can one infer from the sort of phenomena epitomized by the species on Darwin's Galapagos Islands? The evolutionary process is rife with happenstance, contingency, incredible waste, death, pain and horror. . . . Whatever the God implied by evolutionary theory and the data of natural selection may be like, he is not the Protestant God of waste not, want not. He is also not the loving God who cares about his productions. He is not even the awful God pictured in the Book of Job. The God of the

15. S. E. Lawrence, "Sexual Cannibalism in the Praying Mantis, *Mantis Religiosa:* A Field Study," *Animal Behaviour* 43 (1992): 569-83; see also M. A. Elgar, "Sexual Cannibalism in Spiders and Other Invertebrates," in *Cannibalism: Ecology and Evolution among Diverse Taxa*, ed. M. A. Elgar and B. J. Crespi (Oxford: Oxford University Press, 1992).

16. See J. A. Downes, "Feeding and Mating in the Insectivorous Ceratopogoninae (Diptera)," *Memoirs of the Entomological Society of Canada* 104 (1978): 1-62.

17. Olivia Johnson, *Dr. Tatiana's Sex Advice to All Creation* (New York: Holt, 2002).

Galapagos is careless, wasteful, indifferent, almost diabolical. He is certainly not the sort of God to whom anyone would be inclined to pray.[18]

## Darwin's Revolution

Charles Darwin read and enjoyed *Natural Theology* while a student at Cambridge University and found the argument compelling, but this would change later. I have elsewhere suggested that the motivating objective of Darwin's *Origin of Species* was to provide a solution to Paley's problem; namely, to demonstrate how his discovery of natural selection would account for the design of organisms, without the need to resort to supernatural agencies. As Darwin saw it, if his explanation were correct, biological evolution would follow; organisms would have changed over time and diversified, in response to a diversity of conditions in different places and at different times. Darwin, therefore, assembled evidence for evolution because the occurrence of evolution corroborated his explanation of design as a result of natural selection.[19]

The interaction between "chance" processes, such as genetic mutation and recombination, and natural selection yields a creative process that generates novelty (new sorts of organisms) and adaptation. The organisms appear to be designed to live in their environments, and their parts appear to be designed to fulfill certain functions, as a consequence of the incremental, step-by-step dialogue and barter between contingent genetic events and natural selection, exercised over aeons of time. But the process is haphazard, imperfections are pervasive, and the immense majority of species become extinct. The defective and dysfunctional design of organisms amounts to an "argument-from-imperfection" for the origin of organisms by natural processes.

There is a priggish version of the history of the ideas that sees a parallel between Copernicus's and Darwin's monumental intellectual contributions, which are said to have eventuated two revolutions. According to this version, the Copernican revolution consisted in displacing the earth from its previously accepted locus as the center of the universe, moving it to a subordinate place as one more planet revolving around the sun. In congruous manner, this version affirms, the Darwinian revolution consisted in displacing humans from their position as the center of life on Earth, with all other species created for the purpose of humankind, and placing humans instead as one species among many in

18. See D. L. Hull, "God of the Galapagos," *Nature* 352 (1992): 485-86.

19. Francisco J. Ayala, "Intelligent Design: The Original Version," *Theology and Science* 1 (2003): 9-32.

the living world, so that humans are related to chimpanzees, gorillas, and other species by shared common ancestry. Copernicus had accomplished his revolution with the heliocentric theory of the solar system. Darwin's achievement emerged from his theory of organic evolution.

I have proposed that this version of the two revolutions is inadequate: what it says is true, but it misses what is most important about these two intellectual revolutions, namely, that they ushered in the beginning of science in the modern sense of the word. These two revolutions may jointly be seen as the one scientific revolution, with two stages, the Copernican and the Darwinian.[20] Darwin is deservedly given credit for the theory of biological evolution, because he accumulated evidence demonstrating that organisms evolve, and he discovered the process, natural selection, by which they evolve their functional organization. But *The Origin of Species* is important because it completed the Copernican revolution, initiated three centuries earlier, and thereby radically changed our conception of the universe and the place of mankind in it.

The Copernican revolution was launched with the publication in 1543, the year of Nicolaus Copernicus's death, of his *De revolutionibus orbium celestium (On the Revolutions of the Celestial Spheres),* and bloomed with the publication in 1687 of Isaac Newton's *Philosophiae naturalis principia mathematica (The Mathematical Principles of Natural Philosophy).* The discoveries of Copernicus, Kepler, Galileo, Newton, and others, in the sixteenth and seventeenth centuries, had gradually ushered in a conception of the universe as matter in motion governed by natural laws. It was shown that the earth is not the center of the universe, but a small planet rotating around an average star; that the universe is immense in space and in time; and that the motions of the planets around the sun can be explained by the same simple laws that account for the motion of physical objects on our planet (laws such as $f = m \times a$, force = mass $\times$ acceleration, or the inverse-square law of attraction, $f = g\ (m_1,\ m_2)/r^2$). These and other discoveries greatly expanded human knowledge, but the conceptual revolution they brought about was more fundamental yet: a commitment to the postulate that the universe obeys immanent laws that account for natural phenomena. The workings of the universe were brought into the realm of science: explanation through natural laws. Physical phenomena could be accounted for whenever the causes were adequately known.

Darwin completed the Copernican revolution by drawing out for biology the ultimate conclusion of the notion of nature as a lawful system of matter in motion. The adaptations and diversity of organisms, the origin of novel and

20. Francisco J. Ayala, "Darwin's Devolution: Design without Designer," in *Evolutionary and Molecular Biology,* pp. 101-16.

highly organized forms, the origin of mankind itself, could now be explained by an orderly process of change governed by natural laws.

The advances of physical science had driven mankind's conception of the universe to a sort of intellectual schizophrenia, which persisted into the middle of the nineteenth century. Scientific explanations, derived from natural laws, dominated the world of nonliving matter, on the earth as well as in the heavens. However, supernatural explanations, depending on the unfathomable deeds of the Creator, were accepted in order to account for the origin and configuration of living creatures — the most diversified, complex, and interesting realities of the world. It was Darwin's genius to resolve this intellectual inconsistency. Darwin completed the Copernican revolution by drawing out for biology the notion of nature as a lawful system of matter in motion, which human reason can explain without recourse to extranatural agencies.

The conundrum faced by Darwin can hardly be overestimated. The strength of the argument-from-design to demonstrate the role of the Creator had been forcefully set forth by Paley. Wherever there is function or design, we look for its author. Paley had belabored this argument with great skill and profusion of detail. It was Darwin's greatest accomplishment to show that the complex organization and functionality of living beings can be explained as the result of a natural process, natural selection, without any need to resort to a Creator or other external agent. The origin and adaptation of organisms in their profusion and wondrous variations were thus brought into the realm of science.

Darwin agreed that organisms are "designed" for certain purposes; i.e., they are functionally organized. Organisms are adapted to certain ways of life, and their parts are adapted to perform certain functions. Fish are adapted to live in water, kidneys are designed to regulate the composition of blood, the human hand is made for grasping. But Darwin went on to provide a natural explanation of the design. The seemingly purposeful aspects of living beings could now be explained, like the phenomena of the inanimate world, by the methods of science, as the result of natural laws manifested in natural processes.

## Darwin's Explanation of Design: Evolution as By-Product

In *The Origin of Species,* Darwin argues that hereditary adaptive variations ("variations useful in some way to each being") are likely to appear in organisms ("seeing that variations useful to man have undoubtedly occurred," as in the selection of domestic animals and plants). He summarizes the argument for natural selection and its definition as follows: "If such [useful variations] do occur, can we doubt . . . that individuals having any advantage, however slight, over others, would have the best chance of surviving and of procreating their kind? . . . [The] preservation of favorable variations and the rejection of injurious variations, I call Natural Selection."[21]

The success of pigeon fanciers and animal breeders clearly evinces the occasional occurrence of "useful" hereditary variations. Useful variations are those that may make possible or improve some function, such as vision, fleetness, gathering or processing food, and the like. Individuals with more useful variations will generally have higher probability of surviving and procreating than individuals with less useful variations. Over the generations favorable variations will be preserved, multiplied, and conjoined; injurious ones will be eliminated. In one place Darwin adds: "I can see no limit to this power [natural selection] in slowly and beautifully adapting each form to the most complex relations of life."[22]

Darwin's argument addresses the same issues as Paley's: how to account for the adaptive configuration of organisms, the obvious "design" of their parts to fulfill their particular functions. Darwin proposed natural selection not to account for the evolution of organisms, but to account for their being designed — configured to carry out certain functions, a certain way of life, and made up of composite parts suited for performing those functions. According to Darwin, evolutionary change through time and evolutionary diversification (multiplication of species) are not necessarily promoted by natural selection (hence, the so-called evolutionary stasis noted by Darwin and emphasized by the theory of punctuated equilibrium), but they often ensue as by-products of natural selection fostering adaptation.

One possible reading of Darwin's *Origin of Species* sees it, first and foremost, as a sustained effort to solve Paley's problem within a scientific explanatory framework. This is indeed how I interpret Darwin's masterpiece. The introduction and chapters 1–8 explain how natural selection accounts for the adaptations and behaviors of organisms, their "design." The extended argument starts in chapter 1, where Darwin describes the successful selection of domestic plants and animals and, with considerable detail, the success of pigeon fanciers seeking exotic "sports." This evidence manifests what selection can accomplish using spontaneous variations beneficial to man. The ensuing

21. See Charles Darwin, *On the Origin of Species,* a facsimile of the first edition of 1859 (New York: Atheneum, 1967). Quotations from Darwin in this paragraph are from the 1967 edition, pp. 80-81.

22. Darwin, *Origin of Species* (1967), p. 469.

chapters extend the argument to variations propagated by natural selection (i.e., reproductive success) for the benefit of the organisms, rather than by artificial selection for traits desirable to humans. Organisms exhibit design, but it is not "intelligent design," imposed by God as a Supreme Engineer. It is the result of natural selection promoting the adaptation of organisms to their environments. Organisms exhibit complexity; however, this is not an "irreducible complexity" that has emerged all of a sudden in its current elaboration, but one that has arisen gradually and cumulatively, step-by-step, promoted by the adaptive success of individuals with incrementally more complex elaborations.

If Darwin's explanation of the adaptive organization of living beings is correct, evolution necessarily follows, as organisms become adapted to different environments and to the changing conditions of environments, and as hereditary variations become available at a particular time that improves the organisms' chances of survival and reproduction. *Origin*'s evidence for biological evolution is central to Darwin's explanation of "design," because his explanation necessitates the occurrence of biological evolution, which he, therefore, adduces in order to support his argument of design by natural selection. He proffers this evidence of evolution in most of the remainder of the book (chapters 9–13), returning to the original theme in the concluding chapter 14. In the last paragraph of *Origin,* Darwin eloquently returns to the dominant theme of adaptation or design:

> It is interesting to contemplate an entangled bank, clothed with many plants of many kinds, with birds singing on the bushes, with various insects flitting about, and with worms crawling through the damp earth, and to reflect that these elaborately constructed forms, so different from each other, and dependent on each other in so complex a manner, have all been produced by laws acting around us. . . . Thus, from the war of nature, from famine and death, the most exalted object which we are capable of conceiving, namely, the production of the higher animals, directly follows. There is grandeur in this view of life, with its several powers, having been originally breathed into a few forms or into one; and that, whilst this planet has gone cycling on according to the fixed law of gravity, from so simple a beginning endless forms most beautiful and most wonderful have been, and are being, evolved.[23]

23. Darwin, *Origin of Species* (1967), pp. 489-90.

## Natural Selection and Mutation

The modern understanding of the principle of natural selection is formulated in genetic and statistical terms as differential reproduction. Natural selection causes some genes and genetic combinations to be transmitted to the following generations with a higher probability than their alternates. Such genetic units will become more common in subsequent generations, and their alternates less common. Natural selection is a statistical bias in the relative rate of reproduction of alternative genetic units.

Natural selection acts in the filtering way of a sieve, by eliminating harmful genetic variants and retaining beneficial ones, but it is much more than a purely negative process, for it is able to generate novelty by increasing the probability of otherwise extremely improbable genetic combinations, as it proceeds stepwise. Natural selection is thus a creative process. It does not "create" the entities upon which it operates, but it produces adaptive (functional) genetic combinations that could not have existed otherwise.

Natural selection has no foresight, nor does it operate according to some preconceived plan. Rather it is a purely natural process resulting from the interacting properties of physicochemical and biological entities. Natural selection is simply a consequence of the differential multiplication of living beings, as pointed out. It has some appearance of purposefulness because it is conditioned by the environment: which organisms reproduce more effectively depends on which variations they possess that are useful in the place and at the time where the organisms live. But natural selection does not anticipate the environments of the future; drastic environmental changes may be insuperable to organisms that were previously thriving. Species extinction is the common outcome of the evolutionary process. The species existing today represent the balance between the origin of new species and their eventual extinction. More than 99 percent of all species that ever lived on Earth have become extinct without issue. These may have been more than one billion species; the available inventory of living species has identified and described less than two million out of some ten million or more estimated to be now in existence.

Natural selection does not strive to produce predetermined kinds of organisms, but only organisms that are adapted to their present environments. Which characteristics will be selected depends on which variations happen to be present at a given time in a given place. This in turn depends on the random process of mutation (broadly understood; see below), as well as on the previous history of the organisms (i.e., on the genetic makeup they have as a consequence of their previous evolution). Natural selection is an "opportunistic" process. The variables determining in which direction it will go are the environment, the preexisting constitution of the organisms, and the randomly arising mutations.

The process of mutation that provides the raw materials for natural selection is now known to be much more complex than it was thought a few decades ago. There are the point mutations, changes of a single nucleotide by another in the DNA, which in protein-coding genes may or may not change the encoded protein; some mutations involve DNA segments within a single gene or that implicate more than one gene; genes and DNA segments change locations; there are chromosomal mutations that involve exchanges between chromosomes (and, thus, involving many genes), and that fuse, split, duplicate one or more chromosomes, even a complete chromosome complement, as in the polyploidy; genomes are very dynamic, continuously experiencing additions, duplications, deletions, and all sorts of changes, implicating from very small to huge DNA segments; full genomes may be acquired, even within a preexisting genome, or in the form of organelles, such as the mitochondria and chloroplasts that characterize eukaryotic organisms, such as animals and plants. Now we know that lateral transfer of genes among distantly related organisms went on for millions and millions of years, to the extent the early evolution of the three domains of life (bacteria, archaea, and eukarya) may have formed not just a genetic bush of interconnected branches, but a "ring of life," which nevertheless preserves the prokaryote-eukaryote divide.[24]

Mutations are said to be accidental, undirected, random, or chance events. These terms are often used as synonyms, but there are at least three different senses in which they are predicated of the mutation process. *First,* mutations are accidental or chance events, in the sense that they are rare exceptions to the regularity of the process of DNA replication, which normally involves precise copying of the hereditary information, encoded in the nucleotide sequences. *Second,* mutations are accidental, random, or chance events also because there is no way of knowing whether a given gene or genome will mutate in a particular cell or in a particular generation. We cannot predict which individuals will have a new mutation and which ones will not, nor can we predict which gene will mutate in a given individual. This does not imply that no regularities exist in the mutation process; the regularities are those associated with stochastic processes, to which probabilities can be assigned. There is a definite probability (although it may not have been ascertained) that a given gene will mutate in any given individual. Moreover, it is not true that any mutation is just

---

24. M. C. Rivera and J. A. Lake, "The Ring of Life Provides Evidence for a Genome Fusion Origin of Eukaryotes," *Nature* 431 (2004): 152-55; see also in the same volume W. Martin and T. M. Embley, "Early Evolution Comes Full Circle," pp. 134-37.

as likely to occur as any other mutation. *Third,* mutations are accidental, undi-rected, random, or chance events in a sense that is very important for evolution: they are unoriented with respect to adaptation. Mutations occur independently of whether or not they are adaptive in the environments where the organisms live. In fact, newly arisen mutations are much more likely to be deleterious than beneficial. It is easy to see why this should be so. The genes occurring in a popu-lation have been subject to natural selection. Genetic variants that occur in sub-stantial frequencies in a species are therefore adaptive; they are common in the species precisely because they are favored by natural selection. Any newly aris-ing mutation is likely also to have arisen earlier in the history of the population; if such a mutation does not already exist in substantial frequencies, it is because it has been eliminated or kept at low frequencies by natural selection, owing to its harmful effects on the organisms. But this point should not be carried too far. It is important to realize that mutations are not beneficial or harmful in the abstract, but rather with respect to some specific environment, at some specific time, and in some particular organism.

## Contingency and Determinism

Natural selection accounts for the "design" of organisms, because adaptive vari-ations tend to increase the probability of survival and reproduction of their carriers at the expense of maladaptive, or less adaptive, variations. The argu-ments of Paley against the incredible improbability of chance accounts of the adaptations of organisms are well taken as far as they go. But neither Paley nor any other author before Darwin was able to discern that there is a natural pro-cess (namely, natural selection) that is not random, but rather is oriented and able to generate order or "create." The traits that organisms acquire in their evo-lutionary histories are not fortuitous but determined by their functional utility to the organisms, "designed" as it were to serve their life needs.

The process of mutation cannot by itself account for adaptation or de-sign. Mutations occur in single individuals; even if a mutation occurs repeat-edly in a species consisting of many individuals, it will never extend, not even nearly, to all members of the species because particular mutations will be, over time, counteracted by other mutations and dissolve. Natural selection — i.e., differential multiplication — can accomplish adaptation because a favorable mutation that has occurred in one individual may thus spread to the whole spe-cies in a few generations, few in the scale of evolution, and with high probabil-ity in the scale of the low probability of mutations.

Chance is nevertheless an integral part of the evolutionary process. The mutations that yield the hereditary variations available to natural selection arise at random, independently of whether they are beneficial or harmful to their carriers. This random process (as well as others that come to play in the great theater of life) is counteracted by natural selection, which preserves what is useful and eliminates the harmful. Without mutations, evolution could not happen because there would be no variations that could be differentially conveyed from one generation to another. But without natural selection, the mutation process would yield disorganization and extinction, because most mutations are disadvantageous and occur erratically. Mutation and selection have jointly driven the marvelous process that starting from microscopic organisms has yielded orchids, birds, and humans.

The theory of evolution conveys chance and necessity intricately conjoined in the stuff of life. Contingency and determinism interlocked in a natural process that has produced the most complex, diverse, and beautiful entities in the universe: the organisms that populate the earth, including humans, who think and love, are endowed with free will and creative powers, and are able to analyze the process of evolution itself that brought them into existence. This was Darwin's fundamental discovery, that there is a process that is creative though not conscious. And this is the conceptual revolution that Darwin completed: that everything in nature, including the "design" of living organisms, can be accounted for as the result of natural processes governed by natural laws. This is nothing if not a fundamental vision that has forever changed how mankind perceives itself and its place in the universe.

## 3. *Reduction, Emergence, Naturalism, Dualism, Teleology: A Précis*

FRANCISCO J. AYALA

In the pages that follow I convey my understanding of the meaning of various philosophical terms, which appear in various places in the present volume. Terms such as "reduction," "emergence," "naturalism," and "dualism" are sometimes used without qualification, yet with different meanings in different places. At best, this essay would show that apparent disagreements may just be apparent. When the disagreements are real, the exercise that follows may help to define the nature of the disagreement.

### Reduction

Organisms are complex self-organizing entities made up of parts: organs, tissues, cells, organelles, and ultimately molecules and atoms. One question that arises concerns the relationship between the whole and its component parts. The issue at stake is sometimes called "the question of reduction" or "the problem of reductionism." Few if any questions in the philosophy of science have received more attention and been more actively debated than the question of reduction. The debates, however, often involve several different issues, not always properly distinguished. Issues about the relationship between organisms and their physical components, or between biology and the physical sciences, arise in at least three domains, which may be called "ontological," "methodological," and "epistemological."

Reduction questions arise, first, in a domain that may be called ontological, structural, or constitutive. The issue here is whether physicochemical entities and processes underlie all living phenomena. Are organisms constituted of the same components as those making up inorganic matter? Or do organisms consist of other entities besides molecules and atoms? Ontological reductionism claims that organisms are exhaustively composed of nonliving parts; no substance or other residue remains after all atoms making up an organism are taken into account. Ontological reductionism also implies that the laws of physics and chemistry fully apply to all biological processes at the level of atoms and molecules. It does not necessarily imply, however, that organisms are nothing but atoms and molecules. The inference that because something consists only of something else it is nothing but this "something else" is an erroneous inference, the "nothing but" fallacy. Organisms consist exhaustively of atoms and molecules, but it does not follow that they are nothing but heaps of atoms and molecules. I shall return to this question below, in my discussion of emergence.

Second, there are reduction questions that might be called methodological, procedural, or strategical. These questions concern the strategy of research and the acquisition of knowledge — the approaches to be followed in the investigation of living beings. An outstanding characteristic of living beings is complexity of organization, recognized in their common name, "organisms." A hierarchy of levels of complexity runs from atoms, through cells and multicellular organisms, to populations, species, and communities. Methodological reductionism is the claim that the best strategy of research is to study living phenomena at increasingly lower levels of complexity and, ultimately, at the level of atoms and molecules. Methodological reductionism in its extreme form would be the claim that biological research should be conducted only at the level of the physicochemical component parts and processes. Research at other levels would not be, allegedly, worth pursuing or would yield at best results of provisional value, since biological phenomena must ultimately be understood at the molecular and atomic levels. Scientists rarely sponsor this extreme form of reductionism, except perhaps rhetorically. Extreme methodological reductionism would imply, for example, the unreasonable claim that genetic investigations should not have been undertaken until the discovery of DNA as the hereditary material.

A moderate position of methodological reductionism points to the success of the analytical method in science and to the obvious fact that the understanding of living processes at any level of organization is much advanced by knowledge of the underlying processes. The analytical method is of great heuristic value; much is often learned about a phenomenon through the investigation of its component elements and processes. In biology, the most impressive achievements of the last few decades are those of molecular biology. But there is little justification for any exclusionist claim that research should always proceed by investigation of lower levels of integration. The only valid criterion of a research strategy is its success.

Investigation of a biological phenomenon in terms of its significance at higher levels of complexity often contributes to the understanding of the phenomenon itself; compositionist investigations are also heuristic. For example, the problem of the specificity of the immune response of antibodies proved refractory to a satisfactory solution as long as antibodies, antigens, and their structures alone were taken into consideration. The natural selection theory of antibody function emerged only when antibodies were considered in their organismic milieu. Although the idea of clonal selection was first logically inadequate and quite vague, it had an enormous heuristic value in helping to understand how the specificity of antibodies comes about.

The third type of reduction question concerns issues that may be called epistemological, theoretical, or explanatory. The fundamental issue here is whether the theories and laws of biology can be derived from the laws and theories of physics and chemistry. Epistemological reductionism is concerned with whether biology may be ignored as a separate science because it represents simply a special case of physics and chemistry. When philosophers of science speak of reductionism, they generally refer to epistemological reduction. In biology, the question of epistemological reduction is whether the laws and theories of biology can be shown to be derived as special cases from the laws and theories of the physical sciences.

Science seeks to discover patterns of relationships among many kinds of phenomena in such a way that a small number of principles explain a large number of propositions concerning those phenomena. Science advances by developing gradually more comprehensive theories, i.e., by showing that theories and laws that had hitherto appeared as unrelated can in fact be integrated in a single theory of greater generality. The connection among theories has sometimes been established by showing that the tenets of a theory or branch of science can be explained by the tenets of another theory or branch of science of greater generality. The less general theory (or branch of science), called the secondary theory, is then said to have been reduced to the more general or primary theory. Epistemological reductions are of great value to science because, as special cases of the integration of theories, they greatly contribute to the advance of scientific knowledge. In biology, the reduction of Mendelian genetics to molecular genetics has been far from completely successful. Yet there can be little doubt that much has been learned from what has been accomplished up to the present. Nagel and Popper[1] have elaborated the conditions that must be met to

1. Ernst Nagel, *The Structure of Science* (New York: Harcourt, Brace and World, 1961); Karl R. Popper, "Scientific Reduction and the Essential Incompleteness of All Science," in *Studies in the Philosophy of Biology,* ed. Francisco J. Ayala and Theodosius Dobzhansky (London: Macmillan, 1974), pp. 259-84.

accomplish epistemological reduction of one theory to another and have analyzed claims of successful reduction (see also Ayala).[2] Indeed, Popper has shown that no major case of epistemological reduction (including such model cases as the reduction of thermodynamics to statistical mechanics) "has ever been completely successful: there is almost always an unresolved residue left by even the most successful attempts at reduction."[3]

## Emergence

The well-known evolutionist Stephen Jay Gould has written that the study of evolution embodies "a concept of hierarchy — a world constructed not as a smooth and seamless continuum, permitting simple extrapolation from the lowest level to the highest, but as a series of ascending levels, each bound to the one below it in some ways and independent in others. . . . 'emergent' features not implicit in the operation of processes at lower levels, may control events at higher levels."[4] Elsewhere he adds, "The hierarchical theory of selection recognizes many kinds of evolutionary individuals, banded together in a rising series of increasingly greater inclusion, one within the next — genes in cells, cells in organisms, organisms in demes, demes in species, species in clades . . . , and we may choose to direct our evolutionary attention to any of the levels."[5]

The world, and not only the world of life, is hierarchically structured; so are many human contraptions. A steam engine may consist only of iron and other materials, but it is something else than iron and the other components. Similarly an electronic computer is not only a pile of semiconductors, wires, plastic, and other materials. Organisms are made up of atoms and molecules, but they are highly complex systems, and systems of systems, of these atoms and molecules. Cellular, physiological, developmental, and other living processes are highly special and highly improbable patterns of physical and chemical processes. I have already pointed out the "nothing but" fallacy that (ontologically) reduces a complex entity to its component elements or to lower levels

2. Francisco J. Ayala, "Biology as an Autonomous Science," *American Scientist* 56 (1968): 207-21; Ayala, "Biological Reductionism: The Problems and Some Answers," in *Self-Organizing Systems: The Emergence of Order,* ed. F. E. Yates (New York and London: Plenum, 1987), pp. 315-24.

3. Popper, "Scientific Reduction," p. 260.

4. Stephen J. Gould, "Is a New General Theory of Evolution Emerging?" *Paleobiology* 6 (1980): 121.

5. Stephen J. Gould, *The Structure of Evolutionary Theory* (Cambridge, Mass., and London: Harvard University Press, Belknap Press, 2002), p. 674.

in a hierarchy. Time adds one additional dimension of the evolutionary hierarchy, with the interesting consequence that transitions from one level to another occur: as time proceeds, the descendants of a single cell may include multicellular organisms and the descendants of a single species may include separate species, genera, families, and so forth.

One way some authors express the irreducibility of the properties of a complex entity to its components is to point out, as Gould does in the quotation above, that organisms, like other complex entities, exhibit "emergent" features. But here again, as in the discussion of reductionism, it may be helpful to distinguish between the ontological and the epistemological domains. Consider the following question: Are the properties of common salt, sodium chloride, simply the properties of sodium and chlorine when they are associated according to the formula NaCl? If among the properties of sodium and chlorine we include their association into table salt and the properties of the latter, the answer is yes. In general, if among the properties of an object we include the properties that the object has when associated with other objects, it follows that the properties of complex systems, including organisms, are also the properties of their component parts. This is simply a definitional maneuver that contributes little to understanding the relationships between complex systems and their parts.

In common practice we do not include among the properties of an object all the properties of the systems resulting from its association with any other objects. There is a good reason for that. No matter how exhaustively an object is studied in isolation, there is usually no way to ascertain all the properties that it may have in association with any other object. Among the properties of hydrogen we do not usually include the properties of water, ethyl alcohol, proteins, and humans. Nor do we include among the properties of iron those of the steam engine.

The question of emergent properties may be formulated in a somewhat different manner. Can the properties of complex systems be inferred from knowledge of the properties that their component parts have in isolation? For example, can the properties of benzene be predicted from knowledge about oxygen, hydrogen, and carbon? Or, at a higher level of complexity, can the behavior of a cheetah chasing a deer be predicted from knowledge about the atoms and molecules making up these animals? Formulated in this manner, the issue of emergent properties is an epistemological question, not an ontological one; we are now asking whether the laws and theories accounting for the behavior of complex systems can be derived as logical consequences from the laws and theories that explain the behavior of their component parts.

This is the proper way of formulating questions about the relationship between complex systems and their component parts. The issue of emergence cannot be settled by discussion about the nature of things or their properties, but it is resolvable by reference to our knowledge of those entities. Assume that by studying the components in isolation we can infer the properties they will have when combined with other component parts in certain ways. In such a case, it would seem reasonable to include the "emergent" properties of the whole among the properties of the component parts. (Notice that this solution to the problem implies that a feature that may seem emergent at a certain time, might not appear as emergent any longer at a more advanced state of knowledge.) Often, no matter how exhaustively an object (or component part) is studied in isolation, we cannot ascertain the properties it will have in association with other objects (or component parts). We cannot infer the properties of ethyl alcohol, proteins, or human beings from the study of hydrogen, and thus it makes no good sense to list their properties among those of hydrogen. The important point, however, is that in the ontological sense the issue of emergent properties is spurious and that it needs to be reformulated in terms of propositions expressing our knowledge. It is legitimate to ask whether the statements concerning the properties of organisms (but not the properties themselves) can be logically deduced from statements concerning the properties of their physical components.

I will further illustrate the distinction between the ontological and the epistemological domains I have made here, as well as above when discussing reduction, with a culinary analogy. Consider my favorite Spanish cold soup, gazpacho, made of tomatoes, peppers, cucumbers, celery, carrots, garlic, and other pureed vegetables mixed with oil, vinegar, a dash of lemon, and so forth. No sensible person would argue that gazpacho is made of anything other than these ingredients (read: ontological reduction or identity at the level of events) or that the flavors of gazpacho come from anything other than its components. A different question is whether we can predict the gazpacho's magic flavors from what we know about the flavors of its ingredients. I do not think so. But be that as it may, my point here is to distinguish the different issues at stake when speaking of reduction or emergence. Are the flavors of gazpacho the same as the flavors of its components? The answer would be yes if among the components' flavors we include the flavors they yield when suitably combined with the other components in gazpacho soup. But if we cannot predict gazpacho's flavors from what we know by tasting each component separately, the appropriate answer would be no. To say that table salt is nothing else than sodium and chlorine (or similarly for organisms or gazpacho that it is nothing else than its components) is to commit, as I have said, the nothing-but fallacy.

## Naturalism/Dualism

Naturalism as a philosophical point of view can be methodological, epistemological, or ontological. Methodological naturalism is the position taken, at least in practice, by scientists. Science seeks to explain the natural world by formulating hypotheses, laws, and theories that can be tested against the world of nature. A scientific explanation identifies the conditions and processes that account for the phenomena it seeks to explain; it establishes general relationships between specific conditions and their consequences or between specific causes and their effects. A scientific explanation must be subject to the possibility of falsification by observation or experiment. A hypothesis is tested by ascertaining whether or not predictions about the world of experience derived as logical consequences from the hypothesis agree with what is actually observed. Scientific explanations include only entities, relationships, and processes that have consequences that can be reproducibly observed. Scientific statements do not include, that is, neither affirm nor deny, entities or processes outside the natural world, that is, the world of experience.

Methodological naturalism does not imply epistemological naturalism; it does not imply that science is the only way of knowing. Science's scope embraces all natural entities, inorganic as well as living, but knowledge about reality can be acquired in ways that do not meet the scientific demand of testing by observation and experiment. Common sense, aesthetic and ethical values and principles, philosophical reflection, and religious experience are valid ways of knowing that enrich human experience, both individually and collectively. Scientific naturalism is compatible with considerations of value, meaning, and purpose in the universe and in human life in particular. Indeed, scientists in general accept aesthetic and ethical values, and many see meaning and purpose in the universe. Moreover, science is compatible with the existence of the supernatural and preternatural. Science does not include any conclusions about the existence of God, souls, or other nonmaterial entities. Science implies neither epistemological naturalism nor ontological naturalism.

Ontological naturalism affirms that there is no reality outside the world of experience. Ontological naturalism is materialism; it denies that there are souls, spirits, Gods, or any nonmaterial reality. In its most extreme form materialism becomes epistemological naturalism; it denies the validity of nonscientific ways of knowing; it denies that values can be objectively discovered or established and that the universe or anything in it has any meaning or purpose. In less extreme forms, ontological naturalism is compatible not only with values, meaning, and purpose, but also with some forms of dualism.

Methodological dualism implies that there are other ways of knowing in addition to science. It is therefore compatible with methodological naturalism (but, of course, not with epistemological naturalism). Ontological dualism affirms that reality exists beyond matter. Many positions might be considered ontological dualism. Some affirm the existence of a supernatural God; others affirm the existence of souls and/or spirits as well, a position known as "vitalism" and associated sometimes with the great Greek philosopher Aristotle (384-322 B.C.), who was also the best biologist of his time. Descartes (1596-1650) famously proposed that animals are nothing else than complex machines, except for humans, who are endowed with spiritual souls. In the twentieth century some biologists were vitalists, notably Hans Driesch (1867-1941), who recognized two components in an animal, a material component and an "entelechy," from which each animal received its distinctive characteristics.

In addition, one version of ontological dualism sees two dimensions in the universe: one material and the other immaterial. The philosophers Henri Bergson (1859-1941) and Alfred North Whitehead (1861-1947), as well as the Jesuit paleontologist P. Teilhard de Chardin (1881-1955), may be included in this category. Teilhard, for example, distinguishes two aspects in any kind of thing: its external complexity (which he defines as "organized heterogeneity") and its interior consciousness. Complexity and consciousness are intimately related; they are two aspects of the same reality, like the two sides of a coin. A greater level of material complexity is always accompanied by a higher degree of consciousness. In the *Phenomenon of Man*, Teilhard writes: "Whatever instance we may think of, we may be sure that every time a richer and better organized structure will correspond to the more developed consciousness."[6] Complexity and consciousness are the two defining characteristics of every natural entity: "Spiritual perfection (or conscious 'centreity') and material synthesis (or complexity) are but the two aspects or connected parts of one and the same phenomenon."[7] Teilhard saw no dichotomy between matter and spirit, but rather a continuum between inorganic and organic reality. He predicates consciousness of all entities, inorganic as well as organic: "The term 'consciousness' is taken in its widest sense to indicate every kind of psychism, from the most rudimentary forms of interior perception imaginable to the human phenomenon of reflective thought."[8]

6. Pierre Teilhard de Chardin, *The Phenomenon of Man* (New York and Evanston, Ill.: Harper Torchbooks, 1961), p. 60.

7. Teilhard de Chardin, *The Phenomenon of Man*, pp. 60-61.

8. Teilhard de Chardin, *The Phenomenon of Man*, p. 57.

## Teleology

Knives, eyes, and mountain slopes are used for cutting, seeing, and climbing. Knives and mountain slopes have in common that they are used for certain purposes, but differ because knives, but not mountain slopes, have been specially created for the purpose they serve. Knives exist at all and exhibit certain features because they have been designed for cutting. This is not so with mountain slopes, which can be used for climbing but do not exist for that purpose. What about eyes? Human eyes share something in common with knives and something with mountain slopes. Like knives, they have been "designed," because were it not for the function of seeing they serve, eyes would have never come to be; and the features exhibited by eyes specifically came to be to serve for seeing. But eyes and mountain slopes both came about by natural processes; the eyes by natural selection, the mountain slopes by geological processes and erosion. Knives, on the other hand, are designed and produced by humans.

In *The Origin of Species* Darwin accumulated an impressive number of observations supporting the evolutionary origin of living organisms. Moreover, and most importantly, he advanced a causal explanation of evolutionary change — the theory of natural selection, which provides a natural account of the design of organisms, or as we say in biology, their adaptation. Darwin agreed that organisms are adapted to live in their environments, and that their parts are adapted to the specific functions they serve. Penguins are adapted to live in the cold, the wings of birds are made to fly, and the eye is made to see. Darwin accepted the facts of adaptation and advanced a scientific hypothesis to account for the facts. It may count as Darwin's greatest accomplishment that he brought the design aspects of nature into the realm of science. The wonderful designs of myriad plants and animals could now be explained as the result of natural laws manifested in natural processes.

Biologists need to account for the functional features of organisms, their "design," in terms of the goals or purposes they serve, which they do by teleological hypotheses or teleological explanations. Physical scientists do not face similar demands. The configuration of sodium chloride depends on the structure of sodium and chlorine, but no chemist is likely to write that sodium chloride has been designed for certain purposes, such as tasting salty. The revolution of the earth around the sun results from the laws of gravity, but astrophysicists do not state that this happens in order to produce the seasons.

A dictionary definition of "teleology" is "the use of design, purpose, or utility as an explanation of any natural phenomenon."[9] The same dictionary

9. *Merriam Webster's Collegiate Dictionary,* 10th ed. (1994).

defines "teleological" as "exhibiting or relating to design or purpose esp. in nature." The Oxford dictionary includes virtually identical definitions: "teleological," "dealing with design or purpose, esp. in natural phenomena"; "teleology," "such design as exhibited in natural objects or phenomena."

An object or a behavior can be said to be teleological, or telic, when it gives evidence of design or appears to be directed toward certain ends, goals, or purposes. For example, the behavior of human beings is often teleological. A person who buys an airplane ticket, reads a book, or cultivates the earth is trying to achieve a certain goal: getting to a given city, acquiring knowledge, or getting food. Objects and machines made by people also are usually teleological: a knife is made for cutting, a clock is made for telling time, a thermostat is made to regulate temperature. In a similar fashion, I argue, features of organisms have come to be because they serve certain purposes or functions, and in this sense they can be said to be teleological: a bird's wings are for flying, eyes are for seeing, and kidneys are constituted for regulating the composition of the blood. The features of organisms that may be said to be teleological are those that can be identified as adaptations, whether they are structures like a wing or a hand, processes like the regulation of temperature in mammals, or behaviors like the courtship displays of a peacock. Adaptations are features of organisms that have come about by natural selection because they increase the reproductive success of their carriers.

Inanimate objects and processes (other than those created by humans) are not teleological because they are not directed toward specific ends; they do not exist to serve certain purposes. The configuration of sodium chloride depends on the structure of sodium and chlorine, but it makes no sense to say the structure is made up so as to serve a certain end. Similarly, the slopes of a mountain are the result of certain geological processes and weather erosion, but they did not come about to serve a certain end, such as skiing. The revolution of the earth around the sun results from the laws of gravity, but it does not exist to satisfy certain ends or goals, such as producing the seasons. We may use sodium chloride as food and a mountain for skiing, and take advantage of the seasons, but the use we make of these objects or phenomena is not the reason why they came into existence or why they have certain configurations.

The previous observations point out the essential characteristics of teleological phenomena, i.e., phenomena whose existence and configuration are determined by the use made of them. This use is the reason why the entity exists at all and exhibits certain features. Teleological explanations apply only to features or behaviors that would not have come about were it not for the particular end or purpose they serve. The end, goal, or purpose served is, therefore, the explanatory reason for the existence of the feature or behavior and its distinctive characteristics. A teleological hypothesis purports to identify the function or purpose that accounts for the evolution of a particular feature.

I want now to introduce two sets of contrasting distinctions: natural versus artificial teleology and bounded versus unbounded teleology. The second distinction primarily applies to natural teleology.

Actions or objects resulting from purposeful behavior may be said to exhibit artificial (or external) teleology. Their teleological features have come about because they were consciously intended by some agent. The teleology of a knife, a car, and a thermostat is artificial, the result of purposeful intent. Systems with teleological features that are not due to the purposeful action of an agent but result from natural process may be said to exhibit natural (or internal) teleology. The wings of birds have a natural teleology; they serve an end, flying, but their configuration is not due to the conscious design of any agent. The development of an egg into a chicken is a teleological process also of the internal or natural kind, since it comes about as a natural process, in both its proximate causation, the concatenation of events by which the egg ultimately develops into a chicken, and its remote causation, the evolutionary process by which chickens and their developmental processes came to be.

Natural teleology is of two kinds: bounded (or determinate or necessary) and unbounded (or contingent or indeterminate). This distinction applies as well to purposeful objects and behaviors, but human actions are predominantly determinate; they are consciously intended for a definite purpose.

Bounded natural teleology exists when a specific end state is reached in spite of environmental fluctuations. The development of an egg into a chicken, or of a human zygote into a human being, is an example of determinate natural teleological processes. The regulation of body temperature in a mammal is another example. In general, the homeostatic processes (developmental or physiological) of organisms are instances of determinate natural teleology.

Indeterminate or unbounded teleology occurs when the end state served is not specifically intended or predetermined, but rather is the result of a natural process selecting one among several available alternatives. For teleology to exist the selection of one alternative over another must be deterministic and not purely stochastic. But which alternative happens to be selected may depend on environmental and/or historical circumstances, and thus the specific end-state is not generally predictable. Unbounded teleology results from a mixture of stochastic (at least from the point of view of the teleological system) and deterministic events.

Many features of organisms are teleological in the unbounded sense. The evolution of birds' wings requires teleological explanation: the genetic constitutions responsible for their configuration came about because wings serve for flying and flying contributes to the reproductive success of birds. But nothing in the constitution of the remote ancestors of birds necessitated the appearance of wings with specified features in their descendants. Wings came about as the consequence of a long sequence of events, where at each stage the most advantageous alternative was selected among those that happened to be available; which alternatives were available at any one time depended, at least in part, on contingent events.

In spite of the role played by stochastic events in the phylogenetic history of birds, it would be mistaken to say that wings are not teleological features. As pointed out earlier, there are differences between the teleology of an organism's adaptations and the nonteleological potential uses of natural inanimate objects. A mountain may have features appropriate for skiing, but those features did not come about so as to provide skiing slopes. On the other hand, the wings of birds came about precisely because they serve for flying.

## 4. Egg-to-Adult, Brain-to-Mind, and Ape-to-Human Transformations

FRANCISCO J. AYALA

### Biology's Three Major Frontiers

Biology in the twenty-first century faces three great research frontiers: ontogenetic decoding, the brain-mind puzzle, and the ape-to-human transformation. By ontogenetic decoding I refer to the problem of how the unidimensional genetic information encoded in the DNA of a single cell becomes transformed into a four-dimensional being, the individual that grows, matures, and dies. Cancer, disease, and aging are epiphenomena of ontogenetic decoding. By the brain-mind puzzle I refer to the interdependent questions of (1) how the physicochemical signals that reach our sense organs become transformed into perceptions, feelings, ideas, critical arguments, aesthetic emotions, and ethical values; and (2) how, out of this diversity of experiences, there emerges a unitary reality, the mind or self. Free will and language, social and political institutions, technology and art are all epiphenomena of the human mind. By the ape-to-human transformation I refer to the mystery of how a particular ape lineage became a hominid lineage, from which emerged, after only a few million years, humans able to think and love, who have developed complex societies and uphold ethical, aesthetic, and other values. The human genome differs little from the chimp genome.

I will refer to these three issues as the egg-to-adult transformation, the brain-to-mind transformation, and the ape-to-human transformation. The egg-to-adult transformation is essentially similar, and similarly mysterious, in humans and other mammals. The brain-to-mind transformation and the ape-to-human transformation are distinctively human; they define the *humanum,* that which makes us specifically human. No other issues in human evolution are of greater consequence for understanding ourselves and our place in nature. In raising these issues, I seek to alert readers of this volume as to where biology is heading, at least according to my viewpoint.

## Ontogenetic Decoding

The instructions that guide the ontogenetic process, or the egg-to-adult transformation, are carried in the hereditary material. The theory of biological heredity was formulated in 1866 by the Augustinian monk Gregor Mendel, but it became generally known by biologists only in 1900: genetic information is contained in discrete factors, or genes, which exist in pairs, one received from each parent. The next step toward understanding the nature of genes was completed during the first quarter of the twentieth century. It was established that genes are parts of the chromosomes, filamentous bodies present in the nucleus of the cell, and that they are linearly arranged along the chromosomes. It took another quarter century to determine the chemical composition of genes — deoxyribonucleic acid (DNA). DNA consists of four kinds of chemical components (nucleotides) organized in long, double-helical structures. The genetic information is contained in the linear sequence of the nucleotides, very much in the same way as the semantic information of an English sentence is conveyed by the particular sequence of the twenty-six letters of the alphabet.

The first important step toward understanding how the genetic information is decoded came in 1941 when George W. Beadle and Edward L. Tatum demonstrated that genes determine the synthesis of enzymes; enzymes are the catalysts that control all chemical reactions in living beings. Later it became known that amino acids (the components that make up enzymes and other proteins) are encoded each by a set of three consecutive nucleotides. This relationship accounts for the linear correspondence between a particular sequence of coding nucleotides and the sequence of the amino acids that make up the encoded enzyme.

Chemical reactions in organisms must occur in an orderly manner; organisms must have ways of switching genes on and off since different sets of genes are active in different cells. The first control system was discovered in 1961 by François Jacob and Jacques Monod for a gene that encodes an enzyme that digests sugar in the bacterium *Escherichia coli*. The gene is turned on and off by a system of several switches consisting of short DNA sequences adjacent to the coding part of the gene. (The coding sequence of a gene is the part that determines the sequence of amino acids in the encoded enzyme.) The switches acting on a given gene are activated or deactivated by feedback loops that involve molecules synthesized by other genes. A variety of gene control mechanisms was soon discovered in bacteria and other microorganisms. Two elements are typically present: feedback loops and short DNA sequences acting as switches. The feedback loops ensure that the presence of a substance in the cell induces the synthesis of the enzyme required to digest it, and that an excess of the enzyme in the cell represses its own synthesis. For example, the gene encoding a sugar-digesting enzyme in *E. coli* is turned on or off by the presence or absence of the sugar to be digested.

The investigation of gene control mechanisms in mammals and other complex organisms became possible in the mid-1970s with the development of recombinant DNA techniques. This technology made it feasible to isolate single genes (and other DNA sequences) and to multiply them, or "clone" them, in billions of identical copies, to obtain the quantities necessary for ascertaining their nucleotide sequence. One unanticipated discovery was that most genes come in pieces: the coding sequence of a gene is divided into several fragments separated one from the next by noncoding DNA segments. In addition to the alternating succession of coding and noncoding segments, mammalian genes contain short control sequences, like those in bacteria, but typically more numerous and complex, that act as control switches and signal where the coding sequence begins.

Much remains to be discovered about the control mechanisms of mammalian genes. The daunting speed at which molecular biology is advancing has led to the discovery of some prototypes of mammalian gene control systems, but much remains to be unraveled. Moreover, understanding the control mechanisms of individual genes is but the first major step toward solving the mystery of ontogenetic decoding. The second major step is the puzzle of differentiation.

A human being consists of one trillion cells of some three hundred different kinds, all derived by sequential division from the fertilized egg, a single cell 0.1 millimeters in diameter. The first few cell divisions yield a spherical mass of amorphous cells. Successive divisions are accompanied by the appearance of folds and ridges in the mass of cells and, later on, of the variety of tissues, organs, and limbs characteristic of a human individual. The full complement of genes duplicates with each cell division, so that two complete genomes are present in every cell. Yet different sets of genes are active in different cells. This must be so in order for cells to differentiate: a nerve cell, a muscle cell, and a skin cell are vastly different in size, configuration, and function. The differential activity of genes must continue after differentiation, because different cells fulfill different functions, which are controlled by different genes. Nevertheless, experiments with other animals (and some with humans) indicate that all the genes in any cell have the potential of becoming activated. The sheep Dolly was conceived using the genes extracted from a cell in an adult sheep.

The information that controls cell and organ differentiation is ultimately contained in the DNA sequence, but mostly in very short segments of it. In mammals, insects, and other complex organisms, there are control circuits that operate at higher levels than the control mechanisms that activate and deactivate individual genes. These higher-level circuits (such as the so-called *homeobox* genes) act on sets rather than individual genes. Many details of how these sets are controlled, how many control systems there are, and how they interact, as well as many other related questions, are what needs to be resolved to elucidate the egg-to-adult transformation. The DNA sequence of some controlling elements has been ascertained, but this is a minor effort helped only a little by plowing through the entire 3 billion nucleotide pairs that constitute the human genome. Experiments with stem cells are likely to provide important knowledge as scientists ascertain how embryonic cells become brain cells in one case but muscle cells in another, and how some cells become the heart and others the liver.

The benefits the elucidation of ontogenetic decoding will bring to mankind are enormous. This knowledge will make possible understanding the modes of action of complex genetic diseases, including cancer, and therefore their cure. It will also bring an understanding of the process of aging, the unforgiving disease that kills all those who have won the battle against other infirmities.

Cancer is an anomaly of ontogenetic decoding: cells proliferate although the welfare of the organism demands otherwise. Individual genes (oncogenes) have been identified that are involved in the causation of particular forms of cancer. But whether or not a cell will turn out cancerous depends on the interaction of the oncogenes with other genes and with the internal and external environment of the cell. Aging is also a failure of the process of ontogenetic decoding: cells fail to carry out the functions imprinted in their genetic code script or are no longer able to proliferate and replace dead cells.

## The Brain-Mind Puzzle

The brain is the most complex and most distinctive human organ. It consists of thirty billion nerve cells, or neurons, each connected to many others through two kinds of cell extensions, known as the axon and the dendrites. From the evolutionary point of view, the animal brain is a powerful biological adaptation; it allows the organism to obtain and process information about environmental conditions and then to adapt to them. This ability has been carried to the limit in humans, in which the extravagant hypertrophy of the brain makes possible abstract thinking, language, and technology. By these means mankind has ushered in a new mode of adaptation far more powerful than the biological mode: adaptation by culture.

The most rudimentary ability to gather and process information about the environment is found in certain single-celled microorganisms. The protozoan *Paramecium* swims apparently at random, ingesting the bacteria it encounters, but when it meets unsuitable acidity or salinity, it checks its advance and starts in a new direction. The single-celled alga *Euglena* not only avoids unsuitable environments but also seeks suitable ones by orienting itself according to the direction of light, which it perceives through a light-sensitive spot in the cell. Plants have not progressed much further. Except for those with tendrils that twist around any solid object and the few carnivorous plants that react to touch, they mostly react only to gradients of light, gravity, and moisture.

In animals the ability to secure and process environmental information is mediated by the nervous system. The simplest nervous systems are found in corals and jellyfish; they lack coordination between different parts of their bodies, so one part is able to react only when directly stimulated. Sea urchins and starfish possess a nerve ring and radial nerve cords that coordinate stimuli coming from different parts; hence, they respond with direct and unified actions of the whole body. They have no brain, however, and seem unable to learn from experience. Planarian flatworms have the most rudimentary brain known; their central nervous system and brain process and coordinate information gathered by sensory cells. These animals are capable of simple learning and hence of variable responses to repeatedly encountered stimuli. Insects and their relatives have much more advanced brains; they obtain precise chemical, acoustic, visual, and tactile signals from the environment and process them, making possible complex behaviors, particularly in searching for food and selecting mates.

Vertebrates — animals with backbones — are able to obtain and process much more complicated signals and to respond to the environment more variably than insects or other invertebrates. The vertebrate brain contains an enormous number of associative neurons arranged in complex patterns. In vertebrates the ability to react to environmental information is correlated with an increase in the relative size of the cerebral hemispheres and of the neopallium, an organ involved in associating and coordinating signals from all receptors and brain centers. In mammals the neopallium has expanded and become the cerebral cortex. Humans have a very large brain relative to their body size, and a cerebral cortex that is disproportionately large and complex even for their brain size. Abstract thinking, symbolic language, complex social organization, values, and ethics are manifestations of the wondrous capacity of the human brain to gather information about the external world and to integrate that information and react flexibly to what is perceived.

With the advanced development of the human brain, biological evolution has transcended itself, opening up a new mode of evolution: adaptation by technological manipulation of the environment. Organisms adapt to the environment by means of natural selection, by changing their genetic constitution over the generations to suit the demands of the environment. Humans, and humans alone, have developed the capacity to adapt to hostile environments by modifying the environments according to the needs of their genes. The discovery of fire and the fabrication of clothing and shelter have allowed humans to spread from the warm tropical and subtropical regions of the Old World, to which we are biologically adapted, to almost the whole earth. It was not necessary for wandering humans to wait until genes evolved providing anatomical protection against cold temperatures by means of fur or hair. Nor are humans biding their time in expectation of wings or gills; we have conquered the air and seas with artfully designed contrivances, airplanes and ships. It is the human brain (the human mind) that has made mankind the most successful, by most meaningful standards, living species.

There are not enough bits of information in the complete DNA sequence of a human genome to specify the trillions of connections among the thirty billion neurons of the human brain. Accordingly, the genetic instructions must be organized in control circuits operating at different hierarchical levels, as described earlier, so that an instruction at one level is carried through many channels at a lower level in the hierarchy of control circuits. The development of the human brain is indeed one particularly intriguing component of the egg-to-adult transformation.

Within the last two decades neurobiology has developed into one of the most exciting biological disciplines. An increased commitment of financial and human resources has brought an unprecedented rate of discovery. Much has been learned about how light, sound, temperature, resistance, and chemical impressions received in our sense organs trigger the release of chemical transmitters and electric potential differences that carry the signals through the nerves to the brain and elsewhere in the body. Much has also been learned about how neural channels for information transmission become reinforced by use or may be replaced after damage; about which neurons or groups of neurons are committed to processing information derived from a particular organ or environmental location; and about many other matters. But, for all this progress, neurobiology remains an infant discipline, at a stage of theoretical development comparable perhaps to that of genetics at the beginning of the twentieth century. Those things that count most remain shrouded in mystery: how physical phenomena become mental experiences (the feelings and sensations, called "qualia" by philosophers, that contribute the elements of consciousness), and how the mind emerges out of the diversity of these experiences, a reality with unitary properties, such as free will and the awareness of self, that persist through an individual's life.

I do not believe that these mysteries are unfathomable; rather, they are puzzles that the human mind can solve with the methods of science and illuminate with philosophical analysis and reflection. And I will bet that, over the next half century or so, many of these puzzles will be solved. We shall then be well on our way toward answering the injunction "Know thyself."

## The Ape-to-Human Transformation

Our closest biological relatives are the chimpanzees, who are more closely related to us than they are to the gorillas, and much more than to the orangutans. (The chimpanzees include two species closely related to one another and equally to humans, *Pan troglodytes*, or common chimpanzee, and *P. paniscus*, or bonobo.) The hominid lineage diverged from the chimpanzee lineage 7-8 million years ago, and it evolved exclusively in Africa until the emergence of *Homo erectus*, somewhat before 1.8 million years ago. The first known hominids are the recently discovered *Sahelanthropus tchadensis*, dated 6-7 million years ago,[1] *Orrorin tugenensis*, dated 5.8–6.1 million years ago,[2] and *Ardipithecus ramidus*, dated 5.2–5.8 million years ago.[3] They were bipedal when on the ground but retained tree-climbing abilities. It is not certain that they all are in the direct line of descent to modern humans, *Homo sapiens;* rather, some may represent side branches of the hominid lineage, after its divergence from the chimpanzee lineage. *Australopithecus anamensis*, dated 3.9–4.2 million years ago, was habitually bipedal and has been placed in the line of descent to *A. afarensis, H. habilis, H. erectus,* and *H. sapiens*. Other hominids, not in the direct line of descent to modern humans, are *A. africanus, Paranthropus aethiopicus, P. boisei,* and *P. robustus,* who lived in Africa at various times between 3 and 1 million years ago, a period when three or four hominid species lived contemporaneously on that continent.[4]

The first intercontinental wanderer among our ancestors was *H. erectus*.

---

1. M. Brunet, F. Guy, D. Pilbeam, H. T. Mackaye, A. Likius, D. Ahounta, A. Beauvilain, C. Blondel, H. Bocherens, J. R. Boisserie, et al., "A New Hominid from the Upper Miocene of Chad, Central Africa," *Nature* 418 (2002): 145-51.

2. B. Senut, M. Pickford, D. Gommery, P. Mein, K. Cheboi, and Y. Coppens, "First Hominid from the Miocene" (Lukeino Formation, Kenya), *CR Academy of Scences* 332 (2001): 137-44.

3. Y. Haile-Selassie, "Late Miocene Hominids from the Middle Awash, Ethiopia," *Nature* 412 (2001): 178-81.

4. For a review of hominid evolution, see C. J. Cela-Conde and Francisco J. Ayala, *Human Evolution: Trails from the Past* (Oxford: Oxford University Press, 2007).

Shortly after its emergence in tropical or subtropical eastern Africa, *H. erectus* dispersed to other continents of the Old World. Fossil remains of *H. erectus* are known from Africa, Indonesia (Java), China, the Middle East, and Europe. The fossils from Java have been dated 1.81 and 1.66 million years ago, and from Georgia between 1.6 and 1.8 million years ago. Anatomically distinctive *H. erectus* fossils have been found in Spain and in Italy, deposited about 800,000 years ago, the oldest known in western Europe.

Fossil remains of Neanderthal hominids *(H. neanderthalensis),* with brains as large as those of *H. sapiens,* appeared in Europe around 200,000 years ago and persisted until 40,000 years ago. The Neanderthals were thought to be ancestral to anatomically modern humans, but now we know that modern humans appeared at least 100,000 years ago, much before the disappearance of the Neanderthals. Moreover, in caves in the Middle East, fossils of modern humans have been found dated nearly 100,000 years ago, as well as Neanderthals dated at 70,000 and 60,000 years ago, followed again by modern humans dated at 40,000 years ago. It is unclear whether the two species repeatedly replaced one another by migration from other regions, or whether they coexisted in the same areas. Recent genetic evidence indicates that interbreeding between *sapiens* and *neanderthalensis* never occurred.

Anatomically modern humans are thought to have originated in Africa between 150,000 and 100,000 years ago. From Africa they spread throughout the world, replacing elsewhere the preexisting populations of *H. erectus* and other hominid species.

Biological heredity is based on the transmission of genetic information from parents to offspring, in humans very much the same as in other animals. The DNA of humans is packaged in two sets of twenty-three chromosomes, one set from each parent. The total number of DNA letters (the four nucleotides represented by A, C, G, T) in each set of chromosomes is about 3 billion. The Human Genome Project has deciphered the sequence of the 3 billion letters in the human genome, that is, in one set of chromosomes. The human genome sequence varies among individuals.

I estimate that the King James Bible contains about 3 million letters, punctuation marks, and spaces. Writing down the DNA sequence of one human genome demands 1,000 volumes of the size of the Bible. The human genome sequence is of course not printed in books, but stored in electronic form, in computers, where fragments of information can be retrieved by investigators. But if a printout is wanted, 1,000 volumes will be needed just for one human genome.

The two genomes (chromosome sets) of each individual are different from one another, and from the genomes of any other human being (with the trivial exception of identical twins, who share the same two sets, since identical twins develop from one single fertilized human egg). Therefore, printing the complete genome information for just one individual would demand 2,000 volumes, a thousand for each of the two chromosome sets. Surely, again, there are more economic ways of presenting the information in the second set than listing the complete letter sequence; for example, by indicating the position of each variant letter in the second set relative to the first set. The number of variant letters between one individual's two sets is about 10 million, about 1 in 300.

The Human Genome Project of the United States was initiated in 1989, funded through two agencies, the National Institutes of Health (NIH) and the Department of Energy (DOE). A private enterprise, Celera Genomics, started in the United States somewhat later, joined the government-sponsored project in achieving, largely independently, similar results. The goal was to obtain the complete sequence of one human genome in fifteen years at an approximate cost of $3 billion, coincidentally about $1 per DNA letter. A draft of the genome sequence was completed ahead of schedule in 2001. In 2003 the Human Genome Project was finished. The sequence has become known with as much precision as is wanted.

Knowing the human DNA sequence is a first step, but no more than one step, toward understanding the genetic makeup of a human being. Think of the 1,000 Bible-sized volumes. We now know the orderly sequence of the 3 billion letters, but this sequence does not provide an understanding of human beings any more than we would understand the contents of 1,000 Bible-sized volumes written in an extraterrestrial language, of which we know only the alphabet, just because we would have come to decipher its letter sequence.

Human beings are not gene machines. The expression of genes in mammals takes place in interaction with the environment, in patterns that are complex and all but impossible to predict in the details — and it is in the details that the self resides. In humans the "environment" takes a new dimension, which becomes the dominant one. Humans manipulate the natural environment so that it fits the needs of its biological makeup; for example, using clothing and housing to live in cold climates. Moreover, the products of human technology, art, science, political institutions, and the like are dominant features of human environments.

Two conspicuous features of human anatomy are erect posture and a large brain. Brain size is generally proportional to body size; relative to body mass, humans have the largest (and most complex) brain. The chimpanzee's brain weighs less than a pound; a gorilla's slightly more. Our hominid ancestors had, since at least 5 million years ago, a bipedal gait, but their brain was small, no more than 450 cubic centimeters, a pound in weight, until about 2 million years ago. Brain size started to increase notably with our *Homo habilis* ancestors, who had a brain about 650 cubic centimeters and also became toolmakers (hence the name *habilis*), and who lived for a few hundred thousand years, starting about 2½ million years ago. Their descendants, *H. erectus,* had adult brains reaching up to 1,200 cubic centimeters in size. (I use the name *Homo erectus,* as it is often used, in a broad sense that encompasses a fairly diverse group of ancestors and their relatives, which current paleoanthropologists classify in several species, including *H. ergaster, H. antecessor,* and *H. heidelbergensis.*) Our species, *H. sapiens,* has a brain of 1,300-1,400 cubic centimeters, about three times as large as that of the early hominids. Our brain is not only much larger than that of chimpanzees or gorillas, but also much more complex. The cerebral cortex, where the higher cognitive functions are processed, is in humans disproportionately much greater than the rest of the brain when compared to apes.

The draft DNA sequence of the chimpanzee genome was published on September 1, 2005. In the genome regions shared by humans and chimpanzees, the two species are 99 percent identical. The differences appear to be very small or quite large, depending on how one looks at them: 1 percent of the total seems very little, but it amounts to a difference of 30 million DNA letters out of the 3 billion in each genome. Of the enzymes and other proteins encoded by the genes, 29 percent are identical in both species. Out of the one hundred to several hundred amino acids that make up each protein, the 71 percent of nonidentical proteins differ by only two amino acids, on the average. The two genomes are about 96 percent identical if one takes into account DNA stretches found in one species but not the other. That is, a large amount of genetic material, about 3 percent, or some 90 million DNA letters, has been inserted or deleted since humans and chimps initiated their separate evolutionary ways 7 or 8 million years ago. Most of this DNA does not contain genes coding for proteins.

Comparison of the two genomes provides insights into the rate of evolution of particular genes in the two species. One significant finding is that genes active in the brain have changed more in the human lineage than in the chimp lineage. Also significant is that the fastest-evolving human genes are those coding for "transcription factors." These are "switch" proteins, which control the expression of other genes, that is, when they are turned on and off. On the whole, 585 genes have been identified as evolving faster in humans, including genes involved in resistance to malaria and tuberculosis. (Malaria is a much more severe disease for humans than for chimps.) Genes located in the Y chromosome (the chromosome that determines maleness; females have two X chromosomes, males have one X and one Y chromosome, the Y being much smaller than the X) have been much better protected by natural selection in the human than in the chimpanzee lineage, where several genes have incorporated disabling mutations that make the genes nonfunctional. Several regions of the human genome seem to contain beneficial genes that have rapidly evolved within the past 250,000 years. One region contains the *FOXP2* gene, involved in the evolution of speech.

Extended comparisons of the human and chimp genomes and experimental exploration of the functions associated with significant genes will surely advance considerably our understanding, over the next decade or two, of what makes us distinctively human. Surely also, full biological understanding will come only from the joint solution of the three conundrums I have identified. The distinctive features that make us human begin early in development, well before birth, as the linear information encoded in the genome gradually becomes expressed into a four-dimensional individual. In an important sense, the most distinctive human features are those expressed in the brain, those that account for the human mind and for human identity. As biological understanding advances, much will surely be left for philosophical insight, as well as theological reflection.

## 5. Neo-Darwinism: Scientific Account and Theological Attributions

JEFFREY SCHLOSS

While the evolutionary history of life is virtually undisputed among modern biologists, various causal explanations and metaphysical interpretations of this process are not infrequently antagonistic. One aim of this book is to explore the possibility of consonance between evolutionary science and theology. Of course, the form of such consonance, and indeed the plausibility of any consonance at all, very much depends on which causal and interpretive perspectives on evolution are engaged. Unfortunately, many theological responses sympathetically focus on a favored position or antagonistically emphasize an easy target, rather than assessing the range and indeed ambiguity evident in contemporary evolutionary theory.

I will structure my essay in three sections. In the first I will comment on the content of neo-Darwinism; in the second I will identify some implications often drawn from neo-Darwinism; and in the third I will briefly describe some contemporary supplements or alternatives to a neo-Darwinian interpretation of evolution.

### Neo-Darwinian Proposals

As Ayala has noted, the term "neo-Darwinism" does not play an important role in the scientific literature. Moreover, even in the philosophical or interpretive literature, there is not a recent tradition of clear definition and unambiguous or extensive employment. Indeed, these days the term itself seems to be used not infrequently as a vague ad hominem by those disagreeing with a particular philosophical implication of some aspect of evolutionary theory.

For all these reasons, I am somewhat reticent even to use the term, but given the current state of interdisciplinary discourse over evolutionary theory, I am not sure we can do without it, or something like it. Merely referring to evolution — the fact of descent with modification — does not address the important issues related to causal mechanisms of evolutionary change. Referring to "Darwinism" — much more frequently used by biologists than "neo-Darwinism," and abundantly used by philosophers of biology — does distinguish the importance of natural selection as the algorithm for change. But it does not address important theoretical enhancements that have been added since Darwin or identify crucial differences between various "camps" within both Darwinian theory and emerging "non-Darwinian" proposals. Nor does it engage the very influential philosophical interpretations of recent refinements to or applications of Darwinian theory.[1] Indeed, the latter enterprise has become a cultural industry.

Whatever ambiguity exists in the meaning of "neo"-Darwinism, it can help engage the above issues in two ways. First, it serves as a tag for the rejection of understandings of evolution that it is not. It is not evolutionary common descent from a first form that was supernaturally designed and front-loaded with information for future forms.[2] It is not evolution directed by God through interruptions of lawlike behavior,[3] nor is it divinely guided, employing mutation and selection noncoercively influenced within quantum uncertainty.[4] It is not evolutionary convergence due to Platonic constraints on morphological possibility space,[5] nor directionality due to a vitalistic driving force,[6] nor — to get closer to the themes of this book — evolutionary history driven or attracted by

1. See Daniel Dennett, *Darwin's Dangerous Idea: Evolution and the Meaning of Life* (New York: Simon and Schuster, 1995); David Hull, "The God of the Galapagos," *Nature* 352 (1992): 485-86; James Rachels, *Created from Animals: The Moral Implications of Darwinism* (New York: Oxford University Press, 1990); Michael Ruse, *Taking Darwin Seriously: A Naturalistic Approach to Philosophy* (Amherst, N.Y.: Prometheus Books, 1994); Tamler Sommers and Alex Rosenberg, "Darwin's Nihilistic Idea: Evolution and the Meaninglessness of Life," *Biology and Philosophy* 18 (2003): 653-68.

2. Michael Behe, *Darwin's Black Box: The Biochemical Challenge to Evolution* (New York: Simon and Schuster, 1996).

3. Stephen Meyer, "The Origin of Biological Information and the Higher Taxonomic Categories," *Proceedings of the Biological Society of Washington* 117, no. 2 (2004): 213-39.

4. Robert J. Russell, "Special Providence and Genetic Mutation: A New Defense of Theistic Evolution," in *Evolution and Molecular Biology: Science Perspectives on Divine Action*, ed. Robert J. Russell, William F. Stoeger, and Franciso J. Ayala (Vatican City: Vatican Observatory Publications; Berkeley: Center for Theology and the Natural Sciences, 1998).

5. Simon Conway Morris, *The Crucible of Creation: The Burgess Shale and the Rise of Animals* (Oxford: Oxford University Press, 1998); Simon Conway Morris, *Life's Solutions: Inevitable Humans in a Lonely Universe* (Cambridge: Cambridge University Press, 2003).

6. Michael Denton, *Nature's Destiny: How the Laws of Biology Reveal Purpose in the Universe* (New York: Free Press, 1998).

symbiogenesis, metaphysical affinities, or even self-organization, although it may be reconcilable with some of these.

Second, it does have identifiable content that distinguishes what it *is*. I posit six characteristics of currently prevalent interpretations of Darwinian evolution, and given the fact that all of them are, or contain, propositions that Darwin himself did not know about, did not commit himself to, or actually disavowed, "neo"-Darwinism sounds just fine. I do want to say in advance that, although I believe the following fairly depict an extant, multifaceted, unified theoretical program, I am aware that wedding them together via any single term compresses interpretive nuance; and I am painfully aware that using a term to refer to proponents rather than the proposed — i.e., "neo-Darwi*nist*" — as if one were either in or out, is systematically unhelpful.

### 1. Non-Lamarckian

Weisman's first formulation of neo-Darwinism: evolution involves the transmission of heritable changes to the germ line (reproductive cells, or gametes, used by sexually reproducing organisms). In cases of asexually reproducing organisms, there is no "germ line," but evolution still involves changes to the genetic material. This provides an explanation of why Lamarck was wrong: evolution cannot involve the transmission of acquired characteristics, i.e., changes to the body alone.

### 2. Explanatory Adequacy of Natural Selection

As formulated by the modern synthesis, and not fully understood by Darwin, the above process occurs according to the two-step process of genetic mutation and selection. Moreover, mutation and selection adequately explain evolution on all temporal and phyletic scales.[7] There is no need to invoke special, alto-

---

7. In this paper I have characterized neo-Darwinism in terms of commitment to an adaptationist paradigm, i.e., affirming that "natural selection is both sufficient and true," which includes the proposition that "we are evolved beings whose every attribute has been produced by an evolution guided primarily by differential reproduction" (R. D. Alexander, "Biological Considerations in the Analysis of Morality," in *Evolutionary Ethics,* ed. M. H. Nitecki and D. V. Nitecki [Albany: State University of New York Press, 1993], p. 175). Not all evolutionary biologists accept this, or accept it in the same way. One alternative to adaptationism is Gould's notion of an "evolutionary spandrel," or a trait that is a nonadaptive by-product or feature of some other structure that is adaptive (Stephen J. Gould and R. C. Lewontin, "The Spandrels of San

gether different, or significantly supplemental causal processes behind major evolutionary changes or long-term trends (if they exist). A provocative but apt reflection of commitment to the all-encompassing adequacy of this process is Richard Dawkins's endorsement of "the simplicity of my colleague Dr. Henry Bennet-Clark, with whom I have discussed these matters: 'All questions about life have the same answer (though it may not always be a helpful one): natural selection.'"[8] However, some would identify themselves as Darwinians and would resist the rhetorical ethos and/or the emphasis of this position.[9]

## 3. Nonprogressive Evolution

Evolutionary change is nonteleological and nonpurposive, and entails no intrinsic progression or indeed directionality of any kind. Contrary to what Darwin himself claimed, there is no general tendency toward perfection of corporeal endowments, and there are no progressive trends at all. There are two reasons for this. First, mutation is random with respect to needs of the organism and demands of the environment, and selection itself is dis-teleological. Second, there is a general rejection of, certainly a de-emphasis on, the idea that evolution might be "guided" by enduring patterns or intrinsically directional changes in environmental information, or by organisms acting as agents in their own evolution by top-down influences of bodily or community function.

---

Marco and the Panglossian Paradigm: A Critique of the Adaptationist Programme," *Proceedings of the Royal Society of London* 205 [1979]: 581-98). The extent to which spandrels characterize the products of evolution is debated, but the existence of "pleiotropy" — incidental or multiple traits emerging from genetic endowments — is well established. Therefore, in cases of pleiotropy, it is possible fully to accept a trait as "emerging from genetically informed characteristics that have been selected for over evolutionary time," and not view that trait as an adaptation. Francisco J. Ayala, "The Difference of Being Human: Ethical Behavior as an Evolutionary Byproduct," in *Biology, Ethics, and the Origins of Life*, ed. Holmes Rolston III (Boston: Jones and Bartlett, 1995), makes precisely this point about morality, which he argues is not an adaptation in itself but a by-product of other cognitive capacities that are adaptive. Although he is one of the few biologists writing on the evolution of the capacity for morality who does not view it as an adaptation, his proposal is important. Moreover, extensive literature in evolutionary cognitive science makes a similar point about the capacity for religious belief, viewing it as a nonadaptive, cognitive spandrel (Scott Atran, *In Gods We Trust: The Evolutionary Landscape of Religion* [New York: Oxford University Press, 2004]; Pascal Boyer, *Religion Explained: The Evolutionary Origins of Religious Thought* [New York: Basic Books, 2002]).

8. Richard Dawkins, *Climbing Mount Improbable* (New York: Norton, 1997), p. 228.

9. Stephen J. Gould, *Wonderful Life: The Burgess Shale and Natural History* (New York: Norton, 1989), and H. Allen Orr, "Dennett's Strange Idea. Natural Selection: Science of Everything, Universal Acid, Cure of the Common Cold . . .," *Boston Review*, Summer 1996.

Instead, the environment constitutes an unpredictable source of contingent and novel adaptive challenges.[10]

### 4. Genes as Biotic Actors

The very meaning of adaptation is reformulated from being understood in terms of organismal function to genetic replication. An adaptation *is* a contrivance for the successful transmission of genes (or informational replicators): "If we wish to speak teleologically, all adaptations are for the preservation of DNA: DNA itself just is."[11] Moreover, after the groundbreaking work of William Hamilton,[12] fitness itself is conceptualized as a property of genes, not, or not just, of organisms. These notions make possible a profound form of reductionism that goes beyond the standard causal reductionism that typically guides the framing and answering of scientific questions, i.e., it is not just that neo-Darwinism attempts to explain the origins or properties of life in terms of the behavior of matter. In a sense, it constitutes "teleological" reductionism,[13] in that it characterizes not just the constitution or operation, but also the very telos or purpose of living organisms and all their endowments (which have always evoked teleonomic attributions in biological science), as being "for" the replication of genes. This dramatic reconceptualization of life itself is expressed in the oft-repeated aphorisms "the organism is only DNA's way of making more DNA"[14] and "[genes] created us body and mind, and their preservation is the ultimate rationale for our existence."[15] Indeed, and highly relevant to theological reflection, this interpretive perspective extends to every aspect of the living world and human experience, e.g., "That simple, biological statement must be pursued to explain ethics and ethical philosophers, if not epistemology and epistemologists, at all depths."[16] Instead of being seen as

10. Albert Bennett, "Evolution and the Control of Body Temperature: Is Warmer Better?" in *Comparative Physiology: Life in Water and on Land,* ed. P. Dejours, L. Bolis, C. R. Taylor, and E. R. Weibel (Padova: Liviana Press, 1987); Gould, *Wonderful Life;* and Stephen J. Gould, *Full House: The Spread of Excellence from Plato to Darwin* (New York: Harmony, 1996).

11. Richard Dawkins, "Replicators and Vehicles," in *Current Problems in Sociobiology,* ed. King's College Sociology Group (Cambridge: Cambridge University Press, 1982), p. 45.

12. William D. Hamilton, "The Genetic Evolution of Social Behavior," *Journal of Theoretical Biology* 7 (1964): 1-16.

13. Henry Plotkin, *Evolution in Mind: An Introduction to Evolutionary Psychology* (Cambridge: Harvard University Press, 1997).

14. E. O. Wilson, *Sociobiology: The New Synthesis* (Cambridge: Harvard University Press, 1975), p. 3.

15. Richard Dawkins, *The Selfish Gene* (Oxford: Oxford University Press, 1976), p. 20.

16. Wilson, *Sociobiology,* p. 3.

agents — biotic or mental — that purposefully pursue ends, living creatures are means to the end of DNA's "drive" for replication.[17]

Thus there arises within the materialist realm itself a strange parody of the Cartesian model of two noncommunicating substances. There is on the one hand the blind automatism of a germ history enacted in the subterranean darkness that no light from the upper world penetrates, and on the other hand the upper world of the soma meeting the world in terms of life, pursuing its destiny, fighting its battles, taking the impress of its victories and defeats — and all this being of no other consequence for the hidden charge than that of its being either continued or eliminated. In a reversal of the classical formula, one would have to say that the developed is for the sake of the undeveloped, the tree for the sake of the seed.[18]

### 5. Rejection of Group Selection

Since George Williams's seminal *Adaptation and Natural Selection*,[19] and the ensuing elaborations of its insight,[20] orthodox neo-Darwinism has firmly, even virulently, rejected the idea that natural selection operates at hierarchical levels of scale, i.e., from individuals, to dyadic or symbiotic assemblages, to groups, populations, or species. Richard Dawkins expresses this quite succinctly: "Group selection of any kind is not Darwinism as Darwin understood it nor as I understand it."[21] To explain this, I should point out that while what is selected for is genes (or reproducing units of information, called "replicators"), what selection "sees," i.e., what interacts with the environment, is of course not genes but their products. Because it is these products that in any given environment "carry" genes into the next generation, they are referred to as "vehicles." Neo-Darwinism is reductive not only in construing organisms as merely vehicles "for" genes (the point of number 4 above), but also in terms of viewing individual traits, or at most the constellations of traits we call organisms, as the highest level of organization that serves as a vehicle, i.e., that is "seen" by natural selection. This means that dyadic associations, groups, etc., are not functionally

17. Plotkin, *Evolution in Mind*.

18. Hans Jonas, *The Phenomenon of Life: Toward a Philosophical Biology* (New York: Harper and Row, 1966), p. 52.

19. George Williams, *Adaptation and Natural Selection* (Princeton: Princeton University Press, 1966).

20. Dawkins, *The Selfish Gene;* Wilson, *Sociobiology*.

21. Frank Miele, "Darwin's Dangerous Disciple: An Interview with Richard Dawkins," *Skeptic* 3, no. 4 (1995): 80-85.

meaningful entities at all, are not in themselves adaptations, and do not have their own qualities that regulate their behavior or are evolutionarily selected for.[22]

### 6. Proposal of Memetic Selection

If points 4 and 5 are true, it is theoretically impossible for forms of group cooperation to evolve that involve reproductive sacrifice of one individual group member for another. And yet, it appears to many that this nevertheless occurs, particularly in human groups. To explain this within a neo-Darwinian context, which rejects group selection, a number of the most ardent advocates of the above interpretations of evolution have invoked another kind of informational replicator — memes (roughly understood as ideas) — which may influence organismal behavior and be replicated in a fashion semi-independent of, and sometimes in opposition to, genetic transmission. At face value this actually seems non-Darwinian since (a) it involves the ostensibly Lamarckian notion of inheritance of acquired (in this case learned) characteristics, and (b) it seems hierarchical, operating on a level of information "higher than" or irreducible to genetic selection. But it turns out to be fully, some would say "hyper," Darwinian by virtue of its emphasis on discrete replicating units that are transmitted by a strictly Darwinian selection mechanism: differential reproduction of particulate information. Moreover, as with genes, the "memes" are the actors or agents in the evolutionary play; the vehicles — human minds — are "just memes' way of reproducing themselves,"[23] or entities that are infected by memetic viral agents.[24] And finally, I should point out that here, as with genes and their organismic vehicles, the highest level of vehicle organization is the individual: a mind, but not interacting minds or "cultures," is the meaningful functional unit. The notion of memetic selection is controversial and by no means uniformly accepted by evolutionary biologists. At the same time, it has come to occupy not only a provocative but also a crucial role in the explanatory program of prominent advocates of neo-Darwinism.[25]

---

22. Dawkins, *The Selfish Gene;* Howard Holcomb, *Sociobiology, Sex, and Science* (Albany: State University of New York Press, 1993).

23. Susan Blackmore, *The Meme Machine* (Oxford: Oxford University Press, 1999).

24. Daniel Dennett, *Breaking the Spell: Religion as a Natural Phenomenon* (New York: Viking Press, 2006).

25. Dawkins, *The Selfish Gene;* Daniel Dennett, *Freedom Evolves* (New York: Viking Press, 2003).

### Neo-Darwinian Implications

I should acknowledge that the above points, at least 2-6, are debatable in several important ways. First, they are of course debatable scientifically; i.e., there can be, and is, disagreement about whether they constitute, individually or jointly, an accurate and adequate account of evolution. I shall say a few things about this in the next section.

Second, they are, in a sense, debatable sociologically; i.e., one could debate the demographic question of whether they fairly represent issues of consensus, indeed orthodoxy, in the evolutionary community, or perhaps merely reflect the views of a few extreme but prominent expositors. My own view is that this differs from point to point and, like most things in science, is also changing with time. But undeniably, an extensive and influential literature advocates each of the above points, and there are highly regarded proponents of the entire package or paradigm.

Third, one could debate the theological and philosophical implications of the above neo-Darwinian constellation. Of course, considerable debate exists on a variety of epistemological, ethical, and metaphysical implications of evolution in general and neo-Darwinism in particular. But interestingly, several religiously significant issues, with a few exceptions,[26] are rather uniformly presented by prominent exegetes of evolutionary theory as necessarily entailing elements of a natural atheology.[27] Indeed, on such points there is striking agreement between these authors and leading antievolutionary creationists.[28] I

26. Francisco J. Ayala, "Biology Precedes, Culture Transcends: An Evolutionist's View of Human Nature," *Zygon* 33, no. 4 (December 1998): 507-23; Kenneth Miller, *Finding Darwin's God: A Scientist's Search for Common Ground between God and Evolution* (New York: Cliff Street Books, 1999); Ronald Numbers, ed., *Creation-Evolution Debates* (New York: Taylor and Francis, 1995); Michael Ruse, *Can a Darwinian Be a Christian?* (New York: Cambridge University Press, 2001).

27. Richard Dawkins, *River out of Eden* (New York: Basic Books, 1995); Dawkins, *A Devil's Chaplain: Reflections on Hope, Lies, Science, and Love* (New York: Houghton Mifflin, 2003); Dennett, *Darwin's Dangerous Idea;* George Williams, "Mother Nature Is a Wicked Old Witch," in *Evolutionary Ethics;* Hull, "The God of the Galapagos"; Rachels, *Created from Animals;* John Dupre, *Human Nature and the Limits of Science* (Oxford: Clarendon, 2001); Gould, *Wonderful Life;* Gould, *Full House;* W. B. Provine, "Progress in Evolution and Meaning in Life," in *Evolutionary Progress,* pp. 49-74.

28. Phillip Johnson, *Darwin on Trial* (Downers Grove, Ill.: InterVarsity, 1993); William Dembski, *Intelligent Design: The Bridge between Science and Theology* (Downers Grove, Ill.: InterVarsity, 2002); Benjamin Wiker, *Moral Darwinism* (Downers Grove, Ill.: InterVarsity, 2002); Cornelius Hunter, *Darwin's Proof: The Triumph of Religion over Science* (Grand Rapids: Brazos, 2003); Henry Morris, *The Long War against God* (Green Forest, Ark.: Master Books, 2000); David Klinghoffer, "Darwin Would Put God out of Business: If You Have Faith in God as

will not discuss here whether these points (1) follow strictly from neo-Darwinism or (2) reflect precommitments that have influenced the content of the theory,[29] the plausibility criteria by which the theory is evaluated,[30] or philosophical implications attributed to it.[31] As with all theories, these alternatives are interactive rather than mutually exclusive. The points I want to emphasize are that the following claims about several religiously significant issues *are* widely made by advocates of neo-Darwinism and that they function "clearly as a rhetorical tool . . . virtual parables of Darwinism that are used not merely factually but representatively: they are intended to present the inner truth of nature."[32]

Before describing them, I should comment on the relationship of the following to materialism. Although neo-Darwinism does reflect a commitment to explanation in terms of material causes, in contrast to its creationist critics, I do not believe this commitment is a necessary and sufficient *input* to generate the theory: there are non-Darwinian materialist accounts, and there are non-materialists of various kinds who fully accept Darwinian biology. On the other hand, and unlike a number of contributors to this volume, I do not believe that the ostensibly atheological implications of neo-Darwinism are ultimately *outputs* from a brute and generic materialism or naturalism. The following points are posited by most proponents to accrue from a *specifically Darwinian* naturalism.

### Altruism

"If natural selection is both sufficient and true, it is impossible for a genuinely disinterested or altruistic behavior pattern to evolve."[33] Given the neo-

the Creator, You Can't Embrace Darwinism Too, Despite What Some Scientists Claim," Beliefnet.com, August 23, 2006.

29. E. Fox-Keller, "Language and Ideology in Evolutionary Theory: Reading Cultural Norms into Natural Law," in *The Boundaries of Humanity: Humans, Animals, Machines*, ed. J. J. Sheehan and M. Sosna (Berkeley: University of California Press, 1991), pp. 85-102; Howard L. Kaye, *The Social Meaning of Modern Biology: From Social Darwinism to Sociobiology* (New Haven: Yale University Press, 1986); M. Midgley, "Gene Juggling," *Philosophy* 54, no. 210 (1979): 108-34.

30. Philip Johnson, *Reason in the Balance: The Case against Naturalism in Science, Law, and Education* (Downers Grove, Ill.: InterVarsity, 1995).

31. David Oates, "Social Darwinism and Natural Theology," *Zygon* 23, no. 4 (1988): 439-54; Jeffrey P. Schloss, "Evolution and Religion," in *Oxford Handbook of Religion and Science*, ed. Philip Clayton (Oxford: Oxford University Press, 2006).

32. Oates, "Social Darwinism and Natural Theology."

33. M. T. Ghiselin, "Darwin and Evolutionary Psychology," *Science* 179 (1973): 964-68.

Darwinian commitment to the truth and sufficiency of natural selection, the view that there is no such thing as genuine altruism is extensively, if not nearly universally, accepted amongst its proponents. But the claim is equally widely misunderstood by those outside of evolutionary biology. The evolutionary notion of "altruism" is one of consequences, not motives: biological altruism, if it exists, would involve the sacrifice of an actor's fitness while benefiting that of the recipient. Natural selection is construed as winnowing out such behavior and favoring the opposite — behavior that enhances fitness of the actor at the expense of others. Because Darwinian fitness is a comparative notion, "enhancement" for one entails concomitant decrement to another. However, this does not imply what it is widely misunderstood to mean — that everyone is intentionally selfish. On the contrary, an act could be "genetically selfish" (i.e., reproductively beneficial) while being entirely unselfish motivationally.

Nevertheless, the implications of this theory do conflict with traditional understandings of love.[34] According to it, even if we have unselfish motives, their operation must be restricted to behaviors that benefit, and do not cost, the actor's reproduction. Moreover, if we think we are capable of unconditional love — extended without compensatory benefit — we are probably deceiving ourselves.[35] In his influential *Biology of Moral Systems,* Richard Alexander concludes that twentieth-century neo-Darwinian supplements to evolutionary theory, which amount to a second Darwinian revolution, have precisely these profound implications for altruism:

> I suspect that nearly all humans believe it is a normal part of the functioning of every human individual now and then to assist someone else in the realization of that person's own interests to the actual net expense of those of the altruist. What this "greatest intellectual revolution of the century" tells us is that, despite our intuitions, there is not a shred of evidence to support this view of beneficence, and a great deal of convincing theory suggests that any such view will eventually be judged false. This implies that we will have to start all over again to describe and understand ourselves, in

---

34. Jeffrey P. Schloss, "Emerging Accounts of Altruism: 'Love, Creation's Final Law?'" in *Altruism and Altruistic Love: Science, Philosophy, and Religion in Dialogue,* ed. S. Post, L. Underwood, Jeffrey P. Schloss, and W. Hurlbut (Oxford: Oxford University Press, 2002), pp. 212-42.

35. R. D. Alexander, *The Biology of Moral Systems* (Chicago: Aldine-de-Gruyter, 1987); Ghiselin, "Darwin and Evolutionary Psychology"; R. Trivers, "Deceit and Self-Deception: The Relationship between Communication and Consciousness," in *Man and Beast Revisited,* ed. M. H. Roinson and L. Tiger (Washington, D.C.: Smithsonian Institution Press, 1991), pp. 175-91; E. O. Wilson, *On Human Nature* (Cambridge: Harvard University Press, 1978).

terms alien to our intuitions, and in one way or another different from every discussion of this topic across the whole of human history.[36]

## Morality

Language, morality, and other fundamental human cognitive and affective capacities are understood by Darwinian biology as genetically informed endowments that have been selected over evolutionary time. That is, they are viewed as adaptations, the "technique by which human genetic material has been and will be kept intact"; indeed — "morality has no other demonstrable ultimate function."[37] In *The Moral Animal,* Robert Wright's best-selling popularization of what he calls the "new Darwinism," he maintains that "'mental organs' are here for a reason. And the reason is that they goaded our ancestors into getting their genes into the next generation. . . . What is in our genes' interests is what seems 'right' — morally right, objectively right, whatever sort of rightness is in order."[38]

Ever since Huxley published his *Evolution and Ethics* in 1894, debate has been ongoing over the moral legitimacy and scientific merit of such claims.[39] To the extent that they are accepted as solid science, their implications for ethics are claimed to be twofold. First, normative ethical claims must be trimmed to fit the reproductively viable (a variant of the altruism problem).[40] Second, it is argued that, in the absence of metaphysical assumptions involving a moral structure of the cosmos that ensures that what is reproductively efficacious leads to what is morally real, the grounds for ethical realism, or at least confidence in moral perceptions, is seriously compromised. "Hence the basis of ethics does not lie in God's will. In an important sense, ethics as we understand it is an illusion fobbed off on us by our genes to get us to cooperate. It is without external grounding. . . . like Macbeth's dagger, it serves a powerful purpose without existing in substance."[41] Amongst religious believers and others, this pro-

36. Alexander, *Biology of Moral Systems,* p. 20.

37. Wilson, *On Human Nature,* p. 167.

38. Robert Wright, *The Moral Animal: Evolutionary Psychology and Everyday Life* (New York: Vintage, 1995), pp. 28, 325.

39. See note 7 above. See also Ayala, "The Difference of Being Human"; George C. Williams, "Huxley's Evolution and Ethics in Sociobiological Perspective," *Zygon* 3, no. 4 (1988): 383-407; Philip Clayton and Jeffrey P. Schloss, eds., *Evolution and Ethics: Human Morality in Biological and Religious Perspectives* (Grand Rapids: Eerdmans, 2004).

40. Michael Ruse, "Evolutionary Theory and Christian Ethics: Are They in Harmony?" *Zygon* 29, no. 1 (1994): 5-24.

41. Michael Ruse and E. O. Wilson, "The Evolution of Ethics," in *Religion and the Natural Sciences: The Range of Engagement,* ed. J. E. Hutchingson (Orlando: Harcourt and Brace, 1991), pp. 310ff.

vokes profound concern (which does not make the claim false). Many believe that "two thousand years of Judeo-Christian ethics cannot simply be replaced with the carte blanche of natural selection. The essential lack of ethical ground prescribed by nature and her ways is almost too frightening to face."[42] Indeed, Huxley had the same concern.

One response to this is to try to put a kinder spin on things and argue that the "universal acid of Darwin's dangerous idea" may nevertheless "turn out to be, in the end, just what we need to preserve . . . the values we cherish."[43] In their essay "Darwin's Nihilistic Idea," Sommers and Rosenberg reject this grasping for "nice nihilism." They distinguish between naturalism or Darwinism and what they call "Darwinian nihilism," which necessarily rejects the truth of all morality. But they argue that the distinction is only rhetorically consoling, not logically sustainable, since to turn the former into the latter one "need only add the uncontroversial scientific principle that if our best theory of why people believe P does not require that P is true, then there are no grounds to believe P is true."[44] This leaves us with the challenge of recognizing that "morality is an illusion foisted upon us by evolution. The naturalistic fallacy is a red herring in this debate, since there is really nothing that counts as a 'fallacy' at all. . . . we may be able usefully to employ a moral discourse, warts and all, without believing in it."[45]

## Purpose

Neo-Darwinism has profound impacts — in two ways — for the understanding of purpose in nature. First, it has eliminated the need to employ purposeful activity or final causation as an explanation for the origin of living things.[46] As Ayala has said in this volume, Darwin "completed the Copernican revolution" by extending to biology the understanding of nature as "a lawful system of matter in motion."[47] Actually, this is simultaneously something of an overstatement and an understatement. It is an overstatement in the sense that Darwin did not find a naturalistic solution for the ultimate biological questions of life's origin or functional stability, and in *Origin* he actually ended up invoking special creation

42. Dorion Sagan and Lynn Margulis, "Facing Nature," in *Biology, Ethics, and the Origins of Life*, ed. H. Rolston III (Boston: Jones and Bartlett, 1995), p. 54.

43. Dennett, *Darwin's Dangerous Idea*, p. 521.

44. Sommers and Rosenberg, "Darwin's Nihilistic Idea," p. 667.

45. R. Joyce, "Darwinian Ethics and Error," *Biology and Philosophy* 15 (2000): 713.

46. Richard Dawkins, *The Blind Watchmaker: Why the Evidence of Evolution Reveals a Universe without Design* (New York: Norton, 1986).

47. Chapter 2.

for the former. In the view of many, biogenesis is not a question for evolutionary biology at all, since the Darwinian mechanism requires life rather than generates it.[48] Nor does contemporary neo-Darwinism explain the reproductively self-relinquishing manifestations of mind. Instead, it must deny their existence or attribute them to unseen memetic entities, the causal leverage of which seems no less magical than divine intervention or soulish dualism.[49] I am not making an argument from ignorance here, suggesting that because we cannot yet explain these things they are inexplicable. But as George Whitesides points out, working on the biophysical chemistry of self-assembling systems, we should not overstate the completeness of our present understanding: "Although I believe that science will ultimately be successful in rationalizing . . . life in terms of physical principles, it should be cautious and claim credit only for the puzzles it has already solved, not those whose solutions still lie in the future. . . . Claiming credit prematurely — claiming, in effect, that current science holds all the answers — may stunt the growth of the new ideas that a resolution may require."[50]

What Darwinism did do is pay down an outstanding promissory note on the origin of life's adaptive diversity that was then held by natural theology. That done, confidence in the explanatory solvency of materialist explanation has become sufficiently robust that there is little doubt it will be profitably employed in addressing these crucial issues — and all others as well. Thus, while Darwinism did not "complete" the Copernican revolution in terms of explanatory adequacy,[51] it did successfully finalize the transfer of power from one epistemological regime to another.

In this sense, then, Darwinism did more than complete the Copernican program of materialist causal explanation. It has been employed to restrict the domain of legitimate questions to those answerable within the materialist framework. Purpose becomes unnecessary for explaining not only the origin of life's diversity but also the nature of life itself: "the lifeless has become the knowable par excellence and is for that reason also considered the true and only foundation of reality."[52] Hans Jonas anticipated this before the ascendance of

---

48. Gould, *Wonderful Life;* Christian de Duve, *Life Evolving: Molecules, Mind, and Meaning* (Oxford: Oxford University Press, 2002).

49. Alexander, *The Biology of Moral Systems;* F. de Waal, *Good Natured: The Origins of Right and Wrong in Human and Other Animals* (Cambridge: Harvard University Press, 1996).

50. George Whitesides, "The Improbability of Life," in *Fitness of the Cosmos for Life: Biochemistry and Fine Tuning,* ed. John Barrow, Simon Conway Morris, Stephen Freeland, and Charles Harper (Cambridge: Cambridge University Press, 2007).

51. For a philosophical account of why even the Darwinian revolution itself is incomplete, see Holcomb, *Sociobiology, Sex, and Science.*

52. Jonas, *The Phenomenon of Life,* p. 10.

what I am calling neo-Darwinism: "Indeed it was the Darwinian theory of evolution, with its combination of chance variation and natural selection, which completed the extrusion of teleology from nature. Having become redundant even in the story of life, purpose retired wholly into subjectivity."[53]

Neo-Darwinism influences perceptions of purpose in a second way as well. In addition to purpose being unnecessary as a causal explanation of nature's behavior or as an attribution of nature's properties, it ceases to be viable as an interpretation of nature's significance. The first point — that nature does not have purposes, only effects — is, strictly speaking, an entailment not of Darwinism but of materialism,[54] the lingering impediments to which Darwin helped clear away. But the second point — that nature does not credibly suggest or intimate purposes beyond nature — is more explicitly an impact of Darwinism, specifically a neo-Darwinian view of evolutionary history. Michael Ruse points out that in the wake of Darwin natural theology did not go extinct, but itself evolved.[55] Instead of employing divine agency as an explanation for the origin of organismic actors on earth's stage, it saw divine wisdom and providence reflected in the themes of the evolutionary play. In light of belief in evolutionary progressivism, natural theology's emphasis switched from biological products to process. Although progressivism has cycled in and out of acceptance by evolutionary biologists, its rejection by contemporary neo-Darwinism has been strongly associated with natural atheology. Even Stephen Gould, who, unlike the more virulent evolutionary atheologists, views science and religion as nonoverlapping magisteria (NOMA) without implications for each other's claims,[56] nevertheless concludes that in light of evolution's radical historical contingency, the idea of providential purpose for the world or humankind makes no sense.[57] He maintains that this represents a profound "Freudian dethronement" in that "we are, whatever our glories and accomplishments, a momentary cosmic accident that would never arise again if the tree of life could be replanted from seed and regrown under similar conditions."[58]

53. Jonas, *The Phenomenon of Life*, p. 44.

54. Jerry Fodor, *In Critical Condition: Polemical Essays on Cognitive Science and the Philosophy of Mind* (Cambridge: MIT Press, 1998).

55. Michael Ruse, *Monad to Man: The Concept of Progress in Evolutionary Biology* (Cambridge: Harvard University Press, 1996); Ruse, *Darwin and Design: Does Evolution Have a Purpose?* (Cambridge: Harvard University Press, 2003).

56. Stephen Jay Gould, *Rock of Ages: Science and Religion in the Fullness of Life* (New York: Random House, 2002).

57. Gould, *Full House*.

58. Gould, *Full House*, p. 18.

Richard Dawkins argues that the very question of cosmic purpose is a "universal delusion" and is illegitimate:

> I have lost count of the number of times a member of the audience has stood up after a public lecture I have given and said something like the following: "You scientists are very good at answering 'How' questions. But you must admit you're powerless when it comes to 'Why' questions." . . . Behind the question there is always an unspoken but never justified implication that since science is unable to answer "Why" questions, there must be some other discipline that is qualified to answer them. This implication is, of course, quite illogical. . . . The mere fact that it is possible to frame a question does not make it legitimate or sensible to do so. . . . at the very least you have no right to assume that the "Why" question deserves an answer when posed about a boulder, a misfortune, Mt. Everest or the universe. Questions can be simply inappropriate, however heartfelt their framing.[59]

### Natural Evil

Darwinism has not only *contributed* to discussion of natural evil, but it also has *employed* discussion of it in three ways. First, it has utilized observations of useless traits, clumsy design, or suboptimal function as a scientific argument against special creation. These aspects of biology are both explainable and predictable by Darwin's theory. Special creation offers no explanation, and can only appeal to the inscrutability of the Creator. To the extent Darwin's mechanism also successfully explains the origin of adaptive elegance, in addition to making sense of ostensible blunders, accepting it over special creation seems to be a fairly straightforward case of inference to the best explanation.

Second, waste, defects, and suffering have been used as a *theological* argument against special creation.[60] Ayala is one of those who argue that God, or at least an all-wise, good, and powerful God, would presumably not do things in such a way.[61] Ayala views the dysfunction and suffering that attend design defects such as the narrow human birth canal as incompatible with action by the biblical God and understandably laments, "Surely we don't want to blame God for this." Fortunately, "science, much to the relief of many theologians, provides an explanation that convincingly attributes defects, deformities, and dysfunctions to natural causes." Thus, in addition to evolution providing a

59. Dawkins, *River out of Eden*, p. 97.
60. Reviewed by Paul Nelson, "The Role of Theology in Contemporary Evolutionary Reasoning," *Biology and Philosophy* 11 (1996): 493-517.
61. Ayala, chapter 2 above.

better scientific explanation of defects (as per the above point), it also appears to offer a more theologically conciliatory opportunity.

I am sympathetic to this line of thinking, but believe things are not so simple on two counts. In the first place, it is not clear that it constitutes an effective or necessary argument against Intelligent Design (ID), or "special action by the omniscient and omnipotent God of Judaism, Christianity, and Islam." Quite ironically, the scriptures of these traditions include stories that attribute precisely the defect of childbirth to God's direct action and also ascribe to it a deluvian biotic decimation far worse than the fossil record, without blaming God. But I will leave aside the questions raised by the biblical narrative. While current advocates of ID may all believe in its omniscient and omnipotent God, they do not explicitly attribute these characteristics to the creating agent they propose. This is reflected by the fact that ID's criteria for inference to design neither require nor imply optimality — only irreducibility. The doubly adequate reasons ID's contemporary design arguments do not work is that their primary examples of complexity have been demonstrated not to be irreducible, and irreducibility itself is not unattainable by evolutionary means. These criticisms suffice to discredit the proposal without appeal to speculations about what the biblical God does or does not seem likely to do.

In the second place, it is not clear how science gets God off the hook. Even if one accepts the distinction between God's shaping the world through "special action" and "natural causes," and understands the defects of creation to have emerged from the latter as described by science, this alone does not better preserve God's goodness. Hiring a drunk to drive you home after an evening's excess at the bar is just as morally reckless as driving yourself. Moreover, attributing defects to natural causes may actually exacerbate the problem, depending on the intrinsic nature of those causes. In evolution, not only do we end up with defective *products,* but in addition the very causal *process* appears deeply morally objectionable — replete with, indeed dependent on, carnage, suffering, brutality, cataclysm. Especially in the absence of a potentially redemptive progressionist understanding of evolutionary history[62] or some explicitly theological rationale for the divine employment of this mechanism,[63] it is difficult to see how evolutionary naturalism, on its own merit, provides a meaningful theodicy.

None of this is lost on the enterprise of evolutionary atheology, however, which represents the *third* employment of natural evil — used as an argument

---

62. John Haught, *Deeper Than Darwin: The Prospect for Religion in the Age of Evolution* (Cambridge, Mass.: Westview Press, 2003).

63. John Haught, *God after Darwin: A Theology of Evolution* (Cambridge, Mass.: Westview Press, 2000).

against not only special creation but also any claim whatever for the existence or goodness of God.[64] I have no intention of minimizing the problem of natural evil, but I do want to say three things about its neo-Darwinian exegesis. One, the litany of evils so often cited by evolutionary theorists entails evident, almost clichéd, aspects of nature that have nothing to do with evolutionary theory: "The total amount of suffering per year in the natural world is beyond all decent contemplation. During the minute it takes me to compose this sentence, thousands of animals are being eaten alive; others are running for their lives, whimpering with fear; others are being slowly devoured from within by rasping parasites; thousands of all kinds are dying of starvation, thirst and disease."[65] While these facts are undeniable, typically unmentioned are Darwin's points that the death of animals often does not entail suffering and natural selection employs pleasure more than pain as an adaptation.

Two, the connection between the problem of evil and evolution, to the extent it is made, often entails a teleological characterization of nature, not infrequently a personification, in terms of the agenda of the gene: "So long as DNA is passed on, it does not matter who or what gets hurt in the process. . . . genes don't care about suffering, because they don't care about anything."[66] In one sense, this could appropriately be said of boulders or lightning or any physical entity or process: given traditional metaphysics, none of these things "care." The difference is that nobody is saying that organisms (or anything) exist *for* boulders. Moreover, there is no "so long as" with these things; there is no metaphysical urgency for them to achieve their telos, at the cost of indifference to anything else or expense to it.

Third and last, there is a fascinating adjunct to the neo-Darwinian elaboration of natural evil: just as suboptimality was an argument against special creation, so natural beneficence becomes an argument against neo-Darwinism, which cannot brook altruism. David Oates points out that for neo-Darwinism, "the familiar problem of evil is turned on its head, and becomes the problem of goodness."[67] The exclusion of beneficence from the representation of nature raises the question, framed by Malthus, of whether this "reflects the author's melancholy spleen of disposition, or the dark hues are in the picture." In this case the absence of "natural goodness" may or may not reflect metaphysical precommitments, but it surely does involve theoretical requirements.

64. Hull, "The God of Galapagos"; Williams, "Mother Nature Is a Wicked Old Witch"; Dawkins, *River out of Eden.*
65. Dawkins, *River out of Eden,* p. 132.
66. Dawkins, *River out of Eden,* p. 131.
67. Oates, "Social Darwinism and Natural Theology."

## Beyond Neo-Darwinism?

The above issues are not easily dismissed as caricatures, and in light of them it is claimed — by both theists and those who reject theism — that "Those who are worried about the clash between science and religion have good reasons for their worries."[68] Indeed, Daniel Dennett claims that "those evolutionists who see no conflict between evolution and their religious beliefs have been careful not to look as closely as we have been looking."[69] ID advocate Philip Johnson agrees, and for this very reason his "strategy requires driving a wedge between the atheistical Darwinists and their dupes in the religious world."[70]

There are, however, at least three alternatives to these claims. First, the above philosophical implications may not necessarily follow from neo-Darwinism. Second, even if they do, or some of them do, there may be theological accommodations that in the long run do not injure, but perhaps even enhance, religious faith.[71] Third, there may be fully evolutionary alternatives or supplements to the neo-Darwinian program I have described here.

Of course, insisting that neo-Darwinism must be inadequate due to unwelcome theological entailments reflects a consequentialist fallacy. Nevertheless, I do want to close this section by enumerating some alternatives or supplements to neo-Darwinian understandings of evolutionary history that have recognized empirical merit. This is not an exhaustive list, but it represents a series of proposals in the current literature that are scalable as enhancements or refinements — not as irreconcilable opponents — to neo-Darwinian theory.

### 1. Hendersonian Notions of Environmental Fitness or Ideas of Physical/Biochemical Fine-Tuning

Darwinian processes emphasize the selection of random variations to fit environmental challenges; notions of fine-tuning or environmental fitness emphasize the preconditional suitability for life, for particular kinds of life, and perhaps for specific trajectories of biological evolution. It is even possible that the abiotic environment itself changes in regular or directional ways, so that evolutionary change is progressively driven or pulled.

68. Ruse, "Evolutionary Theory," p. 5
69. Dennett, *Darwin's Dangerous Idea*, p. 310.
70. Philip Johnson, "Back Home in Mitford," *Touchstone Magazine* 14, no. 1 (2001).
71. Haught, *God after Darwin*.

### 2. Intrinsic Biotic Constraints or Directionality

With the exception of natural selection itself, biological systems have not been successfully described in terms of universal lawlike generalizations. This may be because the behavior of organisms is a historical process contingent upon small differences in starting conditions, or we may yet discover such laws or invariant constraints. There are a number of current proposals for morphological convergence, scaling laws, and life history invariants, in terms of either intrinsic directionality to natural selection or underlying physical first principles.

### 3. Group Selection

Group selection continues to have its advocates,[72] and recent proposals have gained credence as they marshal empirical support and incorporate theoretical refinements that avoid the problems of earlier formulations. Indeed, group selection has recently appeared preferable to a major theoretical alternative, kin selection. Many have thought this ingenious proposal of William Hamilton makes sense of apparent sacrifice on the basis of strict genetic relatedness, thereby avoiding recourse to group selection. However, kin selection has not turned out to be the comprehensive solution originally hoped for. According to E. O. Wilson, a prominent advocate of kin selection from the theory's first introduction, its application to radical cooperativity in social insects has been "a thriving industry for three decades." But he acknowledges that, in light of new work, this theory has now "collapsed." Wilson concludes: "the ongoing shift to group-level selection forced by empirical evidence suggests that it might be profitable to undertake a similar new look at the wellsprings of social evolution in human beings and nonhuman vertebrates."[73]

### 4. Symbiogenesis

The notion of symbiogenesis[74] is that adaptive new traits are created by symbiotic (mutually helpful) association between different species. A relatively

72. E. Sober and D. S. Wilson, *Unto Others: The Evolution and Psychology of Unselfish Behavior* (Cambridge: Harvard University Press, 1998); Christopher Boehm, "The Natural Selection of Altruistic Traits," *Human Nature* 10, no. 3 (1999): 205-43.

73. E. O. Wilson, "Kin Selection as the Key to Altruism: Its Rise and Fall (Eros in the Natural Sciences)," *Social Research* 72, no. 1 (2005): 165.

74. Lynn Margulis, *Symbiotic Planet: A New Look at Evolution* (New York: Basic Books, 2000).

unarguable but important implication of this proposal is that symbiosis can be a source of phenotypic novelty that does not require genetic mutation, and may have a directional bias. As a stronger proposal, symbiogenesis may be creator of altogether new niches that do not require competitive displacement. In some situations, through the amplification of eco-space, it could entail evolution through the relaxation, not employment, of natural selection.

## 5. Directional Interactions among the Above

It is possible that there may be directional interactions and even feedback loops between the above. For example, Williams and Frausto Da Silva argue that the evolutionary escalation of organizational complexity from single-cell, to multicellular, to complex organisms represents an "inevitable progression" due to organisms' increasing oxidation of the environment: "life was in a physical chemical tunnel and there was only one way to go."[75] A more ambitious and controversial form of interaction would involve regulated feedback, in which group adaptations function as agents controlling aspects of environmental fitness (e.g., Gaia).

In my contribution to part IV, I develop theories that are more hospitable to theistic interpretation. This will involve exploring interactions between points 1 and 2 above as they relate to the question of directionality or progressive trends in evolutionary history.

75. R. Williams and J. Frausto Da Silva, "Evolution Was Chemically Constrained," *Journal of Theoretical Biology* 200 (2003): 335.

# II TO BROADEN AND DIVERSIFY EVOLUTIONARY THEORY

## Editor's Preface

Today when one hears the word "evolution," one thinks first and foremost of the evolution of biological species. However, the word has much broader application. To evolve is simply to develop gradually. The whole universe has evolved. Cultures evolve. In the whole process of evolution many factors are involved besides random mutation of genes.

This unquestioned fact does not contradict any teaching of neo-Darwinism, which considers only the evolution of biological species from the eukaryotic cell. Even the evolution of that cell is excluded. It is possible, in principle, that biological evolution does not involve any of the processes that have been present in other forms of evolution, that only selection among randomly mutated genes has any effect in this sphere. Nevertheless, those who view biological evolution in the wider context of cosmic history tend to be skeptical of this restricted view. To them it seems more likely that processes studied by physics and chemistry, as well as the biological process that brought the eukaryotic cell into being, also play a role in biological evolution.

Once the door is opened to this consideration of multiple contributors to evolution in general, observers, including biologists, feel free to note other dynamics that seem to contribute to that part of evolution on which neo-Darwinists have focused their attention. None of this denies the importance of genes and genetic mutations. But it emphatically challenges the idea that this important phenomenon excludes all others from significant roles in biological evolution.

This book is ultimately about the relation of evolutionary theory to religious faith, and especially to theism. However, unlike the contributors to the other three parts of the book, most of the writers in this part propose alternatives to neo-Darwinism without theistic interpretations of evolution in view. Indeed, some of the proposals are as resistant to such interpretation as is mainstream neo-Darwinism. For example, insofar as the theories of Margulis and Dorion have explicitly religious implications, they have to do with Gaia rather than with God. Nevertheless, the approaches represented here open the way to a richer understanding of the evolutionary process and provide ideas with which humanists and theistic believers, as well as scientists, should come to terms.

The essays in part II discuss contributions to evolution neglected by hard-core neo-Darwinism and not integrated into the standard explanations of evolution influenced by it. The theories of Hendersonian fine-tuning, biotic constraints on directionality, and group selection, with which Schloss ended chapter 5, already point in this direction, although they have considerable status in the mainstream community of working biologists. Most of the contributors to part II propose that a full explanation of biological evolution would involve a sharper break with neo-Darwinism and a greater challenge to mainstream biologists. They think that much more is involved in evolution than environmental selection among randomly mutated genes. The alternatives they offer are of two types: one brings in the perspectives of physics and chemistry, the other operates in the context of biology.

1. Explanations of evolution in terms of physics and chemistry are reductionistic in a way that neo-Darwinism is not. Neo-Darwinism reduces explanations of evolution to genes and the environment. In its usual formulations it implies that reduction to matter in motion is possible and ultimately ideal, but it keeps the actual discussion of evolution at the level of biology. As Ayala made clear in chapter 2, most advocates of the standard theory believe that, in principle, genetic changes and natural selection are explicable in terms of chemistry and physics. But the explanations biological evolutionists give do not extend that far. They could accept the view that life is an emergence in the ontological sense without changing anything in their biology.

However, both those who affirm and those who deny the possibility of reducing the laws of biology to the laws of chemistry and physics assert that these latter laws do apply also to living organisms. This is not in dispute. All agree that some features of the behavior of all things, including human beings, are explicable by the laws of physics. What human beings do and what happens to us are compatible with gravitation, even if gravitation by itself cannot explain all human behavior.

One question is: How far can one go in explaining such important matters as genetic mutation in terms of physics and chemistry? Such explanation is part of the program implicit in the way Ayala argues that Darwin has shown that even human beings are ultimately explicable in terms of matter in motion.

A second question is: How far can the direct application of what is known in physics and chemistry explain biological phenomena, specifically evolution? It is with answers to this second question that we are concerned in part II. Do physical or chemical laws suggest accounts of biological evolution other than gene selection?

2. Contemporary studies in biology offer evidence that biological changes are sometimes brought about by the activities of the organisms that evolve in ways not highlighted, or in some cases even allowed, in standard formulations of neo-Darwinism. In the standard formulation, those few among the random genetic changes that prove favorable in the given environment gain ascendancy. The activities of the organisms count for nothing in this account. However, other biologists find evidence that the activities of organisms are important. They select and change the environment and find new ways of operating within it. Which random mutations prove favorable is influenced by the results of these activities of the organism. Instead of regarding all changes in organisms as the result of changes in the genes, it is argued that causality sometimes goes in the opposite direction.

There is also the question of whether all genetic changes leading to new species occur gradually through changes in individual genes or whether some of them occur through the acquisition of genes, or even entire genomes, from other organisms. Regardless of the answer to this important question, there are good reasons to believe that the behavior of organisms can lead to genetic changes. The issue is not whether genetic changes are crucial, but whether the process of genetic change is adequately depicted in the standard account. In fact, it seems that the origin of species is not as simple as depicted by neo-Darwinism.

Part II begins with a survey by A. Y. Gunter of theories that are supplementary to the standard neo-Darwinian account. He identifies six as worthy of serious consideration. The first three of these are of the reductive type. In many ways the most interesting is the most reductive — the quantum alternative. Whereas prior to the development of quantum theory reduction was thought to apply to matter in motion, as many biologists seem still to assume, today the quanta cannot be reasonably conceived as tiny lumps of "matter," and their behavior is not deterministic. When clues to the understanding of organisms and their evolution are sought at this level, organisms may be considered as open systems with indeterminate behavior. Gunter surveys the literature in this field in some detail, especially because it is not discussed elsewhere in this book. He deals much more briefly with two other approaches to evolution from the side of physics: thermodynamics and chaos theory.

The remainder of Gunter's paper treats three theories that arise out of biology itself. He describes evidence for neo-Lamarckian phenomena, which are not discussed elsewhere in this book, at considerable length. The other two are the Baldwinian point that the behavior of organisms affects the selection of genes and the view that organisms acquire genes from other organisms through symbiotic relations. These topics, to which later chapters are devoted, Gunter treats briefly. His main interest is not to argue that one or another of these theories has been decisively proven, but to make clear that there is much evidence for evolutionary changes that does not fit well into the pure neo-Darwinian framework. His point is that the notion that all evolutionary developments occur according to a single pattern is unfortunate and should be dethroned.

The remainder of part II follows the general order of Gunter's discussion. Gunter refers to Dorion Sagan in his account of a thermodynamic explanation of evolution, and Sagan's essay on this topic follows Gunter's chapter. Many of us have regarded the evolutionary complexification of organisms over time as an indication that there is a counterentropic process taking place. No one has supposed that the law of entropy is thereby abrogated. But since entropy leads to a reduction of the capacity to work, and organic developments increase the local capacity for work, the latter appeared to move in the opposite direction from entropy. Sagan, however, sees the second law of thermodynamics, or nature's abhorrence of a gradient, as *explanatory* of evolution! He is impressed by the fact that living things increase entropy faster and more efficiently than do inorganic things. The human case is the most extreme illustration of this point. The primary function of organisms, in his view, is to speed the entropic process. Nature produces organisms for this "purpose." It is not immediately clear just how this idea can influence the formation of specifically biological theories of evolution, but it should be taken into account especially by theists interested in finding direction in evolution.

The academic discipline closest to biology is chemistry. To recognize the importance of this level of analysis, I have included a short paper by Reg Morrison, who has worked closely with Sagan and Lynn Margulis. His comments highlight how completely the whole history of life has depended on, and been shaped by, the availability of particular chemicals. He focuses attention not on how new species evolve but on how the evolutionary process deals with such dangerous species as *Homo sapiens*.

Morrison explains that hydrogen is the primary constituent of the universe and also plays a key role in making life possible. Of course, the other chemicals are important, especially carbon, but he believes that describing life as carbon-based is misleading. To understand the chemical constituents of life is important because the living systems and the environment that makes them possible depend on the appropriate chemical balance, a balance to which the organisms themselves contribute. His paper leads into that of Margulis on the Gaia hypothesis.

Margulis's essay on Gaia defines evolution far more broadly than the way it is usually treated by biologists. This different perspective relativizes the issue of the genesis of new species of multicellular animals on which Darwinians focus. If our interest is in how the world came to be as it is and how it is now changing, she shows that we need to view matters in a quite different way.

She also provides a radically different perspective on the relation of organisms and their environment than that of standard accounts. The latter neglect the effects of organisms on the environment that selects among them. The Gaia hypothesis proposes that the chemical environment of organisms has largely been created by organisms and that planetary temperature is regulated by them. This suggests that organisms play a large role in their own evolution. The Gaia hypothesis also evokes an organic and self-organizing image of the planet and its environment that is very different from the mechanistic one expressed in most scientific accounts, including neo-Darwinism.

The current cultural and political clash between science and religion centers on the relation of evolution to belief in God. Margulis is not interested in that debate. For her the religious implications of cutting-edge science move in a quite different direction. Her depiction of Earth has religious implications, but she does not always appreciate the way they are expressed in New Age spirituality. Sadly, these religious issues are not discussed in this book.

Margulis is also widely known for her work on symbiogenesis. The next essay, which she coauthored with Sagan, is on the importance of symbiosis in the evolutionary process. The authors judge that one reason neo-Darwinians focus on a single mechanism of change is that their inquiry is limited to the period and to the organisms in which this mechanism has played the largest role. When the whole story of life is in view, all must acknowledge the evidence for other mechanisms, including symbiogenesis. Among bacteria the exchange of genes is fluid and rapid and does not depend on neo-Darwinian principles. For most of the history of life, the living things were exclusively bacterial. Hence the omission of this phenomenon is highly restrictive.

Further, the evolution of the eukaryotic cell was the first great step beyond bacterial life. There is widely acknowledged evidence that this single most important event in evolutionary history took place by symbiogenesis, the acquisition of the genes of one bacterium by another. Even after that occurred, instead of transferring all attention to the further developments in the evolution of multicellular organisms through changes in their genes, Margulis continues to attend to the bacteria and to the role they play in the ongoing history of other organisms. What others view as a single organism, such as a termite or a wolf, she sees as a vast multiplicity of organisms, most of them bacteria, in symbiotic relations. Each of these organisms has its own genes. Among the bacteria, genes continue to be exchanged freely. She is convinced that there is extensive evidence that symbiotic relations have led to genetic changes in multicellular organisms.

Mainstream discussion of biology has focused extensively on the fact that change does not occur steadily and gradually but more drastically in relatively brief time periods. This is sometimes taken as a serious challenge to standard neo-Darwinism. Stephen Jay Gould has proposed the theory of "punctuated equilibrium" as, in some sense, an alternative theory. This plays little role in the criticisms of neo-Darwinism elsewhere in this book, but Ayala recognizes it as an important topic and contributes a short chapter on it. He shows that there is no conflict between the facts cited in support of punctuated equilibrium and standard neo-Darwinism.

Gunter briefly discusses the Baldwin effect, an alternative to neo-Darwinian theory that he calls "ultra-Darwinian." This theory depicts the environment as given for the organisms among which it selects. The Baldwin effect has been sufficiently demonstrated so that most evolutionists consider it valid. It shows that there are nuances in the process of evolution not suggested by standard neo-Darwinian formulations. However, most biologists believe that the needed adjustments can easily be made and, indeed, that they have already been introduced into standard evolutionary theory. In the next chapter Francisco Ayala describes the Baldwin effect in that way. He describes it in terms of the impact of the environment on quite simple organisms and how this can lead to favoring different mutations.

However, other examples of the Baldwin effect have more significant theoretical implications. In the chapter following Ayala's, Ian Barbour surveys five scientific developments that put pressure on neo-Darwinism to reshape itself more radically. One of these is the Baldwin effect. Examples of the effect include the way choices made by animals lead to changes that in turn influence the selection among mutations. Examples of this sort suggest that omitting the subject from consideration in evolutionary theory limits its adequacy to the empirical facts. This is a major theme of part III.

The contrasting treatment of the Baldwin effect by Ayala and Barbour is particularly indicative of a difference between the mainstream of biological thought and those who have a process perspective. Both affirm the effect, but what they thereby affirm differs. Ayala defines it as "the hypothesis that the environment affects adaptively the phenotype of an organism . . . and that such adaptive modifications may later become genetically fixed by natural selection." Barbour understands the theory to be that "the initiatives of organisms and their learned behavior play a significant role in evolutionary history." Since, in Ayala's account the organisms themselves remain passive, the difference from standard theory is only that the environment plays an additional role. He finds little problem in expanding neo-Darwinian theory to include this. For Barbour, Baldwin's theory focuses attention on the activity of organisms, which can be intelligent and purposive. To include that in the evolutionary story would require a much more fundamental modification of the standard account, a basic feature of which is the exclusion of purpose of any sort from a role in evolution.

Even so, Barbour's survey of developments requiring theoretical adjustments stays much closer to mainstream biological thinking than do some of the ideas discussed by Gunter and expounded in the chapters that follow his survey. Whereas many biologists feel free to ignore quantum interpretations, thermodynamics, and symbiosis, they are more likely to discuss with Barbour not only the Baldwin effect but also his other topics: "contingency and teleology," "complexity and design," "hierarchical levels and downward causation," and "self-organization and emergence." Barbour also discusses the relation of science to metaphysics, thus offering a transition to part III.

Barbour affirms the congeniality of Whitehead's philosophy to the developments in biology that he describes, implying that a metaphysical shift from seventeenth-century materialism to a process cosmology would improve the ability of biologists to understand their data. He develops his views in part in critical dialogue with another Whiteheadian, David Griffin, who responds to some of the concerns in chapter 17.

Gunter expresses surprise that so many supplementary or alternative theories are formulated with little regard for one another or for the facts expounded in the standard theory. I have added a concluding chapter drawing on the other chapters in this part and suggesting an overarching Whiteheadian view that would be more inclusive of the evidence than is the neo-Darwinian one. The main thesis is one already implied in several of the chapters in part II, that the activity of organisms plays an important role in determining the direction of evolution. I believe that many of the problems with typical current accounts of evolution can be overcome if the activity of organisms is recognized as a fourth variable.

# 6. *Six Scientific Alternatives to Neo-Darwinism*

A. Y. GUNTER

This chapter deals with what are for its author two basic puzzles: the assumption of certainty on the part of contemporary ultra- (or hyper-) Darwinism, and the current harvest of scientific alternatives to reigning Darwinian assumptions. If I am puzzled by the first, it is because its defenders seem oblivious both of late-twentieth-century philosophy of science (whether in a Kuhnian and/or Popperian form) and of putative scientific alternatives. If I am puzzled by the various alternatives to contemporary Darwinism, it is because of the apparent lack of interest of their proponents in each other's proposals as well as because of my uncertainty as to just how far they might succeed. The conclusion of this chapter is that an adequate theory of evolution will be more broadly based and more cohesive than any that is currently available.

## Ultra-Darwinian Gnostics

By "ultra-Darwinism" I mean the view that while organisms do exist, they are essentially means toward reproducing genes. Ultra-Darwinism is the "selfish gene" hypothesis put forward by Richard Dawkins, plus the other classical assumptions of Darwinism. (This is much the same as what most authors in this volume mean by "neo-Darwinism." See, especially, Griffin's chapters.)

It is, among other things, ultragnostic. Dawkins, Crick, Dennett, and their congeners seem not only to know that their theory is true but also to know, beyond any doubt, that it can never be seriously transformed or replaced. Put in these terms — true now, undeniably true forever — ultra-Darwinism turns out to have a strange kinship with Protestant fundamentalism. Though ultra-Darwinists become upset when called "fundamentalists," in the sense in which I use the term, it fits. Utter certainty is utter certainty. And, as with fundamentalism, alternatives are at best not plausible. At worst they are headed for, with biblical fundamentalism, a Protestant hell, with ultra-Darwinism, an epistemological Gehenna.

It is interesting to note the cover story of the September 2004 *Scientific American:* "After Einstein."[1] It is hard to conceive that the presiding genius of twentieth-century physics and the leader of an epoch-making paradigm shift might, in the early years of the twenty-first century, be in danger of being eclipsed. Yet this is a possibility that many contemporary physicists are considering. The defenders of ultra-Darwinism, by contrast, seem sure that their "take" on evolution — their paradigm — can never be overturned or seriously transformed. The response to this prevailing attitude is to point not only to the history of science (including recent science) but also to later twentieth-century philosophy of science. Postpositivistic philosophy of science is associated with such names as Karl Popper, Thomas Kuhn, Imre Lakatos, and Paul Feyerabend.[2] Kuhn's terminology and many of his ideas have been taken over by scientists and the general public, and it is his viewpoint, with the notions of paradigm shift and revolutionary science, that I will use here.

What the newer philosophy of science has brought to bear on our understanding of the sciences is precisely history. From the vantage point of history the sciences do not pursue a simple linear career, piling up truth with remorseless accumulation. Rather, the sciences go through a series of zigzags, unpredictably moving from one "paradigm" to the next, with paradigms providing intelligibility for the empirical data compiled. Anyone seriously aware of the Kuhnian-historical approach, with its rise and fall of central meaning structures, will doubt the possibility of any one paradigm prevailing forever. The absolute persistence (hence, one supposes, absolute truth) of any one paradigm is not to be observed in astronomy, mathematics, or physics. One is driven to wonder what special epistemological status evolutionary biology has that insulates it from the conceptual shifts obvious in the other natural sciences. Barring the demonstration of this special status, must not we admit that such a transformation is at least possible?

Having praised the Kuhnian-historical approach to the sciences, however, I am now compelled to criticize it. If the history of the sciences evidences serious and fundamental conceptual changes, it is clear that these do not always come in simple, dramatic paradigm shifts. The moves from Ptolemaic to Co-

---

1. *Scientific American* (special issue) 291, no. 3 (September 2004).
2. See Thomas Kuhn, *The Structure of Scientific Revolutions*, 2nd ed. (Chicago: University of Chicago Press, 1970), p. 210; Karl Popper, *The Logic of Discovery* (New York: Harper Torchbooks, 1968), p. 479.

pernican astronomy and from Aristotelian to Newtonian physics have such unitary, dramatic contours. Significant changes in other sciences, however, have a different structure.

Thermodynamics, founded in the mid–nineteenth century and codified at the end of the century by Ludwig Boltzmann, remained essentially unchanged for decades. Then, beginning in the 1960s it was transformed, not by being eclipsed but by being broadened and (as I would put it) deepened. From a system understood in linear and equilibrium terms, it came to be founded on nonequilibrium ideas. To be sure, the second law of thermodynamics has not been jettisoned. But its content will never be the same.[3]

A similar history attends quantum physics. Planck's constant (formulated in 1900) still lives. But unlike relativity physics, which is the work of one man, quantum physics is the work of many, and it has gone through several transmutations. We recall the reshaping of early quantum physics resulting circa 1925-1927 in a now-classical formulation. Other changes, some consisting of simple discoveries, others of real conceptual surprises, have followed this significant reformulation. The most recent include Bell's theorem and quantum teleportation, decoherence theory, and the unexpected emergence of the standard quantum effects out of the microcosm into the mesocosm and then into the macrocosm (a point I will return to later).

I have been insisting on an alternative to Kuhn's dramatic notion of paradigm shifts. But another criticism can be lodged against Kuhn and, I think, also Popper, again on the basis of the actual history of physics in the twentieth century. Newtonian physics was one. But physics today is many; it is relativity physics plus quantum physics plus thermodynamics. Though these often overlap on important points, each is inconsistent with the others. Bluntly stated, physics today is not a single shining edifice but a three-ring circus. It is not clear whether or how this Humpty Dumpty can be put back together again. One hopes that the results of paradigm shifts or internal conceptual transformations will lead to unified sciences. But surprisingly, this too can be doubted.[4]

There have been many efforts to falsify Darwinism, efforts springing from assumptions as diverse as those of Marxism, religious fundamentalism, vitalism, and even simple skepticism. It is important to see that over the last few decades the nature of such attempted refutations has shifted radically — has in fact become inverted. If early-twentieth-century critics objected that living

---

3. Ilya Prigogine and Isabelle Stengers, *Order Out of Chaos* (New York: Bantam Books, 1984).

4. John Horgan, *The End of Science: Facing the Limits of Knowledge in the Twilight of the Scientific Age* (New York: Broadway Books, 1996), p. 322.

things and their evolution could not be explained by mere physics and chemistry, some critics now argue that new discoveries in physics and chemistry provide possible nonmechanistic, nonatomistic explanations of life. Far from saying that physics and chemistry cannot explain the living organism, they want to hold that ultra-Darwinism either fails to continue its reductionism all the way (e.g., to quantum reality) or fails to consider alternative reductions (e.g., roughly, to nonlinear phenomena).

I will say more about these latter alternative "reductions" throughout this chapter. It will help at this point to let Brian Goodwin sketch the new world of physics: "[T]he notion of particles as tiny bits of billiard-ball-like matter that get pushed and pulled about by fields external to themselves is a hard one to put to rest. The relatively recent experimental confirmations by French physicist Alain Aspects of the predictions of Einstein and his colleagues has finally forced the realization that mechanical interpretations of basic physical processes have to be abandoned and replaced by a much more integrated, interconnected view of the dynamics of change at the fundamental level of physical reality."[5]

Goodwin goes on to speculate that the new purview of physics amounts to a change in the nature of physics and biology and in their interrelations: "Biology thus becomes more physical and mathematical, putting the insights of genetic, developmental and evolutionary studies into more precise dynamical terms; at the same time, physics becomes more biological, more evolutionary, with descriptions of the emergence of the four fundamental forces during the earliest stages of the cosmic Big Bang, the growth sequences of stars, and the formation of the elements during stellar evolution."[6]

In his depictions of the new relative status of physics and biology, Goodwin goes further than do most contemporary scientists. The Newtonian or Newtonian-like ideas that have dominated modern science, as Goodwin sees it, die hard. He projects not so much the present state of the sciences as a future state, perhaps not so far over the horizon.

For the sake of argument I will sketch six current scientifically based alternatives to standard Darwinian theory: (1) quantum evolution, (2) thermodynamic evolution, (3) "chaotic" or nonlinear evolution, (4) neo-Lamarckian evolution, (5) Baldwinian evolution, and (6) Margulis's genome-capture hypothesis. The first three interpret evolution in light of developments in physics. The second three are more specifically biological.

The most extensive attention is given to quantum evolution, primarily

5. Brian Goodwin, *How the Leopard Changed Its Spots: The Evolution of Complexity* (New York: Simon and Schuster, Touchstone, 1994), p. 173.

6. Goodwin, *How the Leopard*, p. 71.

because it is of great potential importance and is not treated elsewhere in this book. For somewhat similar reasons, neo-Lamarckian theories are also given considerable attention. No claim is made to offering an exhaustive list of non-Darwinian theories.

## Quantum Evolution

A theory that attempts to derive the emergence and evolution of life from fundamental quantum phenomena is found in Johnjoe McFadden's *Quantum Evolution*.[7] Two new factors in quantum physics support McFadden's theory: the discovery of quantum effects in the mesocosm and the development of decoherence theory. Quantum decoherence is a recent permutation of the basic approach to quantum measurement. For the purposes of a quantum biology, decoherence has several advantages, the most important of which is its denial that a human observer is needed for a successful observation. Decoherence theory is thus epistemologically realist. It denies, among other things, the observer-induced collapse of the wave function.

The recent emergence of quantum effects from the microcosm into the mesocosm is unconnected with quantum decoherence. It is less a theory than an experimental achievement. It has been assumed that the well-known quantum effects (wave-particle duality, Heisenberg's relations, tunneling) exist only at the level of one or a few subatomic entities. (I refuse to call them particles.) Recent experiments, however, show that even so weighty an object as buckminsterfullerine ($C_{60}$) can, under the right conditions, exhibit "quantum weirdness." Even a very hefty "buckeyball" ($C_{70}$) behaves à la Heisenberg and shows wave-particle duality.

Two things follow from this, both of very general import (reaching beyond the confines of McFadden's particular approach). First, the new mesoscopic quantum effects must surely put to rest the notion that Heisenberg's uncertainty relations are caused by the impact of the measuring device on the object measured. Photons, protons, electrons cannot have a significant effect on $C_{60}$ or $C_{70}$ sufficient to cause uncertainty in position or momentum. Second, though most biologists (and neurophysiologists) believe that the peculiar quantum effects have nothing to do with brains, organisms, or evolution, this opinion may well have to be revised, and the need for such revision is the point of McFadden's book.

McFadden's attempted restructuring of biology is twofold, touching on

7. Johnjoe McFadden, *Quantum Evolution* (New York: Norton, 2000), p. 338.

the emergence of life from nonliving matter (presently an unresolved problem) and on the subsequent evolution of life. His concept of the first chemical replicator is surprisingly specific. He proposes that the emergence of something that can replicate itself and thus initiate the beginnings of life must have occurred in a relatively protected area (a "protocell"), which could be as simple as a cavity in a rock. The candidate he offers for this first replicator is a short peptide chain, which can function as an enzyme.

A short peptide along with others of its kind in a protected cell need not wait three and a half billion years for a human observer for decoherence to occur. Decoherence would occur when the peptide is, as would happen sooner or later, affected by its environment. The result would be the emergence of the peptide out of the quantum state, into which state it could again drift pending another environment contact and decoherence: and so on indefinitely.

> This process of drifting into the quantum realm, measurement, collapse into a quantum state, and drifting back into the quantum realm, would have continued as the peptide added more and more amino acids. Some amino acid additions — those that did not counter enzymatic activity — would have taken place in the quantum realm, whereas others would have precipitated quantum measurement and a brief return to the world of classical physics. This process would have continued to elongate the quantum superposition of possible peptides until such a time when the system irreversibly collapsed into a classical state. The point at which this irreversible collapse would have taken place is easy to predict: it would have been when the peptide learned to self-replicate.[8]

Thus, McFadden urges, there is a previously unsuspected capacity at the upper limits of quantum reality for quantum phenomena to produce biological order, including the dynamic sort of order exhibited in replication.

McFadden's model thirty-two amino acid replicator, he reasons, would have to undergo a continuing Darwinian test (natural selection), producing a more "fit" replicator through, among other things, the capture of "lipid membranes, peptides, or nucleic acids."[9] The end result — one requiring a considerable stretch of time — would be the first, simplest cell.

I will not attempt to present McFadden's account of the development of cells and multicellular organisms: the grand sweep of biological evolution. This would involve the ability of living cells to "measure" their own quantum states and respond with increasing sorts of complexity.

8. McFadden, *Quantum Evolution*, p. 227.
9. McFadden, *Quantum Evolution*, p. 236.

Two critical comments are needed here. McFadden dismisses contemporary (nonlinear) thermodynamics as having nothing important to do with evolution. His own quantum explanations provide, he says, a negentropic vector for life's history of increasing complexity. But, compared to the linear thermodynamics of Clausius and Boltzmann, for whom natural processes can produce only either relative disorder or static form ("crystallization"), nonlinear thermodynamics *is* negentropic: it creates new levels of dynamic form (hence higher levels of complexity). Hence nonlinear thermodynamics could, and probably does, play a role in biological evolution. What is, for example, to keep the (mesoscopic) nonlinear processes studied in the new thermodynamics from amplifying and continuing near-mesoscopic quantum effects?

Mae-Wan Ho, in *The Rainbow and the Worm*, offers another approach to quantum evolution.[10] Though rich in conceptual content and diverse in subject matter, Ho's biology in fact rests on a few basic claims. In three respects, she argues, the living organism differs from our ordinary understanding of it. (1) Its thermodynamics differs fundamentally from both the linear thermodynamics of Boltzmann and the more recent nonlinear thermodynamics of Ilya Prigogine and his colleagues. (2) Its chemistry is that of the liquid crystal, a chemical state that easily accepts realignment. (3) Its most fundamental causality is not that of DNA, RNA, or the familiar electrical and chemical process that governs nerve function. Rather, quantum coherence directs the organism's activities.

It is tempting to describe Ho's theory (if inelegantly) as a stool that sits on three legs. This image is misleading, however, since it suggests three independent theoretical parts, while (consistently with her organismic viewpoint) her three primary components are profoundly interwoven. Each requires, and is closely involved with, the other.

Ho's thermodynamics rests on some remarkable (but little-noticed) facts. In living organisms essential chemical processes attain remarkable efficiencies: photosynthesis and muscle contraction are 100 percent efficient, while other biochemical processes rival this efficiency. The result is that the organism produces surprisingly little entropy and is thus able easily to store energy and to act without using it up. Ho's understanding of entropy is subtler than these words suggest. Both linear Boltzmannian and nonlinear Prigoginean entropy are necessary conditions of Ho's "third thermodynamics."

The term "liquid crystal" may sound unfamiliar, even self-contradictory, but in fact liquid crystals are common in nature. The kinds of rigid crystals we

10. Mae-Wan Ho, *The Rainbow and the Worm: The Physics of Organisms*, 2nd ed. (River Edge, N.J.: World Scientific, 1998), p. 282.

are used to (salt crystals, quartz crystals) constitute only one limit of a crystal continuum. At the other end are liquids, which are relatively disordered. In between are the liquid crystals, which have some characteristics of crystal lattices and some of ordinary liquids. Being a liquid crystal is a matter of degree: "Unlike liquids which have little or no molecular order, liquid crystals have an orientational order, in that the molecules are aligned in some common direction(s), rather like a crystal. But unlike solid crystals, liquid crystals are flexible, malleable, and responsive."[11]

All major components of living organisms may be liquid crystalline: lipids of cellular membranes, DNA in chromosomes, cytoskeletal proteins, muscle proteins, collagens, and others. Liquid crystals typically undergo rapid changes in orientation and/or phase transitions when exposed to electric and to magnetic fields.

The moral is not far to seek. Living organisms possess stores of energy that science has not fully understood or taken account of. Living organisms, in addition, are neither solid (as we usually conceive of their skeletal material) nor liquid. They are "solid states," held together both within the cell and between cells by omnipresent connective tissues, which make very rapid — unexpectedly rapid — signaling possible from part to part, part to whole, and whole to part.

But what is to create and, where necessary, to direct this ceaseless signaling? The author does not deny that brains, nervous systems, and other standard communicating systems exist and play important roles. She believes that quantum physics, however, introduces an all-important factor that has not been recognized in biology: quantum coherence. We have discussed this new approach to quantum phenomena in reviewing McFadden's quantum biology, noting both that it removes the necessity of the human observer from physics (and biology) and is slowly moving out of the microcosm into the mesocosm. Professor Ho takes advantage of both of these factors. For her "the living system is one coherent 'photon field' bound to living matter. This photon field is maintained far from thermodynamic equilibrium and is coherent simultaneously in a whole range of frequencies that are nonetheless coupled together."[12] That is, the different components of the organism, each with its own tempo (biological rhythm), are made synchronous by a quantum-coherent field.

A coherent system exhibits neither space nor time separation. A change in one part is "instantaneously" communicated to the others, regardless of the distance between them. Yet, paradoxically, coherence can be compared to a

11. Ho, *Rainbow and the Worm*, p. 173.
12. Ho, *Rainbow and the Worm*, p. 152.

"large jazz band, where everyone is doing his or her own thing, yet keeping perfectly in time or in step with the whole."[13] Thus in a coherent system the whole does not ablate the parts; nor can the whole be reduced, atomistically, to the parts.

Professor Ho writes with remarkable brevity, considering the wide diversity of her subject matter. It would be worthwhile to consider, for example, the ways in which quantum-coherent fields may coordinate both the organism's movements and its multiplicity of biological rhythms (which she compares to Bergsonian duration).[14] It would also be helpful to examine the evidence for information transfers in the organism that are faster than the nervous system can account for.[15] Comparison of the views of Ho and McFadden (sometimes in sync, sometimes not) would also be helpful.

Examining the work of Ho and McFadden gives rise to many questions, which critics will be sure to stress. However, it is impossible to avoid a significant conclusion. Only now can quantum physics begin to help us understand the living organism. The results, inevitably, will change many fundamental concepts: in genetics, in neurophysiology, and in evolutionary theory. Some of these changes are likely to be radical.

## Thermodynamic Evolution

In several discussions with Ilya Prigogine concerning the relations of his nonequilibrium thermodynamics to biology, I was surprised to hear him reiterate his belief that nonlinear autocatalytic chemical reactions could be responsible for evolution through their capacity to manipulate the genetic code, producing new genetic information. What he envisages is not chance mutation but a spontaneous creation of dynamic form. This is not a purposeful process in the usual sense, because it is "experimental," that is, vectored toward form but not predetermined in its results. Prigogine's achievements by their very nature invite extension from chemistry to biology; the gap between the two being, today, virtually negligible. In fact, his influence on almost all those who attempt to provide scientific alternatives to ultra-Darwinism is profound — though often not recognized.

13. Ho, *Rainbow and the Worm*, p. 210.
14. Ho, *Rainbow and the Worm*, p. 242.
15. Mae-Wan Ho, "Quantum Coherence and Conscious Experience," *Cybernetics* 26 (1997): 265-76.

Dorion Sagan takes up the case for thermodynamic evolution in the next chapter. He argues that

> *computerized simulations, no less than intelligent humanity itself, are not exemplary or foundational of intelligence, but represent a subset of naturally complex thermodynamic systems in an inherently (if cryptically) intelligent universe.* These complex thermodynamic systems naturally cycle matter in complex ways and undergo spontaneous, elaborate path-building regimes "in order" to come to equilibrium. Please pay attention to this "in order." Such activities, which occur in real time, require no genetic machinations. They are completely natural, and their complexity, as seen below, is a by-product of the entropy-production function implicit in the second law.[16]

Once one considers the possibilities opened by the new thermodynamics, Sagan's views are plausible — I am tempted to say inescapable. The reader of this book will have the opportunity to examine them directly.

## Chaos Evolution

A third approach to evolution from physics is informed by the physics of chaos or nonlinear dynamics. This physics has much in common with thermodynamics and quantum physics. All three involve nonlinearity and the emergence of form. Indeed, it may be that chaos evolution could be developed in such a way as to encompass quantum phenomena and thermodynamics.

Nevertheless, the physics of chaos has its own concepts and should be treated separately. The literature dealing with this field is immense. For the sake of brevity I will mention only two books: *How the Leopard Changed Its Spots* by Brian Goodwin and *At Home in the Universe* by Stuart Kauffman.[17] Both works start not from a specific physics but from a generalized awareness of science's discovery of "self-organization," "spontaneous order," "order for free," and "complexity."

The two books involve very different approaches to their subject matter.

---

16. Emphasis in original. For a full development of this viewpoint, see Eric D. Schneider and Dorion Sagan, *Into the Cool: Energy Flow, Thermodynamics, and Life* (Chicago: University of Chicago Press, 2005), p. 345. Cf. also Eric D. Schneider, "Gaia: Toward a Thermodynamics of Life," in *Scientists Debate Gaia: The Next Century,* ed. Stephen H. Schneider et al. (Cambridge: MIT Press, 2004), pp. 45-56.

17. Stuart Kauffman, *At Home in the Universe: The Search for Laws of Self-Organization and Complexity* (New York: Oxford University Press, 1995), p. 321.

Kauffman's quasi-experimental computer-oriented research rarely descends to the level of specific organisms or specific evolutionary bifurcations. Goodwin, on the other hand, pays special attention to specific organisms, exploring their morphology in geometrical terms. Goodwin describes Kauffman's achievement: "[Kauffman's] focus is on the types of order that can emerge spontaneously in complex systems and the role of natural selection as an external force that drives the system into particular stages of adaptation."[18]

That is, most of the order that we see in living nature is an expression of properties inherent in complex dynamic systems. Simple rules of interaction between large numbers of elements create living order. It follows that natural selection is not all that significant in producing life-forms. There is "order for free," Kauffman insists. It emerges spontaneously without having to be chiseled out gradually by natural selection working on point mutations.

Goodwin happily proclaims that his work and Kauffman's, though they start from different considerations and with different orders of fact, converge in common (non-Darwinian) insights. This is true. But problems still remain.

Does the Goodwin/Kauffman alliance rest on quantum foundations, on thermodynamic foundations, or on both? Or is their "consensus" separate, free-floating? If so, it would seem that physics today is a four-ring circus with the physics of chaos as the fourth ring (not a fifth wheel). A second problem stems from an unresolved tension in the two thinkers. Kauffman's focus is on *time*, Goodwin's on *space*. Neither author suggests a rapprochement between the two. Perhaps some third approach is necessary.

We turn now from theories drawing on wider principles of physics to three theories that arise directly out of the biological data.

## Neo-Lamarckianism

Lamarckianism, a live option around the turn of the last century (1890-1910), has beaten a continuing retreat in biology, being finally expelled from its last stronghold in unicellular organisms by Joshua Lederberg in the 1950s. Several factors have brought it back, as it were, limping from the dead. Some of these include Barbara McClintock's discovery of the dynamic genome and her defense of heretical Lamarckian views,[19] and Howard Temin's discovery of reverse

---

18. See Goodwin, *How the Leopard*, p. 186.

19. For an excellent account of McClintock's life and thought, cf. Evelyn Fox Keller, *A Feeling for the Organism* (New York: Freeman, 1983), p. 235. For a brief but revealing account of her Lamarckian position, cf. Barbara McClintock's Nobel Prize lecture, "The Significance of Re-

transcriptase, with its transmission of protein "backward" from RNA to DNA. Temin's work opened the door to the possibility of further transmission, from protein to RNA. Similarly, though later disproved, John Cairns's 1988 experiments, interpreted as establishing guided mutations, have led to further research in the direction of Lamarckian mutations.[20] (Edward J. Steele's *Lamarck's Signature* contains a spirited defense of neo-Lamarckianism and an account of recent research.)[21] Only one other essay in this volume touches on this topic, that of Reg Morrison, and that only lightly. Accordingly, I will discuss it somewhat fully.

A probe into the literature of recent Lamarckianism provides two interesting insights. The first is that while Lamarck and many of his followers (e.g., Nietzsche) emphasized volition — the effort of the giraffe lengthening its useful neck — contemporary Lamarckians reject voluntarism, speaking of the "stress" that the organism undergoes as the transformative factor. The second is that there appear to be two kinds of Lamarckian inheritance, one permanent, the other "temporary." The existence of permanent inherited acquired characteristics is hotly debated. Even so, some examples are hard to refute. Horny patches on the breast of the emu are embedded in both its skin and its breastplate — and in its genes. Somehow this flightless bird has been able to genetically assimilate an environmentally induced structure. Meanwhile, short-term "Lamarckian effects" are well established. Water fleas, confronted with predatory phantom midge larvae, grow huge helmets, which halve their mortality rates. These helmets are then passed on to the second generation, and in a less pronounced form to the third and fourth generations. Radishes, when chewed on by cabbage butterfly caterpillars, produce 30 percent more spikes on, and ten times more repellent mustard oil glycosides in, their leaves. These are passed on to the second generation and, in diminished degree, to the third generation. That such effects occur is unquestionable. The question is *how* they occur.[22]

---

sponses of the Genome to Challenge," in *The Dynamic Genome,* ed. N. Federoff and D. Botstein (Plainview, N.Y.: Coldspring Harbor Laboratory Press, 1982), pp. 174-93.

20. John Cairns, J. Overbought, and S. Miller, "The Origin of Mutants," *Nature* 335 (September 1988): 142-45. For a brief rundown on the refutation of Cairns's thesis and the resulting research derived from it, cf. "Evolution Evolving," *Scientific American,* September 1997. Available on the Internet under "Genesis of Eden Diversity Encyclopedia," at http://www.dhushara.com/book/evol/evev.htm.

21. Edward J. Steele, Robyn A. Lindley, and Robert V. Blanden, *Lamarck's Signature: How Retrogenes Are Changing Darwin's Natural Selection Paradigm* (Reading, Mass.: Perseus Books, 1998), p. 286.

22. Susan Milius, "Threatened Mothers Have Tougher Offspring," *Science News* 156, no. 10 (September 4, 1999): 151; Gail Vines, "There Is More to Heredity Than DNA!" *New Scientist,* April 19, 1997, p. 16; Susan Milius, "Tadpole Science Gets Her Legs," *Science News* 160 (January

Whether long run or short run, the variety of effects that can be termed "Lamarckian" is hard to corner in detail. In part this is because the exact definition of Lamarckian is hard to come by. Any genomic effect that appears in one generation other than by chance mutation and can be transmitted to the next is, strictly speaking, Lamarckian, since it involves the "heredity of acquired characteristics" (whether this involves transmission of information from protein to RNA to DNA or not). Eva Jablonka and Marion J. Lamb in *Evolution in Four Dimensions* present a powerful marshaling of evidence for Lamarckianism in this broad sense.[23] One cannot recommend a better book than this to bring the reader up to date on current trends in now-blossoming "Lamarckian" biology.

The four "dimensions of evolution" that the authors examine are: genetic, epigenetic, behavioral, and symbolic. Though, as we will see, all four are not found in all types of living organisms, all have the same effect. That is, they account for inheritable effects (and thus for features of the course of evolution) *without having recourse to chance mutations*. The authors modify this claim in dealing with the genetic dimension, which in line with neo-Darwinian orthodoxy does have a place for chance mutations, but, interestingly, not only for these.

It is customary to conceive of variations in the phenotype as entirely a function of the genes, and of changes in the genes as a function of chance mutations alone. The authors believe this approach is outmoded. Not only does the "knocking out" of genes participating in important developmental pathways often not affect the phenotype at all;[24] many changes in the genes take place when bacteria encounter a hostile environment. Some bacteria contain stretches of DNA ("hot spots") whose mutation rate is hundreds if not thousands of times higher than elsewhere. This activity is focused; that is, it is targeted for functions that involve much diversity (like the avoidance of immune system responses). The authors explore what is known about all such processes, noting that at one extreme (the sheer increase in mutations of all sorts) such effects are random, while at others (in which increased mutation rates are limited to genes that influence specific characteristics of the organism) effects are clearly targeted. The authors deny neither the existence of classic "blind" mutations nor their importance. It is surprising to learn, however, that blind mutations are not the only source of genetic variation. Increasingly others are being found, which are, simply, functions of the genes themselves.

---

12, 2002): 26-28. Among the "short-term Lamarckian" organisms are: mice, human beings (inheritable size diminution due to food shortages), several species of tadpoles, and (as noted in the text) water fleas and wild radishes.

23. Eva Jablonka and Marion J. Lamb, *Evolution in Four Dimensions: Genetic, Epigenetic, Behavioral, and Symbolic Variation in the History of Life* (Cambridge: MIT Press, 2005), p. 462.

24. Jablonka and Lamb, *Evolution in Four Dimensions*, pp. 64-65.

The second sort of variation (and of inheritance) is "epigenetic": it is not created by the genes at all, but by factors external to them. The authors describe four EIS (epigenetic information systems), the most impressive of which is termed the chromatin marking system. Chromatin is what chromosomes are made of, and they are spatially complex. They consist of DNA molecules wrapped around histones (small proteins), twisted to make chromatin fiber, which is compacted to make chromosomes. Thus DNA gets "packaged" (the writer is driven in conceptualizing such structures to think of ropes wrapped around ropes, twisted into looplike assemblages). Exactly where a stretch of DNA is in the chromosome "package" determines much about whether/when it will be active. The decisive point here is that non-DNA features of chromatin *can be passed from one generation to the next.* These heritable features are called "chromatin marks," which influence how easily genes can be turned on or off. The results are striking: which genes are expressed, and hence what features the adult organism will have, is never a function of the DNA alone, but also of the "chromatin marks," which may be inherited generation after generation. The genes cannot therefore be as selfish as some would have them be. They are constrained by chromosomal "social" factors surrounding them.

Both genetic variation and epigenetic inheritance systems occur and function in unicellular organisms. It had long been assumed, prior to the 1980s, that in the making of sperm and ova in multicelled organisms the epigenetic past is completely erased. This limitation has been overcome. The authors cite, among other evidence, the part played by chromatin marking in speciation in toadflax and in heredity in laboratory mice. In the latter not only coat color but also obesity, diabetes, and susceptibility to cancer are passed along via "epimutations."

Beyond nonstandard genetic and epigenetic inheritance lie behavioral and symbolic information systems. Behaviorally influenced inheritance will be discussed in the next section, and thus we need not discuss the authors' treatment of it, except to stress their acceptance of a particular form of Baldwinian inheritance, C. H. Waddington's "genetic assimilation" thesis, according to which the genes are surprisingly rich in alternative developmental pathways, many of which are "masked." Behavioral options pursued by the organism may lead to choices of new niches in which hitherto unused genes are brought into action ("unmasked"). Natural selection in the new context will lead to the dying out of organisms less suited to it, thus "fixing" the newly used genes in the population. Behavior thus shapes the effective genome.

Finally, the authors explore the symbolic inheritance system. This is the final step up "evolution mountain." The first step utilizes both Mendelian and non-Mendelian genetics. The second involves these as well as new epigenetic factors, and leads to the emergence of multicellular creatures. The third step involves behavioral alternatives, which become fixed in the genes. The fourth step is limited to human beings, whose capacity to use language allows them to construct cultural niches and hence highly complex societies that are not accessible apart from verbal skills. Like behavioral evolution, evolution that occurs through the use of linguistic symbolism creates new situations favoring some genes, minimizing others. The latter will tend to become genetically fixed. Like behavioral evolution, evolution via symbolic communication falls under the general heading of Baldwinian evolution.

## Baldwinian Evolution

The Baldwin effect refers to the initiative taken by organisms to move into a new, different environment, whose selective pressures may then mold the organism in a new way. It is often understood in terms of speciation. Allopatric speciation is caused by geographical factors: mountain ranges, rivers, deserts, which separate populations, which then drift apart. Sympatric speciation — now beginning to be seriously studied — occurs in the same or overlapping geographical areas. For the former, life appears as passive in the hands of the environment. For the latter, the organism selects a new environment, perhaps by changing what it feeds on. (Maggot) flies that lay their eggs on hawthorn become hawthorn maggot flies. Maggot flies that lay their eggs on apples become apple maggot flies. Apples were introduced into the wild only two centuries ago; genetic differences between the two groups of flies are now being observed.

Other candidates for sympatric speciation are the peppered moth, the Megaohyssa wasps, pitcher plant mosquitoes, crickets, lacewings, and African parasitic finches.[25] As with the Lamarckian option, the many Baldwinian approaches are embroiled in controversy. They cannot, however, simply be dismissed, as would have been the case a few years ago.[26]

25. Mary Jane West-Eberhard, *Developmental Plasticity and Evolution* (New York: Oxford University Press, 2003), p. 793.

26. S. Via, "Sympatric Speciation in Animals: The Ugly Duckling Grows Up," *Trends in Ecology and Evolution* 16, no. 7 (July 1, 2001): 381-90; U. Dieckmann and M. Doebell, "On the Origin of Species by Sympatric Speciation."

## Symbiogenesis

It is no small problem to explain how the first nucleated (eukaryotic) cells arose. If Lynn Margulis is right, we have overcomplicated the problem. Instead of looking for chance mutations and their gradual accumulation via natural selection, we should look at the way in which a host cell can appropriate the genome of a bacterium (prokaryote) and turn the newfound genetic arsenal to its own advantage. Margulis states:

> Any bacterium can pass genes to any other. Restrictions on promiscuous gene flow, and thus to the possibility of speciation, began in the lower Proterozoic Eon, about 2,500 million years ago, when the transformation from bacteria cells to consortia and communities led to integration and boundary-making and finally to the earliest Eukaryotic cells. These cells, as we have explained elsewhere, are themselves symbiotic assemblages. Eukaryotic cell parts such as mitochondria and maybe even cilia and their microtubules originally evolved as free-living organisms.[27]

Symbiogenesis — Margulis's technical term for the creation of new species through the union of previously existing organisms — explains the origin of species in a double way: (1) through the bringing together of organisms in the ancient past to form creatures capable of speciation; and (2) through the subsequent creation of new species by the incorporation of organisms and (eventually) of their genomes.

Margulis provides numerous examples of organisms "appropriating other organisms" in states of symbiosis: a very long list indeed. Equally impressive is the realization of how many organisms contain the genes of other organisms. Some 250 of the more than 30,000 human genes come directly from bacteria.[28] "Every organism that has been studied has some detectable degree of gene duplications: a part of an older gene, a set of a few genes, a chromosome's worth, or — as in yeast — nearly every gene in the cell's little body."[29]

This explains the *dis*continuity of evolution and of the fossil record. Evolution occurs not continuously but dramatically, through the capture of whole new genomes. This process is Lamarckian, but in a way unimagined by McClintock or Steele. It involves the inheritance of acquired genomes.

---

27. Lynn Margulis and Dorion Sagan, *Acquiring Genomes: A Theory of the Origins of Species* (New York: Basic Books, 2002), pp. 65-66.
28. Margulis and Sagan, *Acquiring Genomes*, p. 76.
29. Margulis and Sagan, *Acquiring Genomes*, p. 77.

## Conclusion

Additional theories could be examined, such as various theories of "autopoiesis." Even though these may be understood to fall within the confines of the physics and biology of chaos, it would be interesting to determine how they further diversify the field of chaos theories.

What then follows from all this? At least two points, both already stated. First, the abundance — an increasing abundance — of scientific alternatives to neo-Darwinism strongly suggests that this theory as presently constituted is not immune to change. Usually those who talk about such a change talk in terms of dramatic Kuhnian shifts or grand Popperian falsifications. But there are also significant permutations within a science in which, though the original terms remain (as in thermodynamics and quantum physics), their meanings are significantly transformed. If neo-Darwinism is to survive, it needs to go through change of this sort.

Second, the sheer plurality of scientific alternatives constitutes a problem in itself. The overlap between various standpoints is complex and unresolved. Equally puzzling, it becomes hard, once this plurality is recognized, to accept any one, no matter how well argued, as a full explanation. There is always the nagging suspicion, entirely justified, that something has been left out.

# 7. Evolution, Complexity, and Energy Flow

DORION SAGAN

*Energy is the only life.*

WILLIAM BLAKE

## Importance of Thermodynamics to Darwinism and Process Philosophy

Students of evolution should not ignore thermodynamics, the study of energy systems, as it provides the greatest single source of scientific observation about progress, purpose, and complexity. In contrast to algorithmic studies of chaos, artificial life, complexity, and emergent behaviors, which reconstruct lifelike patterns as computer graphics programs by iterating instructions, the designs studied by thermodynamics occur without human oversight. Although evolution by the neo-Darwinist mode of accumulated mutations must have been crucial during the evolution of bacteria, thermodynamic factors such as increasing energy efficiency may have provided a direction to evolution that was far from random.

Although no cases of evolution by the gradual accumulation of point mutations have been observed, the time periods (or numbers of generations) involved would preclude easy observation. Nonetheless, accumulated mutations themselves are not exceptional but expected on the basis of the randomizing tendencies of the second law of thermodynamics. What is more remarkable is not biological variation, organisms' tendency toward randomizing, but their complexity and stability. Such stability makes sense only from a thermodynamic perspective, as complex energy-processes serve as "stable vehicles of degradation"[1] by which entropy

---

1. J. Wicken, *Evolution, Thermodynamics, and Information: Extending the Darwinian Program* (New York: Oxford University Press, 1987).

can be produced at greater rates, and in a more effective, longer-lasting manner than can be done in the absence of such natural complex systems.[2] Philosophically, one can argue that *computerized simulations, no less than intelligent humanity itself, are not exemplary or foundational of intelligence, but represent a subset of naturally complex thermodynamic systems in an inherently (if cryptically) intelligent universe.* These complex thermodynamic systems naturally cycle matter in complex ways and undergo spontaneous, elaborate path-building regimes "in order" to come to equilibrium. Please pay attention to this "in order." Such activities, which occur in real time, require no genetic machinations. They are completely natural, and their complexity, as seen below, is a by-product of the entropy-production function implicit in the second law.

The deists saw the universe as a clock; we see the universe as a computer. But post-Copernican science shows a different path — not reflection of our cleverest current artifact (or God as a version of ourselves), but a return to study of things themselves. When we do this we find that naturally occurring energy systems, without selection or evolution (neo-Darwinian or otherwise), maintain themselves in designlike forms for considerable periods, even growing to make use of available energy sources.[3] In theory, energy-using life, including human life whose "intelligence" may be reaching a crescendo with the global plunder of nonrenewable fossil fuel resources (collected by "stupid" microbes), is a particular form of naturally complex, naturally purposeful, thermodynamic matter. At the very least it behooves us to be suspicious of any unsubstantiated claims of unique divinity, and to balance claims of unparalleled human consciousness, or relationship to God, or grand place within the scheme of earthly or cosmic development, with the astonishing evidence, accumulating in science for hundreds of years now, showing our remarkable likeness, both in substance and process, to the cosmos around us.

## Purposeful and Protoconscious Behavior in Inanimate Systems

Thermodynamics focuses on energy and matter changes in systems at the size realm of everyday life between the cosmic and the microscopic. The history of thermodynamics is marked by its initial concentration on systems closed to

2. Eric D. Schneider and Dorion Sagan, *Into the Cool* (Chicago: University of Chicago Press, 2002).

3. Dorion Sagan and Eric D. Schneider, "The Pleasures of Change," in *The Forces of Change: A New View of Nature* (Washington, D.C.: National Geographic Society, 2000), pp. 115-26.

both matter and energy exchange, called isolated systems. Such systems inevitably reach equilibrium, the maximization of entropy. The most important observation of classical thermodynamics is that heat flows from a hotter to a cooler body, and cannot be recovered — the essence of the second law of thermodynamics that says that entropy (originally heat divided by temperature, but later given a statistical formulation) inevitably increases in isolated systems. Nonequilibrium thermodynamics, although historically an offshoot of statistical thermodynamics, and academically a specialty of thermodynamics, treats systems of a more general nature — open systems that exchange both energy and matter across their borders. (In thermodynamics a closed system is technically one that is open to energy flux but closed to the exchange of matter.)

Eric D. Schneider has rephrased the second law of thermodynamics in a more general form that not only applies to open, as well as closed and isolated, systems, but also subsumes the elusive entropy quantity, which is difficult to measure in open systems. This broader form of the second law is: "Nature abhors a gradient."[4] A gradient is simply a difference across a distance, such as a temperature, pressure, or electron potential (chemical concentration). Areas (or, more precisely, volumes) of energy flow are marked by gradients. Energy in a steam engine for instance derives from the thermal difference across a space between a hot boiler and a cold radiator; this is a temperature gradient. It is always the quantitative difference, the gradient, which provides energy as the second law is obeyed. The second law describes a drive toward randomization.

Complex systems produce *nondeterministic* chaos (i.e., not "chaos" in the sense of chaos theory, which is generated by computer programs) around them in the wake of order, as time goes forward. The big discovery of nonequilibrium thermodynamics was that in volumes of energy flux organized structure can be spontaneously generated, maintained, and increased. A more recent major discovery is that complex systems, regions where "matter cycles" and "energy flows,"[5] can be more effective than mere random particulate arrangements at meeting the second law's mandate of producing entropy. A complex, cycling system, although internally highly organized, efficiently produces atomic and molecular chaos in its wake. It either does so more quickly or more ably over longer periods of time. The production of such entropic waste is arguably its natural reason for being. Consider a barometric pressure gradient in the atmosphere: a great cycling tornado, certainly not a random system, comes into be-

---

4. Eric D. Schneider and J. J. Kay, "Nature Abhors a Gradient," in *Proceedings of the 33rd Annual Meeting of the International Society for the Systems Sciences* 3, ed. P. W. J. Ledington (Edinburgh, 1989), pp. 19-23.

5. Harold J. Morowitz, *Energy Flow in Biology: Biological Organization as a Problem in Thermal Physics* (Woodbridge, Conn.: Ox Bow Press, 1979), p. 33.

ing to reduce the pressure difference between high and low air masses. Similarly, a "tornado in a bottle," a whirlpool formed when a 1.5 liter soda bottle filled with water is inverted and attached to another such bottle with a small column of punctured plastic, much more effectively drains via organized cycling than the slow drip that occurs when it does not. Such cycling reduces temperature and other gradients, including gravitational or potential energy gradients at the mesocosmic scale. The complex system, the cycling whirlpool of air or water, is *more effective* at dissipating the preexisting gradient, which represents, from a Boltzmannian or statistical mechanic sense, unexpected previously existing order. The swirling form that spontaneously appears has a natural function, or purpose — to reduce the preexisting gradient.

## Purposeful and Conscious Behavior in Living Systems

By hypothesis, the natural purposeful behavior of nonliving systems, to reduce ambient gradients, becoming fixed in living beings, has evolved into consciousness. Conscious beings, modeling themselves and their surroundings, of which they are intrinsically "aware" — to which they respond — are better equipped to seek out the energy gradients upon which they depend. Archaebacteria and bacteria literally swim toward sweetness and light, that is, up (and down) sugar and light gradients. Indeed, there are multiple lines of evidence for life's origin from ancient subsea sulfur gradients, where sulfide, bubbling up with magma from Earth's interior, is oxidized in complex reactions forming pyrite and key enzyme reactions before nucleic acids such as DNA and RNA.[6] Although an "RNA world" and thoughts of genes coming before proteins still dominate within science, the thought experiment of rapidly replicating genes hampering their reproductive growth by the development of bodies is itself enough to seriously question the genes-first view in favor of a metabolic, gradient-based origin of life.

In fact, the genes-first and metabolism-first camps overlap more than is generally recognized.[7] The pressure-gradient-reducing function of the sponta-

6. Freeman Dyson, *Origins of Life* (Cambridge: Cambridge University Press, 1999).

7. Wicken, *Evolution, Thermodynamics, and Information*, p. 104. Organisms are not just genetic machines, but energy transformers sensing in real time. The near-instantaneous reactions, and proactive activities (even bacteria swim toward sweetness and light — that is, along sugar and energy gradients!), of organisms who have stored energy at their continuous disposal must affect the thermodynamic flows in the environments of which they are part in nongenetic ways. Genes themselves likely appeared secondarily, after metabolically sustaining energy systems. It was their ability to further stabilize already relatively continuous centers of energy deg-

neously forming complex systems we call tornadoes, hurricanes, whirlpools, and dust devils (and perhaps even Jupiter's Great Red Spot)[8] applies also to chemical cycling systems. Chemical "clocks," such as the Belousov Zhabotinski reactions, reduce chemical gradients as they produce surprising, suggestively lifelike structures. Although these systems do not replicate, they do maintain and grow more complex. Because nature "selects" at a prebiological level for complex systems that are more effective than simple systems at reducing preexisting gradients, it seems clear that replication would have aided, and eventually helped stabilize, complex systems whose normal function, to reduce ambient gradients, could now be prolonged. As such systems maintained and developed over time, their abilities would continuously construct themselves to favor systems more adept at accessing energy.

Consciousness, if related to making internal models of ways to access various energy paths, would tend to increase. Agglutinating foraminifera (large single-celled protozoa) select and discard different-sized and different-colored glass beads for use in constructing their silicon skeletons. Such protoconscious "choice" forms the physiological infrastructure from which consciousness "proper" (that is, as we know it in ourselves) likely evolved. Physiological organs, sometimes said (particularly the sexual ones!) to have a "mind of their own," anticipate consciousness in that they clearly display functions — functions that are not contested in biological discourse because they have obvious "mechanical" explanations. The function of the heart is to pump blood, the kidneys to purify the blood, the eyes to see. Such functionality is explained (away) as the result of natural selection.

But there is no need to invoke natural selection to explain functionality. The basic purpose of living beings, the one from which the variegated physiological organs arise during the course of bacterial, protozoan (protoctist), and later animal, fungal, and plant evolution, is to degrade gradients. Complexity in nature, which we so narrowly associate with the product of our own minds, requires neither humanlike creation — epitomized by the "mechanical" process of putting things together from constituent parts — nor the operation of natural selection; rather, designlike structures and processes can appear spontane-

---

radation, favored without natural selection by the second law, that allowed genes the chance to arise in the first place. Consider an effective replicator hobbling its reproductive success by growing a great, protein-studded body. Why would such a replicator shoot itself in the foot? Nonmetabolizing replicators would easily replace it. This thought experiment proves that thermodynamic complexity, in the form of relatively stable but not yet fully replicative metabolizing bodies, must have appeared before naked DNA, or the (popularly postulated) RNA world.

8. The shape of spiral galaxies, and of the DNA double helix, is also suggestive of gradient-reducing processes.

ously as ambient gradients break down. *Organisms, the biosphere, whirlpools, and other natural complex systems are functional arrangements of matter that belong to the general class of second law–friendly molecular chaos producers.* By hypothesis human global technical intelligence, with its necessary thermodynamically derived biological focus on energy sources, is in no way an exception to, but part and parcel of, a much older, deeper "intelligence," rife with functionality, which may or may not display "humanlike" consciousness at various levels.

## Gaia

Gaia, the proper noun for the biosphere as a planet surface system that moderates its atmospheric composition, ocean salinity, alkalinity, acidity, global mean temperature, and other factors, has been criticized as teleological. Despite the evidence for global regulation, such global complexity has been by turns cavalierly and cleverly dismissed because it seems to require an unacceptable biotic coordination indistinguishable from consciousness. Moreover, because there is only one Earth, natural selection — the one causative mode acceptable in modern science for the production of truly functional systems, and the accepted neo-Darwinian means of accounting for the appearance of complexity in a cosmos governed by the second law — cannot account for the data. Thus traditional evolutionists have tended to dismiss Gaia as a retro-religious fantasy of a controlling Earth goddess. Damning by association, they have pointed out how Gaia has been embraced by New Age deists and animists.

But the natural functionality of gradient breakdown also suggests why it is not necessary to invoke natural selection to explain the regulation of temperature, atmospheric chemistry composition, marine salinity, and other variables in the biosphere.[9] Just as nucleic acids hone gradient reduction through replication, so natural selection hones physiological regulation. But neither is necessary for the origin of functional behaviors. Purposeful behaviors thus need not be divine, if by divine we mean conscious in a human way. Rather, the maintenance and expansion of complexity in the service of gradient breakdown appear eminently natural. Ironically, although Aristotle's focus on teleology in combination with the appropriation of his philosophy by the church made scientists reject talk of purpose as unscientific, Aristotle himself separated purposeful behavior from a hands-on creator, considering it, rather, to be deeply

---

9. Dorion Sagan and Jessica Whiteside, "Gradient-Reduction Theory: Thermodynamics and the Purpose of Life," in *Scientists Debate Gaia: The Next Century*, ed. Stephen H. Schneider, James R. Miller, Eileen Crist, and Penelope J. Boston (Cambridge: MIT Press, 2004), pp. 173-86.

natural. Aristotle observed that organisms did not develop randomly, but toward a telos, or end. Over two millennia ago Aristotle, recognized as "the first biologist," wrote: "In natural products the sequence is invariable, if there is no impediment. . . . *It is absurd to suppose that purpose is not present because we do not observe the agent deliberating* (emphasis added). Art does not deliberate. If the ship-building art were in the wood, it would produce the same results *by nature* (emphasis in McKeon translation). If, therefore, purpose is present in art, it is present also in nature. . . . It is plain then that nature is a cause, a cause that operates for a purpose."[10]

Aristotle defends teleology as inherent in living beings in 2.1 and 2.8 of *The Physics*. In chapter 2 he likens the purposefulness of organisms to a doctor who happens to treat himself: although made of matter (everybody can be a patient), organisms work on themselves (like a doctor operating on himself). Because for Aristotle organisms seem to be the only examples of the phenomenon they display, it is difficult to find analogies for their peculiar behavior. But Aristotle says his self-treating doctor is "the best example," returning to it in chapter 8 of book 2 of *The Physics*. Because art often imitates nature, and sometimes completes what nature starts, Aristotle is also interested in looking at art to understand natural teleology. In animals, Aristotle argues, front teeth for cutting and molars for grinding do not occur simply by chance; they serve a discrete purpose, chewing food prior to digestion. Similarly, plant roots do not just happen to move down into the ground; they orient themselves that way for the purpose of nourishment (hydration). Aristotle argues that the parts of nonliving things are different from those of living things, since living things are purposefully organized. He even goes so far as to say that, far from being reducible, living beings are prior to those parts. This makes sense thermodynamically when we consider that the ur-purpose, the original goal of the systems we call living, was to gain energy through the reduction of gradients: the downward-seeking of roots and the grinding teeth of animals are offshoots of an energy function — to gain materials to preserve the gradient-reducing, molecular chaos-producing, second law–friendly form. The natural function, or purpose, is to reduce gradients in accord with the second law. The fact that the free will of God intervening in nature is incompatible with the scientific search for eternal laws should not distract us from viewing clearly the thermodynamic roots of our purposeful, energy-based behavior, nor from speculating that consciousness, far from belonging to a completely different realm, is an outgrowth of such natural, complexity-building thermodynamic behavior.[11]

---

10. *The Basic Works of Aristotle*, ed. Richard McKeon (Princeton: Princeton University Press, 2001), p. 251.

11. Sagan and Whiteside, "Gradient-Reduction Theory."

Life's stuff, its carbon and oxygen atoms, was forged in the centers of stars that then exploded in a recycling process older than the sun. But life is not just stuff — it is also a process. An organism is, as the philosopher Immanuel Kant astutely observed, "both cause and effect of itself." Far from linking life with anthropomorphic notions of creationism, still current in religious thought, in his 1790 *Critique of Judgment* Kant describes life in terms that seem to develop Aristotle's description of a purposeful process without any deliberate, humanlike maker. Wicken writes,

> In Kant's conception an organism was a "natural purpose," in which each part and process was jointly cause and effect, end and means, of the operation of the whole. This remains an extremely useful definition. First, it states explicitly the circularity of biological causation and teleonomic organization with which any theory of emergence must come to terms. Second, it can be brought readily into the framework of contemporary science in a way that makes contact with the *ecological* identity of organisms. In this definition, Kant had pithily captured the concept of *informed autocatalysis*. A "natural purpose" is an informed autocatalytic system or AO — a system with an internal organization of kinetic relationships able to maintain itself by pulling environmental resources into its own production. The fact that an organism behaves as its own end and means through participation in the dissipative flow of nature suggests a deep connection between self-organization and the Second Law.[12]

As Kant points out, organisms have an "inner natural perfection"; an organism is a natural end that, unlike a watch or any machine, produces itself. It has not "only a motive power" but also a "self-propagating formative power." Organized beings are thus "not thinkable and explicable in accordance with any analogy to any . . . natural capacity that is known to us; indeed, since we ourselves belong to nature in the widest sense, it is not thinkable and explicable even through an exact analogy with human art. . . . Organized beings are thus the only ones in nature which . . . must . . . be thought of as possible only as its ends, and which thus first provide objective reality for the concept of an end that is not a practical end but an end of nature, and thereby provide natural science with the basis for a teleology."[13]

Yes, we and all life are ends of nature or, more properly, means by which nature reaches its ends, of molecular and atomic chaos as mandated by the second law. While even thoughtful modern commentators on evolutionary theory,

12. Wicken, *Evolution, Thermodynamics, and Information*, p. 31.
13. Immanuel Kant, *Critique of the Teleological Power of Judgment*, §65.

such as Michael Ruse,[14] lump William Paley (who famously compared living beings to a watch designed by a Designer) with Kant, in fact Kant pointed out that a watch differs from an organism because an organism's parts are not only deeply interconnected but actually produce each other. Thus they cannot have had a human-type designer. Such interconnected, self-productive systems are natural, as Kant suggests, and they have a purpose that is not an anthropomorphic one, as both Kant and Aristotle suggest.

In sum, one may suggest that the naturally purposeful processes inherent in a cosmos governed by the second law set the stage both for the origin of life as a thermodynamic process and for humankind as a peculiar outgrowth of that process. If this suggestion is accepted — that the simple functional behavior of nonliving systems has led to the more complex functional behavior of living ones — then a corollary would be that the roots of simple thermodynamic behavior can still be glimpsed within the heights of seemingly greatly different human consciousness. In fact, despite the lofty connotations of consciousness, our mental processes are most often concerned with money, sex, relationships, and food — subsidiaries of reproduction and self-maintenance — means of continuing gradient breakdown.

## The Scientific Roots of the Antipurpose Taboo and a Characterization of "God"

Descartes made the world safe for scientific investigation by arguing that most of it was devoid of life and consciousness, and could be dismantled without causing pain. He divided the world, in a way congenial to religious authorities, between the realm of mechanically acting matter, *res extensa,* and the realm of mind, *res cogitans.* The realm of spirit and free will, thought to be unique in humans, he connected to the body through the pineal gland, a light-sensitive organ then known only from the brains of humans. He described the world of nature, including the human body, as subject to mechanical laws imposed by God and discoverable by scientific inquiry.

Descartes, like Newton and most of the scientists of that period, thought God was not bound by the laws he imposed. They also supposed that the world of mind or spirit functioned on entirely different principles from the world of matter. Spinoza followed and one-upped Descartes by unifying the lawful, timeless aspects of spirit and matter. Further, Spinoza said the realm of cause

14. Michael Ruse, *Does Evolution Have a Purpose?* (Cambridge: Harvard University Press, 2003).

and effect, of nature free of the miracles of divine intervention, could not be limited, as Descartes had done, to the realm of matter, the *res extensa*. Rather, the human mind, despite its feeling free, was deluded and was also under the control of eternal, scientifically specifiable laws. But in following and ratcheting up Cartesian materialism, mechanism, and determinism — by philosophically making science, as it were, more scientific by eliminating the realm of free will even from God — Spinoza arguably dealt the notion of purpose a final death blow. In a letter explaining his views to two correspondents, Spinoza writes, "So the infant believes that he freely wants the milk; the angry boy that he wants vengeance; and the timid, flight. Again, the drunk believes it is from a free decision of the mind that he says those things which afterward, when sober, he wishes he had not said. Similarly, the madman, the chatterbox, and a great many people of this kind believe that they act from a free decision of the mind, and not that they are carried away by impulse. Because this prejudice is innate in all men, they are not easily freed from it."[15]

We feel free because we don't know the causes determining our behavior. This hyper-Cartesianism is important, because the God of Spinoza is the God of Einstein. It is a God who does not, as Einstein wrote to Max Born, "play dice." It is a God who is not made in man's image. In short, their God is indistinguishable from nature. No wonder that Nietzsche, who aimed barbs at virtually all his philosophic predecessors save Spinoza,[16] said we killed God without realizing it. God as a transcendent Will, imposing law on the world and then intervening in the course of events, is dead. God as a lawful eternal being of which we are part, is still consonant with science.

Life belongs to a class of open thermodynamic systems that maintain and, where applicable, increase their complexity in regions of energy flux. Aside from thermodynamics, the emphasis on energy, as opposed to genetic determinism, has received alternate formulations, such as the "metabolic,"[17] opposed to genetic theories of the origins of life. Although evolution and thermodynamics are sciences of connection, linking us to other organisms and to other energy systems, there is a lingering tendency to consider ourselves special. This itself is perhaps thermodynamically based because of the necessity of successful energy systems to focus energy streams upon themselves, with the consequent literal self-centeredness that such focus entails. The Protagorean "man is the measure of all things," and is thus opposed to the Copernican ten-

15. *A Spinoza Reader: The Ethics and Other Works by Benedict de Spinoza*, ed. and trans. Edwin Curley (Princeton: Princeton University Press, 1994), pp. 267-68.

16. Steven Shavel, personal communication, July 2004.

17. Iris Fry, *The Emergence of Life* (Piscataway, N.J.: Rutgers University Press, 2000).

dency to demote us, to drag us down to the level of ordinary cosmic stuff and process.

Evolution belongs to the non-Protagorean category. Sociobiology and evolutionary psychology have attempted to insist on the absolute naturalness, based on genetics, of the human enterprise. Human beings, however, due to the cortical parts of the brain governing symbolic behavior, have a materially accelerating culture. Neocortex-based symbol manipulation explains the huge difference between 120,000-year-old hunter-gatherers and global technological humanity.[18]

Evolution, thermodynamics, and the success of Copernican-style scientific revolutions in general link human processes to those of all life, and living processes in general to those of the universe. The processes in ourselves may not be essentially alien from those outside us. However, the processes that link our brains and bodies to those of the cosmos do not appear so much genetic as thermodynamic (energetic, metabolic, etc.). Our real-time responses to the world, our physiological reactions, such as an increase in one's heartbeat when one reads or hears one's name, are too quick to be genetically mediated. Such processes, whether or not they involve conscious awareness, clearly occur in simpler organisms, such as bacteria swimming toward the light or magnetic north; and these real-time responses entail real-time energy flow in materially cycling, highly sensitive systems. Thus the thermodynamic (the metabolic or energetic) offers an alternative scientific domain for explanations of biological complexity.[19]

Finally and parenthetically, since there is little time to explore such connections here, one might consider the theories of Samuel Butler, enumerated in works such as *Evolution, Old and New, Luck or Cunning,* and the section of *Erewhon* entitled "Darwin among the Machines." Butler, originally enchanted by Charles Darwin's theories, became disillusioned with the lack of consciousness ascribed to naturally selected organisms. Making an ironic contrast, he presented machines as also evolving by natural selection, and as doing so more successfully than organisms. He was motivated in part by the desire not to excise the phenomenologically glaringly obvious data of awareness and purposeful behavior, which he noted had been included in pre-Darwinian descriptions of evolution, from an account of the evolutionary process. I suggest that real-time thermodynamic flow patterns may provide the nongenetic mechanism, associated with organisms' (often minor) influence upon their environment,

18. John Skoyles and Dorion Sagan, *Up from Dragons: The Evolution of Human Intelligence* (New York: McGraw-Hill, 2002).
19. Sagan and Schneider, "The Pleasures of Change."

which Butler intuited as missing from the account of evolution given by Darwin. Perhaps due to the social need to link a science of life with the already-accepted Cartesian mechanical paradigm, Darwin, as Butler quipped, "took the life out of biology."[20]

Whether we believe in free will, whether we entertain a paradoxical compatibility of free will and scientific determinism, whether we explain or explain away consciousness without which we are rendered as curiously deluded zombies or automatons, the evidence for direction over evolutionary time is unequivocal. The direction of organisms in their growth, evolution, and conscious, purposeful behavior cannot be denied. Although not all seemingly progressive trends continue (e.g., increase of brain-to-body-mass ratios has decreased in some lineages), the naive intuition that evolution has a direction (which is not the same as saying that it is directed in an anthropomorphic or divinity-based way) has proven correct. Over time life has increased its real extent, its taxa, its metabolic modes and levels of energetic efficiency, and its ability to tap into, store, and deploy new energy sources. (The problem and promise of the human species can be traced to its prowess in this last area.) These trends can be objectively, not just subjectively, enumerated. For example, the number of different chemical elements involved in the biospheric circulation at Earth's surface has increased over the last three billion years. Now nuclear elements (e.g., neptunium, plutonium, bohrium, dubnium, mendelevium, californium, americanium, einsteinium, etc.) with fleeting isotopes, never before seen on Earth, have appeared.

The tendency of complex thermodynamic systems is to grow to a point of maximum continuous entropy production, to maintain their complexity as they produce atomic and molecular (not algorithmic) chaos. Ecosystems undergo rapid growth via pioneer species at first, and then become more diverse and slower-growing in their so-called climax phase. Satellite and airplane measurements show the most complex rainforest ecosystems to be the most effective at reducing the solar gradient, the thermal difference between Sun and Earth (or space).[21] Humanity has turned liquids beneath the crust into gases in the atmosphere, releasing and deploying energy in powerful new ways. The biosphere has not reached the equivalent of a steady-state climax ecosystem. Whether humans will be involved in such a proximal end state remains to be seen.

In summary, the qualities we recognize, honor, and fear as living and human seem not to be unique but manifestations of an energetic cosmos.

20. *Shrewsbury Edition of the Works of Samuel Butler,* ed. Henry Festing Jones and A. T. Bartholomew (New York: Dutton, 1923-26).
21. Sagan and Schneider, "The Pleasures of Change."

# 8. Hydrogen: Humanity's Maker and Breaker

REG MORRISON

The primary molecular ingredients of earthly life are carbon, hydrogen, nitrogen, oxygen, phosphorus, and sulphur (CHNOPS). All six play vital and particular roles in the structure and behavior of organisms, but I believe that the traditional emphasis on carbon obscures a more accurate, cosmic view of the biota, the biosphere, and our place within it. This skewed perspective effectively conceals the magnitude and immediacy of the threats we face on this hydrogen-regulated planet.

As a crucial component of all living organisms, carbon is essential, but it is primarily a structural element and a heavy haulage vehicle that plays no executive role in life's imperatives: growth, reproduction, and self-maintenance. Carbon is the brick and mortar that sustains life's mansions, but adds no "vital spark" that switches on and off the light inside those mansions. Hydrogen, not carbon, executes that genetic order.

The Russian geochemist Vladimir Vernadsky proposed life as a geological force — a dynamic extension of the earth's crust and an inevitable by-product of the energy gradient that forms the interface between the body of the planet and the matrix of space.[1] Since hydrogen is the basic energy unit of the cosmos, this proposition supports the contention that life, too, is hydrogen-based.

Our species' recent population explosion and its massive impact on the planet's biosphere were both fueled by fossil hydrocarbons, and the environmental and energy crises that we now face will be orchestrated by the vast quantity of hydrocarbons that we have already transferred from the crust to the atmosphere. Oil-dependent and vulnerable to methane-triggered climate change, we are staring down the barrel of hydrogen's loaded gun.

1. Vladimir Ivanovitch Vernadsky, *The Biosphere* (New York: Copernicus Springer-Verlag, 1998); originally published 1926.

## Hydrogen's Crucial Roles

The primacy of the hydrogen atom is due to its cosmic abundance and its unique structure. Approximately 90 percent of the atoms in the measurable universe are hydrogen — a weakly charged proton attended by a solitary, promiscuous electron. This structure makes it impetuously reactive and gives it a major role in all chemistry, especially organic chemistry.

The tiny relic of big bang energy in hydrogen's solitary proton enables it to forge bonds that are only 5 percent as strong as the weakest chemical alliance between other elements. It is the weakness of this hydrogen bond that enables the four nucleotide bases of DNA to build, disengage, and rebuild their partnerships repeatedly during reproduction and protein manufacture. If the hydrogen bond were any stronger, it would prevent DNA from unzipping to replicate and administer protein sequences; any weaker, and DNA's double helix would disintegrate. Without hydrogen's peculiar bonds the helix could not unzip, its sequence could not be "read" by RNA, proteins could not be synthesized, and replication could not occur. Without hydrogen chemistry, life could not exist.

Hydrogen also shapes the biota via an epigenetic (external to the genetic code) switching mechanism. Whether genes are expressed or silenced largely depends on a pattern of hydrogen-loaded carbon tags ($CH_3$) that may become attached to the nucleotide base cytosine (also adenine in some bacteria). Contrary to Darwinian theory, certain environmental factors have been shown to alter the pattern of these epigenetic attachments, thereby altering the pattern of protein production within the organism. These epigenetic tags, known as methyl groups, turn genes on or off by reshaping the three-dimensional structure of the genetic material at the attachment points. Here, too, carbon is the vehicle for hydrogen and appears to play no executive role.

The altered pattern of methylation is particularly significant where it occurs within the X or Y chromosomes since the reshaping of the chromosome appears to be heritable and may persist for several generations. Certain environmental pollutants, especially those whose breakdown products resemble the sex hormones estrogen, progesterone, and testosterone, have been shown to interfere with the normal pattern of methylation, and thereby with the complex process of gender determination and sexual behavior. (The social significance of such interference in the human genome is discussed later in this text.)

Hydrogen's third major role lies in the establishment of biological identity. Without hydrogen no semi-waterproof membranes could form and no organisms could exist.

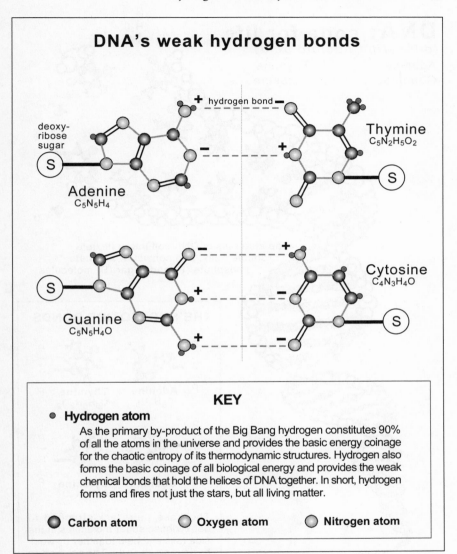

Figure 1. DNA's weak hydrogen bonds

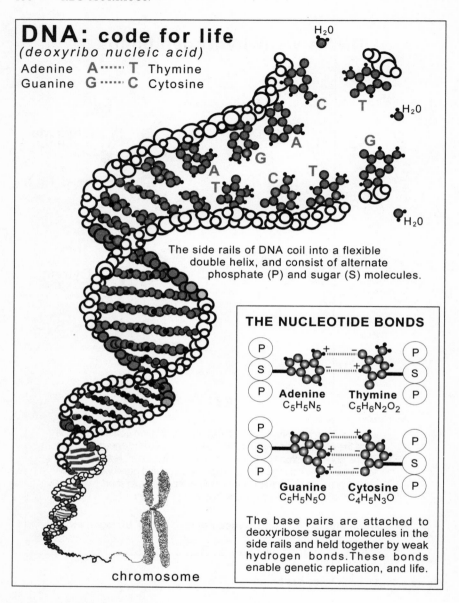

# DNA: code for life
*(deoxyribo nucleic acid)*

Adenine   A ······ T  Thymine
Guanine   G ······ C  Cytosine

The side rails of DNA coil into a flexible
double helix, and consist of alternate
phosphate (P) and sugar (S) molecules.

## THE NUCLEOTIDE BONDS

**Adenine**
$C_5H_5N_5$

**Thymine**
$C_5H_6N_2O_2$

**Guanine**
$C_5H_5N_5O$

**Cytosine**
$C_4H_5N_3O$

The base pairs are attached to
deoxyribose sugar molecules in the
side rails and held together by weak
hydrogen bonds. These bonds
enable genetic replication, and life.

chromosome

**Figure 2. DNA: Code for life**

Genes cannot survive and replicate outside membrane-bounded sacs. These manufacture themselves from sheets of molecules that are water compatible (hydrophilic) on one side and water repellent (hydrophobic) on the other. Such molecular sheets are known as lipids. The hydrophobic side consists of a forest of densely packed carbon chains loaded with hydrogen atoms. (Carbon alone is not hydrophobic.) In a watery environment this hydrophobic side survives only if it floats with its hydrophobic side facing upward. Oil is a perfect illustration.

When floating sheets of lipid molecules become fragmented by water turbulence or the impact of rain or hail, they tend to fold their hydrophobic faces together to form bilipid membranes (fig. 3). Submerged during severe turbulence, such bilipid membranes resolve into a multitude of microspheres that are impermeable and very strong — their internal and external lipids glued together by their hydrocarbon filling. If the membrane spheres are small enough, they may remain suspended within the watery medium indefinitely, forming an emulsion, like milk. Four billion years ago membrane-bounded microspheres enabled the existence of RNA, DNA, genetic replication, the manufacture of protein, and the continuation of growth.

Hydrogen's fourth executive role is empowerment of the world's smallest engine, the rotary motor that drives the flagella of swimming bacteria. Its fuel is subatomic protons mined from hydrogen nuclei that have been stripped of electrons. It takes up to 1,000 protons to drive the rotor through a single revolution, yet this molecular engine may achieve speeds between 300 and 400 revolutions per second.[2] If scaled up, the flagellar motor can produce a torque that is roughly equivalent to an eight horsepower electric engine. Its fuel is generated by an electron-stripping process that occurs within the bilipid cell membrane and ejects a torrent of positively charged hydrogen protons outside the cell membrane. Too large to return unaided through the bilipid membrane, the protons pass easily through the "stator" array that surrounds the rotor. When a significant charge gradient builds up between the proton-rich positive exterior and the hydrogen-depleted negative interior, the rush of protons reentering through the stator spins the rotor and its flagella (fig. 5).[3]

2. M. Meister, G. Lowe, and H. C. Berg, "The Proton Flux through the Bacterial Flagella Motor," *Cell* 49, no. 5 (1987): 643-50; also H. C. Berg, "The Rotary Motor of Bacterial Flagella," *Annual Review of Biochemistry* 72 (2003): 19-54.

3. Keiichi Namba, "How Proton Flow Drives Molecular Motors," *Foresight* Update, 32 (1998): 5. Also David Blair, 2005, at http://www.bioscience.utah.edu/bc/bcFaculty/blair/blair.html. Rotor speeds of almost 1,700 revolutions per second have been recorded in some specialized bacteria, but their motors are driven by sodium ions rather than hydrogen protons. They represent an exception to the hydrogen rule.

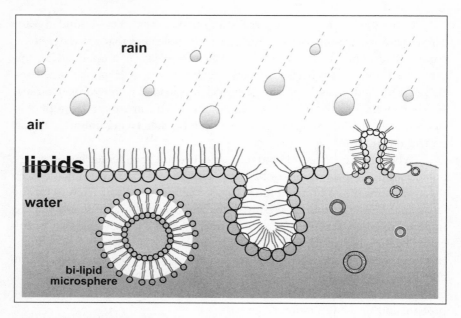

**Figure 3. Lipid sheet reflexes to become bilipid**

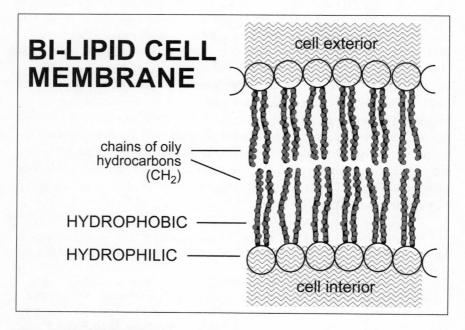

**Figure 4. Bilipid membrane immersed in water**

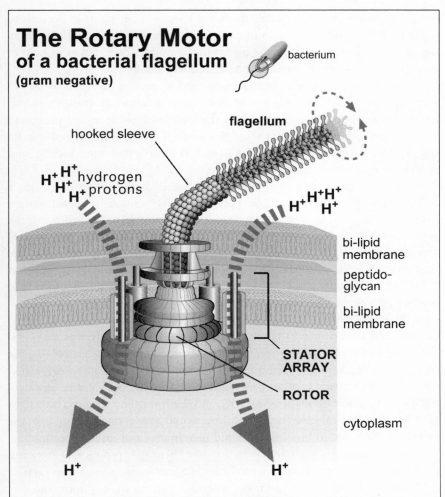

# The Rotary Motor
## of a bacterial flagellum
### (gram negative)

bacterium

flagellum

hooked sleeve

$H^+ H^+$ hydrogen
$H^+ H^+$ protons
$H^+$

$H^+ H^+ H^+$
$H^+$

bi-lipid
membrane

peptido-
glycan

bi-lipid
membrane

**STATOR
ARRAY**

**ROTOR**

cytoplasm

$H^+$           $H^+$

The rotor spins in either direction according to chemical stimuli.
Speeds of up to 400 revolutions per second have been recorded.

*based on Keiichi Namba, Osaka, and David Blair, Utah (pers.comm.)
and on microscopy by David DeRosier et al, Brandeis.*

**Figure 5. The rotary motor of a bacterial flagellum**

The hydrogen-powered flagella motor enables many kinds of bacteria to move swiftly toward nutrients and away from potential threats. This mobility has enabled them to colonize the planet to the point where they now help to modify the earth's crust, its atmosphere, and its climate.

Another aspect to the flagella motor and its proton fuel reaches far beyond the microscopic world. By virtue of eubacterial relicts (mitochondria) embedded in our cells, we use precisely the same proton-harvesting process to manufacture our body's primary cellular fuel, ATP (adenosine triphosphate) (fig. 6). Like bacteria, our cells use ATP to fuel growth and reproduction, and this enables us to breathe, move, feel, and think.

ATP consists of a genetic nucleotide, usually based on adenine, plus a two-part phosphate tail. Its usable energy lies in its "semitrailer" construction. Although the phosphate modules are not directly coupled by hydrogen, the same electron-stripping process that supplies hydrogen protons to flagella motors also supplies protons to trigger the coupling of the phosphate tail to the adenosine "tractor." The coupling is achieved via an enzyme, ATP synthase. When the cell requires a burst of energy, it can be obtained by detaching each of the two phosphate modules.

The twin processes of stripping electrons and protons from atomic hydrogen appear to be common to all organisms, but most significantly, they are essential features of energy production in methane-producing archaebacteria. As the probable primogenitors of earthly life, such methanogens would have originated when the young planet's atmosphere was largely composed of volcanic gases, especially water and carbon dioxide ($CO_2$), and the young Sun shed too little light to support photosynthesis. These organisms would have extracted from $CO_2$ the carbon they needed to build their bilipid membranes and internal scaffolding, but they could have done it only with the aid of hydrogen proton fuel extracted either from water, from hydrogen sulphide ($H_2S$), or from hydrogen gas (2H).

Even today, clustered about the volcanic vents on the sea floor, and distributed throughout the planet's crustal material to a depth of almost four kilometers, descendants of those primal organisms continue to thrive without light. They too reduce $CO_2$ to cell material, extracting the necessary energy from hydrogen bound to carbon in the form of methane ($CH_4$) or bound to sulphur in the form of hydrogen sulphide ($H_2S$).

## Photosynthesis

All hydrogen enters Earth's biota via autotrophy (bacterial self-manufacture from inorganic elements), but it is the fast, efficient, photosynthetic version of

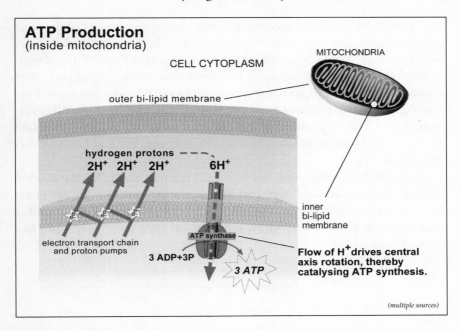

**Figure 6. ATP production in mitochondria**

this process, mediated by two forms of chlorophyll, that now underpins almost all surface life. It enables cyanobacteria and their chloroplast descendants (embedded in green algae and green leaves) to extract hydrogen from water molecules and dump the oxygen as waste. This process, which first appeared more than three billion years ago, was destined to change the course of evolution.

As photosynthetic bacteria began to thrive in Earth's warm primordial seas, their oxygen waste reacted with the seas' vast store of soluble iron, turning it into insoluble rust. The rust settled to the seabed and the oxygen began to leak into the atmosphere. This is the oxygen that we harvest with each breath that we draw, the highly reactive molecule that ultimately enables us to move, see, feel, and think. Originally, however, oxygenation of the biosphere represented a catastrophic pollution event and the greatest threat that life had ever faced. The source of that crisis was life's intrinsic hunger for hydrogen, and that primordial link between hydrogen efficiency and reproductive success remains unequivocal and undiminished today. It is as rigid as the link between reproductive success and environmental degradation. Such is the entropic nature of our hydrogen-based cosmos.

Finally, life's enabling medium is water, another by-product of the weak hydrogen bond. The peculiarly flexible attraction between molecules allows water to remain "watery" over a huge temperature range (4°–100° C), making it an invaluable medium of transport for life's nutrients and ingredients. Most crucially, the weak hydrogen bond causes water to lose density and expand between 0°–4° C. This property makes ice float. If water behaved like other solvents and its density increased as it froze, ice would sink and the seas would freeze from the bottom upward. In such circumstances life may not have survived at all.

To summarize: hydrogen not only fires the stars and lights the dustiest corners of the cosmos, it also performs a similar function in the moist microcosmos of Earth's biota. The spark of life and the "vital force" that has been sought by philosophers, sages, and scientists since the time of Plato and Aristotle is hydrogen.

---

Editor's note: The foregoing text is an extract from a larger essay on the future of our species. It goes on to propose that our consumptive fecundity has so perturbed Earth's finely balanced energy gradient that we must expect to be automatically culled by the standard evolutionary mechanisms that maintain this gradient. Displaying a population graph typical of all plague species, we appear to have triggered the same kind of hydrogenous hormonal backlash that brings most mammal plagues to a halt, namely, the General Adaptive Syndrome (Hans Selye, 1936).

Significantly, Morrison argues, the coup de grace will also be delivered by hydrogen. When the imminent decline in hydrocarbon fuel production combines with the inevitable degassing of abyssal methane, it will provide evolution with a lethal pincer movement of dearth and surfeit that will surgically remove the bulk of our troublesome species.

Earth's methane-charged "Greenhouse" will abruptly overheat, and our hydrogen-starved technoculture will collapse in confused disorder.

Immobilized, meanwhile, by a resurgence of conflicting spirituality and religious fundamentalism, humanity will be unable to mount a collaborative defense, and judging by historical examples such as Easter Island, civilization will then implode in an orgy of mystical discord and vengeful aggression.

# 9. Gaia and Machines

## Lynn Margulis

## Gaia

The Gaia hypothesis, invented by James E. Lovelock over thirty years ago, explains the tendency of the Earth's lower atmosphere, including the oceans, to regulate, within rather narrow limits as well as for millions of years, its concentration of oxygen and of other atmospheric gases, its temperature, and its alkalinity. The self-maintaining properties of cells, organisms, communities, and ecosystems, and the evolution, including death and extinction, of these entities through time, are intrinsic to the Gaia regulation system. Gaian modulation of the environment that applies to the atmosphere and surface sediments of planet Earth is consistent with the legacy of Charles Darwin or Darwinism. This mode of thought is distinguishable from neo-Darwinism. The over 30 million extant species are components of the huge Gaian regulation. But so are their extrasomatic structures and artifacts that include our machines. Although not by themselves alive, like viruses, snail shells, tree bark, termite mounds, beehives, and other animal-built structures,[1] our machines reproduce. Even though they are not wet, membrane-bounded cellular systems, machines evolve.

Knowledge of the Gaia hypothesis and its implications aids in an under-

---

The author acknowledges the indispensable aid of Celeste Asikainen, Carmen Chica, Professor Ricardo Guerrero, Reg Morrison, Bruce Scofield, Mercé Piqueras, and especially Dorion Sagan in the preparation of this chapter. The author is grateful to the Graduate School of the University of Massachusetts-Amherst, the Alexander von Humboldt Stiftung Prize, Abraham Gome, the Tauber Fund, and the Rockefeller Foundation Study and Conference Center for their support of this work.

1. See J. Scott Turner, *The Extended Organism: The Physiology of Animal-Built Structures* (Cambridge: Harvard University Press, 2000) and *The Tinkerer's Accomplice: How Design Emerges from Life Itself* (Cambridge: Harvard University Press, 2006).

standing of our living planet. The Gaia idea transcends traditional biology: to understand it requires knowledge from geology, thermodynamics, chemistry, microbiology, atmospheric science, and other specialties. The Gaia concept, whose development requires scientific research at many levels, can shed great light on the evolutionary process. In this essay I try to put "evolution of life," the changes populations of living beings have undergone through time, in a Gaian context. I try to show why the narrow, neo-Darwinist views should be replaced with far more informed, sensitive, and knowledgeable views of life and its environment.

This planetary worldview was promulgated by Lovelock in his first book, *Gaia: A New Look at Life on Earth*.[2] He explained the history of the new global thought style in his autobiography, *Homage to Gaia*.[3] Lovelock, an independent atmospheric chemist and biological theorist, was aided by chemical oceanographer Michael Whitfield and eclectic physical scientist Andrew Watson, both of the Marine Biological Association, Plymouth, England, and by Stephan Harding of Schumacher College, Devon. The original Gaia hypothesis has been refined, restated, and extended over the years. The definition I prefer is:

> The composition of the reactive gases, their oxidation state, the ocean's acidity/alkalinity and the temperature of the lower atmosphere, i.e., troposphere, of the planet Earth are dynamically regulated by the growth, metabolism, ecological and other interactions of living organisms. Differentially reproducing cells and organisms made of cells dwell as communities in ecosystems, their activities modulate the composition, temperature, and other properties of the atmosphere, surface sediments and waters of the Earth.

An exciting multifaceted debate about the Gaian science exposition is now available.[4] Two recent books critically examine Gaian concepts. One factors Gaia into a broader planetary and geological view of the history of the Earth.[5] The second is more ecological and contemporary in its scientific outlook.[6] Both are immensely informative. Lowman critically and imaginatively reviews the geological history of the Earth as revealed by the application of

---

2. James E. Lovelock, *Gaia: A New Look at Life on Earth* (London: Oxford University Press, 1979).

3. James E. Lovelock, *Homage to Gaia: The Life of an Independent Scientist* (New York: Oxford University Press, 2001).

4. Stephen H. Schneider, James R. Miller, Eileen Crist, and Penelope J. Boston, eds., *Scientists Debate Gaia: The Next Century* (Cambridge: MIT Press, 2004).

5. Paul Lowman, *Exploring Space, Exploring Earth* (New York: Cambridge University Press, 2002).

6. Vaclav Smil, *The Earth's Biosphere* (Cambridge: MIT Press, 2002).

space technologies, whereas the current state of the biota (flora, fauna, and microbiota) and the extent of the biosphere are discussed by Smil. And now Harding examines scientific Gaia in a personal way that is cognizant of ancient intuitive responses of many peoples to the natural world.[7]

A whole Gaian style of thought that supersedes narrow neo-Darwinism emerges. Perception of the environment through time is seen as a participatory phenomenon. The Gaian view, ironically, is more consistent with the muddled, humble, and inquisitive original nineteenth-century Darwinism than with the current form of neo-Darwinism.

I suspect and hope that the number of scientists and others who participate in the Gaian "whole Earth approach" is increasing. The very existence of the new oratorio by Nathan Currier,[8] performed by 170 musicians, supports my hope. In the Gaian view we people are linked inextricably, and in subordinate fashion, to the rest of the biota. Science provides absolutely no evidence that the world was made for man. For Gaia, humans are easily dispensable. *Homo sapiens* is a latecomer on the evolutionary stage, about 2 million years ago. Gaia thrived for 3,500 million years prior to humans. Indeed, humans are only one small part of the web of life of this planet, a tangled net comprised of plant, microbial, and other animal life-forms.

The modern Gaian thought style is not really unique or new — in fact, it represents a partial return to an older, naturalistic way of seeing the world. Modern Gaian science represents an enlightened return to science as a tiny, experimental part of nature's greater whole. Gaian philosophy returns us to healthier ways of relating to our planetary home without denial of the logic and efficacy of modern scientific thought.

Unfortunately, Judeo-Christian beliefs are still widely entrenched among the diverse, energetic peoples of western Europe and northern North America. The monotheistic concept that identifies the paternal family control with nationhood is an inculcating "meme" that resonates with modern written history. Those partaking of this meme or its variations, for example, Third Reich Nazism, apparently felt no responsibility for actions that were vindicated by their God, a fatherlike power. This corporate or superorganism lack of accountability occurred despite the fact that, at certain junctures in history, for example, during the Reformation, the same omnipotent father-god was invoked by both warring sides.

---

7. Stephan Harding, *Animate Earth: Science, Intuition, and Gaia* (Dartington, U.K.: Green Books; White River Junction, Vt.: Chelsea Green, 2006).

8. Nathan Currier, *Gaian Variations,* an oratorio presented on Earth Day in April 2004 at Avery Fisher Hall, Rockefeller Center, New York.

Even cosmopolitan thinkers, evidence-seeking scientists, and scholars who criticize excessive tribal loyalty do not necessarily repudiate, or even recognize, their anthropocentrism. Most educated people admit there is overwhelming evidence that we belong to the mammalian order of primates, but they still believe that we humans are the "highest" species of animals. Even as the Bible maintains Jews to be the "chosen people," humans take it to be self-evident that "people are superior to all other life-forms." But these and other traditional ideas of Western civilization contrast, indeed conflict, with Gaian perception.

## Thought Styles

Prevailing thought styles have the advantage of momentum. The weight of Western history and its success attach to social groups that fervently promulgate the idea that man dominates nature. The Gaian thought style, however, extends "horizontally" to other organisms and "vertically" beyond mere human history to natural history writ large. Human beings and technology in the broad Gaian view are intrinsic, rather than superior, to activities of the biosphere. The biosphere, with a vertical dimension of about twenty kilometers (from twelve kilometers below in the ocean abyss to some eight kilometers at the tops of the mountains), is supported by uncountable numbers of life-forms that indulge simultaneously in great growth rates and in equally immense death rates.

This teeming mass of interacting life unconditionally depends on food, i.e., on the production of organic chemicals by photosynthetic and chemosynthetic processes. The energy for metabolism derives from the sun or, in the dark, chemical oxidation of hydrogen, methane, or hydrogen sulfide, and it is distributed through the intricacies of food sharing. What we humans reject as "spoiled food" is healthy growth for the dense populations of yeast, bacilli, and other microbes that colonize our bread and meat. Though waste to us, the dung of cattle is both food and shelter to the dancing *Pilobolus* mold and to dung beetle larvae. Uneaten cheesy crusts stuffed down a kitchen sink garbage disposal are not "wasted"; they become the source of life for vast populations of ciliates, mastigotes, germinating bacterial and fungal spores, and so on.

The consortial quality of the individual preempts the notion of independence. What appears to us to be a single wood-eating termite insect is in fact a multitude of organisms. A single termite is comprised of millions of microbes, protists that ingest wood chips and bacteria that produce acetate, for example. Very few kinds of these actually digest the tough cellulose fibers of wood. The insect ingests the wood of the consortium but is totally incapable of digesting it. Gaia is the same sort of consortial entity as a single wood-ingesting termite, but of course, she is far larger and far more complex. Consortia, communities, associations, syntrophies, partnerships, symbioses, and competitions — many bizarre and specific interactions between different organisms — extend to the global scale. Living and nonliving matter, self and environment, are inextricably interconnected.

A Gaian view increases public awareness of human dependence upon more-than-human life and is extremely valuable in the battle against the prevalent ideology of selfishness: "Nature is pristine and should be preserved." "Nature is simply a huge resource for man to plunder." These admonitions and ideologies are ignorant. The truth is that we are deeply connected to myriad other organisms, and simply by living we cannot help altering them and their environment. We are barely conscious of our actions. Removal from Gaia is not independence; it is death.

The news media, indeed human psychology in general, is oriented toward crisis. Responses of the press and the reading public to many Gaian processes have been arbitrary. The distorted biases of "hot topics" have included carbon dioxide increase, water pollution, acid rain, genetically modified food, and ozone depletion. By failing to respond until crisis is upon us, we run risks of violently positive feedback processes that tend toward cultural disintegration as Lovelock has admonished.[9] Money and scientific expertise are arbitrarily thrown at perceived problems in isolated attempts to buy easy solutions. Gaia herself has never been seen by any granting agency or philanthropic organization as an entity worthy of scientific study. Research on biospheric self-regulatory mechanisms has been neglected or, at best, woefully underfunded. Gaia refuses to fit neatly into any single academic field; she forms no circumscribed budget category as do, for example, atmospheric science, biology, environmental chemistry, geology, and wildlife management. Yet life, as a planetary-level phenomenon, and the effect of life as a geological force are nonetheless vital topics that impinge on all of Earth's inhabitants.

## Scientists' Resistance

Most scientists seem still unaware of the Gaian point of view. Some familiar with professional literature have criticized it. W. Ford Doolitle of Dalhousie University in Halifax, for example, finding no scientific basis for a "Gaian mechanism," denies the existence of the Gaian regulatory phenomenon. Rich-

9. James E. Lovelock, *The Revenge of Gaia* (London: Penguin Books, 2006; New York: Basic Books, 2006).

ard Dawkins of Oxford University denies Gaia on the basis of lack of competition for survival of Earth relative to the flanking planets of Mars and Venus; he also finds no "mechanism," and he denies that life regulates environments. A third critic, Heinrich D. Holland of Harvard University, finds the Gaia hypothesis "charming but unnecessary." He invokes a variation of the anthropic principle; namely, had the biosphere not evolved for millions of years, we would not be around to marvel at its putative regulation mechanism. Advocating the position that only physical and chemical processes regulate temperature, acidity/alkalinity, and chemical composition of reactive gases of the lower atmosphere, Holland, as a geochemist, denies environmental homeorrhesis by the biota.

Against such a backdrop, students of nature inclined to detailed investigation of the physiology of the biosphere are impeded. We do not simply advocate a belief in the unproven assertion that "Gaia is the modulated biosphere"; rather we call for open investigation into this claim. We value the new, wider viewpoint and suggest replacement of outmoded, overly reductionist, thought styles. No perception is possible without some assumption and/or belief system, and all science results from perception. The Gaia hypothesis recognizes the perceptive capacity of all live beings.

## People and Biosphere

We humans are embedded in the biosphere, as are all life-forms. The biosphere, its resident biota, and their metabolic products and energetic transformations flow through and around us. We have arisen from within this biosphere that has enjoyed continuity through at least 3 thousand million years. As technologically dependent on nonhuman life-forms, we humans have as much independence from the rest of the biosphere as a cancer virus has from the dividing cell in which it dwells. Those twin delusions of human grandeur, our natural superiority and unique scientific objectivity, are spectacularly successful strategies for human survival. But they are illusions, even if scientists and scholars share them.

The trial-and-error method of science, the formulation and testing of hypotheses, and the rapid transmission of the results of scientific investigations through culture resemble natural selection through mutation and bacterial gene transfer. Science, that is, is both unconsciously imitative and well within the scope of older biotic processes. Reproduction occurs not only in animals but also in their component cells. Even communities, such as those comprising millions of microbes in the termite hindgut, reproduce. Neither science nor art is uniquely human: both imitate and come from nature. Science, like all cultural activities, indulges in anthropocentrism while ignoring or denying it.

The great ape, *Homo sapiens,* in its present state is a singularly technological creature. Human beings today are obligate techno-beings. We are weak bodies entirely dependent on the rapid harvest of agricultural grasses (e.g., corn, wheat, barley) and on milking, slaughtering, and packaging domesticated artiodactyls (e.g., sheep, goats). Today humans must extract huge quantities of buried organic materials, fossil fuels, which are remnants of vast communities of ancient algae, tropical oxygenic photosynthesizers. We now depend absolutely on electromagnetic communication satellites. We can hardly survive without our telephones, automobiles, and airplanes. In short, the human species and those that have coevolved with it (e.g., *Triticum sativum, Zea mays, Bos dometicus, Equus equus, Canis domesticus,* and *Blattera cunis*) all depend on machines.

Nature itself, unfortunately for us, is not dichotomous in a way that matches our speech. It fails to conform to our definitions. There is a dynamic continuum between the living and the nonliving. A fertile egg, a fetus, and even a tiny ejaculated human sperm have always been alive and have always been human. Life and humanness do not come in at the fetal stage, age twenty-one, or even at the two-cell stage. Life is always already there.

Living systems, from their smallest limits as bacterial cells to their largest extent as Gaia, are autopoietic: they are self-forming, or at least self-maintaining and invariably connected to a source of energy and of matter. As autopoietic systems, cells and organisms made of cells are bounded by membranes generated by the system itself. All living systems retain their recognizable features even while they undergo a dynamic interchange of parts and radical developmental changes. All known autopoietic systems on Earth are composed of certain specific forms of matter: carbon, nitrogen, phosphorus, sulfur, and hydrogen compounds bathed in water. All, without exception, are composed of cells that are bounded by membranes composed of lipids (fatty materials) and proteins. The minimal autopoietic system documented as a living cell is smaller than one-millionth of a meter in diameter. But it is organization and function, and not composition, that distinguish the living. A recent corpse and a lively man have nearly identical composition: DNA, RNA, protein, salts, lipid, water, and so forth are all present; yet the two differ profoundly in organization, energy flow-through, and fate. The self-assembly, self-maintenance, incessant metabolism, continuous exchange of energy and matter of the nonstop self-maintenance, i.e., autopoietic, state distinguish the living from the dead.

Autopoiesis is a prerequisite to reproduction. If life is defined as a system that reproduces and mutates, then a barren woman is not alive. Of course, fertile or sterile, lively or docile, a woman is an autopoietic system. Autopoietic systems, whether single-celled individuals or organisms or multicelled, as are all plants and animals, are not platonic, clearly defined, logically consistent entities. All are interdependent and connected. Because of these requisite connections, there may be no completely autopoietic system smaller than Gaia herself. But components and products of autopoietic systems, whether cells in a cancerous tumor, a pair of lovers, or the big red-and-yellow *M* over the McDonald's restaurant, can and do reproduce.

That machines and other animal artifacts can and do reproduce is evident. They do not self-assemble unaided — but neither do infants. They do not self-maintain. Machines alone, insufficient for reproduction, form parts of autopoietic systems. Despite the African machineless past of human life, nearly all current human autopoiesis now depends on machines. This new sort of dependency on machinate extrasomatic structures, i.e., on machines, fossil fuels such as coal and oil, and machine reproduction, is analogous to the way the reproduction of the component cells of our bodies depends on human organization. Our anatomy, physiology, behavior, and social dependencies in supportive environments are essential to the persistence of our body's cells.

## Machine Reproduction

Biological precedents for machine reproduction abound. When proteins are synthesized on mitochondrial ribosomes, protein synthesis is part of the autopoiesis of the cell. When cells reproduce, their reproduction is part of the autopoiesis of the animal. When human animals reproduce, our reproduction is part of the autopoiesis of a technological society. The reproduction of technological societies and their components is part of the autopoiesis of the entire biosphere, the twenty kilometers in diameter hollow sphere at the Earth's surface. Indeed, when a technological society, as part of a phenomenon of global life, reproduces by, for example, the establishment of a colony on the moon, the machines within them, as well we the people with our coevolved fellow organisms, also will have reproduced.[10] Only DNA and RNA molecules replicate, but we are surrounded by machines required for our own reproduction. Neither a DNA molecule nor a machine is autopoietic — both are required for autopoietic systems.

The Gaian biosphere with its multitudes and bizarre histories may, we

10. Lynn Margulis and Oona West, "Gaia and the Civilization of Mars," *GSA Today,* vol. 3 (1993), pp. 277-80; see also Dorion Sagan, *Notes from the Holocene* (White River Junction, Vt.: Chelsea Green, 2007).

reckon, persist at least 3 thousand million more years, namely, until the death of the Sun. Our ancestors were chimplike apes. If we saw them today, we would probably wonder if they had escaped from some local zoo. Our descendants may find themselves in a similar predicament with machines, some of which — or rather whom — may become our descendants. This being the case, we hope that Butler's humorous comment of 1863 will not be simply a statement of the near future of our self-centered species: "We treat our horses, dogs, cattle and sheep, on the whole with great kindness, we give them whatever experience teaches us to be the best for them, and there can be no doubt that our use of meat has added to the happiness of the lower animals far more than it has detracted from it; in like manner it is reasonable to suppose that the machines will treat us kindly, for their existence is as dependent upon ours as ours is upon the lower animals."[11]

## Reinstatement of Environment and the Fallacy of the Gene-Centric Hegemony

Those who tout the ability of the accumulation of DNA gene sequences to solve the problems of disease, overcrowding, food production, and other biological threats are dangerously naive. An enlightened return to our senses literally, to the understanding that people are a minuscule and very recent part of the Gaian system, must lead to a rejection of modern molecular biology and the reductive population modeling of neo-Darwinism and its gene-centered preoccupation with DNA molecules. Complete genome sequences are useful for medicine, forensics, microbial ecology, and evolutionary reconstruction. But it is a delusion to seek in them an explanation for most of physiology and evolutionary change. We have seen the enemy; alas, it is us. We destroy "the environment," and in the same act we destroy ourselves. Gaia existed 3 thousand million years prior to the evolution of the talking ape and is predicted to persist another several thousand million after this ape's demise. An Earth strewn with automobiles, plastic baby diapers, and doodads will correlate precisely with the junkyard on the basaltic surface of the Moon, and a Martian regolith replete with its peculiar plethora of rovers as machinate fossils. These together may serve as late Holocene stratigraphic markers. Indeed, this three-way correlation of Mars, Moon, and Earth sedimentary deposits may even be useful as clues to extinct life-forms for the inquisitive, if any, among our descendants.

11. Samuel Butler, "Darwin among the Machines," letter to the editor of the *Press,* Christchurch, New Zealand, June 13, 1863.

# 10. The Role of Symbiogenesis in Evolution

## Lynn Margulis and Dorion Sagan

## Some Definitions

When we view "evolution" in a Gaian context, we see the word's meaning has expanded. Evolution means "change through time." Stars evolve. The planet's surface, with its continents that are the raised portions of its tectonic plates, also evolves. Animals, including humans of course, and fungi evolve too, and indeed, so do our machines. Although for many "evolution" has come to mean only biological evolution or even only the neo-Darwinist tradition of biological evolution, that in fact is only a tiny part of the whole evolutionary process.

Neo-Darwinism was invented as an early-twentieth-century attempt to reconcile Mendelian genetic stabilism with dynamic population genetics phenomena to explain change in organisms through time as posited by Charles Darwin (1809-82). The neo-Darwinian tradition defines evolution as "change of gene frequencies in natural populations over time." This limited, mammalocentric definition is inadequate — not so much wrong as intellectually anachronistic. A doctrinaire and obsolete formalism, neo-Darwinism as a body of esoteric knowledge has impeded the wider study of the evolution of life. Even as a description of changes in life-forms over four billion years of Earth's history, this new Darwinism is ready to be replaced. Except as a technique to trace gene flow in Holocene primate (including human), avian, and other vertebrate and tracheophyte plant populations, it is an unhelpful analytical tool.

Even though in a Gaian context the evolution of multicelled organisms is a limited part of the whole of evolution, it still remains important. Hence we will also contribute the results of our research to that topic as well. We are convinced that major changes are more attributable to symbiogenesis than to neo-Darwinistic "beneficial random mutations."

Neo-Darwinism recognizes three major components of the evolutionary process. It teaches that all populations of all organisms at all times grow by survival and reproduction. Indeed, all tend to outgrow the capacity of their immediate environment to sustain that growth. Secondly, observable heritable change may be measured in all populations. For neo-Darwinism heritable changes mainly occur as random mutation in DNA. Then natural selection, measured as differential reproduction of offspring of the mutant (changed) organism, tends to lead to observable evolutionary change both in modern organisms and in the fossil record. A hefty body of literature supports all three generalizations. All are logical, verifiable outgrowths of nineteenth-century Darwinism.

However, there are problems. Neo-Darwinism postulates evolutionary change into new species via the accumulation of inherited random mutations. This may well be the case, although no verified cases of random mutation-producing new eukaryotes (animals, plants, or fungi) have ever been observed. The textbook example, "industrial melanism," concerning melanin change in moths to provide dark camouflage against newly sooty trees in industrial England, has been disputed on a number of grounds, including researcher fraud. The one documented case of laboratory speciation in animals, Dobzhansky's work with fruit flies bred at different temperatures that then could no longer interbreed, was attended by the loss of a bacterium in one of the laboratory-evolved species. This suggests that the one nontheoretical example of neo-Darwinism in fact has a better, symbiogenetic explanation: the presence or absence not of a mutation or series of mutations, but of an entire mycoplasm, a bacterium whose genome conferred the ability to live at different temperatures. The presence of *Wolbachia*, a bacterium that has been microphotographed nestling against chromosomes in insect eggs, dramatically alters the animal's animal biology: the presence of this bacterium leads to sex changes in adults.

We do not argue that the lack of observation of random mutation-based speciation is compelling evidence against the neo-Darwinian theory, as the time periods necessary for such speciation would preclude observation in the laboratory. Nevertheless, while evidence for species origin by random mutations is lacking, we do not think evolutionary theorists should ignore the fact that evidence abounds that the acquisition of new positive heritable features has occurred by symbiogenesis.[1]

---

1. Lynn Margulis and Dorion Sagan, *Acquiring Genomes: A Theory of the Origins of Species* (New York: Basic Books, 2002). See also *Insect Symbiosis*, vol. 2, ed. K. Bourtzis and T. A. Miller (Boca Raton, Fla.: CRC Press, 2006).

## Symbiogenesis

Symbiogenesis is a development that takes place in the context of the common phenomenon of symbiosis. Symbiosis, an ecological phenomenon, is defined as organisms belonging to distinct taxa living together in physical contact for much of their life history. Symbiosis, as physical association, was first defined this way by the German scientist Anton de Bary.[2] The partners in protracted symbiosis change. This change can lead to symbiogenesis.

Symbiogenesis, an evolutionary term, refers to the appearance in the symbiotic partners of new behaviors, new metabolism, new tissues, new organs or organelles, and new gene products, etc. Usually they appear in this sequence. Symbiogenesis, we have argued, is the major source of inherited variation in the evolution of the first nucleated cells and of their descendants.[3]

Thermodynamically open systems, i.e., organisms, may merge bodies, cells, and genes in sexual, parasexual, and symbiotic mixtures. From bacteria symbiotically aggregating into cells with nuclei to animals organizing into hives, termite mounds, and cities, individuals can and do lose parts of themselves as they behave in groups that prove their mettle by their efficacy in managing energy flow. Rampant lateral transfer of genes has been well documented and is now recognized as a means of evolutionary change. The cells of plants, animals, fungi, and protoctists (nonbacterial organisms that don't fit into these other taxa), it is now agreed, are the result of genetic mixtures of bacteria that took up residence in each other, mutually managing energy and resources.[4] Viruses, plasmids, and other genetic elements transfer genes among bacteria that belong to different species. Bacteria metabolize arsenic, hydrogen gas, and sulfide, to name just a few substances. Such metabolic virtuosity has been whittled down in familiar surface life-forms. Although people tend to think well-known organisms are more diverse and "higher," oxygen-metabolizing plants and animals suffer in comparison to the chemical prowess of our more numerous, and ecologically important ancestors.

Bacterial metabolic virtuosity likely evolved, not by symbiosis, but by the transmission of genetic elements, combined with fortuitous mutations, in rampantly reproducing bacteria. Bacteria are metabolically more advanced (or di-

---

2. Jan Sapp, *Evolution by Association: A History of Symbiosis Research* (Cambridge: Cambridge University Press, 2000).

3. Mitchell B. Rambler, Lynn Margulis, and Lynn Fester, *Global Ecology: Towards a Science of the Biosphere* (New York: Academic Press, 1989). See also Margulis and Sagan, *Acquiring Genomes*.

4. Lynn Margulis and Dorion Sagan, *Microcosmos: Four Billion Years of Microbial Evolution* (Berkeley: University of California Press, 1997).

verse) than plants and animals and even than human industry — compare biological room-temperature nitrogen fixation to the high temperatures of fertilizer factories. However, our emphasis[5] on symbiosis as a means of speciation must be qualified by the realization that bacteria are arguably not classifiable into species. The original buildup of metabolic diversity in bacteria was likely by neo-Darwinian mutation — combined with the lateral "sexual," but not reproductive, transfer of genes that have recently been borrowed by humans in genetic engineering. This has been, clearly, a major means of evolution.

The classical example of symbiosis is between fungi and algae or, alternatively, fungi and cyanobacteria. The rock-clinging abilities of fungi, combined with the light-using abilities of photosynthetic organisms, hone these organisms into a new unit — lichens — with combined capacities to take energy from the environment, turn it into the stuff of life, and degrade ambient gradients. Although the idea was initially ridiculed, no modern biologist now disputes the fact that lichens are not plants but symbiotic organisms, which are part fungi. Also, the theory that all eukaryotic cells, cells with nuclei and chromosomes, are products of symbiosis (or symbiogenetic mixtures) has been genetically proven and is taught in textbooks.

The main organelles (cell parts) that evolved from bacteria include the mitochondria, which evolved from oxygen-users, bacteria that grew to cover the planet as the release of free oxygen by cyanobacteria continued. Cyanobacteria had mutated to use water as hydrogen source. The mitochondria, which "live" outside the nucleus but cannot grow on their own anymore, are inherited in humans only from the mother, because those in the sperm break off with the tail upon fertilization. Mitochondria are found in all plants and animals; they need oxygen to generate chemical energy for physiological function.

Latter-day symbionts that can no longer live outside the plant or animal, the mitochondria, found outside the nuclear membrane, likely evolved from small invasive oxygen-respiring bacteria. The small bacteria ancestral to mitochondria could have invaded larger cells used to living in a nonoxygen atmosphere. These larger cells are thought to be Archaea, perhaps similar to *Thermoplasma,* a hardy sulfur bacterium that survives in scalding hot springs. The ancestors of mitochondria, after invading entirely different larger cells in the manner of a disease, survived.

The second major class of symbiotic organelles is plastids, which when green are called chloroplasts. The green, purple, and yellow plastids of algae (eukaryotic photosynthetic organisms that are not plants as they don't form embryos) have been definitively traced, by genetic techniques, to free-living

5. Margulis and Sagan, *Acquiring Genomes.*

photosynthetic bacteria. Photosynthetic bacteria were probably not the first form of life to evolve, but they were very successful, especially when they developed means to take hydrogen from water. The result of this was the planet's first big pollution crisis, the production of oxygen gas. The gas was (and is) very reactive, and further evolution was required to tolerate it, and then to use it. The new atmosphere rich in free oxygen that arose two thousand million years ago is a profound example of the thermodynamic waste that results from a rapidly spreading population. Such rapid growth leads to many deaths, and puts selection pressure on developing new means of waste disposal, detoxification, etc., which involves the evolution of new biochemical pathways, kinds, and species of life. The ancestors of mitochondria were among those lucky few that evolved not just to tolerate but also to make use of the energetic potential of originally almost universally hazardous oxygen gas. Their success in the new oxidizing planetary surface environment is attested by the near universal mitochondrial presence of oxygen-using organelles in the bodies of plants, fungi, and animals. (Some protoctists, although they have cell nuclei, do not possess mitochondria; they are the equivalent of microbial living fossils harking back to before the steep rise in atmospheric oxygen levels.)

The ancestors of plastids — the colorful parts of plant and algal cells that originated from cyano-bacteria — were probably not invaders but rather were devoured. Because microbes do not have immune systems, some of the devoured organisms successfully resisted digestion. In cases where they did, the continued metabolism of the swallowed photosynthetic bacterium sometimes conferred an evolutionary advantage. The swallower received a continuous food supply; the swallowed, a safe haven.

Apart from the accepted symbiotic mergers of mitochondria and plastid ancestors, a third, arguably more prevalent symbiosis is postulated to be a root infection, now constitutive of the basic identity and abilities of all eukaryotic cells. The proposed agents are spirochetes, among the fastest movers in the microbial world, and which today are seen attached, sometimes permanently, to larger microbes to which they provide a means of movement through the viscous media of water and mud. Spirochetes also often penetrate cells, reproducing inside them. By hypothesis, but not yet by the sort of genetic sequencing proof that has led scientists to accept the free-living symbiotic origin of plastids and mitochondria, spirochetes invaded ancient sulfur metabolizers. There they helped evolve the complex cytoplasmic streaming, chromosomal movement, and nuclear apparatus that are observed in eukaryotic cells but not in bacteria.

By hypothesis the kinetochores, the attachment sites on the chromosomes, are a part of the spirochetal heritage. Because different, closely related species of mammals, such as dogs and wolves, and pigs and boars, are characterized by inferably different chromosome numbers, it is suggested that the tendency of the spirochetal remnants to reproduce on their own may lead species to generate chromosomal number differences that lead to new intrabreeding populations. This would be an example of symbiogenesis, the evolution of new species, not just in microbes, but also in larger organisms on our own scale.

Another example of the extensive effects of symbiosis on multicellular organisms is *Convoluta roscoffensis*. This is a flatworm that does not eat because it depends on algae that photosynthesize beneath its translucent skin. When the surf pounds, or researchers stomp, the worms burrow into the sand out of harm's way. They save their own skin as well as that of their photosynthetic guests. The parallel to the relation of algae to photosynthesizing ancestors of their plastids is remarkable.

Finally, those hesitant to consider symbiogenesis as credible in larger beings are encouraged to consider the bizarre results of Donald Williamson, a real-life Dr. Moreau on the Isle of Man. Williamson has shown that chordate sperm *(Ascidia)* can fertilize echinoderm eggs *(Echinus)*. Unlike mules, the hybrids are, on rare occasion, fertile; they retract their arms, begin metaphorosis, and survive. Apparently, in these invertebrates the barriers to interspecies fertilization we see in vertebrates do not exist.[6] We need to be wary about extrapolating from species like our own to evolution as a whole.

There is a hypothesis that explains such cross-species fertilizations. University of Hawaii symbiosis expert Margaret Ngai-McFall stresses the huge concentrations of microbes in the waters in which our ancestors evolved. Some of these bacteria are necessary symbionts for normal digestion processes of the animals in whose guts they live. She points out that immune systems may have originated from the advantage of systematically recognizing needed intestinal symbionts in the aqueous medium. According to this idea, the relative rarity of symbiogenesis in "higher" organisms, insofar as it exists, is ironically an offshoot itself of the need to preserve still other, earlier, symbiotic associations in our animal ancestors.

## The Wider Phenomena

The tendency to look at things from our own scale hampers us in contemplating evolution. In this regard we are not so much anthropocentric as zoocentric. Thus, when we contemplate how symbiosis might act to produce species in large, familiar organisms such as animals in the way it has clearly done in mi-

---

6. D. I. Williamson and Sonya E. Vickers, "The Origins of Larvae," *American Scientist* 95 (November-December 2007): 509-17.

crobes, we forget something rather basic: speciation itself is a eukaryotic phenomenon. The merging of different kinds of bacterial cells to make cells with
nuclei was a major evolutionary event, and it set up the conditions, too involved to summarize here, by which conspecific cells evolved cycles of fertilization and meiosis, leading to sexual reproduction. Only in sexually reproducing
organisms does speciation begin in the familiar sense we imagine it to occur in
animals. So symbiogenesis, while it can clearly lead to new species, also set up
the conditions for speciation itself. Clearly, symbiotic effects are not confined
to microbes and medieval bestiaries.

From a process philosophy perspective, another point of interest is that
choices made by organisms — what to eat, where to live, and with which organisms to associate — seem to be able to translate directly into the genetic effects of
evolution. This is fairly well accepted already in Darwin's sexual selection, where
females, by choosing males on the basis of certain traits, including theoretically inheritable behavioral ones, such as charm or fighting prowess, can have significant
genetic effects. Evolution has been half-jokingly called a great breeding experiment run by females. The brighter plumage and generally greater variety of
shorter-lived, sexually less discriminating, and biologically more expendable
males suggest that in most species they are the ones more often chosen than choosing. There is even the theory that consciousness itself, insofar as it is not directly related to survival — for example, the presence of poetic wit and artistic imagination
— is the result of females choosing males on the basis of their speech, thus encouraging the thinking that speech expresses. This might explain why human intelligence seems to be bloated beyond what is necessary for survival.

But the effects of choice extend beyond whom one is to mate and associate with. More importantly, from a symbiogenetic standpoint, they extend to
whom one wishes to merge with genomically, most obviously by the open thermodynamic process of eating. For example, a starving herbivore may find that
by eating some sort of special yogurtlike substance it can appropriate the enzymes necessary for meat digestion. This behavioral lark may have serious evolutionary consequences. By what is a ridiculously simple "mechanism" in principle, eating, it can influence its genetic destiny in a potentially permanent way.
Exercising its desires in a certain direction in its partly edible environment can
have potent, permanent, genetically based evolutionary consequences. Although Darwin made evolution palatable by focusing on the indubitable mechanism of natural selection, he also ascribed choice to worms, to female insects
and birds choosing mates, and so on. In sum, animal choices — not just in sexual selection, but also via eating and by social association leading to symbiosis
and potentially to symbiogenesis — would seem to have a real role in evolution.

Moreover, genetic elements can alter our behavior virtually instantaneously, as in the development of propulsive sneezing after catching a cold, a tendency to bite after getting rabies, and, perhaps, a tendency for increased promiscuity coincident with the contraction of certain venereal diseases. Infection, after all, is another name for lateral genetic transmission of the kind that led to nucleated cells after invasion of anaerobes by ancestors of cilia and mitochondria. Sickness and health are relative, and may trade places over evolutionary time.

An important question to ask seems to be: In what ways do infectious agents, genetic elements, change host behaviors to advance their own spread or insure their own survival? Some of the effects may turn out to be quite subtle, not deleterious at all, and indeed a constituent part of what we formerly were inclined to think of as our impregnably independent identities. Dogs with rabies slaver and bite, transferring their genetically conferred "madness." But increased biting, among other things, means increased exposure to genetic change through acquisition of foreign proteins, hormones, and genomes. James Joyce, Oscar Wilde, Vincent van Gogh, Gustave Flaubert, Abraham Lincoln, and Ludwig van Beethoven were also "mad" according to many of their contemporaries — although now they are recognized as geniuses afflicted with *Treponema pallidum,* the syphilis spirochete. Over evolutionary time, sickness can morph into health, as attested by the origins of the animal cell via bacterial infection!

Clearly a new science, which might be called "medical symbiotics,"[7] should study health from a microecological standpoint that jettisons the idealistic nonsense of the organism as an isolated, genetically impregnable system, a pure culture of one. Genomic acquisition is to be associated with change and growth — and bursts of evolution — as well as infection and illness.

At a conference on symbiosis and consciousness in Bellagio, we even suggested a symbiosis-related theory for the origins of tool-using humanity from more apelike ancestors. Physical anthropologists most often explain our relative hairlessness as a trait concomitant with our ancestors' long treks while hunting game on the plains. Over long distances humans are the fastest animal, and loss of hair helped sweat to evaporate. Because of our relative hairlessness, the grooming instincts, which play a major part in social interaction in the primates most like us, may have been deprived of their main object — insects. In the absence of body hair, there would have been few insects to groom, and so the fine motor coordination of opposable thumb and forefinger, used to discern and remove possible disease-carrying insects, would have been freed up for other uses. This is not symbiogenesis per se, but it shows how ecological be-

---

7. Jessica Hope Whiteside, "Towards Ecological Medicine: Spore-Formers in Fossil and Extant Intestines," in *Chimera and Consciousness: Evolution of the Sensory Self,* ed. Lynn Margulis, Wolfgang E. Krumbein, and Celeste Asikainen (White River Junction, Vt.: Chelsea Green, 2008).

havioral alterations in our species could have led from grooming to tool fashioning and use, activities that also make use of fine coordination.


## Conclusion

We have described two phenomena ignored in the standard formulations of the neo-Darwinian synthesis. First, symbiogenesis is observed, where new organisms evolve not slowly but rapidly on the geological scale, by a "genome at a swallow." Symbiogenesis must be moved to front and center away from curious evolutionary marginalia. Symbiont merger and integration should always be suspected at the major evolutionary transitions. The infection of microbes, and their eating of one another without digestion, was the Dionysian forerunner to the Apollonian order of organisms discreetly speciating via putative overcredited "neo-Darwinian mechanisms" — e.g., random mutation.

Second, choice (even if a Spinozistic illusion) cannot be ignored. Darwin spoke of sexual selection, but culinary or gustatory selection must also operate in organisms that choose one part of their largely edible environment over another. With whom we decide to associate in eating and living seems crucial, and likely influences subsequent evolution — perhaps even, through amplification, events millions of years in the future. If sexual organisms can influence the shape and behavior of their offspring by choosing their mates, they can also influence their evolution by choosing to associate with and eat some life-forms and avoid others, thereby favoring or inhibiting certain feedback loops and thermodynamic flow. Such loops and flow patterns operate in real behavioral, not just drawn-out, geological time.[8] Charles Darwin ably presented natural selection as a Cartesian-like "mechanism," thereby making it scientifically acceptable. The "life" that Butler suggests Darwin thereby took out of biology now returns, in a scientific fashion, when we appreciate the near instantaneous actions and responses of organisms as naturally complex agents of their own energy and matter transformations.

8. Williamson and Vickers, "Metamorphosis: Small Larvae Change the Paradigm of Animal Evolution," in *Chimera and Consciousness*.

## 11. *Punctuated Equilibrium and Species Selection*

FRANCISCO J. AYALA

### The Argument

The fact that there are large gaps in the fossil record and that the emergence of new species does not appear to have been as gradual as Darwin expected is sometimes regarded as in conflict with mainstream evolutionary theory. The most influential theory, critical of traditional gradualism, is called punctuated equilibrium (PE). This theory was first advanced in 1971 by Niles Eldredge and received its moniker in 1972 in a paper coauthored by Eldredge and Stephen J. Gould.[1] It has been the subject of some argumentation among scientists and of much misrepresentation by the media, by fundamentalist creationists, and occasionally by philosophers and theologians.

The PE theory proposes that the frequently observed scarcity or absence in the fossil record of specimens that are intermediate in morphology between successive fossil forms is not always, or even generally, due to the incompleteness of the record. According to PE theory, the record should be taken at face value. The abrupt appearance of new fossil species reflects their development in bursts of evolution, after which species remain unchanged in their morphology for the species' duration, which may extend for millions of years. The theory proposes that the prevailing view, that morphological evolution is predominantly gradual, must be replaced with a model of speciation with two distinct sequential components, a burst of change during the origination of a species, followed by a long period of stasis for the remaining duration of the species. Gould acknowledges that gradual change and punctuational change both are

1. Niles Eldredge and Stephen J. Gould, "Punctuated Equilibria: An Alternative to Phyletic Gradualism," in *Models in Paleobiology,* ed. T. J. M. Schopf (Cooper, Colo.: Freeman, 1972), pp. 82-115.

represented in the fossil record, but he affirms that the punctuational mode appears at a much higher frequency.

The PE theory provides Gould with the foundation on which he builds the claim that macroevolution (i.e., evolution on the large scale, as studied by paleontologists) is an autonomous subject of evolutionary investigation. This is because the punctuational pattern is not predictable on the basis of the small and gradual genetic changes investigated by population geneticists and other students of microevolutionary processes that occur in living organisms. In his monumental treatise *The Structure of Evolutionary Theory*, Gould says I support this claim of macroevolutionary autonomy and quotes me at length:

> I have particularly appreciated the fairness of severe critics who generally oppose punctuated equilibrium, but who freely acknowledge its legitimacy as a potentially important proposition with interesting implications, and as a testable notion that must be adjudicated in its own macroevolutionary realm. Ayala has been especially clear and gracious on this point: "If macroevolutionary theory were deducible from microevolutionary principles, it would be possible to decide between competing macroevolutionary models simply by examining the logical implications of microevolutionary theory. But the theory of population genetics is compatible with both punctualism and gradualism; and, hence, logically it entails neither. Whether the tempo and mode of evolution occur predominantly according to the model of punctuated equilibria or according to the model of phyletic gradualism is an issue to be decided by studying macroevolutionary patterns, not by inference from microevolutionary processes. In other words, macroevolutionary theories are not reducible (at least at the present state of knowledge) to microevolution. Hence, macroevolution and microevolution are decoupled in the sense (which is epistemologically most important) that macroevolution is an autonomous field of study that must develop and test its own theories."[2]

My position here would not come as a surprise to those who read my brief philosophical introductory essay in the present volume, "Reduction, Emergence, Naturalism, Dualism, Teleology: A Précis," but I want now to make two conceptual clarifications.

In sexually reproducing organisms, species are groups of interbreeding

---

2. Stephen J. Gould, *The Structure of Evolutionary Theory* (Cambridge: Harvard University Press, Belknap Press, 2002), p. 1023. The quotation of mine Gould quotes is from "Microeveolution and Macroevolution," in *Evolution from Molecules to Men*, ed. D. S. Bendall (Cambridge: Cambridge University Press, 1983).

organisms that are reproductively isolated from any other such groups. Speciation involves, by definition, the development of reproductive isolation between populations previously sharing in a common gene pool. But it is in no way apparent how the fossil record could provide evidence of reproductive isolation. Paleontologists recognize species by their different morphologies as preserved in the fossil record. New species that are morphologically indistinguishable from their ancestors (or from contemporary species) go totally unrecognized. Sibling species, that is, species that are morphologically indistinguishable from one another, are common in many groups of insects, marine bivalves, rodents, and other well-studied organisms. Thus, when Gould uses evidence of rapid phenotypic change in favor of the punctuational model of speciation, he commits the fallacy of definitional circularity. Speciation as seen by the paleontologist always involves morphological change because paleontologists identify new species by the eventuation of morphological change.

The second clarification concerns the "sudden" appearance of new species in the fossil record. The succession of fossil forms is associated with the succession of stratigraphic geological deposits, which accumulate for millions of years, separated by discontinuous transitions. The discontinuities reflect periods that typically last from 50,000 to 100,000 years or longer, during which sediments failed to accumulate.

Creationists have argued that punctuated evolution manifests the intervention of God in the evolutionary process. The sudden appearance of new species would indicate divine acts of special creation. In *The Structure*, as he had done many times before, Gould negates this implication and reiterates that the geological "instants," during which "sudden" change occurs, typically encompass from 50,000 to 100,000 years, and that these bursts of change result from the well-known processes studied by evolutionary geneticists, genetic mutation and natural selection, yielding adaptive evolutionary change.

The creationist claim is based on an additional and truly monumental misunderstanding, and this misunderstanding is shared by some otherwise thoughtful philosophers and theologians. The bursts of morphological change noticed by Gould and others does not involve new body plans, the emergence of radically different kinds of organisms, or the appearance of new limbs or organs, such as wings or lungs. Rather, the traits manifesting punctuated evolution are traits such as the shell flatness of oysters, irregular patterns of coiling in ammonites, or the configuration of the head bones in lungfishes.

## An Example

This observation deserves to be elaborated for those unfamiliar with the fossil record, whether they be scientists, philosophers, theologians, or others interested in the evolutionary process. I can see no better way of illustrating the fossil patterns of evolutionary change than by reproducing the figure chosen by an eminent paleontologist, James W. Valentine, a supporter of punctuated equilibrium, for an evolution textbook.[3]

The trait examined is rib strength in a group of brachiopods. These are marine animals with shells, abundantly represented in ancient fossil beds; "rib strength" is the ratio (ranging from 0 to 60 percent, as shown at the bottom of the figure) of the height to the width of the shell ribs. The figure spans from 415 million to 405 million years ago (see dates on the left). There are thirteen samples (obtained from four stratigraphic sites) at the times indicated by the dots on the right. The observations are summarized in the middle of the figure. For each sample, three numbers are graphically given (I will refer in parentheses to the values in the bottom sample, by way of example): range of variation of individuals in the sample, represented by the horizontal line (observed values ranging from about 22 to 54 percent); the mean or average value for all individuals in the sample, represented by the vertical line (about 45 percent); and the confidence interval of the mean, represented by the box (from about 39 to 52 percent). The confidence interval is a statistical statement that, on the basis of the sampled individuals, the true mean value of the population sampled has 95 percent probability of lying somewhere within the confidence interval. That is, for the bottom sample, we are 95 percent "confident" that the mean lies somewhere between 39 and 52 percent.

I shall now follow the logic of the paleontologist seeking to identify how many species can be defined among the thirteen samples. The mean of the five bottom samples oscillates between 41 (middle sample) and 49 percent (second sample from below), but the five confidence intervals considerably overlap. That is to say, these five bottom samples are not statistically different from one another, and thus they are identified as members of one species, *Eocoelia hemisphaerica* (see label sideways on the left). The species so defined persists without (statistically evinced) change for about 2 million years, between 415 million and 413 million years ago. The sixth sample from the bottom has a mean displaced to the left and, although statistically it is not different from three of the samples below (their confidence interval boxes overlap), it overlaps

3. Theodosius Dobzhansky, Francisco J. Ayala, G. L. Stebbins, and J. W. Valentine, eds., *Evolution* (San Francisco: Freeman, 1977), p. 329.

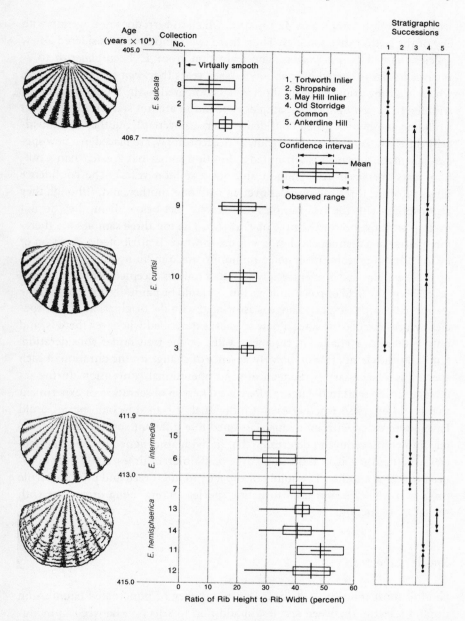

**Evolution of rib strength in the brachiopod *Eocoelia* between 415 million (bottom of diagram) and 405 million (top of diagram) years ago.**

with the seventh sample just on top of it, which in turn does not overlap with any of the bottom five samples. Thus, these two samples are considered a new species, named *E. intermedia*. The transition from *E. hemisphaerica* to *E. intermedia* has occurred over about 200,000 years (between samples 5 and 6), which is a time span relatively short when compared to the 2 million years attributed to *E. hemisphaerica*. Samples 8, 9, and 10 are not statistically different from one another (i.e., their confidence intervals overlap), but they are statistically different from all samples below and, accordingly, are placed in a new species, *E. curtisi*, to which is attributed a duration somewhat greater than 5 million years (between 411.9 million and 406.7 million years). The confidence intervals of the three top samples overlap with one another, and, although they also overlap with the two samples of *E. curtisi* just below them, they do not overlap with the bottom sample of *E. curtisi*. The top three samples are therefore placed in a distinct species, *E. sulcata*, to which is attributed a duration of nearly 2 million years (from 406.7 million to 405.0 million years ago).

The logic used is scientifically sound. It follows accepted conventions and practices in the field of paleontology. But it should be painfully obvious that the claim that morphological change is associated with the origination of new species evinces circularity, since a new species is described whenever there is, and only if there is, a change in the mean value of the trait under consideration. Similarly, the claim of stasis, namely, absence of change for the duration of each species, is a necessary consequence of an operational convention. In the sequence represented in the figure, there is no known observation or experiment that could establish whether or not individuals assigned to one species could have intercrossed with individuals assigned to a different species. Nor is there any known procedure to determine that individuals assigned to the same species, whether they lived at the same time or at different times, could have interbred with one another. The ability or capacity to interbreed and produce fertile progeny is the criterion used to define species among living organisms with sexual reproduction.

## Species Selection

Gould's most innovative claim is that the theory of punctuated equilibrium implies selection between species, in addition to selection between individuals, as the driving process of evolutionary change. By reference to the figure, the PE claim would be that, whatever evolutionary shift we perceive in the evolution of *Eocoelia* from 415 million to 405 million years ago is not primarily the outcome of natural selection acting among individuals but rather is a consequence of species selection, that is, the survival of some species and the extinction of others.

The claim of species selection as an important evolutionary process has been repeated for thirty years now by Gould and other proponents of punctuated equilibrium. But where is the evidence that species selection occurs? This certainly cannot be convincingly inferred from the observations displayed in the figure, which are more parsimoniously interpreted as outcomes of individual selection. Nor can it be inferred (and for the same reason) from any typical descriptions of fossil morphological evolution. Instances of species selection have been proposed over the last three decades, but in no case known to me — or known to Gould, he admits in his 2002 treatise — have they survived critical scrutiny. Gould argues that this is because scientists have not looked hard enough. So the case needs to be made by hypothetical examples, of which he provides one.

Gould's one hypothetical example that I have often used to illustrate this issue and to argue for species selection proceeds as follows:

> Suppose that a wondrously optimal fish, a marvel of hydrodynamic perfection, lives in a pond. This species has been honed by millennia of conventional Darwinian selection, based on fierce competition, to this optimal organismic state. The gills work in an exemplary fashion, but do not vary among individual organisms for any option other than breathing in well-aerated, flowing water. Another species of fish — the middling species — ekes out a marginal existence in the same pond. The gills don't work as well, but their structure varies greatly among organisms. In particular, a few members of the species can breathe in quite stagnant and muddy waters.
>
> Organismic selection favors the optimal fish, a proud creature who has lorded it over all brethren, especially the middling fish, for ages untold. But now the pond dries up, and only a few shallow, muddy pools remain. The optimal fish becomes extinct. The middling species persists because a few of its members can survive in the muddy residua. (Next decade, the deep, well aerated waters may return, but the optimal fish no longer exists to reestablish its domination.)[4]

The decisive characteristic in his example is the different degree of variability within each hypothetical species. Natural selection, Gould says, acts among species, because the species that survives is the one with the greater variability, while others go extinct. The character — variability within each species — "*does not exist* at the organismal level, and each species develops only one

4. Gould, *Structure of Evolutionary Theory*, pp. 665-66.

state of the (emergent) character because the character belongs to the species as a whole. Therefore, selection for this character can only occur among species."[5]

I fully disagree with Gould. Because of changed environmental conditions, natural selection has favored the few individuals of the "middling species" capable of breathing in muddy waters. Other individuals of this species and those of the other species have not survived because they lack such capacity. The middling species has survived not because it had more variability but because some of its individuals are capable of surviving in muddy waters. The trait under selection is not degree of variability within species, but the breathing properties of individual fish. Indeed, if there had been a species without any variability but made up of individuals fit to survive in muddy waters, the species would have handsomely survived.

If this is the best "evidence" that Gould and other PE proponents can marshal in support of species selection, which is PE's distinctive theoretical claim, readers should not be surprised that evolutionary biologists have largely, if not completely, lost interest in PE as a scientific theory. In any case, the point that may be of greater interest to philosophers and theologians is that PE refers to morphological changes that are trivial and irrelevant in order to account for transitions between major groups of organisms. It provides no support whatever for creationists, although they have sometimes mistakenly appealed to it.

---

5. Gould, *Structure of Evolutionary Theory,* p. 665, emphasis in original.

# 12. *The Baldwin Effect*

Francisco J. Ayala

The evolutionist J. M. Baldwin formulated a hypothesis in 1896, which he further developed in 1902. Later it became known as "the Baldwin effect." Simply stated, the hypothesis asserts that the environment affects adaptively the phenotype of an organism, that is, its configuration, so that the organism can survive and reproduce under conditions that are unusual or even extreme, and that such adaptive modifications may later become genetically fixed by natural selection. Baldwin's hypothesis was formulated at about the same time by other evolutionists, such as C. L. Morgan in 1896 and H. F. Osborn in 1897. The hypothesis was elaborated and made more precise during the twentieth century, in conjunction with the advance of genetic knowledge. The hypothesis became incorporated into the modern ("synthetic") theory of evolution, largely through the work of the Russian evolutionist I. I. Schmalhausen, whose main book was translated into English in 1949 by Theodosius Dobzhansky, a principal author of the synthetic theory of evolution. A central conceit of Schmalhausen's book is the notion that Dobzhansky had named in 1937 the "norm of reaction," which refers to the possible configurations that the genotype of an organism may express as it becomes exposed to different environments. Distinctive of the Baldwin hypothesis is the claim that natural selection will favor mutations that yield phenotypes that perform well in a particular environment. Thus, adaptation to an unusual environment may first be accomplished by phenotypic adaptation, but become all the more likely and more effective owing to mutations favored by natural selection, so that the adaptation becomes genetically fixed.

The Baldwin effect has been confirmed in numerous cases in all sorts of organisms. More significant is that our knowledge of how it happens is now much more detailed and precise, as a consequence of the great advances of molecular genetics and developmental biology. Recent excellent and extensive reviews can be found by M. J. West-Eberhard[1] and M. W. Kirschner and J. C. Gerhart.[2] B. J. Weber and D. J. Depew have edited a volume that treats the Baldwin effect from multiple perspectives.[3] One case that I find particularly fascinating is the chromosomal mechanism of sex determination in animals. In some animals the sex of an individual depends on the environment. In many species of lizards and turtles the ambient temperature at which the egg develops determines sex. In some alligator species, eggs invariably produce females when incubated at up to 86° F and males when incubated at 91° F or above. Early in development the sex organs (gonads) are similar in all individuals. During a critical week within the nine-week development period, the gonads differentiate into testes that produce spermatozoa (so that males develop) or into an ovary with eggs (so that females develop), depending on the temperature. At temperatures between 87° and 90° F, intermediate proportions of males and females are produced, not hermaphrodites or intersexes.

The process is under hormonal control. If alligator eggs developing at a male-yielding temperature are exposed to the hormone estradiol, they develop into females; similarly, inhibiting estradiol yields males from eggs developing at the female-determining temperature. This effect is due to a circuit switch gene, SF-1. At high levels of the SF-1 protein, enzymes are produced that synthesize testosterone, and males result. At lower levels of the SF-1 protein, an enzyme is made that converts testosterone to estrogen, and females result. In mammals and birds the mechanism determining sex is also under the control of factors like the SF-1 protein, but it has become genetically fixed. In mammals, including humans, females have two identical sex-determining chromosomes (XX) while in males they are different (XY). The Y chromosome is a relic of an ancient X chromosome that began to lose most of its genes millions of years ago. The much-reduced Y chromosome retained male-determining genes, so that individuals inheriting the Y chromosome invariably develop into males. In the evolution of birds the diminishing chromosome retained female-determining genes, so that the females have an unequal pair of sex-determining chromosomes (called ZW), while the males have two identical chromosomes (ZZ). As the evolutionary lineages evolved, one leading from reptiles to birds and the other to mammals, sex-determining genes became fixed, so that sex was no longer dependent on the vagaries of the environment.

1. Mary Jane West-Eberhard, *Developmental Plasticity and Evolution* (Oxford and New York: Oxford University Press, 2003).

2. M. W. Kirschner and J. C. Gerhart, *The Plausibility of Life: Resolving Darwin's Dilemma* (New Haven and London: Yale University Press, 2005).

3. B. J. Weber and D. J. Depew, eds., *Evolution and Learning: The Baldwin Effect Reconsidered* (Cambridge, Mass., and London: MIT Press, 2003).

The Baldwin effect has been ascertained in many other instances, including cast-determination in social insects (ants, termites, and honeybees) and the affinity of hemoglobin for oxygen. Indeed, the Baldwin effect has been generally involved in the origin of evolutionary novelties.[4] Evolutionary novelties are reorganizations of preexisting phenotypes, which first arise in response to environmental challenges (given that all genotypes have enormous plasticity, that is, a wide norm of reaction), but eventually become genetically determined if the particular environmental challenges persist and the adaptation importantly contributes to survival and reproductive success. Kirschner and Gerhart explain in considerable detail that the genetic changes that account for evolutionary novelty involve gene control circuits (numerous but very short DNA sequences), rather than changes in the enzymes encoded by genes.[5]

---

4. West-Eberhard, *Developmental Plasticity and Evolution.*
5. Kirschner and Gerhart, *The Plausibility of Life.*

## 13. Evolution and Process Thought

IAN G. BARBOUR

In 1942 Julian Huxley gave the name "the modern synthesis" to the systematic integration of evolutionary theory and population genetics. Among its proponents were Gaylord Simpson, Theodosius Dobzhansky, and Ernst Mayr. They insisted that the formation of new species is determined exclusively by variation and natural selection, whereas Darwin himself had been open to the possibility that other factors contributed to evolutionary change. Advocates of the modern synthesis also defended gradualism, the thesis that major evolutionary changes are the result of the accumulation of many small changes. They held that random genetic mutations and recombinations resulted in individuals with adaptive advantages better able to survive and reproduce in their local environments, resulting in gradual shifts in gene frequencies in populations.[1]

In the 1970s Stephen Jay Gould and Niles Eldredge challenged such gradualism and defended "punctuated equilibrium," the thesis that there have been long periods of stability interrupted by brief periods of rapid change. Gould also challenged "panadaptationism," the thesis that all evolutionary changes were the product of adaptive advantages. He asserted that many changes conferred no advantage and were simply the accidental by-products of other changes that were adaptive. Instead of the earlier stress on individual genes and separate traits, he took a more holistic approach, claiming that most physiological structures and behavioral patterns are the product of many genes. He said directions of change are determined by the possibilities of developmental reorganization in the growth of embryos as well as by selective forces acting on organisms in environments.[2]

1. Julian Huxley, *Evolution: The Modern Synthesis* (London: Allen and Unwin, 1942); Gaylord G. Simpson, *The Meaning of Evolution* (New Haven: Yale University Press, 1949).

2. Stephen J. Gould and Niles Eldredge, "Punctuated Equilibria," *Paleobiology* 3 (1977): 115-51; Stephen J. Gould and Richard C. Lewontin, "The Spandrels of San Marco and the Panglossian Paradigm: A Critique of the Adaptationist Programme," *Procedings of the Royal So-*

Most biologists — including such highly respected scientists as Francisco Ayala — insisted that an expanded neo-Darwinism could account for all these phenomena.[3] Yes, dramatic and far-reaching changes such as those that occurred in the pre-Cambrian period took place very rapidly on a geological timescale, but they spanned an enormous number of generations, sufficient for speciation and even the formation of new phyla with differing body plans to occur by familiar mechanisms. Yes, physiological structures are the product of many genes and complex embryonic developmental systems, but the operation of regulatory genes is increasingly being understood at the molecular level. Natural selection, they said, is still the main factor in determining the direction of evolutionary changes.

I will look at five areas of recent research and propose that each of them suggests the need for new ways of thinking that go beyond the refinement of neo-Darwinism. I will also argue that in each case people open to the process philosophy of Alfred North Whitehead should welcome these new ideas. The five topics are: (1) contingency and teleology, (2) the Baldwin effect and interiority, (3) complexity and design, (4) hierarchical levels and downward causation, and (5) self-organization and emergence. In the final section I will consider the broader question of the relation of science to metaphysics.

## Contingency and Teleology

Stephen Jay Gould has emphasized the role of contingency in evolutionary history. If a small isolated population happens to have a distribution of gene frequencies different from the distribution in the original population, a new species can be formed relatively rapidly. Catastrophic events such as the impact of comets have drastically and unpredictably altered the course of evolutionary history. If the tape of evolution were replayed on Earth — or on another planet — the outcome would not at all resemble the forms of life with which we are familiar. Gould maintained that our presence on Earth was entirely a matter of chance and that it is highly improbable that anything resembling human beings, or even intelligent life, would occur more than once. He was critical of all ideas of directionality or progress in evolutionary history.[4]

---

*ciety of London* 205 (1979): 98; Stephen J. Gould, "Darwinism and the Expansion of Evolutionary Theory," *Science* 216 (1982): 380-87.

3. G. Ledyard Stebbins and Francisco J. Ayala, "Is a New Evolutionary Synthesis Necessary?" *Science* 213 (1981): 167-71, and "The Evolution of Darwinism," *Scientific American* 253 (July 1985): 72-89.

4. Stephen J. Gould, *Wonderful Life: The Burgess Shale and the Nature of History* (New York: Norton, 1989).

The Cambridge biologist Simon Conway Morris vehemently disagreed with Gould, first in *The Crucible of Creation*[5] and more recently in *Life's Solution*.[6] He shows that very dissimilar species have independently evolved similar structures and functions. For example, camera-like eyes have evolved in squid, jellyfish, snails, and vertebrates. The protein rhodopsin has functions other than response to light, and it could repeatedly be co-opted for a new function, vision. The transition from egg laying to the live birth of the young has evolved independently at least 100 times. The many parallels between marsupial and placental mammals on distant continents have long been noted. Conway Morris shows that dolphins and chimps show striking similarities in brain size, communication systems, and social organization, despite the dolphin's unique paralimbic brain lobe and sonarlike abilities in echolocation.

Conway Morris describes in detail the similarities in the social organization of colonies of bees, ants, termites, and mole rats. He argues that, even at the lowly level of bacteria, adaptation along preestablished lines far outweighs either chance or history in evolutionary change. He cites experiments by Richard Lensky in which a population of E. coli was divided into a number of samples, which diversified over the course of 2,000 generations, and were then subdivided into thirty-six populations, which diversified for another 1,000 generations. But when transferred from glucose to maltose nutrients, the populations converged on the same adaptive changes despite their differing histories. Conway Morris concludes: "Despite differing starting points, different lineages converge on particular destinations."[7]

Whereas Gould held that intelligent life on other planets is highly improbable because of the dominant role of chance in evolutionary history, Conway Morris concludes that once life has started, intelligent life is virtually inevitable, though he thinks that planets with physical conditions hospitable to life may be very rare (hence his subtitle, "Inevitable Humans in a Lonely Universe"). "The principle aim of this book has been to show that the constraints of evolution and the ubiquity of convergence make the emergence of something like ourselves a near-inevitability. Contrary to received wisdom and the prevailing ethos of despair, the contingencies of biological history will make no long-term difference to the outcome."[8] The directionality of evolution is con-

5. Simon Conway Morris, *The Crucible of Creation: The Burgess Shale and the Rise of Animals* (Oxford: Oxford University Press, 1998). See also the exchange between Gould and Morris in *Natural History* 107 (1998): 48-55.

6. Simon Conway Morris, *Life's Solution: Inevitable Humans in a Lonely Universe* (Cambridge: Cambridge University Press, 2003).

7. Conway Morris, *Life's Solution*, p. 124.

8. Conway Morris, *Life's Solution*, p. 328.

sistent with Conway Morris's religious beliefs as a Christian, though he grants that science does not provide any proof of theism.

> Life is also pervaded by inherencies by which I mean that much of the template of complex life is assembled long before the structures themselves evolve. Following on, we can also see that, far from being a contingent muddle, life is pervaded with directionality; by no means everything is possible, but what is possible will evolve repeatedly. Finally, life constantly surprises us with its elegance and economy of construction, yet all of it emerges from a common and seemingly unremarkable substrate. None of this can be used to prove the activity of the Creator, but it seems consistent.[9]

I would argue that Gould has overemphasized the role of contingency and Conway Morris has underemphasized it. It is, of course, rather speculative to estimate probabilities with a sample of only one evolutionary history on one planet. There seems to be more directionality in evolution on Earth than Gould acknowledges but less than Conway Morris portrays. Conway Morris interprets convergence as the fulfillment of a detailed plan — whether preordained by God or predetermined by formal relationships that limit the range of viable possibilities. In his view, contingencies do not alter the outcome. Gould thinks life on other planets will have little in common with life on Earth; Conway Morris expects life on other planets (if suitable ones exist) to closely resemble life on Earth. A middle position would lead us to expect creatures with intelligence and consciousness, but not with ten fingers and ten toes.

I suggest that a middle ground between Gould and Morris would also be consistent with process philosophy, which envisages a broad directionality and teleology in cosmic history but not a detailed preordained goal. In traditional Christian thought, history was taken to be the realization of a preexisting divine plan, but in process thought the future is always unpredictable and never inevitable. God presents new possibilities to the world in each new context but leaves alternatives open, eliciting the response of entities in the world. This is a God of persuasion rather than coercion and a world of freedom and novelty as well as of order and structure. God is not the transcendent Sovereign of classical Christianity, but interacts reciprocally with the changing world, an influence on all events though never the sole cause of any event. Process metaphysics

---

9. Simon Conway Morris, "The Paradoxes of Evolution: Inevitable Humans in a Lonely Universe?" in *God and Design: The Teleological Argument and Modern Science*, ed. Neil A. Manson (London: Routledge, 2003), p. 334.

understands every momentary entity to be jointly the product of past causes, divine purposes, and the entity's own activity.[10]

Scientists have been understandably wary of concepts of purpose. The idea of divine purpose in nature, especially the assumption of a precise design or plan, has sometimes cut short the search for natural causes. Reference to the purposes held by natural agents has also hindered the progress of science. Aristotle, for example, said a falling body seeks its natural resting place and an oak seed seeks to become an oak. But process thinkers avoid these pitfalls. They argue that concepts of anticipation and purposeful behavior can in attenuated form be extended to lower life-forms, but this does not exclude the presence of efficient causes. The resistance of some biologists to any reference to purposes may be partly a legacy of atomistic and materialistic assumptions of the past.

## The Baldwin Effect and Interiority

Bruce Weber and David Depew have recently edited an interesting collection of essays, *Evolution and Learning: The Baldwin Effect Reconsidered.*[11] Depew's opening chapter suggests that interpretations of the Baldwin effect and reactions to it have been strongly influenced by the changing conceptual assumptions of the dominant evolutionary theories. In 1896 James Baldwin proposed that the initiatives of organisms and their learned behavior play a significant role in evolutionary history.[12] At that time August Weismann had dealt what seemed a deathblow to the Lamarckian claim that traits acquired during an organism's lifetime could be inherited by later generations. Weismann showed that germ-line cells are sequestered from somatic cells and are not affected by any changes during the life of the organism. In Weismann's view all changes are initiated by random genetic variations, which are subsequently selected by the environment.

In reacting to Weismann, Baldwin acknowledged that learned behaviors cannot be directly inherited, but he proposed an indirect route by which the

---

10. Ian G. Barbour, *Religion and Science: Historical and Contemporary Issues* (San Francisco: HarperSanFrancisco, 1997), pp. 293-97.

11. Bruce Weber and David Depew, *Evolution and Learning: The Baldwin Effect Reconsidered* (Cambridge: MIT Press, 2003).

12. J. M. Baldwin, "A New Factor in Evolution," *American Naturalist* 30 (1986): 441-51, and *Development and Evolution* (New York: Macmillan, 1902). See also Robert J. Richards, *Darwin and the Emergence of Evolutionary Theories of Mind and Behavior* (Chicago: University of Chicago Press, 1987), chapter 10.

initiatives of organisms could lead to genetic changes and affect the direction of evolutionary change. A new behavior initiated by an individual organism could be imitated by other individuals and socially transmitted for a long enough period that genetic mutations supportive of that behavior could occur. Natural selection would then perpetuate genetically what had been initiated behaviorally. Moreover, though environments select organisms, organisms also select environments. Lamarck's emphasis on the agency of organisms could still be maintained, but without the Lamarckian belief in direct inheritance. Baldwin also defended the role of mind in evolutionary history, but without any implication that organisms consciously choose to evolve in a particular way.

Depew shows that by the time of the modern synthesis, forty years later, natural selection was understood as a change in the survival and reproductive rates of populations rather than in terms of the life and death of individuals. In this new context Julian Huxley defended the Baldwin effect as a way in which habitats could be extended and behavior modified and subsequently supported by the selection of favorable mutations. Mayr completely dismissed the effect, while Simpson held that it was a possible mechanism but not necessary to explain the spread of learned behaviors in social interactions. Meanwhile C. H. Waddington had proposed a theory of "genetic assimilation" that had some features in common with the Baldwin effect.[13] He found that environmental shock, such as extreme heat, applied to fruit flies in the early stages of development produced new phenotypes that were inherited in subsequent generations. Destabilizing a developmental system, he said, revealed alternative genetic patterns at a deeper level that could be passed on. This was a rather different mechanism from Baldwin's, though they are often conflated. However, recent theorists have again picked up Waddington's interest in embryology, which was ignored by most evolutionary theorists in his day.

The chapters in the Weber and Depew volume reflect a recent interest in Baldwin's ideas, reinterpreted in new conceptual frameworks. A chapter by Daniel Dennett describes the evolution of an organism as the exploration of its "fitness landscape" in the "design space" of possible modifications.[14] Behavioral plasticity and the capacity to learn from trial and error accelerate the discovery of design improvements. A "good trick" that solves a pressing adaptive problem can be socially shared until a subsequent change in gene frequencies

13. C. H. Waddington, *Organisers and Genes* (Cambridge: Cambridge University Press, 1940), and *The Strategy of the Genes* (New York: Macmillan, 1957).

14. Daniel Dennett, "The Baldwin Effect: A Crane, Not a Skyhook," in *Evolution and Learning*.

enhances its effectiveness. Dennett considers this a version of the Baldwin effect. In an earlier book, he wrote, "animals by dint of their own clever activities might hasten and guide the further evolution of their species."[15] Redesign at the level of genes will follow the lead and confirm the direction taken by individual organisms in their successful explorations. For Dennett, however, mentality and consciousness are just ways of talking about information-processing systems. He views natural selection as an algorithm for exploring a potential fitness landscape, and he thinks it can be described in computational terms without any distinctive role for mind.

Two chapters by Terrence Deacon support what he calls "Baldwinian ideas."[16] Here, as in his book *The Symbolic Species*,[17] he questions the insistence in the modern synthesis that changes in gene frequency must precede phenotypic inheritability. He argues that variant behaviors can be established before any shift in gene frequencies support such behavior. Like Baldwin, he stresses the initiative of organisms in seeking and even constructing new environments ("niche construction"). In the human case these niches involve both ecological and cultural changes, as in the advent of agriculture, which alters the environment and then the human genes (for example, sickle-cell anemia as a response to the spread of malaria following changes in agricultural methods). Deacon is particularly interested in the interweaving of neurological and social factors in the evolution of human language. For him the capacity for symbolic representation and communication, accompanied by changes in the organization (and not just the size) of the brain, is the key to the distinctive human capacity to imagine alternative futures. Deacon, like Baldwin, defends the role of mental life in evolutionary history.

Weber notes that Gerald Edelman credits Baldwin with being the first person to emphasize the importance of plasticity in developmental processes. Edelman has shown that the structure of the brain in the embryo and in the growing organism is not genetically determined or hardwired, but is in fact strongly influenced by its experience. Connections are strengthened by use and weakened by disuse; cells not making synaptic connections simply die off in large numbers. Edelman says feedback pathways are selected that support the ongoing experience of the organism. In evolutionary history, he holds, this

15. Daniel Dennett, *Darwin's Dangerous Idea* (New York: Simon and Schuster, 1995), p. 77, emphasis in original.

16. Terrence W. Deacon, "Multilevel Selection in a Complex Adaptive System: The Problem of Language Origin" and "The Hierarchic Logic of Emergence: Untangling the Interdependence of Evolution and Self-Organization," in *Evolution and Learning*.

17. Terrence W. Deacon, *The Symbolic Species: The Coevolution of Language and Brain* (New York: Norton, 1997).

leads to the emergence of social relationships, consciousness, language, and subjective self-consciousness.[18]

Susan Oyama discusses developmental systems extensively in her contribution to the Weber and Depew volume.[19] She maintains that Baldwin and many of his defenders reacted to prevailing mechanistic views and sought a way to insert mind as an independent source of evolutionary change. They portrayed a separate channel for the flow of information between generations in addition to that provided by the genes. Oyama thinks this perpetuates a dualistic view of body and mind that leads to a dualism of inherited versus acquired characteristics (or in broader terms, a contrast of nature versus nurture). She proposes that if heredity is seen as a spatially and temporally extended process, we do not have to introduce internal mental forces to supplement purely external selective forces.

Oyama acknowledges that evolution requires stable repetition and variation, but she holds that these are provided not just by genes but also by repeated developmental cycles involving the whole organism and its environment. Development is a multilevel process of construction using resources that are transmitted from generation to generation in diverse ways. She describes the context-sensitive dynamics and ecological embeddedness of developmental systems. Evolutionary change is not defined by genetic change and does not have to be initiated by genetic change. Like Baldwin, she insists that active organisms alter the contexts of their development and selection so the construction of organisms and environments is mutual and interactive. But by describing an integral many-leveled process, she hopes to avoid any tendency to contrast acquired and inherited traits or mental and physical causes as if they could be considered separately.

I suggest that process thinkers should welcome this renewed interest in the Baldwin effect, even though it is found in only a minority of evolutionary biologists. Process metaphysics postulates at least a minimal novelty and creativity in integrated entities at all levels. In this framework, one would expect the initiatives of organisms to have significant long-term consequences. Process thought postulates that every integrated entity has a momentary inwardness or subjectivity in addition to the external objective causal influences it receives from the past and exerts on other entities in the future. The evolution of interiority, like the evolution of physical structures, is characterized by both continuity and change. The forms taken by interiority vary widely, starting from rudi-

18. Gerald W. Edelman, *Bright Air, Brilliant Fire: On the Matter of the Mind* (New York: Basic Books, 1992).

19. Susan Oyama, "On Having a Hammer," in *Evolution and Learning.*

mentary memory, sentience, responsiveness, and anticipation in simple organisms, going on to consciousness with the advent of nervous systems, and then self-consciousness in the case of primates and human beings. As David Griffin suggests, it is preferable to describe such interiority as a moment of experience (panexperientialism) rather than as a form of mind (panpsychism) because the latter term still carries for most people a legacy of mind-body dualism.[20]

## Complexity and Design

Griffin acknowledges the Baldwin effect. "It is well accepted that organisms by purposefully adopting a new pattern of behavior, can bring about genetic changes in their species, insofar as the new behavior means that certain random mutations, if and when they occur, will be selected for." But Griffin would like to go further than this. He says Whiteheadian metaphysics "can allow that an organism's need or desire might more directly lead to change in the genome."[21] He accepts Michael Behe's claim that the "irreducible complexity" of living systems shows that they cannot be the product of gradual evolution. Behe argues that complex biological structures and long chains of molecular reactions could not have had simpler functional precursors because they would not have worked if even a single component had been missing. Behe offers the analogy of a mousetrap with five parts. If one part, such as the spring, were missing, the trap would not work at all. It is an all-or-nothing system that must have been designed all at once, not by stages.[22] Griffin says that, when he has defended Behe, biologists have often responded that evolutionary explanations of many of these complex phenomena have been given, but he asserts that he has been unable to find any such accounts. "That such accounts exist seems to be something that is widely known, but I have yet to find anyone who knows where they exist."[23]

This is a puzzling statement because at that time there was already an impressive literature replying to Behe, and it has grown considerably since then. Previous claims of "the God of the gaps" were vulnerable if those gaps were

20. David Ray Griffin, "Some Whiteheadian Comments," in *Mind and Nature: Essays on the Interface of Science and Philosophy,* ed. John Cobb, Jr., and David Griffin (Washington, D.C.: University Press of America, 1977).

21. David Ray Griffin, *Religion and Scientific Naturalism* (Albany: State University of New York Press, 2000), p. 299.

22. Michael Behe, *Darwin's Black Box* (New York: Free Press, 1998).

23. Griffin, *Religion and Scientific Naturalism,* p. 287 n. 23.

later filled in, but Behe insists that evolutionary explanations of "irreducible complexity" are in principle impossible. To refute this claim it is not necessary to find historical evidence of the particular series of evolutionary steps that was actually followed. One need only provide detailed scientific evidence for a plausible series of possible steps. Many evolutionary advances can be understood as a combination of components already available rather than as the introduction of a total system designed from scratch.[24] For example, an enzyme that initially served one function could have been co-opted for a new function in a different context. One of Behe's most dramatic examples is the rotation of the hairlike flagella of bacteria by which they move around. The biologist Kenneth Miller shows that structures providing motility on other types of cells lack two or three of the components that Behe says are essential. He also shows that many proteins in the structure of bacterial flagella are identical or very similar to proteins that serve other functions elsewhere in the cell, such as secretion or contraction rather than motility.[25] Such evidence is particularly important because Behe's writing has been used by evangelical Christians to support their efforts to have "Intelligent Design" included as an alternative to evolution in biology texts and classes in the public schools.

Though Griffin supports Behe's criticisms of evolutionary theory, he rejects Behe's belief that coordinated design was intermittently introduced by supernatural intervention, either with the first cell or in subsequent history. According to Griffin, God continually presents every momentary entity with new relevant possibilities to which it can respond. He asks: "What is it that holds many groups of animals to an astonishingly constant form over millions of years?"[26] And what produces "well-integrated changes" when they occur? He suggests that God introduces new ideal forms or archetypes. He describes Whitehead's theory of "eternal objects," which assumes the reality of preexisting Platonic forms. Griffin says we have intuitions of eternal forms of beauty, mathematics, and logic. He argues that Whiteheadian metaphysics would allow a novel form prehended by the psyche of an animal to be taken directly into its genome and passed on to its descendants.

---

24. Collections of essays for and against Intelligent Design are identified in Neil A. Manson, ed., *God and Design: The Teleological Argument and Modern Science* (London and New York: Routledge, 2003), and Roland T. Pennock, ed., *Intelligent Design Creationism and Its Critics: Philosophical, Theological, and Scientific Perspectives* (Cambridge: MIT Press, 2001). A bibliography of recent articles can be found on the Web site of the National Center for Science Education at www.ncseweb.org.

25. Kenneth Miller, "Answering the Biological Argument from Design," in *God and Design.*

26. Griffin, *Religion and Scientific Naturalism*, p. 289 (quoting William Thorpe).

I believe that such essentialism does not do justice to the dynamic character of evolutionary systems in which organisms continually respond to each other and to changing environments. It seems to minimize the role of contingency in evolutionary history, as Conway Morris does in describing "convergent evolution." I would argue, with Susan Oyama, that an organism's desires influence the genes not directly but indirectly through the developmental systems, behavioral activities, and ecological contexts of embodied and embedded organisms. I suggest that the divine influence, rather than being passed on within the organism directly to the genes, is mediated through the many-leveled systems of which they are a part.

## Hierarchical Levels and Downward Causation

Many-leveled systems are prominent in many fields of science today: ecosystems in ecology, developmental systems in embryology, neural networks in neuroscience, computer networks designed to simulate natural processes, and so forth. A level identifies a system that is relatively integrated, stable, and self-regulating (such as a cell), even though it interacts with other systems at the same level (such as other cells), lower-level subsystems (molecules), and higher-level systems of which it is a part (an organism with other organisms in an ecosystem). Interdependence, holism, and feedback between levels are characteristic of such systems.

A recent symposium on systems in *Science* includes articles on bacteria, neural networks, electrical networks, and ant colonies.[27] The behavior of individual ants — the route followed in search of food, for example, or the division of time between tasks such as food storage and defense of the colony — is governed by their response to particular molecules (pheromones) laid down by other ants. Their behavior can be simulated on a computer screen by a program that follows a few simple rules. The integrated behavior of the colony apparently arises from simple rules for local interactions. Compared to the complexity and many levels of organization of the individual ant, the social organization of the colony is relatively simple and inflexible and has very limited channels of communication. But the colony itself has its own life cycle and is of course the product of a long and many-leveled evolutionary history.[28]

27. "Life and the Art of Networks," *Science* 30 (September 26, 2003): 1863-74.
28. See Steven Johnson, *Emergence: The Connected Lives of Ants, Brains, Cities, and Software* (New York: Scribner, 2001).

I have discussed elsewhere[29] the distinction between three kinds of reduction between levels.

1. *Methodological reduction.* This is a research strategy: the study of lower levels in order to better understand relationships at higher levels. Analysis of molecular interactions has been a spectacularly successful strategy in biology, but it is not incompatible with multilevel analysis and the study of larger systems.

2. *Epistemological reduction.* This is a relation between theories: the claim that laws and theories at one level can be derived from laws and theories at lower levels. I have argued that biological concepts are distinctive and cannot be defined in physical and chemical terms. Distinctive kinds of explanations are valid at differing levels. But interlevel theories may connect adjacent levels, even if such theories are not derivable from the theories applicable to either level alone. The concepts used at any level may change over time as interlevel theories are developed. A series of overlapping theories and models unifies the sciences without implying that one level is more fundamental or real than another.

3. *Ontological reduction.* This is a claim about the kinds of reality and the kinds of causality that exist in the world. I have defended ontological pluralism, a multileveled view of reality in which differing (epistemological) levels of analysis are taken to refer to differing (ontological) levels of events and processes in the world, as claimed by critical realism.

Bottom-up causation occurs when subsystems influence a system. Top-down causation is the influence of a system on its subsystems. Higher-level events impose boundary conditions on chemical and physical processes at lower levels without violating lower-level laws. The state of the upper-level system is specified without reference to lower-level variables. Network properties may be realized through a great variety of particular connections. Correlation of behaviors at one level does not require detailed knowledge of all its components. The laws of chemistry limit the combinations of atoms that are found in DNA but do not determine them. The meaning of the message conveyed by DNA is given not by the laws of chemistry, but by the interaction of the proteins expressed by the DNA within their wider organismic context.[30] Theo Meyering describes top-down causation as follows:

> [Levels] are related by higher-level principles organizing lower-level events into systemic patterns of interaction. As a result, certain context-dependent

29. Ian G. Barbour, *Issues in Science and Religion* (Englewood Cliffs, N.J.: Prentice-Hall, 1966), pp. 327-37, and *Religion and Science*, pp. 230-35.

30. On top-down causation, see Arthur Peacocke, *Theology for a Scientific Age*, enlarged ed. (Minneapolis: Fortress, 1993), chapter 3.

causal pathways of physical activities will be selectively activated rather than others. . . . Higher-level patterns of organization are themselves genuine causal factors actually operative in channeling and orchestrating the lower-level flux of microphysical events to yield stable recurrent patterns of macrocausation that are self-sustaining or self-reproducing as a result of the systemic organization of their parts.[31]

Among process thinkers, Charles Hartshorne has developed most fully the idea of a hierarchy of levels. His holistic outlook directs attention to system properties that are not evident in the parts alone. Process philosophy has always insisted on contextuality and relationality. But Hartshorne recognizes that various levels may be integrated according to different principles of organization, so their characteristics may be very different. In a complex organism, downward causation from higher to lower levels can occur because every entity is what it is by virtue of its relationships. The atoms in a cell behave differently from the atoms in a stone, and cells in a brain behave differently from those in a plant. Every entity is influenced by its participation in a larger whole. But causal interaction between levels is not total determination; there is some self-determination by integrated entities at all levels, but not in stones and other aggregates in which there is no integration above the level of molecules.[32]

Hartshorne calls an organism "a society of cells." In some societies (for example, a sponge or a tree) the integration occurs at a relatively low level. An ant colony has some coordination and division of labor but no central agent. Other societies are well-unified wholes with dominant members and complex internal organization. Only when a nervous system is present can the unification of the experience of the whole organism be achieved. Even in human beings, however, each cell has considerable independence; various organs and subsystems (heart, endocrine, digestive systems, etc.) function apart from conscious control. In general, patterns of activity at any level are influenced by patterns of activity at both higher and lower levels. One can say that part and whole mutually influence each other, without implying that the whole is somehow an entity existing independently of the parts.

Hartshorne's thought thus combines dipolar monism and organizational pluralism. It is a monism because in contrast to a dualism that postulates two kinds of enduring substances (such as mind and matter), it postulates only one kind of event with two phases. Dipolar monism makes an ontological claim,

31. Theo Meyering, "Downward Causation," in *Encyclopedia of Science and Religion*, ed. J. Wentzel Vrede van Huysteen (New York: Macmillan Reference, 2003), p. 229.
32. Charles Hartshorne, *Reality as Social Process* (Glencoe, Ill.: Free Press, 1953), chapter 1, and *The Logic of Perfection* (La Salle, Ill.: Open Court, 1962), chapter 7.

not merely an epistemological distinction as proposed by some advocates of two-aspect monism. Organizational pluralism indicates recognition that in multilevel processes events can be organized in very diverse ways. All integrated entities at any level have an inner reality and an outer reality, but these take radically different forms at different levels. In contrast to a mind-body dualism of just two substances, process thought allows for many levels of activity in the human organism between molecules and personal selfhood.

## Self-Organization and Emergence

The previous section dealt with the relation between levels in an organism at one point in time. We must now consider the appearance of new levels in the lifetime development of an organism and in evolutionary history. Examples of self-organization in which disorder at one level leads to order at a higher level are found already in the physical world. In unstable systems far from equilibrium, new levels of collective order will appear and achieve stable forms — for example, in the formation of vortices in the turbulent flow of a river or convection cells in a heated liquid. Ilya Prigogine showed that the new higher-level order often cannot be predicted from the behavior of the components.[33] Nonlinear instabilities in dissipative systems have multiple possible outcomes that diverge from each other. Stuart Kauffman finds common patterns in the integrated behavior of systems that appear very different, such as living cells, neural networks, ecosystems, and technological and economic systems. In each case feedback loops and nonlinear interactions make cooperative activity possible in larger wholes. The systems show emergent systemic properties not present in their components.[34]

In one of his contributions to the Weber and Depew volume[35] and in other writing,[36] Terrence Deacon has distinguished three kinds of emergence. In first-order emergence new properties appear in an aggregate, but they can be predicted from lower-level laws and configurational relationships among the components, without knowledge of the previous history of the system. For ex-

33. Ilya Prigogine and Isabelle Stengers, *Order out of Chaos: Man's New Dialogue with Nature* (New York: Bantam Books, 1984).

34. Stuart Kauffman, *At Home in the Universe: The Search for Laws of Self-Organization and Complexity* (New York: Oxford University Press, 1995).

35. Terrence W. Deacon, "The Hierarchic Logic of Emergence," in *Evolution and Learning*.

36. Bruce H. Weber and Terrence W. Deacon, "Thermodynamic Cycles, Developmental Systems, and Emergence," *Cybernetics and Human Knowing* 7, no. 1 (2000): 21-43.

ample, the liquidity of water can be explained by the laws governing hydrogen, oxygen, and their combination into water molecules. Thermodynamic laws for the behavior of gases can be derived from the statistical mechanics of gas molecules. In second-order emergence, system-wide configurations change across time and affect lower-level interactions. Higher-order regularities can become unpredictably unstable and new causal architectures are formed. Chaos theory and complexity theory show critical sensitivity to initial conditions and to historical contingencies. Every falling snowflake is unique because its past history of growth under conditions of variable temperature and humidity constrains its future possibilities.

In third-order emergence, according to Deacon, levels of causality are linked across wider spans of time and space. When features of the state of a system can be represented as a historical memory, the information can be repeatedly reentered at lower levels of the ongoing system. This occurs in differing ways in the development of an embryo, in biological evolution, and in the cultural transmission of information. In the continuing interaction between genes, organisms, populations, and environments, causality is distributed across time and space, forming multilayered systems of great complexity. Adaptation is itself a holistic concept, a complex of traits selected in a wider context. Representation, memory, and reference are crucial features of cognitive processes expressed in global configurations of neural activity in the brain. Deacon defends a "progressive holism" of "top-down configurational causes" in addition to bottom-up causes that have a discrete location in time and space.

Philip Clayton has explored the theological implications of emergence. Genuinely new properties have appeared in later stages of evolutionary history, which cannot be explained by theories applicable to earlier stages. We should therefore accept explanatory pluralism rather than (epistemological) reductionism. But Clayton also advocates ontological pluralism as "the best explanation of explanatory pluralism." Patterns of activity at higher levels are causally effective, exerting a top-down influence on activity at lower levels.[37] Clayton traces three broad stages in evolutionary history and assigns differing roles to God in each.[38]

1. *The physical level.* Though there may be some indeterminacy at this stage, lawfulness predominates and can be seen as an expression of God's constancy. Clayton does not accept the thesis of process thought that there is an in-

37. Philip Clayton, "Neuroscience, the Person, and God: An Emergentist Account," in *Neuroscience and the Person: Scientific Perspectives on Divine Actions*, ed. Robert John Russell, Nancey Murphy, Theo C. Meyering, and Michael Arbib (Vatican City: Vatican Observatory; Berkeley: Center for Theology and the Natural Sciences, 1999).

38. Philip Clayton, "The Emergence of Spirit," *CTNS Bulletin* 20, no. 4 (Fall 2000): 3-20.

wardness in integrated entities at all levels to which God can offer relevant pos-sibilities. But Clayton insists that deism can be avoided because, according to the panentheism that he defends, God is always present in the world — even if only as the upholder of order and regularity.

2. *The biological level.* Here information, function, and form are crucial. In this context it makes sense to speak of the role of information as formal causality. Moreover, the historicity of organisms and their changing evolutionary environ-ments are important; Clayton cites Deacon's view of third-order emergence. With more complex living organisms, purposiveness mentality and protomentality are present. Clayton holds that divine intentionality can influence the drives and un-conscious goals of organisms, as process philosophers hold. He says, "process thinkers do not respond adequately to what we have learned about the emergent structure of the natural world."[39] He claims that biology shows that purposive-ness mentality and protomentality are present only after the emergence of life.

3. *The human level.* Mental properties differ in kind from properties at lower levels, and mental activities exert a distinctive type of causality. Clayton writes: "I have argued the real existence and causal efficacy of the conscious or mental dimension of human personhood."[40] Ideas and intentions can change history. God can influence our thoughts and motives at the mental level with-out violating lower-level laws. Human/divine interaction in religious experi-ence, human history, and culture goes far beyond anything previously possible. Prehuman life reveals little of the personal character of the divine, but human life can be an expression of God's personal agency.

In his contribution to the recent Festschrift honoring my eightieth birth-day, Clayton indicates many points of agreement between his views and mine.[41] But he holds that process thought does not allow for genuine novelty because it extrapolates interiority down to the lowest levels. He says that despite White-head's frequent reference to novelty and creativity, there can be no real emer-gence if the same ontological categories apply to events all the way down. Now Clayton does quote my statement that "Whitehead himself was so intent on a set of metaphysical categories applicable to all events that I believe he gave in-sufficient attention to the radically different ways in which those categories are exemplified at different levels."[42] But Clayton does not discuss my claim that this defect is remedied by Hartshorne's defense of organizational pluralism — which makes possible the emergence of significant new phenomena such as re-

39. Clayton, "The Emergence of Spirit," p. 15.

40. Clayton, "Neuroscience," p. 211.

41. Philip Clayton, "Barbour's Panentheistic Metaphysics," in *Fifty Years in Science and Religion: Ian Barbour and His Legacy,* ed. Robert John Russell (Aldershot, U.K.: Ashgate, 2004).

42. Ian G. Barbour, *Nature, Human Nature, and God* (Minneapolis: Fortress, 2002), p. 37.

sponsiveness, purposiveness, sentience, consciousness, and self-consciousness, each of which is causally effective in a distinctive way.

Clayton balances continuity and discontinuity in evolutionary history, but for him discontinuity prevails at the transitions between physical, biological, and human stages. The contrast he draws between the three major stages is so strong that it seems to exclude the possibility of intermediate stages that might help us to explain the transitions between them. And by limiting God's role in the physical world to that of upholding lawful regularities, Clayton denies any possibility of divine action before the advent of life. Such a limitation of God's power in cosmic history is an even more radical departure from the biblical tradition and classical theism than the limitation of God's power that is defended by process thought.[43]

## Science and Metaphysics

Clayton and I both acknowledge a two-way interaction between science and metaphysics.[44] On the one hand, science influences metaphysics. Philosophical reflection must take well-established theories into account. On the other hand, metaphysical assumptions influence the interpretation of scientific theories and even the theories themselves — especially in the choice among competing models and among paradigms reflecting alternative conceptual frameworks. A similar two-way relationship exists between religious beliefs and metaphysics, though conceptual frameworks in religion are much more influential because of their role in the interpretation of religious experience within particular historical traditions.[45] Both Clayton and I therefore give an epistemological privilege to science over religion, but I think that for him that privilege is more heavily weighted toward science.

Clayton claims that the findings of science are "incompatible" with the presence of interiority before the appearance of life.[46] I would agree that the effects of interiority at the physical level are indeed negligible, though indeterminacy, holism, and top-down causality are already evident at that level. But I would argue that a minimal interiority can be postulated even at the physical level for the sake of metaphysical consistency and generality. New phenomena and new properties emerge historically, but we should seek fundamental cate-

---

43. Ian G. Barbour, "God's Power: A Process View," in *The Work of Love: Creation as Kenosis*, ed. John Polkinghorne (London: SPCK, 2001).

44. Clayton, "Barbour's Panentheistic Metaphysics," p. xx.

45. Ian G. Barbour, *Myths, Models, and Paradigms* (London: SCM, 1974).

46. Clayton, "Barbour's Panentheistic Metaphysics."

gories that are as universal as possible — though I have suggested that White-head's application of them did not do justice to isolated particles at the lowest level or human selfhood at the highest. Our categories must also represent the continuity of developmental processes and of evolutionary history, and the impossibility of drawing any sharp lines between stages.[47]

Moreover, we have immediate access to human experience. I know myself as an experiencing subject. We are part of nature; even though human experience is an extreme case of an event in nature, it offers clues as to the character of other events. To be sure, we must avoid the dangers of anthropomorphism, the assumption that other creatures are just like us. But we must also avoid the dangers of mechanomorphism, the assumption that other creatures are just like machines.[48]

Is the subjective experience postulated in process thought accessible to scientific investigation? Does not science have to start from objective data accessible to all observers? Whitehead sometimes stresses the selectivity of science and the abstractive character of its concepts. He calls the temptation to think that scientific concepts provide an exhaustive description of the real world "the fallacy of misplaced concreteness." He writes: "Science can find no individual enjoyment in nature; science can find no aim in nature; science can find no creativity in nature; it finds mere rules of succession. These negations are true of natural science; they are inherent in its methodology."[49] On this reading, we must accept the limitations of science and supplement it by including it in a wider metaphysical synthesis that integrates diverse kinds of experience. This view would also limit the contribution that process metaphysics might make to science.

After discussing Teilhard de Chardin's concept of "the within," John Haught concludes:

> This does not mean that theology must reject science's methodological bracketing of the fact of subjectivity in nature. Science has every right to leave out all considerations of subjectivity as long as its practitioners remain aware of this self-limitation. It is of utmost importance that a theology in dialogue with science have available to it a metaphysics fully aware that science, in its attempt to be clear and distinct, has left behind what is truly fundamental in the natural world, including the possibility of a vein of subjectivity inaccessible to scientific objectification.[50]

47. Barbour, *Religion and Science*, p. 290; Barbour, *Nature*, pp. 37, 99.

48. Barbour, *Nature*, p. 99.

49. Alfred North Whitehead, *Modes of Thought* (Cambridge: Cambridge University Press, 1938), p. 211.

50. John F. Haught, *God after Darwin: A Theology of Evolution* (Boulder, Colo.: Westview, 2000), pp. 178, 179.

By contrast, Griffin has pointed to other passages in which Whitehead says that adequate metaphysical categories are in the interest of science itself and that scientific concepts are after all reformable. Griffin suggests that if every entity is for itself a moment of experience, one would expect this to be reflected in observable behavior. As noted earlier, he accepts the idea that the initiative and creativity of organisms have initiated evolutionary changes (the Baldwin effect). He points out that ethologists use explanatory concepts referring to the mental life of birds and animals. As we consider lower levels, he asks, how can we draw a sharp line at any point? He holds, moreover, that scientists adopting a process metaphysics would be likely to redirect research to problems neglected by other scientists, and they might propose new concepts and theories and ways of testing them observationally.[51] I am inclined to agree with Griffin here, though I agree with Haught that we must be aware of the limitations of science and the need to draw from diverse forms of human experience.

I have suggested five topics in the interpretation of evolutionary history in which I believe we need new concepts that go beyond the refinement of neo-Darwinism: contingency and teleology, the Baldwin effect and interiority, complexity and design, hierarchical levels and downward causation, and self-organization and emergence. The new concepts I discussed were introduced by people who were not familiar with process philosophy, though they shared many of its ideas. I have tried to show that these concepts are supportive of the central tenets of process philosophy, especially in Hartshorne's version. I have said also that philosophical assumptions inevitably influence the formulation of scientific theories, even though theories must always be tested against empirical evidence. Process thought encourages an interest in these five topics that may have been too readily dismissed by scientists influenced by the prevalent philosophies of reductionism and materialism. Hopefully the dialogue can be fruitful between philosophers or theologians well informed about current evolutionary theories and biologists open to alternative philosophical assumptions.

---

51. David Ray Griffin, "On Ian Barbour's *Issues in Science and Religion,*" *Zygon* 23 (1988): 57-81.

# 14. *Organisms as Agents in Evolution*

John B. Cobb, Jr.

## A Whiteheadian Alternative

Whitehead thought human thinking is prone to commit "the fallacy of misplaced concreteness."[1] He explained that we cannot think at all without abstractions. As a mathematician he was aware of the enormous gains that have been made with the use of abstractions. There is no doubt that neo-Darwinian theory, for example, has brought about great advances in evolutionary biology by directing attention to important features of the history of living organisms. However, the inevitability and usefulness of abstractions carry the danger that we neglect those elements in the concrete world that are left out of our most fruitful abstractions. We then treat our abstractions and the complex theories that we derive from them as if they accurately described reality. This leads to overstatements that direct attention away from other potentially fruitful lines of inquiry. These overstatements can become so rigid that they are in fact false. The thesis of this chapter is that neo-Darwinian theory commits the fallacy of misplaced concreteness.

In Whiteheadian perspective, the development of life on this planet has been extremely complex. There is no way of telling the complete story about even any portion of it, because the simplest organism is already more than any set of abstractions can describe. But this is not a counsel of despair. Within all this complexity there are repetitive patterns that can be described accurately in abstractions. Scientists can provide rigorous definitions and theories that have wide application and allow for extensive predictions. If they do not suppose

---

1. Alfred North Whitehead, *Science and the Modern World: Lowell Lectures, 1925* (New York: Free Press, 1967), p. 51; Whitehead, *Process and Reality: An Essay in Cosmology,* corrected edition by David Ray Griffin and Donald W. Sherburne (New York: Free Press, 1978), p. 7.

that they have then described the actuality of things in their concrete reality, no fallacy has been committed. However, there is a widespread tendency to forget that much has been left out or to think of what is left out as unimportant.

In the history of evolutionary theory one great achievement was the discovery that the complex and highly functional systems that characterize organisms can be produced by natural selection. A second great discovery was that the organisms among which nature selected were shaped by their genes, and that significant changes in the organisms occurred when genes replicated imperfectly. This showed that evolution is expressed in genetic changes that govern phenotypical ones. A third discovery was that genes are remarkably well insulated from environmental effects. A fourth was that the imperfect replication of genes generally had deleterious effects, so that they were clearly not designed in themselves to improve the chances of the organism to survive and reproduce. It was, however, this random mutation of genes that occasionally led to improved reproductive success and eventually to new species.

These discoveries led to quite simple explanations of evolution that were explanatory of many phenomena. The picture that emerged and that still dominates the standard explanation of evolution to the public is somewhat as follows. Individual genes have the characteristics once attributed to atoms. They are basically self-contained, and any influence by their environment could be neglected. These genes generally reproduce themselves exactly, but occasionally there are random changes not affected by their cellular or organismic environment. These changes affect the phenotype of the organism in which they occur, and on the rare occasions on which they enable the organism to adapt more successfully to its environment, the organism survives longer and reproduces more. The changed or new gene is then transmitted to a larger portion of the next generation. Thus a process that involves no purposeful activity, indeed no subjectivity of any kind, explains the course of evolution. The significant causal relations are unidirectional — from the gene to the organism and from the environment to the organism. The organism is described as the recipient of causal forces and not as an agent.

In this volume Francisco Ayala represents the scientific side of neo-Darwinism, the side to which part II is dedicated. In part I, chapter 2, he offers the following statement about the determinants of evolution: "The variables determining in which direction [natural selection] will go are the environment, the preexisting constitution of the organisms, and the randomly arising mutations." He goes on to explain the meaning of "randomly." Mutations are accidental or chance events in three senses: (1) "they are rare exceptions to the regularity of the process of DNA replication, which normally involves precise copying of the hereditary information, encoded in the nucleotide sequences";

(2) "there is no way of knowing whether a given gene or genome will mutate in a particular cell or in a particular generation"; and (3) the mutations "are unoriented with respect to adaptation."

To eyes informed by Whitehead's thought, this picture looks too much influenced by a materialist model. Whitehead calls his position a philosophy of organism. Rather than modeling organisms on mechanisms constituted of matter in motion, as most biology tends to do, Whitehead thought science should model the basic units of physics on organisms. The primary difference is that, unlike matter, which is inert and related to other bits of matter only externally, organisms are agents of action as well as recipients of the actions of others. Their relations with other organisms are internal, that is, they influence what the organism becomes. In Whitehead's view, everything interacts with its environment. Nothing is what it is or acts as it does apart from its relations to other things. Accordingly, the Whiteheadian is prejudiced toward the belief that the simplistic picture of the evolutionary process, still so widely presented to the public, commits the fallacy of misplaced concreteness in quite serious ways.

Indeed, Whitehead makes strong statements about the inadequacy of materialism as a basis for explaining evolution. He wrote that "a thoroughgoing evolutionary philosophy is incompatible with materialism. The aboriginal stuff, or material, from which a materialistic philosophy starts is incapable of evolution. . . . Evolution, on the materialistic theory, is reduced to the role of being another word for the description of the changes of external relations between portions of matter. There is nothing to evolve, because one set of external relations is as good as any other set of external relations."[2]

Whitehead, writing in 1925, assumed that the advocates of evolution saw it as a way of explaining the rise of more valuable entities from less valuable ones. Darwin himself thought he had explained the emergence of creatures of greater value from lesser ones by this theory, and the general public as well as most biologists shared in this assumption. Accordingly, some notion of progress was part of the meaning of evolution. Whitehead pointed out the inconsistency of making such an assumption while adopting a materialist science and philosophy.

However, the commitment to materialism by biologists has proved stronger than the belief that evolution explains an advance of any kind. Instead of adopting a philosophy of organism that could explain evolution in the sense of how more valuable organisms arose, they chose to accept the consequences of their materialism and redefine evolution. Today, exponents of neo-Darwinism typically accept and even emphasize that they are not describing an evolutionary as-

2. Whitehead, *Science*, p. 107.

cent or any kind of progress. They are simply explaining changes. The only sense of "better" that they affirm is in relation to adaptation to environment. Hence, a chimpanzee would be an advance over a paramecium only if it were better adapted to its environment than the paramecium was to its. Accordingly, the fact that materialism precluded the value judgments Whitehead took for granted does not count now as an argument against the adequacy of materialism.

The issue, then, is philosophical. Should we accept a materialist philosophy and its rejection of all judgments of value, or should we adopt an organismic philosophy that can affirm such judgments? This kind of question belongs to part III of this book. There it becomes clear that judgments about what is of value in itself are about subjects, whereas neo-Darwinism, in common with most of science, limits itself to the study of objects. We all know that some of our experiences are of greater value than others, and we can examine the characteristics of these experiences that lead us to this judgment. Whitehead showed us how we can integrate reflection about our subjective experience with our study of the objective world.

For something to have value in itself, it must have existence or reality for itself. That which exists only as an object for other things can have only instrumental value for those other things. Whiteheadians believe that all the unitary entities that make up the world have reality in themselves as well as for others. Therefore, all have some intrinsic value. But we believe that the value may be very slight or very considerable. We believe that animals with central nervous systems have far richer experience than unicellular organisms or the cells that make up plants and animals, although these cells are not valueless. For this reason we believe that evolution began with entities of very modest intrinsic value and has produced creatures of much greater value. Overall, therefore, there has been enormous progress.

From the perspective of process thinkers, then, the inability of thoroughgoing neo-Darwinians to speak of progress is a weakness. It leads them in the direction of nihilism. But since they agree that their position is incompatible with judgments of greater or lesser value, and since they sometimes celebrate the consequences, which include the rejection of any claim that human beings are superior to other creatures, for us to point out this omission is not an argument against them. They can understand their topic to be the rearrangements of bits of matter and their task as explaining how these occur.

Accordingly, the adequacy of the standard formulation of the neo-Darwinian model must be judged in a different way. Its adequacy is to a large extent a factual question, and factual questions cannot be settled by metaphysical biases. We must ask whether there are scientific reasons to think that their account of how evolution has occurred is too limited.

Actually, Ayala and most other neo-Darwinian biologists readily acknowledge full awareness of many complications, complications that their own research has brought to light. Indeed, between his summary of the variables operative in evolution and his explanation of what is meant by randomness, Ayala has inserted a paragraph that shows his comprehensive knowledge of the complexity of the actual process.

> The process of mutation that provides the raw materials for natural selection is now known to be much more complex than it was thought a few decades ago. There are the point mutations, changes of a single nucleotide by another in the DNA, which in protein-coding genes may or may not change the encoded protein; some mutations involve DNA segments within a single gene or that implicate more than one gene; genes and DNA segments change locations; there are chromosomal mutations that involve exchanges between chromosomes (and, thus, involving many genes), and that fuse, split, duplicate one or more chromosomes, even a complete chromosome complement, as in the polyploidy; genomes are very dynamic, continuously experiencing additions, duplications, deletions and all sorts of changes, implicating from very small to huge DNA segments.

The issue is, then, whether all these changes are "random" in the sense Ayala describes above. The impression given there is that mutations are imperfect replications, and that it is these that are random. The argument for randomness is normally directed only to these inexact replications. That all these other ways in which genes and genomes change are random in the same sense would have to be shown in detail. Near the end of this chapter, I will revisit the randomness of all genetic change.

Before pursuing the issue of randomness further, I will build on the preceding chapters in part II to identify the most important omission from Ayala's list of variables responsible for evolution. In particular I will argue that the activity of organisms plays a large role in determining the direction taken by evolution. Whereas Ayala's formulation follows standard neo-Darwinism in depicting the multicellular organism as an object shaped by randomly mutating genes and selected by the environment, I will argue that the relations of such organisms both to their environment and to genes are reciprocal. The actions of organisms, directly or indirectly, affect both the environment and the genomes. This means that the actions of organisms constitute an independent variable that cannot be reduced to the three specified by Ayala.

Furthermore, the actions of organisms do not share in the purposelessness that characterizes random mutation and environmental selection. Although this is obviously true only in animals with complex brains, Whiteheadians speculate, in light of the continuity that evolutionary thinking emphasizes, that a telic element characterizes cells and even quanta, and all the organisms in between. Indeed, process thinkers see the world as made up of organisms interacting with one another rather than of matter in motion. We believe that a theory of evolution formulated in these terms is both more adequate to the evidence and more congenial to deep-seated humanistic and religious values.

## The Wider Setting

Earlier chapters in this part gave considerable attention to the relation of biology to physics. We should note that whereas the standard formulation is generally reductive, the process of reduction stops at the level of genes. No scientist questions that genes are complex entities ultimately composed of subatomic entities. A great deal of work has been done in physics with respect to these entities. In chapter 6, A. Y. Gunter summarizes ideas about evolution to which quantum theory has given rise.

Further, as Dorion Sagan emphasizes in chapter 7, much work in physics has been done on self-organization and the second law of thermodynamics. He believes that what has been learned on these topics can illumine the process of evolution. Many phenomena that have seemed unique to living things have analogues in the inanimate world.

## The Role of Organisms

Thus far I have argued that the physical analysis of both genes and organisms may prove illuminating of the evolutionary process. However, this book deals chiefly with specifically biological phenomena. In this connection, we have noted, Ayala identified three variables operative in evolution: the genes or genomes, the environment, and the organisms that evolve. However, he specifies only the preexisting condition of the organisms. He says nothing about how their activity contributes to evolution. The primary topic of this chapter is to criticize this exclusion and to call for the inclusion of the activity of organisms as a major factor in evolution.

Few neo-Darwinists reject all evidence for the role of the activity of organisms, but they do not give it any significant place in their theory and rarely mention it in presenting this theory to the public. Even mating, a form of activity with obvious genetic consequences, is often not mentioned as a factor in evolution. From the point of view of process thought, the neglect of the activity of organisms, including intelligent and purposeful activity, is a serious weakness in neo-Darwinian theory.

The argument involves several stages, most of them uncontroversial. First, genes by themselves do not fully determine phenotypes. Second, "natural selection" is of phenotypes rather than directly of genes. Third, the environment affects the phenotype. Fourth, the activity of organisms (phenotype) is not all genetically programmed. Fifth, unprogrammed activities of organisms affect natural selection. Sixth, the activity of organisms affects the environment, so that the environment that selects among phenotypes that will survive and reproduce is itself in part the result of the activity of organisms. Seventh, even the genes are affected by the activity of organisms. Eighth, this activity is sometimes intelligently purposeful.

I will develop the argument in three stages: by considering the importance for evolutionary theory of the first three points above; by arguing that the relationship of the environment and the organism is affected by unprogrammed activities of the organism; and by pointing out that in some instances the action of the organism on the environment involves intelligent purposiveness.

For the first stage I have the full support of Francisco Ayala. Although his formulation of what directs evolution followed by his discussion of random mutations suggests that the variability of the organisms among which the environment selects comes only from random mutations, elsewhere he makes clear that this is by no means his intention. The concluding paragraph of his essay on the Baldwin effect (chapter 12 above) points to a quite different understanding of what is involved in the evolutionary process. "Indeed, the Baldwin effect has been generally involved in the origin of evolutionary novelties. Evolutionary novelties are reorganizations of preexisting phenotypes, which first arise in response to environmental challenges (given that all genotypes have enormous plasticity, that is, a wide norm of reaction), but eventually become genetically determined if the particular environmental challenges persist and the adaptation importantly contributes to survival and reproductive success."

Ayala defines the Baldwin effect as the theory "that the environment affects adaptively the phenotype of an organism, that is, its configuration, so that the organism can survive and reproduce under conditions that are unusual or even extreme, and that such adaptive modifications may later become genetically fixed." This contribution to evolutionary change was not in view when neo-Darwinism was first developed, and the usual formulations of neo-Darwinian theory, including the one I have quoted from Ayala, do not lead one to expect this. Not only does the environment select among genotypes, as neo-Darwinian theory emphasizes, but it also affects organisms of the same genotype differentially.

Ayala seems to say that evolutionary novelties normally come about in this way. I do not know whether by evolutionary novelties Ayala means new species, but it is hard to see how these novelties can be irrelevant to the emergence of new species. If I do not misunderstand Ayala, accordingly, the changes effected in organisms by the impact of the environment play a large role in evolution. Adaptive changes in the phenotype precede and determine the selection of genes. This is quite distinct from the selection by the environment among genetic mutations those that cause phenotypes to be adaptive, but it seems to be of equal importance.

This doctrine, Ayala assures us, was incorporated into the "modern ('synthetic') theory of evolution," which I have called neo-Darwinian. No doubt this is true, but two points should be noted. First, the usual presentations to the public, including his formulation, quoted above, do not convey the enormous plasticity of the genotype and the consequent importance of the environment's effect on the phenotype for the evolutionary process. Although Ayala's summary quoted above did not exclude a role for the environment in shaping the organism, most readers, conditioned by standard neo-Darwinian formulations, will assume that the environment selects only the organisms made fit by their randomly mutating genes.

My suggestion is that after asserting that "the variables determining in which direction [natural selection] will go are the environment, the preexisting constitution of the organisms, and the randomly arising mutations," Ayala should add another sentence: "The environment plays two roles: it affects the organisms of a particular genotype differentially according to their phenotypes in ways that affect their survival and reproduction, and it selects among genotypes for those that have favorable mutations."

Clearly, my difference with Ayala up to this point is not about the empirical facts. It is about what is important. Ayala assures us that the Baldwin effect as he defines it has been assimilated into the dominant theory. My objection is that when the dominant theory is summarized, this new feature is omitted. Ayala, presumably, does not consider it important enough to make explicit. I judge that it is. I also judge that once this is included, additional modifications are needed.

## The Effect of Organisms on the Environment

At this point I proceed to the second step in the argument. Once it is acknowledged that the organism plays a role in evolution, the question arises whether some of this role is active. It is my judgment that it is.

Here I cannot appeal to Ayala for support, although I am not sure he would deny anything I will say. Ayala's definition of the Baldwin effect still locates all causality in the environment and the genes. In his definition and examples the activity of the organism plays no role — only its preexisting condition. However, other phenomena, usually regarded as examples of the Baldwin effect, involve the behavior of the organisms. Barbour's discussion of the Baldwin effect, in chapter 13, focuses on these.

An example of how the behavior of organisms affects evolution can be found in the codlin moth. This moth was a pest for apple growers, since it laid its eggs on apples. However, nearly a century ago some codlin moths began laying eggs on walnuts. These have evolved through genetic selection into a distinct species. No one knows why some of the moths chose walnuts as hosts, but that this choice had evolutionary effects is indisputable.[3] This is an example of host selection. It clearly introduces genetically unprogrammed behavior of the organism into the evolutionary picture.

As we have seen, the emphasis of neo-Darwinian theory is on the effects of the environment on the organism. Yet all biologists know that organisms modify their environment. Richard Lewontin has opposed the machine metaphor that blocks attention to this fact, and has strongly emphasized the role of organismic activity. In John Greene's contribution to this volume (chapter 1), he summarized Lewontin's important contribution:

> In biology, Lewontin argued, it was time to stop conceiving the organism as the passive nexus of independent environmental and genetic forces, the changing environment generating problems for the organism in its struggle to survive, and random genetic mutation providing solutions to these problems. Instead of conceiving the organism as adapting to a randomly changing environment in this random fashion, biologists should recognize that the organism *constructs* its environment by its activities, and that the effective environment consists of those aspects of the external world that are relevant to those constructive activities.[4]

3. Birch, chapter 15 below.
4. See also Richard Lewontin, "The Dream of the Human Genome," *New York Review of Books,* May 28, 1992, pp. 32-39.

Lewontin's general point can hardly be denied. It would be difficult to doubt that when new species of plants and animals enter an ecosystem, they change the environment for other organisms and then also for themselves. As the environment changes, so do the selective pressures that determine which mutations will be transmitted to new generations.

Unfortunately, thus far, his obviously correct point has had little influence in the community of evolutionists. As Lewontin understood, this reflects the mechanistic bias of neo-Darwinism and is a clear example of the fallacy of misplaced concreteness. That is, by abstracting from the actual complexity those features that fit the machine model, which means those that materialism favors, evolutionists have learned much. This makes them loath to pay attention to those aspects of the world omitted from their abstractions. They do not deny the reality of these aspects, but they do not give them attention in their research, admit them into their theoretical formulations, or acknowledge that, if they were admitted, the theory would be affected.

The materialist bias into which the dominance of neo-Darwinist thinking has socialized most biologists leads to favoring unidirectional causality. The bias of process thinkers is to expect causal efficacy to flow in all directions. Such questions should not be settled by metaphysics but by empirical evidence. I believe that the evidence strongly favors the view that the relations of organisms and their environment are reciprocal.

Indeed, from a Whiteheadian perspective, the distinction between organisms and environment is not sharp. Strictly speaking, the environment is composed entirely of other organisms, and every organism is part of the environment of the others. We can distinguish living organisms from those that are not alive, and we could then consider the possibility that only the nonliving organisms in the environment are important in natural selection among phenotypes of living organisms. We could then also consider the possibility that living organisms have no effect on the inorganic ones, or no effect of evolutionary importance.

Here again the argument should not be based on deductions from metaphysics. We need to examine the evidence. Do the effects of organisms on the environment make a significant difference in the course of evolution as process thinkers expect? Or can evolution be adequately understood without reference to such effects, as theories influenced by neo-Darwinism continue to imply?

That organisms interact with their environments to some degree is hardly disputable. Indeed, this activity plays a considerable role in evolutionary accounts despite its omission from the standard neo-Darwinian summary statements, including that of Ayala quoted above. The question is again about importance. If the features of the environment that are truly important in the process of natural selection are independent of the organisms among which they select, then the omission from evolutionary theory of the influence of organisms on the environment is not a serious one. But if organisms affect features that are important in natural selection, this variable should be included. In that case organisms affect the nature that then "selects" the ones that survive and reproduce. The relation is genuinely reciprocal.

Obviously some features of the environment are little affected by organisms. The sun is one such feature. Although Whiteheadian metaphysics declares that organisms have *some* effect on the sun, it is negligible for our purposes. The impact of the sun on organisms fits the neo-Darwinian model.

Yet this effect cannot be isolated from other effects. The sun plays an important but not exclusive role in determining local climate. It is that climate as a whole rather than the sun in separation from it that functions directly in natural selection. The question is, therefore, whether organisms play a role in determining the climate. Local weather, including both temperature and precipitation, is obviously affected by vegetation, which in turn is often affected by animals. Clearly the relations between organisms and climate are reciprocal.

Another example is the composition of the atmosphere, which certainly plays a role in selection. Is it simply given for the organisms among which it selects, or do these organisms affect it? The answer is that relations over evolutionary time are reciprocal. There is no doubt that during the course of evolution the atmosphere has been affected by living organisms in important ways. The oxygen produced by ancient organisms was toxic to many of them and led to dramatic genetic changes.

Beyond these indubitable facts there are strong indications that the biosphere plays a *regulatory* role on the chemical composition of the atmosphere. The Gaia effect is still disputed, but considerable evidence speaks in its favor. If in fact the biosphere has affected its chemical environment in ways favorable to the continuation of life, this has obviously been important for evolution. This cosmic role of the biosphere would carry the interaction among all the constituents of reality even further than Whiteheadians might have anticipated.

Another way living organisms dramatically change their environments is through symbiosis. Two species initially independent of one another develop a relation of mutual dependence. Some functions of one or both that were previously essential for survival then become unnecessary. Over time the genetic basis for those functions is likely to erode and perhaps disappear. At that point separate existence becomes impossible.

Symbiosis can lead to symbiogenesis. This is the acquisition by one organism of the genes of another, sometimes of the complete genome. In this case genetic change takes place without any direct involvement of random mutation.

It is obvious that today human beings are making dramatic changes in organisms by introducing genes from one species into the germ lines of another species. In this sense symbiogenesis is probably now the main cause of the evolution of new species. The question is whether this mechanism of evolution depends on human intervention or has occurred earlier in natural ways.

Ayala certainly assumes the latter. The quotation cited above from chapter 2 continues:

> Full genomes may be acquired, even within a preexisting genome, or in the form of organelles, such as the mitochondria and chloroplasts that characterize eukaryotic organisms, such as animals and plants. Now we know that lateral transfer of genes among distantly related organisms went on for millions and millions of years, to the extent that the early evolution of the three domains of life (bacteria, archaea, and eukarya) may have formed not just a genetic bush of interconnected branches, but a "ring of life," which nevertheless preserves the prokaryote-eukaryote divide.

One of these instances of symbiogenesis may be the single most important step in the evolution of life, namely, the emergence of the eukaryotic cell. It is now thought that it acquired its nucleus by consuming a bacterium that retained its genome in the context of the larger cell.

Accordingly, symbiogenesis was clearly an important factor in evolution in the early days, and also is currently. Why is it ignored by most biologists in their explanation of evolution? The answer is that evolutionists generally focus attention on the emergence of new species of multicellular organisms apart from human intervention. In this realm, most are convinced, natural selection among mutations is the major mechanism involved. They treat examples of the role of symbiogenesis here as rare exceptions not worthy of integration into basic theory.

A quite different picture has considerable empirical support. A different theory is possible that would go far to explain the lack of intermediate forms between species. It may be that new species appear most often when natural selection operates among organisms that have acquired new genes from other organisms, chiefly bacteria. Margulis believes that the neglect of the role of bacteria in the whole evolutionary process is a serious limitation (see chapter 9).

There seem to be instances of symbiogenesis also between multicellular organisms. Lichens are the example most commonly proposed.[5] It is plausible that the common phenomenon of symbiosis leads more often than now recognized to a transfer of genes from one organism into another.

5. Sagan, chapter 7.

The literature on evolution often gives the impression that new species come into being through imperfect replication of genes. We have seen that this is an exaggeration. It also gives the impression that there is clear empirical evidence for the rise of new species in this way. This is not actually the case either. That selection among random mutations affects intraspecies development is indeed well established. That the same process leads to new species is a plausible theory, but not one for which there is much empirical evidence. Sagan recognizes that the absence of empirical demonstration by no means invalidates the theory. But he also points out that the one experiment cited in its support, that of Waddington with fruit flies, can easily be interpreted to support symbiogenesis instead.[6] Until the importance of the role of bacteria in transmitting genes to host organisms is ruled out by careful and open-minded scientific research, the symbiogenetic source of new species should be recognized as a plausible alternative.

In their joint chapter (10), Lynn Margulis and Dorion Sagan discuss thoroughly the role of symbiosis in evolution. They give examples such as the flatworm, *Convoluta roscoffensis,* which no longer eats because it receives the needed energy from photosynthesis through the presence within it of algae. One cannot doubt that the actions of organisms that lead to such changes, for example, in the internal "environment" of the flatworm, have genetic consequences.

Whereas the Baldwin effect and symbiogenesis are acknowledged and then largely ignored, Lamarck is systematically discredited. Some even define neo-Darwinism in terms of its rejection of Lamarckian explanations of evolutionary change.[7] Lamarck thought that acquired characteristics could be directly inherited. Neo-Darwinism rejected this, arguing that only genetic changes could lead to new, heritable characteristics. These genetic changes are thought not to be affected by anything in other parts of the body or in the wider environment. For the most part it is now clear that what appears to be the inheritance of acquired characteristics can be explained in neo-Darwinian ways. Much of this chapter has been devoted to showing that "acquired characteristics" can indirectly, and over time, have an effect on the genetic constitution of the species. My complaint has been that the usual formulation of neo-Darwinian theory neglects this important fact, introducing it only when needed to counter Lamarckian theories.

Nevertheless, there are reasons to question the *absolute* exclusion of the direct inheritance of acquired characteristics without the intervention of ge-

6. Sagan, chapter 7.
7. Clayton, chapter 18.

netic change. In the first chapter in this part (6), Gunter cites examples of epigenetic inheritance. Reg Morrison, in chapter 8, also refers to the role of the epigenetic in evolution. He spells out one example in some detail in his discussion of the role of hydrogen.

> Hydrogen also shapes the biota via an epigenetic (external to the genetic code) switching mechanism. Whether genes are expressed or silenced largely depends on a pattern of hydrogen-loaded carbon tags (CH3) that may become attached to the nucleotide base cytosine (also adenine in some bacteria). Contrary to Darwinian theory, certain environmental factors have been shown to alter the pattern of these epigenetic attachments, thereby altering the pattern of protein production within the organism. These epigenetic tags, known as methyl groups, turn genes on or off by reshaping the three-dimensional structure of the genetic material at the attachment points. Here, too, carbon is the vehicle for hydrogen and appears to play no executive role.
>
> The altered pattern of methylation is particularly significant where it occurs within the X or Y chromosomes since the reshaping of the chromosome appears to be heritable and may persist for several generations. Certain environmental pollutants, especially those whose breakdown products resemble the sex hormones estrogen, progesterone, and testosterone, have been shown to interfere with the normal pattern of methylation, and thereby with the complex process of gender determination and sexual behavior.

I have given reasons to think that the role of "random" changes in genes has been exaggerated, that genetic change occurs in other ways, and that the changes are not exclusively of the genes themselves. I have emphasized that the activity of the organism plays a role in determining (1) the character of the natural environment, (2) which genetic mutations will be selected, (3) how lateral transfer of genes occurs, and (4) the occurrence of epigenetic influences on evolution. The neglect of all these factors and, therefore, of the activity of organisms suggests that the materialist assumptions so widely operative in scientific theory make it difficult for biologists to give full weight to some aspects of the empirical evidence. The typical exposition of neo-Darwinian theory presents random mutation as the only source of the genetic changes from which the natural environment selects. This picture commends itself to materialists because of its comfortable fit with their metaphysical bias. It falls far short of adequacy in explaining the known facts.

To say this is not to deny the important roles of the other three variables, including randomly mutating genes. We can agree that those phenotypes that are best adapted to the environment reproduce more and that their genes are inherited. We can agree that the occasionally adaptive mutations are the ones that are thereby multiplied and that this leads to evolutionary change. I have argued only that the activity of organisms is also an important variable in determining the direction taken by evolution, and that it should be added to Ayala's list.

## Enter Purpose

Baldwin himself was interested in the activity of organisms. As noted by Ian Barbour in chapter 13, Baldwin thought there was clear evidence that "the initiatives of organisms and their learned behavior play a significant role in evolutionary history." As long as the focus of attention is exclusively on randomly mutating genes and natural selection as a purposeless activity, the role of purpose in evolution is excluded from consideration. However, once we acknowledge the important role of organisms and their actions in evolution, the inclusion of the purposes of organisms as a variable in setting the direction of evolution seems eminently plausible.

In the course of exploratory behavior, an animal may, perhaps quite by chance, find a new way to procure food. Having found this behavior successful, the animal is likely to repeat it. Other animals of the same species, seeing the success of this behavior, imitate it. This improves the relation to the environment without any genetic change. However, genetic change may well follow. If the new source of food proves important for the species, random mutations favorable to acquiring food in this way will lead to the disproportionate reproduction of those in whom it occurs. Intelligent and purposive action will have played a role in evolution.

I have avoided attributing purposive intelligence to the discovery of the new method of obtaining food, although this may well be a factor. However, since it is also possible that the discovery may be entirely by chance during exploratory behavior, I set this aside. My point is that the repetition of this activity when its results are favorable as well as its imitation by other members of the species is not a matter of chance but an intelligent effort to attain the same results. Animals do not in the same way repeat and imitate behavior that has no results they desire.

We can speak of all such action as affected by cultural factors, that is, by factors that depend upon animals learning how to act by observing others. Animals that are not distinguished genetically behave differently in different places.

This means that a good deal of animal behavior is culturally influenced rather than genetically determined.

Much of this learning occurs by observing and imitating parents. This clearly involves the subjective experience of the animals involved, such as seeing. However, it may be thought that such learning is simply a matter of genetically programmed imitation. To avoid debate about how far such imitation can in fact be programmed by the genes, I will point to imitation that cannot reasonably be interpreted in this way.

The clearest examples occur when members of a species discover a new way to acquire food. In chapter 15 Charles Birch reminds us of how tits learned to open milk bottles. One may suppose that the first tit that opened a milk bottle did so by chance, thus avoiding the attribution of learning by trial and error. However, that this tit repeated its behavior and that other tits quickly learned this skill can hardly be considered a matter of chance behavior. Of course, imitation was involved. But tits are not programmed to copy all behavior of other tits. The positive outcome of this behavior was what led to its widespread imitation. Any reasonable interpretation of what happened will include the idea that tits learned to open milk bottles in order to get milk. This is purposive, intelligent behavior.

The role of intelligent purpose is highlighted by the fact that when the caps of milk bottles were changed to protect the milk from the birds, the birds learned to open the new caps as well. This is most plausibly understood as the result of purposeful effort on their part. Random exploratory behavior might have led to the first discovery, but it is unlikely that the activity that led to success in the second case was purely random.

Given that there is clear evidence that animals can learn new behavior that improves their chances of survival and reproduction, it is reasonable to think that much of the cultural behavior that is now characteristic of animals developed in this way. It is also reasonable to suppose that some, perhaps most, of the behavior that is now genetically determined was first cultural. New ways of procuring food or avoiding danger favor the retaining of some mutations rather than others and thus eventually change the genetic constitution of those species of which some members have adopted these practices. Natural selection will also favor those who engage in some of these practices instinctively rather than having to learn them from other members of the species. From the point of view of process thought, learning new things has probably played a large role in the evolution of vertebrate animals, and this learning is in part a purposive activity expressive of intelligence.

It is obvious that intelligent behavior is not a factor in all evolution! We are not likely to use the word "intelligent" beyond the sphere of vertebrate animals, and perhaps not with all of those. Whitehead emphasized the difference between organisms in which one member coordinates the work of all the others to some degree and other organisms that lack any such member. The presence of a brain is indicative of such coordination. It is in the evolution of organisms with central nervous systems and brains that intelligent learning plays a significant role.

Nevertheless, Whitehead sees continuity as well as discontinuity between such organisms and simpler ones. Both types of organisms are made up of cells. Unicellular organisms are also purposive in their behavior and can even be said to learn from past experience. They are, presumably, not conscious or intelligent in any usual sense. But in Whitehead's words, they aim to live, to live well, and to live better. Cells do not lose this teleological character altogether when they combine into larger organisms. Plants as plants do not learn or act intelligently. They have no purposes of their own. But they are not machines made up of purely material parts. They are organisms made up of living cells, which have their own unified response to their environments. Without the creativity of cells, plants and other such multicelled organisms would not evolve.

Process thought understands that organisms are composed of momentary events or occasions, and that every occasion is a creative synthesis of its relations with other occasions. Every occasion then becomes part of the creative syntheses that constitute subsequent occasions. Every occasion, in the moment of its occurrence, is a "subject," which then immediately becomes an "object" for other occasions. It is as subject that the occasion receives and acts. Hence, the activity of organisms, even very simple organisms, involves their subjectivity. Further, we judge that subjective experience is always purposive in a very general sense.

From this perspective the activity of the codlin moth also expresses its subjectivity. This subjectivity has a purposive character to it. The moth aims to survive and to reproduce itself. These purposes, especially in this abstract sense, are not part of the moth's experience. But the moth is nevertheless seeking an apple tree. As long as it can find such a tree, its genetic programming suffices to account for its purposive actions. But when it cannot find such a tree, it is doubtful that the genetic constitution predetermines exactly what it will do. The choice of a walnut tree is purposive without being programmed.

## The Role of Emergents in Evolution

I have presented culture as an emergent in the process of evolution. It emerged earlier than human beings, but only with human beings has it acquired enormous importance. I have argued that cultural phenomena should be considered in their own terms rather than reductively. This does not mean that culture lacks an essential genetic basis that is relevant to its explanation. This is useful in explaining the occurrence of culture, and perhaps why cultures vary. It does not help in explaining the specific differences among cultures. For that purpose, quite different explanatory categories are needed.

Neo-Darwinists are generally resistant to thinking in terms of emergents of this kind, but inconsistently so. On the one hand, they take for granted that the phenomena they analyze are emergent from inanimate ones. That is, they treat organisms on their own terms rather than as illustrations of the "laws" of physics and chemistry. On the other hand, they do not give serious attention to the possibility that within their field there may be additional emergents. Let me explain.

Ayala is representative of neo-Darwinism in arguing that, from a scientific point of view, human beings are part of nature, which in turn is constituted by matter in motion. The idea of the world as so constituted comes from physics. It is ironic that the idea of matter in motion no longer works for physicists in their analysis of the constituent elements of the universe. In any case, Ayala does not want his use of this language to commit him to a metaphysical materialism (see chapter 2); so it seems to function chiefly to indicate that in principle biological and human phenomena can be explained by the "laws" of physics.

Yet, in fact, neo-Darwinists show little interest in the efforts reported by Gunter and illustrated by Sagan to throw light on evolution from the perspective of quantum physics, self-organizing systems, and the second law of thermodynamics. On the contrary, for all practical purposes they assume that the study of living things is not to be conducted as a subdivision of the study of the inanimate world. They treat life as an emergent property that requires that living things be studied on their own terms.

There is nothing especially problematic about this assumption that life introduces emergent characteristics worthy of study on their own terms. The idea that there are emergent characteristics of this kind at other levels in the physical world is widely accepted. For example, many scientists recognize that chemistry deals with emergent characteristics of molecules.[8] That life introduces additional emergent characteristics worthy of study in their own terms is an entirely reasonable assumption, one that has the full support of Whiteheadians.

Practically speaking, this idea is taken for granted by biologists. Theo-

8. Clayton, chapter 18.

retically it makes good sense. Its full acceptance invalidates the idea that evolution demonstrates that living things are composed of only what physicists regard as the ultimate constituents of the world. This opens the door to thinking about the other constituents of the world besides quanta. Genes can be taken seriously as a unit of analysis that is not exhaustively explained in terms of quantum phenomena.

Further, if one acknowledges that there are emergent properties at various levels, then one should be open to the possibility that there are additional emergent characteristics within one's field of study. Especially in the study of evolution, it would be reasonable to suppose that what has evolved sometimes has such properties. For example, one might propose the hypothesis that at some point the ability to learn emerges. Once learning is possible, culture enters as a new variable into the evolutionary process. It requires attention in its own terms.

## Implications for Human Self-Understanding

One reason for introducing the activities of organisms and the idea of emergents into the explanation of the evolutionary process is that it enables us to include human beings within that evolution without the dramatic break that is characteristic of most accounts. Few evolutionists deny that human activity that is intelligently purposive has an effect on evolution. But when it is held that nothing of this sort occurs with any other animal, it is hard to avoid reintroducing the dualism that evolutionary thinking intends to overcome. If we recognize that other animals have rudimentary language and use of tools, then the elaboration of language and tools among human beings fits evolutionary thinking. If we recognize that intelligent purposive activity of other animals plays some role in evolution, then the fact that the intelligent purposive activity of human beings now plays a large, indeed the major, role in current evolution does not violate the inclusion of human beings within nature that is essential to evolutionary thinking.

At the same time that recognizing more continuities between human beings and other animals supports the inclusion of human beings within nature, it also removes the negative implications of that inclusion. When nature is defined as matter in motion, the inclusion of human beings in nature is profoundly demeaning. But if the nature in which we understand ourselves to be included has the properties of life as emergent elements, and if it contains subjectivity, learning, purpose, and intelligence, then viewing ourselves as part of nature need not be reductive and dehumanizing at all. We are free to study which features of human behavior are fully controlled by genes and which have a considerable cultural aspect. We can take the latter at face value as constituting a distinctive cultural realm that is far more developed among human beings than are comparable realms among other species. This realm can be studied on its own terms without questioning that it could not exist without a genetic basis. We can also affirm that the freedom or self-determination that can be discerned in the activities of other animals is more fully developed in us.

## A Focus on Genes

I have completed my main task in this chapter. I have argued that when we recognize the important role that organisms play in evolution, we can formulate a theory that includes creaturely subjectivity, purpose, and intelligence in the evolutionary process. Given this view of evolution, the recognition that we human beings are part of evolving nature no longer is demeaning. Much of the conflict between an evolutionary understanding of human beings and a humanly satisfying one is overcome.

The resulting picture is one of extensive interaction between the activity of the organism, the environment, and the genome. Nevertheless, most of what has been said is consistent with the widely held view that the individual genes themselves are not affected by the activity of the organisms or the environment. I came closest to implying the effect of the environment on the genes by quoting Ayala on how gene control circuits arise through the Baldwin effect. I assumed, however, that these control circuits are better considered as epigenetic rather than genetic. The remainder of this chapter is devoted to closer attention to the genes to suggest that they too have their being in interaction with the rest of the world. Genes are not exempt from the flux of interrelations that are basic to reality as a whole.

In common formulations of neo-Darwinian theory, genes are presented as more of less isolated and self-contained entities unaffected by their environments. They control the organism but are not affected by its activity. We were once led to think, in some formulations, that individual genes were not even affected by the other genes constituting the genome.

Biologists have long known that this is not the case. However, there has been a strong tendency to deny that the interaction of genes with other genes and with other elements in their environments makes a significant difference. G. C. Williams wrote in 1966 as follows:

> No matter how functionally dependent a gene may be, and no matter how complicated its interaction with other genes and environmental factors, it

must always be true that a given gene substitution will have an arithmetic mean effect on fitness in any population. One allele can always be regarded as having a certain selection coefficient relative to another at the same locus at any given point of time. Such coefficients are numbers that can be treated algebraically, and conclusions inferred for one locus can be iterated over all loci. Adaptation can thus be attributed to the effect of selection acting independently at each locus.[9]

Genes appear in this account to be individual entities whose functions can be abstracted from other influences and treated as decisive causes of the nature and behavior of multicellular organisms. Richard Dawkins has popularized this view, deriving from it the idea that organisms are the gene's way of making more genes. Although most neo-Darwinians would not speak in this way, the formulations they present to the public still imply that genes exist as distinct entities with causal powers whose functioning can be treated apart from the consideration of whatever interactions are taking place. This is a clear example of misplaced concreteness with highly misleading results.

Both random mutation and symbiogenesis treat the role of genes as central, and the Baldwin effect does not challenge this. These theories differ on the way genetic change occurs. For symbiogenesis and the Baldwin effect, this change is initiated at the level of the phenotype and its activity, whereas neo-Darwinism largely ignores this.

## What Are Genes?

Usually genes are spoken of as if their existence and nature were quite unproblematic. There is very little discussion of this question in this book. Nevertheless, the topic is of sufficient importance to warrant a brief consideration. Let me say, however, that I am qualified to report only on what a few students of the subject have said. I find this sufficient to reject some of the common conceptions of the genes, shared probably by few scientists, but nevertheless too easily communicated by their common formulations. I am particularly influenced by two essays, one by Peter John Beurton and the other by Barry Commoner.[10]

9. G. C. Williams, *Adaptation and Natural Selection* (Princeton: Princeton University Press, 1966), pp. 56-57.

10. Peter John Beurton, "A Unified View of the Gene, or How to Overcome Reductionism," in *The Concept of the Gene in Development and Evolution*, ed. Peter John Beurton, Raphael Falk, and Hans-Joerg Rheinberger (Cambridge: Cambridge University Press,

My general thesis is that the earlier view, still too widely supported by popular expositions of neo-Darwinism, that genes are self-enclosed physical entities hardly affected by their environment is seriously misleading. A more accurate picture sees them as remarkably stable combinations of other entities that nevertheless come into being and function in complex processes of inter-action. In my current understanding, genes are as much the products of the ac-tivities of phenotypes as they are the causal explanation of phenotypes. If this is true, additional changes are needed in standard accounts of evolution.

Mendel hypothesized the existence of genes to account for his empirical observations. His hypothesis has proved extremely fruitful. The modern theory that we call neo-Darwinian integrated his hypothesis with Darwin's theory of natural selection. Interpreting natural selection as operative on phenotypes controlled by genes proved to be a richly explanatory theory. Nevertheless, it re-quires many qualifications.

We quoted Ayala on the point that the relation between genes and pheno-types is far less fixed than was once thought. The environment and the activity of the organisms play a much larger role than is usually recognized in deter-mining the phenotypes that are selected from, as well as the nature that does the selecting. Nevertheless, there is no question but that the genes play a crucial role in determining the phenotype.

What are these genes? They are not, as once thought, little bits of matter comparable in their identity and self-containedness to molecules or atoms. They are instead segments of DNA consisting of nucleotides. In close study nothing is visible to allow one to determine where one gene ends and another begins. This is decided by the way they function in determining the phenotype, not by anything apparent in them. Furthermore, a single nucleotide may be part of more than one gene, and a single gene may consist of noncontiguous nucleotides.

The gene is the smallest unit of natural selection. That is, nothing smaller than the gene makes the kind of difference in the phenotype that affects natural selection. This is true, however, not on the basis of information learned about an entity definable on some other basis, but because the gene is defined in this way. The definition then allows for empirical search to determine what combi-nations of smaller elements constitute genes.[11] It is, accordingly, misleading to speak of DNA as composed of genes. It is composed of nucleotides some com-

---

2000). Quotations from Beurton in this section are from this essay. The Williams quote, cited above, is also taken from it. The other essay is Barry Commoner, "Unravelling the DNA Myth: The Spurious Foundations of Genetic Engineering," *Harper's Magazine,* February 2002.

11. Beurton, "A Unified View of the Gene, or How to Overcome Reductionism."

binations of which constitute genes by virtue of the way they function in relation to the phenotype.

Beurton supposes that DNA existed before there were genes. The question is, then, how genes arose. Remember that this is not a question of how a new physical particle arose. It is a question of how patterns of nucleotides became fixed as constituting units of natural selection. His answer is complex and startling.

> This is not a unit *encountered* by natural selection. Rather, it is an *emergent* unit or one *generated* in the process of natural selection from a background of never-ceasing variation contained in the genome. The more ultimate source for the coming into being of such a unit of selection, or gene, is a specific difference in adaptive performance among individuals which triggers differential reproduction and keeps it going. Difficulties in identifying genes or their locations have led frequently to the assertion that a gene is simply that "what makes a difference" between any two individuals. I am turning this around and saying, a physical difference among organisms, when perpetuated through populations, is what makes a gene. Schroedinger was stunned by the genes' stability because he saw them instrumental to the stability of the organism. It is, however, the other way around; differential reproduction of organisms due to some particular overall differences in adaptive performance is the most important source for the coming into being of stable units that deserve to be called genes.

Obviously, this does not negate the role these stable units play in the evolutionary process, but it gives a very different picture than the usual one of how they are related to the activities of organisms. Beurton summarizes as follows: "Not only are the selective values of genes emergent properties, but the genes *themselves* are emergent particles resulting from the interactive processes of populations." Dorion Sagan makes a similar point.[12] In the language used in previous sections of this essay, we can say that genes have been created by the Baldwin effect.

It is important to note also that the genes by themselves can do little. It is in combination with various proteins that they have their effects. When speaking of the genes, it is appropriate to focus on segments of DNA and to exclude the other components of the DNA molecule, but exclusion does not mean lack of relationship. Genes function as they do because of their environment in the molecule.

12. Sagan, chapter 7, note 7.

## DNA, RNA, and Proteins

There are other misleading features of the still too common public presentation of evolution. It seems to suggest that the only source of the variations among which nature selects is the DNA genome. It describes a simple one-way causality from DNA to RNA and from RNA to protein. It implies that there is a one-to-one relation between the genomes in DNA and those in proteins. In Ayala's summary statement, RNA and proteins are not mentioned as variables influencing the direction of evolution. As Ayala and other biologists know well, the reality is much more complex. A single gene, instead of encoding one type of protein, can give rise to hundreds, or even thousands, of different types.

According to Barry Commoner:

> This results from splicing, which occurs in the transmission of the information from DNA to RNA. A specialized group of fifty to sixty proteins, together with five small molecules of RNA — known as a "spliceosome" — assembles at sites along the length of the messenger RNA, where it cuts apart various segments of the messenger RNA. Certain of these fragments are spliced together into a number of alternative combinations, which then have nucleotide sequences that differ from the gene's original one. These numerous, redesigned messenger RNAs govern the production of an equal number of proteins that differ in their amino acid sequence and hence in the inherited traits that they engender.[13]

Commoner describes other functions of proteins. Clearly they are not the passive outcomes of DNA but significant contributors to genetic functioning. Proteins play a role, for example, in reducing the number of mutations. They can be "misfolded" and fail to function properly, thereby introducing their own errors into the process. In short, important as genes and their mutations may be, the process of evolution is affected only by genes and proteins interacting in complex ways.

## How Random Are Mutations?

Much of the discussion above indicates that the imperfect replication of genes is not as determinative of the evolutionary process as the standard formulations of neo-Darwinian theory imply. Actually this is recognized by mainstream biologists, although this recognition does not affect their summary

13. Commoner, "Unravelling the DNA Myth."

statements about the mechanism of evolution. The concluding sentence in Ayala's essay on the Baldwin effect (chapter 12 above) suggests that genetic changes occur in response to the environment in ways not mediated by random variation: "Kirschner and Gerhart explain in considerable detail that the genetic changes that account for evolutionary novelty involve gene control circuits (numerous but very short DNA sequences), rather than changes in the enzymes encoded by genes." It seems from this that changes in gene control circuits are at least as important as changes in the genes themselves. In the passage from which this sentence is taken, Ayala notes that changes that account for "evolutionary novelty" occur in response to the environment.

There is clearly a tension between all this and the continued insistence on the randomness of all the mutations productive of genotypes among which the environment selects. Perhaps the explanation is that gene control circuits randomly mutate and that certain mutants are selected in accord with the Baldwin effect. However this passage is to be understood, it attributes to the interaction of the organism and the environment a more direct role in shaping the genome than has usually been supposed. Genes are not as insulated from the environment as has been supposed.

I have made the case for a theory of evolution with quite different implications from those of standard neo-Darwinism. I have followed Beurton in describing the coming into being of genes as brought about by factors operating at the level of populations. There is no question but that the way genes *function* is dependent on many environmental factors that include the activity of organisms. Through symbiosis the constitution of a genome can change without dependence on imperfect replications of genes. Also, epigenetic factors play a large role in evolutionary developments.

On the other hand, Beurton emphasizes with neo-Darwinism that once the genes, as units of selection, are established, they are remarkably independent and stable. And none of this denies that imperfect replications of genes play an important role in providing the mutations among which the environment selects. There still remains the question of the senses in which these imperfect replications are completely "random" and the limitations of this randomness.

The doctrine of randomness was introduced in rejection of the notion that genetic change responds to the needs of organisms in any direct way. It also rejects any idea that God intervenes to bring about genetic changes as needed to advance evolutionary development. The indubitable fact that most of these imperfect replications are harmful is sufficient grounds for supporting the doctrine of randomness against these ideas.

On the other hand, it is important to remember that most biologists do not mean that these mutations are random in the sense of being uncaused. Some have speculated that cosmic rays may play a role. Other causal explanations at the level of atoms and subatomic entities are not excluded. The teaching of the randomness of mutations of this type is not a rejection of the determinism to which most scientists subscribe. Presumably the "laws" of physics are not suspended.

Given agreement on the above points, the area that requires more study has to do with another common understanding of the randomness of imperfect replication. This is the idea that genes and the process of their replication are not affected by their environment. No one now supposes that the genes and their functioning are unaffected by other elements within the genome. But Weismann asserted, and many biologists have agreed, that the genome as a whole is insulated from any external influence. This lack of influence on mutation is part of what is meant by asserting that imperfect replications are random.

Some of what has been said above requires qualification of Weismann's thesis. The fact that the stress experienced by some organisms accelerates the process of mutations indicates that the genome is not as completely sequestered from the larger organism as was supposed. We noted that the epigenetic elements in the genome are responsive to some features of the environment. If the influence of the environment on the gene becomes a frontier of scientific research, it is my guess that other effects on replication from outside the genome will be found.

For a Whiteheadian, the possibility of some entities being well insulated against the influence of others is entirely acceptable. The idea of total insulation is not. Presumably, for example, the quanta that are constituents of genes are related to quanta in other parts of the body, but whether this influences the nature of mutations is an empirical question. Whitehead taught that the molecules in the living body "exhibit certain peculiarities of behavior not to be detected outside an animal body."[14] More directly, they are part of a cell, which is part of an organ, which is part of a body. We know that very different kinds of cells develop from the same DNA according to their location in different parts of the body. We look for ways in which cells affect their constituent molecules. We believe that evidence that Weismann exaggerated will increase. We expect that "randomness" in the sense of lack of influence by environmental factors will be further qualified. We prefer the formulation of anthropologist Tim Ingold, who proposes that we shift from what he calls the decontextualizing population thinking of contemporary neo-Darwinian theory to seeing the gene

14. Whitehead, *Process and Reality,* p. 106.

"not as a discrete, pre-specified entity but as a particular locus of growth and development within a continuous field of relationships."[15]

Process thinkers are not opposed to the idea of randomness in general. Far from it. We believe that chance plays a large role in the world. We also believe that there is an element of spontaneity in the energy events that constitute the world, including genes. We would favor an explanation of imperfect replication that combined physical causes with some small element of spontaneity. This would give a certain ontological ground for "randomness." On the other hand, by undercutting the materialist metaphysics that underlies neo-Darwinian formulations, it would change the whole picture. I will return to this topic in my chapter in part IV.

## Conclusions

These brief pointers hardly begin to describe the complexities of what transpires in the real world. I have provided no facts of which neo-Darwinists are ignorant. Much of the complexity I note is mentioned in the paragraph cited from Ayala. The problem is that neo-Darwinists regard this complexity as unimportant to the basic understanding of the evolutionary process. They continue to describe this process in materialistic and reductionistic terms, abstracting from the interrelationships the existence of which they acknowledge.

My view, on the other hand, is that a materialistic treatment of evolution is profoundly inadequate and misleading. It is far closer to the facts to envision a field of events in which significant patterns can be discerned. The events are much better conceived in organismic than in mechanistic terms. They are what they are in and through their relations with one another.

Much of what is abstracted from in the usual formulations of neo-Darwinism can be grouped together under the heading of the activity of the organism. I have argued that this is an independent variable that must be added to the nature that selects, the preexistent organism, and the genome. The activity of organisms affects both the environment that selects and the genetic constitution of future organisms. It also affects genes.

Once the role of organisms is acknowledged, it is reasonable to think that their influential activity is sometimes intelligent and purposive. We find it so in ourselves. It appears to be so in other animals. The rejection of the role of purpose in evolution is metaphysical, not scientific. A better metaphysics is available.

15. Tim Ingold, "Beyond Biology and Culture: The Meaning of Evolution in a Relational World," *Social Anthropology* 12 (2004): 218.

# III THE PHILOSOPHICAL CHALLENGE TO NEO-DARWINISM

# Editor's Preface

Part II surveyed proposals for thinking scientifically about evolution in ways that were different from the almost exclusive focus on random mutation of genes and natural selection of neo-Darwinism. Few if any scientists dispute that random mutation occurs and is an important factor in evolution, and no one questions that favorable mutations are more likely than unfavorable ones to be transmitted to offspring. But we saw in part II that a good number of scientists point out other factors that affect the course of evolution.

Although some of the proposals in part II fit poorly into the metaphysics of matter in motion that underlies neo-Darwinism and most scientific theories, this was not the concern of most of the authors. Sagan is an exception, but it is Barbour's essay that, while it focuses on questions of science, begins a transition to the explicitly philosophical concerns of part III. Beyond that, my essay in part II and that of Birch in part III involve both the empirical concerns of part II and the philosophical concerns of part III. Hence the shift between the two parts is not sharp.

A central issue — perhaps *the* central issue — between the model employed by most scientists and the Whiteheadian one is the exclusion of the subject from the former and its inclusion in the latter. Not only science, but also a great deal of contemporary philosophy, excludes subjectivity from consideration as an important part of reality, at least when dealing with the nonhuman world. The recognition that human beings have evolved from nonhuman ancestors brought the human species into the province of natural science, and this has led to the treatment of human beings as objects only. When scientists give the impression that they can explain the phenomena of human behavior adequately without reference to human subjectivity, humanists and religious people find this both unrealistic and dehumanizing. If those who study human beings in this purely objective way also affirm that this mode of study yields the only available truth, the dehumanization is thoroughgoing.

Charles Birch, as a biologist, adopts most of the neo-Darwinian synthesis as a description of how new species arise. He expresses little interest in most of the proposals of alternative ways in which evolution can be thought to have occurred. Nevertheless, he sees that the standard theory, like almost all scientific theories, fundamentally omits the subjective side of reality from its purview, treating its objects as if they were only objects. He notes that nothing in this dominant account requires any subjectivity on the part of the organisms that evolve. This includes human beings. Biology as now typically taught provides us with no explanation as to why we are not zombies. The fact, in his view, that we are not zombies raises a fundamental question about the adequacy of the account.

Birch does discuss one way in which evolution occurs that does not fit the neo-Darwinian model. It is the Baldwin effect as discussed in part II by Barbour; I made use of his examples in chapter 14. This was treated also by Ayala, but he selected examples that could be interpreted in a purely objective way. Barbour's examples show that animal behavior plays a role in evolution, and that this behavior may be intelligently purposeful. This suggests that a fully adequate account of evolution needs to recognize that animal subjectivity exists and affects the course of events. Obviously, if this is true for other animals, it applies to human beings as well. Birch concludes his essay by challenging process theologians to clarify the relation of God to the evolutionary process. Some of the writers in part IV try to respond, but the theistic issue is not thematically considered in part III.

The mathematician-scientist-philosopher Robert Valenza understands the theoretical issues clearly. Accordingly, his essay deals exclusively with this topic. The issue is about the nature of science in general and its relation to the subjective sphere rather than about biology or interpretations of evolution as such. Nevertheless, the issue comes to a head around the inclusion of human beings in the world studied by science. If the world studied by science both omits subjects and also is self-enclosed, and if, in principle, science provides a complete account of the world, then the subjective world of thought and feeling and purpose has no actual role in the course of events.

Previous generations often discussed the relation between the subjective and objective in terms of causality. They asked whether what happens subjectively is exhaustively caused by what happens objectively or has some autonomy, and whether the subjective can affect the objective. The view that all causality is physical led to what can be called epiphenomenalism. This is the doctrine that the subjective is exhaustively caused by the objective and that it has no causal power of its own.

A similar discussion today is informed by the idea of supervenience.

Valenza enters the discussion in these new terms and introduces original formulations in conversation with leading contemporary thinkers. In the end he parts company with them, affirming the need for something like a Whiteheadian inclusion of the subjective in a comprehensive understanding even in science. His essay is long, not directly focused on evolution, and more technical than most of the content of this book. For contemporary philosophers it is likely to be the most important contribution of this volume. It is published as the appendix to this volume. Part III includes only a brief introduction to the full essay, stating its major theses in a form fully accessible to the general reader. These theses are evidently of crucial importance for evolutionary theory.

The other two chapters in part III, by David Griffin and Philip Clayton, are of a quite different character. Both recognize the central importance of the issue emphasized by Birch and Valenza, but they approach this in wider philosophical contexts. In Griffin's case this context is an exhaustive account of the basic teachings of Darwinism and of neo-Darwinism. In Clayton's case it is an account of the alternative theories of emergence.

Both Griffin and Clayton recognize that neo-Darwinism involves a strong emphasis on the random mutation of genes, but neither emphasizes this point. Accordingly, neither shows much interest in most of the theories presented in part II about other factors in evolution. These would become important for either of them only as they affected the more philosophical aspects of neo-Darwinian theory. Griffin identifies some twenty doctrines of neo-Darwinism, of which this is one. Clayton, on the other hand, considers any theory to be neo-Darwinian if it limits its explanations to what is observable and rejects Lamarckian inheritance of acquired characteristics.

The difference is not quite as great as that seems. What Clayton means by neo-Darwinism's refusing to go beyond the empirical evidence is what Griffin means by positivism. Many of the other teachings that Griffin lists as definitive of neo-Darwinism follow from, or are closely related to, this positivism. Perhaps the main difference is that Griffin sees neo-Darwinists, consciously or unconsciously, as associating this positivism with a materialistic metaphysics, whereas Clayton thinks they eschew metaphysics. In consequence Clayton finds that the refusal to engage in metaphysics limits the ability of neo-Darwinists to recognize the full range of emergence in the world of life that evolutionists study. For Griffin the need is to free biologists from the straitjacket of a materialist metaphysics and provide them with a better one in the process tradition. Clayton's task is to persuade biologists to see the value of metaphysics. Griffin's task is to persuade them that the metaphysics to which they are now committed is a bad one and that science can be improved by employing a better one. Griffin, explicitly, and Clayton, implicitly, offer ways out of the current dilemma about the teaching of evolution in public schools. This dilemma arises because, to many people, the main way in which the problem of science and religion has been resolved is not now convincing. This is the dualistic way discussed in the introduction to this book and exemplified by Ayala but rejected by most of the other contributors. For advocates of the dualistic way, there is no problem for science to describe a world from which humanistic and religious concerns are completely excluded. Science is just one way of knowing. Ethics and religion constitute other ways of knowing.

A practical problem with this dualism is that in the United States science is taught in public schools while ethics and religion are not. Hence formal education subjects children only to the reductionistic and dehumanizing views offered by the sciences and coming especially to expression in typical teaching of evolution. A theoretical problem is that dualisms of this kind run counter to actual human experience and are hard to defend philosophically. Both Griffin and Clayton believe that evolutionary theory can be presented in a way that makes this dualism unnecessary.

Griffin fully agrees that evolution is certainly "fact" and not "theory" in the pejorative sense. However, the Darwinian and neo-Darwinian teachings not only affirm and describe the fact but also clothe it in elaborate theory that should be recognized as such. Theory construction of this sort is quite legitimate as long as it recognizes its hypothetical character. The problem, however, is that many teachers of evolution teach this theory as if it also were fact. Griffin makes clear that neo-Darwinism carries a lot of baggage that goes far beyond what is scientifically demonstrated. If the basic science is separated from its unnecessary neo-Darwinian metaphysical interpretation, its teaching will not have the implications that are so disturbing to many humanists and religious people.

Clayton finds especially promising the extensive discussion of emergence among scientists in many fields. Much of the strong objection to the teaching of evolution stems from its reductionist formulations, such as the idea that human beings are reduced to being parts of a nature that is itself understood as matter in motion. Since subjective experience is denied to nature, human beings as parts of nature are also to be explained on purely objective grounds. But emergence theory cuts against all this. As new phenomena emerge, they must be treated on their own terms rather than as "nothing but" the effects of lower-level entities. This kind of thinking opens the way to understanding that life is not simply a new form of matter in motion and, especially, that the emergent subjectivity, which we all know to be present in ourselves, also plays a role in nature. To understand human beings as emerging in that kind of nature is not a dehumanizing thought. Clayton is convinced that current trends in the sciences open the way to teaching evolution scientifically in this nonreductionistic way.

Clayton is puzzled that Whiteheadians have played so small a role in the discussion of emergence. He rightly notes that Whitehead saw the emergence of novelty everywhere. This should make emergence theory thoroughly congenial to Whiteheadians, and indeed it does. On the other hand, emergence theory tends to draw sharp lines between the places where emergence occurs and others. A Whiteheadian sees some emergence in all interactions. Of course, in most instances the emergent novelty is negligible and not transmitted to subsequent occasions; so we could eliminate this from the discussion of emergence in which Clayton is interested. And even within the sphere where there is some transmission of novelty through what Whitehead calls "hybrid feelings," there is value in identifying the places where it is important enough to be highlighted by scientists. We process thinkers should have invested ourselves more in this enterprise, and we can only be grateful to Clayton for his important contribution.

A second difference is that Whiteheadians see most of the current discussion of emergence as descriptive rather than explanatory. It is, of course, important to have an adequate description, but assuming that there is emergence everywhere, Whiteheadians have focused on understanding the nature of the entities whose relations give rise to this emergence. For us it is important to recognize that to be truly related to something is to be affected by it, so that, for example, a molecule or gene (we would prefer to say a molecular or genetic event) in close relation to one set of other molecules or genes is not the same as it would be when closely related to a different set of molecules or genes. For us the doctrine of internal relations is fundamental for understanding evolution.

A third difference is that Whiteheadians make a distinction between the kinds of changes that can come about through emergence and those that cannot. Clayton thinks of subjectivity or experience in general as emerging from a world in which it was long absent. Whiteheadians think that complex forms of subjectivity have emerged from very simple ones. In Whiteheadian metaphysics the idea of an actual entity that is nothing in and for itself, one that exists only as an object for others, is completely empty. Hence the idea of a world in which there was a complete absence of subjects does not make sense. Whether there is ultimately a sharp metaphysical disagreement with Clayton, or whether the issue is more terminological, is hard to tell. Clayton sometimes speaks of the preexperiential character of things before there are experiential subjects. What he considers preexperiential may correspond to what process thinkers consider the lowest grade of nonconscious experience.

## 15. Why Aren't We Zombies?
## Neo-Darwinism and Process Thought

CHARLES BIRCH

Neo-Darwinism is the dominant biological theory accounting for order in the living world. More particularly it is a theory of the origin of the diversity and adaptiveness of living organisms. Neo-Darwinism is Darwinism in the light of modern genetics. It emphasizes three propositions: chance genetic variation, struggle for existence, and natural selection. It is from the pool of genetic variation derived from the mutation of genes, together with the recombination of genes in sexual reproduction, that natural selection in the struggle for existence changes the type and eventually the species. An accurate definition of natural selection is that it is the differential survival and reproduction of individuals in the population. It moves the genetic constitution of the population in the direction of greater adaptiveness.

Neo-Darwinism, like all biological theories, is strictly mechanistic, no more and no less than the theory of DNA. Its entities, be they genes or organisms, are treated as objects and not as subjects. The dominant framework in which biologists discuss evolution is mechanistic and materialistic. What then is the possible role of process thought in this discussion? I think it is twofold. First, it claims to provide a framework for interpreting the accepted facts of neo-Darwinism that is better than the purely mechanistic one now employed. Second, and more problematic, is its claim to incorporate evidence that does not fit well into the currently dominant model.

### The Philosophical Framework of Neo-Darwinism and Its Limits

The dominant philosophical framework is mechanistic and materialistic. This is the way the science of biology works. Its method has been highly successful in answering the questions it asks. It has led some of its most famous exponents to atheism. But neo-Darwinian theory does not necessarily imply atheism. It does, like Darwinian theory in general, make irrelevant the dominant concept that people have of God's role in nature. It leaves no room in nature for an interventionist, supernatural God. However, neo-Darwinism does not exclude the possible relevance of other concepts of God. If it is not to lead to complete atheism, it cries aloud for another view of divine action.

The questions neo-Darwinism asks are clear. It is highly successful in explaining the emergence of such things as legs from fins and complex organs from simpler ones. An example of the latter is the evolution of the complex eye of vertebrates. Opponents of neo-Darwinism like to tell us that there is no possibility of getting together at the same time all the necessary components of the eye. Only a miracle would do that. But this is to misstate the problem. Given time and successive changes, the evolution of the complex eye becomes credible. Dawkins contrasts the two views with his vivid metaphor of climbing "mount improbable." The miracle view "faces the sheer cliff of improbability. There must be a ramp of step-by-step progress."[1] Darwin made this clear in the last chapter of *The Origin.* I have asked students to make a list of eyes of organisms starting with the pigment spot of a single-celled organism such as the paramecium, moving to single-celled organisms that had added a cup around the pigment spot and over that a lens, and so on, to more complex eyes. Here we can see the sort of succession that might have occurred over time in evolution. We get further clues by studying the successive stages in development of the eye in the developing vertebrate embryo.

At one time gaps in the fossil record were presented as a case against Darwinian evolution. For most paleontologists this is no longer a major problem.[2] Questions about complex organs and fossils are questions to which biologists can provide credible answers. They are the easy questions.

But other questions are difficult, and neo-Darwinism has up to now avoided them. They have to do with intangible but essential aspects of the living organism. They revolve around consciousness. There is no problem in attributing survival value to consciousness. But why are we not zombies? Zombies are fictitious creatures devoid of any conscious experience and yet having behavior identical to that of their conscious counterparts. They could get along all right provided they had inbuilt programs to avoid dangers and be attracted to favorable environments such as those that provide food and energy. I know of no ar-

1. See Richard Dawkins, *A Devil's Chaplain* (London: Weidenfeld and Nicholson, 2003), p. 212.

2. See J. Maynard Smith and E. Szathmary, *The Major Transitions in Evolution* (Oxford: Freeman Spektrum, 1995).

gument in the mechanistic model of neo-Darwinism as to why all living creatures, including us, are not zombies. What in principle is the merit of conscious
behavior over unconscious robotic behavior of the same survival value? I know
of none. The question remains unanswered by neo-Darwinism, but it has an
answer in process thought as discussed below.

Consciousness has, in recent years, been added to biologists' considerations. But their questions are based on mechanistic models. Much study has
been made of the experience of redness. The question asked is: In what part of
the brain is redness registered and what happens to the neurons there in terms
of electrical and chemical changes? These are neurological correlates of the experience of redness. But we are still left with the difficult question as to what is
the inner experience of redness. That can be broadened to the question: What is
the nature of the subjective? Biologists tend not to ask such questions. They
leave them to philosophers.

One of the founders of neo-Darwinism, biologist Sewall Wright, did indeed ask such questions, and he found that the most satisfactory answer was
not ultimately mechanism but what he called panpsychism (panexperientialism). However, he also concluded that "science must restrict itself to the
external aspects of things. . . . science is a limited adventure, concerned with
the external and statistical aspect of events and incapable of dealing with the
unique creative aspect of each individual event."[3] Wright achieved fame as an
evolutionary biologist, but his philosophy of biology was almost completely
ignored by his fellow biologists. Yet another distinguished biologist was W. E.
Agar, who, like Wright, became a supporter of panpsychism or what may
better be called panexperientialism. Under the influence of Alfred North
Whitehead he held that all living organisms were subjects. He concluded that
it *was* the job of biologists to study them as subjects as well as objects. He
made his case for this kind of study with respect to evolution, embryonic development, and behavior. He did not believe that science should restrict itself
to the external aspects of things. Like Wright, he achieved distinction as a biologist, but his fellow biologists largely ignored his philosophy of biology. I
know that this greatly concerned him. Another evolutionary and Whiteheadian biologist was C. H. Waddington. He claimed that his metaphysical beliefs had a definite influence on his research "both in the types of problems I
set myself and the manner in which I tried to solve them."[4] I incline to the

3. See Sewall Wright, "Biology and the Philosophy of Science," in *Process and Divinity*, ed.
William L. Reese and Eugene Freeman (La Salle, Ill.: Open Court, 1964), pp. 123-24.
4. See C. H. Waddington, "The Practical Consequences of Metaphysical Belief on a Biologist's Work," in Waddington, *Towards a Theoretical Biology 2: Sketches* (Edinburgh: Edinburgh
University Press, 1969), p. 72.

view that evolutionary biologists should at least be aware of the philosophical problems in their work even though they may not be moved to explore them as much as did Wright, Agar, and Waddington. Alas, at present most biologists are strict mechanists and take the view that the philosophy of biology is as useful in their work as ornithology is for birds!

## Questions Posed by Process Thought to Biologists

Process thought asks critical questions about the overall mechanistic picture of the world and life that much science assumes. What it finds missing is an understanding of what it is to be a living subject. Life is bound up with an urge to live. This principle is far more basic to life than the principle of survival of the fittest. The triumph of neo-Darwinism is within limits. Life is more than mechanics. Mechanistic procedures are entirely justifiable provided there is recognition of the limitations involved. What they ignore is experience, some of which at the human level is conscious. Experience is the inner aspect of entities. It has to do with feeling, valuing, purposing, and deciding.

How did experience in general at the human level arise in the evolutionary process? Why aren't we zombies? I think the answer lies in the nature of the building blocks of organisms. If science acknowledges human experience at all, it must ask from what it has evolved. If it is acknowledged that it has evolved from animal experience, the question is pushed further back. At some point, does experience, mentality, or subjectivity emerge from entities that are totally lacking in these properties, entities that are simply objects for other subjects? If the basic constituents of the physical world are purely material, then the answer must be yes. But to believe this is to affirm a miracle. Unless you believe in miracles, you would expect mindless atoms to evolve into zombies. But this does not seem to happen. Griffin provides cogent and detailed arguments against the common view that mentality evolves from that which has no mentality at all.[5]

What meaning could subjectivity have for atoms and quarks? In process thought the concept of panexperientialism involves "feeling" influences from the past such as occurs in memory and feelings toward possible futures. As Whitehead has said somewhere, "the present is the fringe of memory tinged with anticipation." Even at the elemental level he posited some degree of self-determination. I have a high view of the amoeba and a still higher view of my cat. In this model, evolution is not just change in material bodies but the evolu-

5. See David R. Griffin, *Unsnarling the World-Knot* (Berkeley: University of California Press, 1998), pp. 64f.

tion of experience, which is the inner aspect of things. Whitehead makes it clear that there could be no evolution in a world made up of purely material entities.

> The aboriginal stuff, or material, from which a materialistic philosophy starts, is incapable of evolution. This material is in itself the ultimate substance. Evolution, on the materialistic theory, is reduced to the role of being another word for the description of the changes of the external relations between portions of matter. There is nothing to evolve, because one set of external relations is as good as any other set of external relations. There can merely be change, purposeless and unprogressive . . . the doctrine cries aloud for a conception of organisms as fundamental for nature.[6]

To think even of other people in terms of their subjective experience requires imagination. This is even truer when we think of other animals in this way, and especially of the simplest among them. There is required what Wordsworth called "the inward eye." We do not even have the experience of any other human directly, let alone that of a honeybee. And what of the electron? That is remote indeed. Yet the discoverer of the electron, J. J. Thomson, had some notion of the electron as a subject. He said someplace that to know what an electron *is* you would have to be one. The actual course of evolution involves the whole organism both in its subjectivity and in its appearance to others. The partly conscious experience that probably occurs in all animals with central nervous systems evolved, along with those nervous systems, from the presumably nonconscious subjectivity of unicellular organisms.

On what basis can we believe all this? There is, of course, no proof. But to some of us the theory that all things are subjects as well as objects for other subjects gives a more credible concept of a nature that includes our human experiences and us than does the mechanistic view that is still so widely accepted. We cannot really believe that we are zombies. But if we are not, and if we are part of nature, then why should we suppose that other parts of nature are zombies? It makes more sense to understand our relations with other natural entities as a communion of subjects.

Indeed, philosophically the case is stronger still. Without subjects there can be no objects, since to be an object is to be such for some subject. Whitehead said that "apart from the experience of subjects there is nothing, nothing, nothing, bare nothingness."[7]

---

6. See Alfred North Whitehead, *Science and the Modern World* (Cambridge: Cambridge University Press, 1933), pp. 134-35.

7. Alfred North Whitehead, *Process and Reality,* ed. David Ray Griffin and Donald W. Sherburne, corrected ed. (New York: Free Press, 1978), p. 167.

Up until now science has largely limited itself to nature as object of human experience, especially of sense experience. The feeling and valuing and purposing and deciding that also occur in others are largely ignored. We know that these aspects, whether we are conscious of them or not, are causative in our experience and for our bodies. We may conjecture that similar things, conscious or not, are causative in the rest of the entities of nature, providing these entities with their particular experience and therefore their very being.

In psychology, behaviorism is giving way to the inclusion of human experience as worthy of study. Something similar is happening in the study of other animals, including insects. The process thinker is asking for an alternative model to mechanism that recognizes that all the individual entities we study are subjects as well as objects. Whitehead called this the theory of organic mechanism. It incorporates both the outward and the inward nature of entities from quarks to humans. He anticipated that the first-person experience and the third-person description could become part of an extended form of science. Our present dichotomy between them would eventually be overcome. Its importance? "As we think, we live."[8]

## The Challenge of Process Thought for Neo-Darwinism

Neo-Darwinism has been brilliantly successful. Unless process thought in the Whiteheadian tradition can accept and incorporate the explanations provided by neo-Darwinism, it cannot be adequate to explain evolution. If it can do this, however, then it may also show that still more can be understood about evolution when the entities that evolve are understood to be not only objects for the scientific observer but also subjects in their own right. I will first discuss the compatibility of process thought with the three basic components of neo-Darwinism: chance gene mutation, struggle for existence, and natural selection. I will then consider ways in which process thought, guided by its sense of the subjective side of things, may add something to the usual formulations of neo-Darwinism.

## Mutation of Genes

When genes replicate, the daughter genes are not always identical with the parent gene. Mistakes in replication occur but are rare. They are mutant genes.

8. Whitehead, *Process and Reality*, p. 36.

Furthermore, most of them, by far, are deleterious to the organism that possesses them. Mutations are called random or chance occurrences. The meaning of these terms is that mutations are not biased in favor of adapting the possessor to its environment. Most are deleterious. Some few of these deleterious mutations can be preserved in combination with other genes, which do confer adaptability in certain environments. Mutation can be caused by components of the environment of the gene, such as radiation. The process of mutation is understood on a mechanistic basis. There is neither sense, nor can there be, that the direction of mutation is guided by some outside force such as God.

When the original French edition of Monod's *Chance and Necessity* was published, I happened to be teaching a course on evolution at UC Berkeley. At the same time, Charles Hartshorne was in Berkeley. So I passed on the book to him. He was delighted with Monod's emphasis on chance, as it fit well with his process thinking that the world is not strictly deterministic. It has elements of chance and accident. These have always been difficult for orthodox religious thinkers to accept since they suggest that God is not in control to the extent these thinkers would like. According to their view, God is omnipotent and there is no element of chance in nature. Everything is precisely arranged by divine wisdom and power. Yet that is not how the world works nor, in particular, how evolution works.

## The Struggle for Existence

It has been said that Darwin lost his faith with the help of a wasp. "I cannot persuade myself," Darwin wrote, "that a beneficent and omnipotent God would have designedly created the Ichneumonidae with the express intention of their feeding on living bodies of caterpillars."[9] No doubt also known to Darwin were wasps that paralyze their prey but don't kill them. This way the meat keeps fresh.

Darwin's concept of the struggle for existence includes predators and anything that affects the chance to survive and reproduce. Darwin used the phrase in a metaphorical sense. It included not only predators and disease and shortage of food but also a plant on the edge of a desert, which is said to struggle for life. Much of the struggle would seem to involve suffering, as more offspring are produced than can possibly survive. Again, this is a problem for the

9. *The Life and Letters of Charles Darwin*, ed. Francis Darwin, vol. 2 (London: John Murray, 1888), p. 312. The quotation is in a letter from Charles Darwin to Asa Gray, the Harvard botanist.

orthodox theist whose God is said to be omnipotent and loving. This is not a problem for process thought, which recognizes a cost at every level of creation, with that cost becoming greater at the level of humans. The greater the capacity for sensitivity, the greater the capacity for suffering. The God of process thought is not indifferent to the suffering of the creation but shares in it. Such a God feels the creation in its suffering. The question then to be asked is: Would the world be a better one if all its creatures were insensitive to the higher values and free from the accompanying suffering? It would be like a dead man who has no chance of suffering, nor any of enjoyment.

## Natural Selection

Natural selection is the differential survival and reproduction of individuals in the population. It moves the population in the direction of greater adaptiveness. It is a consequence or necessary result of the struggle for existence between different genotypes. This elemental process would, Darwin argued, lead to the origin of new species. Darwin did not witness natural selection in nature. He knew about artificial selection in pigeons and other animals, which he regarded as a parallel process, engineered by humans. With appropriate techniques we can witness natural selection in almost any population biologists' study. The evolution of resistance of bacteria to antibiotics is a classic example of what is called microevolution. Most biologists think microevolutionary changes can eventually lead to the origin of new species. Evolution creeps. But it also leaps when natural selection is severe. A minority view is that leaps are due to sudden macrochanges.

Natural selection does not require any intervention from outside, such as that of a deity. That is not to say that it is simply a sievelike process of sorting the good from the bad genes that have arisen by chance.

## Enter Purpose

Thus far we have considered only the well-established positions of neo-Darwinism and how process thought can accept them. We turn now to whether, approaching evolution from the process perspective, we can find evidence that the subjectivity of the creatures also plays a role in the total process.

Purposive processes enter the picture. "Host selection" in insects is adaptive behavior that is not initially programmed by genes. The codlin moth was a pest of apples in the United States. Not until 1918 did it become a pest of walnuts.

This new "race" had a preference for walnuts over apples. It appeared to be an example of "host conditioning" leading to a genetic fixation called genetic assimilation. The process has been experimentally demonstrated in the fruit fly drosophila. Larvae of the fruit fly fed on peppermint-flavored food turn into adult flies that, given a choice, prefer laying their eggs on peppermint-flavored food. The fly is conditioned to choose the smell of the food on which it was raised. We may suppose that in the case of the walnut race of the codlin moth there were genetic differences among the original individuals bred on apples in their flexibility of behavior. Some may never have made a mistake. They always chose apples. But some were more flexible in their behavior and found walnuts. Having started their lives on walnuts, they would have been kept in this new environment by "host conditioning." This is adaptive behavior, initiated by exploration, that leads the animal into a new environment where selection is different.

Another interesting example is the story of tits and milk bottles. The first tit to open a milk bottle was presumably engaged in random exploration. However, the repetition of this behavior and its imitation by other tits all over Europe are best understood as expressions of intelligent purpose. When the cardboard tops were replaced by metal ones, the tits learned to open these also. Unless one's metaphysics requires one to explain all this in strictly mechanistic terms, one will assume that the subjective experience of the tits has been involved.

This example is relevant to evolutionary theory. If the tits continue to open milk bottles and drink milk over several generations, this new behavior will give selective advantage to some tits over others. Their genes will be transmitted in larger numbers. Some mutations may also prove to be advantageous that would not otherwise have been so. In this way the purposive behavior of tits could affect the course of evolution. Whether it has actually done so is not important. It is safe to assume that the tits are not the first birds to have learned new skills that have an effect on the selection of genes. It is also safe to assume that birds are not the only living things that learn new skills. Neo-Darwinian theory needs to be expanded to take account of purposive behavior on the part of animals as a contributor to evolution.

Purposive behavior is readily recognized in human beings. We recognize ourselves as creative agents rather than as simply patients that are acted upon. Process thought seeks indications that something of this sort is also true of much simpler entities. This is not the question that neo-Darwinians typically raise on the basis of their metaphysical assumptions. They prefer to think from the bottom up and to explain apparent agency in mechanistic terms. But it is an open, empirical question whether biology provides any evidence of real agency at lower levels.

## Self-Organization

That there is such agency is suggested, although not proved, by the recently emphasized idea of self-organization. This is well developed in physics but is only now being appreciated in biology.[10] An example of self-organization at the molecular level is the local interaction among amino acids that gives rise to complexly folded protein molecules. When this complex molecule is dissociated from a three-dimensional state and associated with a simpler linear state, this is followed by spontaneous reassembly. The molecules are not always able to so self-organize without the help of "chaperone" proteins, which guide the three-dimensional folding of proteins.

A notable example of self-organization of a more complex organism is the slime mold, which starts life as spores, which become amoeboid cells that repel one another. When food becomes scarce, the cells no longer repel each other but aggregate to form a sluglike creature that slithers over the surface of the soil. From this undifferentiated mass of cells a stalk grows, at the top of which is formed a fruiting body that develops spores. The fruiting body bursts and the spores are distributed, and so the life cycle is repeated time and time again. It is clear that a slime mold cell has the potentiality to be an amoeba, a stem cell, a fruiting body cell, and a spore. What causes it to change from one to the other? A chemical called acrasin, which the organism secretes, forms a gradient in the environment. It is the number of surrounding cells and this chemical component of the environment that cause one sort of cell to transform itself into another.

There is no reason to suppose that there are genetic differences between the different cells. Accordingly, what this shows is the remarkably varied potential within one cell to self-organize into different cells. How it organizes itself depends on what is happening in its neighboring cells and on a chemical component of the environment. This example shows how what an entity is and does depends on the environment in which it finds itself. This is very different from the classical idea of a material atom that remains wholly unchanged through time regardless of its relation to other entities.

A much more complex example of self-organization is the ordering process in the development from a single cell, such as the fertilized human ovum, into an adult human. The fertilized ovum has the potentiality to differentiate after cell division into a variety of cells — muscle cells, nerve cells, and many others. These become organized into tissues such as sheaths of muscles. The tis-

10. See Charles Birch, *Biology and the Riddle of Life* (Sydney: University of New South Wales Press, 1999).

sues become organized into organs, such as kidneys, and these are assembled into a working body. The genetic capacities of the original cell are turned on or off depending on the changing environment of the cell in embryonic development. It is then possible to consider every cell in embryonic development as a behaving entity. I know of only one attempt to interpret embryonic development this way, namely, that of Agar.[11] This theory is supported by some experimental studies, but the success of molecular biology in giving mechanistic explanations has pushed this approach into the shadows.

One line of investigation of self-organization is to try to make computer models of its processes. These are necessarily mechanistic models. Some of the processes can indeed be replicated on a computer, but this does not mean that the behaving entities are in all respects like machines. They may partake in something like the purpose-motivated creativity of humans. Determinism by genes is not an all-or-none affair. There can be different degrees of freedom. There is all the difference in the world between 100 percent determination and 99 percent determination. One provides no room for choice and purpose. The other does.

It is impossible to prove that any instances of apparent agency in entities at any level are inexplicable in mechanistic terms. It is possible to create zombies whose artificial intelligence and behavior closely resemble the natural intelligence and behavior of human beings who, we know, actually are subjects as well as objects. That entities at many levels seem to take account of their environment and to act in appropriately responsive ways will never prove that they are not in fact machines. However, noting the many such instances will make clear that the reason for viewing them as machines, rather than as agents, is metaphysical, not empirical.

If one adopts a process perspective, one can examine all the mechanical aspects of behavior, including human behavior, without the compulsion to assert that the mechanical model exhaustively explains what is going on. One can use what we know of human experience to interpret aspects of other levels of the natural world, just as we use what we learn about these levels to explain aspects of ourselves.

## Evolution and God

I have taught many courses on evolution with an emphasis on neo-Darwinism. The difficult question for me has always been what difference should my com-

---

11. W. E. Agar, *A Contribution to the Theory of the Living Organism* (Melbourne: Melbourne University Press, 1951).

mitment to process thought make in teaching such a course. There is no problem in indicating what neo-Darwinism does to the supernatural theism that Darwin was brought up in. It no longer has a leg to stand on.

However, my students have little or no background in philosophy or theology. So it is difficult to say in class anything about a more sophisticated concept of God's activity. I deal with that problem by accepting an invitation from the students' Student Christian Movement to give two lunch hour lectures that are not part of the course. The first is titled "What Darwin Did to God"; the second, "What God Does to Science."

The problem then comes when a bright student asks what specific observable consequences in biology can be attributed to divine causality. I may tell the student that "God acts by being felt by his creatures" (Daniel Day Williams). I find that credible when thinking of human behavior. But what, for example, about the codlin moth? It normally lays its eggs on apples. We may say that the smell of apples gives the moth a particular feeling that makes it lay its eggs there. But on rare occasions the moth seems to exhibit a more exploratory behavior and, when passing walnut trees, stops and lays some eggs on walnuts. The eggs hatch and the larvae, if given the choice, preferentially feed on walnuts rather than apples. These larvae produce moths that have a preference for laying eggs on walnuts. After several generations this behavior becomes genetically fixed through genetic assimilation, and we have a new race of walnut codlin moths. The process is interpreted by geneticists as completely Darwinian. Where does God come into the picture? One response from John Cobb is: "Unprogrammed purposive behavior results from God's internal work. This has an effect on the course of evolution. I think God lures creatures into exploratory behavior, which then leads to the enrichment of the biosphere."[12] I am happy to go along with the idea that the moth is not completely programmed and that it has its degree of freedom to sometimes lay its eggs in the "wrong" place. Further, I am happy to call this purposive behavior. The walnut lures the moth (perhaps by smell) to stop over and lay some eggs there. But why bring God in as a lure for the moth to explore and then settle on walnuts? Biology tells the story without positing God as a cause. What is missing, if anything, in the biological story? I do not know the answer.

I tend to stress self-organization, which is the extent to which the creature itself appears to be programmed or perhaps a consequence of creative freedom. The main point is, as Charles Kingsley once said, that "God makes things that make themselves." Can we be more specific than that, especially concerning nonhumans?

12. John Cobb, personal communication.

Look now at the three components of neo-Darwinism: mutation, struggle for existence, and natural selection. Mutation is built into the nature of DNA. It is not an act of God. If it were, why would God make so many mistakes! Natural selection is a mechanical selective process with one known exception, and that is genetic assimilation (Waddington), as in the case of the codlin moth. Genetic assimilation could be more widespread than we know at present. Struggle for existence is a consequence of harsh environments.

Apart from purposive processes, I have difficulty being specific about divine activity in biological evolution. Does process thought have specific answers? If so, what are they?

# 16. Introduction to "The Metaphysics of Consciousness and Evolution"

Robert J. Valenza

In the appendix to this volume the reader will find my essay "The Metaphysics of Consciousness and Evolution." It moves from abstract metaphysical and epistemological issues to some general considerations about science and the nature of consciousness, and only then enters upon a specific connection with evolution. Here I offer a brief statement of its major conclusions. Before dismissing these conclusions, I ask the reader to consider carefully the detailed argument in the full essay.

The essay was written for the conference on evolution and religion out of which this book has developed. A good preparatory question might be this: Why did our conference not address, for instance, religion and the periodic table (which, in a sense, represents the evolution of elements) rather than religion and the evolution of life-forms? In both cases enormous yet well-structured complexity arises from comparative simplicity, and the process is not completely understood. In both cases a kind of scientific dogma applies: it's just a matter of time until we do have it all figured out.

The key difference, of course, is that we are part of the latter process, and, moreover, an extraordinary part that has direct access to certain elements of the world that seem hopelessly beyond the mechanistic domain of science, among them consciousness, intent, and conceptual creativity. Thus one might say that evolution would not be nearly so much of a problem without consciousness, and in large part this is why we were not merely concerned with the periodic table. We sense that in its account of the evolution of animals Cartesianism — reductionism, mechanism, atomism — is trying to ensnare something special, and some of us are not persuaded that it will or can succeed. The orthodox dogma of science — and absolutely nothing pejorative is intended here — drawing on centuries of astounding, accelerating success, says, "But of course it will! Why would anyone think otherwise?" Yet as firsthand experiencers, we sense an impenetrable boundary, the boundary that is the very root of classical dualism. Meanwhile, science in its forward march, ignoring blatantly all of Kuhn's cautions, optimistically disagrees.

Let us now expand this basic conflict into a more explicit dichotomy, and in so doing introduce some of the basic assumptions and developments of the essay in question. The first pair of tenets, which, to some extent, presage the entire conflict, are these:

1. Experience is both private and real. For some time philosophers tried to distinguish this domain by its incorrigibility (to seem to be in pain is to be in pain), but that doesn't matter here. The point is only that there are elements of private (unsharable) knowledge.

2. Science is public: its terms, measurements, explanations are to a high degree unambiguously sharable, and herein lies the essence of their objectivity. As such, at best science can only make the private elements of reality supervenient on (and not identical with) the public elements. Many philosophers would call this epiphenomenalism and, moreover, would be most uncomfortable with it.

Two key technical terms have occurred in this second assertion that are worthy of brief explanation; neither is all that difficult. Let C be some class of facts or properties of the world. (For instance, C might consist of the laws of physics.) Let D be some other class of facts or properties. Then one says that D is supervenient on C if the C properties necessitate the D properties. Put another way, once the C facts of the world are fixed, so are the D facts. (For instance, in the prevailing view in science, the laws of chemistry are supervenient on the laws of physics: in principle, if not in practice, to know physics is to know chemistry.) Thus supervenience is a matter of entailment, and as such admits two refinements, as noted in the fifth section of the essay in the appendix, with regard to the distinction between natural and logical supervenience.

The only point we need to emphasize here, however, is that assertions of supervenience need not make any reference to causal categories, either of traditional or novel species, and it is precisely this lack of causal encumbrance that lends the notion such effectiveness in the context of the mind-body problem. One may indeed maintain that consciousness, or more generally experience, is supervenient on the physical facts of the world without assuming the burden of causal explanation. One might hold also that the experiential domain exercises no causal efficacy whatsoever on the physical. Such a world is then physically closed, which is to say that everything that happens has a purely physical explanation, and yet possesses this persistent experiential component that is completely defined by its physical configuration while exerting no reciprocal effect. This position is called epiphenomenalism, and it has a kind of inevitability about it if one wants to maintain physical closure without denying the very existence of consciousness.

The key argument in my essay is a denial of the supervenience of consciousness on the physical and of the ensuing epiphenomenalism. To prepare for this denial, I introduce a number of simple mathematical models — involving no more than elementary arithmetic! — to illustrate the attendant metaphysical notions. These models are the so-called Petal Worlds, and the reader is urged to work through the details with pencil and paper. The main point, which is built upon the work of David Chalmers (1996), may be summarized as follows.

3. Epiphenomenalism is incoherent owing to the so-called paradox of phenomenal judgment: it seems wildly absurd that our phenomenal states are irrelevant to our physical reports of our phenomenal states.

We will let the paper speak for itself to explain this, except to say that it seems to reveal a radical incompleteness in science insofar as science addresses exclusively what is physical; we would seem to be at an utter loss to reconcile the facts of experience with any methodology that we would recognize as scientific.

An abstract framework to defeat this incompleteness is suggested by the paradox of phenomenal judgment itself.

4. An attractive metaphysical alternative would lay the foundations of public (scientific) and private (experiential) knowledge on one unified metaphysical base.

Accordingly, I construct a model for this alternative via the introduction of a final version of Petal World, and I note that Whiteheadian metaphysics is an example of just such a unification program. This concludes the first half of the paper; these general considerations are now brought to bear specifically on the problem of evolution.

Insofar as consciousness arises in higher life-forms, a complete biophysical theory of evolution must entail an explanation of consciousness, just as it must explain how complex wings and eyes could develop from simpler, prototypical structures. But is such a theory possible? A kind of categorical argument (reminiscent of a much earlier analysis of Lindsay and Morgenau)[1] operates here that brings us squarely back to the general problem of epiphenomenalism; it is founded on the public-private distinction.

5. Science is self-limiting through its insistence on physical closure and public observables. We do not accept a scientific explanation as complete if it is not closed causally and grounded in public variables. Thus when physical real-

---

1. Robert Bruce Lindsay and Henry Morgenau, *Foundations of Physics* (New York: Wiley, 1936; New York: Dover Publications, 1963).

ity sets limits on causation and observation, such as in quantum theory, science responds to these limits by changing its ways and means. Put another way, experience, insofar as it is ultimately private, is by definition irrelevant to scientific discourse.

The conclusion is clear: science as we know it cannot yield a complete description or explanation of any experiential component of reality — in other words, science as we know it commits us to the incoherence of epiphenomenalism — and therefore must also be essentially incomplete in describing the evolution of systems that manifest experience and consciousness.

This leaves us to speculate on what might serve as an appropriate complement for science in describing a unified basis for both the public and the private domains. My proposal begins with the following observation. We operate more or less successfully in the nonscientific domain of, say, interpersonal transactions by making narrative maps: assessing the beliefs, intentions, feelings of others by their actions and the relationships among our beliefs, intentions, feelings, and actions. We are often wildly wrong, but we have never had much choice. Insofar as we do succeed, it is largely because Alice can answer the question, "What is it like to be Mary?" As the answer to that question degrades in moving away from things more or less like ourselves, so does our success at making narrative maps, until finally when we ask something like, "What is it like to be a water molecule?" we have essentially no good narrative map and must rely almost entirely on science for what to expect of it.

Into what kind of an epistemic stance does this lead us? If we accept, as did Whitehead, that the public and the private, or the scientific and the experiential, both derive from some common metaphysical fabric, then neither the scientific nor the narrative maps can separately be comprehensive. We would expect the purely scientific explanations to become more and more complex and limited exactly where the narrative explanations are most natural, and of course vice versa. How can we transcend the limits of these domains? Scientific discourse will continue as it is so long as its limits are acceptable in managing reality. Narrative discourse probably has the better hope for near-term expansion if we make an effort to ask those what-is-it-like-to-be questions in search of an underlying metaphysical system. There is no sharp reason why the splendid pliability of human intelligence should not extend narrative discourse into wider and wider domains. A myriad of examples from religion and art should be vastly encouraging. (The title character in *Anna Karenina* and the plays of Shakespeare come immediately to mind as evidence of this pliability.) That the phrase "artistic truth" has even been conceived is perhaps already a cause for optimism.

What if this all were to succeed? What would it be like to understand a process like evolution in this context? In this vision, there would be no fully sharable, public answer, but each of us, perhaps drawing on a more developed comprehension of religion and art, might say something like this: "I see that this process entails experiential elements that I can only vaguely encompass, but I begin grasping the truth insofar as my narrative understanding now reaches beyond human experience. I know, too, that I may discard this narrative and that then there remains a closed physical explanation entirely within the limits of public, scientific discourse. But such an explanation is doubly limited, both in its way of speaking and its domain of application. In any case, it is hardly, for me, the most satisfying way of knowing the world."

This last bit of speculation was better framed by Tolstoy:

> From the moment Levin saw his beloved brother dying and for the first time looked at the problems of life and death in the light of what he called the new convictions that between the ages of twenty and thirty-four had imperceptibly taken the place of the beliefs of his childhood and youth, he was horrified not so much by death as by a life without the slightest knowledge of where it came from, what it was for, and why, and what it was. The organism, its dissolution, the indestructibility of matter, the law of conservation of energy, evolution — these were the words that had replaced his former faith. These words and the concepts associated with them were very useful for intellectual purposes, but they made no contribution to life, and Levin suddenly felt he was in the position of a man who had exchanged a warm fur coat for a muslin blouse, and who the first time he finds himself in the frost is persuaded beyond question, not by arguments but by the whole of his being, that he's no better than naked and is inevitably bound to perish miserably.[2]

---

2. Leo Tolstoy, *Anna Karenina,* trans. Joel Carmichael, classic edition (New York: Bantam Books, 1981), p. 834.

# 17. Neo-Darwinism and
## Its Religious Implications

DAVID RAY GRIFFIN

The presently dominant form of evolutionary theory is widely known as "neo-Darwinism." This term is widely used, at least by historians, philosophers, and theologians. According to Francisco Ayala,[1] most working biologists do not use the term. When speaking of the viewpoint they and most of their colleagues hold, most refer simply to "evolution" or "evolutionary theory." Be that as it may, these terms are, from both historical and philosophical vantage points, inadequate, because there have been, and still are, several theories of evolution, and it is even possible that some new theory, quite different from today's dominant view, will become ascendant in the future. For clarity of thought we need a name to distinguish the presently dominant evolutionary theory from other theories — past, present, and possibly future.

Insofar as working biologists do recognize the need for a more specific name, they are evidently inclined simply to use "Darwinism," without the "neo." However, although the presently dominant view clearly developed from Darwin's own position, it is significantly different in several respects. Being a new form of Darwinism, it is appropriately called "neo-Darwinism."[2] So, even

---

1. See Ayala, chapter 2.

2. As Ayala points out in chapter 2, the term "neo-Darwinism" was at one time used to refer to the position of August Weismann. But I am using it, in accord with widespread practice, to refer to the position that originated with the "modern synthesis" achieved in the 1930s and 1940s, which historian William Provine calls the "evolutionary constriction," as discussed in the text below. By looking up "neo-Darwinism" on Google, one can see that the use of this term for the modern synthesis is very common. For example, one encyclopedia article begins: "Neo-Darwinism is the modern version of Darwinian evolutionary theory: the synthesis of Mendelian genetics and Darwinism" (http://www.iscid.org/encyclopedia/Neo-Darwinism). Another begins: "The modern evolutionary synthesis (often referred to simply as the modern synthesis), neo-Darwinian synthesis or neo-Darwinism . . ." Still another entry begins: "Neo-Darwinism is synonymous with the Modern Synthesis" (http://www.everything2.com/index.pl?node=neodarwinism). Turning to *The*

if this term has not been used much by working biologists, it is useful for distinguishing the presently dominant theory of evolution from Darwin's own theory as well as from non-Darwinian theories.[3]

That said, I move to my substantive discussion, which I begin by pointing out that neo-Darwinism has been widely regarded — by advocates as well as detractors — as having negative consequences for both religion and morality. Some detractors also regard it as inadequate even from a scientific point of view, claiming that it has hindered the scientific study of evolution.[4]

Advocates have responded in various ways. Some, while maintaining that neo-Darwinism, at least with some recent additions and refinements, is perfectly adequate, at least in principle, for the scientific study of evolution, say, in effect, "so much the worse for religion and morality." Other advocates, while taking the same position on neo-Darwinism's scientific adequacy, say its deleterious consequences for religion and morality have been exaggerated — that a neo-Darwinian worldview can support robust religious and moral lives.

In this chapter I give an account of the basic tenets of the neo-Darwinian theory and draw forth what I, together with many others, judge to be its religious implications when it is carried to its logical conclusions. Because these implications are extremely negative, it is not surprising that the theory evokes strong opposition. This opposition is often embodied in worldviews that are unacceptable in principle from a scientific perspective. I, however, will suggest a kind of criticism that could, at least in principle, be acceptable to the scientific community. In a second chapter, later in this volume,[5] I spell out a Whiteheadian alternative to neo-Darwinism that is meant to be superior for scientific purposes as well as from moral and religious perspectives.

---

*American Heritage Dictionary of the English Language* (4th ed., 2000), I found this definition of neo-Darwinism: "Darwinism as modified by the findings of modern genetics."

3. The distinction between Darwinism and neo-Darwinism, besides being ignored by many working biologists, is also obscured by some philosophers. For example, in a book titled *Darwin's Dangerous Idea: Evolution and the Meaning of Life* (New York: Simon and Schuster, 1995), Daniel Dennett claims that Darwin's dangerous idea "is that Design can emerge from mere Order via an algorithmic process that makes no use of pre-existing Mind" (p. 83). Whereas John Locke thought design inconceivable without Mind, Darwin's idea "that evolution is a mindless, purposeless, algorithmic process," claims Dennett, allowed him "to overthrow Locke's Mind-first vision" (pp. 83, 320). However, in a few more historically accurate passages (pp. 67, 149-50, 164, 180), Dennett mentions that Darwin himself, being a deist (see point 12 in the text, below), believed in divine design as the basis of the laws of nature behind the evolutionary process. He had, in other words, a "Mind-first vision." A more honest title for Dennett's book, therefore, would have been "Neo-Darwinism's Dangerous Idea."

4. See most of the chapters in part II above.

5. See chapter 22 below.

It is important, in discussing neo-Darwinism, to realize that many biologists working on issues related to evolution do not worry about whether their ideas are neo-Darwinian. Most of them are probably quite eclectic, combining ideas that follow from this theory with others that supplement it and still others that more or less strongly contradict it. It is important, therefore, not to equate the current study of evolution with neo-Darwinism or to assume that most working biologists subscribe to all the doctrines here ascribed to it. It is especially important to realize that most working biologists probably do not endorse what I will describe as the deleterious moral and religious implications of neo-Darwinism.

At the same time, it is equally important to realize that a fairly strict orthodoxy is enforced by those who hold positions of power in the scientific community — such as the heads of granting agencies and the editors, including the book review editors, of leading journals. Those who wish to bring about a change in the way evolution is taught in schools and explained to the public, therefore, need to confront this thing called neo-Darwinism.

That statement presupposes, of course, that there is such a thing. All my reading and experience in this area convince me that there is — that, in spite of many developments in the tradition and some disagreements among neo-Darwinists about the implications of the core doctrines, there *is* a set of core doctrines that has defined the neo-Darwinian tradition. I will now lay out my understanding of what those core doctrines are.

Since, as the name neo-Darwinism indicates, it is a form of Darwinism, I will first summarize the basic doctrines of Darwinism as such. I will begin with two doctrines that can be considered the basic scientific doctrines, then move to the more metaphysical doctrines, and then give a derivative scientific doctrine.[6]

## Basic Scientific Doctrines of Darwinism and Neo-Darwinism

1. Microevolution. This doctrine affirms the occurrence of minor genetic and sometimes phenotypical changes within a species (or even the transformation of members of one species into a new species in one technical sense of that term). Sometimes called Darwin's special theory of evolution, this doctrine, which contradicts the idea that all species are absolutely fixed, is now uncontroversial.

6. This summary draws heavily from chapter 8, "Creation and Evolution," of my *Religion and Scientific Naturalism: Overcoming the Conflicts* (Albany: State University of New York Press, 2000).

2. Macroevolution. This doctrine says that all present species of living things have in some way descended from previous species over a very long period of time. Darwin said this doctrine — through which the idea of the separate creation of each species was replaced by the idea of descent with modification — was his primary concern, with his distinctive doctrine of natural selection being of secondary importance.[7] This doctrine rules out not only standard creationism but also "progressive creationism" — the view that accepts the current consensus on the dating for the rise of bacteria, eukaryotic cells, and so on, but maintains that each species was created ex nihilo.

I turn now to the Darwinian doctrines that, even if they are often considered part of Darwinism as a scientific doctrine, are more properly considered metaphysical doctrines. Although some scientific readers may be tempted to skip over these as "merely metaphysical," it is important to recognize that these metaphysical doctrines, held by Darwin and his early followers, were presupposed when later followers turned Darwinism into neo-Darwinism, which contains scientific doctrines and religious-moral implications that Darwin himself did not endorse.

## Metaphysical Doctrines of Darwinism and Neo-Darwinism

3. Naturalism$_{ns}$. This doctrine stipulates that the explanations for microevolution, whatever they may be, must be entirely naturalistic, with "naturalism" here understood only in the minimal sense, which stipulates that there are never any miraculous, supernatural interruptions of, or interjections into, the normal causal processes. Naturalism in this minimal sense can be called naturalism$_{ns}$ (with "ns" standing for "nonsupernaturalist").

This naturalism is to be distinguished from a much more restrictive doctrine to which the term "naturalism" is now widely attached. This more restrictive doctrine, which has a sensationist doctrine of perception and entails an atheistic, materialistic worldview, can be called naturalism$_{sam}$ (with "sam" standing for "sensationist-atheistic-materialistic"). It is extremely important to make this distinction, because naturalism$_{ns}$, ruling out nothing but supernatural interruptions, can be part of a worldview that is nonmaterialistic, affirms theism, and allows for the possibility of genuine religious and moral experience.[8]

7. Neal C. Gillespie, *Charles Darwin and the Problem of Creation* (Chicago: University of Chicago Press, 1979), p. 130.

8. I have developed and illustrated this point in *Religion and Scientific Naturalism* and, somewhat more fully, in *Reenchantment without Supernaturalism: A Process Philosophy of Religion* (Ithaca, N.Y.: Cornell University Press, 2001).

4. Uniformitarianism. This doctrine stipulates that only causal factors operating in the present can be employed to explain past developments. In Darwin's own mind, this stipulation involved two dimensions: ontological uniformitarianism, which rules out (among other things) supernatural divine interventions, and geological uniformitarianism, which rules out occasional catastrophes. Today, geological uniformitarianism is no longer affirmed, but ontological uniformitarianism, which is simply another term for naturalism in the minimal sense, is absolutely presupposed.

5. Positivism-Materialism. Positivism (as used in discussions of the evolutionary philosophy) is the doctrine that all causes of evolution must be at least potentially verifiable through sensory observation. This insistence is virtually identical with the insistence on exclusively physical or material causes, in that only such causes are in principle detectable through the physical senses. Positivism and materialism, accordingly, have the same implications, so we can combine them into one doctrine, positivism-materialism.

6. Predictive Determinism. To Darwin, says historian Charles Gillespie, "materialism" primarily meant the doctrine that the world is, without exception, a deterministic system of causes and effects.[9] This point was central to Darwin, because he accepted the idea that science requires absolute predictability (in principle), which, of course, required complete determinism. This doctrine of complete determinism required, in turn, the exclusion of all teleology, or "final causation" in the sense of purposive causation. As Frederick Gregory says, "Scientific explanation had come more and more to mean mechanical explanation, so much so that even reference to 'naturalistic' explanation could be intended to connote the exclusion of final cause."[10] As Gillespie puts it: "The essence of the positive science was predictability: caprice had no place in its cosmos."[11]

Darwin's acceptance of this ideal meant that no exception could be made for human beings, which implied that "free will . . . fell under his ban" because it would introduce "an element of caprice." Indeed, materialism for Darwin meant primarily that the brain determines human thoughts and decisions, as did the brains of all other animals.[12] Accordingly, when later Darwinists rejected Darwin's own distinction between natural selection and sexual selection,

9. Gillespie, *Charles Darwin*, pp. 138-41.

10. See Frederick Gregory, "The Impact of Darwinian Evolution on Protestant Theology," in *God and Nature: Historical Essays on the Encounter between Christianity and Science*, ed. David C. Lindberg and Ronald L. Numbers (Berkeley: University of California Press, 1988), pp. 369-90, at p. 370.

11. Gillespie, *Charles Darwin*, p. 152.

12. Gillespie, *Charles Darwin*, p. 139.

because the latter involved a choice, they were only making Darwin's own position more self-consistent.[13] Today, William Provine, a historian of Darwinism, says evolutionary biology teaches us that "free will, as traditionally conceived, the freedom to make uncoerced and unpredictable choices among alternative possible courses of action, simply does not exist. . . . [T]he evolutionary process cannot produce a being that is truly free to make choices."[14]

7. Nominalism. This doctrine entails the rejection of "Platonic realism," according to which forms, archetypes, or ideas are really real, being somehow inherent in the nature of things. Nominalism — from the Latin *nomen*, meaning "name" — is the doctrine that the names for these forms are merely names. They do not point to entities that really exist in any sense. Darwinism is fully nominalistic, rejecting the realism about forms upon which the typological approach of Georges Cuvier and other traditionalists, such as Linnaeus, was based. Ernst Mayr, for example, has said: "I agree with those who claim that the essentialist philosophies of Plato and Aristotle are incompatible with evolutionary thinking. For the typologist, the type (eidos) is real and the variation an illusion, while for the populationists (evolutionists) the type (average) is an abstraction and only the variation is real."[15]

## A Derivative Scientific Doctrine

8. Gradualism: This doctrine stipulates that macroevolution proceeds gradually, through a process comprised of tiny steps. As Darwin famously said: "Natural selection acts only by the preservation and accumulation of small inherited modifications, each profitable to the preserved being. . . . [N]atural selection [will] banish the belief of the continued creation of new organic beings, or of any great and sudden modification of their structure."[16]

Richard Dawkins has recently reaffirmed this approach. Asking how living things, which are "too improbable and too beautifully 'designed' to have come into existence by chance," did come into existence, Dawkins says: "The

13. See Helena Cronin, *The Ant and the Peacock: Altruism and Sexual Selection from Darwin to Today* (Cambridge, U.K., and New York: Press Syndicate of the University of Cambridge, 1991), pp. 267-68.

14. William Provine, "Progress in Evolution and Meaning in Life," in *Evolutionary Progress*, ed. Matthew H. Nitecki (Chicago and London: University of Chicago Press, 1988), pp. 49-74, at pp. 64-66.

15. Ernst Mayr, *Populations, Species, and Evolution* (Cambridge: Harvard University Press, 1970).

16. Charles Darwin, *The Origin of Species* (1872) (New York: Mentor Books, 1958), p. 100.

answer, Darwin's answer, is by gradual, step-by-step transformations from simple beginnings. . . . Each successive change in the gradual evolutionary process was simple enough, relative to its predecessor, to have come into existence by chance."[17] Although gradualism is a scientific doctrine, because it is empirically testable, it is a derivative scientific doctrine, because it is based less on empirical evidence than on the previous metaphysical doctrines.

This dimension of Darwin's proposal, in any case, was doubly radical. On the one hand, it went against the traditional typological view, which said that tiny changes would result in incoherent, unviable organisms. According to Georges Cuvier (1769-1832), who articulated this typological position most fully, the principle of the correlation and interdependence of parts rendered the evolution of one species into another improbable. As John Brooke summarizes Cuvier's position: "There simply could not be a gradual accumulation of variation in any one part, unless all could change in concert. And that, for Cuvier, was simply too fanciful."[18] On the other hand, Darwin also had to deal with the empirical evidence, and the fossil record simply did not support the idea of gradualistic evolution, because it revealed almost nothing but well-defined types, with few if any intermediate varieties. Darwin handled this problem by claiming that the geological record must be "imperfect to an extreme degree."[19]

Further paleontological research has, furthermore, evidently not lessened the problem. George Simpson wrote in 1944 that the "regular absence of transitional forms . . . is an almost universal phenomenon."[20] In 1959 Norman Newell, the curator at the American Museum of Natural History, said: "Many of the discontinuities tend to be more and more emphasized with increased collecting."[21] In 1991 Michael Denton wrote that "the fossil record is about as discontinuous as it was when Darwin was writing the Origin."[22]

Darwin was warned against his gradualism by several fellow scientists, including his advocate Thomas Huxley. In response to Darwin's acceptance of the dictum "nature does not make jumps,"[23] Huxley wrote: "You have loaded your-

17. Richard Dawkins, *The Blind Watchmaker: Why the Evidence of Evolution Reveals a Universe without Design* (New York and London: Norton, 1987), p. 43.

18. John Hedley Brooke, *Science and Religion: Some Historical Perspectives* (Cambridge: Cambridge University Press, 1991), p. 246.

19. Darwin, *The Origin of Species*, p. 438.

20. George G. Simpson, *Tempo and Mode in Evolution* (New York: Columbia University Press, 1944), pp. 106, 107.

21. Norman D. Newell, "The Nature of the Fossil Record," *Proceedings of the American Philosophical Society* 103, no. 2 (1959): 264-85, at p. 267.

22. Michael Denton, *Evolution: A Theory in Crisis* (London: Burnett Books, 1991), p. 162.

23. Darwin, *The Origin of Species*, pp. 181, 191, 256, 435.

self with an unnecessary difficulty in adopting natura non facit saltum so unreservedly."[24]

Huxley, however, evidently did not understand that, given the various philosophical principles behind Darwin's theory, the difficulty was not "unnecessary." As Robert Wesson says, "Darwin insisted on gradualism as the essence of naturalism and the repudiation of divine intervention."[25] Darwin, points out Gillespie, considered any suggestion of evolution *per saltum* (by jumps) to be a disguised appeal to miraculous creation.[26] As Howard Gruber put it, for Darwin "nature makes no jumps, but God does. . . . [N]ature makes no jumps, therefore if something is found in the world that appears suddenly, its origins must be supernatural."[27] Darwin, recognizing that his whole theory was at stake, said: "If it could be demonstrated that any complex organ existed, which could not possibly have been formed by numerous, successive, slight modifications, my theory would absolutely break down."[28]

Given his principles, Darwin could not "save" his theory by allowing divine insertions here and there to explain the apparent jumps in the record. In response to Charles Lyell's belief that an exception to ontological uniformitarianism was required to account for the human mind, Darwin wrote: "If I were convinced that I required such additions to the theory of natural selection, I would reject it as rubbish. . . . I would give nothing for the theory of Natural Selection, if it requires miraculous additions at any one stage of descent."[29]

Having quoted this passage, Dawkins adds: "This is no petty matter. In Darwin's view, the whole point of the theory of evolution by natural selection was that it provided a non-miraculous account of the existence of complex adaptations. For Darwin, any evolution that had to be helped over the jumps by God was not evolution at all. . . . In the light of this, it is easy to see why Darwin constantly reiterated the gradualness of evolution."[30]

Darwin's rejection of saltations, moreover, reflected his rejection not only of miraculous, supernaturalist interruptions of the normal causal processes but also of any form of (ongoing) theistic influence whatsoever. The doctrine of

---

24. *Life and Letters of Thomas Henry Huxley*, ed. Leonard Huxley, 2 vols. (London: Macmillan; New York: A. Appleton, 1901), 2:176.

25. Robert Wesson, *Beyond Natural Selection* (Cambridge: MIT Press, 1991), p. 38.

26. Gillespie, *Charles Darwin*, p. 82.

27. Howard Gruber, *Darwin on Man: A Psychological Study of Scientific Creativity*, 2nd ed. (Chicago: University of Chicago Press, 1981), pp. 125-26.

28. Darwin, *The Origin of Species*, p. 171.

29. *The Life and Letters of Charles Darwin*, ed. Francis Darwin, 2 vols. (New York: D. Appleton, 1896), 2:6-7.

30. Dawkins, *The Blind Watchmaker*, p. 249.

nominalism is here the link. Antinominalists, affirming the real existence of forms or archetypes in the nature of things, could suppose that they might serve as "final causes" or "attractors," so that the jump from one coherent type to another would not be entirely accidental. They could, thereby, believe that it might occur occasionally.

But it is hard to affirm the influence of forms in the world while rejecting theism, because it is difficult to think of Platonic forms as, all on their own, exerting any influence, even of an attractive sort. These intuitions lay behind the medieval doctrine that the forms, or ideas, subsist in God, who gave them not only a home but also ongoing efficacy. Platonic theists can, as antinominalists, reject extreme gradualism in favor of occasional saltations. But Darwin's deism (to be discussed below) limited divine influence to the original creation of the world and hence was effectively nominalistic. (Neo-Darwinism, by rejecting deism as well as theism, is even more emphatically nominalistic.) Darwinian evolution must, therefore, be gradualistic.

## Interlude: The Neo-Darwinian Constriction and the Exclusion of Purposes

Given the above scientific and metaphysical doctrines, we will look at the distinctively neo-Darwinian doctrines that they have been used to support. First, however, it is important to understand what occurred in the creation of what is usually called the "modern synthetic theory" or the "evolutionary synthesis," which resulted in the view that is now widely called neo-Darwinism.[31] Although, as these names indicate, it is usually described simply as the synthesis of original Darwinism with Mendelian genetics, William Provine says it "would be better termed the 'evolutionary constriction,' because it was not so much a synthesis as it was a vast cut-down of variables considered important in the evolutionary process. . . . What was new in this conception of evolution was not the individual variables . . . but the idea that evolution depended on relatively so few of them."[32]

As Helena Cronin points out, Darwin himself had been more pluralistic. Rather than limiting the causes to random variations and natural selection, he allowed for other factors, including the inheritance of acquired characteristics, insisting only that natural selection was the primary factor.[33]

31. See note 1, above.
32. Provine, "Progress in Evolution," p. 61.
33. Cronin, Ant and the Peacocke, pp. 82-83.

Furthermore, much that passed for "Darwinian evolutionism" from the 1860s to the 1930s was even more pluralistic, allowing for various types of purposive causes, both divine and nondivine.[34] The modern construction, says Provine, primarily involved the agreement that "purposive forces played no role at all."[35] Evolution was declared to be nonpurposive in every possible sense, reflecting the purposes of neither a universal creator nor any local creatures. This exclusion of purposes was of course entailed by the doctrines of naturalism$_{ns}$, positivism-materialism, and predictive determinism.

Now, given these metaphysical doctrines — naturalism$_{ns}$, uniformitarianism, positivism-materialism, predictive determinism, nominalism, and the exclusion of all purposes — we are in better position to understand the strictly scientific doctrines that are unique to neo-Darwinism, distinguishing it from earlier Darwinism.

## Uniquely Neo-Darwinian Scientific Doctrines

9. The Reduction of Macroevolution to Microevolution. According to this doctrine, all macroevolution is to be understood entirely in terms of the processes involved in microevolution (which, as the next doctrine points out, are limited to random variation and natural selection). Douglas Futuyama declares that "the known mechanisms of evolution [provide] both a sufficient and a necessary explanation for the diversity of life."[36] Richard Dawkins says Darwinism "has no difficulty in explaining every tiny detail."[37] Some more candid, or perhaps more circumspect, Darwinists admit that this has not been shown. Walter Bock says: "One of the major failures of the [neo-Darwinian] synthetic theory has been to provide a detailed and coherent explanation of macroevolution based on the known principles of microevolution." Even Bock believes, however, that macroevolution can in principle be explained in terms of microevolution.[38]

10. The Restriction to Random Variations and Natural Selection. According to this doctrine, which resulted from the "evolutionary constriction," all

34. Gregory, "Impact of Darwinian Evolution," pp. 179, 383; Provine, "Progress in Evolution," p. 60.

35. Provine, "Progress in Evolution," pp. 64-66, 70.

36. Douglas Futuyama, *Evolutionary Biology* (Sunderland, Mass.: Sinauer, 1979), p. 449.

37. Dawkins, *The Blind Watchmaker*, p. 302.

38. Walter J. Bock, "The Synthetic Explanation of Macroevolutionary Change: A Reductionistic Approach," *Bulletin of the Carnegie Museum of Natural History* 18 (1979): 20-69, at p. 20.

subsequent species of life have come about through evolutionary descent from the first forms of life solely through natural selection operating upon random (or "chance") variations — with the latter understood primarily, albeit not exclusively, in terms of random ("chance") genetic mutations.

Given some of the connotations of the word "random," and especially of the word "chance," some writers have been misled into assuming that evolution is, for neo-Darwinism, not fully determined. Holmes Rolston, for example, assumes that mutations are random in the sense of being "without necessary and sufficient causal conditions," and thereby completely contingent.[39] But Darwin, as we saw, held to predictive determinism. Accordingly, declaring that "the variations of each creature are determined by fixed and immutable laws,"[40] Darwin said "chance" means "our ignorance of the cause."[41] Likewise, in an essay titled "Chance and Creativity in Evolution," Theodosius Dobzhansky denied that there is any "principle of spontaneity inherent in living nature." To say that mutations are "chance events," explained Dobzhansky, is only to say that we are ignorant of the causes.[42] Richard Dawkins, singing from the same page, says: "Mutations are caused by definite physical events; they don't just spontaneously happen."[43] Niles Eldredge agrees, saying: "Mutations have definitive, deterministic causes."[44]

What Darwinists mean by calling mutations "random" is that they are not biased in favor of the adaptation of the organism to its environment. In Eldredge's words, "mutations are random with respect to the needs of the organisms in which they occur."[45] As Stephen Jay Gould put it, genetic variation is "not preferentially directed towards advantageous features."[46] We can therefore call randomness in this sense "randomness$_{na}$" — with "na" standing for both "not advantageous" and "not adaptational." This doctrine rules out, among other things, any need-induced mutations.

This doctrine is important, at least to some Darwinists, because the con-

39. Holmes Rolston III, *Science and Religion: A Critical Survey* (Philadelphia: Temple University Press, 1987), pp. 104, 91.

40. Charles Darwin, *The Variation of Animals and Plants under Domestication* (New York: Orange Judd and Co., 1868), pp. 248-49.

41. Gillespie, *Charles Darwin,* p. 55.

42. Theodosius Dobzhansky, "Chance and Creativity in Evolution," in *Studies in the Philosophy of Biology,* ed. Francisco J. Ayala and Theodosius Dobzhansky (Berkeley: University of California Press, 1974), pp. 307-38, at pp. 313-14, 329.

43. Dawkins, *The Blind Watchmaker,* p. 306; Niles Eldredge, *Reinventing Darwin: The Great Debate at the High Table of Evolutionary Theory* (New York: Wiley, 1995), p. 133.

44. Eldredge, *Reinventing Darwin,* p. 133.

45. Eldredge, *Reinventing Darwin,* p. 133.

46. Stephen Jay Gould, *The Mismeasure of Man* (New York: Norton, 1981), p. 325.

trary idea — that variation is somehow directed toward adaptation — would reduce the importance of natural selection, which many have considered the central Darwinian conception. The "essence of Darwinism," said Gould, "is the creativity of natural selection."[47] Behind this claim is the notion that natural selection creates new organs and species by scrutinizing all variations, the overwhelming majority of which are deleterious, selecting out the very rare one that just happens to give the organism an edge over its rivals in the competition for survival. However, if variations themselves were directed toward adaptation, natural selection would be unnecessary or would at least play a less central role.[48] Dawkins, expressing Darwinian orthodoxy on this point emphatically, says: "It is selection, and only selection, that directs evolution in directions that are non-random with respect to advantage."[49]

11. Evolution as Wholly Undirected. The desire to regard natural selection as virtually the sole creator of all living forms leads to a tendency to insist that mutations are random in an even stronger sense. Gould sometimes said variation was random in the sense of being wholly "undirected," of "aris[ing] in all directions," of having "no determined orientation."[50] Randomness in this sense, which we can call "randomness$_{eps}$" (for "every possible sense"), says that, besides not being directed toward adaptation to the immediate environment, mutations are also random in every other possible sense of the term (except, of course, in the sense of not being fully determined by antecedent causes). This doctrine rules out, for example, the idea that mutations might be biased toward the production of beauty, or greater complexity, or richer experience. This stronger meaning of randomness is intended to rule out the idea of any type of cosmic directivity. The idea that variations are random in every possible sense supports the idea that Gould calls the "cardinal tenet" of Darwinism: "that selection is the creative force in evolution."[51] The resulting doctrine is the idea that evolution is wholly undirected. This doctrine rules out not only supernaturalistic theism (which allows for supernatural interruptions) but also naturalistic theism (which does not).

As Phillip Johnson sees, furthermore, this metaphysical exclusion of ongoing divine activity is not simply an optional interpretation of the scientific doctrine of Darwinism. Rather, "the metaphysical statement is . . . the essential

47. Stephen Jay Gould, *Ever Since Darwin* (New York: Norton, 1977), p. 44.

48. Gould, *Ever Since Darwin*, p. 44; Stephen Jay Gould, *Hen's Teeth and Horse's Toes* (New York: Norton, 1983), p. 138.

49. Dawkins, *The Blind Watchmaker*, p. 312.

50. Stephen Jay Gould, *The Panda's Thumb* (New York: Norton, 1982), p. 79; Gould, *Hen's Teeth*, pp. 138, 334.

51. Gould, *Hen's Teeth*, p. 138.

foundation for the scientific claim."[52] The "scientific doctrine," in other words, does not involve merely a methodological atheism, according to which scientists exclude "God" from their scientific theories without thereby implying that God is not real or fails to exert any causal influence. Rather, the Darwinian theory of macroevolution, according to which it involves nothing but natural selection operating on random variations, is intended as an explanation of how the world got the way it is on the assumption that there has been no divine influence.

For many thinkers in the Darwinian tradition, moreover, this metaphysical-scientific doctrine is not an optional element. Gould, for example, declared the idea that evolution is completely "undirected" to be "the central Darwinian notion."[53] It should be noted, however, that this doctrine has a different meaning in neo-Darwinism than it had for Darwin himself. Darwin, as a deist, held that God had, in creating the world's original molecules, given them a propensity to evolve into the more complex beings (see point 12 below). A kind of directedness was hence built into the evolutionary process from the beginning. The doctrine that evolution was undirected meant only that, after instilling this original directedness, God provided no more help. For neo-Darwinians, by contrast, no direction was provided even at the beginning of the process. Neo-Darwinism excludes theism of every type, including that type usually called deism.

## Some Religious and Moral Implications of Neo-Darwinism

Now, having discussed the core metaphysical and scientific doctrines of neo-Darwinism, I deal with some implications for religion and morality. Although it is only the metaphysical and scientific doctrines that, strictly speaking, constitute the core doctrines of neo-Darwinism, these religious and moral doctrines can also be included, insofar as they are logically entailed by the metaphysical and scientific doctrines.

12. Atheism. If Darwinism rules out all theistic influence — naturalistic as well as supernaturalistic — it might seem to follow, as writers such as Dawkins, Gould, and Provine indicate, that it is completely atheistic. Darwin himself, however, was not an atheist. Rather, as indicated earlier, he endorsed, if somewhat waveringly, what is now usually called deism. Darwin wrote, for example,

---

52. Phillip E. Johnson, *Darwin on Trial*, 2nd ed. (Downers Grove, Ill.: InterVarsity, 1993), p. 168.

53. Gould, *The Panda's Thumb*, p. 38.

of "the laws impressed on matter by the Creator,"[54] saying that "some few organic beings were originally created, which were endowed with a high power of generation, & with the capacity for some slight inheritable variability."[55] Elsewhere, rejecting the idea of a special creation of each species, Darwin quoted with approval the statement that "it is just as noble a conception of the Deity to believe that He created a few original forms capable of self-development into other and needful forms."[56] In a personal letter in 1881, Darwin wrote that the universe cannot be conceived to be the result of chance, "that is, without design or purpose."[57]

What is arguably true, however, is that Darwin should have been an atheist, given his other principles. His naturalism$_{ns}$ and uniformitarianism are violated by the unique divine act that creates our universe. His deism also violates his materialistic positivism. In this sense, those followers who try to portray him as an atheist are right, because self-consistency would have led to the complete atheism characteristic of later Darwinists. In any case, this move from deism to atheism by neo-Darwinists implies some other philosophical implications that Darwin himself, because of his deism, would have rejected.

13. The Universe as Meaningless. One of the things modern evolutionary biology teaches us, says Provine, is that "[t]he universe cares nothing for us. . . . Humans are as nothing even in the evolutionary process on earth. . . . There is no ultimate meaning for humans."[58] Gould agreed, saying we have to create our own meaning because there is none in nature.[59]

14. Amoralism. This is the doctrine that the universe contains no moral norms. Provine says evolutionary biology, along with modern science in general, "directly implies that there are no inherent moral or ethical laws."[60] Gould again agreed, saying that "there is no 'natural law' waiting to be discovered 'out there.'"[61] Helena Cronin reflects a similar position: "Man's inhumanity to man may indeed make countless thousands mourn. But it is man's humanity that

54. Darwin, *The Origin of Species,* p. 449.

55. Darwin, *The Origin of Species,* p. 449. See also Robert C. Stauffer, ed., *Charles Darwin's Natural Selection: Being the Second Part of His Big Species Book Written from 1856 to 1859* (Cambridge: Cambridge University Press, 1975), p. 224.

56. Darwin, *The Origin of Species,* p. 443.

57. See the discussion in Gillespie, *Charles Darwin,* pp. 140-45, where this statement is quoted.

58. Provine, "Progress in Evolution," pp. 64-66, 70.

59. Gould, *Ever Since Darwin,* p. 13; Gould, *The Panda's Thumb,* p. 83; Gould, *Hen's Teeth,* p. 93.

60. Provine, "Progress in Evolution," pp. 64-66.

61. Stephen Jay Gould, "Impeaching a Self-Appointed Judge," *Scientific American,* July 1992, pp. 118-21, at p. 118.

gives Darwinians pause. . . . Human morality . . . presents an obvious challenge to Darwinian theory."[62]

15. Nonprogressivism. This doctrine is the insistence that there is no general trend behind or within the macroevolutionary process to produce organisms that are in any significant sense "higher," "better," or "more valuable" than those that came earlier. As a result of the felt need of many "to distinguish the consequences of neo-Darwinian natural selection from the older progressivist theories," says Matthew Nitecki, "the concept of progress has been all but banned from evolutionary biology."[63]

Gould especially rejected the idea of evolutionary progress, calling it "noxious."[64] Neo-Darwinism rules out progress, Gould saw, because it portrays macroevolution as proceeding solely in terms of random-in-every-possible-sense variations and natural selection, which together could provide no basis for saying that some of the later products are in any sense higher than some of the earlier ones. In Gould's words, "if an amoeba is as well adapted to its environment as we are to ours, who is to say that we are higher creatures?"[65] Darwin's criterion of adaptation, Gould conceded, was "improved fitness," but this meant only "better designed for an immediate, local environment," not improvement in any "cosmic sense."[66]

Others agree. Provine points out that although some neo-Darwinists have tried to hold on to progress, this attempt has been self-contradictory. "The difficult trick was to have the progress without the purpose. The problem is that there is no ultimate basis in the evolutionary process from which to judge true progress."[67]

In the essay "Can 'Progress' Be Defined as a Biological Concept?" Francisco Ayala likewise says a criterion for progress depends upon a standard not provided by Darwinism. "The concept of progress contains two elements: one descriptive, that directional change has occurred; the other axiological (= evaluative), that the change represents betterment or improvement."[68] Ayala concludes that because the notion of progress is axiological, "it cannot be a strictly scientific term," because "value judgments are not part and parcel of scientific discourse."[69]

62. Cronin, *Ant and the Peacock*, p. 267.

63. Nitecki, *Evolutionary Progress*, p. viii.

64. Stephen Jay Gould, "On Replacing the Idea of Progress with an Operational Notion of Directionality," in *Evolutionary Progress*, pp. 319-38.

65. Gould, *Ever Since Darwin*, p. 36.

66. Gould, *Ever Since Darwin*, p. 45.

67. Provine, "Progress in Evolution," p. 63.

68. Francisco J. Ayala, "Can 'Progress' Be Defined as a Biological Concept?" in *Evolutionary Progress*, pp. 75-96.

69. Ayala, "Can 'Progress'?" p. 81.

Unlike many of his fellow neo-Darwinists, however, Ayala does believe that if one carefully qualifies the term, speaking only of particular and net progress, not general and uniform progress, one can come up with a meaningful standard of progress, such as "the ability of an organism to obtain and process information about the environment."[70] Given this standard, animals are more advanced than plants, vertebrates are more advanced than invertebrates; mammals are more advanced than reptiles, which are more advanced than fish. The most advanced organism by this criterion is doubtless the human species.[71]

Ayala is quick to add, however, that "there is nothing in the evolutionary process which makes the criterion of progress I have just followed best or more objective than others."[72] What he means, of course, is that nothing in the evolutionary process as interpreted in neo-Darwinian terms makes this criterion more objective than any others.

Darwin himself did not deny progress. Dov Ospovat showed that "Darwin never seriously doubted that progress has been the general rule in the history of life."[73] Robert Richards agrees, saying, "Darwin crafted natural selection as an instrument to manufacture biological progress and moral perfection."[74] The final paragraph of *The Origin of Species* says: "Thus, from the war of nature . . . the most exalted object which we are capable of conceiving, namely, the production of the higher animals, directly follows."

Ospovat, agreeing with John Greene's characterization of Darwin as an "evolutionary deist," shows that this conception of the universe lay behind Darwin's belief in progress.[75] In Richards's words, Darwin's belief in evolutionary progress was "a direct consequence of Darwin's . . . regarding natural selection to be a secondary cause responsive to the primary cause of divine wisdom."[76] In his autobiography, Darwin included the existence of human beings as a reason for believing in divine purpose, saying that it is impossible to conceive "this immense and wonderful universe, including man with his capacity of looking far backwards and far into futurity, as the result of blind chance or necessity."[77] Although Darwin

70. Ayala, "Can 'Progress'?" pp. 80-81, 90.

71. Ayala, "Can 'Progress'?" p. 92.

72. Ayala, "Can 'Progress'?" p. 95.

73. Dov Ospovat, *The Development of Darwin's Theory: Natural History, Natural Theology, and Natural Selection, 1838-1859* (Cambridge and New York: Cambridge University Press, 1981), p. 212.

74. Robert J. Richards, "Moral Foundations of the Idea of Evolutionary Progress," in *Evolutionary Progress*, pp. 129-48, at p. 131; see also p. 146.

75. Ospovat, *Development of Darwin's Theory*, p. 72.

76. Richards, "Moral Foundations," p. 142.

77. *The Autobiography of Charles Darwin*, ed. Nora Barlow (New York: Norton, 1969), p. 92.

did give up his early theological view that the details of the world reflected a divine plan, he continued to accept the view, Ospovat showed, that beings with moral and intellectual qualities were intended.[78]

## Implications for the Debate about Teaching Evolution in the Public Schools

I have sought, through this discussion of eleven core doctrines and four implications for moral and religious questions, to characterize what neo-Darwinism is. This characterization could be challenged by arguing that it reflects an untenable essentialism, and that we should instead understand neo-Darwinism as a dynamic movement that has already left some of these doctrines behind and will surely transform itself even more radically in the future. My reply would be that although such an understanding of itself might well be preferable, this "essentialism" about neo-Darwinism seems to be strongly embedded in the ideological leaders of the neo-Darwinian tradition. It is, as I suggested earlier, employed by these leaders to portray other approaches as unscientific and, therefore, unworthy of funding and publication.

Of the core doctrines, furthermore, it seems that thus far only the doctrine of predictive determinism has been widely rejected (largely under the impact of quantum physics). Even here, moreover, the dominant approach seems to be to minimize the implications of the rejection of complete determinism. For example, as we saw, historian William Provine still holds that the (neo-Darwinian) evolutionary account of human beings does not allow for human free will. Some other core doctrines have, to be sure, been modified in terms of emphasis. It seems, for example, that the earlier focus on mutations as the primary source of random variations has been modified. Beyond such changes, however, my reading suggests that the core doctrines as summarized above are still widely held.[79]

That said, I will now briefly point out the relevance of my analysis of neo-Darwinism for the current cultural debate about the teaching of evolution in our public schools. Although the issues are quite complex, because there are many participants with quite diverse perspectives, the public debate has primarily been between two factions, which are poles apart.

One faction claims that from a scientific perspective, evolution is at best

---

78. Ospovat, *Development of Darwin's Theory*, pp. 72-73, 226.

79. I should perhaps add that many people who are orthodox on the core doctrines may not accept what I take to be the consistent "philosophical implications."

unproven, at worst woefully inadequate to relevant evidence, and that from a religious-moral perspective it is very destructive. These people argue, therefore, that the teaching of an alternative understanding of how our world came about, now often under the name "Intelligent Design," should be mandated or at least allowed by the state. The other faction holds that Darwinian evolution is now so well supported by scientific evidence that the idea of having it presented simply as one of two equally viable theories is absurd.

The debate between these two factions has thus far seemed irresolvable, because there has been found no mediating position acceptable to both sides. The analysis of Darwinian and neo-Darwinian interpretations of evolution presented in this chapter, however, can be used both (1) to understand why the debate has thus far seemed irresolvable and also (2) to point to the possibility of a mediating position that could be accepted, even if with less than complete enthusiasm, by advocates from each of the hitherto warring camps.

One reason the debate has been irresolvable thus far is that there has been truth on both sides. A second reason, closely related, has been the failure to get clear, in debates about the position alternatively called "evolution," "Darwinism," and "neo-Darwinism," exactly what position is being discussed.

For example, when some scientists say that "evolution is a fact, not merely a theory," they have in mind merely the first two doctrines, which affirm the reality of both microevolution and macroevolution. And they are right; the reality of evolution in this twofold sense has been established about as well as any view could be. There is simply no legitimate basis for claiming that evolution in this sense should be taught only as one possible theory about how the present world has come about.

However, when opponents retort that "evolution is not a fact but just a theory," they may well have in mind all fifteen doctrines of neo-Darwinism, or at least all eleven of its core doctrines. And they are right. The metaphysical doctrines — namely, naturalism$_{ns}$, uniformitarianism, positivism-materialism, determinism, nominalism, and undirectedness — have not been scientifically established. The same is true of the distinctively neo-Darwinian doctrines that are considered scientific doctrines, namely, gradualism, the reduction of macroevolution to microevolution, and the restriction of the causes of evolution to random variations and natural selection — partly because these doctrines, although scientific in the sense that they are empirically testable, have been, at least in part, deduced from questionable metaphysical doctrines. So, insofar as critics, in claiming that evolution (or Darwinism, or neo-Darwinism) should not be taught as fact in the public schools, have in mind "evolution" in the sense of all or at least many of the core doctrines of neo-Darwinism, they are right.

Finally, when critics of the teaching of evolution claim that it is destructive from a religious-moral perspective, they usually have in mind the neo-Darwinian doctrines 12, 13, and 14, which portray an atheistic, meaningless, amoral universe. (The fifteenth doctrine, which says that the universe is nonprogressive, seems to play a much smaller role in these debates.) These critics are doubly right: These doctrines are destructive. And, being deduced from doctrines that are not empirically established, they cannot claim the imprimatur of science. Critics of the teaching of evolution in the public schools are, accordingly, completely justified in maintaining that "evolution" or "Darwinism" in this sense should not be taught as if it were somehow scientifically established.

Given this analysis, a mediating position, which could in principle be accepted by both sides, can be articulated. This mediating position would contain the following elements:

1. Evolution (or evolutionism, or the evolutionary worldview) would not be equated with either Darwinism or neo-Darwinism. Rather, "evolution," used without adjectival qualifier and presented as a scientifically established idea, would be limited to the first two doctrines, which declare microevolution and macroevolution to be facts.

2. The only other items in the list to be included in "evolution as a scientific doctrine" would be doctrines 3 and 4: naturalism$_{ns}$ and uniformitarianism. Teachers and students, it would be explained, are free to understand this inclusion in one of two ways. On the one hand, they could hold that the rejection of supernaturalism, which implies the affirmation of naturalism$_{ns}$ and ontological uniformitarianism, has been the fundamental ontological presupposition of the scientific community since at least the middle of the nineteenth century, so that it is now considered essential to the scientific worldview as such. Evolution as a scientific doctrine, thus understood, would rule out all supernaturalistic doctrines of creation.

On the other hand, teachers and students could understand the refusal to allow any appeals to supernatural causation in scientific explanations as a methodological principle inherent in the discipline known as "natural science," previously known as "natural philosophy," which by definition limits itself to the study of natural (as distinct from supernatural) explanations. This methodological restriction on what can count as a "scientific explanation," teachers would point out, does not necessarily mean a denial that supernatural causation ever occurs.

But, whichever explanation be accepted, it would be agreed that the scientific doctrine of evolution, which would be taught in our public schools, would include the first four doctrines, and only the first four doctrines, in the list.

3. It would be taught — as long as it is true — that the neo-Darwinian interpretation of evolution is the one that is now dominant in the scientific community. It would be emphasized, however, that doctrines 5-11 do not have the authority of "science" behind them and are in fact rejected by many philosophers and scientists, including some who endorse alternative theories of evolution. It would also be pointed out, of course, that doctrines 12-15, the negative religious-moral implications that follow from neo-Darwinism, are not implied by the evolutionary worldview that has been discovered and verified by scientific methods. It would not be suggested that the evolutionary worldview as vouchsafed by scientific methods somehow uniquely supports a Darwinian or neo-Darwinian explanation of the evolutionary process. Indeed, it would be pointed out that alternative theories of evolution embody the first four doctrines and that some of those theories are theistic (but not of course supernaturalistic, since they embody the third and fourth doctrines).

This teaching would provide a mediating position that could, in principle, be supported by both Darwinists and anti-Darwinists, including antievolutionists. I stress the qualifier "in principle" because another factor that has made the debate so intractable has been dogmatism on both sides. On the one side, some antievolutionists are so dogmatically committed to supernaturalistic creationism that they would not agree to a position that teaches macroevolution as a scientific fact and insists that scientific explanations must be naturalistic$_{ns}$. On the other side, some evolutionists are just as dogmatically committed to neo-Darwinism and consider the entire neo-Darwinian worldview, as articulated by at least most of the fifteen doctrines, to be scientifically established. They would not be happy with a position that included only four of the fifteen doctrines, thereby failing to rule out positions they consider scientifically disproved.

A mediating position cannot, however, expect to appeal to everyone, especially the most extreme believers on both sides. It can only aim to be accepted by reasonable, circumspect persons on both sides, who can then forge an alliance that may, in the long run, win the allegiance of the majority. I believe that the position suggested above could function in this way.

# 18. Process and Emergence

PHILIP CLAYTON

Process thought and emergence theory would seem to be natural allies. After all, Alfred North Whitehead seems to embrace a philosophy of pervasive novelty and emergence. Samuel Alexander, long acknowledged as an important process figure, is one of the authors most frequently cited in histories of emergence theory, particularly his Gifford Lectures, *Space, Time, and Deity*. Henri Bergson's *Creative Evolution* is a foundational text in the philosophy of emergence, yet Bergson is himself one of the core process thinkers of the late nineteenth and early twentieth centuries.[1] Teilhard de Chardin also qualifies as a central emergentist thinker and a foundational process philosopher.

Why then has the reemergence of emergence theory in the last several decades not been more strongly identified with process philosophies? Most works on the topic develop emergence theories in the context of mainline philosophy of science and analytic (Anglo-American) philosophy. In these presentations emergence becomes a theory about the relations between specific scientific disciplines and about new developments in scientific theory. What conceptual steps are necessary if the sciences that describe emergent phenomena are to be linked more closely with process metaphysics? And what compromises will be necessary on both sides to make this marriage work?

These questions set an obvious agenda for this chapter. We must first trace the reemergence of emergence theory in the second half of the twentieth century and describe its scientific support. An in-depth analysis of at least one sophisticated theory of scientific emergence will give the notion a level of conceptual depth and rigor usually missing in more popular presentations of the

---

1. See the excellent chapter on Bergson by Pete Gunter in David Ray Griffin et al., *Founders of Constructive Postmodern Philosophy: Peirce, James, Bergson, Whitehead, and Hartshorne* (Albany: State University of New York Press, 1993), pp. 133-63.

topic.[2] But a second sort of analysis is also necessary. Too often advocates of one metaphysical position or another charge bravely into the territory of the sciences, arguing that theirs is the best higher-order interpretation of the scientific data. But until one can carefully lay out the whole range of metaphysical interpretations, contrasting one's favorite theory with its competitors, one cannot really make a credible case for the superiority of one's position to its rivals. To foster a more sophisticated dialogue among the various metaphysical interpretations of the phenomena of biological evolution, the final portion of this chapter offers a detailed typology of the twelve major metaphysical positions one can take on the nature of evolution.

## The Concept of Emergence: A First Approximation

The concept of emergence is often presented by contrasting it with two alternative (and still widely held) views. Although this technique is useful as a first approximation, its limits will soon become clear. According to *reductionist theories,* the phenomena studied by a given discipline are only scientifically (read: truly) understood when they can be expressed using the laws of a lower-level discipline. When scientific reduction is successful, the phenomena become a special case of the more general explanatory framework represented by those laws. If one seeks to reduce any given level to the level beneath it, one must eventually come down to the fundamental laws of physics, the bedrock of all else.

According to *dualist theories,* by contrast, there are gaps in the relations between the various disciplines, such that the reductionist ideal is impossible. Not only can phenomena of *mind* or *spirit* not be explained in terms of any lower-level laws, but dualists also challenge the claim that mind depends essentially on any of its physical or material substrates. Thus dualists have classically held that minds are essentially different from bodies and can continue to exist without them. Minds do not rely on the physical energies that sustain bodies and allow them to move; instead they belong to a different ontological order altogether.

Emergence theories attempt to split the difference between these opposing positions. They grant the downward dependence of the reductionists, but they challenge the achievability of downward explanatory reduction. Rather, they maintain that it is a contingent fact of natural history that new levels of or-

2. See Steven Johnson, *Emergence: The Connected Lives of Ants, Brains, Cities, and Software* (New York: Scribner, 2001).

ganization emerge, which because they are novel are not predictable or explainable in terms of any lower-level laws, forces, or particles.

This framework, though useful, is not sufficient. Contrast it with an alternate way of defining the concept. Emergence is a theory about evolution. Specifically, it is a theory about how the various scientific disciplines that study cosmic evolution are related to one another. Suppose we list the various disciplines that study the natural world according to the order in cosmic history in which the phenomena that each studies first arose: quantum physics, classical physics or macrophysics, physical chemistry, biochemistry, genetics, cell biology, anatomy, etc. Let's label the resulting list using A, B, C, etc., to stand for the specific disciplines. We can then number the particular relations between any two neighboring disciplines using 1, 2, 3, etc., yielding something like the following diagram:

Emergence Studies

∧ ∧ ∧

1 2 3 4

∧ ∧ ∧ ∧

A B C D E

As the diagram shows, emergence theory thus becomes a sort of third-order theory: a theory about the relations between the relations between scientific disciplines.

## The Reemergence of Emergence

A special issue of the *Proceedings of the National Academy of Sciences* explores the principles of self-organization and the formation of complex matter, asking, "what are the steps and the processes that lead from the elementary particle to the thinking organism, the (present!) entity of highest complexity?"[3] Complexity, the authors argue, is inherently a systemic function; it involves the interaction between multiple components of multiple kinds and the principles that affect their correlation, coupling, and feedback relationships. The goal of

3. See the introduction to the collection in Jean-Marie Lehn, "Toward Complex Matter: Supramolecular Chemistry and Self-organization," *Proceedings of the National Academy of Sciences* 99, no. 8 (April 16, 2002): 4763-68.

the sciences of complexity is "to progressively discover, understand, and implement the rules that govern [matter's] evolution from inanimate to animate and beyond, to ultimately acquire the ability to create new forms of complex matter."[4] Emergent complexity spans the entire spectrum of cosmic history, "from divided to condensed matter then to organized and adaptive matter, on to living matter and thinking matter, up the ladder of complexity."[5]

This vision clearly forms the core of research programs currently running in most, if not all, the major natural sciences, from the emergence of classical physical systems out of quantum physical systems, through the emergence of chemical properties and the origins of life, and on up to the higher cognitive behaviors of the great apes. Indeed, Adelman and Tononi are not doing anything different when, in their widely cited *Science* article, "Consciousness and Complexity," they offer a theory of consciousness as an emergent property of the brain.[6]

Examples of emergence do not start at the level of life or mind but arise in scientists' attempts to explain the very earliest stages of cosmic evolution. Classical physics has been described as emergent out of quantum physics.[7] And recently Stephen Adler has argued that quantum theory itself is an emergent phenomenon.[8] The recent physics Nobel laureate Robert Laughlin drew significant attention to the emergence debate within the sciences by arguing that scientific reduction is a dogma and that his field, condensed matter physics, could be grasped only by using the paradigm of emergence.[9] Among his examples of emergent phenomena are superconductivity, the quantum Hall effect, phase transitions, crystallization, collective instabilities, and hydrodynamics.

Other studies of complex matter in which nonlinearities dominate, such as soft materials, come to similar conclusions. Elbio Dagotto, for example, recently reported the "spontaneous emergence of electronic nanometer-scale structures"

4. Lehn, "Toward Complex Matter," p. 4768.

5. Lehn, "Toward Complex Matter," p. 4768.

6. Giulio Tononi and Gerald M. Adelman, "Consciousness and Complexity," *Science* 282 (December 4, 1998): 1846-51.

7. Wojciech Zurek, "Decoherence and the Transition from Quantum to Classical — Revisited," *Los Alamos Science* 27 (2002): 14; cf. Zurek, "Decoherence and the Transition from Quantum to Classical," *Physics Today*, 1991, p. 44.

8. See Stephen Adler, *Quantum Theory as an Emergent Phenomenon: The Statistical Dynamics of Global Unitary Invariant Matrix Models as the Precursor of Quantum Field Theory* (Cambridge: Cambridge University Press, 2004). If string theory is correct, quantum mechanics would be an emergent property of strings.

9. Numerous examples are offered by Laughlin in his recent book, *A Different Universe: Reinventing Physics from the Bottom Down* (New York: Basic Books, 2005). See also the review by Philip Anderson, "Emerging Physics: A Fresh Approach to Viewing the Complexity of the Universe," *Nature* 434 (April 7, 2005): 701-2.

in transition metal oxides: "In complex systems the properties of a few particles are not sufficient to understand large aggregates when these particles strongly interact. Rather, in such systems, which are not merely complicated, one expects emergence, namely the generation of properties that do not preexist in a system's constituents. This concept is contrary to the philosophy of reductionism, the traditional physics hallmark. Complex systems spontaneously tend to form structures (self-organization) and these structures vary widely in size and scales."[10]

Chemists have long held up their discipline as a model of emergence. Pier Luigi Luisi, for example, maintains that chemistry is "the embodiment of emergence" because it studies properties that, although rooted in physical structures, cannot be explained without the help of a new conceptual framework. Chemical properties emerge only in sufficiently complex natural systems, and one requires a level of analysis distinct from physics to understand them.[11] Luisi also endorses downward causation: "chemical examples show that emergence must go hand in hand with downward causation — one is the consequence of the other, and the two phenomena take place simultaneously."[12] He adds finally that "life can be seen as a particular kind of emergent property" and "life itself is indeed the most dramatic outcome of emergence."[13]

This new perspective goes under multiple names within specific sciences; "emergence" is, as mentioned above, only an overarching rubric to describe many different research programs in many different sciences. Molecular biologists speak, for instance, of the emergence of a "network perspective," which is necessary for describing how particular types of chemical reactions are cata-

---

10. Elbio Daggoto, "Complexity in Strongly Correlated Electronic Systems," *Science* 309 (July 8, 2005): 257-62, at p. 257.

11. Pier Luigi Luisi, "Emergence in Chemistry: Chemistry as the Embodiment of Emergence," *Foundations of Chemistry* 44 (2002): 183-200. See also his book *The Emergence of Life: From Chemical Origins to Synthetic Biology* (Cambridge: Cambridge University Press, 2006). An earlier case for the importance of emergence in chemistry was made by the process thinker Joseph Earley: "Far-from-Equilibrium Thermodynamics and Process Thought," in *Physics and the Ultimate Significance of Time*, ed. David R. Griffin (Albany: State University of New York Press, 1985), pp. 251-55; "The Nature of Chemical Existence," in *Metaphysics as Foundation*, ed. Paul Bogaard and Gordon Treash (Albany: State University of New York Press, 1992); "Self-Organization and Agency in Chemistry and in Process Philosophy," *Process Studies* 11 (1981): 242-58; "Towards a Reapprehension of Causal Efficacy," *Process Studies* 24 (1995): 34-38; and "Collingwood's Third Transition: Replacement of Renaissance Cosmology by an Ontology of Evolutionary Self-Organization," in *With Darwin beyond Descartes — the Historical Concept of Nature and Overcoming "the Two Cultures,"* ed. Luigi Zanzi (Pavia, Italy, forthcoming).

12. Luisi, "Emergence in Chemistry," p. 195.

13. Luisi, "Emergence in Chemistry," p. 197.

14. Rui Alves, Raphael A. G. Chaleil, and Michael J. E. Sternberg, "Evolution of Enzymes in Metabolism: A Network Perspective," *Journal of Molecular Biology* 320 (2002): 751-70.

lyzed by evolutionarily related enzymes.[14] The analogue of metabolic networks in the study of cells is *systems biology,* one of the largest growth areas in contemporary biology. Hiroaki Kitano describes its core assumption: "While an understanding of genes and proteins continues to be important, the focus [of systems biology] is on understanding a system's structure and dynamics. Because a system is not just an assembly of genes and proteins, its properties cannot be fully understood merely by drawing diagrams of their interconnections."[15]

In cell biology, what was at first merely a way of expressing reservations about purely gene-driven analyses ("epigenesis" or "epigenetic factors") has become a rigorous study of "system-level insights" in its own right.[16] As Kitano writes, "a transition is occurring in biology from the molecular level to the system level that promises to revolutionize our understanding of complex biological regulatory systems and to provide major new opportunities for practical application of such knowledge."[17] And in an interesting review in *Science,* Kevin Laland baptizes the new approach as "the new interactionism," which describes "how genes are triggered into action by environmental events; how they switch other genes on and off; how they guide neurons to build brains; and how learning operates through gene expression."[18]

The new interactionism goes between the horns of the classical dilemmas, "genes versus environment" and "nature versus nurture." Indeed, these new perspectives may defuse one further classical dilemma: the dilemma between "upward" and "downward" causation. Reductionists have generally held that all causal influences occur at the level of microphysics; these effects, taking place within highly complex systems, are said to account for the deceptive appearance that distinctively biological or psychological causes exist. In opposition to them, idealists and Cartesian dualists protested that a distinct type of cause, a mental one, is different in kind from physical causes, is not dependent on them, and exercises its own agency in the world. But from the systems or interactionist perspective, the entire dichotomy appears to be mistaken. Causality is "circular"; it involves interacting effects between different levels of natural organization, e.g., between the microscopic and the macroscopic. This new framework, as Moreno and Umerez note, "makes it possible to talk properly about the appearance of new kinds of causal relationships. . . . Thus, what enables us to speak in terms of

15. Hiroaki Kitano, "Systems Biology: A Brief Overview," *Science* 295 (March 1, 2002): 1662-64.

16. Kitano, "Systems Biology," p. 1664.

17. Kitano, "Systems Biology," p. 1664.

18. Kevin Laland, "The New Interactionism," *Science* 300 (June 20, 2003): 1879-80, drawing on Matt Ridley, *Nature via Nurture: Genes, Experience, and What Makes Us Human* (New York: HarperCollins, 2003).

a double causal action — upward and downward — is precisely the conjunction of a circular causality with [at least] two different levels of organization, one of which is constituted by informational components. . . . [This] special, downward kind of causation appears just when very complex (interwoven) meta-networks of recursive reaction networks arise in Nature."[19]

Harold Morowitz likewise denies that the notion of downward causation is speculative, describing it instead as a "key feature" that is characteristic of all biological emergence. He describes two classes of molecules that are produced by the metabolic network, both of which contribute to the building of structures: monomers and amphiphiles (including micelles, bilayer membranes, and liposomes or vesicles). A vesicle, which is a higher-level process emerging from intermediate metabolism, provides a straightforward example of downward causation: "by isolating a space and introducing trans-membrane phenomena, it alters the chemical kinetics and local equilibria of the molecules that are the lower-level entities."[20]

One can trace examples of emergence along the path of natural history from the first cells to the great apes.[21] Morowitz identifies twenty-eight distinct levels of emergence in his monograph *The Emergence of Everything.*[22] In a recent article in *Physics Today,* the astrophysicist George Ellis describes the emergent features of quantum measurement, DNA coding, social creations, and economics. And I have not even begun to trace the construal of consciousness as an emergent phenomenon from sufficiently complex brains and central nervous systems.[23]

## What Makes Emergence Scientific?

It is one thing to speculate about emergence as part of a metaphysical theory, and something else to claim scientific support for the framework of emergence.

19. Moreno and Umerez, "Downward Causation at the Core of Living Organization," in *Downward Causation: Minds, Bodies, and Matter,* ed. Peter Bøgh Andersen, Claus Emmeche, Niels Ole Finnemann, and Peder Voetmann Christiansen (Aarhus, Denmark: Aarhus University Press, 2000), pp. 112, 115.

20. Harold Morowitz, "The Emergence of Intermediary Metabolism" (unpublished paper), p. 8.

21. Barbara Smuts, "Emergence in Social Evolution: A Great Ape Example," in *The Reemergence of Emergence,* ed. Philip Clayton and Paul Davies (Oxford: Oxford University Press, 2006).

22. Harold Morowitz, *The Emergence of Everything: How the World Became Complex* (New York: Oxford University Press, 2002).

23. Clayton, *Mind and Emergence: From Quantum to Consciousness* (Oxford: Oxford University Press, 2004).

Although I believe such claims are justified, they bring with them unique challenges.

As long as one continues to do science, one attempts to draw the closest possible connections between the set of phenomena that one is studying and the lower-level laws that are available. The scientific study of chemistry is impossible, for example, without its connections to physics; to study the origins of life *means* to try to explain the transition from nonreproducing biochemical molecules to reproducing life-forms (and if one could understand life in terms of biochemistry, so much the better); and to understand an animal's behavior scientifically *just is* to explain as much of it as possible in terms of the body's morphology, hormone releases, selective pressures, and the like. The quest to explain phenomena in terms of reconstructible, testable causal systems is so basic to the project of science that we could almost use it as *the* defining characteristic of science.

The phenomenon of emergence makes this project more difficult, but it does not eliminate it. If it had turned out to be possible to explain higher-order phenomena in terms of lower-order laws across the scientific disciplines, then science would be in the position fully to achieve the goal in terms of which it is defined. Even if, as emergence theorists believe, the natural world is such that this downward reduction is often impossible in principle, the goal does not simply disappear, to be replaced by a happy-go-lucky holism. One can still determine the scientific or nonscientific status of a theory about the world by the presence or absence of this goal, viz., to connect the phenomena of one level as closely and precisely as possible with the phenomena at the next lower level.

Consider two concrete examples. Walter Elsasser, in his classic *Reflections on a Theory of Organisms,* makes the case for the autonomy of biological explanations. Elsasser believes that the "information stability" of living things cannot be reduced to the physicochemical stability of molecules. Alongside this emergentist manifesto, however, Elsasser is careful to show how the scientific study of life-forms is still possible. He does not argue for the untestability of biological theories, for example, but rather for the necessity of utilizing different kinds of tests. It is just that biological causality "cannot be fully verified by the standard procedure of the physicist or chemist," that is, by "measurement followed by mathematical extrapolation, technically called integration, of the equations of quantum mechanics that govern molecular motion."[24]

Moreover, Elsasser gives very precise, empirical reasons for a certain autonomy of biology. Thus his fourth chapter demonstrates how an immense

24. Walter Elsasser, *Reflections on a Theory of Organisms* (Quebec: Editions ORBIS Publishing, 1987), p. 142.

number of molecular configurations are compatible with a given set of physicochemical constraints. Even if the structure and dynamics of all molecules can be understood by applying quantum mechanical principles, "a cell is much too complex to admit of meaningful analysis in such terms."[25] Because of this "combinatorial explosion,"[26] it is demonstrably impossible to compute cell behavior in quantum-physical terms. Likewise, in a later chapter Elsasser describes how physicists study stable systems (those in which each mode of motion is stable) and then come to understand what happens when the system is perturbated. All biological systems, by contrast, are massively unstable; they are, in Stuart Kauffman's beautiful expression, always existing "at the edge of chaos." Hence it is not possible to understand them by extrapolation from stable systems and through computation of each perturbation — which is to say: it is impossible to understand them physically. "Owing to the amplificatory effect, the ultimate changes are no longer predictable."[27] Elsasser concludes that "the morphological future of such [biological] systems [is] unpredictable on the basis of physics and chemistry."[28]

Finally, Elsasser remains committed to the scientific study of biological phenomena, even in light of this unpredictability. He emphasizes that biological results "cannot differ from any known rule of physics and chemistry." He continues to emphasize the importance of structure (morphology) and function as basic to testable biological theories. And he does not advance biological holism as a way of avoiding tests and experiments, but rather as representing a call for a new type of testability: "if the holistic properties are to be verified experimentally, a different type of experiment from that conventionally used by physicists and chemists is required."[29]

Elsasser thus represents a paradigm example of scientific emergence. The leading biophysicist, Harold Morowitz, heavily influenced by Elsasser, comments, "emergence requires pruning rules to reduce the transcomputable to the computable. . . . [I]n both Elsasser's approach and Holland's view, biology requires its own laws that are not necessarily derivable from physics, but do not contradict the physical foundations."[30] Similar examples of scientific emergence could be drawn from the work of Paul Davies, George Ellis, Harold Morowitz, John Holland, and others.

Contrast Elsasser's strictures with the approach to emergence taken by

25. Elsasser, *Reflections*, p. 52.
26. Cf. Morowitz, *The Emergence of Everything*, for details on this notion.
27. Elsasser, *Reflections*, p. 105.
28. Elsasser, *Reflections*, p. 142.
29. Elsasser, *Reflections*, p. 148.
30. Morowitz, "Emergence of Intermediary Metabolism," p. 4.

B. C. Goodwin and Rupert Sheldrake. Both thinkers wish to appeal to what they call "morphogenetic fields" and "morphic resonance." Goodwin explicitly refuses to interpret the morphogenetic field in terms of any known forces: "electrical forces can affect it . . . but I would not wish to suggest that [it] is essentially electrical. Chemical substances" can affect it, yet it is not "essentially chemical or biochemical in nature." He is nonetheless certain that morphogenetic fields "play a primary role in the developmental process."[31] Similarly, Sheldrake postulates "patterns of oscillatory activity" throughout the world, which he calls morphic resonance.[32] Resonances are strongest, he is sure, with one's own past, somewhat weaker with genetically similar animals, and weaker still with animals from other races. Apparently, though, some resonance still exists between all living things. A genuinely scientific theory of morphic resonances looks unlikely, however, since, like Goodwin, he is loath to tie them to any known forces.

Sheldrake does claim that his theory has "testable predictions," though he admits that his predictions "may seem so improbable as to be absurd." For example,

> if thousands of rats were trained to perform a new task in a laboratory in London, similar rats should learn to carry out the same task more quickly in laboratories everywhere else. If the speed of learning of rats in another laboratory, say in New York, were to be measured before and after the rats in London were trained, the rats tested on the second occasion should learn more quickly than those tested on the first. The effect should take place in the absence of any known type of physical connection or communication between the two laboratories.[33]

Unfortunately, this kind of testability may still not be sufficient to make a theory scientific. (One thinks of Nancey Murphy's "replicable" test that one can find out whether the Holy Spirit wishes to be called by the feminine pronoun by utilizing feminine language in speaking of the Spirit and then seeing whether the religious community that speaks and prays in this way thrives or stagnates.)[34] It is also crucial that the theories in question specify their connec-

---

31. B. C. Goodwin, "On Morphogenetic Fields," *Theoria to Theory* 13 (1979): 109-14, cited in Rupert Sheldrake, *A New Science of Life: The Hypothesis of Morphic Resonance* (Rochester, Vt.: Park Street Press, 1995).

32. Sheldrake, *New Science of Life,* p. 170.

33. Sheldrake, *New Science of Life,* p. 14.

34. Nancey Murphy, *Theology in an Age of Scientific Reasoning* (Ithaca, N.Y.: Cornell University Press, 1990), pp. 167f.

tions with the existing body of scientific knowledge. In addition to meeting this condition, a theory of scientific emergence must provide details, given as much as possible in terms of lower-level theories, that show why a given set of phenomena would be irreducible to those theories. When somebody suggests, as Sheldrake does, that there are both energetic and nonenergetic fields, it is difficult to see how connections can be drawn with any scientific field theory.

## The Logic of Scientific Emergence

Terrence Deacon offers the clearest expression of the logic of scientific emergence available today; it is therefore valuable to consider his recent proposals in some detail. Deacon begins with the empirical evidence that "complex dynamical ensembles can spontaneously assume ordered patterns of behavior that are not prefigured in the properties of their component elements or in their interaction patterns."[35] On his view, only emergence theories can adequately interpret and explain this type of self-organization.

In section order, however. Deacon was the first to identify three distinct "orders" of emergence. First-order emergence involves the appearance of new properties in the aggregate that are not present in the individual particles. Deacon draws his primary examples from quantum theory and statistical thermodynamics, though he admits that even simpler examples can be adduced, such as how the properties of water molecules produce liquid properties. "Although the nature of the wave and its detailed underlying dynamical realization in each [particular wave] may differ depending on whether the fluid is water, air, or an electromagnetic field, the ability to propagate a wave is a first-order emergent feature they all share in common." As with the other two "orders" of emergence, Deacon is careful to specify exactly what are the conditions under which this kind of emergence will occur. Thus he argues, for example, that "it is only when certain of the regularities of molecular interaction relationships add up rather than cancel one another that certain *between-molecule* relationships can produce aggregate behaviors with ascent in scale."[36]

In second-order emergence, specific perturbations of a system are amplified, resulting in types of causal effects not seen in the first order. In the formation of snow crystals, for example, the specific temperature and humidity pres-

35. Terrence Deacon, "The Hierarchic Logic of Emergence: Untangling the Interdependence of Evolution and Self Organization," in *Evolution and Learning: The Baldwin Effect Reconsidered*, ed. Bruce H. Weber and David J. Depew (Cambridge: MIT Press, 2003), pp. 273-308.

36. Deacon, "Hierarchic Logic of Emergence," p. 288.

ent at each stage of the crystal's descent through the air are "recorded" in the emerging structure of the crystal as it evolves; these features then influence its subsequent structural formation. The structural features emerging at a given point are amplified, in other words, such that they affect all subsequent crystal growth. These "feed-forward circles of cause and effect" are distinctive of this new type of emergent property. Deacon offers detailed examples, drawing from "self-undermining (divergent) chaotic systems, as in turbulent flow, and self-organizing (partially convergent) chaotic systems."[37] Second-order emergence is also found in the so-called autopoietic systems. This type of emergence works not just by aggregating individual components (say, molecules); here systematic features play a causal role. Put differently, forms or structures, and not merely particles, become the operative links in the feed-forward cycle.

Third-order emergence shares this feature from the previous order. Yet now what is passed on is *information* or *memory,* not merely forms and structures. As a result, Deacon argues, "third-order emergence inevitably exhibits a developmental and/or evolutionary character. . . . It occurs where there is both amplification of global influences on parts, but also redundant 'sampling' of these influences and reintroduction of them redundantly across time and into different realizations of the same type of second-order system."[38]

The classic example of third-order emergence is the self-reproducing cell.[39] Cells exhibit features not present in prebiological physical systems; they contain information — specifically, information sufficient for building other cells like themselves. The information is isolated by a boundary (the cell wall), which allows the cell as a whole to function as an entity in its own right on which environmental forces act. Because cells can make copies of themselves in ways that prebiotic structures cannot, the forces of natural selection can begin to operate for the first time. A cell thus becomes a sort of hypothesis about what informational structure will survive and reproduce most effectively in a given environment. If the cell exists in an environment congenial to it, it will make more successful copies of itself than its rivals and come to dominate its ecosystem. Deacon describes this process as "a sort of self-referential self-organization, an autopoiesis of autopoiesis."[40] As a result, cells can be understood only through "a combination of multi-scale, historical, and semiotic analyses. . . . This is why living and cognitive processes require us to introduce

37. Deacon, "Hierarchic Logic of Emergence," p. 295.
38. Deacon, "Hierarchic Logic of Emergence," p. 299.
39. Deacon has developed the notion of the "autocell" in "Reciprocal Linkage between Self-Organizing Processes Is Sufficient for Self-Reproduction and Evolvability," *Biological Theory* 1, no. 2 (2006): 136-49.
40. Deacon, "Hierarchic Logic of Emergence," p. 299.

concepts such as representation, adaptation, information, and function in order to capture the logic of the most salient emergent phenomena."[41]

By introducing the framework of semiotics, derived from the work of C. S. Peirce, Deacon implicitly claims that the cell is an interpreter of the world: it stands in an informationally mediated relationship to its environment. Emergent entities at this level refer to or represent their world; they are themselves hypotheses about how best to survive and thrive in a particular environment. Despite his occasional reticence about antireductionist language, Deacon's position clearly stands as a sharp alternative to reductionist analyses of the natural world: "Life and mind cannot be adequately described in terms that treat them as merely supervenient because this collapses innumerable convoluted levels of emergent relationships. Life is not mere chemical mechanism. Nor is cognition mere molecular computation."[42]

If Deacon is right — and I think recent origins-of-life research, systems biology, and ecosystems theory all offer empirical support for his analysis — then to understand life scientifically means to understand it according to different principles than those that pertain to purely physical or chemical systems. Only third-order emergent processes in evolution have the capacity "to progressively embed [other] evolutionary processes within one another via representations that amplify their information-handling power."[43] Indeed, the process of emergence does not stop with the first self-reproducing cell. Under evolutionary selection pressures, natural systems continue to increase in complexity, discovering ever new ways of "making a living" (as Stuart Kauffman likes to say) in the world. In Deacon's masterful study *The Symbolic Species*,[44] for example, he traces the coevolution of brains and language or culture. Language use, of course, remains dependent on a complex brain and central nervous system, but language can never be reduced to an instinct (Pinker) or a mere by-product of brain processes; the two evolving phenomena mutually influence one another. The result is a continual growth in complexity of both of

41. Deacon, "Hierarchic Logic of Emergence," p. 300.
42. Deacon, "Hierarchic Logic of Emergence," p. 304.
43. Deacon, "Hierarchic Logic of Emergence," p. 305.
44. Terrence Deacon, *The Symbolic Species: The Co-evolution of Language and the Brain* (New York: Norton, 1997). See also Zoltán N. Oltvai and Albert-László Barabási, "Life's Complexity Pyramid," *Science* 298 (October 25, 2002): 763-64. Barabási is best known for his popular presentation *Linked: The New Science of Networks* (Cambridge, Mass.: Perseus Books, 2002); for a more technical presentation see Barabási and Reka Albert, "Emergence of Scaling in Random Networks," *Science* 286, no. 15 (October 15, 1999): 509-12. Note that embracing the core principles of network theory does not mean that it will lead to "an accurate mathematical theory of human behavior," as Barabási claims in "Network Theory — the Emergence of the Creative Enterprise," *Science* 308 (April 29, 2005): 639-41.

them. For example, Deacon argues, language moves from the "iconic" mode of representation to a more complex form of reference involving indexicals, and finally (in *Homo sapiens*) to the rich symbolic modes of representation that are the bread and butter of human cultural existence.

## Emergence, Evolution, and Metaphysics

This volume encompasses a number of the leading options for interpreting evolutionary theory today. I have argued that emergence theory occupies a sort of middle ground between strongly gene-centered interpretations of the evolutionary process (represented in this volume by Francisco Ayala, but known to most outside the field through the work of Richard Dawkins) on the one hand, and the process-philosophical understanding of evolution, which emphasizes that all existing entities are centers of experience ("panexperientialism") that are able to respond to the pervasive lure of God, on the other.

In a debate broad enough to include Dawkins, emergence theory, and process theism, there is clearly a significant danger of equivocation, of incommensurable theoretical frameworks, and of attacks and defenses that merely sail past one another. It is therefore crucial for the success of the project that one step back for a moment to reflect on the whole range of options represented within the contemporary debate about the nature of evolution. Since the various positions are *interpretations of* evolution, and since many of them involve claims about what does (or does not) "ultimately" or "really" exist, the debate is correctly classified as metaphysical (whether the participants like to admit it or not).

In these closing pages, then, I attempt to lay out the twelve major positions on biology and metaphysics. As it turns out, one discovers a relatively clear continuum of positions leading from physicalist-reductivist approaches to the biological sciences, through the varieties of neo-Darwinism, through emergentism and stronger and stronger teleological views, including process metaphysics, on to dualism and Intelligent Design. Obviously, the more fine-grained one makes the analysis, the more overlap one can demonstrate between the various positions. Still, to get a sense of the (sometimes subtle) conceptual differences between the positions, it is useful to distinguish about a dozen different varieties.[45] Because the typology represents a rational reconstruction

45. I am grateful to Jeffrey Schloss for extensive comments and criticisms of an earlier draft of this typology, which have, I believe, greatly improved the accuracy of the result, and for some crucial bibliographical references.

rather than a sociological study, and so as not to induce unnecessary squabbling, I have omitted names wherever possible.

1. *Reductionist-physicalist approaches to biology.* Although these approaches may use the language of genetics and molecular biology, it is a part of their position, metaphysically speaking, that all the higher-order structures one finds in biology are manifestations of fundamental physical laws and forces (ontological reductionism). Further, they hold, in a "completed science" the higher-order structures could and would be reduced to explanations given in terms of fundamental forces and laws, presumably those of microphysics (epistemological reductionism).

2. *Neo-Darwinian genetic theory.* This view dominated the middle third, or even the latter half, of the twentieth century and continues as the metaphysical commonsense view of very many, but certainly not all, leading molecular and cell biologists. Historically it arose in two stages. The "modern synthesis" in the 1940s and 1950s brought together Darwin's theory of natural selection with Mendel's work on inheritance, though it predated the 1953 discovery by Watson and Crick of the double helix structure of DNA, the key molecular structure for transmitting genetic information. The strong "gene-centrism" of contemporary evolutionary theory arose during the two decades that followed, building on the work of George Williams,[46] William Hamilton, and Maynard Smith, and then popularized by Richard Dawkins and others in the 1970s.[47]

What characterizes these views metaphysically is the preeminence of gene-level analysis. Dawkins, with his talk of "gene machines," is probably the best-known representative of this standpoint writing today. Like (1), it is a reductivist position, but here the bottom line is not physical particles and forces but rather genes, which are seen as the foundational building blocks of biology. All higher-order structures, processes, and behaviors within organisms are, finally, manifestations of the genetic dynamics (ontological reductionism) and are to be explained ultimately in terms of random genetic variation and selective retention of the resulting biological structures by the environment.

3. *Systems biology.* Probably the biggest growth industry in molecular biology today, systems biology studies the interactions between genes and cell structures, hence between genetic evolution and broader organic structures. Because of the extremely precise nature of molecular- and cell-level accounts — even though the molecules in biochemistry are, from a physicist's point of

46. See George C. Williams, *Adaptation and Natural Selection: A Critique of Some Current Evolutionary Thought* (Princeton: Princeton University Press, 1966).

47. The two stages should be distinguished since, for example, proponents of systems biology (point 3 below) adhere to the modern synthesis but not to the radical gene-centric claims of Dawkins and others.

view, massive, almost hopelessly complex, and hence messy — the interactions being studied are extremely specific, relatively isolated, and highly precise. The emphasis now lies on the biochemistry of single cells, on particular transduction cascades or particular protein interactions that lead to (or inhibit) gene expression. Systems biology does not mean mushy holism; it does not include, for example, speculations on the effects of the (human) body as a whole on its individual cells.

The empirical preciseness of systems biology makes (3) much more similar to (2) than, for instance, to classical "systems theory" (Ervin Laszlo, Ludwig von Bertolansky). Yet (2) and (3) are metaphysically distinct, because the latter is committed metaphysically to an equal causal and explanatory role for genes and their cellular or multicellular environment. The interaction of these two codependent factors is understood to work in both directions without metaphysical priority being given to the one or the other side.

4. *Emergentist neo-Darwinism.* Here the metaphysical priority is placed on the emergent entities, at whatever level they occur. This view is (generally) not reductionist in either the ontological or epistemological sense. There is no overarching teleology that guides the evolutionary process. But the laws of nature are such that the evolutionary process gives rise to more and more complex entities. These emergent entities then become basic to explanations of biological phenomena at more and more complex levels of structure and function.

Note that positions 2, 3, and 4, though otherwise distinct, are all neo-Darwinian. (For example, much talk of emergence by scientists trained in biology can be fit into the framework of neo-Darwinism.) This fact helps to explain the rampant confusion surrounding the use of the term. When someone speaks of a position as "neo-Darwinian," it should suggest two limits. First, neo-Darwinian explanations are those that are not Lamarckian; that is, they do not allow for the inheritance of acquired traits. Second, the term implies that one cannot say more than the empirical science by itself allows; all more robust metaphysical positions are excluded — or, better, they are seen as lying beyond the parameters of what the scientist qua scientist can say.

Much parental training is Lamarckian: you can teach your children things that you learned after they were born, and they can pass these ideas on to their children. Indeed, it would appear that cultural evolution is fundamentally Lamarckian. This means that the big battle now being fought concerns the relationship between biological and cultural evolution. Is culture just a means used by genes to increase the selective advantage of certain organisms, or does it represent a new pattern in natural history, explainable only in terms of causes and "entities" (e.g., ideas, institutions, ideologies) that transcend the neo-Darwinian framework?

5. *Terry Deacon's emergence.* Deacon's position stands as a bridge between (4) and (6). I list it here because it is so well developed scientifically, conceptually, and metaphysically, and so significant as a standpoint, that it needs to be covered on its own. Deacon's metaphysical commitments are clearly Buddhist, and he has worked them out with some precision. In most respects his view would fall under heading 4, but there are exceptions. He wants to defend a form of real teleology in biology, but when he explains this metaphysically, he appeals to the negating metaphysics of traditional Buddhist thought. (This means accepting some paradoxes along the way, e.g., in his slogan "something more from nothing but.") Also, he introduces the idea of coevolution, derived from the work of William Durham (and ultimately from Gilbert and Raven),[48] which connotes a level or type of emergence that goes beyond what one ordinarily finds within (4).

In general, there are complex and fascinating metaphysical differences between (4), (5), (6), and (7). Distinguishing between these four different interpretations of contemporary biological theory may just be the single most important task for any discussion of biology and metaphysics today. The issues raised are not foreign to the actual "bench science" in biology but arise directly out of current work; hence one does not have to prove biologists wrong in order to start raising the pertinent metaphysical issues. This makes for conversations with greater mutuality, and greater fruitfulness, than one finds in some of the earlier and later categories.

6. *Neo-Aristotelianism.* In recent decades a variety of philosophers of biology have attempted to conceive the role of structures in biology in a manner inspired by Aristotle's theory of formal causation. As I define these positions, they resist final causation and vitalism; more on that in a minute. But by advocating formal causation — that is, speaking of the *causal* role played by forms, structures, morphologies, aggregates, and systems — these theorists move beyond what modern empirical science has been willing to countenance as "real" instances of causation.

The distinction between formal and final causation brings us to the heart of the contemporary emergence debate: the distinction between "weak" and "strong" emergence.[49] Science is about explaining, and scientific explanations

48. The coevolution concept can be traced back to Lawrence E. Gilbert and Peter H. Raven, eds., *Coevolution of Animals and Plants: Symposium V, First International Congress of Systematic and Evolutionary Biology, 1973* (Austin: University of Texas Press, 1975), which predated by almost two decades William Durham's famous *Coevolution: Genes, Culture, and Human Diversity* (Stanford: Stanford University Press, 1991).

49. The history of the distinction and its role in the current discussion are central themes in my *Mind and Emergence.* In fact, one of the main themes of the book is to defend strong

are *causal* explanations. Moreover, whatever does the causal work in science is what is taken as "really" existing; to know the preferred causal account for some field of study is to know that field's ontology. Hence the level(s) of phenomena to which one ascribes causal efficacy is (are) the level(s) that really counts. Take (4), for example. It is an emergentist position — something genuinely new emerges — and yet it holds that the properties of emergent levels are explainable in terms of the lower levels out of which they arise. Given its causal account, and thus its ontology, it must be classified as an instance of "weak" emergence. By contrast, (6) ascribes real causal efficacy, and hence real existence, to emergent structures in biology, making it an example of strong emergence. Deacon's position, (5), stands on the boundary between these two views; I have argued that it is strongest when developed in the direction of strong emergence, but at other points Deacon continues to be drawn (unfortunately) toward the framework of weak emergence.

7. *From teleonomy to teleology: emergent agents.* Teleonomy has dominated biology in the twentieth century. Philosophically, one might say that teleonomy takes a Kantian approach to higher-order functions in the biosphere. Life-forms within the universe *act as if* there were purposes, intentions, goals, agents, and thoughts. One takes these appearances as seriously as possible and works intensely to explain them, but one never asserts the actual existence of purposive systems.

Approach 7 removes the Kantian "as if." It is willing to speak of these teleological systems as real. The "strong emergence" position in biology — the view that emergent agents exercise "downward causation" on their constituent parts — is committed to a metaphysics at least as robust as (7). Since this is such a huge step, I list it as a separate option in the metaphysical hierarchy.

Probably the positions that fall in this category are best defined as those that accept agents and purposes in the biosphere as real but that seek to provide the metaphysically most minimalist account of such agents and purposes that is possible. Thus Stuart Kauffman and I have recently sought to define the conditions for the most minimal agent in biology, with important similarities to, but also contrasts with, Terry Deacon's recent article in *Biological Theory* on "autocells."[50] We clearly go beyond Deacon's position in degree of metaphysical robustness in our understanding of agency, and yet we explicitly hold back

---

emergence against its detractors. Note that "strong" and "weak" are not evaluative comments; many hold that weak emergence is the empirically more adequate account of the world.

50. Stuart Kauffman and Philip Clayton, "On Emergence, Agency, and Organization," *Philosophy and Biology* 21 (2006): 501-21; Deacon, "Reciprocal Linkage between Self-Organizing Processes Is Sufficient for Self-Reproduction and Evolvability."

from any commitment to the reality of intentional agents in the sense in which folk psychology speaks of human agents.

8. *The Platonic school in biology.* One might question placing this school here, since it might not seem that Platonic approaches are more metaphysical than Aristotelian approaches. But there are good reasons to think that one ends up with a more emphatically metaphysical system when the formal constraints are taken to be abstract possibilities or forms rather than specific structures actually existing in specific organisms.

Several books and at least one article in *Nature* by Michael Denton fall in this category.[51] The recent and highly influential book by Simon Conway Morris of Cambridge University, *Life's Solution,* tends in this direction as well.[52] Denton's work is particularly representative of this school of thought because he explicitly interprets evolution as traversing a predefined conceptual space of probability, indeed even inevitability. A priori forms structure the evolutionary process. One thinks of his claim that at the big bang it was already inevitable that intelligent animals would eventually evolve within the universe that had an opposable thumb and forefingers. Platonists argue, similarly, that random variation and selective retention do not tell the whole story about evolution. Evolutionary outcomes are also (and equally?) constrained by the preexistence of formal possibilities for protein structures, and the constraints imposed by these preexisting forms explain why evolution was able to "discover" the life-supporting protein structures in such a short time. These thinkers not only hold that evolution inevitably tends toward intelligent life; in addition, they adduce Platonic arguments to defend this view.[53]

9. *Bergson and the life principle.* Vitalist positions are metaphysically more robust than (8) because now the guidance for the evolutionary process comes not just from an abstract Platonic possibility space that constrains the process, but also from an unfolding immanent force that develops itself (or "comes to itself," to use language that Samuel Alexander borrowed from Hegel) over the

51. Michael Denton, *Evolution: A Theory in Crisis* (Bethesda, Md.: Adler and Adler, 1986); Denton, *Nature's Destiny: How the Laws of Biology Reveal Purpose in the Universe* (New York: Free Press, 1998); Michael Denton and Craig Marshall, "Laws of Form Revisited," *Nature* 410 (March 22, 2001): 417.

52. Simon Conway Morris is even more overt about the possible Platonist connection in his earlier book, *The Crucible of Creation: The Burgess Shale and the Rise of Animals* (Oxford: Oxford University Press, 1998).

53. At the same time, Denton is also explicit in his most recent work in connecting with the vitalist traditions and attempting to rehabilitate them. To the extent that he intends this as a constructive metaphysics of biology and not merely as an exercise in iconoclasm, Denton's position tends toward (9).

course of evolution. The later passages of Bergson's *Creative Evolution* are strongly teleological, as is, on my reading, Bergson's position as a whole. Other parts of Bergson's overall system move him closer to (10) or even (11), but his defense of the life principle is a quintessential example of (9).

10. *Whiteheadian and neo-Whiteheadian process philosophies.* I take this category to be metaphysically more robust than (9) because here the creative agents are understood to be present from the very beginning, whereas Bergson maintains (at least in *Creative Evolution*) that experiencing agents arise over the course of evolution. Clearly nontheistic forms of process thought, where Creativity functions as a sort of Life-Force, are metaphysically more minimalist; theistic forms in which God presents distinct initial aims to each actual occasion are metaphysically more robust. Similarly, those process views that distinguish the mode of God's existence from that of all finite actual occasions employ a larger metaphysical superstructure than those that understand God to be an actual occasion exemplifying exactly the same metaphysical principles as all other occasions. Not only do purposive agents actually exist, *pace* the teleonomists, but everything that exists is either a teleological system (an actual occasion) or its by-product.

11. *Dualism.* I concur with David Griffin that process metaphysics stands closer to most forms of modern naturalism than does dualism, which postulates a distinct type of substance in the world. Not all dualisms are identical, however. Cartesian dualism — the belief that a purely spiritual substance influences physical bodies and is influenced by them, even though it is an essentially different type of reality — stands at perhaps the greatest distance from (10). William Hasker's *The Emergent Self* stands much closer to (10), and Thomistic dualisms (hylomorphisms) that reject Hasker's emergentist arguments stand somewhere between the two.

One might challenge this construal, arguing that, e.g., Hasker's dualism is not very different from strong emergence, that is, emergence theories with top-down mental causation. In fact, one might argue, any dualism is *functionally* equivalent to top-down mental emergence, since both hold that to explain behavior we must take account of the causal influence of thoughts, and thoughts themselves are not explainable in terms of the material forces from which they emerge. But this is not quite right. Hasker emphasizes the importance of understanding mind as mental substance — that is, in terms of a robust substance metaphysics — whereas the strong emergentists in the philosophy of mind defend the causal powers of mental *properties,* which may be properties of things that are not different in their essence from other natural things. Of course, some are skeptical whether those of us who argue in this way will be able to make our case in the end. Still, our *intention* is to provide a metaphysically less substantial account (as it were) of mental causation, and this different intention justifies the different placement in the typology.

12. *Classical philosophical theism in the West.* Classical philosophical theism (CPT) adds to the dualism of embodied mental substances within the world an omnipotent, omniscient being who is pure Spirit, one who precedes the world and influences its development from a purely spiritual realm. CPT thus adds to the dualist's teleology (agents with purposes exist) two other metaphysical forms of purpose: a fully purposive divine agent who sets things in motion and guides them toward his goals, and, as a result, a genuine purpose to the entire cosmic evolutionary process. This more robust metaphysic is shared by virtually all strictly orthodox theologies within the three Abrahamic (Western monotheistic) traditions.

## Conclusion

One could nuance the preceding account in a variety of ways, but certainly as it stands it provides a good sense of the range of positions.

Assuming that this analysis is basically correct, it follows that those who wish to defend a process account of evolution will need to argue that the best metaphysical interpretation of contemporary biology will involve a metaphysics at least as robust as (10). Accounts less robust than that, they must argue, are too metaphysically thin to be adequate. For instance, perhaps thinner accounts do not explain human experience in the world, or perhaps they leave metaphysical questions unanswered that we have reason to think should be answered. The proponents of a process metaphysic of evolution must also argue that holding (10) is not antiscientific: process metaphysics, they must show, is consistent with scientific results, while placing them within the best available metaphysical framework. By contrast, the process metaphysician will seek to show, (11) and (12) *are* antiscientific and should therefore be rejected by anyone interested in integrating contemporary science and metaphysical reflection.

# IV EVOLUTION AND GOD

## Editor's Preface

Often the primary focus of a discussion of science and religion is the question whether one can still affirm a role for God in a world explained by science. If a favorable answer is proposed, the question becomes *how* God acts in the world. These are important topics for this book as well. Often the discussion assumes that science and its worldview are given and that theology must adjust to that. But from a Whiteheadian point of view, the question is not so much how to adapt theological formulations to the currently dominant scientific theory of evolution as how to develop or change that theory to make possible fruitful integration with a revised formulation of theology.

That is what most of the book has been about to this point. Part II dealt with scientific criticisms and proposed changes in the currently dominant theory. Part III dealt with philosophical changes. Part IV builds on both biological alternatives to neo-Darwinism and a different philosophy.

The emphasis on scientific and philosophical critiques of neo-Darwinism has not excluded reflection about God all along the way. All writers had the whole scope of the discussion in view and were free to express the full range of their interests. Indeed, the word "God" may appear as often in some of the earlier chapters as in some of the chapters here. Nevertheless, it is only in this part that thematic discussion of the question is the primary focus.

Contributors to the book represent a variety of viewpoints on this topic. A few are antitheistic, indifferent or neutral. The widespread view among religious people that science and faith should be kept quite separate has also been represented by Francisco Ayala. But the organizers of the conference out of which this book developed and I, as editor of the book, want to make positive connections between faith and science. As a result, those seeking to modify both theology and science to integrate them into a unified vision of reality are overrepresented in comparison with their role in the national and international discussion. All those included in this part belong to this group, although they vary in the extent to which they are prepared to modify either discipline.

Consider the problem faced by anyone who wants to describe God as actually involved in what happens in the world. The importance of the issue for persons of theistic faith is highlighted by the fact of evolution, since this brings human beings fully into the world studied by science. The neo-Darwinian account of evolution accomplishes this naturalization of humanity by integrating human beings into a mechanical world. It depicts evolution as coming about, not through the creative interaction of organisms, but through mechanisms that ignore the purposive activities of living beings. In an extreme formulation, some have said that the organism is only the gene's way of reproducing itself. Since neo-Darwinism is now the leading theoretical influence among biologists, the current teaching of evolution in our schools typically implies that human beings are part of the world machine, nothing but matter in motion.

This in itself does not exclude a role for God. It is not impossible to relate God's activity to a mechanical world. Indeed, one reason scientists initially adopted the mechanical model was that it made clear the need of a divine Creator in a way that organic models of the world did not. Throughout the eighteenth century most people were persuaded that the need of an intelligent and purposeful Creator was obvious. A machine cannot make itself. More generally the laws obeyed by matter had to be imposed upon it. They cannot be understood as inherent in the matter itself.

Further, in those preevolutionary days human beings, or at least their minds, were believed to be located outside the machine. They were viewed as a separate creation. They could be understood as subjects in communion with the divine subject. God was seen as creator and lawgiver of a mechanical nature. For human beings God was understood to provide a moral law along with sanctions for obedience or disobedience. Since the human mind or soul did not participate in the condition of the material world, it made sense to suppose, as Plato and Descartes both did, that it participated in immortality.

In that context theologians disagreed on whether God acted in the world in other ways. Many believed that the God who created the world and its laws could suspend or break them. Many thought that to demonstrate the truth of the Christian gospel God had indeed intervened from time to time to work miracles. God had done this in the ministry of Jesus and in the early church. But most Protestant theologians supposed that once the Bible had been accepted as authoritative, miracles ceased. Others thought miracles had never occurred — that any suspension of natural law would imply that God's laws were imperfect. They held that the world operated fully in terms of these perfect laws, without exception.

The use in science of the term "natural law," still widely current, reflects the thinking of that period. A world of material particles cannot account for its own regularities of behavior. These must be imposed. The imposition of particular patterns of behavior is like the law of a sovereign ruler. Actually it is stronger than that, since this natural law cannot be disobeyed.

The machine model is not as popular today as it once was. Philosophers of science are more likely to use other language. But for the most part they believe that occurrences in the natural world, the world that now includes human beings, are fully conformed to the "laws" discovered by scientists. These "laws" in combination with boundary conditions are thought, in principle, to describe or explain everything. These philosophers do not affirm an added realm of subjectivity, freedom, spontaneity, responsibility, or value as playing any role in the real world. If these exist at all, these philosophers teach, they exercise no causality and therefore have no real significance.

For the most part, those who operate in science and the philosophy of science today see no place for God. They see no need for a creator, since the world has been creating itself ever since the big bang. The cause of that explosion is mysterious, but positing God seems, to most, to explain nothing.

To avoid the implication of a lawgiver in our antitheistic age, many scientists and philosophers today speak of "lawlike" behavior, but many still speak of "obeying" laws. It is sometimes thought that when the occurrences of nature can be predicted in terms of the "laws" or "lawlike" behavior of nature, any reference to God is precluded. But that there are "laws" at all, and what their nature may be, is rarely explained.

If God can be assigned any role at all in this picture, it is likely to be giver of natural law. The alternative seems to be that the regularities of behavior, or at least the particular regularities found in our world, are a matter of chance. However, the notion of chance as the ultimate ground of what is has its problems. The "laws" that govern the self-unfolding of this cosmos and of life on this planet are quite wonderful. Yet there seems to be no natural necessity for just these "laws." Attention focuses today especially on the physical "constants." They seem to be arbitrary in the sense that one can discern no deeper scientific reason why they are just what they are. Yet if they had been significantly different, the conditions necessary for the emergence of life would have been lacking.

It is as if a supremely powerful and intelligent being, desirous of shaping the universe in such a way that there would be living things and an evolution of very complex ones, chose just these constants and imposed them on the world. This has led some scientists to belief in God. Most scientists, however, resist this move. Some have gone to great lengths to posit many universes, successive or simultaneous, so that the remarkable character of this one can more easily be attributed to chance.

None of the contributors to this part of the book make use of this simple deistic argument for God. They are not primarily interested in this deistic God who acted only once by imposing order on a passive matter. They see much more agency in nature itself than materialists can acknowledge. Regularities of behavior do not all depend on the imposition of order from outside. Yet they want to discern God's hand in the course of natural and historical events.

Unfortunately, this is not possible if each such event is exhaustively caused by antecedent events, as so much philosophy of science implies. The proposals in part II are important because most of them put some emphasis on the activity of organisms. This opens the way to considering how the subjectivity of animals may play a role in the evolutionary process. And that, in turn, opens the door to another way of envisioning God's role, that of divine influence in subjective experience.

John Haught recognizes that efforts to show divine purpose at work at particular steps in the evolutionary process have been unsuccessful. He rejects the idea of Intelligent Design as that has recently been systematically developed. The apparent designs can be explained without reference to any special imposition of order. The same forces that are at work elsewhere can explain the appearance of design.

Instead of viewing the universe, including biological evolution on this planet, in terms of design, he employs the category of narrative. Narrative requires both necessity and contingency. It is not compatible with an imposed end. The fact that some biologists emphasize the necessity of events, and others, their contingency, makes it plausible for him to assert that reality is in fact just that mixture of necessity and contingency that is required for a story. It is the overarching story of evolution that most interests him. However, the story would lack interest if cosmic evolution has no directionality. Haught finds the needed direction in the increase of beauty, which involves ordered novelty and heightened consciousness.

Haught believes that the actual course of events has both the overall direction required for a story and the many twists and turns that one would expect in view of the large role of contingency. God acts persuasively, not coercively. Much that happens does not advance God's purpose of increasing beauty. Nevertheless, beauty has increased.

Haught does not directly challenge those biologists who deny that they can find directionality in biological evolution. He argues from a still broader perspective, that of cosmic evolution. Jeffrey Schloss shares much of this interest with Haught, but his work is more narrowly focused on biological phenomena. His theological question is whether the course of *biological* evolution is compatible with belief in God. This compatibility depends, for him, on scientific evidence that there is a direction in evolution. Hence, whereas Haught locates biological evolution in the context of that of the whole universe, Schloss focuses on the specific question of whether those biologists who deny any directionality to evolution are justified in doing so. He judges that they are not.

Schloss undertakes to show on purely empirical grounds that there is directionality in biological evolution. He does this in the face of the majority judgment among contemporary evolutionists that there is no direction to be found. Some conclude this on the basis that what happens is simply the outworking of necessity; others, that it is purely contingent. Both groups tend to derive the negative conclusion from their a priori assumptions rather than from detailed study of the course of events. Schloss demonstrates from the empirical data that there are long-term trends or directions.

The theological conclusions of Haught and Schloss are remarkably similar. Both look for signs of divine purpose in the direction taken by evolution as a whole. Schloss seeks them in biological evolution. Haught emphasizes the entire cosmic history. In this difference they are complementary rather than opposed.

To assert that there *is* a direction puts them in conflict with dominant evolutionary theory; so they must make their case carefully. Both see the category of narrative as fruitful for understanding the overall course of events. Both see God as the author of the narrative as a whole rather than as controlling the actions of the individual characters.

There is another question. *How* does God affect the course of events? One view would be that this is by the basic structure or order imposed by God upon the universe. Schloss seems open to that view, but does not develop it. Haught refers to Whitehead's doctrine of divine persuasion as compatible with his narrative account of evolution.

The remaining essays focus more on this second question from a Whiteheadian point of view. Van Till comes to the topic from physics, but he has long recognized that the major problems about science for Christians have arisen because of the theory of evolution. Conservative Christians have strongly opposed this theory not only because it is in tension with the creation story in the Bible but also for the reasons frequently mentioned in this book. It undermines human freedom and responsibility as well as excluding God from any role in the course of events. Their response has often been to look for gaps in the naturalistic account of evolution. They could then posit divine interventions to explain what happens at these points.

As a scientist Van Till did not find these gaps. He was convinced that God had not intervened in the course of events. God had provided all that was needed for the wonderful developments that were to come. Van Till called this the Right Stuff Universe Principle. That the universe would be so formed that the wonderful development of life and its many forms could take place, he emphasizes, is a truly remarkable fact, taken for granted by science but unexplained by any naturalist principles. At that time Van Till believed that God *could* act supernaturally in the world, but he could not point to any instances where God had done so. Accordingly, his account of God and the world seemed deistic. As a Christian believer, he was not comfortable with this position.

He received a critique of his work from David Griffin, who opened up to him another option. If God is understood in a supernatural way, then God is seen as normally external to the world. Such a God could only act in the world by intervening in its natural processes. Van Till saw no evidence of such intervention. But if God is always in the world, working for order and novelty, for novel order and ordered novelty, then God never intervenes but is always a factor in what is happening. Van Till now sees God as a contributing cause in the world rather than one that unilaterally determines the outcome of any event.

Whitehead's philosophy is of central interest to those of us who organized the conference out of which this book developed. By far its fullest explanation is found in the chapter by Griffin that follows that of Van Till. Griffin expounds Whitehead's understanding of reality in general, but with a special focus on how God affects the course of worldly events. Based on this account, he picks up from his chapter in part III where he identifies fifteen doctrines of neo-Darwinism and the philosophy that informs it. He shows that Whitehead can provide an account of evolution that accords well with the data but rejects most of these doctrines.

The astute reader will notice that not all who are influenced by Whitehead hold to exactly the same views. In his chapter in part II, Barbour criticizes Griffin's support of Behe's argument that neo-Darwinian mechanisms do not suffice to explain particular evolutionary phenomena. Griffin's response in part IV shows that he and Barbour are not as far apart as they seemed.

Probably, the greatest difference has to do with Griffin's way of describing Whitehead's doctrine of forms or "eternal objects." Whitehead identifies himself, along with the whole history of Western philosophy, as Platonic. Plato noted that we cannot understand the world apart from reflection on the recurrent forms within it. Plato saw them as having a transcendent reality. Aristotle located them more in the natural world. Whitehead followed Plato in attributing to the forms some element of transcendence vis-à-vis the actual occasions that constitute the world. However, his ideas about these transcendent forms were shaped by a different logic and mathematics from that available to Plato.

Plato connected the forms closely with normative ideas. Whitehead saw them as pure potentials or forms of definiteness that inform everything, good and bad alike. However, they are ordered in such a way as to encourage the increase of value. Hence, they do play a normative role.

For Plato there are forms corresponding to each species of animals. Individual animals participated in these forms. For Whitehead they are forms corresponding to every member of every species as well as to all possible animals and to everything else, actual or possible, as well. The forms in themselves cannot therefore explain why animals are so clearly grouped with so few intermediate instances. However, Whitehead also held that the forms do not function neutrally. They are ordered in their relevance to the situations in the world. This ordering can lead to the phenomena Conway Morris has emphasized. Given particular situations, certain potentials function as attractors. This applies at every level of unitary actuality, including both cells and the organisms.

Accordingly, it is possible either to emphasize the close connection between Whitehead and Plato or the sharp differences. Griffin emphasizes the former and finds places where Whitehead does recognize that the forms play a normative role. I would argue, with Barbour, I think, that it is not the forms as such that play such a role but the divine ordering of the forms that tilts the world toward the actualization of value. Again, the difference may not be very great.

My chapter, with which part IV ends, explains *my* view of how God orders the forms or eternal objects to provide regularity and novelty and to make possible the self-determination of the entities that constitute the world. My understanding, like that of other Whiteheadians, is that relevant forms offer alternative ways of self-constitution to the energy events that make up the world. This works in the process of their becoming, that is, in their subjectivity determining just what form the subject will take. This determines also what these events will be as objects for future subjects. To the necessity and chance emphasized by Barbour, Haught, and Schloss, I add what is usually called freedom but is more precisely described as self-determination. God's role is at once to make this self-determination possible and to lure creaturely events to actualize what value is possible in their acts of self-organization.

Whitehead's conceptuality leads one to expect long-term changes of the sort that Haught and Schloss emphasize as well as a narrative quality in the course of events. It also supports Van Till's emphasis on the Right Stuff Universe Principle. But as Van Till appreciatively recognizes, it also shows that God is differentially contributory to the coming into being of each creature in ways that Griffin explains.

Whitehead describes not only God's influence on events in the world but also how God is affected by what happens in the world and saves it. In the final paragraphs of his magnum opus, *Process and Reality,* he even writes of how God provides a particular providence for particular occasions. There is rich potential for understanding much religious experience in these terms without coming into conflict with scientific thought. However, this possible direction of thought has little relevance to the issues dealt with in this book.

# 19. *Darwinism, Design, and Cosmic Purpose*

John F. Haught

## Classical and Contemporary Cosmologies

Religions, for the most part, have taught that the universe is the embodiment of a transcendent wisdom. The cosmos is a "great teaching" permeated with purpose.[1] Such a belief gives meaning to people's lives as well as a context for ethical aspiration. The good life, accordingly, consists of conforming ourselves to the transcendent value incarnate in nature. The universe of traditional religions is pedagogical, though still mystifying. It is riddled with ambiguity, but it is ultimately benign and not indifferent. It is sacramental, that is, revelatory of the sacred mystery in which it is enfolded. A dominant world-picture in Western thought after Plato has portrayed the universe as a Great Chain of Being, running vertically from lowly matter at the bottom to God at the top.[2] The distinct levels between matter and God consist of plants, animals, humans, and angelic beings. In this venerable cosmology every being has its divinely assigned station and mission. And, because humans occupy a relatively high level in the hierarchy of beings, they can assume that they are endowed by God with an exceptional dignity.

But this picture emerged in our history long before modern science came along. Its adherents knew nothing of evolution and astrophysics. The science of today requires new imagery to represent what the universe looks like. Imagine, for example, thirty large volumes on your bookshelf, each tome 450 pages long, and every page standing for 1 million years. Let this set of books represent the scientific story of our 13.7-billion-year-old universe. The narrative begins with

---

1. Jacob Needleman, *A Sense of the Cosmos* (New York: Dutton, 1976), pp. 10-36.
2. Arthur O. Lovejoy, *The Great Chain of Being: A Study of the History of an Idea* (New York: Harper and Row, 1965).

the big bang on page 1 of volume 1, and the first twenty-one books show no signs of life. The earth story begins in volume 21, 4.5 billion years ago, but life doesn't appear until volume 22, about 3.8 billion years ago. Even so, living organisms do not become particularly interesting, at least in human terms, until almost the end of volume 29. There the famous Cambrian explosion occurs, the patterns of life suddenly bursting out into an unprecedented array of complexity and morphological diversity. Dinosaurs come in around the middle of volume 30 but are wiped out on page 385. Only during the last sixty-five pages of volume 30 does mammalian life begin to flourish. Our immediate hominid ancestors start showing up several pages from the end of volume 30, but modern humans don't appear until the bottom of the final page. The entire history of human intelligence, ethics, religious aspiration, and scientific discovery takes up only the last few lines on the last page of the very last volume.

Now compare the classic hierarchical cosmology to the greatly enlarged picture of the universe that today's sciences suggest. Can we ever hope to unwind the vine of purposiveness that attached itself so comfortably to the vertical, hierarchical cosmology and rewind it around the expansive thirty-volume horizontal drama of a world still coming into being? Such a project seems impossible to many modern scientific thinkers, and so they are happy to let go of humanity's spiritual past altogether. They see no reason to save the ancient religious and ethical sensibilities that were so carefully refined in the context of prescientific worldviews. Even committed religious thinkers today often wonder how much of the older Wisdom traditions could possibly survive and perhaps find new applications in terms of the picture of the cosmos now emerging. The Darwinian chapters — volumes 22-30 — of the new cosmic story seem especially puzzling.[3]

## Darwinism as a Special Problem

Evolution, after all, has the effect of "temporalizing" the Great Chain of Being, turning the hierarchy on its side, as it were, and allowing its content to spill out only gradually — first matter, then life, then mind. By itself this horizontalizing is not necessarily a threat to traditional teleological (purposive) visions of nature. The principle of plenitude, according to which every level in the cosmic hierarchy must be filled with some kind of being, could in principle be implemented by a gradualistic "program" for the world's creation.[4] However, much

---

3. For further discussion see John F. Haught, *God after Darwin: A Theology of Evolution* (Boulder, Colo.: Westview, 2000).

4. Charles Coulston Gillispie, *Genesis and Geology: A Study in the Relations of Scientific*

harder to match up with the earlier purpose-filled hierarchical portraits is the Darwinian recipe for the diversification of life over the last nine volumes of our new story.

In the simplest terms, biological evolution is made up of three generic elements: (1) contingent events such as the accidents involved in the spontaneous origin of life, random genetic variations (mutations) that constitute the raw material of evolutionary diversity, and undirected occurrences in natural history, e.g., climatic changes or meteorite impacts, that shape the pathways of evolution in unpredictable ways; (2) lawful constraints: these include not only "natural selection" but also other physical, mathematical, and biological factors that keep contingency within bounds and make scientific prediction possible; and (3) deep cosmic time, the billions of years that the universe has made available to evolution for its extravagantly diverse and abundant experiments with life.

A major question for religious thought, as much today as in Darwin's time, is how to reconcile the brute impersonality and blindness of the three items in evolution's recipe with a religious sense of cosmic purpose.[5] There is also the struggle and predation that often offend human ethical sensibilities. Of course, there is much more to evolution than all of this. It is not all competition, pain, and waste, but also symbiosis and cooperation. And yet, as scientific information of natural history has accumulated after Darwin, religious purpose and biological evolution have not become any easier to tie together.[6] Life's long journey, as we now realize, has left such a wide and drawn-out trail of contingency, loss, and pain that many sensitive people have given up trying to make religious sense of the universe at all. For some, the Darwinian account of life has stretched to the breaking point the persistent problem of theodicy — that is, the problem of how to reconcile the ideas of divine goodness and power with suffering and evil. The idea of cosmic purpose has generally been associated with a divine "plan" or "design," but such a comforting concept seems to bear little relationship to the Darwinian map of life's journey.

Design, moreover, can now be explained apparently without invoking any notion of divine intentionality. Any claim in an age of evolution that nature's designs can lead the mind directly to God, or that pure reason can discern a providential plan for nature, is no longer easy to defend. To many scientists and

---

Thought, Natural Theology, and Social Opinion in Great Britain, 1790-1850 (Cambridge: Harvard University Press, 1996), p. 18.

5. Gillispie, *Genesis and Geology*, p. 220.

6. For a discussion of some previous attempts to connect God and evolution in England, see Peter Bowler, *Reconciling Science and Religion: The Debate in Early Twentieth-Century Britain* (Chicago: University of Chicago Press, 2001).

philosophers today, evolutionary mechanisms are enough to account for the adaptive design that previously seemed to be either direct or indirect divine handiwork. Because of its adaptive complexity, the eye, for example, may seem to be divinely designed, but it is really the unintended outcome of a process of blind Darwinian selection.

So the evolutionary naturalist will take any suggestion that purpose is operative in the life process, or in the universe at large, to be a rival account to the suggestions of science. Final causal explanations seem to be a potential threat to the explanatory power of the notion of natural selection.[7] If we allow purpose to get its foot in the door, the naturalist claims, then the quest for true causes is over and science will lose its bearings. Even a commonsense usage of the idea of purpose must be discarded as cognitionally worthless. As the Harvard biologist Richard Lewontin states:

> Our willingness to accept scientific claims that are against common sense is the key to an understanding of the real struggle between science and the supernatural. We take the side of science . . . because we have a prior commitment, a commitment to materialism. It is not that the methods and institutions of science somehow compel us to accept a material explanation of the phenomenal world, but, on the contrary, that we are forced by our a priori adherence to material causes to create an apparatus of investigation and a set of concepts that produce material explanations, no matter how counterintuitive, no matter how mystifying to the uninitiated. Moreover, that materialism is absolute, for we cannot allow a Divine Foot in the door.[8]

For Lewontin material causes are explanatorily sufficient, and any talk about purpose counts for nothing. As he concedes, however, the statement just quoted is not a scientific one, but instead a profession of faith. Perhaps this concession makes it appropriate to say, therefore, that it is not science per se but scientific materialism that contradicts a theological (or teleological) understanding of nature.

---

7. See Michael R. Rose, *Darwin's Spectre: Evolutionary Biology in the Modern World* (Princeton: Princeton University Press, 1998), p. 211, and Gary Cziko, *Without Miracles: Universal Selection Theory* (Cambridge: MIT Press, 1995).

8. See Richard Lewontin, "Billions and Billions of Demons," *New York Review of Books,* January 9, 1997, p. 31.

## Does Evolution Rule Out Cosmic Purpose?

Charles Darwin himself, especially in light of the excessive amount of pain he observed in life's evolution, eventually abandoned his earlier belief in divine purposiveness. He was taken aback by the way the life process seems to have worked. His favorite example was the wasp that laid its eggs inside of living caterpillars, making it possible for the freshly hatched larvae to start consuming their host before it died. How could such phenomena be reconciled with trust in a creative and purposive God? Likewise, Sir Charles Sherrington, in his 1940 Gifford Lectures, was puzzled at the disproportionate amount of suffering caused by lowly parasites:

> There is a small worm (Redia) in our ponds. With its tongue-head it bores into the lung of the water-snail. There it turns into a bag and grows at the expense of the snail's blood. The cyst in the snail's lung is full of Redia. They bore their way out and wander about the body of the snail. They live on the body of the snail, on its less vital parts for so it lasts the longer; to kill it would cut their sojourn short before they could breed. They breed and reproduce. The young wander within the sick snail. After a time they bore their way out of the dying snail and make their way to the wet grass at the pond-edge. There amid the green leaves they encyst themselves and wait. A browsing sheep or ox comes cropping the moist grass. The cyst is eaten. The stomach of the sheep dissolves the cyst and sets free the fluke-worms within it. The worm is now within the body of its second prey. It swims from the stomach to the liver. There it sucks blood and grows, causing the disease called "sheeprot."[9]

The worms then lay eggs that make their way down the animal's bile ducts and finally exit into the wet pasture. "Thence as free larvae they reach the meadow-pond to look for another water snail. So the implacable cycle rebegins."

What does all of this mean? Sherrington does not have a satisfying answer: "it is a story of securing existence to a worm at cost of lives superior to it in the scale of life as humanly reckoned. Life's prize is given to the aggressive and inferior of life, destructive of other lives at the expense of suffering in them, and, sad as it may seem to us, suffering in proportion as they are lives high in life's scale."[10]

Even if liver flukes and ichneumon wasps exhibit a kind of ingenuity, it is

9. Charles Sherrington, *Man on His Nature* (Cambridge: Cambridge University Press, 1951), p. 266.

10. Sherrington, *Man on His Nature*, p. 266.

not easy to trace it to divine design. Before Darwin it seemed easy to justify belief in cosmic purpose by examining instances of adaptive design in many living beings and processes. Afterward, however, it has seemed sufficient to invoke the mechanism of natural selection — along with, of course, accidents and deep time — to account for design. It now appears that there has been more than enough time for Darwin's recipe to do the work of creating new forms of life and adaptive design without the presence of any overarching purposive agency. The vast amount of time in which change can occur randomly and stepwise in evolutionary history rules out the need for any divine plan for life and the universe.[11]

What justification then could there possibly be for clinging to a sense of cosmic purpose amidst the darkness of evolution? If an overarching purpose were to manifest itself palpably anywhere in nature, would it not be in the lifeworld? Yet Darwinian biology finds at best only an apparent purposiveness in the adaptive living design that reportedly came about without being intended in any way.[12] Even the most materialistic evolutionist will admit, of course, that humans have "purpose on the brain."[13] But our habit of looking for purpose can apparently be accounted for in Darwinian terms alone. Our religious tendency to attribute purpose to the universe is an evolutionary adaptation, or at least the by-product of other adaptations.[14] Today many biologists, social scientists, and philosophers would explain it in terms of human genes striving for immortality. Construing the universe as purpose-filled is a habit that is ultimately explainable by biology rather than theology. Religious ideas of cosmic purpose are nothing more than heartwarming fiction, "noble lies" that help humans adapt but are empirically unfounded.[15]

However, what would constitute evidence of purpose if it did indeed exist? And could any conclusive evidence for final causes ever show up in, or be ruled out by, scientific inquiry? Moreover, what does "purpose" really mean, anyway? Unfortunately, antireligious evolutionists, not unlike some of their re-

11. Richard Dawkins, *Climbing Mount Improbable* (New York: Norton, 1996).

12. See Michael Ruse, *Darwin and Design: Does Evolution Have a Purpose?* (Cambridge: Harvard University Press, 2003).

13. See Richard Dawkins, *River out of Eden* (New York: Basic Books, 1995), p. 96.

14. Edward O. Wilson, *Consilience: The Unity of Knowledge* (New York: Knopf, 1998), p. 262; Walter Burkert, *Creation of the Sacred: Tracks of Biology in Early Religions* (Cambridge: Harvard University Press, 1996), p. 20; Scott Atran, *In Gods We Trust: The Evolutionary Landscape of Religion* (New York: Oxford University Press, 2002), pp. 78-79; Pascal Boyer, *Religion Explained: The Evolutionary Origins of Religious Thought* (New York: Basic Books, 2001), p. 145.

15. See Loyal Rue, *By the Grace of Guile: The Role of Deception in Natural History and Human Affairs* (New York: Oxford University Press, 1994), pp. 261-306.

ligious opponents, typically reduce the religious sense of purpose to that of "intelligent design." Then, after demonstrating that biological adaptations came about without any intelligent guidance, and that adaptations are merely "designlike" rather than intentionally designed, it seems easy to conclude that there is no underlying purposiveness in life or the universe.[16] Design turns out to be nothing more than the outcome of an unintelligent and unintentional process.

In my own view, however, design is too brittle a notion to absorb all that is implied in the idea of meaning or purpose, at least theologically speaking. Here I shall take purpose to mean not design, but (following Alfred North Whitehead) an overall aim toward the actualizing of value.[17] What makes a process purposive is that it is bringing about or aiming toward something self-evidently good. For example, I consider my writing this essay to be purposive since it has the intended goal of accomplishing something I consider worthwhile. One may suppose that even evolutionary naturalists consider their own work to be purposeful since it is apparently undertaken to serve the self-evident value of truth. If they did not consider truth to be a value worth pursuing, they would hardly be bothered by those recalcitrant religious readers who disagree with them, nor would they bother to invest so much effort in writing books informing the rest of us that religion is nonsense. Clearly, evolutionary naturalists do care. They also have "purpose on the brain." For them the work of science is itself thoroughly purpose-driven.

Most scientific naturalists will not deny that humans are a purpose-driven species. They will allow that our lives and works can be made meaningful when dedicated to something of undeniable value. But can the same be said of life in the cosmos prior to our own late emergence in evolution? Was purpose operative in the natural evolutionary fashioning of organisms in the biosphere during the billions of years before conscious purpose-on-the-brain organisms appeared? It is impossible to avoid tying this question to that of cosmic purpose. Life, after all, is inseparable from the universe; and so, to avoid a vital-

---

16. See Dawkins, *River out of Eden;* Daniel C. Dennett, *Darwin's Dangerous Idea: Evolution and the Meaning of Life* (New York: Simon and Schuster, 1995); Ruse, *Darwin and Design,* pp. 268-70 and 325.

17. Alfred North Whitehead held that the universe is constituted of momentary events rather than enduring bits of matter. The unit events he called "actual occasions." These are largely constituted by their incorporation of their past, but they enjoy some element of self-creativity in the way they integrate the past. In this act of integration they aim at attaining some value in themselves and in their relevant future. This aim is grounded in the deepest nature of the cosmos. His theory of value is most fully developed in part 4 of *Adventures of Ideas* (New York: Free Press, 1967).

ism that contrivedly separates life from nonliving stuff, the question of purpose in biological evolution must be connected to that of purpose in the universe as a whole.

So, is there purpose in the universe? Definitely not, the pure naturalist responds. Yet this does not necessarily mean that an individual person's life is pointless. Some naturalists (people who believe that nature is all there is and that the universe itself can have no overall purpose) even claim that the absence of meaning in the universe as a whole provides the opportunity for the individual's life to have a purposiveness that would otherwise be impossible.[18] For if the cosmos is thought of as inherently pointless, we humans can think of ourselves as the authors of whatever meanings and values actually exist. The ensuing sense of our own radical creativity can boost our self-esteem, whereas the idea of a purposive universe would diminish us.

The ethical and ecological implications of such an anthropocentric perspective are well worth considering, but I cannot dwell on them here except to say that I believe they are at best dangerous for life on earth and humanity's future. Instead I want to focus on the credibility of the modern claim that evolutionary biology rules out cosmic purpose. Now that most evolutionists explain design in a purely naturalistic way, cosmic teleology, which to them is reducible to design, seems to be nothing more than a religious illusion. The combination of blind chance and impersonal selection, along with the enormity of cosmic time, is sufficient to account for the gradual — and hence nonmiraculous — emergence of complex living design. There is no need for, or any sign of, divine influence either in life or in the universe as a whole.

Other understandings of evolution, such as that of Lynn Margulis, can also be viewed in such a way as to render the notion of cosmic purpose unnecessary in the explanation of life. Even though post-Darwinian portraits of evolution may differ in detail from those of strict Darwinians, they usually feature essentially the same generic set of ingredients that have always challenged traditional religious understandings of nature. Accidental occurrences, impersonal natural selection, and huge amounts of time make up all the main versions of the evolutionary recipe, even though the relative proportions may vary from one evolutionist to another. Consequently, from a theological point of view, the task still remains one of showing how the three underlying components of evolution are compatible with a religious trust in a purposive universe. In other words, theology needs to give a credible account of why the universe as such

---

18. See E. D. Klemke, "Living without Appeal," in *The Meaning of Life*, ed. E. D. Klemke (New York: Oxford University Press, 1981), pp. 169-72; Stephen Jay Gould, *Ever Since Darwin* (New York: Norton, 1977), pp. 12-13.

would set the table for biological evolution by so exquisitely weaving together the elements of contingency, lawfulness, and deep time.

My proposal is that this blend of ingredients is precisely such as to give a narrative character to the cosmos. Contingency mixed with some degree of predictability and irreversible time — this is the stuff of story. And if the cosmos is at heart a story, it is not inconceivable that it could also be the carrier of a meaning. Purpose, therefore, does not have to be narrowly construed in terms of "intelligent design." Design alone would be noxious to narrative, freezing all events in the ice of unsuspense. That life does not appear to be tightly engineered is completely consistent with nature's being a meaningful story. If design dominated in natural process, it would lock nature into eternal stasis — death, in other words. There would be neither life nor a life story. Nature must be open to the future if it is to avoid metamorphosing into hard-rock necessity, and it is the ingredient of contingency in nature that opens it to a future in which life and the life story can find their abode.

Order without novelty is meager monotony, as process thinkers have often emphasized. But, blessedly, there is an openness to possibility that always pierces through the armored consistency in natural process. To an earlier and now past brand of Darwinism, it was a theological scandal that many adaptations seemed imperfect, since imperfection spoiled the idea of intelligent divine design. But the idea of intelligent design is itself just another abstract idea originating in our human tendency to disassociate order from the contingency and openness that allow nature to be a narrative. As it turns out, the element of accident and the imperfection of organic adaptation are essential if the story is to keep going and remain interesting. If nature is narrative, we must remark at how fortunate it is that adaptation and "design" are never comfortably complete.[19]

On the other hand, openness to transformation does not mean absolute indeterminateness either, as the phenomenon of biological convergence shows.[20] There is a finite set of realizable possibilities, and evolution unfolds within constraints. These constraints — the laws of physics and chemistry along with the rules of selection — prevent the life story from utterly aimless meandering. The configurations that life assumes appear to be numerically finite. The story is open to unpredictable novelty, but relevant new possibilities are not limitless. Any story must have some degree of coherence and consis-

19. Margulis's important work excels in telling the story in such a way as to overcome any temptation to follow those who view evolution in terms of either design or algorithmic determinism (e.g., Daniel Dennett).

20. See Simon Conway Morris, *Life's Solution: Inevitable Humans in a Lonely Universe* (Cambridge: Cambridge University Press, 2003).

tency. My point, then, is that evolution weaves itself into a narrative fabric already resident in the more fundamental cosmic reality. Darwinism and its post-Darwinian variants cannot explain, but can only presuppose, this narrative matrix. Any story requires some degree of habituality or redundancy, and not just novelty, to keep from dissolving moment by moment into final confusion. And it needs contingency, or accident, to add historicity and dramatic suspense to otherwise routine occurrences. Finally it needs adequate spans of irreversible time. It seems to me that the universe is just such a narrative basis and that the question of the meaning of biological evolution cannot be approached apart from that of a deeper purposiveness in the universe itself.

## What's Going On?

What overall meaning, then, could the narratively endowed cosmos, along with the story of life that it is supporting, possibly be carrying? What is really going on in the universe story? I believe there are a number of ways to answer this question from a theological perspective. Perhaps, though, the cosmological vision of the great mathematician and philosopher Alfred North Whitehead can help us here. Whitehead's expansive vision situates life's evolution into an overall cosmic process whose general orientation is that of bringing about more and more intense versions of beauty. Beauty is a difficult notion to define, but it implies, at the very least, a "harmony of contrasts" or an "ordering of novelty." Without the novelty of contrast there would be only bland order. But without order the elements of novelty and contrast would dissolve into chaos. Beauty is a delicate balance of coherence and complexity, unity and diversity. It embraces local shades of disharmony, bringing them to aesthetic resolution within an ever widening cosmic vision.[21]

It is toward composing more expansive and more intense beauty that our life-bearing universe seems always to have been aiming. It has not succeeded in this objective at every turn, but overall the natural world has in fact made its way from simplicity to complexity, from triviality to more intense versions of ordered novelty — that is, beauty.[22] In its aiming toward beauty, the most sublime of all values, the universe story shows itself, therefore, to be something

21. Whitehead, *Adventures of Ideas*, pp. 252-96. See also Whitehead, *Process and Reality*, ed. David Ray Griffin and Donald W. Sherburne, corrected ed. (New York: Free Press, 1978), pp. 62, 183-85, and 255ff.; Whitehead, *Modes of Thought* (New York: Free Press, 1968), pp. 8-104; and Charles Hartshorne, *Man's Vision of God* (Chicago and New York: Willett, Clark and Co., 1941), pp. 212-29.

22. Whitehead, *Adventures of Ideas*, p. 265.

more than mindless thrashing about. It is not unwise, in my opinion, to propose that the cosmic story carries at least this "loose" kind of teleology. Darwinian evolution, in all its waywardness, fits quite comfortably into such an aesthetically narrative setting. Although Darwinian process leads toward the intensification of beauty in ways that may not conform to human ethical criteria, this need not obscure the fact that the universe, at least in a generally directional way, is in the business of narratively promoting the reign of beauty.

But, one might inquire, why does the universe have this urge to move beyond the status quo at all? Why the impetus for so much novelty, contrast, and diversity? And why is the cosmic creation of so many shades of ordered novelty spread out over so many billions of years? Why has there been so much evolutionary drama, including not only the bringing of beauty into being, but also great tragedy and extravagant loss? And why did the life story take so long to burst into consciousness and the capacity for goodness and worship?

Whitehead's aesthetic cosmology may help locate such puzzling features of the cosmos, including Darwin's recipe. These are completely consonant with the notion of a God whose narrative "design" for the universe is the maximizing of beauty.[23] And if God is also infinite love, then divine love would act most effectively, not by forcing its will onto the cosmos, but by allowing the universe to unfold spontaneously, according to its own narrative rhythms. Moreover, if God is a compassionate and empathetic redeemer, able to heal the tragedy and suffering that do occur in evolution, the cosmic story acquires considerable depth of meaning. Thus the sometimes troubling Darwinian picture of life turns out to be consonant with a purposive God whose power consists of a persuasive love that cannot be expressed in a dictatorial way. A God who loves and cares for the world's narrative coherence would concede to it an autonomy that would allow it to emerge as its own distinct reality — and at its own pace. Such an understanding of nature would in no way contradict Darwin's science, but would instead provide a cosmological and theological context that can make very good sense of it.[24]

---

23. For this and other aspects of "process theology," see John B. Cobb, Jr., and David Griffin, *Process Theology: An Introductory Exposition* (Philadelphia: Westminster, 1976), pp. 123-24.

24. In making these points, I need to emphasize that I am not embracing every aspect of Whitehead's philosophy.

## 20. Divine Providence and the Question of Evolutionary Directionality

JEFFREY P. SCHLOSS

With the demise of natural theology's design arguments for the special creation of individual organisms, theological understandings of creation came to emphasize the process rather than individual products of God's creative activity. Much was made of the directional character of evolution, held to reflect God's goal of bringing into being more and more complex creatures and finally human beings as the purported culmination of the process. In this way God's creation of the world was reinterpreted as an ongoing process rather than an event or series of events that took place once for all in the distant past. Moreover, divine providence was seen as employing historical process and honoring the endowments of nature rather than violating them.

However, whether such attributions of purpose are consonant with either the data or the proposed causal mechanisms of evolutionary history has been a matter of vigorous debate. Indeed, theological considerations of purpose aside, there has been ongoing scientific disagreement over whether the course of evolution can be interpreted as progressive or even as having any directionality at all. In this chapter I will describe the grounds for interpretive difficulty, assess several key proposals for evolutionary directionality, and conclude with some theological comments.

### Interpreting Evolutionary History

One of population biology's most evocative phrases, coined by G. Evelyn Hutchinson over a generation ago, alludes to "the ecological theater and the evolutionary play."[1] Evolution is a drama involving a cast of organismic actors

1. G. Evelyn Hutchinson, *The Ecological Theater and the Evolutionary Play* (New Haven: Yale University Press, 1965).

interacting with one another, and themselves changing, over time. But it occurs in the context of an environmental theater, which not only supports and constrains it but also is itself changed by the activity of the actors and by other factors as well. How the interactions between play and theater influence the "plot development" of evolution — and whether or not such a thing even exists — is a complex and contested issue.

Contemporary neo-Darwinian accounts tend to view that play as lacking any kind of thematic directionality, including even enhancement or maintenance of fitness.[2] Like improvisational theater, it utilizes ad-lib responses to props that appear or disappear by accident. From this ostensibly empirical description of historical trajectory and theoretical account of causal interaction, a number of prominent commentators[3] have developed a metanarrative that conjures Macbeth's lament on life, as that which "struts and frets his hour upon the stage . . . it is a tale told by an idiot, full of sound and fury, signifying nothing."

Whether such nihilistic conclusions necessarily or even reasonably follow from neo-Darwinism is open to debate. They may represent thin overlays or even immiscible impositions upon the science. Or, like David embedded in Michelangelo's block of marble, they may emerge out of the deep structure of neo-Darwinian theory. Even if that is the case, it need not betoken a necessary connection: in the stone there might well be another David, or another character altogether, to be sculpted by a different artist, or for a different cultural patron.[4] But philosophical implications aside, there remains the question of whether the standard neo-Darwinian account is adequate. There are two kinds of questions, related to Clayton's continuum.[5] First is whether the empirical data are consistent with claims of comprehensive adirectionality. Second is the theoretical question whether posited neo-Darwinian mechanisms provide an adequate causal explanation. We can also consider this issue from the opposite inferential vector: Are there credible, and testable, theoretical options that make

2. K. D. Bennett, *Ecology and Evolution: The Pace of Life* (Cambridge: Cambridge University Press, 1997).

3. S. J. Gould, *Wonderful Life: The Burgess Shale and Natural History* (New York: Norton, 1989); Richard Dawkins, *River out of Eden* (New York: Basic Books, 1995); Daniel Dennett, *Darwin's Dangerous Idea: Evolution and the Meaning of Life* (New York: Simon and Schuster, 1995).

4. B. Voorzanger, "No Norms and No Nature: The Moral Relevance of Evolutionary Biology," *Biology and Philosophy* 2 (1987): 253-70; Jeffrey P. Schloss, "Sociobiological Explanations of Altruistic Ethics: Necessary, Sufficient, or Irrelevant Perspective on the Human Moral Quest," in *Investigating the Biological Foundations of Morality*, ed. James Hurd (New York: Edwin Mellen, 1996), pp. 107-45.

5. See Clayton, chapter 18.

directionality plausible, even likely? I enumerated several toward the end of chapter 5, and I want to concentrate here on the first two, involving the design of the abiotic "stage" and/or biotic "actors" to support, perhaps even to direct, the drama of life.

This could occur in two ways, each with noninteractive and interactive versions (table 1). First, traditional "fine-tuning" arguments posit that abiotic cosmic, geological, or chemical environments may be uniquely fit to provide the necessary conditions to make possible[6] — and perhaps also the sufficient conditions to make probable or inevitable[7] — life's emergence and directional elaboration. This could involve fundamental aspects of initial environmental conditions, or it could entail interactive influences of organisms upon their environment, making it progressively more fit for greater diversity and developmental depth of living beings.[8] Gaia theory entails a strong version of this view, arguing that biotic influence upon the environment is not only directional but also homeostatically regulated.[9] A more modest version of this approach is that living systems influence the environment in ways that are life-facilitating,[10] and in so doing may entail positive feedback and "biotic escalation." Life may bootstrap its own phylogenic development by adapting to the life-promoting changes that its biochemistry induces.[11]

Second, organismal function may entail intrinsic biotic constraints that lead to directionality in the evolutionary elaboration of life. Metabolic or developmental first-principles may not only limit what is possible, but also determine what is likely by efficiencies of size, energetics, or life history characters.[12]

6. L. J. Henderson, *The Fitness of the Environment: An Inquiry into the Biological Significance of the Properties of Matter* (New York: Macmillan, 1913).

7. Simon Conway Morris, *Life's Solution: Inevitable Humans in a Lonely Universe* (Cambridge: Cambridge University Press, 2003).

8. R. Williams and J. Frausto Da Silva, "Evolution Was Chemically Constrained," *Journal of Theoretical Biology* 220 (2003): 323-43.

9. James Lovelock, *Gaia: A New Look at Life on Earth* (Oxford: Oxford University Press, 1978).

10. Carl Sagan, *The Demon-Haunted World: Science as a Candle in the Dark* (New York: Ballantine Books, 1997).

11. This involves the issue of environmental fitness or fine-tuning not just at biochemical scales.

12. Geoffrey B. West, James H. Brown, and Brian J. Enquist, "A General Model for the Origin of Allometric Scaling Laws in Biology," *Nature* 276 (1997): 122-26; West, Brown, and Enquist, "The Fourth Dimension of Life: Fractal Geometry and Allometric Scaling of Organisms," *Science* 284 (1999): 1677-79; West, Brown, and Enquist, "Growth Models Based on First Principles or Phenomenology?" *Functional Ecology* 18, no. 2 (2004): 188-96.

Or biotic interactions may generate evolutionary escalation in competitive investment[13] or other directional trends in life strategies.[14]

In the rest of this chapter my purpose is not so much to juxtapose entirely the emphasis on contingency by neo-Darwinism and the emphasis on constraints by other perspectives, as to affirm both by exploring the ways in which interaction between "players" and "set" may drive character development — what evolutionary ecologists refer to as life-history strategies — in predictable, even valued, directions. In short, I want to explore proposals for a discernible plot to the evolutionary play, and how this plot — like the relationship of Shakespearian drama to economic constraints on Elizabethan theater companies — may relate to intrinsic bioenergetic constraints. In contrast with widespread polemics on both sides, I shall argue not only that these questions are profoundly complicated, but also that their answers are intrinsically ambiguous. Moreover, for those who view the history of life as revealing a sacred drama, this ambiguity is central to the plot.

In what follows I will make some general comments about inferences of direction and purpose from such trends. I will survey three major domains of evolutionary trend, consider their interactions, and describe their possible relationship to intrinsic constraints. I will conclude with some theological comments on the issue of "plot" or purpose.

## The Question of Directional Trends

To justify the affirmation of purposiveness in cosmic history, three things must be true. First, there must be directionality, or at least pattern, over the course of change. Second, this pattern must arguably be due to developmental constraint (intrinsically entailed or extrinsically imposed) rather than random contingency. Third, purpose, as opposed to brute directionality, must involve "progress," which is not a judgment that biology, or the sciences at all, can make.[15] Progress entails movement toward a teleological end point, or as John Haught has said, "the actualization of value." This can entail functional value, as in the attainment of a thermoregulatory set point, or ethical/aesthetic value. Indeed,

13. Geerat Vermeij, "The Evolutionary Interaction among Species: Selection, Escalation, and Coevolution," *Annual Review of Ecological Systematics* 25 (1994): 125-52.

14. E. L. Charnov, *Life History Invariants: Some Explorations of Symmetry in Evolutionary Ecology* (New York: Oxford University Press, 1993); J. Kozlowski, "Energetic Definition of Fitness? Yes, but Not That One," *American Naturalist* 147 (1996): 1087-91.

15. Francisco J. Ayala, "Can 'Progress' Be Defined as a Biological Concept?" in *Evolutionary Progress*, ed. M. Nitecki (Chicago: University of Chicago Press, 1988), pp. 75-96.

theologies of nature typically explore the nuances of tension and overlap, if not convergence, between the two. In this section I comment briefly on each of these issues, then in the next section I look at some data.

Because an ongoing theme in neo-Darwinian and fine-tuning perspectives on life is the interplay between contingency and constraint, I want to make an observation about their relationship to inferences of purpose in general and providence in particular. Historic discussions of these issues have often reflected Jesus' critique of discerning divine presence: "I played you a dance and you wanted a dirge; I played you a dirge and you wanted a dance." With the rise of Newtonian mechanism, it was argued, there was no room for providence in a deterministic world. With the rise of Darwinian contingency, it has been argued, there is no room for providence in a happenstance world. On the other side, a number of recent approaches to natural theology reflect the same double-mindedness. Some attempt to argue that biochemical necessity reflects divine destiny; others argue that an impossibly unlikely convergence of contingencies demonstrates divine design, and view the idea that the phenomenon of self-organization suffices to account for these outcomes as a theological enemy.[16]

But purpose — the actualization of value — entails interplay between necessity and contingency. On the one hand, even fine-tuning arguments for providential design do not work if fundamental constants are not themselves ultimately contingent, i.e., if God had no choice in fashioning the world. It is one thing to say this is the only world that could produce life; it is another to say this is the only world that could have been produced. On the other hand, if all is contingency, then the appearance of design or even direction must be illusory. One of the problems with design inferences made on the basis of improbable convergences is the lack of a "lever of necessity" for the instantiation of purpose.

Kierkegaard has a wonderful reflection on these themes in *Sickness unto Death*,[17] where he argues that actualization is not the other pole of a directional continuum from possibility; instead, actuality results from the synthesis of dialectical tension between possibility and necessity. This is precisely what is at work in the interplay between the novelty of mutation and the constraint of selection. Vital possibility must submit to the pruning of necessity (which Ezra Pound argues doesn't happen until age forty in humans!). If one eclipses the other, we have the despair of becoming.

16. See Dembski, *No Free Lunch: Why Specified Complexity Cannot Be Purchased without Intelligence* (Lanham, Md.: Rowman and Littlefield, 2001).

17. Søren Kierkegaard, *Works of Love*, ed. and trans. H. V. Hong and E. H. Hong (Princeton: Princeton University Press, 1995).

## Directionality versus Adirectionality

The notion of directionality in evolution has oscillated in and out of acceptability from before Darwin,[18] but since the emergence of the modern synthesis it has been in eclipse. The notion of "trends," and even more, "progress," has been viewed with skepticism for both ideological and scientific reasons. Ideologically, the misuse of the idea of evolutionary progress by both social Darwinism and eugenics generated recalcitrance to the notion.[19]

Scientifically, there are actually three issues. First, the origin of variation through mutation is held to be entirely random both with respect to the needs or environmental challenges faced by the organism and with respect to any particular trajectory of change. Second, the differential retention of variation through natural selection is posited to be fundamentally dis-teleological. Natural selection is not pitched toward the "perfection of characters" (a Darwinian phrase) or anything except reproductive output; moreover, it does not necessarily optimize even that.

Third, natural selection itself may not exert determinative influence on evolutionary history, the long-term sweep of which may reflect contingency trumping adaptation. One version of this notes that adaptive equilibrium to ecological conditions is disrupted by variation in environmental structure due to cyclic changes in the axis of the earth's rotation or tectonic events occurring at macroevolutionary timescales.[20] Another more radical but not incompatible view is that utterly contingent and massively influential events change the course of evolution in a way that could never be replicated. Stephen Gould's famous claim is that "our origin is the product of massive historical contingency, and we would probably never arise again even if life's tape could be replayed a thousand times."[21] Gould clearly recognizes the philosophical implications of such a claim, and argues against scientific accounts of "survival for cause" — i.e., thematic sense to evolutionary change — by which we might "wake up from this nightmare."[22]

These assertions are primarily theoretical, and I will argue that the empirical record testifies, on the contrary, to significant evolutionary trends. Before doing so, I need to acknowledge the complexity of inferring trends, which en-

18. See Michael Ruse, *Monad to Man: The Concept of Progress in Evolutionary Biology* (Cambridge: Harvard University Press, 1996).

19. Ruse, *Monad to Man*; Stephen J. Gould, *The Mismeasure of Man* (New York: Norton, 1981).

20. K. D. Bennett, *Ecology and Evolution.*

21. Gould, *Wonderful Life*, p. 233.

22. Gould, *Wonderful Life*, p. 234.

tails at least three difficulties. One, many important characters — like certain aspects of physiology and behavior — are difficult to infer biostratigraphically (though we might make inferences based on phylogenies). Second, there is currently little agreement on how to quantify many of the most frequently discussed characters, like biological complexity or adaptedness.[23]

Third, if we have a preserved character and a reliable way to measure it, it is still not clear how to evaluate a "trend." A trend could be entailed by a change in mean or median character, or a change in character maximum. And such changes could be assessed anagenically or cladogenically, that is, within or across various taxonomic groups or lines. Moreover, trends can involve the convergent appearance of particular characters, the selective retention of characters in the geological record once they appear, or the sequential intensification of characters through major evolutionary transitions. And in quantifying increase or persistence, it is not clear what to count. Should it be number of individuals, amount of biomass, number of taxa? Patterns may also be interactive or even countervailing. For example, a trend "against" large body size involving biased extinction of larger organisms could result in repeated evolutionary change away from smaller sizes that typically survive and start a line, resulting in a "trend" for convergent size increases across phylogenies.[24] And finally, there is the interpretive question whether trends reflect intrinsic evolutionary directionality or merely track contingent tectonic or climatic events as mentioned above.[25] Nevertheless, and quite significantly, in his seminal review McShea concludes, "None of the list of candidates for largest-scale trends invokes contingent properties of life on earth as the principle cause of increase."[26]

## Directionality versus Diffusion

Finally, if we have evidence of a persistent trend that is not merely due to an unlikely series of coincident changes, there is still room to question whether it represents a truly directional or a random process. The language used to describe

23. Daniel W. McShea, "Possible Largest Scale Trends in Organismal Evolution: Eight 'Live Hypotheses,'" *Annual Review of Ecology and Systematics* 29 (1998): 293-318.

24. Richard D. Norris, "Biased Extinction and Evolutionary Trends," *Paleobiology* 17 (1991): 388-99.

25. Christine M. Janis, "Tertiary Mammal Evolution in the Context of Changing Climates, Vegetation, and Tectonic Events," *Annual Review of Ecology and Systematics* 24 (1993): 467-500.

26. McShea, "Possible Largest Scale Trends," p. 306.

this entails the distinction between "driven" and "passive" trends.[27] On the one hand, a trend would be considered driven if there is a selective bias toward a directional change in a particular character. On the other hand, a trend would be considered passive if it involved merely a random increase in variation of a trait, which happened to start out at a certain minimal (or maximal) value and then "diffused" away. For example, if most lines of organisms start out at small sizes, and then randomly increase in variability of size, there will be an increase in maximum, but no true directionality or evolutionary "preference" for larger sizes.

Stephen Gould's image for this is a drunk stumbling aimlessly down the street with a wall on one side and a gutter on the other. If he hits the wall, he bounces off and continues his stagger. If he staggers to the other side, "he falls down into a stupor."[28] Given this situation, it is inevitable that "the drunkard falls into the gutter every time, but his motion includes no trend whatever toward this form of perdition. Similarly, some average or extreme measure of life might move in a particular direction even if no evolutionary advantage, and no inherent trend, favor that pathway."[29]

Like the prior issue of whether there is directionality, this interpretive question of whether directionality constitutes an "inherent trend" is beset by both ideological and scientific tensions. The image and even the very language seem chosen for the cause of bleak provocation, reminiscent of Bob Dylan's first and famous interview, "Reality? It's a tramp vomiting in the gutter." But the underlying ideological concern prompting the assertion of randomness is that proposals of an "evolutionary preference for" or "natural tendency toward" a particular characteristic have so often been used both to justify and to marginalize aspects of variation in human groups. This is part of a comprehensive, and understandable, rejection of trends' existence,[30] or, in cases where they appear to exist, the rejection of their intrinsic directionality.[31] But there are scientific tensions here too. First is whether major trends have causes and distributional structures consonant with this account. Second is the issue that — even if the account is applicable to certain trends, and there is no "evolutionary advantage" to a directional change — it is *not* the case that there is no "inherent trend." The inherency of the trend is entailed in the very structure of the envi-

27. Steve C. Wang, "Quantifying Passive and Driven Large-Scale Evolutionary Trends," *Evolution* 55 (2001): 849-58.

28. Stephen C. Gould, *Full House: The Spread of Excellence from Plato to Darwin* (New York: Harmony, 1996), p. 149.

29. Gould, *Full House*, p. 150.

30. Gould, *Wonderful Life*.

31. Gould, *Full House*.

ronment. Indeed, it is a very special environment that would invariably resist or reflect change in one direction and fix it in another. To say that there is no inherent trend would be equivalent to saying of an amusement park ride for children, where the motorcars are directed on tracks, that there is no inherent path of travel — just because there was no agent *inside* the car directing it.

If we wish to employ the passive/driven distinction and the attendant metaphor of random diffusion — and in my view its utility is open to debate — then to do so meaningfully entails three questions intrinsic to diffusive flux. First, what is the "driving force" away from the minimum wall and toward increased variance?[32] "Natural selection" is not the driving force for the twofold reason that it is, strictly speaking, not a driving force at all but a filtering or resistance term; and even if excessive and differential fecundity is construed as a force, it does not work toward inexorable diffusional radiation, but may, depending on the environmental fitness, promote stasis or even reduced variance. One proposal for a diffusional driving force along thermodynamic lines involves increasing informational entropy over evolutionary time. As a function of the second law, organismal phenotypes expand to fill morphospace.[33] Evaluating such proposals is beyond the scope of this paper, but their implications are, as is the very question of a driving force, that the distinction between passive and "driven" trends is somewhat misleading: any invariant trend is, in some sense, "driven."

The second question entails the morphospace into which a trend — diffusional or biased — moves. Now one reason a trend may be biased is that there may be intrinsic constraints on available morphospace that occur across lineages. But even without such biases, there must exist fundamental biomechanical and biochemical prerequisites to generate biological possibilities. All-too-common talk of moving into "empty ecological niches" begs both the metaphysical question of whether there even is such a thing as an empty (Platonic) niche prior to an occupying organism, and the mechanistic question of the process by which possibility space "opens up." For example, the metazoan niches or morphospace was not just "empty" in the biochemical and

32. McShea, "Possible Largest Scale Trends in Organismal Evolution"; Stephen J. Gould, "On Replacing the Notion of Progress with an Operational Notion of Directionality," in *Evolutionary Progress,* pp. 319-38; Gould, "Trends as Changes in Directionality in Evolution," *Journal of Paleontology* 62 (1988): 319-29.

33. D. R. Brooks and E. O. Wiley, *Evolution as Entropy,* 2nd ed. (Chicago: University of Chicago Press, 1988); D. R. Brooks, J. Collier, B. A. Maurer, J. D. H. Smith, and E. O. Wiley, "Entropy and Information in Evolving Biological Systems," *Biology and Philosophy* 4 (1989): 407-32; J. Collier, "Entropy in Evolution," *Biology and Philosophy* 1 (1986): 5-24; and Stanley Salthe, *Development and Evolution: Complexity and Change in Biology* (Cambridge: MIT Press, 1993).

abiotic environment of the Archaean — it simply did not exist. This space was *created* by the atmospheric and chemical changes driven by organisms that then evolved to inhabit it. Is, then, the expansive range of size, shape, and organizational and functional complexity, over evolutionary time, something that was determined to emerge given the initial abiotic conditions and nature of life on Earth, or was the possibility itself vulnerable to contingencies? Even a diffusional or "passive" trend may entail the former. For example, Williams and Frausto Da Silva[34] argue that the reductive chemistry of primitive cells inevitably opened up possibility space by driving the oxidation of the environment and providing new sources of chemistry and energy; moreover, organisms were driven into this possibility space by the initial need to develop cellular structures that enabled them to avoid the toxic effects of new oxidized chemicals. Third, there is the issue of environmental resistance or conductance to diffusional movement into possibility space, which is to say, natural selection. Phenotypes will not diverge away from a minimum wall, even if the forms are biomechanically and biochemically possible, unless the physically possible is also reproductively favorable. That does not mean reproductive advantage must exist across all or even most lineages and environments, so as to induce eliminative change away from the minimum. But phenotypic changes must have repeatable success across lineages and environments to result in sustained or convergent trends. The structure of the environment, the stage, must be fit for or conducive to such change. So even "passive" or diffusional trends are shaped or biased by the structural receptivity, the "fitness," of the environment.

## Proposals for Evolutionary Trends

Although there are numerous widely discussed proposals for major evolutionary trends,[35] I will describe three trends, posited to be causally interrelated, that involve fascinating unsolved questions and end up relating to "the actualization of value."[36]

---

34. Williams and Frausto Da Silva, "Evolution Was Chemically Constrained."

35. Daniel W. McShea, "Complexity and Evolution: What Everybody Knows," *Biology and Philosophy* 6 (1991): 303-24; McShea, "Possible Largest Scale Trends in Organismal Evolution"; J. Maynard Smith and E. Szathmary, *The Major Transitions in Evolution* (Oxford: Freeman, 1995).

36. Jeffrey P. Schloss, "Is There Venus on Mars? Bioenergetic Constraints, Allometric Trends, and the Evolution of Life History Invariants," in *Fitness of the Cosmos for Life: Biochemistry and Fine Tuning*, ed. John Barrow, Simon Conway Morris, Stephen Freeland, and Charles Harper (Cambridge: Cambridge University Press, forthcoming).

*Size*

The empirical generalization that organismal size increases in most groups is often referred to as Cope's Law.[37] Because Cope himself postulated generalizations involving both specialization and size across evolutionary time,[38] and because the "law" designation begs the very question of determinative versus contingent constraint, the generalization is probably better referred to as "Cope's Rule."[39]

The observation itself is widely confirmed. Maximum body size has progressively increased since life's origin, and the largest animal and nonclonal plant that has ever existed lives today.[40] Multicellular bacteria; single and multicellular eukaryotes; and algal, fungal, plant, and animal lineages all manifest increases in both maximum and mean size.[41] Looking just at animals, the largest representatives of annelids, gastropods, crustaceans, pelecypods, echinoderms, cephalopods, and vertebrates are currently living species.[42] In an analysis of forty-one Jurassic lineages of bivalves and nineteen of ammonites, Hallam found many had increased from threefold to fivefold in size, and 69 percent had at least doubled.[43] An exhaustive analysis of birds and mammals on the four major continents reveals a rechtokurtic skew of body mass distributions, by both species and genera.[44] In a landmark matched-pair study of over fifteen hundred North American mammal species, Alroy found older species were larger than younger species within a line;[45] a comprehensive reanalysis of the widely discussed horse lineage reveals a similar trend.[46] The trend toward increased body size is seen so regularly, within and between so many indepen-

37. Bruce J. McFadden, "Fossil Horses from 'Eohippus' *(Hyracotherium)* to Equus: Scaling, Cope's Law, and the Evolution of Body Size," *Paleobiology* 12 (1986): 355-69.

38. Paul D. Polly, "Cope's Rule," *Science* 282 (1998): 47.

39. John Alroy, "Cope's Rule," *Science* 282 (1998): 47.

40. J. T. Bonner, *The Evolution of Complexity by Means of Natural Selection* (Princeton: Princeton University Press, 1988); Gould, "On Replacing the Notion of Progress with an Operational Notion of Directionality"; Gould, *Full House*; McShea, "Possible Largest Scale Trends in Organismal Evolution."

41. Sean B. Carroll, "Chance and Necessity: The Evolution of Morphological Complexity and Diversity," *Nature* 409 (2001): 1102-9.

42. N. D. Newell, "Phyletic Size Increase, an Important Trend Illustrated by Fossil Invertebrates," *Evolution* 3 (1949): 103-24.

43. A. Hallam, "Evolutionary Size Increases and Longevity in Jurassic Bivalves and Ammonites," *Nature* 258 (1975): 493-96.

44. Brian A. Maurer, James H. Brown, and Renee D. Rusler, "The Micro and Macro in Body Size Evolution," *Evolution* 46 (1992): 939-53.

45. John Alroy, "Cope's Rule and the Dynamics of Body Mass Evolution in North American Fossil Mammals," *Science* 280 (1998): 731-34.

46. McFadden, "Fossil Horses from 'Eohippus' *(Hyracotherium)* to Equus."

dent lineages, that there is warrant for viewing it as one of the most significant cases of directional and convergent evolution in the history of life.

Nevertheless, though extensively apparent, it has been widely debated whether the trend is passive or driven. Cope himself seemed to understand the trend as merely reflecting random divergence from the size (and specialization) minima that give rise to most lineages.[47] The notion of passive diffusion away from a minimum wall has been posited on more recent theoretical grounds as well.[48] However, a number of seminal empirical studies have given compelling evidence for an active trend toward increased body size. One way to assess this is to look at anagenic versus cladogenic evolution, i.e., to assess size differences reflecting selection within lineages as opposed to extinction between lineages.[49] Another way is to look at size distributions, to see if patterns conform to random diffusion away from a minimum threshold.[50] In Alroy's study of pair-matched North American mammal species, his finding of increased size in older species within a line is consistent with a driven trend but inconsistent with a noneliminative, purely passive trend. McFadden's similar finding in horses also reflects a driven trend.[51] The pronounced rightward skew in bird and mammal sizes on continental landmasses also appears inconsistent with a passive trend, nor is it accounted for by models of diffusion away from a minimum size that survives extinction events.[52] The distribution pattern of morphological maxima in the late Proterozoic appears less plausibly explained by passive than active processes.[53]

47. E. D. Cope, *Primary Factors of Organic Evolution* (Chicago: Chicago University Press, 1886); Cope, "The Method of Creation of Organic Forms," *Proceedings of the American Philosophical Society* 12 (1871): 748-50.

48. Newell, "Phyletic Size Increase, an Important Trend Illustrated by Fossil Invertebrates"; S. M. Stanley, "An Explanation of Cope's Rule," *Evolution* 27 (1973): 1-26; Norris, "Biased Extinction and Evolutionary Trends"; Gould, *Full House*; A. H. Knoll and R. K. Bambach, "Directionality in the History of Life: Diffusion from the Left Wall or Repeated Scaling of the Right," *Paleobiology* 26 (supplement) (2000): 1-14; Daniel W. McShea, "The Minor Transitions in Hierarchical Evolution and the Question of Directional Bias," *Journal of Evolutionary Biology* 14, no. 3 (2001): 502-18.

49. Alroy, "Cope's Rule"; D. Jablonski, "Body Size Evolution in Cretaceous Molluscs and the Status of Cope's Rule," *Nature* 385 (1997): 250-52.

50. Daniel W. McShea, "Mechanisms of Large-Scale Evolutionary Trends," *Evolution* 48, no. 6 (1994): 1747-63; McShea, "The Minor Transitions in Hierarchical Evolution and the Question of Directional Bias"; McShea, "Complexity and Evolution"; Daniel W. McShea and Mark A. Changizi, "Three Principles in Hierarchical Evolution," *Integrative and Comparative Biology* 43 (2003): 74-81; Wang, "Quantifying Passive and Driven Large-Scale Evolution Trends."

51. McFadden, "Fossil Horses from 'Eohippus' *(Hyracotherium)* to Equus."

52. Maurer, Brown, and Rusler, "The Micro and Macro in Body Size Evolution."

53. McShea and Changizi, "Three Principles in Hierarchical Evolution."

The most widespread explanation of this has emphasized the selective advantages of large body size.[54] Both theoretical work and empirical work have posited the adaptive value of large body size to intra- and interspecific competition,[55] predator defense, increased resistance to food or thermoregulatory stress,[56] increased brain size and concomitant behavioral flexibility,[57] increased visual acuity,[58] resistance to short-term environmental fluctuations,[59] increased longevity, and increased fecundity for females and mate access in males — "widely agreed" to be the most significant selective forces favoring larger body size.[60] There are still problems with attributing intrinsic selective advantage to size — impressively widespread as evolutionary size increases are, the trend is neither universal nor eliminative.[61] Nevertheless, in his review Blanckenhorn concludes that "the evidence for selection favoring larger body size is overwhelming."[62]

In contrast to the above approaches, Demetrius has developed an innovative proposal to explain trends in body size evolution that appears to be consistent with many other kinds of observations.[63] His proposal entails a general "theory of evolutionary directionality" that integrates population genetic notions of genotypic fitness with demographic understandings of age-related heterogeneity in reproductive output and energy consumption within a population, through the concept of evolutionary entropy — a statistical measure of age variability in a population. Demetrius posits a relationship between evolutionary entropy and body size that "predicts a tendency toward an increase in

54. Reviewed in D. A. Roff, *Evolution of Life Histories* (New York: Chapman and Hall, 1992), and Wolf Blanckenhorn, "The Evolution of Body Size: What Keeps Organisms Small?" *Quarterly Review of Biology* 75 (2000): 385-407.

55. J. H. Brown and B. A. Maurer, "Body Size, Ecological Dominance and Cope's Rule," *Nature* 324 (1986): 248-50.

56. Stephen Stearns, *The Evolution of Life Histories* (Oxford: Oxford University Press, 1992).

57. Mark A. Changizi, "Relationship between Number of Muscles, Behavioral Repertoire Size, and Encephalization in Mammals," *Journal of Theoretical Biology* 220 (2003): 157-68.

58. R. A. Kiltie, "Scaling of Visual Acuity with Body Size in Mammals and Birds," *Functional Ecology* 14 (2000): 226-34.

59. Brown and Maurer, "Body Size, Ecological Dominance and Cope's Rule."

60. Blanckenhorn, "The Evolution of Body Size."

61. J. Damuth, "Cope's Rule, the Island Rule and the Scaling of Mammalian Population Density," *Nature* 365 (1993): 748-50.

62. Blanckenhorn, "Evolution of Body Size," p. 385.

63. Lloyd Demetrius, "Directionality Principles in Thermodynamics and Evolution," *Proceedings of the National Academy of Science* 94 (1997): 3491-98; Demetrius, "Directionality Theory and the Evolution of Body Size," *Proceedings of the Royal Society of London, Biological Sciences* 267 (2000): 2385-91.

body size within most phyletic lineages,"[64] a driven trend consistent with Cope's Rule. Quite interestingly, his general theory of evolutionary directionality can be applied to size trends described not only by Cope's Rule but also by the Island rule (evolutionary increases and decreases in body size for colonists of small and large islands) and Bergman's rule (the increase in body size with latitude or decreasing environmental temperature).

### Energy and Allometry

There are several evolutionary trends in organismic energy expenditure. First, to the extent that there is a trend toward larger body size, there is also a concomitant trend toward higher energy utilization: you have to buy more food to feed a pet dog than a pet mouse. Second, there is a general increase in energetic intensiveness across the taxa representing major evolutionary transitions: energy use per gram goes up from unicellular, to ectothermic ("cold-blooded") multicellular, to homeothermic organisms. And third, even within homeotherms body temperature and energy utilization go up from monotreme (egg-laying) to marsupial to eutherian (placental) mammals, and from nonpasserine to passerine birds.

What "drives" this trend? A variety of studies provides evidence for the selective advantage of increased body temperature. Even though they spend more time basking, cooler-latitude lizards that maintain higher body temperatures, increase velocity of movement, foraging distance, and net food intake.[65] Growth rates increase with interconnected increases in thermoregulatory time, body temperature, and food consumption.[66] Snakes that maintain higher temperatures catch more prey.[67] And predation *on* lizards decreases for prey with higher body temperatures.[68] As most children who like to try to catch lizards or bees know quite well, "in regards to locomotion, warmer ap-

---

64. Demetrius, "Directionality Principles," p. 3497.

65. R. Avery, J. Bedford, and C. Newcombe, "The Role of Thermoregulation in Lizard Biology: Predatory Efficiency in a Temperate Diurnal Basker," *Behavioral Ecology and Sociobiology* 11 (1982): 261-67.

66. R. Avery, "Physiological Aspects of Lizard Growth: The Role of Thermoregulation," *Symposium of the Zoological Society of London* 52 (1984): 407-24.

67. O. Greenwald, "Thermal Dependence of Striking and Prey Capture by Gopher Snakes," *Copeia*, 1974, pp. 141-48.

68. Keith Christian and C. Richard Tracy, "The Effect of the Thermal Environment on the Ability of Hatchling Galapagos Land Iguanas to Avoid Predation during Dispersal," *Oecologia* 49 (1981): 218-23.

pears to be better."[69] Similar arguments exist for the maintenance not of higher, but of constant body temperature.[70] What is interesting for our purposes is that while the very appearance of homeothermy and the energetic escalation within homeotherms are still topics of discussion, nearly all current proposals emphasize its connection to increases in parental care (as reflected in the above sequence).

In addition to *directional* increases in energy utilization over evolution, however, there also exists a remarkable *convergence* in how energy use proportionally scales or allometrically varies with body mass. Of course, energy use increases with mass, but it does so in a less than linear fashion: on a per gram basis, it is "cheaper to be big." This was described in mammals before Darwin, and because mass-specific metabolic rate seemed to scale with body mass in a fashion close to that of surface area, the prevailing explanation entailed metabolic replacement of heat loss. It was Julian Huxley who first refuted this, a century later,[71] by fitting surface area and metabolic rate to body mass, via a power function with two-thirds and three-fourths exponents respectively. Moreover, since that time we have found that a similar relationship obtains for ectotherms, plants, even unicellular organisms, none of which replace heat loss with their metabolism. There is an ongoing flurry of hypothesizing about why this fundamental nonlinear relationship between mass and metabolism exists. In a series of groundbreaking papers, West and coworkers argue for the existence of universal scaling laws — perhaps the first proposal for "laws" in biology — that may entail a "master equation" based on physical first principles.[72] "Does some fixed point or deep basin of attraction in the dynamics of natural selection ensure that all life is organized by a few fundamental principles and that energy is a prime determinant of biological structure and dynamics among all possible variables?"[73]

On the other hand, critics point to the inability of this deterministic model to explain the huge and often systematic deviations from its predictions,

---

69. Albert Bennett, "Evolution of the Control of Body Temperature: Is Warmer Better?" in *Comparative Physiology: Life in Water and on Land,* ed. P. Dejours, L. Bolis, C. R. Taylor, and E. R. Weibel (Padova: Liviana Press, 1987), pp. 421-31.

70. Brian McNab, *The Physiological Ecology of Vertebrates: A View from Energetics* (Ithaca, N.Y.: Cornell University Press, 2002).

71. See Julian Huxley, *On Relative Growth* (London: Methuen, 1932).

72. West, Brown, and Enquist, "A General Model for the Origin of Allometric Scaling Laws in Biology"; West, Brown, and Enquist, "The Fourth Dimension of Life"; West, Brown, and Enquist, "Growth Models Based on First Principles or Phenomenology?"; Geoffrey B. West and James H. Brown, "Life's Universal Scaling Laws," *Physics Today,* 2004, pp. 36-42.

73. West and Brown, "Life's Universal Scaling Laws," p. 42.

and another approach is to explain the relationship in terms of a statistical outcome from disparate selection pressures.[74] The bottom line, at this point, is that we don't know. It is one of the most provocative mysteries of biological constraint, and, with some drama though no lack of warrant, Heusner claims it "remains the central question in comparative physiology."[75]

As we shall see, it ends up being profoundly important for issues of life history, and it entails one possible influence on the trend toward larger body size. Although the total metabolic demands of larger organisms are greater, and they require more food, the per gram needs are lower, and therefore in the absence of food they will consume stored biomass at a lower proportionate rate.[76] It costs more to feed a dog than a shrew, but leave for a week and you'll still have your dog when you return.

Another notable concomitant of body size, with cascading influence for other life history characteristics, is life span. Longevity appears to scale positively and logarithmically to body mass, across a variety of lineages. There are two differing explanations for this and, in fact, for the issue of death and senescence in general. First, the "rate of living" hypothesis suggests that the existence of death reflects intrinsic and negotiable constraints on biological systems, which are subject to progressive deterioration through accumulation of mistakes in cellular replication or buildup of metabolic toxins. Although repair occurs, there is an upper limit to reparability, and the faster one lives (i.e., the higher the metabolic rate), the faster one dies. The countervailing perspective, the "evolutionary explanation," posits no such constraint, but views senescence as a nonnecessary by-product of "antagonistic pleiotropy" — a situation where a characteristic increases fecundity (perhaps through earlier reproduction) while carrying a phenotypic piggybacker that reduces longevity.

While often presented as mutually exclusive, both of these mechanisms could be operating simultaneously and independently; or they could be operating interactively (e.g., increased reproduction could cause increased mortality, reflecting intrinsic constraints — see the next section). Interestingly, these positions reflect the themes of constraint and contingency. In any case, for sound empirical reasons I will make the case that allometric scaling of life span does

74. J. Kozlowski and J. Weiner, "Interspecific Allometries Are By-Products of Body Size Optimization," *American Naturalist* 149 (1997): 352-80; J. Kozlowski and M. Konarzewski, "Is West, Brown, and Enquist's Model of Allometric Scaling Mathematically Correct and Biologically Relevant?" *Functional Ecology* 18, no. 2 (2004): 283-89.

75. See A. Heusner, "Size and Power in Mammals," *Journal of Experimental Biology* 160 (1991): 34.

76. See McNab, *The Physiological Ecology of Vertebrates.*

reflect fundamental biotic constraints, which themselves drive other character-istics of life history with implications for issues of purpose.[77]

## Life History Trends

Life history strategy involves the investment of resources in growth, mainte-nance, reproduction, and the developmental timing of these processes. Issues related to life history — such as the existence of senescence, early life versus late life mortality dynamics, systems of mating, and the minimal investment in nu-merous offspring with no postnatal care at the end of life versus the lavish in-vestment in and affective bonding with a few offspring over a long life span — seem closely related to themes we would associate with "the actualization of value." However, trends in these areas are also quite complicated to discern.

I regret to say that there has been a good deal of either outright nonsense or dubious oversimplification in numerous attempts to extrapolate life history evolution to a kinder, if not utopian, end.[78] Contrary to the claims of some evo-lutionary eschatologies or ecotheologies, there is no indication of a singular coevolutionary trend toward reduction of pathogenic virulence, an attenuation of competition between species, a reduction of aggression between members of the same species, or minimization of sexual or intergenerational conflict. In-deed, several plausible though not uncontested theories point to an evolutionary escalation of investment in competitive and defensive armaments[79] and a trend of decline in social cooperation.[80] It is interesting that, in this view, humans are not an extension of this tendency but are seen as "reversing the downward trend of social evolution in general . . . the culminating mystery of all biology."[81]

There are complicated life history trade-offs in all these areas that make di-rectional resolution difficult. However, it may be fair to generalize about one fea-ture of life history, an increase in maximal parental investment. This rather gen-eral but by no means invariant evolutionary trend entails greater investment in a smaller number of offspring. This is evident at a gross level from invertebrates, to poikilothermic vertebrates, to birds and mammals (though there are also evo-

77. For a more extended discussion, see Schloss, "Is There Venus on Mars?"

78. Jeffrey P. Schloss, "From Evolution to Eschatology," in *Resurrection: Theological and Scientific Assessments,* ed. Ted Peters, Robert J. Russell, and Michael Welker (Grand Rapids: Eerdmans, 2002), pp. 56-85.

79. Vermeij, "The Evolutionary Interaction among Species."

80. E. O. Wilson, *Sociobiology: The New Synthesis* (Cambridge: Harvard University Press, 1975).

81. Wilson, *Sociobiology,* p. 382.

lutionary trends and ecological differences within taxa). This reproductive strategy represents a continuum, which is often positively correlated with body size, life expectancy, total metabolic rate, and investment in maintenance and competitive defense. The union of these factors has been referred to as a "K" strategy. The relationships scale allometrically, and there are some proposals for explaining them in terms of bioenergetic first principles.[82] This may contribute to, but it by no means entirely explains, the patterns observed, since there are striking relationships between timing and intensity of parental investment even after the effects of body size are controlled for. There is warrant for viewing an increase in "K-ness" as an important trend in its own right across both ecological and evolutionary (i.e., community succession) timescales. It is not eliminative: there are vastly more non-K (r) individuals, species, and total biomass. Nevertheless, even Stephen Gould affirmed this trend, noting tripartite increase in body size, complexity, and time to maturity or parental investment: "Evolutionary trends toward greater size and complexity form the classical subject matter of 'progressive' evolution as it is usually conceived — the slow and gradual fine tuning of morphology under the continuous control of natural selection. These trends display three common features marking them almost inevitably as primary products of K-selective regimes."[83] Finally, I will comment on the relationship of trends in parental investment to other issues of life history and social organization. Of course, high parental investment is accompanied by enlargement of the limbic brain in mammals and the capacity for behavioral and affective attachment. Such attachment has itself been demonstrated not only to evoke nurture and protection, but also to mediate both homeostatic regulation and ontogenic development, reflecting an emergent deepening of capacities for exchange between organisms. In cases of very high parental investment, pair-bonding, or attachment between parents, also emerges. Moreover, capacity for such attachments lays the groundwork for patterns of social cooperation that go beyond kin selection to reciprocal altruism. This entails discrimination between individuals of the same species on the basis of relational history. This phenomenon is especially noteworthy in two mammalian groups with unique patterns of energetic investment — bats and primates.

To be candid, but hopefully not saccharine, all of this relates to laying a biological foundation for caring or relational attachment. However, it involves capacities and not inevitabilities. In fact, increased capacity for parental care

---

82. West, Brown, and Enquist, "Growth Models Based on First Principles or Phenomenology?"; West and Brown, "Life's Universal Scaling Laws."

83. Stephen J. Gould, *Ontogeny and Phylogeny* (Cambridge: Harvard University Press, Belknap Press, 1977), p. 42.

co-varies with other things to which most of us would ascribe negative value. It ushers in the effects of maternal deprivation and, significantly, the capacity to feel emotional pain in the midst of loss. Maternal separation cries are a mammalian universal, as is physiological evidence of depression in both parent and offspring in the face of separation. In some mating structures, infanticide makes more reproductive sense where investment is higher. Intergenerational and sibling conflict can be more pronounced when parents invest at significant expense in few young across their lifetime.

## Directionality and Destiny?

I want to close with two comments on the relationship of biotic constraint, evolutionary contingency, and teleonomic trend or destiny. First, if by destiny one means not just brute inevitability but telos or valued purpose, I have been suggesting all along that this is not orthogonal to contingency, but rather contingency constrained by necessity is what produces telos. This is vastly different — and I would argue more scientifically credible and more existentially desirable — than either unbounded accident or unyielding inevitability.

Daniel Dennett has provided an apt metaphor for this with his distinction between cranes and skyhooks.[84] Skyhooks involve teleological pulleys, transcendently uncoupled from earthly influences. Cranes are fully grounded on earth, and involve movement on the basis of this grounding. It turns out that the metaphor actually does not entirely serve his purposes, but it serves mine. Something moving up on a crane is not like something riding a geyser; the former involves being drawn from above by a structure whose constraints reflect a telos. But unlike a skyhook, a crane requires grounding — and is subject to earthquakes, compaction, topographic relief, i.e., contingent variation in that ground. The picture I am painting of evolutionary history may be like that, involving a directional telos that is not transcendentally floating but materially grounded, directionally constrained by the operation of life itself, and vulnerable to the contingent influences of random genetic and environmental variation. Life's crane, like Milton's Adam, is "sufficient to stand, but free to fall."

Second, I want to argue that this is as it needs to be if we are to become who we should be. Here I wish to invoke a distinction between two senses of destiny. One involves fatalistic necessity: one may be "destined" to a terrible end as cows are. During the Shoah German Jews were destined for slaughter. But in

---

84. Daniel C. Dennett, *Darwin's Dangerous Idea: Evolution and the Meaning of Life* (New York: Simon and Schuster, 1995), p. 1195.

another sense this is not that for which these beings were ever truly "destined." The other sense of destiny involves a valued or intended end. Some say we are "born to shop" or "made for the perfect wave." The Westminster Confession affirms that our true destiny is "to love God and enjoy Him forever." Attaining such a destiny entails, to use Haught's phrase again, the "actualization of value." But such actualization is not inevitable, and a factual end at variance with this destiny is tragedy. I want to assert that the natural world provides enough evidence to infer destiny in the deeper sense, but it entails enough causal ambiguity to leave open the possibility of tragedy.

Finally, there may even be occasions when, or perspectives from which, the first sense of destiny overrides the second, and the tragic missing of telos appears fatalistically inevitable. Or at least, there may appear to be no assurance of bridging from the first to the second. One response might be to go back to the blackboard and recalculate vectors — I mean this fairly literally — to search for a basis to a kind of scientific confidence in the fate of the cosmos or humanity or oneself. To the extent that distortions of, or impositions upon, science are used to promote a false nihilism, such corrections are perhaps necessary, though employing science to bolster a mechanistic optimism has its own risks. A second response, one truer I believe to both science and religion, is to identify cosmic ambiguity as part of the plot, urging us to theological hope rather than calculative assurance.[85] That hope is in a destiny that drives rather than is driven by necessity, and in a Being who employs contingency for the astonishingly unlikely but ultimately reliable redemption of tragedy.

> All who rest in nature either find no light to satisfy them or come to form for themselves a means of knowing God and serving him without a mediator. Thereby they fall either into atheism, or into deism, two things the Christian religion abhors almost equally. If the world existed to instruct man of God, his divinity would shine through every part in an indisputable manner: but as it exists only by Jesus Christ, and for Jesus Christ, and to teach men both their corruption and their redemption, all display the proofs of these two truths. . . . He must not see nothing at all, nor must he see sufficient for him to believe he possesses it; but he must see enough to know that he has lost it. For to know of his loss he must see and not see; and that is exactly the state in which he naturally is.[86]

85. Fraser Watts, "Subjective and Objective Hope: Propositional and Attitudinal Aspects of Eschatology," in *The End of the World and the Ends of God: Science and Theology on Eschatology*, ed. John Polkinghorne and Michael Welker (Harrisburg, Pa.: Trinity, 2000), pp. 47-60.

86. Blaise Pascal, *Pensees*, trans. W. F. Trotter (Grand Rapids: Christian Classics Ethereal Library, 2002), #1670, p. 90.

| | Non-Interactive | Interactive |
|---|---|---|
| **Abiotic Constraints** | Cosmological Fine Tuning (Corey, 1993) | Biotically Driven Geochemical Evolution (Williams and Frausto de Silva, 2003) |
| | Geological Fine Tuning (Ward and Brownlee, 2000) | |
| | Chemical Fine Tuning (Henderson, 1913) | Biotically Regulated Geochem Homeostasis (Lovelock, 1978) |
| **Biotic Constraints** | Bioenergetic Constraints (West et al., 1999) | Life History Invariants (Charnov, 1993) |
| | Mechanical & Developmental Constraint (Smith et al., 1985) | |

**Table 1. Evolutionary Constraints in the Origin and Diversification of Life**

## BIBLIOGRAPHY

Charnov, E. L. 1993. *Life History Invariants: Some Explorations of Symmetry in Evolutionary Ecology.* New York: Oxford University Press.

Corey, M. A. 1993. *God and the New Cosmology: The Anthropic Design Argument.* Lanham, Md.: Rowman and Littlefield.

Henderson, L. J. 1913. *The Fitness of the Environment: An Inquiry into the Biological Significance of the Properties of Matter.* New York: Macmillan.

Lovelock, James. 1978. *Gaia: A New Look at Life on Earth.* Oxford: Oxford University Press.

Smith, F. A., J. H. Brown, J. P. Haskell, S. K. Lyons, J. Alroy, E. L. Charnov, and T. Dayan. 2004. "Similarity of Mammalian Body Size across the Taxonomic Hierarchy and across Space and Time." *American Naturalist* 163: 672-91.

Ward, Peter, and Donald Brownlee. 2000. *Rare Earth: Why Complex Life Is Uncommon in the Universe.* New York: Copernicus Books.

West, Geoffrey B., James H. Brown, Brian J. Enquist. 1999. "The Fourth Dimension of Life: Fractal Geometry and Allometric Scaling of Organisms." *Science* 284: 1677-79.

Williams, R., and J. Frausto Da Silva. 2003. "Evolution Was Chemically Constrained." *Journal of Theoretical Biololgy* 220: 323-43.

## 21. *From Calvinism to Claremont: Now That's Evolution! Or, From Calvin's Supernaturalism to Griffin's Theistic Naturalism*

HOWARD J. VAN TILL

### My Story

I was thoroughly trained in a staunch Calvinist community, rooted in the Netherlands, which treasured its carefully crafted and comprehensive world-and-life-view. From that experience I "knew" that we Christians were up against a tough enemy out there in the larger North American world, especially in the secular academy. That enemy's name was "naturalism," the contentious problem child of the Enlightenment.

All naturalism, as I was conditioned to think of it, denied the reality of God and put nature in God's place. This generic naturalism had no room for God, no room for the supernatural, no room for the sort of divine action that was so often highlighted in the telling of the Judeo-Christian story. I was told the stories about God parting the Red Sea and making ax heads float. I was told the stories about Jesus turning water into wine and multiplying a few loaves and fish into food for thousands. I was told the stories of all manner of supernatural miracles that demonstrated God's power over all creatures and God's authority over the entire universe.

But when I was told that the natural sciences were closely allied with God-denying naturalism, I was puzzled. In the course of earning degrees in physics and doing research in astronomy, I had gained a high respect for the sciences. The scientists I saw were exemplary in exhibiting both professional competence and intellectual integrity. How could the science I loved be associated with a worldview so detested in my community? It made no sense to me.

Fortunately, it seemed to me at the time, I also learned that there were ways to get around the appearance of conflict between a naturalistic science and my traditional Calvinism. One way was to rest in the comfort that the particular kind of naturalism actually employed by the sciences was merely methodological naturalism and not ontological naturalism.

Ontological naturalism is a statement about the ultimate nature of reality. Methodological naturalism, however, is a statement only about the way the natural sciences have chosen to go about their business. Ontological naturalism (we will also call it materialism) says that matter, or the physical/material universe, is all there is to reality, period. There is no such being as God. There is, therefore, no divine action of any sort, supernatural or otherwise, in the universe. Neither is there any ultimate purpose being expressed in what the universe is, or in what the universe does. Ontological naturalism is explicitly atheistic.

Methodological naturalism, on the other hand, is a statement only about the character of the natural sciences. It says that when these sciences formulate theories about how the universe works, they include only natural causes. Supernatural causes (that is, coercive or overpowering interventions by some nonmaterial divine agent) are beyond science's competence either to propose or to test. Because of this limitation in competence, the natural sciences must remain silent about divine intervention. Given this limitation, the sciences can say nothing about the being or nonbeing of God. Science is agnostic regarding God. Traditional theism, then, is safe from threat by a scientific enterprise that can say nothing about the power or authority of divine intervention.

But, alas, the most vocal Christian critics of science were seldom persuaded by this appeal to methodological naturalism. After all, it was commonly argued (or at least strongly implied), the ultimate source of methodological naturalism was really ontological naturalism. As seen through the eyes of its religiously energized critics, methodological naturalism was little more than a deceptively camouflaged version of materialism. Its real agenda, some suspected, was to allow the wolf of materialism to sneak into the public educational system mischievously dressed in the sheep's clothing of a harmless statement about scientific methodology. Naturalism's critics were, of course, far too smart to be fooled by so simple a disguise. The foul-smelling presence of the wolf was still detectable, and a wolf disguised could be considered even more dangerous and repugnant than one who dared to come in plain view. In the face of such rhetoric, you will not be surprised to hear that I generally chose not to use the term "methodological naturalism."

The relatively conservative Christian audience to which I most frequently addressed my critique of the creation-evolution discussion was often very skeptical of modern science. It was especially skeptical of its theories regarding the evolutionary development of the universe and of "all creatures great and small" within it. The roots of this skepticism were clumped mostly in two areas. (1) There was a concern that faithfulness to the Bible (taken to be divinely authored) required the employment of some form of supernaturalism in portraying divine creative action. (2) There was a close association of the natural sciences, especially their theories of evolutionary development, with materialism (ontological naturalism).

Given that circumstance, and given my grounding in the Calvinist world-and-life-view, my strategy for encouraging a more constructive and mutually informative relationship between Christian theology and natural science was directed toward the task of correcting what I judged to be misunderstandings in each of those two areas. For a combination of scientific and theological reasons I crafted an approach that avoided both extremes of the usual creation/evolution shouting match.

From the theological and biblical side I saw no reason to insist on any form of "special creation" or "episodic creation." Special creationism arose nearly two centuries ago in the context of envisioning God to have separately formed each individual species (or some broader classification category) of living things. Today the emphasis has shifted to the idea that God formed at least some life-forms, or parts of life-forms, by a succession of episodes of form-conferring supernatural intervention. Accordingly, the term "episodic creationism" names this position more accurately.

From the scientific side I saw no reason to doubt that continuing empirical work would eventually lead to the discovery of all the formational resources, potentialities, and capabilities that would have been needed to actualize not only inanimate physical structures, from atoms to galaxies, but also the whole array of biological systems that are participants in the universe's formational history. In other words, I was never hesitant to use the word "evolution" in a friendly manner.

At the same time, however, and still content to operate within the spirit of my Calvinist heritage, I saw no reason to rule out the possibility of supernatural divine action. My usual way of presenting my position at that time was to say that, although I judged that supernatural interventions were wholly unnecessary for the actualization of new structures and life-forms in the course of the universe's formational history, I did not categorically rule out the possibility for God to act supernaturally.

My understanding was that God was free to act in any way consistent with God's being and God's will. I posited that supernatural intervention was unnecessary, for the formation of new creatures did not change that state of affairs. I eventually called this approach the "fully gifted creation" perspective. I posited that the creation to which God gave being (*ex nihilo,* from nothing, I presumed) was fully gifted by God from the outset with all the formational resources, potentialities, and capabilities that would have been required to make its evolutionary development possible, without need for any episodes of form-conferring supernatural intervention.[1]

Not surprisingly, reactions to this approach were highly varied. Conservative Christians prone to biblical literalism have found it difficult to accommodate any approach that accepted the 14-billion-year timescale generated by the historical natural sciences. Furthermore, in North American culture the word "evolution" has become so closely associated with materialism that any approach that accepts the scientific concept of evolutionary development, as my approach did, is perceived as one that has the equivalent of 2.999 strikes against it.

Nonetheless, a significant fraction of traditional supernatural theists is not committed either to biblical literalism or to the rejection of evolutionary theorizing in science. Many members of the Calvinist community fall into this category, as do numerous members of the broader evangelical Christian community.[2] For many of these people, the fully gifted creation perspective (sometimes called the evolving creation perspective) functions fruitfully as a means of placing Christian belief and scientific investigation into a nonadversarial and mutually informative relationship.

Many others, however, remain very skeptical. They seem to be looking for a perspective that is more clearly distinguished from deism and its acceptance of a distant or inactive God. The most common response of my conservative Christian critics can be represented by comments like these: "I know you're not a deist, but this sure sounds like deism to me." "The rhetoric sounds nice, but how does this differ from deism?" "This is just a subtle form of deism, isn't it?" "I smell deism lurking around the corner."

Lurking beneath this suspicion of deism, I presume, are troubling questions: Where is there any explicit reference to divine action in the process of actualizing novel structures? Is there no empirical evidence that God has been active in the actualizing of new forms of life? Does God do nothing to form new creatures? Has God become nothing more than an inactive and unnecessary adornment to standard scientific theorizing about evolution?

---

1. My development of this approach can be found in several publications. See, for example, "The Fully Gifted Creation," in *Three Views on Creation and Evolution*, ed. J. P. Moreland and John Mark Reynolds (Grand Rapids: Zondervan, 1999), pp. 161-247; "Science and Christian Theology as Partners in Theorizing," in *Science and Christianity: Four Views*, ed. Richard F. Carlson (Downers Grove, Ill.: InterVarsity, 2000), pp. 196-236; "The Creation: Intelligently Designed or Optimally Equipped?" *Theology Today*, October 1998, pp. 344-64; and "Is the Creation a *Right Stuff* Universe?" *Perspectives on Science and Christian Faith* 54, no. 4 (December 2002): 232-39.

2. For several representatives of this category, see Keith Miller, ed., *Perspectives on an Evolving Creation* (Grand Rapids: Eerdmans, 2003). My chapter, "Is the Universe Capable of Evolving?" presents the fully gifted creation approach as one that evangelical Christians could find acceptable.

These are among the core questions at issue in this book. Let me now state them in another way by defining a new term that I have found helpful in reflecting on these matters. I define the "formational economy" of the universe to be the set of all the universe's physical resources, structural and functional potentialities, and formational capabilities that have ever contributed to the actualizing of new physical structures and new life-forms in the course of its formational history.[3] In the context of discussions regarding the role of divine action in this history, the following fundamental question inevitably arises: Is the universe's formational economy sufficiently robust (amply equipped) to make possible the actualization of every type of physical structure and life-form that has ever existed, without need for occasional episodes of form-conferring divine intervention? To answer yes to this question is to affirm what I call the Robust Formational Economy Principle (RFEP). If that sounds too formal or difficult to remember, just think of it as the Right Stuff Universe Principle (RSUP) — the universe has the "right stuff" to make the natural evolution of atoms, stars, starfish, and human stargazers possible.

This Right Stuff Universe Principle includes such concepts as the "fine-tuning" of the universe — the idea that the values of the fundamental physical constants (speed of light, universal gravitational constant, fine structure constant, etc.) are just right to make possible the development of carbon-based life somewhere in the universe — but its concerns are at once more basic and more comprehensive. To speak of a universe whose basic parameter values are fine-tuned for life already assumes the existence and character of things like elementary particles, atoms, planets, stars, and galaxies in an expanding spatial framework. The "fine-tuning" feature applies to the particular values of the physical constants associated with this set of entities.

But the RSUP does not take such entities for granted, and it calls attention to the fact that the very existence and nature of these various components are by no means self-explanatory, and that they must be recognized as unexplained features of our universe. That there should exist the specific array of elementary particles that we observe is not self-evident. That they should interact in the particular manner they do is not self-evident. That they should possess the formational capabilities to actualize functional structures like stars or starfish is not self-evident. It is remarkable enough that there exists something rather than

---

3. In this definition "resources" refers to such things as elementary particles, their modes of interaction, and the space-time context in which they interact; "capabilities" refers to what things can do, such as the capabilities of atoms to organize into molecules; and "potentialities" refers primarily to structures that would, if assembled, be sustainable or functional. In a sense the "formational economy" of the universe is the sum of what the universe *is,* how it can *change,* and what it is able to *become.*

nothing. Far more remarkable, I am suggesting, is that the something that exists would be a universe characterized by a robust formational economy — a universe that has all the "right stuff" to self-organize into atoms, molecules, planets, stars, galaxies, and myriad forms of life. We are members of a remarkable universe. Even what we call "ordinary" or "natural" is deserving of our awe.

One feature of this "right stuff universe" deserves more attention than it usually gets — the diverse set of structural and functional potentialities that has been present from the beginning. For instance, given the character of the universe, triple-quark structures like protons and neutrons were always possible in principle but could not become formed or assembled until the circumstances were suitable. These structural potentialities were present from the beginning but could not be actualized until some time later. Similarly, the heavier atomic nuclei were structural potentialities from "time zero" but could not be actualized until the environmental conditions for thermonuclear fusion could be maintained. The formation of atoms and molecules falls into exactly the same pattern. Atoms and molecules were potential structures from the beginning, but they could not become actualized (that is, self-assembled from the resources at hand) until the environmental conditions allowed certain formational capabilities to be exercised fruitfully.

Moving beyond inanimate physical structures to living organisms, I find it useful to employ the idea of a potentiality space in which each potentially viable organism is represented by a point in an imaginary, multidimensional "space." Each viable species (with some degree of variation among its members) would be represented by a cluster of nearby points in potentiality space. Closely related species would appear as clusters of clusters in this hypothetical space of potential organisms. In the spirit of our discussion so far, this potentiality space would have to be recognized as an essential part of the universe's being that was present from the very beginning. In the course of time different portions of it would become occupied as new life-forms become actualized. What happens in the course of time is not so much the creation of new species as the actualization of certain potentialities for the first time.[4] What is new is the fact that some particular portion of the potentiality space of life-forms becomes occupied for the first time.

As I see it, the unimaginably vast array of potentialities for both physical

4. Atheists and Christians have engaged in a lot of confusing talk about atoms, molecules, and cells having the ability to "create" new species of living organisms. I find it far more accurate, however, to speak about the appearance of new species as the *first actualization* of a potentiality that was an integral part of the universe's being from the beginning of time. Using the verb "create" in this context invites confusion with its more theologically profound meaning of "to give being" to *something* in place of an authentic *nothing* that excludes even potentiality.

structures and living forms is an enormously important aspect of the universe's being that needs to be appreciated far more than it has been. These potentialities were part of its being from "time zero." Actualized structures and forms came later. Potentialities are a part of the universe's being. Actualization — the assembling of these structures — is part of the universe's formational history. For the universe to satisfy the RSUP, just having resources that can be organized by formational capabilities is not enough. The universe must also possess a vast set of potentialities for all the functional structures and configurations that are essential to life as we know it. To expect the universe to have those potentialities is an extraordinarily high expectation!

Nevertheless, the natural sciences today do presume that the universe does satisfy the Right Stuff Universe Principle. This principle is a seldom stated but nonetheless profoundly basic presupposition of the historical natural sciences. Presuming the universe to satisfy the RSUP has, I suggest, been the foundation for the astounding fruitfulness of the historical natural sciences. Fruitfulness of this degree goes a long way toward building warranted confidence in any principle or physical law. As for the laws of thermodynamics, so also for the Robust Formational Economy Principle.

But scientific fruitfulness is not the only reason for accepting the RSUP as likely to be true. The fully gifted creation perspective, as outlined above, also presumes that the universe satisfies the RSUP. What would that signify? In that religious context the RSUP would serve as a manifestation both of the Creator's creativity (in conceiving of such a system that would work so well) and of the Creator's generosity (in giving being to such a richly equipped system). However, and here's the rub, the Right Stuff Universe Principle is also presumed true by proponents of ontological naturalism. Given its exclusion of any form of deity, materialism has little choice but to take the universe's robust formational economy as an unexplained given. Now, if the fully gifted creation perspective makes the same basic assumption as does ontological naturalism (materialism) regarding the applicability of the RSUP, then has all reference to divine action in the formational history of the universe been made unnecessary, superficial at best? If there are no gaps (missing elements) in the universe's formational economy, is divine action categorically ruled out? In effect, this is the same question we asked a moment ago: Does God do nothing to form new creatures?[5]

Anxious Christian critics of the fully gifted creation perspective have never been hesitant to point out to me that the Right Stuff Universe Principle seems to

---

5. At this point in the story the distinction between *coercive* and *noncoercive* divine action is not yet functioning. Without that distinction, traditional Christians are likely to see the RFEP as effectively equivalent to materialism.

lack any specific or positive reference to the need or nature of divine action in the evolution of forms in the course of time. In my responses to these critics, I have generally attempted to settle their anxieties with the following observations:

1. The RSUP does not categorically rule out all divine action; it merely posits that one form of divine action (episodic, form-imposing intervention) is unnecessary for the actualization of new creaturely forms.

2. Traditional supernatural theism (including the Calvinist theology in which I was brought up), building on the concept of *creatio ex nihilo*, maintains that God's continuing action of sustaining the being of the creation is just as essential as God's action of giving it being in the first place. The RSUP does not at all negate either the possibility or the necessity of God's sustaining action.

3. Orthodox Christian theology has never, to my knowledge, posited that divine action was possible only within gaps (opened up by missing elements) in the creation's formational economy. That being the case, the absence of such gaps constitutes no theological loss whatsoever.

After offering these and other considerations in defense of the fully gifted creation perspective or the Robust Formational Economy Principle that it entails, I have found that the most common response from traditional Christians remains: "I know you're not a deist, but this sure sounds like deism to me." "The rhetoric sounds nice, but how does this differ from deism?" "This is just a subtle form of deism, isn't it?" "I smell deism lurking around the corner." Some stories move toward a conclusion; some just give you another dose of "instant replay."

This instant replay of concerns about deism and divine inactivity is a telling response. The message it conveys to me is this: remove the need for occasional episodes of form-conferring supernatural intervention, and the majority of Christians today become fearful that the possibility of any divine action has been surrendered to materialism. Supernaturalism is deeply embedded in contemporary Christianity, and any attempt to make even one portion (specifically the episodic creationist portion) of that action unnecessary will be met with intense resistance, or at least deep skepticism. That is, I believe, the driving force of the Intelligent Design (ID) movement, the most recently devised form of episodic creationism, especially of its agenda for finding empirical support for rejecting the RSUP and for positing the need for episodes of form-conferring divine intervention to compensate for an inadequate system of natural formational capabilities. After all, if ID theorists could demonstrate scientifically that the system of natural causes is inadequate, then the case for supernatural intervention would seem to be quite strong, right? Whether I like it or not, that approach has a lot of appeal to North American Christianity today.[6]

---

6. Having studied the literature of the Intelligent Design movement extensively, I have

## Good Advice for a Better Solution

As I noted earlier, I stood for a long time on what felt like a narrow ledge at the perimeter of the mountain of majority Christian supernaturalism. (Some of my critics might add that this ledge was located just above the slippery slope into heresy, but having discovered that "heresy" is simply the name for "holding a view different from the received majority view," I no longer worry about such charges.) Standing on that peripheral ledge, I found supernatural intervention to be unnecessary as a means of forming novel creatures, but I was not yet prepared to exclude supernaturalism categorically. This is where I found David Griffin's critical engagement of my work especially helpful.[7] In fact, as I have told many audiences in the last couple of years, I found his criticism to be the most helpful that I had ever received. To summarize it as succinctly as I can, these are the two principal challenges he offered for my consideration:

1. Dare to be consistent in regard to supernatural divine action. If, as I had already maintained for some time, supernatural action is unnecessary for something as astounding as the formational history of the entire universe, then why hold to the need, or even to the possibility, for occasional episodes of coercive supernatural action in any other arena? Griffin's carefully crafted development of a concept of variable and effective, but noncoercive, divine action struck me as an attractive alternative to the traditional concept of supernatural action held by the majority of Christians today. Not only does it offer a way to appreciate the ubiquity of noncoercive divine action in the natural world, it also offers a way to avoid some of the dreadful problems of theodicy that inevitably accompany traditional supernaturalism and its doctrine of divine omnipotence.

2. Naturalism and theism need not be enemies: naturalism comes in significantly differing forms that must be carefully distinguished from one another. Maximal naturalism (I have been calling it both ontological naturalism and materialism) does indeed preclude the existence of God, and it builds its worldview on the premise that nature (taken to be no more than a physical/material system) is all there is. Other forms of naturalism, however, require no

---

concluded that the strongest case that ID proponents can make is this: *In the absence of a detailed, laboratory testable, step-by-step scientific account of how biotic structure X came to be actualized for the first time, it is logically permissible to posit that the first actualization of X required, in addition to all relevant natural causes, one or more episodes of nonnatural, form-imposing intervention by an unidentified, unembodied, choice-making agent.* That might well be true, but it is of no scientific value whatsoever. Furthermore, it does *not* establish the *need* for form-imposing intervention, but only a sliver of logical space for positing it.

7. See David Ray Griffin, *Religion and Scientific Naturalism* (Stony Brook: State University of New York Press, 2000).

such denial of God and no categorical rejection of divine action. Minimal naturalism, for example, rejects only supernatural (coercive) divine action and remains agnostic on noncoercive divine action. Griffin's recommendation to spokespersons for science is to rid the sciences of their recently acquired association with maximal naturalism and to recognize that minimal naturalism is sufficient for the work of the natural sciences. Naturalistic theism — yet another form of naturalism — joins minimal (scientific) naturalism in rejecting supernaturalism but then proceeds to develop an enriched concept of natural phenomena by incorporating purposeful and effective but noncoercive divine action as an essential component of all natural processes.

Griffin's two challenges to my earlier strategy have been essential to my continuing theological odyssey. His criticism of the "fully gifted creation" approach has stimulated me to try different approaches for making theological sense out of the human experience, including the experience of scientific investigation and theorizing about biological evolution. It has also stimulated me to craft a thesis concerning why my earlier efforts in the traditional Christian community to promote the Right Stuff Universe Principle, and the fully gifted creation perspective that incorporated it, experienced only limited success.

That thesis consists of three parts. (a) The rejection of the RSUP by a majority of the traditional Christian community is an indication that traditional Christian supernaturalism may have an inadequately developed concept of noncoercive divine action. (b) The RSUP's inclusion of a negative reference to (coercive, supernatural) form-conferring divine intervention is, consequently, likely to be heard as a negation of all divine action. (c) In that context, my failure to posit any effective role for noncoercive divine action in the evolution of new forms, especially of biological forms, has functioned to reinforce the judgment of my critics that the RSUP constitutes a sellout to either deism or materialism. In fact, I am now inclined to think that my failure to include any specific proposal regarding the form-evoking role of noncoercive divine action may indicate that my own concept of divine action was just as inadequate as that of my critics.

If this analysis is correct, then perhaps I should reformulate the RSUP in a way that explicitly welcomes the contribution of noncoercive divine action to all natural processes. Perhaps the RSUP should be restated in the vocabulary of process theology to read as follows: "The formational economy of the universe is sufficiently robust to make possible the actualizing, by wholly natural processes and events, of every type of physical structure and life-form that has ever existed — with the understanding that natural processes and events, while they do preclude any form of coercive divine intervention, may nonetheless include noncoercive divine action as an effective factor."

Would this reformulated Right Stuff Universe Principle be welcomed by traditional supernaturalists? I must confess a bit of skepticism here. In recent months I have tried to get a number of evangelical Christians who are trained in, or at least well informed by, the natural sciences to appreciate the distinction between coercive and noncoercive forms of divine action. My most common strategy has been to invoke the problem of theodicy, arguing that once you posit that God is both able and, on occasion, willing to perform coercive supernatural interventions — either to make $x$ happen or to prevent $y$ from happening — then God becomes accountable for all the suffering and tragedy that occur in the human experience. Not a pretty picture of God![8]

But the very terminology of "coercive" and "noncoercive" divine action has its shortcomings. Whenever I would refer to coercive divine action, members of the discussion group would react negatively because the term "coercive" seemed to carry with it the unattractive connotation of God acting over the objection or against the resistance of some creature. It seems that the word "coercive" cannot easily be disassociated from the idea of a hostile, dictatorial action. Thus, my speaking of coercive divine action was heard as a sleazy rhetorical device in which a prejudicial bias against a concept was built into its very name. Similarly, designating other forms of divine action simply as "noncoercive" is just plain dull; although this designation might benefit from having no negative connotations, it also fails to provide any positive connotations to make it attractive on its own merit.

Could other choices of terminology accomplish the essential distinction we wish to make without inviting resistance of this sort? Let me propose one possibility. If I understand correctly, one of the fundamental (and, to process theology, highly objectionable) features of coercive divine action is that God's action becomes wholly determinative of the outcome of some event. The chain of natural causation is broken and the outcome of some event becomes determined, not by the free and creative interplay of natural causes, but solely by divine decision either (a) to overpower some natural system and to force it to do something contrary to its natural capabilities, or (b) to impose on a creaturely system one particular outcome among several otherwise possible outcomes (as might be the situation for quantum transitions). That being the case, let us call this kind of action "determinative" divine action, hoping that "determinative" does not carry the same negative connotation that "coercive" seems to entail.

8. One way of dramatizing the problem is this: If God were both able and willing to break the chain of natural causation and to install, by form-conferring intervention, a rotary propulsion system on E. coli bacteria (as proposed by ID theorists), then why did God not also intervene to install auxiliary rotary propulsion devices that would divert the hijacked planes away from the World Trade Center towers on 9/11?

The other category of action could, then, be called "nondeterminative," but that would fail to make explicit the positive idea that this is a form of divine action that, while not wholly determinative, nonetheless makes some effective contribution to the outcome of any creaturely action in a manner similar to the way in which persuasion might make a nondeterminative contribution to the outcome of human action. Process theologians often call this "persuasive" divine action. Critics, however, are likely to balk at the idea of a DNA molecule responding to divine persuasion. Many see the term "persuasion" as being so deeply tied to the behavior of sentient, rational, decision-making creatures that they find it awkward to use in reference to atoms, molecules, or genes.

My suggestion, then, is to employ the term "contributive" as the category name for nondeterminative divine action. Calling this "contributive divine action" not only sets it apart from "determinative divine action," but also calls positive attention to the idea that we are envisioning a category of divine action that can make an effective contribution to the outcome of creaturely action in the nondeterminative manner that process theologians designate by the term "persuasion."

Employing this new terminology, perhaps we should edit the RSUP lightly to read: "The formational economy of the universe is sufficiently robust to make possible the actualizing, by wholly natural processes and events, of every type of physical structure and life-form that has ever existed — with the understanding that natural processes and events, while they do preclude any form of determinative divine intervention, may nonetheless include noncoercive or contributive divine action as an effective factor."

## Concluding Remarks

In closing, let me call attention to what has taken place in this presentation. I began with the story of my efforts to accommodate my concept of the formational history of the universe to the worldview I inherited from my Calvinist community. Although the success of this was limited, I still think the fully gifted creation perspective could be maintained with integrity, and persons within the evangelical Christian community are welcome to do so. If a person wishes to maintain both the possibility of supernatural divine action and a respect for what the natural sciences have learned, I recommend this as the way to go.

However, for a variety of reasons, not all of which were considered here, I have found it necessary to explore a different theological territory, beyond traditional supernaturalism, in my quest to make sense of life's experiences. The first steps of that new exploration formed the end of the story told in this presentation — my first steps in employing some of the conceptual vocabulary of process theology to reformulate my thoughts about the formational history of the universe and of the nature and role of divine action in that remarkable cosmic drama. These were my first steps on a journey from John Calvin's supernaturalism to David Griffin's naturalistic theism, my first steps from Calvinism to Claremont.

## 22. Whitehead's Naturalism and a Non-Darwinian View of Evolution

DAVID RAY GRIFFIN

### The Whiteheadian Third Way

In my previous contribution to this volume, chapter 17, I spelled out fifteen doctrines that, as I see it, constitute the theory of evolution generally known as neo-Darwinism. I had two motives, beyond simply seeking understanding, for doing this. One was to provide a basis for showing that evangelical and fundamentalist theologians, in maintaining that neo-Darwinism is objectionable on moral, religious, and even empirical grounds, are not entirely wrong.

My second motive was to provide a basis for understanding why the opposition between these critics and the mainstream evolutionary community has been so total and, seemingly, so incapable of mediation. One reason is that these critics, increasingly under the banner of Intelligent Design, want to replace scientific naturalism with a supernaturalist worldview.[1] Given that naturalism — in the generic sense of the rejection of the possibility of supernatural interruptions of the world's basic causal principles — has become almost universally regarded as an essential presupposition of science, this attack on naturalism is seen as an attack on science itself. From the perspective of advocates of

1. William A. Dembski, generally considered the intellectual leader of the Intelligent Design movement, sometimes claims that this movement is not committed to a supernatural designer; see *Intelligent Design: The Bridge between Science and Theology* (Downers Grove, Ill.: InterVarsity, 1999), pp. 107, 247, 252, 259, and *The Design Revolution: Answering the Toughest Questions about Intelligent Design* (Downers Grove, Ill.: InterVarsity, 2004), pp. 25, 169, 176. These claims cannot be taken seriously, however, in the light of other statements in which Dembski argues that only the Christian God, understood as having created the world ex nihilo, and hence capable of performing miracles, can fully account for the world and the design evident in it; see *Intelligent Design*, pp. 16, 18, 51, 66, 102, 214, 224; *The Design Revolution*, pp. 174-76.

Intelligent Design, however, neo-Darwinists are illegitimately using the prestige of science to promote an atheistic, amoral worldview.

A second reason for the total opposition between these two communities is that the advocates of Intelligent Design reject neo-Darwinian evolutionism almost in its entirety. They accept only the first doctrine, which refers merely to the reality of microevolution. These critics, therefore, reject the very heart of the evolutionary account of the world, the doctrine of macroevolution, according to which the present species of living creatures have evolved, through "descent with modification," from earlier species.[2] From the point of view of the mainline evolutionary community, however, the doctrine of macroevolution is as well established as any scientific theory of such scope could possibly be, and it is simply presupposed in most scientific work. From this perspective, the critics, far from rejecting some particular theory, are rejecting science as such.

A crucial factor in this total opposition is the failure, on both sides of the debate, to distinguish between scientific naturalism in the generic sense (naturalism$_{ns}$) and the specific version of naturalism embedded in neo-Darwinism, which I have called naturalism$_{sam}$ (with "sam" standing for "sensationist-atheist-materialist"). Because of this failure, which makes it seem as if naturalism as such entailed atheism and hence an amoral, meaningless universe, the only alternative seems to be a supernaturalist worldview, in which miraculous interruptions occur or are at least possible.

But naturalism in the generic sense (naturalism$_{ns}$), with its rejection of the possibility of supernatural interruptions, is widely and justifiably considered an essential presupposition of science as such. As long as the only recognized challenge to the overall worldview of neo-Darwinism is perceived as coming from supernaturalists, therefore, it will understandably be met with total rejection.

If this analysis is correct, the total opposition between these two positions involves fault on both sides. On the one hand, as I have shown in chapter 17, the neo-Darwinian construal of evolution combines its well-grounded evolutionary naturalism, as embodied in the first four doctrines, with highly dubious metaphysical doctrines having highly problematic scientific, religious, and moral implications. I hold with Ian Barbour, therefore, that we need "new ways of thinking that go beyond the refinement of neo-Darwinism."[3]

2. Dembski has sought to differentiate Intelligent Design from its parent, scientific creationism. One element in this effort has been the refusal to insist on the rejection of the doctrine of macroevolution, or common descent, as essential to his movement; see *Intelligent Design*, pp. 113, 250, 252. Thus far, nevertheless, the movement has been widely presented and understood as rejecting this doctrine.

3. Barbour, chapter 13.

On the other hand, the valid points made by supporters of Intelligent Design need to be separated from their rejection of both naturalism and evolution. People will more likely take these valid criticisms of neo-Darwinism seriously when made on the basis of a position that endorses evolutionary naturalism. If we understand "intelligent design" (without capitalization) to refer simply to the idea that the universe reflects intelligent purpose of some sort or other, this can be discussed, and is discussed in this book, without any threat to the integrity of science. This does not involve support of "Intelligent Design" (capitalized) as the school of thought that promotes a supernaturalist, antievolutionary worldview.

Whitehead's major contribution to this issue was to provide a philosophical worldview that, while radically different from the worldview of naturalism$_{sam}$ presupposed by neo-Darwinism, likewise embodies naturalism in the generic sense (naturalism$_{ns}$). Whitehead's philosophy embeds this generic naturalism in a specific type of theistic naturalism that provides a middle ground, and hence a potential mediating position, between neo-Darwinism and Intelligent Design.

In my attempt to demonstrate this point, I will begin by discussing Whitehead's basic criterion for adequacy. I will next discuss several doctrines of Whitehead's naturalism that have direct relevance to evolution, religion, and morality. I will conclude by briefly reviewing, from the perspective of Whitehead's theistic naturalism, the fifteen doctrines of neo-Darwinism discussed in chapter 17.

## Inevitable Presuppositions as a Crucial Test of Adequacy

To be intellectually acceptable, any theory must be self-consistent and adequate to the relevant facts. These "facts" are usually limited to particular empirical facts, such as evidence that the earth is over four billion years old. Whitehead suggests, however, that our theories must also avoid "negations of what in practice is presupposed."[4] In other words, we should not contradict in theory any ideas that we inevitably presuppose in practice. The "metaphysical rule of evidence," he said, is "that we must bow to those presumptions which, in despite of criticism, we still employ for the regulation of our lives."[5]

In adding "in despite of criticism," Whitehead recognized that we might

---

4. Alfred North Whitehead, *Process and Reality: An Essay in Cosmology* (1929), ed. David Ray Griffin and Donald W. Sherburne, corrected ed. (New York: Free Press, 1978), p. 13.

5. Whitehead, *Process and Reality*, p. 151.

explicitly deny certain ideas while implicitly presupposing them. It is widely recognized, for example, that we cannot help presupposing that we make free decisions. As John Searle puts it, "we can't act otherwise than on the assumption of freedom, no matter how much we learn about how the world works as a determined physical system."[6] Whitehead himself said our sense of freely making decisions is "too large to be put aside merely as misconstruction. It governs the whole tone of human life."[7] We must not, therefore, affirm a completely deterministic worldview, because we would be presupposing our freedom in the very act of denying it. We would thereby be guilty of what Jürgen Habermas and Karl-Otto Apel call a "performative contradiction," in which the performance of making the statement contradicts the meaning of the statement.[8] To be considered adequate, accordingly, a philosophical position must be adequate to freedom and all the other inevitable presuppositions of practice as well as to the various empirical facts that have been discovered.

## Organisms and Causation

Whitehead referred to his position as "the philosophy of organism" because he held the actual world to be composed entirely of things best thought of as organisms. "Science . . . is becoming the study of organisms. Biology is the study of the larger organisms; whereas physics is the study of the smaller organisms."[9]

One of the main respects in which this switch is important for the philosophy of evolution involves the nature of causation. "A satisfactory cosmology," Whitehead said, "must explain the interweaving of efficient and final causation."[10] This explanation is needed, he added, because unless we can "explain the diverse senses in which freedom and necessity can coexist, . . . we have to explain away one or other of the most obvious presuppositions of our daily thoughts."[11] As I showed in chapter 17, however, neo-Darwinism has no tools

6. John R. Searle, *Minds, Brains, and Science: The 1984 Reith Lectures* (London: British Broadcasting Corporation, 1984), p. 97.

7. Whitehead, *Process and Reality*, p. 47.

8. See Martin Jay, "Debate over Performative Contradiction: Habermas versus the Poststructuralists," in Jay, *Force Fields: Between Intellectual History and Cultural Critique* (New York and London: Routledge, 1993), pp. 25-37.

9. Alfred North Whitehead, *Science and the Modern World* (1925) (New York: Free Press, 1967), p. 103.

10. Alfred North Whitehead, *The Function of Reason* (1929) (Boston: Beacon Press, 1968), p. 28.

11. Alfred North Whitehead, *Modes of Thought* (1938) (New York: Free Press, 1968), p. 7.

for doing this, given its rejection of final or purposive causation on the part of the world's entities.

The switch to the concept of organism is crucial for this issue because, as Dorion Sagan reminds us, Kant observed that one of the unique features of an organism is that it is "both cause and effect of itself."[12] An organism is, in other words, partly self-causing, self-determining. Whitehead's particular doctrine of organisms, as Barbour points out, explains how this purposive, self-determining activity of organisms does not exclude the exercise of efficient causation on them by other organisms.[13]

This explanation involves the idea that all enduring individuals — such as quarks, electrons, atoms, molecules, macromolecules, bacteria, organelles, eukaryotic cells, and animal psyches — are really temporally ordered societies of momentary organisms. In Whitehead's philosophy the momentary organisms are the actual entities, meaning the entities that are *actual* in the fullest sense of the term. Whitehead also called them "actual occasions" to emphasize that the fully actual entities are not individuals that endure through time but momentary events. An enduring individual is a series of these momentary events or, to be more precise, a temporally ordered society of actual occasions by virtue of sustaining a character through time. In emphasizing this point, Whitehead said: "The real actual things that endure are all societies. . . . [T]he mistake that has thwarted European metaphysics from the time of the Greeks [has been] to confuse societies with the completely real things, which are the actual occasions."[14] The durations of these events can vary enormously. At the subatomic level, each actual occasion would constitute less than a billionth of a second; at the level of the human psyche, each one might constitute more like a tenth of a second.

In referring to these momentary events as actual entities or actual occasions, Whitehead is saying that they are the entities that act. What kind of action are they capable of? In the type of naturalism embodied in neo-Darwinism, actual entities can exert nothing but efficient causation, that is, causation on other things. Final or purposive causation, in which they would act on themselves, perhaps to help make themselves, is excluded. But in Whitehead's worldview, all actual entities, being organisms, have at least some elementary capacity for self-creation as well as for receiving and exerting efficient causation.

---

12. Immanuel Kant, *Critique of Judgment, Part 2: Critique of Teleological Judgment*, trans. W. S. Pluhar (Indianapolis: Hackett, 1987), p. 64, quoted by Dorion Sagan, in this volume, chapter 7.

13. Barbour, chapter 13.

14. Alfred North Whitehead, *Adventures of Ideas* (New York: Macmillan, 1933), p. 204.

## Dipolar Monism and Perpetual Oscillation

Barbour helpfully refers to this aspect of Whitehead's position, according to which actual entities exert final causation as well as receive efficient causation, as his "dipolar monism." It is monism because all actual entities are of the same basic type: Whitehead rejected the Cartesian dualism between physical and mental actual entities. This is Whitehead's way of emphatically asserting that human beings, including their conscious experiences, are fully natural. But it is *dipolar* monism because each actual occasion has two poles, which can be called the physical and the mental poles. The mental pole, to the extent that it exists, emerges out of the physical pole, with which the occasion begins.

### *Physicality and Mentality*

To understand this doctrine we need to avoid the Cartesian meaning of those terms, according to which "physical" means "devoid of experience" and "mental" means "having experience." Actual occasions are experiential through and through. Whitehead's other technical term for them is in fact "occasions of experience." I discuss this doctrine, which I call "panexperientialism," below. The point for now is to clarify the distinction between physical experience and mental experience.

The idea that an occasion begins as physical means that it simply repeats forms of energy received from prior occasions. Physicality means receptivity from the past. Whitehead's technical term for this receptivity is "physical prehension." Each actual occasion begins by prehending prior occasions. In a positive physical prehension, also called a "physical feeling," the occasion appropriates something from those prior occasions. An occasion that belongs to a low-level temporally ordered society, such as an electron or a molecule, for the most part simply repeats the prior occasions in that society.

While physicality refers to receptivity and repetition, hence lack of originality, mentality refers to self-determination, wherein lies a possibility, whether great or slight, for originality. The mental pole begins with a conceptual prehension, which is a prehension of possibilities, in light of which the occasion will complete its moment of becoming. To say that an occasion's physical pole is followed by a mental pole is to say that, having been partly constituted by the efficient causation from the past, the occasion completes itself by deciding, in light of the possibilities open to it, precisely how to integrate the material it has received from prior actualities and hence how to influence the future. In low-grade actual occasions, this element of mentality or self-creation is vanishingly small, even if never completely absent. In higher-grade occasions, the role of the mental pole is greater.

### Subjectivity and Objectivity

Given this distinction between the physical and mental poles of actual occasions, Whitehead then explained the "interweaving of efficient and final causation" in terms of a doctrine he called "perpetual perishing" but, because that terminology has proved perpetually confusing, is better called "perpetual oscillation."[15] This doctrine involves a distinction between two modes in which an occasion of experience exists: as a subject and then as an object. (This distinction should not be confused with the distinction between the physical and mental poles of an occasion.) As each occasion is coming into existence, it is a subject of experience (with its physical and mental poles). It is during this subjective existence that it can exert final causation, thereby being self-causing. But as soon as its moment of self-creation is completed, it becomes an object — and to be an "object" is to be such for subsequent subjects. As an object, therefore, it exerts efficient causation on those subsequent subjects (which prehend it). In losing its subjectivity, Whitehead wrote, an actual entity "loses the final causation which is its internal principle of unrest, and it acquires efficient causation."[16]

Accordingly, any enduring individual, such as a proton or a psyche, perpetually oscillates between subjectivity and objectivity, and hence between final and efficient causation. Each occasion arises out of efficient causation from the past; it then exerts final causation in completing its self-creation; and then, by becoming an object prehended by the subsequent occasions, it exerts efficient causation on them, and so on.

## Panexperientialism with Organizational Duality

By showing how the world's actual entities can exercise final as well as efficient causation, Whitehead has overcome one of the main reasons in modern thought for assuming that our sense of freedom must be *only* a sense — that is,

---

15. For a discussion of this confusion, see David Ray Griffin, *Reenchantment without Supernaturalism: A Process Philosophy of Religion* (Ithaca, N.Y.: Cornell University Press, 2001), pp. 115-16.

16. Whitehead, *Process and Reality*, p. 29.

an illusion. But there has been another reason for this widespread thought among those who reject Descartes's dualism. This is the doctrine called "identism," according to which the brain and the mind are numerically identical — that what we call "the mind" is simply certain aspects, functions, or properties of the brain. Whitehead showed how we can avoid this assumption without lapsing back into Cartesian dualism.

## Identism and Determinism

The main basis for identism has been the assumption that the brain is composed of entities that are physical in the Cartesian sense — meaning they are insentient, devoid of experience. Given this assumption, there is only one way to avoid the dualistic idea that what we call "the mind" is a "nonphysical" entity, different in kind from the brain cells: to declare the mind to be numerically identical with the brain. John Searle expresses this view by saying of the human head, "the brain is the only thing in there."[17]

Identism virtually implies determinism. The brain is, of course, a very complex entity, being composed of tens of billions of neurons. It is very difficult to conceive how such an entity could, any more than a rock, be capable of exercising self-determination. Daniel Dennett, expressing this identist position, says the head contains billions of "miniagents and microagents (with no single Boss)," and "that's all that's going on."[18] If that is really all, then there is no agent that could coordinate the billions of microagents to produce a unified, intentional action. And that is, indeed, Dennett's contention.

## Panexperientialist Monism and Nondualistic Interaction

But Whitehead's philosophy, with its switch from materialist monism to panexperientialist monism, overcomes this problem. Higher-grade occasions of experience can arise out of more elementary ones. This idea has already been implied in saying that not only quarks but also, for example, electrons, atoms, macromolecules, and eukaryotic cells are enduring individuals comprised of series of actual occasions. Accordingly, just as a DNA molecule has, by hypothesis, a unified, higher-level experience arising out of the experiences contributed by its ordinary molecular constituents, and just as a

17. John R. Searle, *The Rediscovery of the Mind* (Cambridge: MIT Press, 1992), p. 248.
18. Daniel E. Dennett, *Consciousness Explained* (Boston: Little, Brown, 1991), pp. 458, 459.

eukaryotic cell has, by hypothesis, a unified, higher-level experience arising out of the experiences contributed by its various constituents, the psyche arises out of the experiences contributed by the billions of cells constituting the brain.

The occasions of experience constituting the psyche, being fully actual, have the twofold power (1) to finish creating themselves out of the material provided by the efficient causation on them and (2) to act on subsequent occasions. This means that besides receiving upward causation from the brain, they also, as Barbour points out,[19] exert downward causation back upon the brain and, through it, on the body and the world beyond. The psyche is not, in other words, purely epiphenomenal. There is genuine interaction.

Although both dualists and materialists have equated "interaction" with dualism, which materialists can then show to be unintelligible,[20] Whitehead provides a nondualistic interactionism. The brain cells, by consisting, like the mind, of occasions of experience, can be prehended by the mind, which means that they can exert efficient causation on it. And the mind can, in turn, be prehended by its brain cells, whereby it can exert causal efficacy on them.

Moreover, the mind or psyche, far from being unreal or merely epiphenomenal, is the most powerful agent in the total society we call the living animal. Indeed, just as Leibniz referred to the psyche as the "dominant monad," Whitehead calls it the "dominant member" of the society to emphasize its ability both to synthesize the experiences of the other members and then to exercise a coordinating influence over them.[21]

## Organizational Duality without Ontological Dualism

With this idea Whitehead, like Leibniz, was able, within a philosophy that is ontologically monistic, to explain the most obvious duality in the world — that between things that show signs of self-determination and things that do not. Descartes explained this distinction with his ontological dualism, thereby creating most of the distinctive problems of modern philosophy. Whitehead explained it in terms of the idea that "diverse modes of functioning . . . are produced by diverse modes of organization."[22] The basic idea is that once actual

19. Barbour, chapter 13.
20. See David Ray Griffin, *Unsnarling the World-Knot: Consciousness, Freedom, and the Mind-Body Problem* (Berkeley and Los Angeles: University of California Press, 1998), pp. 49-51.
21. Whitehead, *Process and Reality*, p. 102; Whitehead, *Adventures of Ideas*, p. 206.
22. Whitehead, *Modes of Thought*, p. 157.

occasions are organized into enduring individuals, these enduring individuals can be organized in two basic ways: into societies in which a dominant member emerges and into those in which that is not the case.[23]

If we follow Charles Hartshorne in calling the former type "compound individuals,"[24] we can say that the organizational duality is between societies that are compound individuals and those that are not. Of course, the world is not that simple. For example, although Whitehead referred to a tree as a "democracy" to bring out the fact that it has no dominant member,[25] a tree is enormously different from a rock in organization and functioning. Barbour is right, accordingly, to speak of "organizational plurality."[26] However, because of the special importance of the distinction between societies with a dominant member and those without one, I speak of "panexperientialism with organizational duality," listing it elsewhere as one of ten core doctrines of process philosophy.[27]

## Emergence without Supernaturalism

One of the reasons for affirming panexperientialism is that it is the only intelligible basis, within a system that eschews miraculous transitions that could be effected only by a supernatural deity, for explaining how creatures such as ourselves could have arisen. Charles Birch, paraphrasing a statement by Sewall Wright, says that "to propose that no-mind gave rise to mind" is "to posit a miracle." Birch also mentions that I have used the notion of "category mistake" in arguing against the contrary position.[28]

The most serious problem shared by dualism and materialism, I have argued, is "how the emergence of experience out of nonexperiencing entities is

23. Charles Hartshorne, emphasizing the importance of this distinction, said that in formulating the contrast "between active singulars and groups of these, only the former of which literally feel; and that between low and high levels or degrees of feeling, . . . Leibniz took the greatest single step in the second millennium of philosophy . . . toward a rational analysis of the concept of physical reality." See Charles Hartshorne, "Physics and Psychics: The Place of Mind in Nature," in *Mind in Nature: Essays on the Interface of Science and Philosophy,* ed. John B. Cobb, Jr., and David Ray Griffin (Washington, D.C.: University Press of America, 1977), pp. 89-96, at p. 95.

24. See Charles Hartshorne, "The Compound Individual," in Hartshorne, *Whitehead's Philosophy: Selected Essays, 1935-1970* (Lincoln: University of Nebraska Press, 1972), pp. 41-61.

25. Whitehead, *Modes of Thought,* p. 24.

26. Barbour, chapter 13.

27. See Griffin, *Reenchantment without Supernaturalism,* p. 6.

28. Birch, chapter 15.

conceivable."[29] As Thomas Nagel famously put it, "One cannot derive a pour soi from an en soi. . . . This gap is logically unbridgeable." It is impossible in principle, argues Nagel, for a conscious being to be created by "combining together in organic form a lot of particles with none but physical properties."[30] The point is that a *pour soi*, by virtue of having experience, has an "inside," meaning that it is something "for itself." An *en soi*, by contrast, having no experience, has only an "outside," because it does not exist for itself but only for others, for whom it is an object. Even if we put a trillion of these mere objects together, with the most intricate set of interconnections possible, a subject would not arise from them.

Many philosophers have nevertheless argued otherwise, using the notion of emergence in an analogical argument. They begin with some familiar type of emergence, in which a thing with property X emerges out of things without property X. For example, neither hydrogen nor oxygen has the property of liquidity, but if we put them together to form $H_2O$, the property of liquidity emerges. Likewise subatomic particles, which do not manifest solidity, can give rise to things with this emergent property. For a third example, one can point out that if things with scales evolved into things with feathers, then featheriness emerged out of things devoid of this property. By analogy, the argument concludes, experience can arise out of brain cells that are devoid of this property.

I call this the "emergence category mistake" because the familiar, unproblematic examples of emergence are different in kind from the alleged emergence of experience out of wholly nonexperiencing entities. As I have argued:

> All of the unproblematic forms of emergence refer to externalistic features, features of things as perceived from without, features of objects for subjects. But the alleged emergence of experience is not simply one more example of such emergence. It involves instead the alleged emergence of an "inside" from things that have only outsides. It does not involve the emergence of one more objective property for subjectivity to view, but the alleged emergence of subjectivity itself. Liquidity, solidity, and [featheriness] are properties of things as experienced through our sensory organs, hence properties for others. Experience is not what we are for others but what we are for ourselves. Experience cannot be listed as one more "property." . . . It is in a category by itself. To suggest any analogy between experience itself and properties of other things as known through sensory experience is a category mistake of the most egregious kind.[31]

29. Griffin, *Unsnarling the World-Knot*, p. 63.
30. Thomas Nagel, *Mortal Questions* (London: Cambridge University Press, 1979), p. 189.
31. Griffin, *Unsnarling the World-Knot*, pp. 64-65.

To illustrate this point, I showed that although Daniel Dennett says that one of the steps in an explanation of the emergence of consciousness cannot say, in effect, "then a miracle occurs," his own argument contains precisely such a step.[32]

My argument, to summarize, is that to have an adequate theory of evolution we need to be able to explain the rise of the kind of conscious experience we ourselves enjoy, and that to do this, within a naturalistic framework, we need to affirm some version of panexperientialism.

## Freedom, Downward Causation, and the Unity of Experience

The distinction between the brain, as a society of billions of cellular experiences, and the psyche, as the unification of these experiences into a temporally ordered society of dominant occasions of experience, allows us to account for three features that we all presuppose in practice: (1) the unity of our experience, (2) our capacity for freedom in the sense of self-determination in the moment, and (3) our responsibility for our bodily actions by the downward causation exerted by our freely made decisions on our bodies.

Materialists, as we saw, make no distinction between the brain and the mind, with Searle saying that the brain is the only thing in the human head and Dennett stating that the head contains billions of microagents but "no single Boss." But if that were the whole truth, the unity of our experience would be difficult to explain, as even some materialists admit. Thomas Nagel says that "the unity of consciousness, even if it is not complete, poses a problem for the theory that mental states are states of something as complex as a brain."[33] Even Searle agrees. After pointing out that "unity" is one of the "structures of consciousness," he says: "We have little understanding of how the brain achieves this unity."[34] By rejecting identism in favor of the view that the mind in each moment is an occasion of experience, which integrates data from various parts of the brain into a complex experience, we can say that "the brain achieves this unity" not by itself but by giving rise to dominant occasions moment after moment.

The distinction between the brain and the mind is equally important for the question of human freedom. Unless the mind in each moment is a single actuality with the power to make decisions that can then guide the person's bodily actions, human freedom cannot be made intelligible. For example, Searle, holding that the brain is the only thing in the head and that the brain, like everything

---

32. Griffin, *Unsnarling the World-Knot*, pp. 69-70.

33. Thomas Nagel, *The View from Nowhere* (New York: Oxford University Press, 1986), p. 50.

34. Searle, *Rediscovery of the Mind*, p. 130.

else, consists exclusively of "particles and their relations with each other," concludes that the scientific worldview leaves no room for freedom.[35]

## Nominalism and Resulting Problems

Nominalism is, as we saw earlier, the rejection of the position often called "Platonic realism," according to which eternal forms exist objectively in the nature of things. Some thinkers date the beginning of modernity with the fourteenth-century rise of nominalism,[36] which was in fact known at the time as the *via moderna*. Nominalism has, in any case, been at the root of many of the distinctive problems of late modern thought — the period in which nominalism became the dominant outlook.

### Philosophy of Evolution

As I pointed out in chapter 17, one of these problems is that if there are no ideal forms that can serve as attractors, any jump from one coherent species to another would have to be purely accidental and hence too improbable to be believable. As a result, neo-Darwinists have needed to maintain that, in defiance of the fossil record, in Dawkins's words: "Each successive change in the gradual evolutionary process was simple enough, relative to its predecessor, to have come into existence by chance."[37]

To reject nominalism only to solve this problem would be ad hoc. But the problem created for evolutionary theory by the Darwinian acceptance of nominalism is merely one of many problems inherent in late modern thought because of its denial of the existence of ideal forms that can, by being apprehended, be causally efficacious in the world.

### Philosophy of Mathematics

The field called the philosophy of mathematics, for example, might not even exist apart from the nominalism of late modern thought. The problem for phi-

35. Searle, *Minds, Brains, and Science,* pp. 86, 88, 92-93, 98.

36. See Richard M. Weaver, *Ideas Have Consequences* (Chicago: University of Chicago Press, 1948).

37. Dawkins, *The Blind Watchmaker: Why the Evidence of Evolution Reveals a Universe without Design* (New York and London: Norton, 1987), p. 43.

losophers of mathematics is set by the following twofold fact. On the one hand, mathematicians in practice behave as "unabashed realists," presupposing that they are "thinking about 'real objects.'"[38] On the other hand, philosophers of mathematics are plagued by what can be called the "Platonic problem" and the "Benacerraf problem."

The Platonic problem is how and where mathematical objects — as nonphysical, merely ideal objects — could exist in an otherwise purely material universe.

The Benacerraf problem — named for Paul Benacerraf, who raised it[39] — is how mathematical knowledge could be knowledge of Platonic mathematical forms. This problem arises because true beliefs can be considered knowledge, Benacerraf pointed out, only if that which makes the belief true is somehow causally responsible for the belief. But to be an abstract ideal form is, as Penelope Maddy puts it, "to be causally inert. Thus if Platonism is true, we can have no mathematical knowledge."[40] Reuben Hersh asks, rhetorically: "How does this immaterial [Platonic] realm relate to material reality? How does it make contact with flesh and blood mathematicians?"[41] However, when philosophers and mathematicians, in the light of these problems, reject the Platonic view of mathematical objects in favor of the view that mathematicians simply invent them, they fail to do justice to the realism about these objects that mathematicians in practice presuppose.

### Philosophy of Logic

Exactly the same problems exist for the philosophy of logic because, as Hilary Putnam points out, "the nature of mathematical truth" and "the nature of logical truth" are one and the same problem.[42] However, if philosophers, because of the Platonic and Benacerraf problems, reject the idea that logical principles somehow exist in the nature of things, they are implying, as Charles Larmore has pointed out, that the idea that we ought to avoid self-contradiction is

38. Y. N. Moschovakis, *Descriptive Set Theory* (Amsterdam: North-Holland Publishing Co., 1980), pp. 605-6.

39. Paul Benacerraf, "Mathematical Truth" (1973), in *Philosophy of Mathematics,* ed. Paul Benacerraf and Hilary Putnam, 2nd ed. (Cambridge: Cambridge University Press, 1983), pp. 402-20.

40. Penelope Maddy, *Realism in Mathematics* (Oxford: Clarendon, 1990), p. 37.

41. Reuben Hersh, *What Is Mathematics, Really?* (New York: Oxford University Press, 1997), p. 12.

42. Hilary Putnam, *Words and Life,* ed. James Conant (Cambridge: Harvard University Press, 1994), p. 500.

merely a preference, with no inherent authority. None of us can really believe, Larmore points out, that the rule that we ought to avoid self-contradictions has no more authority than we choose to give it.[43]

## Moral Philosophy

These same problems have created havoc in moral philosophy. On the one hand, as John Mackie admitted, "most people in making moral judgments implicitly claim . . . to be pointing to something objectively prescriptive."[44] On the other hand, "[t]he difficulty of seeing how values could be objective is a fairly strong reason for thinking that they are not."[45] Accordingly, "There are no objective values."[46] This means, for example, that "if someone is writhing in agony before your eyes," the idea that you should "do something about it if you can" is *not* an "objective, intrinsic, requirement of the nature of things."[47]

Gilbert Harman also uses the Platonic problem to deny objective norms: "Our scientific conception of the world has no place for entities of this sort."[48] Harman appeals to the Benacerraf problem as well, saying that "there does not seem to be any way in which the actual rightness or wrongness of a given situation can have any effect on your perceptual apparatus."[49] He concludes, therefore, that "there are no absolute facts of right or wrong, apart from one or another set of conventions."[50]

## Nominalism and Atheism

The modern acceptance of nominalism has, as we have seen, created problems in many areas of thought besides the philosophy of evolution. Some of the phi-

43. Charles Larmore, *The Morals of Modernity* (Cambridge: Cambridge University Press, 1996), pp. 99, 87.

44. John Mackie, *Ethics: Inventing Right and Wrong* (New York: Penguin Books, 1977), p. 35.

45. Mackie, *Ethics*, p. 24.

46. Mackie, *Ethics*, p. 15.

47. Mackie, *Ethics*, pp. 79-80.

48. Gilbert Harman, "Is There a Single True Morality?" in *Relativism: Interpretation and Confrontation*, ed. Michael Krausz (Notre Dame, Ind.: University of Notre Dame Press, 1989), pp. 363-86, at p. 366.

49. Gilbert Harman, *The Nature of Morality: An Introduction to Ethics* (New York: Oxford University Press, 1977), p. 8.

50. Harman, *The Nature of Morality*, pp. 131-32.

losophers involved in this discussion have pointed out that the rejection of Platonic realism regarding mathematical, logical, and moral principles depends on the presumption of atheism. Reuben Hersh, for example, has said: "For Leibniz and Berkeley, abstractions like numbers are thoughts in the mind of God. . . . [But] the Mind of God [is] no longer heard of in academic discourse. . . . Platonism without God is like the grin on Lewis Carroll's Cheshire cat. . . . The grin remained without the cat."[51] John Mackie, describing his book as "a discussion of what we can make of morality without recourse to God," added: "I concede that if the requisite theological doctrine could be defended, a kind of objective ethical prescriptivity could be defended."[52]

## Whitehead's Platonic Theism

It was precisely because of this twofold problem, which I have called the Platonic and Benacerraf problems, that Whitehead first, after having long been agnostic or even atheistic, came to affirm the existence of an actuality he thought worthy of the name "God." Having long focused on mathematics and logic, he was keenly aware of the need to affirm the real (but nonactual) existence of what he came to call "eternal objects." At first, while holding a somewhat Spinozistic worldview, he suggested that such objects could exist by being "envisaged" by the "underlying eternal energy."[53]

Soon, however, he revised his doctrine on the basis of what he came to call the "ontological principle," which he also called the "Aristotelian principle."[54] According to one version of this principle, "Everything must be somewhere; and here 'somewhere' means 'some actual entity.'" Whitehead's solution to the Platonic problem, therefore, followed the solution pioneered by middle Platonists, after Aristotle's criticism of Plato's ideas — namely, putting them in God. Whitehead hence completed the thought begun in the previously quoted sentence by saying: "Accordingly the general potentiality of the universe must be somewhere. . . . The notion of 'subsistence' is merely the notion of how eternal objects can be components of the primordial nature of God." "[E]ternal objects, as in God's primordial nature," Whitehead said, "constitute the Platonic world of ideas."[55]

51. Hersh, *What Is Mathematics, Really?* p. 12.
52. Mackie, *Ethics,* p. 48.
53. Whitehead, *Science,* p. 105. This passage reflects Whitehead's position when he delivered the Lowell Lectures in February 1925, before he had developed his first doctrine of God, which is reflected in chapters 10 and 11.
54. Whitehead, *Process and Reality,* p. 40.
55. Whitehead, *Process and Reality,* p. 46.

If this first version of his ontological principle solves the Platonic problem, a second version responds to the Benacerraf problem of how these nonactual entities can be efficacious. According to this second version, "the search for a reason is always the search for an actual fact."[56]

Applied to eternal objects, this principle means that eternal objects can supply reasons for the nature and behavior of things because the "primordial nature of God" is "the active entertainment of all ideals, with the urge to their finite realization, each in its due season."[57] As he put it elsewhere, "the agency whereby ideas obtain efficiency in the creative advance" is "a basic Psyche whose active grasp of ideas conditions impartially the whole process of the Universe," thereby making these ideas "persuasive elements in the creative advance."[58]

Although Whitehead named the all-inclusive psyche in which the eternal forms subsist "God," those for whom this term has been ruined beyond repair can use various alternatives. Whitehead himself, in his later books, used other terms, such as the "Eros of the Universe" and the "Divine Eros."[59] The basic idea is that the universe as whole, by having a dominant member, is the ultimate compound individual. One Buddhist who follows Whitehead on this point speaks, accordingly, of "the wholeness of the universe" or, alternatively, of "the universe considered in its unity."[60]

## Physical Prehension as Nonsensory Perception

The Benacerraf problem has another dimension: Even if ideal forms are being presented with causal efficacy to all creatures in the universe, how can those forms be perceived? Our sensory organs are suited only for perceiving aggregational societies of enduring objects — the kinds of things that in common parlance are called "physical things." Just as we cannot see another human psyche, even if we open up the skull, we also cannot see the psyche of the universe.

Whitehead's solution to this problem — along with many other epistemological problems — involves one dimension of his alternative to naturalism$_{sam}$. The subscript "sam," it will be recalled, stands for "sensationist-

56. Whitehead, *Process and Reality*, p. 40.
57. Whitehead, *Adventures of Ideas*, p. 277.
58. Whitehead, *Adventures of Ideas*, pp. 147, 168.
59. Whitehead, *Adventures of Ideas*, pp. 11, 277.
60. Jeremy W. Hayward, *Perceiving Ordinary Magic: Science and Intuitive Wisdom* (Boulder, Colo., and London: Shambhala, 1984), p. 241.

atheist-materialist." We have already seen that Whitehead's version of naturalism replaces materialism with panexperientialism. We have also seen that he replaces atheism with a type of theism that will be called "panentheism" below.

For now the point is that his naturalism also replaces the sensationist doctrine of perception, according to which we can perceive things beyond ourselves only with our sensory organs, with a prehensive doctrine of perception, according to which sensory perception is derivative from a more basic, nonsensory mode of perception. This nonsensory mode of perception is simply that basic operation with which every actual occasion begins, called "physical prehension." Given this doctrine, he can say that there is a "prehension by every creature of the . . . appetitions constituting the primordial nature of God."[61]

On this basis, Whitehead can explain our experience of normative ideals — whether moral, aesthetic, logical, or other types of ideals: "There are experiences of ideals — of ideals entertained, of ideals aimed at, of ideals achieved, of ideals defaced. This is the experience of the deity of the universe. The universe is thus understood as including a source of ideals. The effective aspect of this source is deity as immanent in the present experience."[62]

## Panentheism as Naturalistic Theism

Many scientists and science-based philosophers have, like the pre-Socratic philosophers, assumed that belief in all divine beings had to be rejected to have a worldview that would support science. However, Whitehead, like his hero Plato, reintroduced deity in order to make science possible.[63] That move would have been counterproductive, of course, if the reintroduced deity had been one who intervened in the world, thereby replacing a naturalistic worldview with a supernaturalistic one.

### The Rejection of Creatio ex Nihilo

Many scientists who find belief in God to be in conflict with science come to this judgment because of the doctrine of God they have learned. They understand the term "God" to refer to a supernatural being who can occasionally in-

---

61. Whitehead, *Process and Reality*, p. 207.

62. Whitehead, *Modes of Thought*, p. 103.

63. David Ray Griffin, *Two Great Truths: A New Synthesis of Scientific Naturalism and Christian Faith* (Louisville: Westminster John Knox, 2004), pp. 4-5.

terrupt the world's normal causal principles and processes. This understanding is bound up with the doctrine of *creatio ex nihilo*. Whitehead, however, explicitly rejected the "theology of a wholly transcendent God creating out of nothing an accidental universe."[64] Newton's affirmation of that doctrine, Whitehead pointed out, implied that our world had "a definite supernatural origin."[65]

Whitehead, instead, reaffirmed Plato's view that the creation of our world "is not the beginning of [finite] matter of fact but the incoming of a certain type of social order."[66] In other words, the creation of our world several billion years ago was not the beginning of the realm of finitude; it was merely the beginning of our "cosmic epoch."[67] This means that, rather than thinking of "God" as referring to a wholly independent being, who could exist without a world, Whitehead portrayed not only "the World as requiring its union with God" but also — in the language of the time — "God as requiring his union with the World."[68]

### God and Metaphysical Principles

In harmony with Dorion Sagan's apparent endorsement of the idea of "God as a lawful eternal being of which we are part," Whitehead's panentheism says both that we dwell within the divine being and also that there are principles that this divine being cannot violate. "[T]he relationships of God to the World," Whitehead wrote, should be conceived to "lie beyond the accidents of will," being instead "founded upon the necessities of the nature of God and the nature of the World."[69] The lawfulness of Whitehead's deity is expressed most famously in the dictum that "God is not to be treated as an exception to all metaphysical principles, invoked to save their collapse," but as "their chief exemplification."[70] Whitehead's naturalistic theism, I have emphasized, means "that God cannot occasionally interrupt the world's causal nexus."[71] This is a metaphysical, not merely a moral, "cannot." The reason God does not interrupt is not, as some theologians have suggested, because God has made a moral pledge not to do so, but because it belongs to the very nature of God to be in interaction with a world involving metaphysical principles, and such principles, by definition, cannot be interrupted.

64. Whitehead, *Process and Reality*, p. 95.
65. Whitehead, *Process and Reality*, p. 93.
66. Whitehead, *Process and Reality*, p. 96.
67. Whitehead, *Process and Reality*, p. 91.
68. Whitehead, *Adventures and Ideas*, p. 168.
69. Whitehead, *Adventures and Ideas*, p. 168.
70. Whitehead, *Process and Reality*, p. 343.
71. Griffin, *Reenchantment without Supernaturalism*, p. 230.

Because of the importance of this point, I wish to note that some of the language in John Haught's exposition of Whitehead's theology is misleading. That is, he says God "permits" natural selection ruthlessly to eliminate maladaptive forms of life,[72] as if God could, if God only would, prevent this. One of the most popular solutions to the problem of evil in recent times has indeed been a "voluntary free will defense," according to which God has voluntarily accepted self-limitations in order to allow the creatures to have genuine freedom. But this move, while slightly alleviating the problem of evil, by no means solves it — a point I have made in several places.[73] The Whiteheadian doctrine, in any case, is that it is impossible in principle for God to interrupt the world's basic causal processes. This doctrine is equally important for theodicy and for the relation of science to theology.

## Naturalism$_{ppp}$

On the basis of the above points, we are now in position to give Whitehead's version of generic naturalism a name to distinguish it clearly from naturalism$_{sam}$. The sensationism of that view, we have seen, is replaced by Whitehead's prehensive doctrine of perception; its atheism is replaced by Whitehead's panentheist view of the universe; and its materialism is replaced by Whitehead's panexperientialism. We can, accordingly, name his doctrine prehensive-panentheist-panexperientialist naturalism, or simply "naturalism$_{ppp}$."

Although many thinkers, such as John Haught, often write as if naturalism as such can simply be equated with naturalism$_{sam}$, to do so is to commit the fallacy of equating a genus with one of its species. Naturalism as such — generic naturalism — is simply naturalism$_{ns}$, the rejection of supernaturalism. Naturalism in this generic sense is embodied in naturalism$_{ppp}$ as fully as it is in naturalism$_{sam}$. To continue to write and speak as if naturalism can simply be equated with naturalism$_{sam}$ perpetuates the false notion that to reject naturalism$_{sam}$ is necessarily to advocate supernaturalism.

72. Haught, chapter 19.

73. David Ray Griffin, *God, Power, and Evil: A Process Theodicy* (Philadelphia: Westminster, 1976), chapter 13; *Evil Revisited: Responses and Reconsiderations* (Albany: State University of New York Press, 1991), chapters 1, 2, 5; "Process Theology and the Christian Good News: A Response to Classical Free Will Theism" and "In Response to William Hasker," in *Searching for an Adequate God: A Dialogue between Process and Free Will Theists*, ed. John B. Cobb, Jr., and Clark H. Pinnock (Grand Rapids: Eerdmans, 2000), pp. 1-38 and 246-62.

## Whiteheadian Evolution and the
## Fifteen Doctrines of Neo-Darwinism

I will conclude by pointing out how a theory of evolution based on Whitehead's naturalism$_{ppp}$ could provide a mediating position between neo-Darwinism and Intelligent Design. I will do this by pointing out that such a theory would reject most but not all of the fifteen doctrines of neo-Darwinism, as listed in chapter 17.

### Doctrines 1-4

A Whiteheadian theory of evolution would accept the first four doctrines. The first two, microevolution and macroevolution, are scientific doctrines — in the sense of being empirically testable — and the evidence for each surely leaves the matter beyond any reasonable doubt (even though the doctrine of macroevolution obviously cannot be subjected to the kinds of laboratory tests possible for microevolution). The Whiteheadian worldview is established as a version of evolutionary naturalism, or naturalistic evolutionism, by its acceptance of these two doctrines in combination with the metaphysical doctrines of naturalism$_{ns}$ and ontological uniformitarianism.

### Doctrine 5

Whitehead fully rejected, however, the twofold doctrine we have called "positivism-materialism." According to positivism, only ideas based on sensory perception can be allowed into a theory of evolution. In contrast, Whitehead's prehensive doctrine of perception, while equally insisting that all fundamental notions must be empirically rooted in the sense of being based on direct perception, understands the deepest level of perception to be nonsensory. This doctrine not only explains the origin of our notions about actuality, causation, and the past but also allows notions about mathematical objects, logical principles, and moral norms. By the same token, it allows the notion of a cosmic agent to explain the causal efficacy of these and other eternal objects, usually called Platonic forms.

   As these examples show, the rejection of sensate positivism is likewise a rejection of materialism, understood as the dictum that science's ontology must be limited to material objects (objects that can, at least in principle, excite our sensory organs). This rejection, like the rejection of positivism, opens the way to the affirmation of Platonic forms and of an actual entity — perhaps understood as the universe as a whole — that provides them with a home and agency.

The rejection of materialism in favor of panexperientialism allows, moreover, the replacement of mind-brain identism with Whitehead's nondualistic interactionism. This move, besides providing a basis for explaining both human freedom and the unity of our conscious experience, also allows, in principle, for the survival of the psyche after bodily death. Whitehead suggested, accordingly, that the question of the reality of such survival could be affirmed if there is reliable empirical evidence for it.[74]

### Doctrine 6

Many suppose that science must assume that all processes, including the behavior of humans and other animals, are fully determined by antecedent causes and hence are predictable in principle. That assumption is true of the movements of aggregational societies, the kind of objects studied by Newtonian mechanics. But the doctrine of panexperientialism with organizational duality provides a basis for rejecting the idea in relation to the behavior of compound individuals. This is not predictable, even in principle, and this unpredictability becomes increasingly greater in the higher animals, due to the increased importance of the mental poles of their dominant occasions. This doctrine shows that although the slight degree of self-determination present at the quantum level is canceled out in aggregational societies, such as billiard balls, it is amplified in living compound individuals. It thereby provides the basis for the rational-moral freedom exemplified by human beings.[75]

### Doctrines 7-8

As I have shown at length elsewhere,[76] Whitehead's rejection of nominalism provides a basis for modifying neo-Darwinian gradualism. Although this point

74. Alfred North Whitehead, *Religion in the Making* (1926) (New York: Fordham University Press, 1966), p. 111. I have discussed this question in David Ray Griffin, *Parapsychology, Philosophy, and Spirituality: A Postmodern Exploration* (Albany: State University of New York Press, 1997); *Religion and Scientific Naturalism: Overcoming the Conflicts* (Albany: State University of New York Press, 2000), chapter 7; and *Reenchantment without Supernaturalism*, chapter 6.

75. "Compound Individuals and Freedom," in Griffin, *Unsnarling the World-Knot*, chapter 9.

76. Griffin, *Religion and Scientific Naturalism*, pp. 298-308.

is too complex to be adequately explained here, the basic ideas can be summarized.

As we have seen, neo-Darwinism has ruled out saltational changes because of the extreme unlikelihood that a jump involving several simultaneous changes would ever, just by chance, result in a viable species. A Whiteheadian theory, however, need not regard such jumps as purely accidental. It can hold, instead, that they are made in response to forms that serve as "attractors" by virtue of being appetitively entertained in the primordial nature of God. This divine influence does not involve supernaturalism, because it is formally the same as the divine influence that is involved in all events.

As such, this divine influence is an attempt to lure creatures to actualize the best possibilities (eternal objects) open to them. Whitehead explicitly connects this Platonic doctrine — that creatures participate in eternal forms — with the "well-marked character of nature" illustrated by the "sharply distinguished genera and species which we find in nature," with its "almost complete absence of intermediate forms."[77]

This doctrine is a modification, not a rejection, of gradualism. Saltations occur only in the outer form, the phenotype, which would always involve actual entities as objects — as prehended by others. Divine influence, however, always works on actual occasions as subjects of experience. Insofar as divine influence is able to persuade an organism to actualize new forms, the new forms are always closely related to forms that had been previously actualized by that organism. Accordingly, as I wrote elsewhere under the heading "Inner Gradualism and Outer Saltationism": "Although there is a saltational change in the outer world, the change that has been going on behind the scenes, which is the only change that the divine appetitions can directly influence, has been gradualistic."[78] This doctrine, accordingly, retains Darwin's intuition that change, to be naturalistic, must be gradual.

Ian Barbour is nervous about this part of my suggestion, partly, at least, because I connect it with approval of one aspect of Michael Behe's criticism of neo-Darwinian gradualism, and this is important, Barbour says, because Behe's writing has been used by evangelical Christians to support their efforts to have "Intelligent Design" included as an alternative to evolution. I have made clear my rejection of this use of Behe's idea. But I also maintain that the fact that Behe's point has been used this way (perhaps by Behe himself) does not mean that if we believe there is an element of truth in his position, we should shy away from stating it for fear of guilt by association. And if, as I have suggested,

77. Whitehead, *Process and Reality*, p. 95.
78. Griffin, *Religion and Scientific Naturalism*, p. 304.

there is a position that states an intelligible middle ground between neo-Darwinism and Intelligent Design, it must include at least one element that has been employed by those fostering Intelligent Design. Such an element, I have proposed, is the rejection of neo-Darwinian gradualism, which is an *extreme* gradualism based on nominalism and atheism, in favor of the idea that new forms can come into the world with the aid of divine influence.

This does *not* mean, as Barbour suggests, that I accept "Behe's claim that . . . living systems . . . cannot be the product of gradual evolution." As I said above, I am proposing "a modification, not a rejection, of gradualism." The "inner gradualism and outer saltationism" I have suggested is very different from the kind of divine changes envisaged by proponents of Intelligent Design. Barbour also says, "Many evolutionary advances can be understood as a combination of components already available rather than as the introduction of a total system designed from scratch," as if that were relevant to my position. But surely I have made clear my Whiteheadian rejection of creation out of nothing — that is, from scratch.

Barbour also objects to my position as a form of "essentialism." But the fact that essentialism is now widely rejected does not mean that every doctrine that can be given that name is to be rejected. I have argued that Whitehead, at least, believed that a doctrine of eternal forms — which can be called essences — is necessary to have an intelligible philosophy of mathematics, logic, and morality. I am unclear if Barbour, with his negative comment about essentialism, meant to reject that dimension of Whitehead or only the kind of application of this dimension of Whitehead's philosophy to biological evolution that I have suggested.

Even if it is only the latter, however, I pointed out that Whitehead himself made this application, referring to the "well-marked character of nature," with its "sharply distinguished genera and species." Whitehead's idea may of course be wrong, and further study might show that transitional species are the rule rather than the exception. My point, however, is that since thus far this has not proved to be the case, it may be helpful to have a philosophy of nature that, while being fully naturalistic, allows for the possibility of changes that are larger than those that can be thought, in Dawkins's words, "to have come into existence by chance." Barbour worries that such a doctrine will "minimize the role of contingency in evolutionary history." We should, however, have no a priori commitment to the idea that the evolutionary process is as fully contingent as the neo-Darwinian worldview implies. It may well be that a philosophy of evolution that makes the process a little less contingent might be necessary to make it more intelligible and more in accord with the evidence.

## Doctrines 9-10

A Whiteheadian theory would have no a priori commitment to the assumption that macroevolution must result solely from the processes that occur in the kind of evolution — microevolution — that can be observed in laboratory experiments, which can be assumed to consist simply of natural selection operating on variations that are "random" in every possible sense. One example of an additional causal factor, divine influence, was discussed in the prior paragraphs.

Another example, which Whitehead's philosophy does not rule out a priori, is the kind of change usually called "Lamarckian," in which an inheritable change can be induced by the organism's need or desire.[79] Richard Dawkins, in response to the idea that desires or purposes could introduce a bias toward mutations of a certain sort, has said that "nobody has ever come close to suggesting any means by which this bias could come about."[80] What Dawkins means, however, is that intellectuals who share his materialist-mechanistic worldview would be unable to envisage such a means. From the perspective of Whitehead's notion of compound individuals, however, such a process is not inconceivable, because every entity at every level can be influenced by every other entity at every level. Whitehead even, in response to the idea that a gene is "a pellet of matter [that] remains in all respects self-identical whatever be its changes of environment," referred to evidence that "genes are modified in some respects by their environments."[81] I have elsewhere discussed prima facie evidence for the reality of this kind of change.[82] If this evidence is confirmed, thinkers informed by Whitehead's philosophy would have no a priori reason to reject it.

Ian Barbour, in responding to this discussion, has faulted me for suggesting that Whitehead's philosophy "would allow a novel form prehended by the psyche of an animal to be taken directly into its genome." In the sentence he quoted, however, I said, after discussing the Baldwin effect, only that Whitehead's position "can allow that an organism's need or desire might more directly lead to change in the genome."[83] To be more direct than the very indirect route involved in the Baldwin effect is not necessarily to be altogether direct and hence unmediated. The influence might well be mediated through one or more parts of the bodily system. That this would have been Whitehead's view is suggested by his statement, quoted earlier, that "the plan of the whole influ-

79. See the discussion of neo-Lamarckian phenomena by A. Y. Gunter, chapter 6.
80. Dawkins, *The Blind Watchmaker*, p. 312.
81. Whitehead, *Modes of Thought*, p. 139.
82. Griffin, *Religion and Scientific Naturalism*, pp. 272-76.
83. Barbour, chapter 13.

ences . . . the plans of the successive subordinate organisms." My point was simply that there is nothing in Whitehead's philosophy to exclude the possibility of this more direct kind of influence on the genome, so that if good experimental evidence for such influence is provided, there would be no reason to declare that it could not possibly be what it seems to be.

Barbour's criticism seems to be based in part on Weismann's dogma ruling out such influence. At the outset of his essay, Barbour says: "Weismann showed that germ-line cells are sequestered from somatic cells and are not affected by any changes during the life of the organism." But Whitehead, as I pointed out earlier, explicitly rejected the idea of genes as impervious to influences from the larger organism they are in. Having rejected that idea, Whitehead said: "Thus no a priori argument as to the inheritance of characters can be drawn."[84] From a Whiteheadian perspective, therefore, the question of whether such inheritance occurs should be a purely empirical question, settled by the relevant evidence.

### Doctrine 11

The fact that Whitehead rejected the idea that evolution is entirely undirected is inherent in his theism. On the kind of directedness involved, Whitehead suggested that God, understood as the Eros of the Universe, primarily seeks "beauty," understood as experience that combines harmony with intensity.[85] The more intense the experience, the greater the beauty and hence the intrinsic value (assuming that the experience is able to combine its components in a harmonious way). Luring the world to produce ever more complex compound individuals has been the primary means to this end. In Whitehead's words, "God's purpose in the creative advance is the evocation of intensities. The evocation of societies is purely subsidiary to this absolute end."[86]

### Doctrines 12-15

All four of the moral-religious implications of neo-Darwinism are reversed. Whitehead's panentheism, which replaces neo-Darwinism's atheism, provides two bases for regarding the universe as meaningful. On the one hand, our world

---

84. Whitehead, *Science*, p. 79.
85. Whitehead, *Adventures and Ideas*, pp. 252-53.
86. Whitehead, *Process and Reality*, p. 105.

reflects a divine purpose. On the other hand, every value that is achieved is then preserved everlastingly in God's receptive side, called the "consequent nature of God."[87] Another possible dimension of meaning is provided by the fact, mentioned earlier, that Whitehead's rejection of the materialist identification of the mind with the brain allows life after death to be affirmed, if it is supported by trustworthy evidence.

Besides not being meaningless, the universe is not amoral. Our notions about moral norms can be taken as objective, in the sense of reflecting divinely rooted moral ideals. As we saw earlier, Whitehead, after pointing out that we have "experiences of ideals," added: "This is the experience of the deity of the universe."[88] Also, rather than regarding the world as meaningless because undirected, he described God as "the poet of the world," leading it in terms of a "vision of truth, beauty, and goodness."[89]

Neither is the universe — to come to the fifteenth doctrine — devoid of progress. There is a standard by which to assess progress, thanks to the divine purpose. And by that standard — the emergence of creatures capable of experience characterized by increasingly greater intrinsic value — the evolutionary process has clearly brought about enormous progress.[90]

## Summary

Whitehead's philosophy, I have suggested, provides the basis for a mediating position between neo-Darwinism and Intelligent Design. Like the latter, the Whiteheadian view regards our world as reflecting intelligent purpose. It endorses this idea, however, while fully agreeing with neo-Darwinism that our world came about through an evolutionary process understood naturalistically, with no supernatural assistance at the beginning or anywhere along the way.

87. Whitehead, *Process and Reality*, pp. 345-51.
88. Whitehead, *Modes of Thought*, p. 103.
89. Whitehead, *Process and Reality*, p. 346.
90. As I mentioned in chapter 17, Francisco Ayala has helpfully pointed out that although the progress, measured by such a standard, has been neither uniform nor universal (occurring in all lines), there has been net progress in some lines.

# 23. What God Does

JOHN B. COBB, JR.

This book centers around two questions. First, what is this evolving world really like? Second, if we who worship God are not entirely deluded, what does the One we worship do in this evolving world? Process theists think that, for theists, these two questions must be answered together to arrive at a coherent view of God and the world.

We assume that relative coherence is religiously helpful and scientifically desirable as well. By coherence we mean not merely that our beliefs avoid contradicting one another but also that they fit well with one another, even illumine one another. That is why we cannot rest with dualisms, such as those of Descartes and Kant that disconnect different parts of the world or of knowledge of the world from one another.

## Science and Theology

We think the modern Western world has suffered a great deal from having largely given up the effort to attain coherence a couple of centuries ago. We think that evolutionary thought should have helped to restore the quest for coherence but that, too often, it has exacerbated the problem instead. Too often scientists have committed themselves to metaphysical materialism, and theists, to supernaturalist interventionism.

If the problem is to be eased, theology must be revised in light of science. Beliefs that were reasonable and acceptable in a prescientific world are not reasonable and acceptable now. This is not just a pragmatic and historically relative matter. We have learned a great deal from science that will not prove reversible. This learning is a permanent gain that is to be deeply treasured. To deny it or to ignore it, or even to relativize it as simply the way one culture thinks about the world, means that we choose to live in ignorance or self-deception. The earth really is one of the planets that circles the sun. Atoms really can be broken up into constituent parts. All the living creatures that inhabit this planet are descended from bacteria that lived here billions of years ago. Our rapid use of fossil fuels really is an important factor in global warming.

Of course, we can play the skeptic's game and rightly point out that human knowledge is never complete, exact, or incorrigible. One can note that since motion is relative, it is possible to view the motion of the earth in a different way and say that its motion around the sun is not a perfect circle. The language of "breaking" an atom or "constituent parts" is not felicitous. It is possible that eukaryotic cells have emerged from bacteria more than once. The exact extent of global warming and whether it may actually lead to a new ice age are still unsettled questions. We will adjust our beliefs as more is known. Accordingly, some reformulation may be legitimately required in the formulations above. But should we ever return to prescientific views, that will be because humanity has lost its passion for truth, its capacity for disciplined study and thought, or its ability to learn from the past. Religiously speaking, we must hope that does not occur.

The vast majority of theists accept the vast majority of what scientists teach. It is only occasionally that they resist. Christian theology adjusted to Aristotelian science when that was the best available. It has made many adjustments to modern science as well. Even the acceptance of Kantian dualism, the view that faith and science deal with quite separate spheres, was a drastic revision of theology in response to science. Theologians need the help of scientists in adjusting theology to the growing body of knowledge provided by scientists in many fields. The necessity of change on the theological side can hardly be questioned.

The situation on the scientific side is different. Especially in the seventeenth century, theological beliefs played a large role in motivating scientists and even in formulating scientific findings. Most scientists were deeply religious persons. Today we would view Newton as a religious fanatic. As late as the nineteenth century, many of the leading scientists, at least in England, were clergymen. In general the church was at least as hospitable to modern science as was the university. For the most part, through this long period, churchmen and scientists, even when they were not the same people, shared a common worldview.

As I noted in the introduction, the idea of a long series of battles between scientists and the church is a serious misreading of history. The reality is that the church has been remarkably supportive of science despite its demands for theological adjustments. Further, the toleration of scientific change by the church was not because the church was generally tolerant during that period. Theological heretics were treated harshly, and sometimes tortured. There were religious wars. Tens of thousands of women were slaughtered for supposedly practicing witchcraft. But no scientist was killed for new scientific teaching.

The one story that became famous when scientists began to oppose the church was the silencing of Galileo. But the major quarrel there was among scientists. The scientific establishment thought Galileo was wrong. It refused to examine his evidence. The church wrongly accepted the authority of that establishment. Even today the scientific establishment sometimes refuses to examine evidence for theories that conflict radically with the established worldview. Even today the church sometimes wrongly accepts its authority.

Darwin's theory of evolution brought about the first significant conflict between scientists and the church. Even on that point, this formulation is misleading. Darwin's teaching caused more debates among scientists and within the religious community than between the two communities. Although many believers objected to Darwin's theory, the mainstream Protestant churches accepted the right of scientists to teach it and began the process of adjusting theology to take account of it. During most of the twentieth century, biological evolution as a general fact has been taken for granted by almost everyone teaching in seminaries of what were, until recently, the mainstream Protestant churches.

Still, it is true that many conservative Christians opposed the doctrine as they understood it, and the Protestant denominations that express these antievolutionary views have flourished. Their political influence has increased dramatically in recent decades. Today the conflict between this branch of Protestantism and the dominant scientific community is serious.

## Revising Science

One thesis of this book is that scientists have contributed to this problem in ways not required by science. The dominant formulations of the theory of evolution are in fact offensive to believers. If theological acceptance of evolution as a reality requires complete agreement with hard-core proponents of neo-Darwinism, it would mean self-destruction on the side of theistic faith. That, of course, is what some of the hard-core scientists want. But then they should not complain when believers oppose their monopoly on the teaching of evolution in the public schools. The reason for keeping religion out of public schools is not to give free rein to antireligious teaching.

If the empirical facts could be understood only in the most rigid neo-Darwinian way, then they would indeed require the final surrender of Christian faith. But the reader of this book should understand by now that this is not the case. There are good reasons for asserting that there is in reality much that the purely objectivist scientific method cannot treat. Some of this book has been devoted to showing that there is also *scientific* evidence for much that hard-core neo-Darwinists have failed to integrate into their theory. Further, as Griffin has clearly shown,[1] many of the hard-core neo-Darwinian doctrines follow from materialistic metaphysics rather than from empirical research. The scientific aspects of evolutionary theory could be formulated against the background of a different metaphysics without loss to science. Indeed, it is the belief of process thinkers that science itself would gain from this change.

Unfortunately, the statement that their formulations express a particular metaphysics offends many scientists. Few scientists in the United States are well educated in the history of Western thought, including that of science. Since they were taught science with certain concepts and assumptions, they have assumed that these reflect the inherent nature of science rather than metaphysical convictions adopted by most scientists since the latter part of the seventeenth century. Even the breakdown of these concepts and assumptions in physics has had little effect on biologists. Nevertheless, the restoration of peace between people of theistic faith and teachers of evolutionary doctrine in public schools in the United States depends on reexamination of the metaphysical assumptions that, especially when applied to human beings, are so offensive.

Some process thinkers have long been engaged in showing the value of using a different metaphysics in theology. We have not been successful in persuading large segments of the theological community to adopt process thought as a whole. Yet a good many of the beliefs that process theologians derive from Whitehead's metaphysics have commended themselves to many in the community of believers. This is true of much of what I say in this essay about how God works in the world. Many of our ideas have turned out to be acceptable to other theists on biblical grounds, for example. It is our hope that more scientists will be persuaded that it is scientifically responsible to think of the world as having those characteristics that allow for interpretation in terms of process thought, even if they do not require it.

## Acknowledging the Role of Subjectivity

The first requirement is that scientists acknowledge and affirm that people are subjects and agents who act and are acted upon; who have purposes, hopes, and

---

1. Chapters 17 and 22.

memories; who make decisions and are responsible for what they decide; and who, in and through all of this, influence the behavior of their bodies and, through them, events in their environment. The exact formulation of all this is discussable, but the basic ideas are hardly negotiable for humanists and religious people. The resistance of scientists to these affirmations comes from their metaphysics rather than from their empirical data. Indeed, as human beings, they actually think and act as if all this were so.

The second requirement is for scientists to give up those assumptions and formulations that contradict this view of human subjects. That would be a considerable adjustment for some of them. It would certainly require changes in the way evolutionary theory is taught.

A third adjustment would follow. Since evolution indicates that human beings are part of the natural world and evolved gradually out of it, our kin in the animal world should be studied on the assumption that they, too, are subjects sharing in some of the characteristics of human subjectivity. Of course, much about human beings is no doubt emergent and cannot be generalized to other animals. But evolutionary scientists should acknowledge continuity in the subjective realm as they do in the objective.

An important question here is whether scientists who acknowledge the subjectivity of animals should include it in their science. I will explain below why I think this belief should affect their theories. Nevertheless, inclusion of the subjective in science is not a requirement for peace.

For practical purposes in daily life, virtually all scientists do think in these ways. Therefore, what I ask of them does not seem unreasonable. Unfortunately, in the past two centuries, beginning especially with Hume and Kant, Western thinkers have learned to bracket their personal, ineradicable beliefs in order to achieve philosophic and scientific rigor. Hume taught us that the only reality is what is given to us in sense experience, that is, the world of appearance, consisting of a phenomenal flux. Kant taught us that the human mind is the creator of this world. The metaphysical belief that the world is clocklike was also shared by both thinkers and survived their epistemological changes. Today many tell us that the world is entirely composed of human language, or that reality is purely socially constructed.

No one actually believes any of these things. People know they are bodily, for example, and that their pets have feelings. Whatever language they use and however they construct their worlds, both they and their pets will need food. But some of the most sophisticated do not admit this knowledge into their theories. They have committed themselves to metaphysical principles that are in conflict with lived reality. The current clash between science and humanism is but one symptom. It will not be easy to undo the damage done by bad metaphysics.

Please note that what I take to be the minimum requirement for peace includes the acknowledgment that, at least in the human case, what happens subjectively affects what happens objectively. I decide to type a word, and my fingers generally type it. An explanation of what my fingers do that omits my decision is an incomplete explanation. If scientists choose, as they well may, to continue to omit it, they should recognize that their explanations of what happens in the physical world are incomplete. As long as they then acknowledge that science does not give an exhaustive account of reality, this is a legitimate choice on their part. It is an example of a human decision that profoundly affects the course of events.

Furthermore, if there is as much continuity between human beings and other animals as process thinkers and most evolutionists believe, then scientists should recognize that an account of animal behavior that omits animal subjectivity is also incomplete. From the point of view of process thought, this is true even for bacteria. Indeed, "decisions," in the root sense of "cutting off," can be attributed to quanta. Quanta, too, cut off some possibilities in order to actualize themselves concretely.

Evolutionists might recognize all this and still hold that the purely materialist account of the origin of species is complete. If this account includes only the random mutation of genes and the selective force of a physical environment, then the activity of animals is in effect excluded from relevance. If the activity of animals is excluded as a variable explanatory of evolution, then obviously the subjectivity of animals can play no explanatory role.

I believe that I have shown that there is a great deal of evidence that the activity of organisms plays a significant role in evolution.[2] The fondness for an account that excludes this variable results much more from metaphysical prejudice than from a broad survey of the evidence. If it is then acknowledged that the observable behavior of animals can be influenced by subjective factors, the incompleteness of a materialist account of evolution is apparent. This is true even if we ignore, as we should not, human evolution and human manipulation of the genes of other organisms.

It is the dread of openly acknowledging basic incompleteness that theologians must ask scientists to overcome. It has too often led to denying the existence of what scientists cannot measure, or at least to asserting that what is omitted cannot have any effect on what they study. It is not given to human beings to have final, exhaustive knowledge of all things, and when the methodology of a discipline is carefully restricted to one range of data, incompleteness is inevitable. A little humility is an essential ingredient in wisdom. The failure in

---

2. See chapter 14.

so much of science to make its limitations clear is, from a Whiteheadian perspective, a massive instance of the fallacy of misplaced concreteness.

Of course, the resistance of many scientists to acknowledging the role of subjective experience is partly a reaction to the dogmatism of many religious people who seek to inject nonscientific ideas into the formulations of science. While the focus of this book is on the dogmatism of scientists rather than on that of religious people, the reality and political importance of the latter are unquestionable. This book must itself be understood as a reaction, and therefore as one-sided. It is a reaction to what appears to be complacency on the side of scientists and many of their liberal supporters about the limitations in their formulations and assumptions. The justification for emphasizing the need for change on the side of scientists is that a careful, scientifically and philosophically responsible critique of the dominant theory of evolution is what is particularly needed at the present juncture.

## Contingency

Haught and Schloss emphasize that evolutionary theory itself requires both necessity and contingency.[3] Some evolutionists prefer to think that the contingency is simply ignorance with respect to necessity. Others believe contingency lies in the actual events, that it is ontological. The worldview Haught and Schloss advocate affirms both epistemological and ontological contingency.

The version of that worldview that I propose distinguishes, in addition, two kinds of ontological contingency. There are, presumably, physical causes of the mutations of genes. The contingency lies in the relative independence of the causal sequences involved. We may say that it is by chance that a particular cosmic ray strikes the earth where a particular gene is located. That does not mean that there is anything contingent about the movement of the cosmic ray or about the location of the gene. But the chains of events involved in the coming of the cosmic ray and in the location of the gene are almost entirely unrelated. Hence their intersection is contingent in relation to either sequence.

There is another kind of contingency. At the quantum level this has been much discussed. In the process view this contingency is a real character of the quanta. Just what a quantum will be and do is decided only when it happens. There is a definite outcome, but what that outcome *is,* is not decided until it occurs. This introduces real contingency into the world.

Process thinkers see human experience in a similar light. Of course, much

3. Chapters 19 and 20.

about what I am and do at each moment is the result of what I have been and done in the past and of my immediate environment. If a scientist knew enough about me and my context, she could predict a great deal. To say that I have freedom is in no way to deny the many causal forces that shape me. I am very largely the product of my social experience, of events in my body, including my genes, and of my past learning.

Nevertheless, I cannot live or act as if that were the whole story. I also organize what I receive from the past in somewhat changing ways. I see alternative paths and take one rather than another. In short, exactly what I become moment-by-moment is decided moment-by-moment. It is not decided until it happens. This means that although forces now at work already determine many aspects of the historical future, exactly what will happen is still open in very important respects. The preparation of this book is motivated by the belief that just how science and religion will relate to each other in the future is still not fully decided. The hope of influencing that relation is not wholly groundless, although any confidence that the ideas in the book will significantly mediate the current disputes would be unrealistic.

There are many instances in which the decision of an individual has had vast consequences. There was a point in time when Socrates did not have to drink the hemlock and Jesus did not have to die on the cross. If they had made other decisions, the course of Western history would have been different. In the twentieth century the decisions of Gandhi and Hitler, of Mandela and George W. Bush, and of Stalin and Gorbachev, to name a few, have made large historical differences. Even though much about the future is already determined, decisions are real, and the actual course of history is radically contingent.

Further, human decisions have a major effect on evolution. The extinction or survival of hundreds of thousands of species depends upon them. The modification of existing species and the creation of new ones do also. These changes will have unforeseen effects on the biosphere as a whole. Scientists may want to ignore all this, since examining it depends on taking human subjectivity into account. But if this is their choice, that decision will also have consequences. These consequences will be much worse if scientists do not acknowledge that they are neglecting much of great importance about the course of physical events. We will all be better off if scientists expand their horizons to include human subjectivity even though this introduces contingency even more forcefully into their calculations.

To introduce subjectivity into science is not wholly unprecedented. Scientific psychology is not limited to behaviorism and physiological psychology. Even in the latter field, some of the leading practitioners have decided that they should recognize that conscious experience is a causal factor in what happens in the brain.[4] Students of animal behavior often cross the line into subjectivity in their formulations.[5] Charles Hartshorne wrote a substantial and thoroughly researched study of birdsong to show that one determinant of how much birds sing is their enjoyment of singing.[6]

But, to repeat, the alternative choice is acceptable. I would prefer that scientists extend their interest to the subjective sphere, recognizing that this heightens the contingency of their conclusions. But the choice to restrict themselves to the world as given to them through their sense organs is acceptable if those who do so recognize that this omits a great deal that is critically important. In either case, they need to acknowledge that what science can explain is still far from all the details of any event. What humanists and religious people cannot accept is the limitation of science to the objective sphere combined with the claim that scientific knowledge deals with the whole of reality.

## Objects, Subjects, and God

What does all this have to do with God? Not much directly, but quite a lot indirectly. If we look for divine causality in the objective world to which science usually limits itself, that is, to the sphere of sense data, we cannot find it. The most we can find are phenomena that are not adequately explained by accounts based entirely on these sense data. This can open the door to positing God as intervening at these points. But the only evidence that God does so is that a gap currently exists in the explanatory account. Actually we can form no intelligible concept of God's acting as an agent in this objective sphere in such a way as to fill this gap. God's act would have to be in competition with natural causes and yet of an order wholly different from them. Any such explanation is necessarily offensive to scientists and hardly intelligible to believers.

In any case, it usually turns out, on further study, that an explanatory account of these phenomena can be found, or at least posited, much like those provided for other phenomena. The real explanatory gaps get larger as we move to more complex animal organisms, and especially to human beings. The "scientific" account of my typing these words, as long as it omits any reference to

4. Roger Sperry, *Science and Moral Priority: Merging Mind, Brain, and Human Values* (New York: Columbia University Press, 1983).

5. Donald Griffin, *The Question of Animal Awareness: Evolutionary Continuity of Animal Experience* (New York: Rockefeller University Press, 1976).

6. Charles Hartshorne, *Born to Sing: An Interpretation and World Survey of Bird Song* (Bloomington: Indiana University Press, 1973).

my subjectivity, leaves a large gap. But it seems more reasonable, at least initially, to posit my thinking and deciding as explanatory than to fill the gap with an act of God.

Nevertheless, this does bring us into a sphere where assigning a role to God is intelligible. In the subjective world the possibility, even the plausibility, of affirming God's efficacy is much greater. Many factors other than physical causes seem to influence our decisions. These include the thinking and feeling of other people. Subjects affect subjects. I think and feel as I do largely because of the way other people have thought and felt. To locate God in a world of subjects is much more intelligible than to try to locate God in a world of objects. Even ancient scriptures warn against the latter effort, and all serious theists reject any idea that God is to be understood as an object of human sense experience. For the theist, God is a subject. We do have some idea about how one subject influences another.

As long as basic habits of thought are materialist, relegating God to the sphere of subjects is virtually to dismiss the relevance of God to the "real" world. But there are good reasons to reverse that judgment. What are thought of as objective are appearances to the sense organs of others. In other words, to be an object is to be an object for some subject. Objects cannot exist simply in and of themselves. As Kant saw, science, if it limits itself to objects, studies only appearances or phenomena, not reality.

Kant also saw that in the world of appearances causes of any kind do not appear. That we cannot avoid attributing efficient causes to the events in the world, Kant taught, is because of the structure of the human mind. Whitehead taught that efficient causes are real, but they operate in the subjective sphere of actuality, not in the objective sphere of appearance. My present experience comes into being only as past events participate in shaping it. They are efficient causes of my present experience. Whitehead generalized this model. Every event in the physical world is what it is by virtue of the way past events participate in constituting it. But this moment of the constitution of the event does not appear to us as an object. Our sense organs are affected only by the completed event.

Accordingly, from the point of view of process thought, the actual world, the world in which efficient causality operates, is the world in which events come into being, the world of subjects. What appears to subjects are, at the most fundamental level, past subjects. It does not make sense to think of God acting on these appearances. If God acts in the world, it is in the actual world of subjects. This action will indirectly affect the way these subjects appear to future subjects, hence, indirectly, God, like other efficient causes, affects objects as well.

Whitehead taught that God is a factor in the becoming of every subject. If God acted in some and not in others, this might lead to gaps, but if we reflect seriously on the nature of the divine contribution to the ongoing processes in the world, this makes no sense. God may be a subject as we are subjects, but God is not one finite subject among others. All other subjects are momentary occasions of experience. God is the subject that grounds all others. There can be no finite subjects apart from God.

## God and Natural Law

This idea of God as the ground of all things has been central to the Abrahamic theological tradition, although it is explained in many ways. Whitehead's account is both rich and distinctive. I will offer a brief pointer to his thinking about God and the world, starting with the idea of natural "law."

We begin with our own experience in the present moment. There is, actually, nowhere else that any reflection can begin. However, most reflection begins with very limited elements of this immediate experience. Whitehead calls for an effort to understand it as a whole.

For the most part the present occasion of my experience is a synthesis of all the events in its past. These include past personal experiences along with the neuronal events taking place in my brain. These mediate many other influences from other parts of the body and, through them, from the external world. There may also be some direct experience of other people, especially of their emotions. For the most part, what my experience in that moment becomes will be the outgrowth of all of that.

Most of science is a study of the way in which the past determines the present. But science does not study this on a case-by-case basis as if no regular patterns were exemplified in this causality. On the contrary, much of science is a search for these patterns or "laws of nature." When the particular event is subsumed under the "law," it is understood to be scientifically explained.

Actually "law" is a very mysterious and misleading term. It comes from politics, the judicial system, and theology. The ruler makes laws. In the seventeenth century it was supposed that God also made laws. The subjects obey. It was thought at one time that God was the ruler of the universe, and that all things obeyed God's laws. It could then be supposed that through these laws God directly compelled every physical entity to act according to the divine will. The notion of physical laws made sense.

But that idea works for few scientists today. They do not want to include God in their sciences. So what do they mean when they say that something "obeys" the "laws" of physics? Probably there is some vague notion that the laws exist somewhere and exercise some force upon the physical entities. But that makes little sense. A "law" as such is far too abstract to exercise force. What is most directly meant is that entities of certain sorts consistently behave in certain ways. Careful philosophers of science speak of "lawlike" behavior. How is this to be explained?

Whitehead thought that many laws were descriptive generalizations. They summarize the habits of nature and are statistical in character. This is true of "laws" of animal behavior. These habits may first come into being culturally but later be genetically fixed.[7]

Whitehead thought "habits" applied to aspects of the behavior of lower-grade entities as well. A member of an electromagnetic field acts in terms of what all the other members of the field have been doing for billions of years. Their lawlike behavior is the fixity of the well-established "habits" of electrons and protons inherited by each new member of the electromagnetic society. Efficient causes play the overwhelmingly dominant role.

Still, these "habits" are developed within a limited range of possibilities. Those limits still remain to be explained. Some may be derived from larger fields or societies of which the events are members. But the limits of possibility are given for all entities in the cosmos. We cannot explain all regularities simply as contingent habits of species of natural entities.

The extreme case of limits is found in the cosmological constants. These are not derivable from the behavior of creatures but rather set limits to what these creatures can be and do. They are given for the creatures. Thus what we call "laws" lie on a continuum between unconditional limits that are simply given and statistical generalizations based on how creatures of a certain sort behave within those limits. Although even the latter presuppose some givenness of limits, they can basically be understood in terms of the causality of the past shaping the present. This is fundamental to Whitehead's vision, but it does not explain all regularities of behavior. What is the status of the "laws" that are more than descriptive of the results of efficient causation, the "laws" that are "given"?

My formulation of these questions points to the same aspect of reality that Van Till treats more fully in chapter 21. The universe has all the potentialities needed for the remarkable welter of living things to appear and function. It is "fully gifted," having all the "right stuff." We should marvel at this fact. Nothing in "nature" explains it; instead, it explains "nature." It is taken for granted by scientists.

---

7. I discussed animal culture in chapter 14.

Whitehead's understanding of this right stuff was in terms of a sphere of potentiality, which might today be called a potentiality space, distinguished from the sphere of actuality but informing it. Every form exhibited in the actual world is included in the potentiality space, but so are many forms that have never been actualized. These potentialities are ordered and, consequently, give rise to regular patterns of behavior.

So far we are speaking only of "laws" that must be "obeyed." This would suggest that every real possibility relevant to the situation in which an event is coming to be includes some one pattern even though, in pure abstraction, alternative patterns are possible. This ordering of what is abstractly possible to exclude most of it from any relevance to what happens is what Whitehead called the principle of limitation. Without limits nothing could happen. Concrete actuality always involves a limitation among abstract potentialities. Therefore, the ordering that limits can also be called the principle of concretion. Thus the principle of limitation or of concretion is the ground of order in the sense of regularity.[8]

For Whitehead, however, order is not primarily regularity; it is that arrangement that enables values to be actualized. The order among the molecules in a cell cannot primarily be described in terms of regularity. It is this order, primarily, that is supported and encouraged by the patterning of the forms or abstract potentials.

However, there is still a problem. The order of potentialities is introduced to explain the limits of what is possible in the actual world. But pure potentials are purely abstract. How do abstractions have an effect on what is actual? One might say that, in the human case, we can imagine them and be attracted or repelled by them, but at best we are influenced only occasionally by such imagination, whereas the potentials are constantly shaping our existence. And they are shaping every photon and quark as well. The order of potentiality must have agency.

Whitehead solves this problem by naming the ordering of potentialities and its agency in the world "the Primordial Nature of God," and interpreting God as an *actual* entity, and therefore a subject. The immanence in the world, in every event as it comes into being, of this supreme subject makes the order of potentiality effective. It provides every creature with its potentialities and its limits on the basis of an ordering that has always been and will always be. This order is not temporal; it is primordial. But it functions differently in each instance according to the actual situation in that moment. This order is radically transcendent in the sense that it does not depend on, and is not limited by, the actual world. But it gives direction to the world only by its radical immanence.

8. Alfred North Whitehead, *Science and the Modern World* (New York: Free Press, 1925).

This understanding of the grounds of "law" explains both the absolute laws, the constants, and also the conditional laws. The "laws" of molecular behavior came into being only when there were molecules. They arose out of the actions of molecules within the limits established by preexisting stable patterns or "laws" combined with the primordial constants. Accordingly, new "laws" are coming into being as evolution proceeds, but they do not require that God think up new laws when the situation changes. The order of possibility, or what is possible under what circumstances, remains unchanged.

## God and Self-Determination

Thus far I have spoken only of regularity and established patterns. Yet my formulations suggest that exact regularity is not the most interesting feature of the order. If, as Whitehead and I and, for practical purposes, almost everyone believe, human beings are not totally determined in our behavior, if we make decisions, then the ordering of possibility establishes some range of possibilities as relevant to the situation in which we find ourselves moment by moment. The range remains very limited in relation to the totality of what is abstractly possible. But it establishes that there is more than one way in which one can integrate what one receives from the past and orient oneself to the future. The primordial order renders relevant to the particular situation possibilities that one does not derive from the past. Hence there is genuine novelty in life. One decides among real alternatives. One is responsible for that decision. Thus the primordial ordering of potentials, the principle of limitation and concretion, is also the source of novelty, of self-determination, and of responsibility.

If the alternative possibilities were merely neutral, this would still not explain our sense of making decisions that are better and worse. Whitehead's response is that the primordial ordering is for the sake of eliciting value, that is, richness of subjective experience. The possibilities are weighted accordingly. The best choice may be experienced as threatening and costly. One may not decide for it. Then one may be aware of having missed a real opportunity. Whitehead judged that a transcultural experience of human beings is the sense of "a rightness in things, partially conformed to and partially disregarded."[9] There is no dualism of good and evil, but there are real differences between better and worse.

Our actual resultant experience is of a great flood of influence from our world and our past combined with responsibility as to how we deal with it. We have freedom within narrow limits. We have deeply entrenched habits, but we

9. Alfred North Whitehead, *Religion in the Making* (New York: Macmillan, 1926), p. 66.

are not completely bound by them. This is because in addition to the causality of the past we also experience God's influence, and this both limits us and frees us within those limits. How we use our capacity for self-determination, limited as it is, makes a real difference for us and for others. Any account of human behavior that denies or obscures the role of decision is truncated, even though it may throw light on real causal factors otherwise ignored or neglected.

I have presented God's role in regard to self-determination chiefly in human experience. But, once again, the assumption is that human beings are fully part of the natural world. What God does in human beings, God does, in some analogous way, for all animals. All conform to the constants and to other more conditional laws as well. But do all also derive from God, moment by moment, some alternative potentials for self-determination? Whitehead's answer is affirmative. Every actual occasion of animal experience has possibilities for self-constitution among which it decides.

Whitehead's understanding of evolutionary continuity goes further still. The entire world is constituted of actual occasions. At present these may be thought of primarily as the quanta. These, like animal experiences, are constituted largely by their relationships. Yet exactly how they are constituted does not seem to be predecided. It is decided only when it happens. If we can use the idea of self-determination without any suggestion of conscious choice, we can follow Whitehead in attributing self-determination to quantum events as well.

It would be dangerous to exaggerate the similarity between a human experience and a quantum of energy, but at a very fundamental level, Whitehead emphasizes, they are both instances of what he calls "creativity." In both, the many (past events) become one; that is, they are freshly synthesized. The new event is then part of the past for later ones. Both quanta and human experiences thus receive from the past, integrate what they receive, and contribute to the future. In doing this, both are affected by God's ordering of potentials.

## Directionality in Evolution

I have not tried to prove the existence of God to any who do not want to believe. I have only described an extremely important functioning of God in the world that is coherent with, even explanatory of, what scientists find and postulate and, at the same time, has rich meaning for the believer. So far as I can see, it offers no threat to the integrity of science. But it would lead one to expect and look for some directionality of the sort sought by Haught and Schloss,[10] some

10. Chapters 19 and 20.

tendencies to convergence in different evolutionary lines, and a considerable contingency in the course of events.[11] In Whitehead's view, God's aim in ordering potentials is the evocation of value in the world of subjects. The balance of necessity and contingency and of regularity and novelty provided by God is directed to that end.

Religious people may see some modest analogy to an earthly parent. A good parent sets some limits for children, but over time these limits are expanded. The results vary greatly. Children make many mistakes. Some end up in self-destruction. But maintaining tight control too long also has negative, sometimes disastrous, consequences. The analogy is to God's role in bringing into being species with greater and greater capacity for self-determination, culminating, as far as this planet is concerned, with human beings. The risk is great. Humans may render the planet uninhabitable. But the possibility of increased value in the universe is also great.

Schloss goes to great lengths to show that there are discernible trends in biological evolution.[12] He is viewing matters objectively. For a Whiteheadian any such objective trends reflect the fact that God's aim at the realization of value introduces into every actual occasion the aim to achieve some immediate value. Intrinsic value characterizes all subjects. But the experience of some subjects is more complex than that of others, and accordingly is capable of attaining greater value.

Before proceeding with the description of how value increases, it may be important to note important qualifications. Two are especially important because they play major roles in the actual course of events. First, the achievement of value in one momentary event and thereby in the organism of which it is a part is often at the expense of losses by other organisms. This is dramatically illustrated in the predator-prey relationship, which is very important in evolution. When the predator is successful, it attains valuable experience for itself. However, the prey suffers, and the possibilities of future valuable experiences are cut off. In this instance, over time it seems that there may be some increase in the capacity of members of both species for the realization of value. But any depiction of the whole process that neglects the suffering that is central to it would be profoundly misleading.

Second, the parasitical relationship, which is also common in the biological world, is still more destructive of any simple notion of the goodness of the process. In the predator-prey relationship one may console oneself by supposing that the time of the suffering of the prey is short compared with its life as a

---

11. See Barbour, chapter 13.
12. Chapter 20.

whole and that usually the predator kills those members of the species that are past their prime. No such consolation is possible for the parasitical relationship. The host, which would otherwise be healthy and strong, often suffers protractedly as it unwillingly provides habitat and food for the parasite. There are no counterbalancing gains for the affected species. Further, the degree of value in the parasite's experience may be much less than that of which the host would otherwise be capable.

Third, the actual attainment of greater value depends on physical conditions that may end. Life, where much greater value is found than in the inanimate world, can emerge only under particular physical conditions. A Whiteheadian expects that, given God's role in the universe, where such conditions obtain, life will in fact appear, and that where the physical conditions allow, it will proliferate and evolve. But conditions change, and these changes may be profoundly unfavorable to life. There is nothing about the way God functions in the world that prevents massive loss of life, including whole species of life. There have been global catastrophes in the past. Eventually, presumably, life as such will end on this planet. Human activity could bring about this end billions of years before physical changes in the cosmos cause it. God calls and urges us humans to cease our suicidal behavior, but there is no assurance that we will follow this lead.

It is extremely difficult if not impossible to reconcile facts of these kinds with some features of traditional theism. A God who controlled the world and acted in these ways can hardly be described as loving all the creatures. Many scientists reject this kind of God for excellent reasons and then understand themselves to be atheists. If this is atheism, we Whiteheadians are also atheists. But simply rejecting God leaves unexplained the basic character and functioning of nature. It also leaves unexplained many of the profound experiences and intuitions, moral and spiritual, that characterize the theistic traditions.

We believe that God is one factor in the subjective becoming of every occasion of experience. This factor establishes the constants to which all events conform. Beyond this its role is to enable that occasion to integrate its past in a way that achieves some immediate value. What can happen in the inanimate world is almost entirely a function of just the past that is integrated. Hence, most of what happens in the visible events in the inanimate world tells us very little, in any direct way, about the character of God. An earthquake is exhaustively explained as geologists are wont to do. God's presence in the individual quanta has a negligible effect on these vast movements of the earth in which trillions of quanta are involved.

On the other hand, at the opposite extreme, we can discern God's influence in history in the decisions of individual saints to act sacrificially for the sake of others. Most such decisions, of course, are hardly noticed; but others, such as those of Mahatma Gandhi, Martin Luther King, and Nelson Mandela, change the course of history. To recognize that God does not control earthquakes is not to declare God irrelevant to the course of events. Between these extremes we discern God's influence in much less dramatic, but quite pervasive, ways in all living things.

That living things try to continue to live is widely recognized. For Whitehead this aim is derived from the divine aim at the realization of value. He adds that organisms aim not only to live but also "to live well, and to live better." This means that they do not aim simply to repeat the past. Their aim to live well and to live better opens them to novel decisions that contribute to the possibility of realization of greater values. This general character of living things underlies the role of the activity of organisms in biological evolution. I emphasized this role in chapter 14. God's role in ordering the sphere of potentials to limit and to guide the self-determination of actual occasions operates here.

In general we theorize that there is a positive relationship between complexity of organization and the amount of value it supports. In plants we suppose that the value is realized in the individual cells. In many animals the order supports the emergence of a central experience distinct from that of the cells. This central experience, as in the case of the human psyche, is of much greater value than any individual cellular experience.

Further, the more valuable experiences have greater variability. More novelty is possible. This means that the divine urge to realize value can have a greater effect in more complex organisms. A Whiteheadian expects to find an acceleration of evolutionary change as time passes.

The influence of the subjective on objectively observable events greatly increases as the role of learning becomes more important. There is evidence that bacteria learn, but we judge that learning plays a far more important role in vertebrate animals. It expresses the aim to live better, that is, to realize greater value.

## Science and God

Theists should not ask scientists to say anything about the grounding of either necessity or contingency. They can simply assert them, or seek explanations of them that do not involve God. They can continue to talk about "laws" without asking how they function. They certainly do not need to speak of God, and they can point out difficulties in this metaphysics.

On the other hand, scientists do not need to attack this understanding of God and of how God works in the world in order to defend their freedom as scientists to follow their evidence to the end. Scientists do not need, for the sake of science, to repeat metaphysical views that exclude the possibility of freedom, novelty, decision, and responsibility, and, hence, morality. They do not need to deny that God is a factor in creaturely experience. In short, they do not need to commit themselves to a materialistic metaphysics with all its problems. As long as they exclude subjectivity from their purview, that kind of metaphysics may work reasonably well. But if they insist on affirming this metaphysics, then they must expect opposition from those who believe that the acceptance of their position would entail denial of all human values.

## Whitehead and a Theistic Understanding of God

Van Till noted that his idea that God provided a universe with all the right stuff seemed to many of his believing hearers closer to deism than to theism. Much of what I have said resembles this teaching of a right stuff universe. It is like deism in that it focuses on a unique act of God that is presupposed by all that takes place, and it rejects supernatural intervention in the course of events.

Yet, even here Whitehead's thinking differs from common formulations of deism in that the act is "primordial." Deists locate God's one act in the remote past, so that God seems very distant from us now. For Whitehead God's act is taking place *now,* in every now. God is *now* the giver of order and novelty, of the ability and necessity of self-determination or freedom, and of the grounds of morality. God's gift is different in every moment and founds every new event. How God acts in each moment depends on how creatures have acted. The biblical images of interaction between God and creatures are justified.

Another important difference is in Whitehead's understanding of how this one act affects individual creatures. Deistic imagery suggests that laws operate externally. For Whitehead God operates internally to each creature. God is "prehended" or felt by each creature in and through those possibilities relevant to that creature's unique situation. This immediate experience of God is foundational to every creature and directs every creature in a distinctive way. This is rarely conscious even among those creatures in which consciousness occurs. When this profound reality of God's presence within each of us does tinge consciousness, that experience takes on a religious character of a theistic type.

The theistic aspect of Whitehead's cosmology goes beyond this. For Whitehead there is more to God than the ordered realm of potentiality, which he names the "Primordial Nature." He speaks also of the consequent nature.

God as an actual entity is "consequent" with respect to the course of creaturely events in the sense that as they happen, God is affected by them. God is compassionate with every emerging occasion, feeling its feelings.

God is not only the organ of order and novelty for the world, God also takes the world into the divine life. We experience God. God experiences us. We are affected by God. God is affected by us. In God we live and move and have our being. In God nothing is lost. What is ephemeral in the world is everlasting in God.[13]

Once again such a belief is not scientifically or philosophically proven. Far from it. No scientist is required to accept it. But nothing in this belief restricts the freedom of the scientist or conflicts with scientific findings and theories.

Whitehead shows that his idea of God's consequent nature is not only consistent with his speculations about the nature of all things, from quanta to human beings, but is also coherent with them. All actual entities are affected by other actual entities. If God is an actual entity, it is plausible to suppose that this applies to God as well.

Further, the affirmation of God's consequent nature is explanatory of some aspects of widespread religious experience. It saves us from the always-threatening nihilism. It provides us with the assurance that God rejoices with us in our joy and suffers with us in our suffering. In Whitehead's words, "God is the great companion — the fellow sufferer who understands."[14]

At the very end of *Process and Reality*, Whitehead's magnum opus, he suggests that there is still more to the divine-human relation. He never develops the idea, and even process theologians do so somewhat hesitantly. Nevertheless, the idea remains as a lure for development where the evidence of religious experience supports it.

Whitehead writes that the consequent nature of God floods back into the world as "the particular providence for particular occasions."[15] No longer are we thinking only of how we benefit from God's primordial ordering of potentiality with a view to the maximization of value in the world in general. Whitehead is here pointing to a far more intimate and personal relation.

There is much in the Bible and the Christian tradition with which this resonates. The main problem is that there have been so many irresponsible claims to special revelation and special guidance that any idea of "particular

13. Alfred North Whitehead, *Process and Reality: An Essay in Cosmology* (1929), ed. David Ray Griffin and Donald Sherburne, corrected ed. (New York: Free Press, 1978), part 5, chapter 2.

14. Whitehead, *Process and Reality*, p. 351.

15. Whitehead, *Process and Reality*, p. 351.

providence" has fallen under suspicion. Even seemingly authentic cases raise the question why God seems to act in such a way more in some instances than in others. Also, the idea could be developed in a way that might seem to conflict with the proper claims of science.

This book is not the place for a serious theological discussion of this topic. I mention it here only to say that those for whom this intimate personal relation with God is religiously important should know that accepting White-head's metaphysics is not an obstacle to belief that such relationships are real. Although his metaphysics does not imply them, it does not exclude their possibility.

I noted earlier that this kind of thinking about God emerges in other contexts than the study of Whitehead's philosophy. I want to end this chapter and the book by quoting from the concluding paragraphs of an essay by Niels Henrik Gregersen, professor of systematic theology at Copenhagen University. He is far better versed than I in the literature of biology and especially of the philosophy of biology and the science/theology dialogue. Accordingly, he uses the contemporary language of information and self-organization, which was not available to Whitehead, but which is certainly congenial to his thought.

> At any moment God is co-experiencing and remembering the experience of the trial-and-errors of God's creatures, and at any moment God is present for the creatures in their coping with the future. . . .
>
> A naturalistic orientation to theology is driven by the intrinsic commitment of Christian faith, that there is only one source of being and life: God, and that God is actively present in and for all natural events.
>
> The unity of God and nature [implies] that from the moment of creation, God cannot be subtracted from the world of nature. *Finitum capax infiniti:* The finite is capable of hosting the infinite, as an old Lutheran maxim says. The transcendence of [God] is . . . displayed . . . especially in the features of openness and self-transcendence. . . .
>
> In this view, the place of God as creator is not outside nature but within nature. The more self-productive the creatures are, the more God is at work in and through these creatures. Even though God cannot be confined to scientific informational structures in matter, God should not be thought as working as an external agent in relation [to] such local patterns of information. Rather God is the Divine Pattern that is the wellspring of any concrete pattern-formation in evolution, and hence is the underlying source of novelty during evolution.[16]

16. Niels Henrik Gregersen, "The Complexification of Nature," *Theology and Science* 4, no. 1 (March 2006): 22, 25-26.

# Appendix: The Metaphysics
of Consciousness and Evolution

ROBERT J. VALENZA

I hope, in the first half of this paper, to bring the classical metaphysical boundary that divides the physical from the mental, spiritual, or merely experiential into sharper relief so that we can watch more carefully for anything sneaking across it. More specifically, we begin by looking at the notion of supervenience in the abstract, using a slightly complex but elementary illustration of the concepts that serve as background for what follows. We move on from there to the critical matter: the separation of the physical (here meaning the domain of discourse of physics) from whatever might be its complement, in part by appeal to basic notions of process metaphysics. In this context the issue of consciousness as it has been approached recently by David J. Chalmers yields a key insight that becomes the point of departure for the second half of our analysis. It is here that I attempt to introduce a general framework for the possible resolution of the problem of dualism, one that is almost inevitably structurally congenial to Whitehead and makes use of insights gleaned from within science itself. Not in the least coincidentally, the proposed framework accommodates a speculative discussion of the metaphysics of evolution, and it is with this that we conclude.

## Supervenience and Dualism in the Abstract

We begin with an example and variations of sufficient clarity and complexity to help us fix terms and concepts that will be much needed later. In this spirit, let me introduce Petal World I, which is no more than an ever-changing sequence of repetitions of the same flowerlike symbol. For example:

```
          * * *
      * * * * * * * * *
        * * * * *
    * * * * * * * * * * * * *
      * * * * * * * *
        * * * *
          * *
           *
        * * * *
```

**Fig. 1. Petal World I**

One should think of each line fully representing the state of this neat little world at each succeeding tick of some discrete master clock: sometimes more flowers, sometimes fewer flowers, and so the pattern evolves. The flower characters themselves seem structured, but this feature is, for the moment at any rate, beside the point. All we have at each stage is the barest individuation (by position) of otherwise identical symbols. Thus Petal World I, with regard to its constituents at least, could hardly be simpler.

An easy exercise in counting shows that Petal World I could hardly be simpler with regard to its evolution (or state trajectory) either! In fact, I have here shamelessly co-opted a numerical sequence that will be familiar to most students of computer science. Starting with whatever seed count (initial state), one proceeds thus: if the count is odd, multiply by 3 and add 1; if it is even, divide by 2. This particular instance of Petal World I begins with 3 and grows and shrinks as we see. Its evolution is thus fully determined by its initial state and an underlying law. To use a word that will seem more appropriate subsequently, Petal World I is fully supervenient on these two properties, and we shall say accordingly that they serve as a supervenience base for this world.

Let us now pass to the closely related universe of Petal World II, which, in at least one incarnation, might look like the illustration on the following page.

Look closely at the petals. What has happened here? We have the same skeletal process, but suddenly the symbols reveal two distinct internal or fine structures, albeit held constant across all objects that appear in any given cohort. In the first stage of this revised example, each solid petal has been replaced by a domino version; in the second stage, we find an alternation of solid and

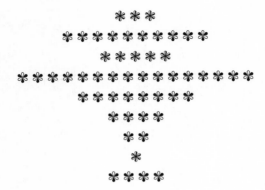

**Fig. 2. Petal World II**

"hollow" petals. Note carefully that to an observer unable to discern these newly introduced fine structures, Petal World II would be utterly indistinguishable from Petal World I: the underlying count sequences are identical.

While something new has indeed been added here, one sees almost immediately that the rule that determines the fine structure is almost trivial: even object counts maintain the alternating pattern; odd object counts maintain the domino pattern. It is clear that the totality of Petal World II remains fully supervenient on the same two properties cited above, augmented only by the odds and even rule; put otherwise, it admits essentially the same supervenience base as previously insofar as the new rule is still dependent on that same object count property.[1]

Let the genesis of our next construction, Petal World III, commence. At first blush, this looks pretty much like its predecessor, but clearly the rules governing the fine structure have changed. Since it is key to the basic point of these examples, I hope the reader will not find too tedious the explanation of just

---

1. More generally, I will say that a collection of properties $B$ serves as a supervenience base for a class of properties $C$ (which might include the entire world state) if $C$ is supervenient on (completely entailed by) $B$. (See David J. Chalmers, *The Conscious Mind* [New York: Oxford University Press, 1996]. Note that in this paper I do not need his distinction between logical and natural supervenience except incidentally below.) Students of linear algebra are no doubt in a state of high alert at this choice of terminology, and thinking about the mathematical terms' linear independence, spanning set, basis. (See, for instance, Robert J. Valenza, *Linear Algebra: An Introduction to Abstract Mathematics* [New York: Springer Verlag, 1993].) On this analogy, I might have used the term "spanning set" where I speak of a supervenience base and might have called a minimal spanning set a supervenience basis. These refinements do seem worthwhile to me, but unnecessary to present purposes.

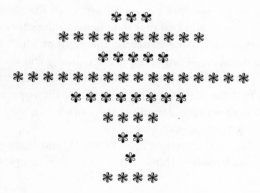

**Fig. 3. Petal World III**

what defines the internal structure of Petal World III. If *A* denotes the alternation variant and *D* the domino variant, the sequence is this:

> *A, D, A, D, A, D, A, A, D* . . .

This is hardly enough to determine any underlying rule uniquely, but let me nonetheless describe the rule I did use, for it is far removed in form from that used to generate the object counts. Recall that an integer greater than 1 is called composite if it admits a proper factorization and prime if it does not. Thus, for example, 6 is composite because it admits the factorization $2 \times 3$, but 5 is prime because it only admits trivialities like $5 = 1 \times 5$. The sequence of primes begins with 2 and, while it may not be obvious, it is nevertheless elementary that it goes on forever:

> 2, 3, 5, 7, 11, 13, 17, 19, 23, 29, 31, 37, 41 . . .

The trick of the fine sequence structure of Petal World III is to jump into this sequence at 5, to divide every subsequent entry by 3, and then to record the remainder (which must be 1 or 2):

> 2, 1, 2, 1, 2, 1, 2, 2, 1, 1, 2 . . .

At this point we need only substitute *D* for 1 and *A* for 2 to obtain the sequence above. In this case we definitely cannot, in any plausible sense, say that we have the same supervenience base, since the fine structures are governed by something entirely novel; in fact, in a clear sense this secondary property does not depend on a single number but on an aspect of the natural numbers in their entirety. We have to add two new data items to the supervenience base of Petal World I to explain the fine structure: the point at which we enter the sequence of prime numbers — anything greater than 3 will do — and the rule that associates a prime with one of the two possible fine structures. This is not to say, however, that the two items that constitute the supervenience base of Petal World I are without considerable explanatory value: they still entirely determine the object counts at each stage.

We pass to our final variation, Petal World IV, and again I ask the reader's patience, in this case because I think we need two subexamples. Consider then Petal World IV-a:

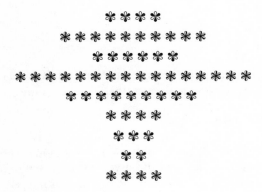

**Fig. 4. Petal World IV-a**

This looks like Petal World III but fattened up a bit, and it is not at all difficult to understand the rules. Object counts belonging to stages that manifest fine structure A have been augmented by 1; object counts belonging to stages that manifest fine structure D are left as previously. The underlying count structure is thus more or less the same, but now only approximately supervenient on the two properties that define Petal World I.

The last and more radical case is Petal World IV-b. (Note that we were forced to a multiline display on the final iteration, and the final result is this beautiful pagoda-like figure; the last two object counts are 29 and 88.) Indeed, amazingly little has changed by way of the underlying rules. But whereas in Petal World IV-a we applied an adjustment that depended on the fine structure to the underlying sequence (3, 10, 5, 16, 8, 4, 2, 1, 4) used to define Petal World I, in this modified case the adjustment was incorporated into the next iteration of the ba-

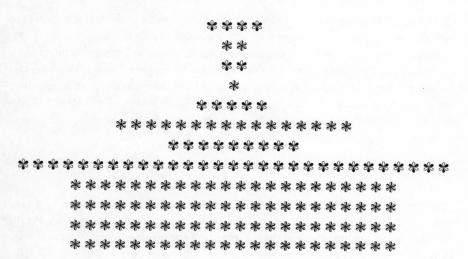

**Fig. 5. Petal World IV-b**

sic transformation. We can describe this more precisely by walking through and comparing the object count calculations for the first few iterations of Petal Worlds IV-a and IV-b. Keep in mind the basic principle for the count transitions from Petal World I: if odd, multiply by 3 and add 1; otherwise, just divide in half.

## Calculations for IV-a

In its initial state the seed number is 3, but the fine structure state is *A*, and hence object count is incremented to 4. Nonetheless, the underlying 3 is passed on to the next iteration of the process and yields the number 10. Since the fine structure is in state *D* for this iteration, the object count remains at 10. In any case, 10 is passed on to the next iteration of the algorithm and yields the number 5. The fine structure is back in state *A*, so the object count is incremented to 6. Nonetheless, it is the number 5 that is passed forward.

## Calculations for IV-b

As above, the seed number is 3, the fine structure state is *A*, and hence object count is incremented to 4. But in this case it is the resulting 4 that is passed on to the next generation. This yields 2, which remains unadjusted because we are in state *D*. This 2 is passed on to the next iteration, where it yields the number 1, which in this case is incremented to 2 by virtue of the fine structure state. The number 2 (not the number 1) is passed forward. That small change renders the two items that previously served as a supervenience base for at least the object count property radically ineffective: one must absolutely reckon with the fine structure to make any sense of this world. Yet, in its totality, Petal World IV-b has very nearly the same supervenience base as instance IV-a.

## What Is This All About?

The time has come to bundle these flowers into a small bouquet of metaphysical positions. If we allow that the object count aspect of the various Petal Worlds stands for the physical (again, meaning the domain of physics) and the fine structure aspect for the experiential (including, of course, but not limited to consciousness), then Petal World I illustrates materialism at its dreariest. There is nothing but physical mechanism, in this case layered on one uninspired decision with regard to the initial population of the world and an only slightly more inspired transformational rule. Indeed, if Petal World I had deep thinkers — which it clearly cannot! — they would certainly have to regard God as a very dull dog indeed.

Petal World II is dualistic and perhaps by metaphor at least occupies the same ground held by epiphenomenalism. Experience arises in causal connection with physical properties and in this one sense is no more than another aspect of it. (Note well that Petal Worlds I and II have essentially the same supervenience base!) Yes, there is something new in the world, but almost as if God appended it as an afterthought — and, again, not as a terribly creative one.

Petal World III is likewise dualistic, and comparing it with its metaphysical neighbors becomes a somewhat subtle engagement. One can hardly describe it as epiphenomenal insofar as the experiential side runs independently of the physical side, so that the supervenience base must be broadened. Moreover, it is possible here (although our example doesn't go on long enough to demonstrate this) that identical physical states may have distinct experiential states. This seems to me to bring it beyond the realms of what Chalmers calls natural supervenience or property dualism,[2] despite the still modest size of its supervenience base. Suffice it to say that in Petal World III the physical does not entail the experiential.

Petal Worlds IV-a and IV-b both exemplify the position of interactionist

2. See Chalmers, *The Conscious Mind.*

dualism, or what I prefer to call efficient dualism. In both cases the physical world is not closed in the sense that physical data do not suffice to determine its trajectory; put otherwise, a supervenience base for just the physical properties of both these worlds must implicate the experiential.[3] The difference between worlds IV-a and IV-b is then one of degree. The experiential realm of the former version is tamely efficient insofar as we have a good approximation of how the world will go, knowing only physical data and principles, while for the latter version, in stark contrast, the experiential realm is radically efficient insofar as we cannot get anywhere without it.

The examples above, of course, do not by any means exhaust the space of metaphysical positions on the dualism-monism debate, nor need they for our present purpose. There is one missing variant, however, that I think is worthy of special note: the experiential side (fine structure) of our efficient models (IV-a and IV-b) is, in both cases, built on the same supervenience base as Petal World III and is thus independent of its physical side. What if, instead, we had used Petal World II as a starting point for our examples of efficient dualism? In this case, since the experiential is entirely supervenient on the physical, any reciprocating action is still supervenient on the physical. In other words, the model would be physically closed, and we would not in essence have left the world of epiphenomenalism![4]

## What Counts as Physical?

While the previous section introduced models that were built to illustrate a handful of metaphysical positions relating to classical dualism, they actually illustrate something a bit more general — and this may not be too surprising, considering that both of the defining Petal World properties, object count and

3. In light of the fundamental facts of quantum mechanics, a critical clarification must be made in connection with this point on physical closure. One might feel that the failure of physical closure is already manifest in the indeterminacy aspects of quantum theory, but this disregards a related aspect: the notion of a state vector in quantum mechanics is not defined by simple numbers (as in our Petal Worlds), but by probability distributions, and the reality of the world dictates that this is the best we can do. With respect to this revised notion of a physical state, physical closure is well within reach, and in fact the prevailing expectation would be for its ultimate success. (By the way, it might be an interesting question — and one I haven't settled myself — whether we could implement a physical state vector for at least Petal World IV-a with respect to which it is physically closed.)

4. This is an important and provocative point that Chalmers is at pains to make, without the benefit of the Petal World models, in several places in his book, and one that highlights the subtleties of epiphenomenalism and the notion of physical closure.

fine structure, are in fact manifestly physical. Given any class of properties $C$ for any given world $W$, we might call $W$ *dualistic with respect to $C$* if $W$ is not supervenient on $C$. We might further say that the dualism is *efficient with respect to $C$* if $C$ is not even supervenient on itself, which is exactly to say that closure fails for the class $C$. In the examples above, letting $C$ denote the class of properties that reference only the object count, we find that all our Petal Worlds except the first are dualistic with respect to $C$, and only Petal Worlds IV-a and IV-b are efficiently dualistic with respect to $C$.

Let me introduce another instance of this notion of dualism relative to a class drawn directly from classical physics. I do this not only as a less contrived illustration, but also because I shall need this specific example to illustrate a critical point subsequently. Imagine a world populated by nothing but a vast number of idealized billiard balls that have been set in motion and collide with each other with perfect elasticity (i.e., without loss of kinetic energy). Further imagine a supervenience base for this world that references a comparatively limited subset of the terms and laws of classical mechanics, the Newtonian laws governing unperturbed motion and conservation of momentum most prominent among them. Suppose next that we allow these objects to interact gravitationally, so that beyond the elastic exchanges of momentum we have introduced a perturbing force in the world, with the consequence that the billiard balls no longer move along unaccelerated trajectories. Clearly, then, this world has become efficiently dualistic with respect to its prior supervenience base.

The point of the generalization is that any further progress on dualism in the usual metaphysical sense must in part depend on defining the boundary between the physical and everything else (if there is anything else) in a meaningful way. Now we might take the domain of physics to be an undefined term of transparently clear meaning, but the history of science and Thomas Kuhn clearly show this to be at best an assailable position.[5] My program here is to use an innocent-sounding phrase of Chalmers and central elements of Whitehead to give a plausible characterization of the physical domain. Even if this characterization is ultimately disagreeable to those whose metaphysics is more traditionally founded, I think we can still say something about dualism in the more general sense described in the previous paragraph.

David J. Chalmers's book *The Conscious Mind* argues persuasively, relentlessly, and often brilliantly that the laws of physics can never explain experience.[6]

5. See Thomas Kuhn, *The Structure of Scientific Revolutions* (Chicago: University of Chicago Press, 1962; 2nd ed., enlarged, 1970).

6. Needless to say, this one-sentence synopsis of his thesis does an injustice to this first-

In defending the logical possibility that a nonexperiential world is entirely compatible with physics, he writes, citing an argument of Jackson,[7] the following:

> [T]he argument is concerned with Mary, a neuroscientist brought up in a black-and-white room, who knows all the physical facts about color processing in the brain. Later when she first sees a red object, she learns some new facts. In particular, she learns what it is like to see red. The argument concludes that the physical facts do not exhaust all the facts, and that materialism is false.
>
> This argument is closely related to the arguments from zombies or inverted spectra, in that both revolve around the failure of phenomenal facts to be entailed by physical facts.[8]

So we learn from this brave and shamefully deprived neuroscientist that there are nonphysical facts, including "phenomenal facts." Moreover, elsewhere Chalmers speaks of "private facts." But one might find the use of the term "fact" in this context more than a little curious.

This is not the place to advance the analysis of truth, fact, and meaning, but at least for the coherence theory of truth, the idea of a private fact needs some explication. I believe it was Richard Rorty who characterized the coherence theory in terms of "what your neighbors will let you get away with saying," a sentiment that, whether one agrees or not in the end, certainly carries some weight. My point is that if being true to the facts implicates a public construct like language, how might the notion make sense in private? Why can't we — or don't we — say anything at all we would like to ourselves when speaking of phenomenal facts? What constrains me to say, "Ooh, I'm having a wonderful lavender feel!" at one time and "Ah, another lavender feel!" at another? If there are private facts, such as what it feels like to see lavender, what sort of private coherence might prevail in our phenomenal selves? This would seem to implicate outside referents, but according to Chalmers and much of our intuition, these referents are not to be found in the world of physics.

This argument invites us to seek a theory of phenomenal structure, and I think Whitehead has already given us a candidate for exactly such a theory. To see this we need only the following elements of process metaphysics, which I summarize in the abstract from *Process and Reality:* The actual entities of the world amalgamate into structured entities called nexuses via mutual prehen-

---

rate work, to which this paper owes much of its framework. A more adequate summary would, regrettably, carry us too far afield.

7. See F. Jackson, "Epiphenomenal Qualia," *Philosophical Quarterly* 32 (1982): 127-36.
8. Chalmers, *The Conscious Mind*, p. 140.

sions. These higher-order entities may extend through space and time and in the latter case admit a subspecies called societies, the characteristics of which are governed by prehension of previous generations, and these prehensions manifest subjective form. The perceptive mode that operates across time is called the mode of causal efficacy, and it is in this mode, as distinct from that of presentational immediacy, that entities perceive the past. To quote Sherburne's characterization: "[C]ausal efficacy, the mode of inheritance from the past, transmits, into the present, data that are massive in emotional power, but vague and inarticulate."[9] Of the two modes, it is thus only presentational immediacy that yields a high-resolution picture of the world, and Granville Henry and I[10] have argued elsewhere that the data of science are given only in this latter mode.[11]

The perception by a society of its antecedent stages would then seem to be a foundational kernel from which we might make sense of the coherence of a private phenomenal world. First, within a Whiteheadian society there is an exclusionary, unshared immanence of the society's own past in its present. Second, this immanence has a given structural or formal aspect (which, by the way, in turn implicates the notions of God and eternal forms in process metaphysics). We have thus a plausible boundary between physics and experience, between the unabashedly public and incorrigibly private, or, more simply put, between the outside and the inside of things.

## A Proposed Framework for Reconciliation

In this section I use a central tenet of Chalmers as the point of departure for my own proposal to reconcile the disjunction between the physical and everything else.

The evident irony of Descartes is that of having both introduced dualism and set in motion, via the principles of reductionism, atomism, and mechanism, a program to bring about its demise in favor of materialism, a doctrine

9. See Donald W. Sherburne, ed., *A Key to Whitehead's Process and Reality* (Chicago: University of Chicago Press, 1981), p. 236.

10. See Granville C. Henry and Robert J. Valenza, "The Preprojective and the Postprojective: A New Perspective on Causal Efficacy and Presentational Immediacy," *Process Studies* 26 (1997): 1-2.

11. Two points: (i) I shall use only certain consequent features of this bare-bones abstract synopsis; hence further elaboration is not needed. (ii) Whitehead and his followers have worked out in great detail a world model that indeed satisfies these properties, and thus I am not building on vacuous abstraction.

that has subsequently marched forward on virtually all fronts to surround all things mental. And yet that one kernel remains: those private facts of consciousness, stubbornly resistant to any final surrender. After carefully looking over the situation on the ground, Chalmers has argued for a position of Odyssean subtlety, one that he admits he is forced to by virtue of far worse alternatives, and one that many, including me, must find highly unsatisfying. Let me summarize his position and some critical related points.

Chalmers holds that experience can never be reductively explained by physics insofar as it is not logically supervenient on the physical world. By this he means that one cannot deny the possibility of a conceivable world identical to ours, but without experiencing beings.[12] Nonetheless, he maintains that experience is naturally supervenient on the physical world in that in our particular world two creatures in the same physical state will be in the same experiential state. Chalmers further distinguishes this property dualism from epiphenomenalism, although he does assume physical closure. This suite of assertions leaves him responsible to address what he calls "the paradox of phenomenal judgment," which I shall now briefly recount.[13]

If the private fact of experiencing red is beyond reductive explanation (and so must Miss Mary agree), consider the behavioral act of making the judgment "I'm having a red sensation now." If this is caused by the corresponding phenomenal experience, physical closure fails — radically! — and we have entered the forbidden domain of efficient dualism. But what is the alternative? According to Chalmers, we must rather admit that "consciousness is *explanatorily irrelevant* to our claims and judgments about consciousness."[14] In other words, the words that express phenomenal judgments are causally unrelated to phenomena themselves, but if they are to be believed, they do nonetheless accompany real phenomenal experiences. The latter possibility is not only paradoxical, but even seems to make the expression of such judgments epiphenomenal on experience, rather than the other way around.

---

12. I am not quite sure whether the zombies of Chalmers's imagination are just the Antipodeans of Richard Rorty, *Philosophy and the Mirror of Nature* (Princeton: Princeton University Press, 1979). The zombies by definition have no experience and yet, according to Chalmers, are entirely conceivable; the Antipodeans just might have experience but not know it. In view of certain comments soon to follow the so-called "paradox of phenomenal judgment" two paragraphs below, it looks as if it could be a close call between these two species, but perhaps something can be concluded from my strong intuition that given the choice between them, I would quite prefer to invite an Antipodean to dinner.

13. See Chalmers, *The Conscious Mind*, chapter 5.

13. Chalmers, *The Conscious Mind*, p. 177.

14. Chalmers, *The Conscious Mind*, p. 177.

Chalmers's address of this paradox is remarkable and more compelling than I can do justice to here. He looks over the possibilities, excludes all but one, and is left with this assertion: it is natural that even zombies, who indeed have no phenomenal experience, would nevertheless express themselves as if they did! Now admittedly there is nothing inconsistent in this conclusion, which one might aptly term *coincidental consciousness,* but in some ways it strikes me in the same way as the creationist theory that God created the fossil record of the world along with the living world itself: an explanation of almost pointless improbability and all in all too high a price to pay to maintain the underlying assumptions. Still, the conclusion does bring matters into possibly decisive focus.

I know of two somewhat related instances in the scientific literature — one of them famous and the other likely to be obscure in the extreme to all but a handful of interested experts — that have a similarity in feel or disposition to what we have just considered; the common element in both is gravity. The famous one belongs to Einstein and his general theory of relativity.[15] How very odd, observed Einstein, that the notion of mass comes up in two completely distinct and fundamentally unrelated contexts in classical physics. We have mass as inertia, resistance to change of motion, and mass as the apparent source of gravitation. Einstein held this as all too great a coincidence and concluded that they must be related. Accordingly, he enunciated the "principle of equivalence" that identified gravity with a uniformly accelerated frame of reference. With this deeper unifying principle in place, the coincidence of inertial and gravitational mass ultimately disappeared as such.[16]

The lesser-known example lies in the domain of classical physics, in fact in celestial mechanics. A curious and often neglected feature of Newton's law of universal gravitation — the very law that Einstein superseded — is that if the distance between two masses were ever to be zero, which is to say if two masses were ever "really" to touch, the gravitational attraction between them, according to the model, would grow to infinity. Fortunately, thanks to quantum theory and, specifically, to the Pauli exclusion principle, masses never do really touch, and so we are spared forever the inconvenience of sticking to our mates when kissing good-bye. Nonetheless, this so-called singularity in the classical expression for gravitational attraction causes a good deal of mischief in the workaday world of predicting the trajectories of stars, planets, moons, and

15. See Lincoln Barnett, *The Universe and Dr. Einstein,* rev. ed. (Mattituck, N.Y.: American Reprint Co., 1950).

16. If the coincidence of inertial and gravitational mass was suspect, how much more suspect the coincidence of phenomenal judgment and phenomenal experience!

mere spacecraft. Revisiting the billiard ball example, with the further proviso that the balls never happen to collide, if one wanted to model that world by computer simulation (this is the so-called *n*-body problem), the requisite numerical calculations involving the direct representation of the positions, velocities, and associated forces are vastly complicated by the presence of force terms that vary by all orders of magnitude. This very theoretical and yet very practical problem has received a huge amount of attention, and the approach that is in my view the most creative is also the most apropos to this discussion. Let me now sketch this out in the broadest of strokes.[17] Imagine the introduction of a fourth spatial dimension to supplement the usual three while time continues to have its customary meaning and relevance. This new space may seem clearly fictitious, but now consider the possibility of bodies interacting in this "larger" space in such a way that (i) there is no gravitational singularity and (ii) it is possible to project from this new space to the old such that the resulting trajectories are just what one would have expected using the Newtonian law of universal gravitation. In a definite sense, by pulling back from the space of our ordinary experience, we are able to substitute a kinder, gentler, more tractable dynamical system. One might object again that the price paid for this benefit is too high, insofar as we have introduced a kind of "shadow world." But to do so is to misunderstand shadows, which are no more than projections from three dimensions to two. It is the motion of bodies in ordinary three-dimensional space that is projected from this dimly grasped four-dimensional world, not the other way around. In any case, in the context of either science or engineering, this price is not too high at all, and this turns out to be an elegant and effective cure for the numerical woes introduced by the singularity at zero of Newton's basic law.

The point of my reference to general relativity is to bolster my claim that we should not be satisfied with the coincidence-encumbered resolution proposed by Chalmers to the paradox of phenomenal judgment. The point of my reference to regularization of dynamical systems is to suggest a way out, a way out that might be characterized as an abstract version of what Whitehead has proposed in detail. But, by way of a preliminary illustration, let me first introduce one more construction in the accustomed style. Behold Petal World V, the Final Frontier, on the following page.

I have let this example run longer than the others to allow its comparative complexity to become apparent: neither the sequence of object counts or fine

---

17. With sufficient patience and a good background in multivariable calculus, one can see this worked out in exquisite detail in Ernest L. Stiefel and G. Scheifele, *Linear and Celestial Mechanic* (New York: Springer Verlag, 1971).

**Fig. 6. Petal World V**

structures is all that obvious, and they seem independent of each other. Yet a unified process binds these two together, and it is a mere variation of the fine structure rule for Petal World III! Indeed, I have merely jumped into the sequence of primes at 11 and used the remainder when dividing by 15 to generate both the count and the fine structure in a rather straightforward way, as given by Table 1 on the following page.

Note that the only possible remainders when dividing a prime number larger than 5 by 15 are those shown in the first line of the table.[18] A little study shows that the second line of the table follows from the first by simply recording the remainder of the entry above following division by 5. The third line is similarly obtained from the first by dividing by 3, but in this case we further assign *D* or *A* according to whether the result is 1 or 2, respectively.

Admittedly Petal World V would be a poor illustration of any species of classical metaphysical dualism, but it is rather a simple instance where two projections from the same underlying process resolve an apparently complex relationship. Would one say this is dualistic with regard to the object count property? Yes, in the technical sense introduced above (moreover, one could well assert the same with respect to fine structure), and yet this seems to miss the point because

18. For example, if an integer yields remainder 10 when divided by 15, it must be divisible by 5. The other exclusions are similar. The rule is that only remainders that have no common factor with 3 or 5 can occur.

| Remainder by 15 | 1 | 2 | 4 | 7 | 8 | 11 | 13 | 14 |
|---|---|---|---|---|---|---|---|---|
| Object Count | 1 | 2 | 4 | 2 | 3 | 1 | 3 | 4 |
| Fine Structure | *D* | *A* | *D* | *D* | *A* | *A* | *D* | *A* |

**Table 1. Object Count and Fine Structure Assignments of Petal World V**

there is an underlying process that somehow encompasses both classes of properties at once and renders the deeper sense of dualism inappropriate.

What Petal World V and the examples from physics suggest in the abstract is the plausibility, and perhaps even the wisdom, of looking for a supervenience base for the world that simultaneously underlies both the physical and experiential domains. The attractiveness of process thought in this light is that it provides both a deep functional definition of the division of these domains and exactly the kind of unified framework for an underlying process from which these disjoint domains may be projected. Indeed, Whitehead even speaks of the mental and physical poles of concrescence, but given the technicalities of how the two basic modes of perception enter into the fundamental process of concrescence, it is much too simplistic to identify them with the physical and experiential in the sense we have been using.

Given the reluctance and occasional disesteem with which many philosophers approach Whitehead, it may be worthwhile to identify and to emphasize the essential features of a metaphysical system that supports the kind of framework I am suggesting. It must (i) make sense of the dichotomy between public (physical) and private (experiential) facts; (ii) make sense of the implicated notion of coherence for private facts; and (iii) admit a supervenience base that jointly supports the public and private domains via some appropriate projections.

I think this framework is indifferent to the defining feature of *natural* supervenience of the experiential on the physical, as Chalmers characterizes it, in two senses. First, I can imagine finding a deep supervenience base that either does or does not have the property that the physical projection uniquely picks out the experiential. (That is, the association of an experiential state with a given physical state may or may not be functional in the mathematical sense.)[19] Second, if the physical and experiential are divided along the lines of public versus private, we may never be able to tell the difference.

19. Would not the opposite assertion, that the association of a physical state with a given experiential state is functional, be a possible characterization of idealism?

## Where Does Evolution Fit?

We have been dealing with dualism at its sharpest here, preparing a framework ultimately targeted at the problem of mind, and so far I have done little more than to say it is a good idea to look for a unified and unifying underlying onto-logical deployment and associated formal structures, to point out that White-head has proposed just such a system, and to wring some high-level abstrac-tions out of his work. But what does this have to do with evolution?

Evolution could plausibly have, in part, a process-theoretic basis because the actual way of the world in Whitehead's theory is fundamentally Darwinian in nature, involving elements of inheritance, selection for stability, and novelty (or creativity).[20] In particular, his notion of a society has a basis in a kind of in-heritance of form, and it is hardly difficult to see this extending to the hard ge-netics of biological species developing over time. One might even suggest that the empirical basis for the theory of evolution might be an especially good place to look for some evidence of the radical incompleteness of physics because the biochemical basis for genetics is so much simpler than the neurological basis for the behavior of higher species. True, the timescale for evolution might be a prob-lem, but perhaps with the simplest of life-forms, something might be learned by close observation or experimentation. Still, speaking with no more formal back-ground in biology than my ninth-grade public school science requirement, I bet this would be a dead end for two categorically separated reasons.

First, the scientists tell us it is a dead end. Mayr[21] and Ayala, to name but two, argue vigorously and with an orders-of-magnitude greater knowledge base that evolution is fully supervenient on physics. Ayala could not be more clear or forceful than he is here: "I argue in this paper that science encompasses all of reality and that we owe this universality to Charles Darwin, who completed the Copernican revolution by extending to the realm of life the Copernican postu-late of the natural world as matter in motion governed by natural laws. The Co-pernican revolution had left out the diversity and configuration of organisms, because organisms and their parts manifest to be designed. Natural selection acting on spontaneously arising mutations can account for the diversity of or-ganisms and their design."[22] So the vast weight of scientific opinion — and a

---

20. Granville Henry and I have attempted to analyze the role of form in inheritance in terms of abstract graph theory. See Granville C. Henry and Robert J. Valenza, "The Principle of Affinity in Whiteheadian Metaphysics," *Process Studies* 23, no. 1 (1994).

21. See Ernst Mayr, *What Evolution Is* (New York: Basic Books, 2001), pp. 91-93, and Dominique J.-F. de Quervain et al., "The Neural Basis of Altruistic Punishment," *Science* 305 (August 2004): 27.

22. Ayala, chapter 2.

good deal of the philosophical, I might add — is behind the proposition that the world is physically closed; no help from the outside is needed.

I would, in passing, like to add that this argument from science may be supported by a more philosophically styled argument, as follows. Let us return briefly to a parallel world without experience. Neurological research of the sort described in de Quervain[23] establishes the possibility of evolving creatures in possession of perhaps oversimplified brains with "survival neurons." These neurons fire at a low background intensity when all is well (that is, when all the other sensory data correlates with safety), but sound off like firecrackers on the Fourth of July when things start looking bad. The point is that such neurological hardware could well suffice as survival enhancers without attendant, supplementary emotional feels like "all cozy and secure" or "scared as hell." Put more succinctly, zombies or Antipodeans (see note 12) could evolve, too, and hence the physical is sufficient to explain even the most advanced life-forms.

We come now to the second reason, far removed from the first, that evolutionists may never come to doubt seriously the physical supervenience base for their theories. The argument in fact applies quite generally to science, so I will pull back for the moment to more abstract terms. Assume that there is some deep reality $W$ and two associated projections $W_P$ and $W_E$ into the physical and the experiential.[24] We might think of $W$ as the entirety of the experiential-physical universe, while still retaining the materialist possibility that $W$ really is just $W_P$, or at least is isomorphic to it. Then an absolutely fundamental question of science — if not *the* fundamental question — would seem to be whether $W_P$ is closed. I put this assertion in the subjunctive because it clearly depends on the meaning of the term "physical." If "physical" means whatever is supervenient on whatever supervenience base might be congenial to physics at any given time, then of course the question is tautological. If "physical" means something deeper and less variable, then one could ask whether these deeper features are supervenient on, for instance, the deployment of physical concepts and laws that are accepted at present. This is a legitimate empirical question, but in this relativized form it is neither so fundamental nor nearly so interesting as before, and certainly not the way that science proceeds. So, finally, can we accept some deeper characterization of physics, such as the public-versus-private distinction introduced above, and ask the question again. Let us do just that.

First note that the public-private distinction does not once and for all de-

23. De Quervain et al., "The Neural Basis," pp. 305, 27.

24. It is impossible not to quote the first line of the *Tao Te Ching*, trans. Addiss and Lombardo (Indianapolis: Hackett, 1993): "Tao called Tao is not Tao."

termine the ontological deployment of physics, which expands and contracts according to considerations that become paramount below. Fields of force, electromagnetic waves, gravitons, entanglements, and the ever-elusive neutrino may come and go and even be characterized as somewhat ad hoc, but notice that whatever physics accepts ontologically must be defined relationally with respect to more basic public terms. So, for example, Newton's three laws of motion implicate the entification of forces, but constrain the meaning of the new term to other prior public concepts: a reference body (mass) and the notions of time and distance. At the foundations these relationships might be subtle, and I would not want to claim that physics is as well founded as, say, plane geometry, but it is fair to say that ultimately things resolve unambiguously to the extent that we have no fundamental disagreements among physicists with regard to its terms of discourse. It is at best a small extension of this point that the explanations of physics must also be founded on a public base, and it is right here, I think, the possibility emerges that physical closure is essentially tautological insofar as the limits of physics are the limits of impeccably coherent public discourse. Consider especially quantum theory in this light: it is the failure of even the possibility of certain kinds of measurements that necessitates the transition from states defined by numbers to states defined by distributions, and beyond this physics now dares not go. We might want to talk fancifully about some unseen internal, even intentional state of an electron or photon, but never would we so speak as part of the proper language of physics. Public explanation stops with the public facts, and to the extent to which these are denied we consider our explanations incomplete.[25] The upshot is that the physical closure of the world may not be a matter of empirical fact at all.

## Explanation without Projection

If the closure of the physical world $W_P$ is a sure or almost-sure thing, then perhaps all this talk of a deeper experiential-physical world $W$ can never amount to anything much at all. After all, how can we even begin to know and talk about $W$, in contrast to $W_P$? For one thing, we will never really be sure about what we are saying or, more precisely, hearing. But the failure of the ideal is not a hopeless failure, and we know very well — almost all of us — how to deal with ex-

---

25. See Robert Bruce Lindsay and Henry Margenau, *The Foundation of Physics*, corrected ed. (New York: Dover, 1963), chapter 10. The authors make a compelling argument very similar in form to what I have set forth here in their discussion of causality and the notion of a closed physical system.

actly this sort of thing. We do it all the time on a far lesser scale, and we do it in a way that is essentially consonant with scientific discourse in at least one key aspect of the whole business of explanation.

I am speaking, of course, of the second- and third-person phenomenal judgments or inferences that govern our interpersonal lives. I need spend often only seconds with Miss O before I begin to form firm judgments about her experiential states and modalities: Today she is feeling well, as her posture, brisk movements, and that spirited red dress indicate. Moreover, she is hoping to get away from me as fast as possible, before I can begin discussing metaphysics, all of which she believes is the sheerest nonsense. Note that part of my inference already involves that Miss O is instantly making inferences about me! And what underlies such judgments about this attractive young woman — I mean, potential zombie? A fair but not difficult question. I make a mapping between my own inner states and hers that assumes some common points of contact with the physical, in this case more specifically behavioral, world. What would I be feeling if I were dressing, moving, speaking like Miss O? If she and I have been raised in the same community, the same culture (including language), we have a pretty good chance of getting a fairly coherent picture of each other and therefore of not surprising each other in uncomfortable or even dangerous ways. This coherence and safety might be enhanced by a strong observance of tradition (say, we have both studied the *Analects* of Confucius), a strong observance in religion (say, we both believe that the same God is watching), or a strong agreement about reality (we both believe in the same fundamental truths).[26] Indeed, the success of these private or narrative maps is often what determines our emotional stance toward one another: I often like what I am like and dislike what I am unlike. My ability to make narrative maps is certainly limited: good enough with other humans that I am not viewed as a psychopath, good enough with dogs and cats that I am a responsible pet owner, and trailing off dramatically as we move through bats, worms, flowers, and rocks — including whole planets. Does a fetus want to develop into a baby? Did *Homo erectus* want to evolve into *Homo sapiens?* Is Miss O really feeling well? I don't know the answer to any of those questions, but my narrative map-making function is certainly operating more comfortably in the final case.

For Rorty and his Antipodeans, these narrative operations are inessential insofar as there is no private knowledge: the Antipodeans are disposed to speak accurately in terms of brain states, and their neural anatomy is apparently stan-

---

26. Insofar as one element of the value of truth is that it promotes or facilitates small-scale interpersonal or large-scale social coherence, we can see why it would be difficult to disentangle a correspondence theory of truth from a narrative theory, since both serve this value.

dardized to the extent that their utterances about their various series of fibers are so unambiguous as to count as public, even though the distinction he emphasizes is not along the lines of public versus private states, but corrigible versus incorrigible feels. The world is $W_P$, and further analysis of the mental is a hopeless business. For Chalmers these narrative operations at least do speak about something like phenomenal states, but these states are supervenient on $W_P$. We just don't know quite how yet. In a sense the world is both greater than $W_P$ and determined by it. For me, the paradox of phenomenal judgment latent in this natural dualism is fatal; I cannot accept coincidental consciousness and so call for a more fundamental separation between $W$ and its projections $W_P$. There is no public supervenience base for reality, but I can make helpful maps and even share them with others.

I mentioned that our narrative treatment of the world does have something in common with the operation of science. At the dawn of classical mechanics, astronomers looked into the heavens and saw points of light engaging in some complicated but regular motions. Kepler determined three laws of motion that explained these motions in the sense of reducing their complexity to a base of three laws. When Newton was asked how the planets would behave if his theory of universal gravitation was right, he was able — with considerable work — to reproduce Kepler's laws based on his own, more general laws of motion, but at the expense of introducing forces in general and gravitational force in particular into the ontological base of physics.

Similarly dynamical analysis is often vastly simplified with the introduction of energy (potential and kinetic). What these two cases chosen from many possibilities demonstrate is that the notion of a parsimonious explanation so celebrated by science entwines two separate threads. We have the distinct notions of *ontological parsimony* (Ockham's razor) and — please, excuse me if the ears bleed — *logical parsimony*. A kinematical description of the sky is ontologically more parsimonious than a dynamical one, but the latter is logically more parsimonious in that we must keep track of fewer laws to predict what happens next. So these species of parsimony sometimes lie in opposition. Which should have priority? I don't see how to settle this in the abstract. It seems to me to be a social decision along the lines that Kuhn has famously described. But insofar as even within science we sometimes trade off ontological austerity for logical compactness, we also have good grounds for doing so outside of science. When I attribute phenomenal experience and modalities to Miss O, I have made my ontological stance less tidy, but at least I have some idea of what she's going to do next.

In this light, let us review briefly the elements of Rorty and Chalmers that we have considered above. In Rorty's position, ontological austerity clearly dominates, and what makes the Antipodeans so charming — and so tricky — is that his conservatism seems to cost nothing in the way of logical parsimony: these hypothetical persons without mind step onto the stage of Prof. Rorty's thought experiment equipped, from the very first line spoken to the audience, with a compact logical basis for their behaviors: it's those *T*-fibers or *C*-fibers that explain it all. Chalmers addresses the population of the real world without this sleight and pays the ontological price: he "takes consciousness seriously," to use his often emphasized phrase, and allows for private facts. This price buys something, of course, namely, the undeniable reality of phenomenal experience, but I am not sure he gets his money's worth. It leaves us in an unstable position: instead of simplifying the logic of the world, it saddles reality with an almost incomprehensible coincidence. My proposed framework, which flows from an abstract characterization of Whitehead, is in a way an attempt to drive a harder bargain. This, of course, seems difficult given the limitations we seem to have in making narrative maps, but as Pico della Mirandola once notably asserted in his *Oration on the Dignity of Man,* we alone among the creatures of this earth are free to make what we want of ourselves. So maybe we can extend our narrative maps, and maybe art and religion are precisely such an extension. More importantly, with respect to something like the theory of evolution, on which almost all of life rests, I think we have to make this extension. Here is why:

Let us grant that the world is physically closed, because we are persuaded by the scientists or by the nature of scientific discourse. Then evolution, as described and constituted by science, runs in one form or another from prokaryote to *Homo sapiens,* and perhaps beyond, without the requirement for any ontologically richer or logically more economic basis than physics can give it. Fine, citing Pico again, we are free to see it that way if we so choose. But in a large sense this is a macro analog to the paradox of phenomenal judgment, the problem of explanatory irrelevance of phenomenal experience to phenomenal judgment. Yes, we are logically free to say there is nothing more, to let the limits of public discourse determine the limits of explanation, to explain as well as scientific explanation will allow and to stop there in the miasma of unimaginable happenstance, with anything beyond held as antiscience. But we are also free to hold — and without impeding the urgency or power of science to explain as well as scientific explanation will allow — that if we stop there, we shall then see only part of the full picture of reality. We are free to hold that more exists, is accessible to us in some part, just as the inner selves of certain other lifeforms are accessible to us; that this other way perhaps, for better or for worse, expresses God in the world, and in that respect enhances our experience of the world. We are free to see the expanded ontological commitment that this wider stance entails as enhancement and enrichment, rather than merely a less tidy alternative to materialism. Moreover, to the extent that we need a theory broader than materialism to account for our phenomenal selves in the world, a theory of something deeper than either the physical or experiential world separately, is that theory not implicit in any full explanation of the development of the associated physical forms that seem inextricably linked to these phenomenal selves? Does it seem likely that this broader theory only applies to the end result of the process, and in no way to the process itself? Would we countenance the role of gravity in the development of planets but eschew it in connection with the development of galaxies? I think not.

## Coda

I have argued that the domain of physics respects a public-private boundary that is real, at least in the case of conscious experience, and that in this we have grounds for seeking a deeper metaphysics, such as Whitehead's, that both underlies the physical domain and admits modes of explanation that cannot be entirely public. Moreover, once we accept this alternative, it is difficult not to allow for its application in a deeper understanding of evolution, although our ability at present to be able to describe things in this new way is limited by our ability to make narrative maps across chasms of dissimilarity in structure, scale, and function. Still, it seems possible that we can ultimately develop a less dichotomistic way of speaking of the world than is implicit in classical dualism, and a less limited way than is implicit in the physical sciences. Having said as much, I would like to conclude by putting matters in a somewhat different light.

Late in spring about ten years ago, on a cool but glowing day done in luminescent greens and translucent blues, I had the fine privilege of having lunch with Prof. Joseph Bracken, a marvelous scholar in religion and philosophy, and a Jesuit. I asked him how the world was *physically* different for him in light of the strength and immediacy of his religious beliefs. In response he said, approximately, this: "I see the same world that you do, but it's richer." Accordingly, if, as Charles Hartshorne once observed,[27] the reason to know the truth is indeed to act rightly, and the reason to act rightly is indeed to experience well, then to enrich our world by acknowledging the obvious, that there is more to the natural world than the material of physics, becomes the most natural act of all.

27. See Charles Hartshorne, *Creative Synthesis and Philosophic Method* (Lanham, Md.: University Press of America, 1983).